Cahokia

UNIVERSITY PRESS OF FLORIDA

Florida A&M University, Tallahassee
Florida Atlantic University, Boca Raton
Florida Gulf Coast University, Ft. Myers
Florida International University, Miami
Florida State University, Tallahassee
University of Central Florida, Orlando
University of Florida, Gainesville
University of North Florida, Jacksonville
University of South Florida, Tampa
University of West Florida, Pensacola

Cahokia

A World Renewal Cult Heterarchy

~:~

A. Martin Byers

University Press of Florida
Gainesville/Tallahassee/Tampa/Boca Raton
Pensacola/Orlando/Miami/Jacksonville/Ft. Myers

Copyright 2006 by A. Martin Byers
Printed in the United States of America on acid-free paper

11 10 09 08 07 06   6 5 4 3 2 1

A record of cataloging-in-publication data is available from the Library of Congress.
ISBN 0-8130-2958-9

The University Press of Florida is the scholarly publishing agency for the State
University System of Florida, comprising Florida A&M University, Florida Atlantic
University, Florida Gulf Coast University, Florida International University, Florida
State University, University of Central Florida, University of Florida, University of
North Florida, University of South Florida, and University of West Florida.

University Press of Florida
15 Northwest 15th Street
Gainesville, FL 32611-2079
http://www.upf.com

Contents

Figures

Tables

Preface

The most expansive floodplain of the Mississippi River, located in Illinois and termed the American Bottom, is home to the largest aggregation of monumental earthwork mounds in North America. The largest concentration of this aggregation of mounds is referred to as Cahokia, which is located several kilometers east of East St. Louis, Illinois, about halfway between the eastern upland bluffs overlooking this great floodplain and the Mississippi on the west. Cahokia is known to have at least one hundred mounds; of these, the best known and the largest North American earthwork north of Mexico is referred to as Monks Mound. It is a massive steplike four-terraced earthwork standing about 30 meters high, having its 300-meter-long east–west and 320-meter-long north–south sides oriented to the cardinal points. As social scientists having a strong anthropological orientation, most American Bottom archaeologists have been primarily concerned with revealing as much of the material cultural content of this site as possible, to reconstruct from these findings the cultures and societies of the prehistoric peoples who were responsible for it. That is certainly the purpose of this book. Archaeologists know that Cahokia and its earthworks were built and used between circa A.D. 1000–1050 and circa A.D. 1300–1350, when it was, apparently, rather rapidly abandoned. Indeed, the large population that occupied it and was spread across the American Bottom in small farming households largely abandoned the entire floodplain area.

Cahokia is not the only multiple-mound site of this period in North America, although it is by far the largest. There are several other large sites with which it could be compared and which, for the most part, were contemporary with it. Collectively, they constitute what archaeologists refer to as the Mississippian period culture. Large platform mounds, often paired with conical mounds, along with great plazas and timber buildings probably having religious functions, as well as multiple-dwelling houses, storage pits, and great middens containing the residue of collective feasts and rituals mark what were probably quite complex social systems. The majority of these earthwork sites are found south of Cahokia, many on the lower Ohio River, along river valley bottoms in western Kentucky as well as in Tennessee, Alabama, and so on. In fact, generally, this set of monumental earthwork sites with the residue of buildings, plazas, mortuaries, and storage facilities is termed the Southeastern culture. Most

Southeastern archaeologists characterize these sites as the seats of chiefdoms of various sizes and complexity. This characterization also serves to account for the earthworks and plazas themselves, as researchers generally assume that only social systems having centralized hierarchically structured leadership with strong social and coercive powers could recruit, organize, and direct the massive labor that constructing such earthworks, plazas, and buildings required. Since Cahokia is without a doubt the largest of these monumental sites—easily more than twice the size of its "rival," Moundville, in the Black Warrior Valley of Alabama—many American Bottom archaeologists have argued that it must have been the most complex and largest of North American chiefdoms, possibly rivaling even the power of contemporary rulers in Mexico.

I take a different tack in this book. I argue that it is more accurate to think of Cahokia as marking the coming together of multiple, rather small-scale but ritually specialized non-kinship-based social groups referred to generically in anthropology as sodalities: groups of lifelong same-age/same-gender companions who have come together because they have common interests. In this case, I argue that the primary (but certainly not the only) purpose of these sodalities was to perform world renewal rituals, and therefore they constituted world renewal cult sodalities. These cults were probably internally structured into senior and junior age-grades, each having its own set of sacred ritual and labor tasks to carry out, tasks that, by tradition, were suitable to each respective generation. The cults were also probably organized in complementary female- and male-based groupings, each largely autonomous of the other but collectively working to achieve the common goal of renewing the reproductive powers of the cosmos. The cults, in fact, probably not only were mutually autonomous but also maintained arm's-length relations with the parallel clan organizations (meaning that, much like our own voluntary social groups such as the Optimists and Shriners, individuals would belong to both clans and cults and move from one to the other to perform their duties according to each). The clans, of course, focused their interests and labor on domestic reproduction and therefore occupied the countryside farmsteads. The cults focused their collective efforts on world renewal ritual mediated through the great mound locales that they built and maintained. The social organizations that they constructed through affiliations of cult alliances I have termed world renewal cult heterarchies—and Cahokia, I argue, was the largest of these heterarchies.

This book is written not only for those who are engaged in interpreting the Cahokian and related mound earthwork locales, but also for all those interested in enhancing our understanding of the cultures and societies of the ancestors of the Native American peoples who were occupying this continent when they were unexpectedly confronted with European adventurers. While the nature of social systems of the English, French, Spanish, and Portuguese peoples at that time is well known, very little is known of the social systems of the historic Native American peoples that they encountered. Certainly a great deal of recorded opinion and descriptions of what the conquistadors, missionaries, merchants, and so on, saw and experienced is available to modern scholars. But these descriptions may be—and I suspect largely are—serious distortions of the social world of the Native Americans with whom the Europeans interacted and often aggressively confronted. I work from the not-unusual premise that this Native American social world was profoundly unique, based on cultural beliefs, standards, and principles that were unknown to and possibly the opposite of those of the European social world. Therefore, the view of these societies and their predecessors that we have derived from these European adventurers (and which is still influential among many archaeologists) is probably seriously distorted. I have developed a different perspective derived from modern anthropological studies of foraging and farming societies, both on other continents and in North America; this frame of reference works with a set of premises that is diametrically opposed to those that currently inform much of the interpretation of the Southeastern societies. Hence, I avoid using terms such as *chiefs* and *chiefdoms,* and, as noted above, I prefer to speak of clans and cults organized into complex settlement arrangements based on mutual alliances and enmities and having social structures based on mutual autonomy of responsible parties who interact through collective consensus rather than zero-sum dominance. Such a social world presupposes collective beliefs (cosmology) and structural principles (ethos) that characterize both the natural and the social world in immanently sacred terms. The result is a theoretically well elucidated set of social and cultural models that accounts for the complex archaeological record of the American Bottom more coherently, I claim, than do the current political economic models that postulate that these monumental earthworks were built and controlled by elite-based hierarchies of chiefs that relied on a strategic blend of ideological manipulation and threatened and actual coercion to dominate and direct the great labor of the "commoners."

I want to acknowledge the wonderful moral and scholarly support that Bruce Trigger of the Department of Anthropology, McGill University, has extended to me during my writing of this book. His own publishing career has been an inspiration to me, as it has to many of his colleagues. I especially want to thank the Department of Anthropology of McGill University, Montreal, for its ongoing support enabling me to undertake the research that this book required. The two anonymous (at the time) reviewers are also especially to be thanked for their suggestions. If it were not for their critical, insightful, and kind comments, this book might have been titled "Cahokia as a World Renewal Cult Mall." Of course, I accept responsibility for combining their separate suggestions into the title that it now bears.

This research could not have been possible without the help of the professionals in the McLennan Library of McGill University. I want to thank several of those making up the team that sustains the smooth running of access services out of the stack manager's office—particularly the manager (Carl Eugene) and those of his team whom I have come to know (Geoffery Kibirige, Dolly Rahaman, and Peter Santlal), all of whom helped to ensure that I had use of my study room even during the height of 2004 library renovations, when I was most deeply caught up with the research of this book. Access to the many books and reports that this research depended upon was facilitated by the invaluable work of another team of professionals at the McLennan Library, the interlibrary loans group of Elizabeth Dunkley, Yvonne Mattocks, Janice Simpkins, Maria De Souza, and Francisco Uribe. Their work ensured that even the most difficult-to-access reports were made available to me; I want to thank them for their dedication. Finally, I want to dedicate this book to my wonderful wife, Joy. Without her support and endless patience, this work could not have been written.

1

Introduction

Cahokia is a major archaeological site of the prehistoric Mississippian period in the American Bottom region of the central Mississippi Valley (Figure 1.1). It has an estimated (and to some degree, conventionally recognized) areal magnitude of about fifteen square kilometers. Built and occupied between circa A.D. 1050 and 1300/1350, it consists of over one hundred earthwork mounds, most of which are clustered along the southern bank of Cahokia Creek about seven or eight kilometers east of the Mississippi River (Figure 1.2). While many of these mounds are very large, they are dwarfed by Monks Mound, a four-terrace earthen construction that dominates the local landscape. It is the approximate height of a ten-story building, and the base is approximately 300 meters long east–west and 320 meters long north–south (Figure 1.3). Monks Mound is often pointed out as the largest North American prehistoric earthwork construction north of Mexico. Its stepped construction was built up by the addition of multiple earth strata, often serving as the base for one or more large timber buildings, along with auxiliary facilities, such as marker posts. The upper stages of this earthwork are known to have been completed by means of a series of major additions of a heavy black claylike material, often referred to as "black gumbo" and procured from the margins of the low, swampy ground that richly characterizes the American Bottom. A similar pattern of multiple construction stages with dismantling (sometimes burning, either deliberately or accidentally) and rebuilding of ritual structures is found as a record of the history of most of the major mounds of this complex site referred to as Cahokia.

The northern side of Monks Mound directly overlooks Cahokia Creek and its floodplain. It was (probably) surrounded by four plaza-mound complexes, one each to its immediate south, east, west, and north (Figure 1.4). The southern plaza, often called the Grand Plaza, is the largest of these. Some of the mounds that form the perimeter of the plaza are second only to Monks Mound in magnitude. The northern or Creek Bottom Plaza is the smallest of the plaza-mound complexes that frame Monks Mound. It is delineated by five small mounds. Unlike the other three plaza-mound complexes built on the ridge overlooking Cahokia Creek, the Creek Bottom plaza-mound complex is actu-

Figure 1.1. American Bottom, northern sector. (Pauketat and Emerson 1997a, fig. 1.2, p. 6. Reprinted from *Cahokia: Domination and Ideology in the Mississippian World* edited by Timothy R. Pauketat and Thomas E. Emerson by permission of the University of Nebraska Press. Copyright 1997 by the University of Nebraska Press.)

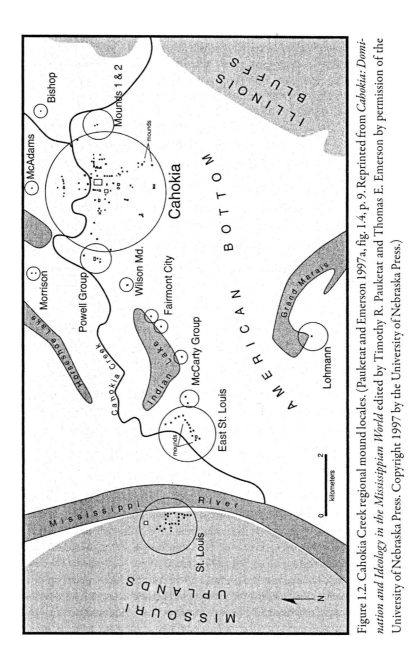

Figure 1.2. Cahokia Creek regional mound locales. (Pauketat and Emerson 1997a, fig. 1.4, p. 9. Reprinted from *Cahokia: Domination and Ideology in the Mississippian World* edited by Timothy R. Pauketat and Thomas E. Emerson by permission of the University of Nebraska Press. Copyright 1997 by the University of Nebraska Press.)

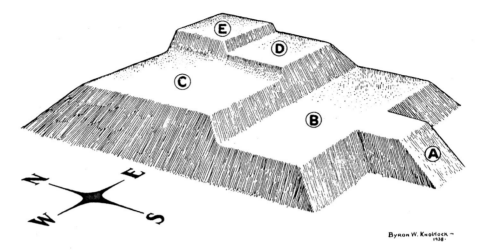

Figure 1.3. Monks Mound. (Fowler 1997, fig. 5.2, p. 89. Courtesy of the Illinois Transportation Archaeological Research Program, University of Illinois. Artist, Byron W. Knoblock.)

ally located on the floodplain of Cahokia Creek. Therefore, the five mounds were probably regularly inundated, either partially or fully, by the seasonal and nonseasonal flooding of Cahokia Creek.

Cahokia is impressively large, but it is only the largest of several other large and contemporaneous multiple-mound groupings nearby (Figure 1.2). The East St. Louis site contains the residue of an aggregation of about forty or forty-five mounds located in what is now the downtown area of that city, making it the second- largest earthwork mound site of the Eastern Woodlands (Emerson 2002, 129). Only the relict bases of some of its many mounds are known to still exist, and these are covered by the modern urban rail, road, and building construction making up the central part of East St. Louis (Kelly 1994, 49–50; 1997, 148). On the western shore of the Mississippi River across from the East St. Louis site, there was another large aggregation of mounds, about twenty-five, that is referred to as the St. Louis site. This was the fourth-largest mound site in the Eastern Woodlands (Emerson 2002, 129). It is also made up of the residue of these mounds. In fact, most of these were cleared away during the construction of downtown St. Louis (Milner 1998, 120).

Besides these latter two multiple-mound sites, both north and south of Cahokia there are a number of other, more or less extant multiple-mound locales. The Mitchell site of Granite City, consisting of ten or eleven mounds, is about

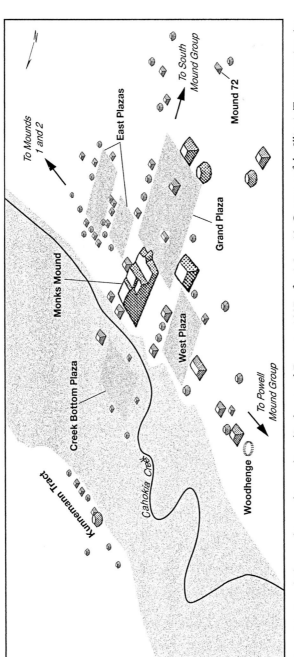

Figure 1.4. Grand Plaza and immediate milieu. (Pauketat and Emerson 1997a, fig. 1.5, p. 13. Courtesy of the Illinois Transportation Archaeological Research Program, University of Illinois.)

eleven kilometers north-northwest of Cahokia (Porter 1969, 137, 159–60). The Lunsford-Pulcher site, also with seven or more mounds, is about twenty-five kilometers south-southwest of Cahokia (Kelly 1993, 434–35). There are also many single-mound sites found distributed linearly north to south across the American Bottom, the best known being the Lohmann site, about halfway between the Lunsford-Pulcher site and Cahokia (Esarey and Pauketat 1992, 3, 13).

THE AMERICAN BOTTOM

The American Bottom is a large east-bank floodplain of the Mississippi River opposite the confluence of the Missouri River. Its northern sector starts at the town of Alton, Illinois, and it stretches south about 125 kilometers to Chester at the mouth of the Kaskaskia River. It can be internally divided into two sectors according to the width of the floodplain. The upper third of the American Bottom is often referred to as the northern expanse. At its widest it is about 19 kilometers east–west along the lower Cahokia Creek, and it is approximately 40 kilometers north–south, narrowing significantly toward the south. From Dupo south to Chester, the floodplain narrows to between 4 and 8 kilometers east–west (Milner 1998, 14, 35).

As would be expected of a floodplain zone, its topography is characterized predominantly by a multiple series of low ridges and swales interspersed by shallow oxbow lakes and broad marshes and swamps. Although in prehistoric times it had both rich wild resources and excellent soil for agriculture, its human occupants were subjected to the considerable risk of either too much or too little water. While regular seasonal floods were expected, unseasonable floods were not uncommon, and, somewhat ironically, the prehistoric populations in the floodplain could also experience summer droughts that could devastate their crops (Milner 1998, 78).

Chronology of the American Bottom

The peoples occupying the American Bottom and responsible for the social systems associated with and realized by these large mound sites and dispersed domestic farmsteads practiced what is often referred to as the Middle Mississippian culture. The period of prehistory is spoken of as the Mississippian period, and it is conventionally dated between circa A.D. 1000 and circa A.D. 1400 (Figure 1.5). More recently, this chronology has been calibrated to circa A.D. 1050 to circa A.D. 1350 (Figure 1.6). Whether the chronology is assessed

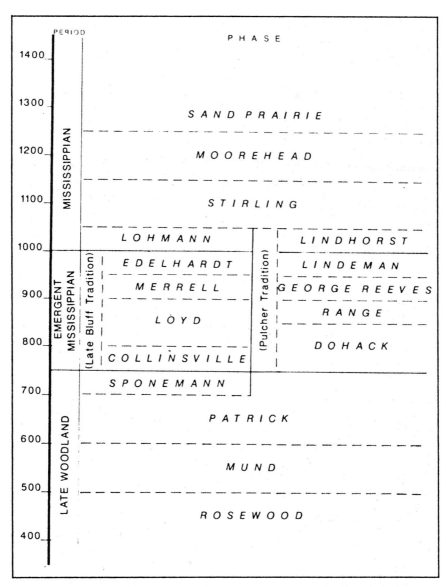

Figure 1.5. Uncalibrated chronology of the American Bottom. (Kelly 1990b, fig. 49, p. 117. From "The Emergence of Mississippian Culture in the American Bottom Region," by John E. Kelly, in *The Mississippian Emergence*, ed. Bruce D. Smith, Smithsonian Institution Press. Reprinted by permission of publisher.)

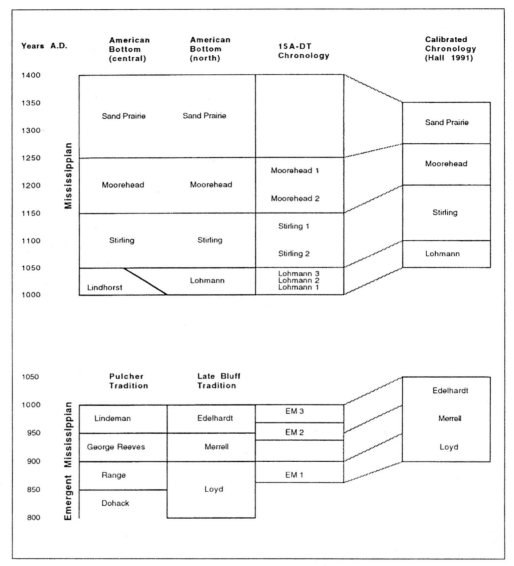

Figure 1.6. Calibrated chronology of the American Bottom Mississippian period. (Pauketat 1994, fig. 3.3, p. 49. Used with permission of the University of Alabama Press.)

in the conventional or in more recent calibrated terms, this is a rather shallow time span. However, the Middle Mississippian culture of the American Bottom had relatively deep historical roots in the region. This is known as a result of a comprehensive series of extensive excavations carried out by the FAI-270 Archaeological Mitigation Project. This project emerged as a result of the planned expansion of the federal interstate highway system in the American Bottom. The FAI-270 project involved surveying along the planned rights-of-way of this proposed highway system, recording all the significant sites, and, finally, conducting a series of full-scale excavations of the most promising and important set of archaeological sites that this survey disclosed. As a result, Illinois archaeology now has a good representative sample of the material residue of the Middle Mississippian culture and its prehistoric roots in the American Bottom.

The archaeologists conducting this project also mapped earlier human occupation of the region, of course, reaching back to the Middle Archaic, or earlier. The bulk of the archaeological material, however, relates to the period from circa A.D. 600, the middle Late Woodland, to circa A.D. 1400, the end of the Mississippian period in this region. This material formed the basis for mapping first a slow and, starting about A.D. 600, a more rapid, although possibly erratic, expansion of population in the American Bottom (Fortier and Jackson 2000, 123–24, 134). As noted above, about A.D. 1050, or even earlier, the great mound locales were initiated, marking the Mississippian period. Then, beginning circa A.D. 1200, the population numbers started to reduce, probably quite rapidly, and by A.D. 1300/1350, the American Bottom was essentially abandoned (Emerson 2002, 138–39). It is this episode—the Mississippian period of the American Bottom between circa cal A.D. 1050 to circa A.D. 1300/1350—that is the primary focus for this book. However, it will be necessary to reach back into the preceding centuries to summarize the archaeological record of the foundational social system out of which the Middle Mississippian culture of the region emerged.

It is widely accepted that, following the Middle Woodland period, the prehistory of the American Bottom can be fairly reasonably divided into three periods between A.D. 300/400 and A.D. 1300/1400. The first is generally referred to as the Late Woodland period, circa A.D. 300/400 to A.D. 800. This is followed by the Emergent Mississippian period, conventionally dated to A.D. 800 to A.D. 1000, and then the Mississippian period, circa A.D. 1000 to circa A.D. 1400 (Figure 1.5). However, this historical framework is based on the older conventional chronology of the American Bottom, which is in the process of being replaced by a more exact chronology based on calibrated radio-carbon dates. For this introductory material, I have chosen the older scheme and terminology, specifically using the term *Emergent Mississippian period* and the dates of A.D. 800–1000 for the period between the Late Woodland and the Mississippian periods. Later, I use the new terminology, referring to the Emergent Mississippian period as the *Terminal Late Woodland period*—and, of course, I shift to using the calibrated dates of ca A.D. 900–1050 (Figure 1.7). The reason for initially retaining the older system is that there is an important theoretical debate about the preferred terminology to use in referring to these pre-Mississippian times. The core issue is whether the sociocultural processes of the post–Middle Woodland period prehistory of the American Bottom leading to the emergence of Cahokia should be characterized in "gradualist" or "rupturalist" terms. At a more appropriate point in this book I summarize the debate and present my own position, which, briefly, is to treat this prehistory as both gradual and ruptural in nature. Indeed, as I indicate shortly, the debate between gradualism and rupturalism obscures what I consider to be a fundamental understanding concerning the nature of the American Bottom prehistoric social systems that is shared among the disputing parties.

In any case, the Late Woodland, Emergent Mississippian, and Mississippian periods are recognized by the particular complex of material cultural attributes that sets each up as "significantly" different from each other. Of course, focusing on the differences leads to the danger of ignoring the continuities that, in the view I develop in this book, link these periods into a coherent, historically developing social system. In this regard, while the Middle Mississippian mound locales are very distinct, I believe that it is important to keep in mind that there is a cultural continuity that links the relatively simple material cultural make-up of the social systems that existed during the Late Woodland period to the much more complex material cultural make-up of the mound locales of the Mississippian period.

In sum, the central theoretical premise of this book is that underwriting the significantly noticeable and quite major material cultural changes that occurred in the American Bottom during this period, there was a profound continuity in cosmology, ethos, worldview, and—in more interactive terms—social structural relations and material practices. To put this another way, the core argument of this book is that the great mound locales that make the Mississippian period distinct represent neither a gradually evolving nor a cataclysmic historic transformation of the American Bottom social system. Rather, the great mounds and their distribution are postulated here to be the monumental

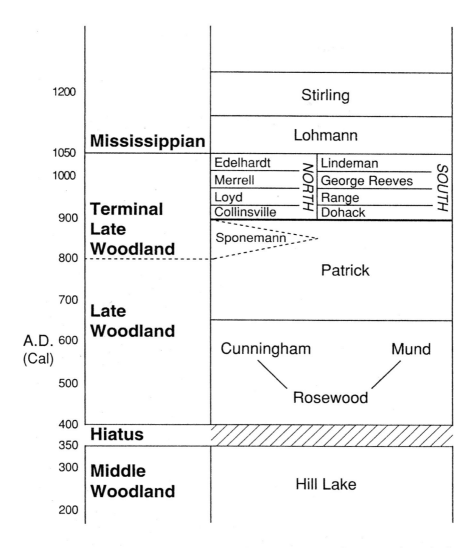

Figure 1.7. Calibrated Terminal Late Woodland chronology. (Fortier and McElrath 2002, fig. 2, p. 181. Used with permission of Alta Mira Press.)

outcome and medium of the transformation of the surface structures and the simultaneous reproduction of the deep structures of the cultural traditions as these were inherited from the earlier Late Woodland period.

The Precursors of Cahokia

Between A.D. 300/400 and 600, the population of the early Late Woodland period of the American Bottom was both rather limited in size and scattered, occupying small, warm-season foraging-gardening sites primarily along the base of the eastern bluffs with the groups probably dispersing and retreating to the uplands during the cold season. About A.D. 600, marking in this general region what is termed the *Patrick phase* of the Late Woodland period, population started to expand into and across the floodplain, probably from both natural growth and increasing migration from the uplands. Indeed, according to Andrew Fortier and Douglas Jackson (2000, 134), circa A.D. 600 marks "a rather spectacular increase in sites in this zone as well as an increase in the diversity of occupied floodplain ecological niches. Similar settlement expansion also occurred in the surrounding upland drainages."[1]

Initially these occupants sustained the mixed gardening and foraging regime of the preceding period. The bow-and-arrow complex was introduced circa A.D. 700, and by circa A.D. 750/800, the cultivation of maize as a subsistence crop was added to the cultivation of the traditional indigenous crops of chenopodium, maygrass, little barley, and erect knotweed, along with several other lesser-used wild plant resources. The introduction of maize to the everyday diet is also taken to mark the end of the Late Woodland period in this region and the beginning of the Emergent Mississippian period. As its name suggests, the Emergent Mississippian period has been characterized as the development of social and cultural processes that culminated in the rise of the Middle Mississippian culture of the Mississippian period of the American Bottom. Among these processes characterizing the Emergent Mississippian was the transformation of the Late Woodland social system of small semisedentary hamlets and villages based on gardening and foraging into a social system of sedentary towns, villages, and hamlets based on mixed gardening, including maize, and possibly some field agricultural practices. By about A.D. 900, deemed the middle of the Emergent Mississippian period, fairly large villages had developed with central plazas and flanking auxiliary plazas (each surrounded by residences with courtyards), which were probably local centers of a network of smaller settlements. Characteristically, the plazas framed large standing posts associated with special-purpose pits having limestone-paved floors. Also, a few specialized complexes of buildings (usually larger than the typical residences) in the larger villages became common, and these were located on one or both sides of the central plazas and also on the periphery of the villages.

The Range site near Dupo in the lower sector of the northern expanse of the American Bottom is archaeologically important because it incorporates the full series of occupations that are relevant to this book, from the terminal Patrick phase of the Late Woodland period, through the Dohack, Range, George Reeves, and Lindeman phases of the Emergent Mississippian period of this sector, to occupations marking the Lohmann and Stirling phases of the Mississippian period (Figure 1.5). John Kelly (1990a, 99; 1990b, 134) has interpreted the changing settlement patterning of this site as mapping the evolution of the Emergent Mississippian social system. For him, the specialized structures, plazas, residential clusters, and ritual posts and pits of the George Reeves phase occupation at the Range site marked a full-fledged ranking of lineage-based residential groups forming possibly a simple chiefdom society.

> The central plaza, its attendant structures and internal features, forms a strong community core. This central plaza is in turn symmetrically flanked by a series of additional courtyards, each with its associated houses. I would postulate that this community pattern reflects the spatial distribution of a series of ranked social groups, and represents the best evidence currently available for the initial emergence by A.D. 900–950 of a *ranked form of sociopolitical organization* in the American Bottom region. (Kelly 1990a, 99, emphasis added)

To support this claim of a "ranked form of sociopolitical organization," he particularly notes the large buildings, one of which he describes as the "chief's house," the pits and posts associated with the plaza area (which he interprets in agricultural fertility ritual terms), and the apparent positioning of smaller plazas as indicating lower or "subordinate social groups":

> Although no mound construction is present, the large rectangular structure at one end of the central courtyard is perhaps the chief's house. The four pits and central post located at the opposite end of the community plaza undoubtedly played the same ceremonial and symbolic role as . . . [the circle-in-square complex of the preceding Dohack phase]. . . . The northernmost and secondary plaza and courtyard are interpreted as separate and subordinate social groups. If the . . . ranking related in any manner to kin relations, the former inhabitants are distantly related to those in the main village. (Kelly 1990a, 99)

Many but not all American Bottom archaeologists agree with Kelly's interpretation that, in general terms, the later Emergent Mississippian period was characterized by internally ranked communities organized into simple settlement hierarchies, constituting probably simple chiefdoms, and that this social structure was the springboard from which the great mound locales such as Cahokia were constructed. Indeed, many are convinced that mound construction started in some of the more favorably situated late Emergent Mississippian towns, such as Lunsford-Pulcher or Cahokia, possibly by or even earlier than A.D. 950–1000, although these archaeologists also quickly note that there are currently no empirical data to confirm this claim (Emerson 1997b, 176; 1997c, 57–58; Kelly 1990b, 135; Milner 1990, 19; 1998, 105–6).[2] Such claims serve partly to account for the apparent "Big Bang" with which the Mississippian period opened. Timothy Pauketat (1997, 31–32) argues that this "Big Bang" occurred at Cahokia and that the rapidity of its occurrence was possible only because of a massive, politically organized and ideologically inspired and planned strategy. This strategy occurred in two steps. The first was a rather short period that saw these simple chiefdoms of the late Emergent Mississippian period forming into competing complex chiefdoms. This brief period, possibly only one or two generations, was terminated by the abrupt and successful emergence of what he terms the *Cahokian paramountcy*. Using calibrated dating in this case, he notes that

> about A.D. 1050, the American Bottom experienced the political and economic equivalent of the Big Bang. I have identified this Big Bang in the Bottom as a consequence of the rapid consolidation of political power or regional control presumably by some subset of the high-ranking Emergent Mississippian population.... The event brought about the abrupt and large-scale transformation of community order, the physical landscape of Cahokia, and the entire northern expanse of the American Bottom floodplain. (Pauketat 1997, 31–32)

While this "Leviathan" (to use his descriptive characterization [Pauketat 1994, 1]) prevailed for about 300–350 years, from circa A.D. 1000/1050 to circa A.D. 1350/1400, the second half of its existence has been characterized (Pauketat and Emerson 1997a, 22–24) as that of a spent "giant," with its final and complete dissolution occurring as the American Bottom essentially became depopulated by A.D. 1400. Pauketat and Emerson conclude, "The significance of its drawn-out ending, however, lies in the transformation of central Cahokia from a political capital to a sacred center and cemetery" (Pauketat and Emerson 1997b, 278).

THEORETICAL VIEWS

The first modern archaeological account of this Mississippian period archaeological record is Melvin Fowler's four-tiered settlement model. Cahokia was treated by him as the singular first-tier site, that is, as the dominant Mississippian period settlement of the American Bottom (Fowler 1974, 27; 1978, 468–74; 1997, 10). As such, it was the center of a hierarchical social system organized as a complex rank-ordered settlement system. In his terms, the smaller multiple-mound sites, such as East St. Louis, Lunsford-Pulcher, and so on, were second-tier centers, politically, economically, and religiously subordinate to Cahokia. The single-mound sites, such as Lohmann, were third-tier centers. The small, multiple, and scattered occupational sites without mounds formed the bottom or fourth tier of the American Bottom social system and consisted of homesteads and hamlets occupied by the mass of the population that served as labor for the leading elite occupants of the hierarchical superstructure.

Since Fowler's initial presentation of this hierarchical model of the American Bottom social system, various other versions have been elaborated. For example, picking up on the central notion of dominance, some archaeologists have claimed that Cahokia had its tentacles reaching well beyond the American Bottom and throughout most of the central and lower Mississippi River drainage. Indeed, as the dominant "city" of the American Bottom, it has been envisioned as a lesser "Teotihuacan-on-the-Mississippi," the core of a widespread "state" or "chiefdom-state" holding direct sway over all the lesser mound centers, each of which may have been the residential capital of a local chief who was subordinate to his paramount chief in Cahokia (Fowler 1974, 26–32; 1997, 10; Kelly 1982, 201; O'Brien 1989, 280–84; Porter 1969, 140, 156–60).

I noted above that there is important ongoing debate over the nature and timing of the transformations that brought about Cahokia (Fortier and McElrath 2002, 173–74; Pauketat 2002, 152–54). However, for the most part the debaters do not question the complex hierarchical nature of Cahokia and the American Bottom social system of the Mississippian period. The latter is taken almost as axiomatic, and the major focus has been on the number of levels of this hierarchical system; the mode of settlement articulation; the geographical scope of the Cahokian political, economic, religious, and social control;

the role of emigration and immigration; how the hierarchical complexity emerged from the prior, simple horticultural village system; and so on (Fortier and McElrath 2002, 173–74). In this regard, the characterizations by Timothy Pauketat and Thomas Emerson are probably the most influential. While they confirm Fowler's claim that Cahokia was the paramount center of the American Bottom, they reject the notion that it was a "lesser" Teotihuacan: "Taken to an extreme by others, Cahokia was characterized as a little Teotihuacan-on-the-Mississippi, a mercantile city crowded with bureaucrats, priests, engineers, craft specialists, peasants, and marketplaces. . . . This extreme view, despite its popular appeal, is not tenable today" (Pauketat and Emerson 1997a, 3). Rather, Pauketat and Emerson settle for a far less specialized, regionally more localized, but still strongly hierarchical social system. Thus, while Cahokia's political and economic power was dominant across the American Bottom, in their view it probably reached only to between thirty and, possibly, one hundred kilometers beyond.

However, they still claim that its cultural influence was geographically widespread and historically extensive (Anderson 1997, 260–61; Pauketat and Emerson 1997a, 2). Hence, they consider that Cahokia's claim to real uniqueness was its long-term cultural impact, one that reverberated across much of the Midcontinent and the Southeast and was still potent when Europeans arrived. For them, this cultural preeminence of Cahokia is attested to "by its size, its massive mounds, its productive residues, and its icons emulated and scattered to the four winds. It was the most expansive political-cultural phenomenon of the Mississippian world. It had a profound impact on other native groups of southeastern and midcontinental North Americans" (Pauketat and Emerson 1997a, 28).

Emerson (1997c, 13–14) has also argued that the Cahokian social and political elite emerged as a result of the collective commitment to monumental construction directed toward religious goals that emphasized *communitas*. Communitas practices suppress social and personal differences and emphasize commonalities and equalities. He goes on to argue that the imperatives of monumental construction worked to contradict the communitas spirit and goals that these religious constructions were intended to gain. This perversion resulted from the construction program's promoting the formation of a leadership that, through its special association with the sacred nature of these constructions, came to be alienated from the very people who had initially chosen these individuals as leaders, thereby becoming self-selected and elitist. Thus, while Cahokia may have been started as the project of peoples constituting a social system having only simple hierarchical tendencies rooted in lineage corporate groups, it quickly and largely unwittingly transformed into a dominance-based hierarchical social system characterized by a ruling, self-selecting elite of chiefs presided over by a supreme chiefly lineage.

Pauketat (1994, 187) effectively argues the same view, except that, in his judgement, the emergence of an elite social stratum was not the unintended consequence of monumental construction but the outcome of an ideological strategy by which the set of elite families of the preexisting simple chiefdoms was able to break the traditional egalitarian commonsense "ideology" of lineage-based kinship systems. The promoting of this self-serving "ideology" by elites was so successful that they were able to constitute the emergent paramount chief as a living god (Pauketat 1994, 17–21). In addition to limiting the geographical scope of Cahokia's political and economic power and influence, which is certainly an important modification of Fowler's four-tiered hierarchical model, Pauketat and Emerson (1997a, 3–4) have made another modification to it. On the basis of settlement data accumulated by the FAI-270 Archaeological Mitigation program, they argue for reducing the settlement hierarchy from a four- to a three-tiered system. They still recognize Cahokia as the only first-tier site. However, they treat all other mound sites, whether these have one or more mounds, as second-tier sites. This means that all the nonmound sites now make up the third tier of the settlement system. Furthermore, basing his detailed analysis of the settlement pattern on the FAI-270 data, Emerson (1997c, 73–79) further reconfigures this level hierarchically. He classifies these nonmound "rural" sites into farmstead sites and nodal sites. The latter he subdivides into nodal household sites retaining a core-complex identifying them as the farmsteads of local "rural commoner" leadership, on the one hand, and the civic, ceremonial-fertility, and ceremonial-mortuary cult nodal sites of the rural elite, on the other. This third or bottom tier of nodal and non-nodal sites constitutes what he refers to as the dispersed village system of the American Bottom region; through the medium of the civic and ceremonial cult nodal sites, in his model this system served as the complex integrative network linking the rural commoners to the spatially distant paramount chief seated at Cahokia.

Mark Mehrer (1995, 15–16) has carried out a comprehensive analysis of the patterning of the rural farmstead locales, focusing on both the residential and related structures and the associated pits that are commonly found in and/ or around them. He also largely accepted a modified version of the view that the Mississippian period in the American Bottom was dominated by a central power (that is, Cahokia). However, he takes a less "ideological" and more materialist, energy-based posture to argue against the view that the "rural" settlements of dispersed villages were fully dominated by the elite occupants of the mound-based settlements. Given that he accepts that the social power residing in the American Bottom was centralized in these latter sites, in my opinion he does not clarify how these dispersed villages could sustain either a fully autonomous or even a semiautonomous arm's-length relation with the mound locales. His suggestion is that the "rural" people became quite adept at hiding their surplus produce from the prying eyes of the chiefs (Mehrer 1995, 140–46). However, this very claim presupposes the acceptance of the authority of the centralized chief. That is, rather than the hiding of surplus being the denial of authority, this action would be an admission and reproduction of this authority—albeit one that would have had serious practical constraints, if Mehrer's claim is correct. Indeed, what this means is that rather than treating autonomy as a principled cultural or social fact, Mehrer reduces it to being a matter of practical limits on control by suggesting that local autonomy was largely a function of the distance between the rural homestead and the mound center: "While social elites assumed control over regional and temple-town matters, village affairs degenerated into household affairs. That is, as temple-town authorities waxed, village authority waned, and considerable autonomy was left to those living in the hinterlands, who were dispersed over the landscape" (Mehrer 1995, 144).

In a later paper he attempts to clarify this reductive model of the "rural/urban" relation by claiming that whereas it has been characterized as hierarchical (as realized by the farmsteads being required to perform corvée duty and contribute tribute to the "urban" centers), the "rural" countryside was actually organized in heterarchical terms, which he defines as a moderate form of ranking mitigated by the face-to-face domestic and wider kinship-based relations. He observes, "The built environment of the dispersed rural communities strongly indicates that some rural contexts were relatively free of centralized control. Most of the rural daily life . . . would have revolved around domestic matters that were of no consequence to regional authority or matters that were best managed by family farmers" (Mehrer 2000, 51).

He appears to be forced to characterize the autonomy of the dispersed farmsteads in practical-based terms, since he also argues that the labor necessary to support Cahokia and similar centers would have been largely derived from the residents of these dispersed "rural" villages and that this contribution would have been added to the labor and surplus produce of the "commoner" lineages permanently resident in the mound locales (Mehrer 1995, 53–54). Hence, he recognizes the essential social nature of the "rural/urban" relation as being one of juridical subordination-dominance, even as he insists that the "rural" peoples would resist this dominance by various practical-based tactics. While I find all this more than a bit puzzling, his characterization of the "rural" settlements challenges the nature of the relationship between the countryside and the mound locales postulated by Emerson and Pauketat by suggesting that it may not have been as hierarchical and dominance-based as they claim. I am in agreement with him in this regard, but for quite different reasons. Indeed, both characterizing the social nature of this relation and giving theoretical and empirical grounds for supporting this characterization are the primary focus of this book. Therefore, I shall return to examining this relationship shortly.

George Milner (1998, 3–13, 168–70) also supports the hierarchical view, but in a temperate form. For him, Cahokia represents neither the political center of a large state or statelike chiefdom nor the economic heart of a widespread interaction sphere. Instead, he argues that the mound centers across the American Bottom and along primarily the eastern side of the central Mississippi Valley were the seats of a multiplicity of competing "quasi-autonomous" complex chiefdoms (Milner 1990, 22–23; 1998, 13, fig. 1.5, 15). These individual chiefdoms waxed and waned in power and presence while, through it all, Cahokia was occupied and was the most important player, being able to sustain the majority of these neighboring chiefdoms as subordinates. In his general overview of the Mississippian period in the Southeast, Jon Muller (1997, 116, 220) takes a similar position, arguing that it is an exaggeration to characterize Cahokia as a major paramount chiefdom supported by a large population dominated by centralized political power. However, Muller seems to equivocate, since he accepts that as a paramount chiefdom, Cahokia's "organization would probably have fluctuated through time between multiple small polities, each surrounding a single small town-center, to much larger but more fragile polities containing several major town-centers within a paramount chiefdom," while also maintaining that at "the highest peak of their power, the chiefs of Cahokia *may* have played important roles in ordering the lives of as many as 20 or 30 thousand people" (Muller 1997, 223, emphasis in the original).[3]

In sum, while each interpretation characterizes the Middle Mississippian social system of the American Bottom slightly differently, the differences are largely quantitative and not qualitative. In qualitative terms, there is substantial agreement that this complex archaeological record dominated by monumental earthwork features was the material outcome of a complex set of hierarchical polities emergent from a preexisting system of simple ranked societies of the late Emergent Mississippian period or, in terms promoted by Andrew Fortier and Dale McElrath (2002, 173), of the Terminal Late Woodland period. While there is currently considerable debate over how these transformations from a simple kinship-based village system to a complex rank-ordered chiefdom system came about, there is little debate or disagreement over the real nature of this social system. That is, whether the social organization is portrayed as a complex, rigidly centralized hierarchical polity or a complex set of loosely interacting hierarchical polities, there is substantial agreement that the core social nature of this settlement system was hierarchical.

The Hermeneutic Spiral: A Critical Method

Hence, there is a profound, largely taken-for-granted unity of understanding of the essential nature and social complexity of this system. This is unfortunate because no competing social system model, as such, has been presented; for this reason, the core claim that the Mississippian period social system was non-egalitarian (with ranked classes of politically and economically dominant elite and subordinate commoners) goes largely, if not completely, unchallenged among those who are most familiar with the American Bottom archaeological record. I consider that this view, in all its variants, reigns hegemonically in American Bottom archaeology, being accepted almost axiomatically. As Emerson confidently states, "I believe that the *hierarchical nature of the Cahokia polity can be accepted as a given,* based on the existing evidence of the archaeological record. Consequently, I assume that, in keeping with the known attributes of such societies and forms of government, the Cahokian chiefly elite emphasized centripetal control of surpluses, labor, religion, and trade" (Emerson 1997c, 188, emphasis added). To reinforce their claim about this basic agreement, Pauketat and Emerson stress the harmony of vision among those who contributed to one of the more recent summaries of the state of Cahokian archaeology, of which they are the joint editors. In their words, "Cahokia, to the authors of these chapters, was about agriculture and appropriation, production and power, ideology and authority, and monuments and mobilization" (Pauketat and Emerson 1997b, 269).

While I know that there are some who would not fully agree (for example, Dean Saitta [1994, 212], who sees Cahokia as a non-exploitative communalistic social system, and Mark Mehrer [1995, 144], who, as pointed out above, argues for at least some surreptitious maintenance of autonomy for the countryside), there is widespread acceptance that the mounds were the residences of powerful and ranked corporate kinship descent groups; that elites in permanent residence at the mound centers mobilized the commoners as clients to provide the corvée labor and tributary subsistence resources required to build the mounds, temples, palaces, and palisades; and that these locales were the administrative centers of polities having defined (and presumably defended) boundaries. When new data are presented, these rarely challenge this social characterization. Instead, their presentation becomes an exercise of conforming the data to this interpretation. For example, a dual mode of building sizes becomes evidence confirming that the Lohmann and Stirling phases of Cahokia were strongly structured into elite (that is, large residential dwellings) and commoner (that is, small residential dwellings) (Pauketat 1992, 36; 1998, 87–88, 136). Similarly, the differential burial treatment displayed in Mound 72 becomes confirmation of this elite/commoner structure and thereby serves to generalize that all mortuary treatment can be divided into and accounted for in these same elite/commoner terms, and so on (Ahler 1999, 104–5; Fortier and McElrath 2002, 199; Fowler 1974, 20–22; 1991, 10; 1997, 145; Fowler et al. 1999, 158, 176–77; Knight 1997, 237; Mehrer 1995, 16; Milner 1990, 27–28; Pauketat 1992, 37; 1994, 177; 1997, 34–35; Rose 1999, 75–76; Saitta 1994, 215–16. However, James Brown [2003] has presented a very interesting counterproposal, which I discuss later).

It is preferred that an interpretive historical approach to the archaeological data have ontological models that contrast in strong rather than weak terms. Models that contrast weakly essentially agree on the fundamental properties of a social system while differing only in the details. Strong models must not only contrast in their essentials, but must also be structured in accordance with the dimensions being addressed, the range of application, and the depth of time, breadth of space, and complexity of content being addressed. Thus, strong models are characterized by having complexes of core, ancillary, and auxiliary models by which they can radically challenge each other at multiple levels and along multiple dimensions. What is shared between them is that they are addressing the same data. Over all, among contrasting strong models, the one that accounts for the same data in the most coherent and least self-contradictory manner is accepted, until another strong model is presented and is seen to do a better job.

Hence, through critical contrasting, the interpretation of the nature of the social and cultural phenomena that are represented in the archaeological record is done in a critical, self-correcting, and knowledge-productive manner. It is critical because part of challenging a model is to show where it is logically

and theoretically inadequate and where it fails to account adequately and coherently for the relevant data. It is self-correcting because, following its critique
of the opposing account, it must present an alternative grounded in the same
data sets. It is knowledge productive because this critical process ensures that
a knowledge vacuum is avoided. A useful term with which to describe this
interpretive method is the *hermeneutic spiral* (Bhaskar 1978, chapter 3; 1979,
11–28, 164–69; Byers 2004, 106–7).[4] The notion of a spiral is useful here since
it suggests that competing models generate a spiralling argument or debate.
Each spiral loop terminates, for the moment, with new knowledge. In these
terms, I will treat the above theoretical characterization of Cahokia and the
American Bottom (in all its versions) as a strong model and will refer to it in
terms of its central themes: the *hierarchical monistic modular polity account* of
the American Bottom. The alternative strong model that challenges it (and is
the purpose of this book) I term the *heterarchical polyistic locale-centric account*.
I initiate the elucidation of these two accounts below by defining the central
concepts of the hierarchical monistic modular polity account, followed by the
heterarchical polyistic locale-centric account.

The Hierarchical Monistic Modular Polity Account

The primary or core concept of the hierarchical monistic modular polity account treats Cahokia and the regional American Bottom social system as having
a dominance-based hierarchy of elites and commoners that largely corresponds
to a settlement hierarchy of ranked mound-and-town locales and subordinated
"rural" dispersed villages. The former are seen as composed of a core of ruling
elite lineages permanently residing in these centers, along with their subordinate client commoner lineages, while the outlying dispersed villages are treated
as permanently occupied by "rural commoners" under local elite supervision
and dominance, mediated largely through the civic and ceremonial-cult nodal
locales. Indeed, the peripheral rural–center core relation might be characterized almost in feudal terms. Certainly, Vernon James Knight Jr. (1997, 237–38)
constantly makes reference to the elites as the nobles or the nobility of Cahokia. Even among those willing to treat this social system in less radically
hierarchical terms, there is general agreement as to the existence of some form
of social stratification of the total population along "rural" commoner and "urban" elite lines (Muller 1997, 119–21, 156–57).

The monistic nature of this orthodox model is another core conceptual
theme by which it characterizes Cahokia and its regional social system. By *monistic* I mean a social system in which a single social structural axis constitutes

the major institutional framework of the society; typically, for preindustrial societies, this is assumed to be anchored by kinship and, in a hierarchical monistic system, constituted as a system of ranked clans, lineages, and extended and nuclear families. This system is ordered into some form of dominant/subordinate class or classlike structure with economic as well as correlated social stratification. As my previous assertion suggests, I believe it is safe to say that this hierarchical monistic view is universally accepted by all interpreters of the Cahokian American Bottom archaeological record: kinship is basic, and the hierarchy is one of ranked kinship groups. If nonkinship social structures are recognized, they are subsumed as cults or warrior orders that serve and are subordinate to the leaders of the elite lineages (Emerson 1997a, 217–18, 225–27; 1997c, 35, 39–40).

Another essential conceptual component of this hegemonic account is the notion that the social system was modular in nature. As I define it, a modular social system is one based on exclusive territories, each territory owned and controlled by the monistic corporate groups that occupy it, thereby forming a polity. Since the polity is also often internally ranked, this suggests a nesting of modular polities making up a complex hierarchically ordered modular territory. In the case of a rigid hierarchical module, the total or near-total region would be embraced by the dominant political authority, such as Cahokia, constituting a single territorial module with defended boundaries and buffering frontier zones. It would be internally divided into ranked and nested boundaried modules ruled by competing and intermarrying chiefly elite lineages. In the case of a flexible, quasi-autonomous set of competing chiefdoms, the nesting of a lower-ranked modular polity within another would be historically contingent with changes, flip-flops, and so on, characterizing the history of intermodular and intramodular polity relations (Milner 1990, 21, 27; 1998, 12–14, fig. 1.5). Whether modules were rigidly or flexibly nested, any given territorial module was, in general, further divided into lands whose lesser owners or tenant lineages owed allegiance to the authorities of the local modular chiefdom system, right down to the individual family with its tenure of local fields ensured by its subordinate attachment to the local landowning or landcontrolling chiefly lineage.

In short, all the different interpretations under this view implicitly or explicitly rely on this hierarchical monistic modular polity theoretical framework. As I pointed out earlier, rather than exhibiting radical disagreement in this area, disputes simply address the extent and degree of the hierarchy (two tiered, three tiered, four tiered), the nature of the monism (ranked lineages, subordinate families linked as clients to elite lineages, non-kin-based cultlike sodalities subsumed to ranked lineages), and the extent and scope of the modular polities (small, competing chiefdoms, a single complex modular polity internally ranked and encapsulating the American Bottom, an extensive centralized modular polity reaching across the central Mississippi Valley, and so on).

When an independent argument is assumed to be needed to justify the basic hierarchical monistic modular polity framework, Cahokia is usually chosen as the major grouping, and the primary tactic is to invoke as prima facie evidence the labor that the mounds must have required. Monks Mound, along with the other hundred-plus mounds, as well as the palisade around the Grand Plaza, the levelling and filling required to construct this plaza, the large buildings that we know were constructed on the platform mounds and those found in more residential areas, as well as the great woodhenge circles, are pointed to as requiring massive amounts of labor. It is then argued that such labor required organization to schedule the labor tasks and discipline the laborers, provide the logistics of procuring food to feed them, and so on. Therefore, the argument goes, this organizational component necessarily required a leadership structure—and this structure, alienated from the mass of workers, would necessarily have had to be authoritative and would have had power over the laborers. Hence, ideological negotiation, imposition, and even coercion are assumed to have been necessary. All this is used to warrant the conclusion that only a strongly stratified, monistic modular political social system with a centralized decision-making power-over authority could have made the existence of Cahokia possible.

This is a persuasive argument, and (unlike Milner, who claims that Cahokia and similar mound sites required only a modest amount of labor for rather short periods by many individuals) I accept the claim that these mounds and associated features and facilities represent major inputs of labor, some of which were rather drawn out, while others were probably rather focused and short term.[5] As such, construction of those sites would have required organization of a high order and the drawing inward of considerable and varied labor resources from across the American Bottom and, in all likelihood, also reaching into areas of the surrounding upland regions. However, it does not follow from this that only a centralized hierarchical monistic modular polity type of social system could support or, more importantly, promote and realize such a monumental construction program. In short, the quantitative aspect of Cahokia cannot be used by itself to sustain a claim of a necessary connection between the archaeological record and the type of social organization that was responsible.

This hierarchical monistic modular polity account in all its versions has another major difficulty, this being accounting for the transformation of the egalitarian, kinship-based social system of the Late Woodland American Bottom into the radically non-egalitarian but still kinship-based hierarchical social system of the Mississippian period. Fortier and McElrath (2002, 176–77) have recently summarized the current status in this regard, arguing that there are two opposed solutions to this quandary. They term these the *gradualist evolutionary* and the *revolutionary historical* solutions, the latter being the one that they favor. They have carried out a comprehensive critique of the former as part of promoting the latter, stressing that the gradualist-evolutionary account has been the dominant framework since the 1980s. In their terms, this approach places primary causal weight on changes in the objective material factors, such as demographic expansion, environmental stresses and changes, and the imperatives of economic exchange. Hence, gradualism assumes that the convergence of changes in these factors is what stimulates human populations to adapt responsively. In these terms, therefore, the gradualist view claims that the abandoning of egalitarianism and the embracing of hierarchy was simply the most efficient social response to the convergence of these particular factors.

Fortier and McElrath then draw on the work of Pauketat and Emerson and (using Pauketat's terminology) present the alternative revolutionary historical approach by characterizing the processes generating the empirical data of the Mississippian emergence in ruptural terms, as mapping and manifesting a rather abrupt and, indeed, socially cataclysmic transformation. They minimize the significance of such exogenous factors as environmental and demographic changes, not by denying the relevance of these factors but by emphasizing that these can only be necessary and not sufficient causes of cultural transformations. Instead, Fortier and McElrath stress the role of ideology—understood as collective beliefs, values, and attitudes—as dominant. Hence for them Cahokia was the material outcome of the pursuit of dominance by an emergent elite promoting elite sectoral interests through ideologically inspired and driven political strategies, simultaneously generating a commoner class. Invoking Pauketat's "Big Bang" thesis, Fortier and McElrath (2002, 203) conclude that the emergence of Cahokia occurred as part of an abrupt and "profound social upheaval."

The approach I favor is also historical, but, as I make abundantly clear in this book, it strongly disagrees with a number of the positions taken by the historical processualist approach, such as the tendency for the latter to deny social developmental significance to the ecological dimension of human culture and society and the contrasting of gradual to ruptural transformation, not simply treating these as mutually exclusive but claiming that only the latter is a realistic account. Furthermore, while historical processualism rests strongly on the necessity of recognizing and treating human agency and practice as central in explanation (certainly a necessary dimension), I contend in this book that historical processualists have inadequately theorized these key notions as well as the importantly related concepts of ideology and cultural traditions. I further contend that this inadequate theorization is at the basis of the denial of historical relevance to the ecological dimension, almost forcing historical processualism to promote a rather radical subject-object dualism, thereby characterizing history as a series of ideologically inspired and abrupt social structural discontinuities and ruptures.

This gradual evolutionary/abrupt historical processual debate does raise an interesting question. Is it possible that I have misconstrued the situation? That is, does the debate itself invalidate my above claim, such that, as disputants, the two groups actually do not share the orthodox view of Cahokia and the American Bottom? I do not think so. In fact, rather than invalidating my claim, the substance of the gradual/ruptural debate confirms my point since at issue is how an egalitarian monistic modular polity type of social system was able to transform into a hierarchical monistic modular polity type of social system. Therefore, the debate presupposes a rather firm agreement on the basic nature of the social system undergoing change.

The Heterarchical Polyistic Locale-Centric Account

The core of this book is the critical presentation and empirical grounding of the heterarchical polyistic locale-centric account. As I define it, a polyistic social system is one that is based on more than one fundamental social structural axis. While kinship certainly will be an essential part of a polyistic system, other socially recognized structural axes, such as gender and generation, also serve as constitutive bases for the formation of social organizations other than and in addition to the kinship-based types. In an important sense, such groups are bound by companionship, the complementary alternative of kinship. Sets of same-age/same-gender peers constitute companions that form groupings generally referred to in anthropology as sodalities. The complementary nature of kinship and companionship sustains and is sustained by an arm's-length relationship between kinship and companionship groups that is best characterized as mutually recognized relative autonomy. The kinship-based and companionship-based groups constituting a polyistic social system recognize each other as autonomous in the sense that each treats the affairs of the other as outside its responsibility or authority. Hence, kinship groups, such as clans, do not typically intervene in the affairs of sodalities and vice versa. This does not mean that there are two separate social systems. Rather, in any given region there is a single social system constituted of the relations between these two autonomous institutions. Therefore, the local regional social system would comprise at least two parallel and autonomous social organizational networks that did, however, share the same population: that is, the individuals making up a population in a given region, such as the American Bottom, typically would participate in and be full members of both types of institutional groups, at least during some part of their lifetime.

Importantly, the mutually recognized autonomy between the two networks, kinship and companionship groups, is at the core of a heterarchical polyistic social system. Since I am arguing that autonomy, and not equality, is the operative principle of a heterarchical polyistic social system, differentiation and inequality not only are recognized but indeed often play a critical role in the organizational interaction. Furthermore, because of the mutual recognition among components of their respective autonomy, successful interaction between them, for example, to effect a regionwide collective activity, entails decision making based on consensus and mutual respect. Without consensus, there can be no effective collective action carried out by the parties constituting the social system. I elaborate on the implications of this core notion of autonomy for understanding heterarchy later.

As I also clarify in detail later, I treat the American Bottom from the Late Woodland through to the Mississippian period as occupied by a heterarchical polyistic social system that historically develops through several stages of settlement orientations, with Cahokia as, in many ways, the culmination of this process. Therefore, in an important sense this characterization already dispenses with the question of how the American Bottom Late Woodland kinship-based social systems could have become complex, since, in fact, a heterarchical polyistic social system is complex in its very nature. The questions that are raised, then, are how does such a system emerge, what kinds of objective and intersubjective properties promote these changes, and what are the empirical data that serve as evidence that such a system actually existed? The rest of this book is the extended answer to these questions.

To sketch out the initial answers, I must first note that a heterarchical social system based upon autonomous kinship and companionship groups typically generates a range of specialized locales, usually domestic-based kinship and ritual-based companionship locales. Generically, I term the former *clans* and *lineages* and the latter *cult sodalities.* Such a social system, complex in its own right, is best conceptualized as multiple, parallel, and autonomous networks of specialized locales. Within this framework, social systems are networks of locales—and, of course, the spatial extension of a social system will tend to be relative to the nature of the groups occupying the locales of these networks. Logically presupposing and underwriting social systems based on open networks of locales linked by paths is the notion that territories are also open or inclusive. That is, in contrast to the notion of exclusive territorialism presupposed by and central to monistic modular polity systems, polyistic locale-centric social systems presuppose the notion (and its realization in practice) of inclusive territorialism. Therefore, in a heterarchical polyistic locale-centric social system, while the organic limitations and imperatives of human biological capacities will define the practical limits of territories for any given population, there will be no juridically defined territories with distinctive, formally recognized boundaries that are intrinsic to one network and that separate one network from the others. Instead, the locales are connected by paths into interrelated networks, and these networks of paths will be only roughly discriminated into zones that come under the responsibility of the occupying groups and, thereby, constitute their domains of active responsibility. Where the responsibility for paths shifts from one locale to the next is always somewhat vague since, in effect, there is always a sense of joint responsibility among locale groups for the paths that link them. A heterarchical polyistic locale-centric social system, therefore, is constituted of autonomous groups responsible for and occupying a range of different types of socially defined locales linked by recognized paths for which they jointly care.

Deontic Ecology

These two accounts constitute complementary opposites of the same archaeological record of the American Bottom. The premises that act as the framework of the hierarchical monistic modular polity account presuppose a more basic framework, the theoretical adequacy of which has rarely even been questioned. I term it the *exclusive territorial/proprietorial domain* paradigm. Similarly, the heterarchical polyistic locale-centric account presupposes an equivalently broad and fundamental theoretical framework, which I term the *inclusive territorial/custodial domain* paradigm (Byers 2004, 9–10, 127–55). The key descriptive terms making up the titles of these two paradigms were carefully chosen to highlight the ecological aspect of the primary theoretical framework while emphasizing territoriality as being socially constructed. That is, I assert here that the relation that humans hold with the land, generally termed *tenure,* is an intrinsic extension of their cultural and social structures. Indeed, the human-environment relation is treated here as always a socialized and enculturated natural relation.

This social approach to ecology draws on Tim Ingold's (1987, 130–64) theoretical insights on tenure among foragers, pastoralists, and farmers. A central part of his thesis is to characterize tenure as the social relation that humans culturally construct with the environment. Taking a cross-cultural, anthropological perspective, he contrasts the typical inclusive territorialism of foragers and pastoralists to the exclusive territorialism of farmers. Inclusive territorialism is based on the premise that land is in the public domain and no party has the right to exclude others from the proper exploitation of the resources. Exclusive territorialism, in contrast, is the basis of treating land as a private domain. These two types of territorialism ground contrasting tenures that can be termed *custodial* and *proprietorial tenurial systems,* respectively, and presupposing these contrasting forms of tenure are contrasting types of world beliefs or cosmologies; contrasting deontic or ethical, moral, legal, and social constitutive principles (that is to say, ethos); and contrasting worldviews and ideologies, that is, in total, contrasting types of cultural traditions.

In these terms, instead of the ecological practices and relations of an occupying population being treated as somehow acultural (or being as natural as the resources that are exploited by them), the occupants are always constrained and enabled in these practices by their cultural traditions. I call this approach *deontic ecology.* Deontics constitute the ethical, moral, legal, and constitutive dimension of social life. Interrelated entitlements, rights, duties, obligations, responsibilities, and privileges—and the socially recognized principles underwriting them—make up the deontic sphere, and from this are generated the social positions that relate parties to each other and to the world around them. Presupposing the deontic sphere are the collective understandings about the world and its nature and of how humans are situated in it. Therefore, the premise that necessarily follows is that a deontic ecology incorporates the ecological practices within the social and cultural structures of a community.

Since I have already given a general overview of the current status of the archaeology of the American Bottom, I will leave more detailed description and analyses as part of the hermeneutic spiral method and focus in the next few chapters on outlining a preliminary theoretical sketch of deontic ecology and the necessary background notions of cosmology, ethos, worldview, and ideology. At the same time I will elucidate the two contrasting paradigms. This will require considerable theoretical discussion. Deontic ecology cannot be treated independently of a theoretical view of action as symbolically constituted, and while certainly fully accepting the instrumental nature of material culture, such a view also requires treating material culture in symbolic terms. This necessitates an outline sketch of a theory of the nature of the symbolic usage of material culture, which I term the *symbolic pragmatic view*. The position that will be presented here is that symbolic pragmatics are constitutive of the action nature of regular ecological behaviors. Therefore, a fuller elucidation of practice requires summarizing a theory of action and agency. Using this as basic, I then develop a general theory of cultural traditions treated as relatively autonomous forms of collective beliefs, desires, perceptions, and intentions, which, respectively, I term *cosmology, ethos, worldview,* and *ideology.* This complex and well-motivated deontic ecological theory can then be used to construct the fundamental theoretical axioms and assumptions of both paradigms.

Following this theoretical elucidation, and to conform to the hermeneutic spiral methodology, the procedure I utilize starts with a critical analysis of the hierarchical monistic modular polity account of the pre-Mississippian period and Mississippian period archaeological records of the American Bottom. This is followed by a presentation of the alternative heterarchical polyistic locale-centric account by means of a series of interpretive models. Each model addresses a particular aspect of the postulated social system and is grounded on the relevant set of empirical data. The book terminates in an overall comparative critique of the two accounts, created by addressing important puzzles that have emerged and examining how each account explains these. The conclusion that follows is that, while still requiring much more work and development, the heterarchical polyistic locale-centric account comes off as a more coherent interpretation and explanation of the American Bottom archaeological record of the Mississippian period and its historical-cultural roots than does the hierarchical monistic modular polity account.

2

The Deontic Ecological Perspective

As I observe in chapter 1, the deontic sphere of a social system is constituted of the moral, ethical, and legal principles and the complex set of rules and protocols that are basic to the social structure of a community. What is rarely noted in most ecological studies, however, is that deontics are also basic to the subsistence and settlement practices of a community and therefore constitute these human-environment interactions as social as well as ecological in nature (Ingold 1987, 130–64; Byers 2004, chapter 6). I argue in the first chapter that the hierarchical monistic modular polity account draws its basic premises from a more general perspective, the exclusive territorial/proprietorial domain paradigm (Byers 2004, 8–9, 141–55). A central notion of this paradigm is exclusive control and use of a territory and/or its resources by an occupying group. Because of this, the group is constituted as the collective "owners," that is, they can be treated as a proprietorial corporation, and the territory over which they have collective use is deemed to be their proprietorial domain.

This paradigm has become almost second nature to many archaeologists in interpreting the patterning of the North American archaeological record generated by settlement and subsistence practices. This influence has been extended to characterizing the relation between mortuary practices and territorialism, as exemplified formally in a series of articles by Douglas Charles and Jane Buikstra elaborating on the social nature of the Archaic burial mounds of the central and lower Illinois Valley (Charles 1985, 223–24; 1995, 78–80, 86; Charles and Buikstra 1983, 121–24; Charles et al. 1986, 458–59, 471). Interestingly, Charles and Buikstra derive their basic premise from the work on Mississippian period cemeteries in the lower Illinois Valley by Lynne Goldstein (1980, 7–8; 1981, 53–54; 1995, 116–18). Goldstein characterizes a cemetery as a site that is used exclusively for funerary-mortuary deposits. As such, she argues, it probably, although not conclusively, marked the group responsible for it as constituting a proprietorial corporate descent group organized, most likely, into a lineage-clan system: "In brief, not all corporate groups that control crucial resources through lineal descent will maintain formal, exclusive disposal areas for their dead. But if a formal, bounded disposal area exists and if it is used *exclusively* for the dead, the society is likely to have corporate groups organized by lineal descent. The more organized and formal the disposal area, the more conclusive this inference" (Goldstein 1980, 8, emphasis in original). Charles and Buikstra (1983, 121–24) develop this claim by identifying the Archaic collective burial locales distributed primarily along the western bluffs overlooking the lower and central Illinois River valley as "cemeteries" marking the territories surrounding each as the corporate property of the living descendants of those buried in them.

The most important point that their analyses implicates for my purpose is not only that there is a linkage between mortuary practices, economy, and ecology, but also that this linkage is deontic in nature. Of course, in this particular approach, a functional or instrumental relation is emphasized. Charles and Buikstra treat the deontic aspect of the mortuary sphere as a way in which a people recruit the symbolic sphere to serve practical ecological and economic needs, namely, stabilizing exclusive control of the resources of defined territories by legitimizing this control. Implicated here, then, is a separation of mortuary and ecological practices along the symbolic/instrumental division, with the assumption being that the deontics of social life properly belong to the symbolic sphere while ecological and related material practices remain firmly in the instrumental sphere. Hence, the "cemetery," a critical institution of the mortuary sphere, is recruited by symbolic means for its deontic meaning, while the ecological engagements it presupposes are assumed to be purely practical. However, as noted above, rather than maintaining this separation of the symbolic and the instrumental, I extend the symbolic-deontic sphere to include the ecological. That is, just as a symbolic treatment constitutes mortuary behaviors as mortuary rituals, so the symbolic sphere also constitutes the ecological behaviors as the (practical) type of social activities they are intended to be. If this is the case, then the symbolic sphere is an intrinsic component of the ecological sphere and, by extension, of economic and political strategies. Therefore, while Andrew Fortier and Dale McElrath, for example, exclude or certainly distance the role that ecological constraints might have as sufficient causes of historical processes (2002, 173, 178–82), the historical approach that I advocate makes these a core symbolic-material causal factor of the transformations that brought about the Mississippian period.

To postulate that a prehistoric people performed mortuary practices by recruiting cosmological beliefs about ancestors and their special powers to warrant exclusive corporate rights to territory simultaneously entails that these same people would also recognize the difference between, for example, hunting as opposed to poaching of animals, gathering as opposed to pilfering of plant resources, and occupying as opposed to squatting on the land. This must be the case, since to claim ownership of territory and its resources entails differentiating between who may and who may not exploit the resources—the former being hunters, gatherers, and dwellers; the latter, poachers, pilferers, and squatters—and this means discriminating between appropriate and unacceptable forms of exploitation of these resources. Therefore, part of being a member-in-good-standing of a proprietorial corporate group entails experiencing ongoing occupation of and foraging on this group's land as dwelling, hunting, and gathering rather than as squatting, poaching, and pilfering. In short, subsistence and settlement practices have irreducibly deontic as well as objective moments.

Critically important here is to note that the foraging behaviors performed by both interlopers and domain occupants are objectively the same. Therefore, the differences that make the interlopers' behaviors count as poaching, pilfering, and squatting and that make the owners' identical behaviors hunting, gathering, and dwelling are purely deontic and intersubjective in nature. That is, although such actions as hunting and poaching are grounded on the same range of objective behaviors, they cannot be reduced to these behaviors. Rather, as I express this concept below, the style with which the behaviors are performed and seen to be performed is what constitutes them and makes them count as the types of actions that they are perceived and experienced to be. For this reason, in general, to have one's objective behaviors recognized and to experience them as hunting rather than as poaching, they must display tangible components that express and manifest the social standing and status of the actors. This is not simply a matter of transmitting deontic information. This is a matter of exercising social powers by means of manifesting or expressing the deontic sources or bases for them. It is these deontic-based social powers that are transformative in nature, and the transformative moment is intersubjective and communicative. What the expressing or disclosing does is elicit from relevant parties the recognition that those performing the behaviors actually occupy the proper social positions that endow them with the social powers in the way of rights and privileges, duties and responsibilities. Furthermore, the expressivity also manifests the appropriate intentions and know-how of the subjects. The simultaneous recognition of the person's social position (member of the proprietorial corporation) and appropriate intentions (hunting, gathering, dwelling) constitute the behaviors as hunting rather than poaching, as gathering rather than pilfering, as dwelling rather than squatting. The recognition by socially relevant others is critical to constituting the action experience itself and therefore to constituting the behavior as the social act intended. Hence actions are normally grounded on actual behaviors performed in social contexts.

Since the dual and simultaneous expressing of the nontangible states of social position and action intention is critical to constituting an agent's behaviors as the types of social acts intended and perceived, as such, then the behavior must disclose or manifest the appropriate deontic position and action intentions of the subjects; this entails that the behavior must display patterning and be mediated by tangible forms that are simultaneously symbolic as well as instrumental. That is, not only must the spear bear properties that afford spearing, as such, but also it must display properties that disclose the intentions and social standing of the user. The latter properties constitute the expressive symbolic moment of material cultural items, and they are critical but not the only media by which to constitute the ecological behaviors as the type of social acts that were intended. Indeed, since both the hunter and the stranger may display the same range of competence, the material behaviors of interlopers may only be able to be perceived as squatting, poaching, and pilfering because they do not display the proper symbolic forms (that is, the ecological instruments bearing recognizable style) that manifest the deontics of domain membership. It also follows that both parties—proprietors and squatters—recognize the existence of territorial boundaries, since these are deontic divisions that exist as symbolically expressed in the cemeteries. Therefore, boundaries expressed in symbolic mortuary media also become the basis for an aggressive posture toward the outer social world as a characteristic aspect of the ethos. Hence, when an exclusive territorial group perceives another as squatting (that is, as transgressing their boundaries), its members will ritually invoke the ancestors for their support while simultaneously arming themselves with the appropriately styled weaponry to punish and eject the interlopers.

SYMBOLIC PRAGMATICS

In the above, I emphasize the way in which materials displaying formal properties are used as symbols, even when these materials have properties designed to serve certain instrumental goals of the users. In trying to make sense of the symbolic utilization of material artifacts, most archaeologists draw an analogy with words, typically treating words as referential symbols. Therefore, since it is assumed that we get at the meaning of an utterance by asking what the utterance is referring to or designating, it is also assumed that we can get at the symbolic meaning of material culture by asking what particular items are used to designate. I term this identification of the symbolic meaning of material culture with the referential meaning of speech the *referential fallacy*. It is a fallacy because it systematically mischaracterizes the way in which humans use the symbolic aspect of material culture, and it therefore leads archaeologists into characterizing material cultural symbolism as a second-class or supplementary form of referring. We might succeed in convincing ourselves that this is plausible with regard to small portable items, such as the styles of arrow points (for example, style A "refers to" a member of Tribe A), but it becomes somewhat unpersuasive when applied to monumental features, such as platform mounds or embankment earthworks.

This is not to claim that speech is a poor guide in this matter. Rather, the root of the referential fallacy is that it uses the wrong meaning of speech by which to model the way in which humans use the symbolic aspect of material culture. Reference is a very important form of word usage, without a doubt. However, we also use words to perform acts—speech acts, such as giving commands and making promises. This major dimension of speech meaning is termed the *pragmatic* or *action usage*. Since archaeologists traditionally analyze material culture in action or pragmatic terms, in that the type of behavioral interventions that items mediated can be inferred through examination of their objective properties, it makes sense to use the pragmatic, not the referential, aspect of language to model the symbolic meaning of material culture. In brief, archaeologists ought to treat material culture not only as instrumental devices but also as symbolic pragmatic or action-constitutive devices.

Under the appropriate and meaningful conditions, by stringing our words together according to standard syntactical rules, we can give orders, make reports, or declare and bring into existence states of affairs, such as wars, peace, marriages, and so on. At the same time, of course, we also convey information by means of reference about war, peace, marriage, and so on. The point is, in speaking, we usually do both simultaneously; that is, we generate both referential and pragmatic meaning. However, these can be analytically separated. To illustrate, note the two following utterances.

1. The soldiers attacked the enemy hill.
2. You soldiers are to attack the enemy hill.

These two utterances can be seen quite clearly to be different and similar at the same time. The similarity is rooted in the semantic content (its referential aspect), which is the same for both, each being about soldiers attacking a hill held by an enemy. Therefore, we can see that the propositional content of the two utterances is effectively the same. Why we also see that they are different is that they do different things. The first utterance is a simple speech act of reporting the activities of the soldiers. The second utterance is an order. That is, it does not report or assert but orders what the soldiers are to do, and the propositional contents are used here to specify to the soldiers just what they are to do. Although the speaker-hearer relation is important in reports, in giving an order the same relation (for example, officer-soldier relation) is critical since it is the deontic constitutive component by which the utterance is endowed with action meaning. In this case, an essential part of the directive speech act is that it is an officer giving an order to soldiers. By the speaker's and hearers' occupying those positions and by the speaker's using the proper syntax, both understand that the utterance counts as an order. Its being an order stipulates its pragmatic meaning. What about the semantic meaning? This is subordinate to or subsumed under the pragmatic meaning in that the officer uses and relies on the semantics of the words to specify what the soldiers are to do by way of fulfilling the order. The meaning that the above two utterances share, then, is the propositional aspect (and this is expressed by the semantic content of the major words), and the meaning they contrast on is the pragmatic aspect, the first being a report, or an assertive speech, and the second being an order, or a directive speech act.

Speech acts are not something we do from time to time. We constantly perform speech activity whenever we make meaningful utterances (vocalized, written, or signed). John Searle (1983, 4–13) argues that there are probably five basic types of speech acts—assertives, declaratives, directives, commissives, and expressives—and each is a real social action in that by performing them in the proper circumstances and according to the appropriate pragmatic rules, the speakers reproduce and/or change the social world, the world of deontic relations. Commissives, for example, are the acts of promising, betting, agreeing, avowing, swearing (oaths), making alliances, and so on, and these are basic forms of constituting and reproducing social relations. By saying "You're on" in response to another's saying to you, "I bet you that X," both speakers have committed themselves to a course of interaction. The betting procedure is a symbolically constructed interaction, and it makes a difference in the social world of those making the bet. That is, the pragmatic rules of language mediated by and reproducing social structures are the means by which we constitute our speech utterances as the speech actions we intend, such as betting, promising, and ordering, and the ongoing performing of the total set of speech acts is a critically important constitutive component of social reproduction and/or transformation.

Unfortunately, if the term *pragmatic* is used at all in archaeology, it is usually synonymous with the term *practical*, so that, in fact, the "pragmatics" of material culture are reduced to the functional-instrumental meanings. However, if we use the term *pragmatic* in the above sociolinguistic sense, then we get to its really useful meaning in archaeology, this being delineating that aspect of material culture by which material behaviors are constituted as intended social activities. Since the constitutive moments of social position and action intention must always be expressed or disclosed by tangible forms, then both must be mediated by an aspect of the artifacts, features, and facilities (including instrumental tools) that we regularly use. Although the term *symbolic pragmatics* is redundant (in that, as defined above, the term *pragmatics* is already conventional), I think that using this terminology to speak of the pragmatics of material culture is justified. Thus what archaeologists usually refer to as material cultural style can be treated as the material mode of symbolic pragmatic expression. Through styles as our expressive symbolic pragmatic media, we manifest the deontics (social position and intentions) that are basic to constituting our material behaviors as the types of material actions that they are.

Pragmatic meaning hinges on expressing collective mental states rather than referring to external objects. This distinction is in accordance with Charles Taylor's (1985b, 248–55) argument that there are two forms of meaning: expressive and designative. The former works by manifesting and invoking what it represents; the latter, as noted above, by designating, pointing to, and referring to what it represents. When we use words to describe the animals we see and where we saw them, we are using words referentially. However, when we smile in response to someone's comments, we are not referring at all. A smile—even when it is simply a "polite" smile—expresses, manifests, discloses, and makes present to relevant others a person's mental and emotional state. "What expression manifests can only be manifested in expression" (Taylor 1985c, 219). It would be a serious mistake, therefore, to claim that the smile and what it is about can be separated, for example, by saying that, in smiling, the person is designating or referring to her/his emotional state. Certainly, one can through descriptive terms make reference to one's emotional state. But smiling, as such, is expressive of a conscious state, and, of course, it works pragmatically in that

the complex of behavioral streams that accompanies the smile is partly constituted as the type of social action it is by the expression, for example, a greeting
(smile) instead of a threat (frown).

I wish to assert that it is precisely in this expressive manner that we use material things as pragmatic symbols. The person legitimately wearing a sheriff's
badge is not referring to the position of "sheriff." Rather, she/he is manifesting
the position and, in manifesting it, is expressing her/his claim to be occupying
it (Byers 1999a, 270–72). Warrants and authoritative documentation are material artifacts that in general have this expressive-pragmatic meaning or sense.
That is to say, the use of symbolic items such as badges, warrants, and other
types of authoritative materials invokes in our collective understanding the
social reality that they represent, and this is the basis of their social as well as
action-constitutive power. Of course, some of the words that are inscribed on
warrants are used referentially. For example, an arrest warrant usually bears the
name of the person who is to be arrested. However, these are part of specifying
the party whose physical seizure will count as an arrest by which to fulfill the
order of the court as expressed in the warrant. That is, as in the above case of
the officer's giving an order, the semantic meaning of the words makes up the
propositional content, and this specifies the conditions that must be realized
for the warrant to be fulfilled. This referential meaning, therefore, has to be
considered in addition to but subsumed under the expressive symbolic pragmatic meaning of the document. The latter is what makes the document what
it is: a court warrant. The warrant is experienced as manifesting and thereby
making present or presencing the authority of the court where and when it is
used. Thus, while referential symbols substitute for that which is not present,
expressive symbols presence that which can only be known but not be seen to
be present.

Since the action or pragmatic nature of the warrant is what I claim is its
relevant expressive symbolic meaning, referring to it as a symbolic pragmatic
device seems appropriate. As I assert above, since any human society will differentiate between hunting and poaching, gathering and pilfering, storing and
hoarding, dwelling and squatting, and so on, it follows that these ecological
practices must be symbolically as well as practically mediated. Thus, tools used
for hunting must not only be efficient practical devices, they must also be effective symbolic pragmatic devices. In this important deontic-constitutive sense,
they are simultaneously hunting tools and hunting "licenses" or "warrants."
Furthermore, strange styles mark persons as interlopers, that is, as potential
poachers, pilferers, and squatters, and the wearers/bearers of such strange ma-

terials carry the onus of proving otherwise. Therefore, in the symbolic pragmatic view, not only are cemeteries and other material features and facilities warrants or, generically, symbolic pragmatic devices, but also all the artifactual categories that bear stylistic variability—hunting gear, pottery, beads, and earrings—are potential bearers of different types and degrees of warranting power. Not only can we not divorce ecological practices from deontics, but also we cannot divorce ecological practices from stylistics, since the deontics are disclosed, endowed, and manifested by means of style, thereby eliciting from all relevant parties recognition and agreement that the killing performed counts as hunting rather than as poaching. If style serves to constitute material cultural items as the primary symbolic pragmatic devices by which deontic, action-constitutive structures are realized in action, not only mortuary practices but even everyday subsistence and settlement practices implicate an ethos, and the latter entails a cosmology or collective world belief. This is the core premise of a deontic ecological approach.

TERRITORIALISM AND TENURE

As noted above, the appropriate term with which to characterize the deontic nature of the social relation a group holds with its territory is *tenure*. If ecological practices cannot be divorced from ethos and cosmology, then neither can tenure. Claiming that people perceive themselves as owning land, a particular form of tenure, presupposes a particular ethos and cosmology that they must also hold. In this case, the central premise that makes "owning" land possible is the cosmological principle that the world is simply a highly complex assortment of essentially inert objects and nonliving states and processes that can be manipulated and used by conscious humans to serve their exclusive interests. Since in this cosmology there is no inherent relation between land and humans, the founder principle or "finders-keepers" principle becomes the basis of usage, and this promotes excluding "second-comers." This transforms into rights of exclusion that are strengthened qualitatively and quantitatively when they can be anchored in a deep history of usage. Thus, under the exclusive territorial/proprietorial domain paradigm, ancestors are the "original" users of the land and therefore the "original" proprietors, and their descendants acquire their preexisting rights merely through ancestral assignment by means of kinship-based inheritance, this assignment being reproduced in the symbolically constituted activity of cemetery burial.

However, we know that preindustrial peoples typically experience the world as having an all-pervasive sacred dimension. Therefore, if they were to experience the world and its elements as separable, divisible, humanly ownable, and exclusive to particular people and parties, then they would also believe that whatever humans can physically do to the world, these interventions modify only its transeunt, objective, tangible properties and not its essential, sacred nature. The latter must be seen as beyond the reach of ordinary human actions. Thus, for a preindustrial people to practice exclusive territorialism and maintain proprietorial domains constituting modular polities, they must also believe in a certain type of world sacredness, since, for ownership per se to be possible, the sacred dimension must be believed to be a transcendent property of the cosmos, a property that, while essential to existence, nevertheless is "out-of-phase" with the transeunt, objective properties with which humans engage in everyday life. If exclusive tenure is to exist in a preindustrial social world, this transcendentalism is particularly critical, because having exclusive control of a part of the natural world is conceivable only if the essential sacredness of the world is believed to be separate from and immune to the mundane, transeunt properties. Only then can humans take themselves to be able to unproblematically manipulate, modify, and even destroy parts of the transeunt, tangible world—since doing so will have no impact on the transcendental sacredness from which the natural order is derived.

I term this type of collective world belief a *transcendental cosmology.* By virtue of having a transcendental cosmology, the people believe that the sacred enters into the relations that humans have with the world in the form of a transcendent Creator/Giver who endows (usually selected) humans with the exclusive right to control particular objective components of the world. Hence, a strong sacred/secular dualism is accepted, and the founder principle comes to be expressed as a special relation between the sacred and the human group. Typically, the transcendental nature of the sacred is key to hierarchical structuring; indeed, the mortuary perspective developed by Charles and Buikstra (1983) presupposes such a hierarchy since the ancestors are not the creators of the world but, in virtue of their original occupancy and usage, have been recipients of the land owing to the beneficence of the Creator, and they, in turn, as spiritual essences, are the givers or assignors of the exclusive access to and use of these particular territories to their descendants. As a mode of sustaining this assignment, their physical aspects (for example, their bones) dwell in the mortuary locale, although their essential spiritual aspects may travel freely, unimpeded by the limitations of the material body.

That prehistoric North American peoples held proprietorial tenure is, I believe, a largely taken-for-granted presupposition that informs much of the interpretation of the social systems of the Late Woodland, Emergent Mississippian, and Mississippian periods outlined in the preceding chapter. Hence, the notions of exclusive territorialism and proprietorial domains (the latter owned and controlled by corporate kinship groups) operate as the conceptual background to the hierarchical monistic modular polity account. Correlated with this proprietorship is the increasing focus on ritual that, in John Kelly's terms (1990a, 92–93), had fertility of the corporate kinship-based community's (exclusive) land as its primary purpose. The fertility rites were carried out in the square or plaza so that, in effect, they operated to legitimize ownership of the surrounding land. With the development of the community plan in the George Reeves phase, the previously implicit hierarchical order was explicitly claimed, again implicating a ranked set of corporate proprietorial domain rights to the surrounding land. Therefore, control of access was not equally distributed; instead it was subject to the decisions of the ranking kin group.[1]

Implicated in this exclusive territorialism, of course, is the existence of domain boundaries. Thus, neighboring chiefdoms would be interacting as peer polities, each with its modular territory having defined boundaries that it would defend. In his focus on the Mississippian period, George Milner (1998, 102, 155–56, 168) particularly picks up on this exclusive territorial notion. For him, the mounds become the locales of simple and/or complex chiefdoms according to the number of mounds displayed. He directly ties the chiefdom to exclusive control of land: the larger the expanse of land that is controlled and the greater the mix of resources it has, the larger the population it can support, and the larger and more powerful and complex the chiefdom can be (Milner 1998, 155–56).

While the correlation of monumental architecture, exclusive tenure, and proprietorial domain modules is theoretically consistent, the critical flaw is the assumption that the deontic nature of tenure must be exclusive. Indeed, exclusiveness seems to become a defining property of the tenure, and therefore, according to the above reasoning, the cosmology of the above social systems must be transcendental in nature and the ethos must be proprietorial. This set of assumptions must be challenged since the notion of a world in which the sacred transcends the mundane is foreign to most historic Native American peoples. Instead, the prevailing belief was, and to a significant degree still is, that the world is immanently sacred. The Osage (who in the seventeenth, in the eighteenth, and during the early part of the nineteenth century occupied the Osage River drainage in south-central Missouri, not that far west of the

American Bottom) are typical of the historic Native Americans of the Midcontinent. According to Garrick Bailey, Francis La Flesche—the Native American anthropologist responsible for most of what we know of the Osage—"went to great lengths to emphasize that *Wa-kon-da* ('God') was a single unified force that manifested itself in various ways in all living, moving things" (Bailey 1995, 9). Bailey elaborated on the notion of Wa-kon-da, pointing out that, for the Osage, "a silent, invisible creative power pervades the sun, moon and stars and the earth, [and] gives to them life, and keeps them eternally in motion and perfect order" (Bailey 1995, 30–31). In short, the sacred is an essential and intrinsic property of the world, inseparable from its transeunt properties. It is essential in the sense that only by virtue of its immanence in the world is the latter sustained in all of the complex activity that transpires. It is intrinsic in that the tangible environment is perceived to be isomorphic with the sacred order, inseparable in that the latter is manifested and presenced in the concrete and tangible makeup of the world. "Every quality and characteristic of *Wa-kon-da* was thought to have its expression or counterpart in the world of the living" (Bailey 1995, 31). Therefore, in an immanently sacred world, all human material interventions in the natural order are simultaneously interventions into the sacred order.

This concept has very important implications for understanding tenure in such a world. No mere mortal can "own" the land, since this means owning the sacred powers immanent in the world. Therefore, there can be no "ownership" in the sense that there can be in a world experienced as transcendentally sacred. Instead, humans are in partnership with the world, and tenure is grounded on this notion of partnership. Humans situate themselves as the "borrowers" of the territories that they exploit. As such, in ideal terms, tenure amounts to a type of usufruct, one in which occupancy is directly tied to survival need, with no party's need being able to be invoked to deny the needs of other parties. Therefore, instead of the squatter being despised, all are squatters. Indeed, squatting is the warranted form of occupying and dwelling on the land—the implication being that all residency is transient and temporary. Hence, while a transcendalist cosmology correlates with a proprietorial ethos, in parallel with an immanentist cosmology, a squatter ethos will prevail. Those who behave in proprietorial terms (that is, those who are perceived as habitually excluding others) become hoarders, and hoarding becomes the "poaching" of this social world and those who do it become "poachers." Hence, in an immanently sacred world, if a party (whether person or group) is perceived as denying to others the same right to occupy and use the land in the same manner as the denier, then the denier is seen as a misappropriator, a person or persons to be despised and scorned.

The immanentist cosmological perspective would appear to be much more appropriately applied to the American Bottom archaeological record than is the transcendentalist perspective that is (as described above) almost second nature to North American archaeologists. In fact, in two recent interpretations of Cahokia, both Melvin Fowler (in Fowler et al. 1999, 183–87) and John Kelly (1996, 106–8) draw upon the Osage as illustrative of the type of cosmology that they claim is presupposed by Cahokia. Although they do not use the term *immanentist* in summarizing the Osage cosmology, their description of the way in which the Osage perceive the world and organize their own settlement clearly conforms to what I summarize above, namely, that the Osage cosmology is immanentist in nature. Interestingly, they do not discuss any possible contradiction between their own characterizations of Cahokia as a paramount chiefdom based on exclusive territorialism and the Osage community based on a type of custodial usufruct tenure.

In any case, in terms of an immanentist cosmology, the world, its objects, and states are autonomous agents, and for this reason, they are not divisible, distributable, and ownable by humans. Indeed, human consciousness would be the model on which this world conception is based. Just as humans are aware of themselves, so are the creatively powerful self-aware and conscious agents that constitute the essences of the multiple aspects of an immanently sacred cosmos: the heavens, middle world, underworld, lakes, rivers, land, trees, animals, and so on. Hence, human interventions in the natural order are always the product and reproduction and/or transformation of social relations that humans hold with the cosmos and its constituent agents. Since the potent spiritual agents of an immanently sacred world also are taken by humans to be self-aware agents, the nature of human–spirit world relations as realized in ecological interaction is also of a social order. Therefore, these relations between humans and nature (that is, human-animal, human-plant, human-land, and so on) would be experienced by the human participants as qualitatively the same as their own human-human relations. In most but not all cases, humans situate themselves as being among the lesser beings of the world, and their relations with other nonhuman beings are seen as relations of negotiation, establishing bonds that are experienced as obligations and duties as well as privileges and qualified entitlements. In short, human-environment relations must be characterized as being as much religious as socioeconomic and socioecological in nature.

Anthropologists have long noted that the subsistence practices of foraging peoples implicate a deontic principle that is the opposite of the principle of exclusive tenure that characterizes proprietorial domain; it is the principle of sharing applied to territory and its resources. The principle of sharing is basic to both kinship and companionship, and it is the core of inclusive territorialism. It is logically consistent with an immanentist cosmology and the squatter's ethos since it presupposes the indivisibility and nonownability of the cosmos and its components. As Tim Ingold (1987, 143–44) puts it, there are

> numerous instances from the ethnographic record of hunters and gatherers in which there is public recognition of demarcated territories but no conception at all of trespass in the form of taking resources from another's area. There can be no such offence as poaching when intruders have the same rights of access as anyone else. If a transgression occurs, it lies in not having asked before taking, not in the taking itself. Though territorial boundaries are generally open to movement across them, such movement should be publicized and not concealed; one does not arrive or leave without advertising the fact. . . . The intentions of persons who do attempt to conceal their movements are bound to be suspect: the suspicion, however, is not that they are out to raid the territory's food resources but that they are planning an attack on members of the resident group. This suspicion, in turn, motivates sometimes violent retribution meted out to such intruders.[2]

Inclusive territorialism hinges on the public, normally taken-for-granted recognition that no one can be denied access to territory simply because it is habitually used by others. Humans are borrowers of or squatters on the land, not proprietors. As borrowers, however, habitual users have important obligations and responsibilities that they must regularly discharge to the land so that those who habitually occupy and use a given area, a practical territory, typically have a special posture toward it. Ingold speaks of them as the custodians of the land, and this human-land relationship constitutes their tenure as custodianship: "Possession . . . is a matter of looking after the country, or tending the creative powers that are thought to reside in its core locales. So-called 'owners' are thus, in reality, no more than the custodians of parts of a world that belongs to all, and they exercise their rights and responsibilities on behalf of the collectivity. . . . [What] an owner possesses, *to the exclusion of others,* is the privilege of custodianship, not that which is held in custody" (Ingold 1987, 224, emphasis in original). Hence, in this world, ownership is subsumed to custodianship, which is transformed into obligations and duties rather than rights and privileges. Custodians of a territory are those who must care for the spaces, places, and paths that they regularly use, and this caring is on behalf of the land itself. This means that the habitual occupants of a territory must ensure that they use it properly, since a territory is part of the public domain, available to all. The habitual users take on this custodial obligation collectively; therefore, they are constituted as a custodial corporation, and the paths and places that they habitually use in the territory constitute their custodial domain.

Ingold (1987, 156–57) thus sees foragers as sectoring the world differently than do farmers. In general, farmers need to control land for long-term exploitation. Therefore, they value two-dimensional extension, that is, the surface of the land. In a world where two-dimensional extension is valued as defining private or exclusive property, one-dimensional extensions across the land are used primarily to define boundaries that sector the land into fields, and the owner-farmer locates his/her residence and facilities in zero-dimensional space, as a place occupied by his/her house and barns. The house and its attached facilities embody the exclusive rights to all of the area as delineated by the one-dimensional lines constituting the domain boundaries. This is the conceptualization of tenure and land that is implicated by exclusive territorialism as described above, and, of course, it is realized by generating a set of separate spatial modules that the occupiers treat as real property.

Foragers do not ignore two-dimensional extension. Rather, they treat it as encompassing the main object of their custodianship. While an obvious point to occupying the land and exploiting its resources is to pursue survival, another legitimate point is to enhance the land through the appropriate use of the locales and paths that ensure all access to these resources. Thus, zero-dimensional extension is identified by them as constituting the places they habitually occupy and reoccupy, that is, their campsites, seasonal locales, and, particularly, the sacred places where the sacred being(s) stopped and rested. In this world, then, one-dimensional extension constitutes not the boundaries that surround the places and cut them off from each other but the paths that link them together and link the custodial domain to all its neighboring domains and, by ramifying extension, to the total cosmos.

Thus, custodial corporations have the heavy burden of ensuring that these paths and places are properly used; this usually means tying their usage into seasonal cycles that are in harmony with the mythical creative travels of the sacred being(s) and the seasonal cycles of nature, as well as the birth, death, and rebirth cycles of human life. Mobility becomes as much a ritual passage along sacred paths, stopping at sacred stations to perform rites of transition and renewal, as it is a practical process of moving to new areas to exploit the resources. A network of paths and places under the responsibility of a custodial corporation has its particular set of prescribed rituals and avoidances that must be respected, and the duty of strangers and those unfamiliar with a region is to approach the custodians to be taught and guided in proper usage. At what point along a path the responsibilities of the custodial group to care for the area becomes the responsibilities of the neighbors is always vague. Thus, the social system of a region is constituted as mutually recognized autonomous custodial groups linked into open social networks based on the shared responsibility to sustain the exploitation of the region in appropriate ways.

Although this elucidation of tenure relates primarily to hunting and gathering groups, it can be extended to underwrite the heterarchical polyistic locale-centric account of Cahokia. Seen in these terms, the prehistoric settlement data of the American Bottom clearly need to be modelled in a radically different way from that envisioned under the hierarchical monistic modular account. I turn to this modelling shortly. Before I do so, however, two revisions to Ingold's theory need to be made.

In the first case, as indicated earlier, Ingold does not consider the possibility that an inclusive tenurial system could also have a form of poaching and pilfering. This may be partly because he does not address the implications of material cultural style for constituting territorialism. Even though access to resources under a regime of inclusive territorialism is largely a matter of practical distances and up-to-date information, it also can be constrained by the style of the tools. In a world where access to resources is open, the role of style would be to constitute subsistence tools as custodial warrants. Therefore, as I suggest above in reference to hoarding, inclusive territorialism would have its own brand of poaching and pilfering, understood generally as the misappropriation and misuse of resources. Of course, among the major media that would prevent ecological behaviors from being perceived in these negative terms is style. Stylistic variation that is perceived by habitual occupants of a region as being outside the norm would probably be a legitimate basis for denying the users the requisite information to exploit the resources and especially denying them the sacred ritual know-how needed to use the paths and occupy the locales used by the local group. Such styles brand them as potential or actual poachers, pilferers, and hoarders.

Thus, the primary grounds for welcoming would be that those entering the territory demonstrate that they can conduct themselves properly. If they are neighbors, their styles will tend to correspond closely, and recognition of the validity of their subsistence intentions will be largely automatic. If the styles of visitors are patently different from those used by local populations, until the visitors can demonstrate that these express the same deontic principles of sharing and cosmological understandings as those used locally, their exploitative interventions could be legitimately denied recognition as fully felicitous acts of resource appropriation, that is, they would be acts of poaching and pilfering.[3] In this regard, in her research among the San of southwestern Africa, Polly Weissner (1983, 269) showed separate groups of adult male !Kung, G/wi, and !Xo the standard range of arrows that each group used. She observed, "A discussion ensued from one small group [of !Kung San] about what they would do if they found a dead animal with such an arrow [G/wi or !Xo styled] embedded in it in their own area, saying that they would be worried about the possibility that a stranger was nearby about which they knew nothing at all." What is particularly interesting is that it was the possible social conduct of the person responsible for an arrow bearing an unrecognized style that concerned them the most. This person is assumed not to have the know-how to conduct himself properly. The onus to prove otherwise is carried by that person: "Although afraid of !Kung strangers as well, they said that if a man makes arrows in the same way, *one could be fairly sure that he shares similar values around hunting, landrights, and general conduct*" (Weissner 1983, 269, emphasis added).

From this, Weissner concluded that one aspect of style is emblemic in the sense that it served to convey information about the ethnicity of the user. The problem with this information-conveyancing view, however, is that it commits the referential fallacy; that is, it characterizes style as making reference to something that is independent of the symbol user and therefore also independent of this user's conduct. Of course, this means that the user of style would be alienated from the very position that she/he is supposed to be occupying! In terms of the symbolic pragmatic view, however, style is expressive, and, therefore, the style manifests and is a constitutive part of the identity of the user. The San feared strangers, and these people were constituted as strangers partly by bearing items of unrecognized style. To them, the meaning of this style was the absence of appropriate hunting etiquette and communal sharing know-how on the part of its bearer.

Furthermore, even if I reconstrue Weissner's notion of emblemic style in expressive and constitutive terms, I still have to disagree with her particular characterization of its meaning as constituting ethnicity. This certainly can be the case, under certain conditions. However, one of these conditions is that ethnicity, as we normally define it, is usually tied to exclusivity. Stylistics under an inclusive regime such as practiced by the San would figure primarily as expressively communicating (that is, presencing) legitimate appropriative intentions and position. As I stressed above, the point to having tools displaying appropriate styles is that—usually implicitly, of course—the users are constituting the social identity of being hunters, and they are doing this by manifesting the know-how required to conduct themselves properly toward the resources that they exploit and also to conduct themselves properly toward their hosts. In short, they know what behaviors would count as a social act of sharing. Hence, different style bearers must demonstrate to each other the warranting equivalence of their particular styles by participating and sharing in collective tasks. When it becomes clear to the custodial group that those bearing strange styles nevertheless know—or have learned—the rules of proper conduct toward the resources they are exploiting and the paths and the places their hosts use and occupy, then the styles will be recognized as equivalent warrants. Out of this might come a sharing of styles and, finally, mutual emulation and possibly transformation into new stylistic variants.

The second modification I must make to Ingold's theory is his tendency to treat deterministically the correlating of zero- and one-dimensional extension with the custodial tenure of hunting and gathering societies and of two-dimensional extension with the proprietorial tenure of farming societies (Ingold 1987, 147–54). Certainly, when applied to Old World societies, this view has considerable empirical support. However, this correlation may be overly deterministic in ecological and economic terms. While not denying Ingold's view that farming will promote exclusive forms of territorial tenure, I must point out that this type of tenure is not necessarily entailed by farming systems. To say that it is, is to ignore the cosmologically informed deontics that give economic and ecological practices an ideological dimension.

How could a regime of custodial domain contend with the "exclusive" imperatives of gardening? That is, despite the immanentist cosmology, would a shift to gardening, or even agriculture, necessarily transform a preexisting custodial domain regime into a proprietorial domain regime, or could the former be modified to sustain its traditional commitments? I will argue that the latter is possible and, indeed, that it is very likely. Even proprietorial domain allows for qualified, quasi-exclusive tenure in the form of renting based on some form of "payment." This is a strongly qualified exclusive tenure of land, of course, constituting the renters as tenants who have a constrained set of exclusive rights termed *usufruct*. It is useful to be explicit here and specify this as a type of usufruct that can be termed *tenancy*. The deontics of tenancy go beyond land usufruct to reinforce the social and political subordination of the tenant to the landowner; in extreme forms of this regime, these landowners become landlords. Indeed, this is the logic behind the hierarchical monistic modular characterization of Cahokia social structure in essentially a dominant-elite/subordinate-commoner manner. Still, as long as tenants fulfil their economic, social, and political obligations to the proprietor-landlords, they usually have first rights of renewing their tenancy when necessary. In some cases, of course—as was quite common in European feudal times—this qualified exclusivity can be enhanced by first rights (and obligations) to tenancy's being inherited by descendants of the tenants.

If proprietorship can be accommodated to the needs of landowners for labor and to the need of the landless to survive by evolving a strongly qualified quasi-ownership, or tenancy, then a modified form of land sharing that accommodates changing ecological and demographic conditions could be anticipated for custodial regimes. Therefore, an emerging farming regime could quite conceivably generate a form of qualified suspension of inclusiveness within a basically custodial regime, producing, in effect, a qualified squatter attitude toward the use of land. This might be appropriately termed *custodial usufruct*. Custodial usufruct would only mimic tenancy since the former would be unlikely to allow for the political and economic subordination that seems inherent in the latter. In an immanently sacred world, custodial usufruct as a qualified suspension of inclusiveness is perfectly consistent for farmers and/or horticulturalists. They cannot exclude others; however, those who habitually use a local range of land for gardening have the first rights to its use as long as they have greater need for it than do others. In keeping with the principles of inclusiveness and autonomy, however, nonresidents would have generalized entitlements to land outside their habitual ranges. As immigrants, they could exercise these, but only as long as the land was not being needfully exploited by those already exercising custodial usufruct. Should increasing demands for land usage emerge through immigration (or natural population growth), given the above principles, the resident custodial gardening group would be pressed to act justly by negotiating and reallocating usufruct to the available gardening land. This would probably result in more intensive exploitation of land, of course, and, therefore, it would provoke compensating innovation in world renewal ritual, a point that figures centrally in my later discussion of deontic ecology.

In a recent discussion of Native American agriculture in a historic context, Douglas Hurt (1987, 67) implicitly acknowledges the existence of custodial usufruct. Since he is speaking from within the Western culture's conceptual framework of tenure, however, he uses the terminology of proprietorship so that he claims that different levels of social categories "owned" different gardens, for example, families "owned" gardens within their lineage fields, lineages "owned" fields within the village's domain, and so on. However, he then states that this "ownership" was qualified by need. Only as long as a family needed the gardening land would it have its rights of use sustained. He even quotes a "Chief Black Hawk" to this effect: "My reason teaches me that land could not be bought or sold. The Great Spirit gave it to his children to live upon, and cultivate as far as necessary for their subsistence, and so long as they occupy and cultivate it, they have the right to the soil—but if they voluntarily leave it, then any other people have the right to settle it" (Hurt 1987, 67).

This translation has to be treated carefully, of course. As in any intercultural case, even the apparently clear statement "The Great Spirit gave it to his children" has to be understood in cultural context. It is likely that the term *children* here refers not to the specific kin group of the chief but to humanity in general. Furthermore, Chief Black Hawk qualified his assertion by saying that "land could not be bought or sold." This terminology of buying and selling land is necessarily situated within the proprietorial perspective. Therefore, the fact that Chief Black Hawk used the negative suggests that he was actually expressing the notions of custodial domain. It is not surprising that Hurt attempts to make sense of this negation by invoking the principle of trusteeship. In his words, "Indeed, Indian land could not be sold because it did not belong to the present generation, which was acting only as trustee of the land for the generations yet unborn. Consequently, the land belonged only temporarily to the generation presently inhabiting it, subject to their good behaviour" (Hurt 1987, 67).

As stated, this would mean that no living generation owns the land. Furthermore, trustees are not custodians. Custodians care for components of public domain; trustees and stewards care for the property of owners who cannot care for it themselves. That is, these terms are part of a proprietorial regime. Therefore, the "generation presently inhabiting it" cannot be stewards or trustees. Rather, they are better understood to be custodians, and, as agriculturalists, their occupying and using the land would have been in the nature of custodial usufruct, as suggested above. This is particularly well and aptly illustrated by George Will and George Hyde (1964, 81), about the use of land for gardening by the Omaha of the upper Missouri during the mid-1800s: "[A]s long as a tract was cultivated by a family no one molested the crops or intruded on the ground; but if a garden patch was abandoned for a season then the ground was considered free for anyone to utilize."

Thus, given an immanentist cosmology, under the proper conditions of population density and technological requirements, a form of custodial usufruct could be expected to emerge, and this would allow for first rights and/or responsibilities to land use while respecting the squatter ethos principles of sharing and inclusiveness. For this reason, the notion of custodial usufruct marks an important theoretical concept by which the analysis of the custodial tenure of hunters and gatherers by Ingold can be assimilated to the analysis of horticultural and agricultural peoples, such as the people occupying the American Bottom before and during the Mississippian period. This notion and the deontic ecological perspective that it entails also explain why I have reservations about Fortier and McElrath's recent (2002, 173, 177–78, 203) critical assessment of the causal role of subsistence and settlement dynamics in accounting for the emergence of the Mississippian period. While they are right to consider material conditions (treated objectively) as insufficient to explain cultural and social changes, by understanding that human populations always actively and strategically engage these conditions through their collective understandings and needs, one can logically deduce that these ecological strategies are fully social phenomena. Thus, through humans' strategically engaging with these objective conditions, they are transformed into historical sociomaterial causes, and a central part of explaining Cahokia entails tracing both the strategic responses of the population as they engage in the everyday pursuit of survival and the unwitting and often perverse consequences of these responses. To advance the development of this theoretical framework, therefore, what now must be addressed is the role of ritual practices in a world that is experienced as immanently sacred, thus showing how these can be understood as a part of ecological processes.

ECOLOGY AND RITUAL

According to the deployment of logic appropriate to an immanentist cosmology, since the natural order is immanently sacred, the regular interventions making up the suite of ecological practices must necessarily have an impact on the sacred order. In an important sense, the observable, tangible changes that human practices cause in the landscape directly express, manifest, and cause changes in the sacred order. These observable or tangible changes can be assessed as either beneficial and sanctifying to the world or costly and sacredly polluting. Above all, this means that populations bearing immanentist cosmologies experience the pursuit of survival as an ongoing potential contradiction. To kill the animals and forage for the foods needed for survival, humans must intervene into the sacred natural order, thereby endangering its reproduction. This endangerment is not something that can occur only if the resources are "objectively" overused, since the wilful use of the resources counts as modifying the sacred order, and, if not conducted properly, this modifying counts as polluting. However, if conducted properly, it is typically perceived as an act of species reproduction and/or enhancement. Therefore, in an immanently sacred world, every ecological act is potentially an act of transgression or an act of creative reproduction and/or enhancement.

Elsewhere I have termed this cosmological notion of immanent sacredness of the natural order the *Sacred Earth principle,* and it grounds what I term the *essential contradiction of human existence* (Byers 2004, 8–9, 132–35). To ensure that their pursuit of survival does not contradict and destroy the very conditions that make this existence possible, humans must conduct this pursuit according to traditional rules by which the destructive moment of exploitation becomes a reproductive moment. In properly killing and reducing the animal, the animal spirit is released so as to be reborn. To fail to ensure that the act of killing is also an act initiating rebirth is to harm the immanently sacred natural world and, therefore, to endanger everyone's survival. The deontic aspect of ecological practices, then, becomes critically important not only to sustain personal survival but also to sustain world survival. Those who come to be known as good hunters earn this recognition by conducting their predatory behaviors while displaying all the signs that disclose their respect for the animals (and plants) that they exploit and their possession of the necessary know-how to ensure that the destructive moment of their behavior is transformed into species reproduction.

Those individuals or groups who come to be seen by others as not respectful quickly gain disrepute, a notoriety that fuels a perception of their being without honor, worth, and trust. This notoriety is partly generated and sustained by failing to use the appropriate warranting devices by which the destructive moment of their exploitative practices is seen as simultaneously reproductive. The result may be that the individuals will suffer ostracism from the community; if a whole group is perceived by others in this way, then the group may also be ostracized. Certainly, feuding could be initiated and fueled by such mutual perceptions. Hence, the ongoing resolution of the essential contradiction of human existence ensures that ecological practices constitute the dual pursuit of organic survival and social survival, the latter being realized as the ongoing pursuit of reputation. Community survival entails ensuring that both pursuits are continuously successful.

Anthony Giddens (1979, 161) has also commented on human existence as grounded on a contradiction. For him it is a "fundamental theorem" that "in all forms of society, human beings exist in *contradictory relation to nature*. . . . [This is] because they are in and of nature, as corporeal beings existing in material environments; and yet at the same time they are set off against nature, as having a 'second nature' of their own, irreducible to physical objects or events" (emphasis in original). What is particularly interesting here is that Giddens goes on to suggest that this "contradiction . . . is perhaps at the heart of all religions," since it "has its universal expression in the finitude of *Dasein* as the negation of the apparent infinity of time-space in which each human life makes its fleeting appearance." However, this view of the contradictory nature of human existence limits the universal nature that he is claiming and therefore makes his theorem inadequate for my purposes. While human culture as "second nature" may be universal such that humans can effortlessly reflect on their own existence in respect to the cosmos, it is an error to assume that this reflection will lead to humans universally formulating a cultural ethos whereby humans are "set off against nature." In fact, in postulating a universal culturally generated attitude toward the world, Giddens is presupposing a particular cultural perspective, that of Western transcendentalism.

Indeed, Giddens (1979, 161) seems to recognize this by immediately citing Claude Lévi-Strauss's view that in "cold societies, the contradictory relation of man and nature is expressed *through its incorporation*" (emphasis in original) and that "nature is not separated from categories of human thought and action, but forms an integral part of their constitution." Giddens then concludes that, in fact, the cultural attitude whereby humans set themselves off from nature emerges only with class-divided societies, the latter being "*administered societies* . . . [in which] centralised control of 'knowledge' or 'information' is a medium of domination" (Giddens 1979, 162, emphasis in original). These societies, of course, are typically monistic modular polities, in my terminology, based on an "*exploitative attitude to nature* . . . [and] associated with *social exploitation,* directly geared into it" (Giddens 1979, 163, emphases in original). The sense that the contradiction of human existence is resolved by pre-class-structured societies through incorporation of nature is the view I am taking here. However, to go one step further, when I speak of this contradiction as "essential," I mean to stress that the human community through its "second nature" (that is, culture) may reincorporate itself into the world by using itself, its own social organization, and the self-awareness of its own members as the model of the world. Thus, just as humans are effortlessly reflexive and embody spiritual powers and also relate to and expressively interact with each other through material symbols by which they exercise deontic principles, rights, duties, and so on, so the world is taken to be the embodiment of spiritual powers having many aspects and is taken to be organized through the same deontic principles. Therefore, its natural processes are forms of expressive interaction whereby the multiple, autonomous components of the cosmos discharge their obligations and duties. Thus, humans are only part of a great society, and their position within it can be construed in different ways by different peoples. At the same time, however, for humans to survive, they must disrupt the social order of nature, thereby disrupting its immanent sacred powers. Hence, as I note above, if humans do not resolve this essential existential contradiction, then they unproblematically assume not only that they might destroy themselves, but also that in doing so they will necessarily disrupt, diminish, and possibly destroy the very condition that made their existence possible: the cosmos itself.

Clearly, therefore, the notion of environmental stress also plays an important role in immanently sacred deontic ecological accounts. However, since the perceptions of the agents are what is important, only when these agents perceive their actions or their numbers as being stressful to the immanent sacredness embodied in the local region will they then modify their conduct. This means that the analyst must assess the possible nature and level of stress to the environment from within a perspective that would make sense to the responsible agents. In short, it means using an emic perspective. Taking an emic perspective means that communities having the same overall objective needs for survival but essentially different cosmologies (for example, transcendental and immanentist), could have different standards by which to assess their own conduct as counting as environmentally stressful or polluting. For example, early European settlers in North America (informed by a transcendentalist cosmology) perceived clear-cutting the forest to be environmentally enhancing by releasing the productive capacity of the land given to them—as the "chosen ones"—by their god for a greater purpose, which was their survival by means of agricultural practices. This assessment, of course, was, in general, not fully in accord with that of the local Native Americans, whose own immanentist cosmology would probably have informed them that such clear-cutting was intrinsically more polluting than sanctifying.

Therefore, this deontic ecological perspective is fully attuned to the rationalist perspective of standard ecological accounts, with three important provisos: (1) an emic perspective must be taken; (2) for the purposes of this book, this must be treated as an immanentist perspective; and (3) the ecological strategies are directed to the dual pursuits of survival and reputation. Deontic ecology does not deny that humans have basic survival requirements, but it also claims that humans uniquely determine the conditions under which these will be pursued.[4] Therefore, this pursuit of organic survival can never be reduced to objective conditions that determine it. Hence, in conditions of perceived environmental stress, a community would have to draw on traditional deontics—both proscriptive and prescriptive rules and principles—to innovate new forms of settlement and subsistence practices that would be perceived as appropriate forms of accommodation to these changing material conditions, thereby simultaneously maintaining/enhancing reputation and survival.

In an immanently sacred world, the logic of proscriptive rules is to minimize (to the degree that is practicable) the impact on the sacred-natural order that ecological interventions must make. Prescriptive rules in an immanently sacred world also have a logic; in this case, they realize the sanctifying attitude, directing the performance of those modifications that must be made to correct the polluting moment of human interventions by rebalancing and, where possible, even enhancing the sacred-natural order. These basic proscriptive and prescriptive deontic attitudes and rules are not alternatives but are reciprocally related so that a particular ecological practice might have built into it both proscriptive rules (expressed as taboos) and prescriptive rules (expressed as imperatives). From this it follows logically that a community would avoid labor that would transgress the sacred boundaries and, if transgression was impossible to avoid, that members of the community would innovate prescriptive rules that would generate forms of behavioral interventions so that, based on traditional know-how precepts and cultural understandings, these would serve to rectify the unavoidable disorder that the pursuit of survival entailed, even if this meant intensifying labor in this area and enhancing the risk to individual and group survival. These greater labor costs and survival risks would be treated as world renewal sacrifices. Perceived as a medium by which to resanctify the sacred order, such world renewal sacrificial conduct would count as reputation enhancing.

The proscriptive/prescriptive deontic aspect of ecological practices would be manifested both at the individual, day-to-day level of environmental interaction and at the collective, public level. In the former case, everyday subsistence and settlement practices would have built-in proscriptive and prescriptive rituals with the point of these being to ensure that in carrying out their everyday tasks, individuals minimize the level and degree of sacred pollution that their subsistence and settlement activities generate while simultaneously enhancing sacred reproduction. This deontic ecological aspect will be termed *midwifery subsistence and settlement ritual* (Byers 2004, 136–39). The collective, group-oriented or public deontic interactive aspect would be organized as community renewal and thanksgiving rituals. The latter would normally be performed in locales that display specialized properties disclosing them as constituted sacred contexts, by which the behaviors performed would count as the type of world renewal ritual intended, thereby rectifying the surplus pollution generated by the everyday pursuit of organic survival and ensuring that the community would maintain good ecological relations with the sacred.

Midwifery Ritual

The term *midwifery* is chosen here because of its association with birth and reproduction. My postulating of midwifery ritual is based on the assumption that in an immanently sacred world, if all material interventions (including those forms necessary for survival) are irreducibly polluting, then the essential contradiction of human existence would be impossible to resolve. Therefore, the working of practical reason would promote construing the destructive moments of subsistence and settlement as having a sacrificial as well as an economic purpose. Subsistence and settlement interventions would be experienced not only as the destructive means of the practical pursuit of survival but also as part of the everyday means of participating in the reproduction of the very species being exploited and of the very places being occupied. The felicity of exploitation and occupation would be dependent on the incorporation of midwifery proscriptions and prescriptions into the practical aspect of subsistence and settlement activities, and these would be seamlessly built into material practices and would not be noted until someone failed to conduct her/himself according to the "traditional" ways. Hence, midwifery ritual would ensure that the destructive moment of exploiting animals and plants was an intrinsic part of the reproduction of these species through exercising practices that were recognized as having reproductive consequences, thereby implicating such beliefs as spirit release, human-guardian spirit reciprocity, sacrifice, and so on. Ingold's (1987, 246–47) comments are very salient in this regard:

> Much of the ritual surrounding the treatment of slaughtered beasts, particularly concerning the careful preservation of bones and other inedible parts, and their deposition in the correct medium and in the precise order

that they occur in the skeleton, is designed to assist the reconstitution of the animals from the pieces into which they have been broken for the purposes of consumption, thus ensuring the regeneration of that on which human life depends. . . . Above all, nothing should be wasted, for this would indicate a casually destructive attitude to nature which would only offend the animal guardians. . . . So as he conducts himself through life, a man must tread with caution, breaking as little as possible, doing what he can to mend what in nature must of necessity be broken, and warding off the equally inevitable and ultimate disintegration of his own person.

Proscriptive and prescriptive midwifery ritual is postulated as basic to the prehistoric Eastern Woodlands (Byers 2004, chapters 5 and 6). The emic perception that subsistence and settlement practices were intensifying would entail modifying midwifery ritual. One manner of doing this would be to innovate and/or emulate a new stylistic dimension, either substituting it for the old or adding it to traditional tools and prescribing their usage. This might hinge on acquiring exotic cherts, and a vision quest might be the innovative source of this insight; that is, in the vision, the quester might have had revealed to her/him that such material resources have special iconic associations with the spirit custodian of the animals or plants, thereby enhancing the sacrificial moment of subsistence.[5] Tools would come to bear new, more potent warranting styles. To further enhance this warranting moment, the vision would associate with these new styles new proscriptions related to their use (for example, only by males of a certain age, only by married females, and so on). Even modes of midden production might be innovated to enhance the spirit release and recycling effect.

Clearly, intensification of subsistence practices would have an impact on settlement practices. Thus, compensatory avoidances or proscriptions might be innovated that would encourage minimizing the concentration of settlement numbers in any given area, just because subsistence intensification was perceived to be increasing and, therefore, greater subsistence-derived disruption of the natural sacred order was being caused by human intervention (that is, pollution). This might lead to promoting the dispersing of the traditional aggregations to smaller locales within a short walk of each other, thereby spreading over a larger area the increasing pollution that greater demographics would cause, while reducing the pollution load per unit area.

There is considerable anthropological support for this view of midwifery ritual. With respect to circumboreal hunting and gathering societies of both Eurasia and North America, Ingold (1987, 217–18) has argued that among the northern tier of societies in both continents, hunting ritual largely identifies the hunting gear, particularly the weaponry, as having a strong sexual-reproductive symbolic pragmatic meaning: "In many cases, the killing of animals is believed to be a means of securing their future reproduction. Hunting . . . is a rite of renewal. Thus, even if the labour expended in the hunt yields an immediate return in the form of kills (not necessarily for immediate consumption), that labour is conceptually equivalent to labour invested in establishing the conditions for the reproduction of the animal resource." He also points out that "hunting peoples . . . base their livelihood upon the products of slaughtered beasts . . . [and] . . . the hunt, just like the sacrifice, is a drama often imbued with religious significance, involving some kind of exchange between mankind and the spirit world" (Ingold 1987, 243). Robert Hall (1977, 510) makes a similar claim for historical Native American peoples, arguing that subsistence and war weaponry was viewed as being endowed with sacred reproductive powers: "The tie between hunters' and warriors' penetrating weapons, the sun father, agricultural fertility, increase of human populations, and animal increase or success in the hunt was both metonym and metaphor in conception but was more than poetic imagery."

World Renewal Ritual

Midwifery ritual is hardly the whole ritual story in an immanently sacred world, however. There is also the inevitable cumulative disordering of the sacredness of the world that arises by the collective nature of human settlement and subsistence (Byers 2004, 139). Collective ritual of a world renewal nature would be causally linked to subsistence and settlement practices as part of reversing the pollution produced by the communal pursuit of organic survival. Therefore, if changing material conditions required intensifying the degree of exploitation and reducing the degree of mobility, then the logical compensatory tactical move would be to innovate and/or intensify world renewal ritual. Hence, world renewal ceremonialism would escalate in proportion to the intensifying of subsistence and settlement. Just as the prescriptive use of new warranting tools and the proliferation of proscriptions reducing the concentration of population in different areas would be embedded in the subsistence and settlement routines, minimizing the degree of material intervention required in public ritual innovations would also apply—at least initially. Such minimizing tactics would encourage "doubling up" of ritual practices. Important preexisting forms of communal ritual, such as mortuary practices, could be co-opted to serve both mortuary and world renewal/thanksgiving goals. Piggybacking one on the other would minimize the overall degree of material disturbance of the natural order that these two ritual forms would require if carried out separately, while also having an overall consequence of enhancing world renewal. Integrating these two tactics would constitute a prescriptive mortuary-mediated world renewal ritual regime.

In an immanently sacred world, this piggybacking would be underwritten by a particular logic of energy exchange. In an important sense, the human life-spirit or life-spirits, often perceived to be intrinsic to the various corporeal parts of the human body (blood, skin, hair, bones, and so on), share the same property with the spirit of the land. Humans perceive themselves as being fed and "raised" by the land, and they view death as entailing the return of the life-spirits to the land, constituting human life and death as the cycling and recycling of cosmic life forces. Hence, mortuary practices can come to have a strong renewal component built into them (Ingold 1987, 154). Further elaboration of this line of thought and its implications for understanding the mortuary practices of the American Bottom Mississippian period are fully discussed after a more detailed elucidation of cultural traditions and their relations to ecology and social systems. This is followed by a discussion of the theoretical understandings of the two different types of social organizations of those communities that are characterized by having exclusive territorialism and proprietorial domains, on the one hand, and those based on inclusive territorialism and custodial domain, on the other. I then return to the symbolic pragmatics of mortuary practices, arguing that two different forms of mortuary spheres are correlated with each type of social system. On the one hand, the hierarchical monistic modular polity account appears to rely on the cemetery perspective, exemplified by Charles and Buikstra's (1983) interpretation of Archaic burial mounds as cemeteries, the latter being markers of proprietorial domain. On the other, the mortuary model that logically fits with the heterarchical polyistic locale-centric account treats mortuary practices as a complex series of funerary, spirit release, and world renewal rituals. I term this mortuary perspective the *Mourning/World Renewal Mortuary model* (Byers 2004, 177–85). Following its full elucidation, I then apply this overall deontic ecological perspective to interpreting the relevant subsistence, settlement, and ceremonial data to reconstruct the trajectory of the Late Woodland, Emergent Mississippian (Terminal Late Woodland), and Mississippian periods of the American Bottom in terms of the heterarchical polyistic locale-centric account.

Cultural Traditions and Prehistoric Archaeology

When prehistoric archaeology moves away from the behavioral moment or aspect of culture and toward the cognitive-normative aspect, culture is usually spoken of as the set of beliefs, values, and attitudes shared by a people and constituting their cultural traditions. When archaeologists give a collective, particularly religious, reading to these notions, terms such as *cosmology* and *ideology* or *ethos* and *worldview* are often used. Typically, an archaeologist will favor the use of one or two of these terms over the others to speak generally about the cultural traditions under the cognitive-normative aspect, without clarifying why one or two are favored. Indeed, it almost seems that we might have a superfluity of terms for this purpose and that one or two could be profitably eliminated. However, in this chapter I argue for the critical necessity of each of the above four terms as delineating real differences within the cultural tradition of a people.

At the general level, then, I use the term *cultural tradition* to refer to this sphere of collective consciousness. I then treat a cultural tradition as structured by four basic relatively autonomous states of consciousness that I term *cosmology, ethos, worldview,* and *ideology.* I treat these states as relatively autonomous forms of collective consciousness in the sense that none is reducible or collapsible into the other, and yet, for example, an ethos can exist only in relation to (that is to say, relative to) a cosmology, and so on. That is, they are not separate and independent forms of "consciousnesses," yet they also do not form a monolithic or fused collective consciousness. Therefore, as I treat it, consciousness is a unitary mental property that has an intrinsic organization of relatively autonomous mental states. I will refer to this as the integrated view of cultural traditions. In addition, individual subjects as active conscious agents experience this integrated form of collective consciousness at both their preconscious or practical level and the fully focused or discursive level of awareness (Giddens 1979, 24–25; for my purposes, I will not discuss the unconscious). Practical and discursive levels of awareness or consciousness are structured by virtue of the mental property of reflexivity that humans have (that is, we have the capacity to be aware of our own consciousness). In fact, it is not simply that we have reflexivity; I have argued that what is unique about human consciousness is that it is characterized as being effortlessly reflexive (Byers 1999b, 30). By this I mean that the human agent can and typically does effortlessly shift mental focus from the extensional (the world outside) to the intensional (the inner mental world), thereby effortlessly bringing the practical self-awareness to the discursive level. This shift in focus is typically mediated through the expressive articulation of the contents of this self-awareness in self-speaking or self- visioning.[1] As cultural traditions, these contents are our shared values, knowledge, and goals. It is the capacity of effortless reflexivity, in my view, that enables us to constitute flexible and integrated cultural traditions (Byers 1994, 372–73).

I have already used the term *cosmology* to refer to the world beliefs shared by a population and the term *ethos* to refer to the shared values and attitudes. As I suggest in chapter 2, the type of ethos that a people share presupposes the type of cosmology that they have. For example, an immanentist cosmology implicates a squatter ethos. However, something is missing here: the mode of connecting these abstract spheres of cosmology and ethos to the everyday life of a people. Everyday life is made up of ongoing perceiving and doing. I refer to the way in which a people perceive their world as their worldview (and this includes both their natural and their social worlds). However, the term *worldview* can be misleading in that, clearly, perceiving is not restricted to the visual experience of "viewing." Therefore, the term *worldview* must be understood as embracing the whole range of perceiving (visual, oral, tactile, and so on) that a people have by virtue of their ethos and cosmology. Complementing the notion of worldview is ideology, defined as the collective prior intentions and their representational contents—rules and protocols—by which a people conduct themselves in their shared worlds. This means that an ethos and an ideology are both deontic. The former operates at the level of standards and principles, the latter at the level of rules and protocols that make up the collective "know-how." Importantly, neither ideology nor worldview can be reduced to ethos or cosmology; nor can they be realized in action and perceptual experiencing independently of cosmology and ethos. That is, they are relatively autonomous collective mental states. Thus, worldview and ideology are realized in those forms of ongoing perceiving and behaving by which the abstract spheres of cosmology and ethos are anchored to human social life, thereby making human existence possible.

INTENTIONALITY

The tendency in anthropology and archaeology is to characterize cultural traditions in passive or descriptive terms, and this is done by focusing on what I refer to above as their representational contents. It might be useful to draw an analogy with speech acts here. In this case, what I refer to as the representational contents of an ideology would be the equivalent to the propositional contents of a promise. However, I want to break with the passive perspective when speaking of cultural traditions. An example of the passive perspective is when the cosmology of a people is described: "The Aztecs believed the world was created by . . . ," and so on. As this example illustrates, the cosmology is usually discussed in terms of the world knowledge or beliefs of a people or, more correctly, in terms of the representational contents of these world beliefs, since it is the latter that are described by the propositional content of the assertive expression, and as such these are intensional descriptive expressions. While the representational contents of cosmologies are certainly important (particularly since humans differentiate among beliefs by their contents), this descriptive approach ignores the phenomenological or dynamic, experiential aspect, that is, the way in which subjects experience believing and having the beliefs that they hold and how these figure in influencing their perceptual experiencing of the world, and so on. The same applies to ethos. In describing an ethos, humans might describe the values and deontic principles that make it up, while overlooking that these principles are what figure in constituting the emotions and attitudes of being proud or ashamed of our actions, and so on.

To clarify the dynamic nature that I want to attribute to cultural traditions, I can draw out the above parallel between the representational contents of cultural traditions and the propositional contents of speech acts, by showing that the pragmatic meaning rather than the propositional meaning of the speech acts is what best models the dynamic nature of cultural traditions. For example, as defined above, an ideology is the complex set of collective prior intentions of a group. These prior intentions constitute the range of collective strategies on which the group, as a group, acts and within which the individual agents of the group operate.[2] A collective or group strategy, of course, is essentially a structured commissive, a self-referring promise or commitment that lays out the organized steps that a group must follow to achieve its goals as predicated in the representational contents of the group strategy; as the publicly promulgated goals of the group, the strategy constitutes a complex promise (or, for those opposed, a threat). In short, as I am using these terms, ideologies, cosmologies, ethos, and worldviews constitute the active experiencing of a people.

Therefore, to describe the dynamic or experiential aspect of these different relatively autonomous aspects of a cultural tradition, we have to use verbs—believing, thinking, guessing, speculating, affirming, desiring, wanting, wishing, shaming, honoring, promising, and so on. Furthermore, all this believing and desiring always entails objects or states of affairs, that is, some thing or things that the believing, speculating, desiring, promising, and so on, are about. The term *intentionality* is used in philosophy generically to refer to this directedness (or "aboutness") that is intrinsic to our beliefs, desires, intentions, hopes, worries, fears, and so on. As philosophers like to say when discussing intentionality, a person cannot simply believe, declare, desire, see, or intend. Rather, a person believes that such and such is the case, or desires X, or sees Y, or intends to do Z, and so on. It is this "aboutness," a mentally embodied reaching out to and engaging with the world, that characterizes intentional states of consciousness; in a very important sense, cultural traditions—as collective forms of consciousness—are always realized in dynamic phenomenological experiences as collective states of believing, wanting, intending, seeing, feeling, doing, making, speaking, and so on.

In John Searle's terms (1983, 26–111), there are four basic forms of intentionality: beliefs, desires, perceptions, and intentions. These terms are used generically for each category. Thus, by *belief* he means beliefs, as such, as well as guesses, speculations, hunches, claims, know-that, hypotheses, theories, and so on. Similarly, by *desire* he means desires, as such, as well as wishes, wants, hopes, fears, and so on. An intentional state, whether a belief, desire, perception, or intention, can be logically analyzed into two components: its dynamic aspect, this being its directedness or psychological mode/attitude; and its formal aspect, this being its representational content. As indicated above, the representational content (or simply stated, the content) can be expressed in words in propositional form, and this specifies what that intentional state is about or directed at, that is to say, what its object is. $S(r)$ is Searle's notation for this structuring of intentional states, where S represents the psychological mode and (r) the representational content. Belief, desire, perception, and intention are notated, respectively, as $Bel(r)$, $Des(r)$, $Per(r)$, and $Int(r)$. Thus, the Bel(r), written as "Henry is an honest man," has a representational content (r) that can be written here in the same words, "Henry is an honest man." This is its sense meaning, and this meaning specifies the object of the belief, that is, what the belief is about: namely, a man known to the speaker and hearers as "Henry," and the attribute, being "an honest man," that is predicated of him.

As stated above, the object of an intentional state, such as a belief, is what that state is about; this is always specified by *(r)*. In Searle's theory, this object (or state of affairs, process, property) is critically important, and he refers to it as the condition of satisfaction of the intentional state. For example, to say in the case of Bel(r) that the contents (r) of Bel(r) specify the object of the belief, or more fully, the conditions of satisfaction of that belief simply means that if the world is the way (r) specifies it is, then the belief fits or corresponds to the world as specified. A simpler way to put this is to say that the belief is true. That is, John's belief "Henry is an honest man" will be satisfied/true if, in fact, there actually is a person "Henry" known by John and this person actually has the property of honesty that John's belief attributes to him. It is notable that truth is a property not of the object—John—but of the belief itself. Therefore, if the content of the belief does not fit the world, then it is not the world that is false, but the belief. John can resolve this problem, of course, by changing the contents of his belief. Hence, while the representational contents of a belief do not determine what the world will be like, they do specify the conditions of satisfaction (that is, what the world must be like) in order for the belief to be true.[3]

So much for the representational content (r) in the notation Bel(r). What about the psychological mode of a belief, notated by Bel? According to Searle's theory, intentional states are not epiphenomenal but real embodied mental properties. As specified above, the psychological mode is the property of mental directedness of a given intentional state. Since Bel is the psychological mode of believing, guessing, asserting, and so on, and since this means that the mental contents (r) of Bel(r) must be "fitted" to the world in order for the belief to be satisfied (that is, for it to be true), Searle characterizes a belief or believing as having the mind-to-world (M→W) direction of fit. That is to say, for the belief to be true, its contents must "fit" the world.

A given belief and a given desire can have the same representational content: for example (expressing these states in words), "I believe that this is a tasty hamburger" and "I want this tasty hamburger." Therefore, we might well ask, since a belief and a desire can have the same contents, what makes them different intentional states? Simply put, they differ in terms of direction of fit. While a belief has M→W direction of fit, a desire has the reverse, or world-to-mind (W→M) direction of fit. That is, for my desire "I want this tasty hamburger" to be satisfied, the world (W) must change (or become changed) so as to fit/

satisfy my desire (M). It is because a particular belief and a particular desire can have the same representational contents while necessarily having opposing directions of fit that these are relatively autonomous and mutually irreducible intentional states.

Of course, beliefs and desires are related. For example, without having the Bel(x), one could not formulate the Des(x), "I want X." But this also means that the belief-want relation is not symmetrical. One could easily have the Bel(x) and never formulate the Des(x), while one could not possibly formulate the Des(x) if one had no belief whatsoever that X existed. Another way of putting this is to say that if a person has the Des(x), then it necessarily follows that the same person must have the Bel(x). This asymmetrical relation is critical to archaeological interpretation since it grounds the view that if the existence and realization of a prehistoric Des(x) is demonstrated in the empirical data, then the people responsible for the behavior that brought about that empirical pattern not only had the Des(x) but also must necessarily have had the requisite Bel(x), since the Des(x) is only possible if the Bel(x) exists.

Wants, desires, hopes, values, and attitudes toward the world are the bases of motives. Therefore, when we do act, we typically have some motivational structure of wants, values, and attitudes, the fulfilment of which we are pursuing. In these terms, the actions that we perform are among the conditions of satisfaction of this motivational structure. However, just as having a belief does not entail formulating certain wants, values, and attitudes, having certain wants, values, and attitudes does not entail acting on them. For example, I might want to eat ice cream. However, knowing that I am lactose intolerant, I suppress the want and never form the intention to eat ice cream; therefore, while certainly sometimes having the ice-cream-eating want, I never formulate or exercise an ice-cream-eating intention. That is, a person can have a want without formulating the intention to perform the action that is the condition of satisfaction of that want. Therefore, while wants and beliefs are necessary for actions to occur, their occurrence requires exercising an additional intentional mental state, commonly referred to as an intention, or Int(r), in the ordinary sense of the word.

Winking and blinking are the same behaviors. But the term *blinking*, as normally used, does not delineate an action as I use that term; it refers to a physiological behavioral response to some object-stimulus. *Winking*, however, while delineating the same physiology, refers to an action because it is the behavior we do in exercising a particular intention. However, as stated above, while clearly some motive or desire is being realized when a person winks, this person might have that same motive or desire at another time and not wink. Therefore, in winking, the agent not only exercises the desire to wink but also clearly forms and exercises the intention to wink.

As I note above, Searle also speaks of prior intentions, which, in structural terms, are notated in the same way as Int(r). The difference is that we can formulate and exercise ordinary intentions at the same time: for example, in becoming angry at a person, one might simply hit out. The whole process of feeling anger, forming a hitting intention, and hitting can occur in a nonreflective manner. However, prior intentions always entail discursive awareness in that they are the bases of planning and necessarily implicate structural frameworks of wants and motives tied to social position and interests. This is why I suggest above that prior intentions make up strategies. Thus, a strategy constituted of a structured plan (which is a logically organized set of prior intentions) will be exercised, and the exercise of prior intentions will cause the formation and exercise of the relevant intentions-in-action. Hence, in many cases desires and in all cases prior and ordinary intentions entail actions as their conditions of satisfaction.

Furthermore, the psychological mode is the same for both desires and intentions, namely, world-to-mind (W→M) direction of fit. This means that, just as the conditions of satisfaction of Des(r) are that the world must change to fit the contents (r), so for our intentions—Int(r)—to be satisfied (fulfilled), the world must change (W→M) to fit the contents (r) of the intentions. This raises the question that if both types of intentional states, Des and Int, have the same psychological attitude (W→M), and if a particular want and a particular intention can have the very same contents so that the same action counts as the condition of satisfaction of both intentional states, how do desires and intentions differ? That is to say, in what way are they relatively autonomous if their contents and directions of fit are the same? Why are they not simply treated by Searle as mutually reductive—all intentions being simply certain types of desires, or vice versa?

The difference, according to Searle, is simple but profoundly important. In the case of a subject A having Des(r), for example, a desire to become wealthy, the desire will be satisfied if the person does indeed become wealthy even without doing anything by way of bringing about this state. That is, desires can be fulfilled without those having them acting to fulfil them. However, the intention to become wealthy requires that the subject who has this intention must actually behave or plan to behave (that is, develop a wealth-production strategy) and be in the situation to be able to exercise that strategy by way of

Table 3.1. Properties of Intentional States

Intentional State	Direction of Fit	Direction of Causality
Belief—Bel(r)	M→W	none
Perception—Per(r)	M→W	W→M
Desire—Des(r)	W→M	none
Intention—Int(r)	W→M	M→W

Source: Derived from Searle 1983, 97.

satisfying this intention. In effect, intentions are causal aspects of their own satisfaction. If one intends to do X, part of the content of the intention is that the person who has that intention must cause her/his doing X.

Searle (1983, 83–98) distinguishes between desires and intentions in precisely these causal terms. Both desires, Des(r), and intentions, Int(r), have the same psychological mode, namely, W→M direction of fit, and a particular want and a particular intention can have the same representational contents, but only intentions have reflexive causality (that is, only intentions stipulate that the holder of the intention must figure as the efficient cause of her/his actions that bring about the conditions of satisfaction of the intentions). Searle characterizes the causality of action intentions in terms of M→W direction of causality. That is, in exercising the intention in behaving in accordance with the contents of his/her intention, the agent changes the world to fit them, thereby satisfying the intention.

Therefore, while both intentions and desires have world-to-mind (W→M) direction of fit, only intentions have direction of causality—and this is always mind-to-world (M→W) direction of causality. Hence, to say that subjects exercise their intentions is to say that they literally move their bodies or components of their bodies in a manner specified but not determined by the content of their own intentions so as to change the world, thereby making the world fit these contents and satisfy their intentions. Of course, subjects may fail to make that fit. That is, intentions can be exercised and still fail to bring about the intended change for many reasons—time runs out, a stronger subject intervenes, a court overrules, and so on. Specifically, Searle is saying that through our mentally controlled embodied engagements with the world, we can cause it to be changed to fit our intentions (Searle 1983, 117–26). The wants and desires that are the motivational background of these intentions, to the degree that they have the same representational contents, are, of course, also satisfied. (To summarize all this, Table 3.1 might be useful.)

Just as desires and intentions are parallel by having the same W→M direction of fit and differ in terms of causality in that only intentions and not desires have reflexive M→W direction of causality, so beliefs and perceptions are equivalently paired. Perceptions, Per(r), and beliefs, Bel(r), share the M→W direction of fit. Just as my belief that "Harry is honest" is true if Harry actually exists and is an honest person, so my seeing the woods and smelling the flowers are real perceptual experiences if my seeing and smelling (mind) "fit" the woods and the flowers (world). If I am having these very same perceptual experiences of seeing the woods and smelling the flowers when in fact no woods or flowers exist there for me to see or smell, then we would say that I am hallucinating, or some such; that is, my perceptions are false, or nonveridical. Like a belief that does not fit the world (false), I am seeing and smelling what is not there (mirage, hallucination). As with false beliefs, to correct the false perception I cannot change the world. Rather, I have to get my perceptions back in order.

Thus, like intentions, real (rather than false) perceptual experiences put us directly and causally in contact with the world in a way that is not the case for beliefs or desires. I can have all sorts of beliefs independently of the world and its objects, just as I can also have all sorts of desires that are unrealistic and incapable of ever being realized. I can think about Caesar, although he is long gone, and I can wish that he had not crossed the Rubicon, although he did, according to historical accounts. In contrast, if I really see the woods and smell the flowers, it is because they cause these perceptual experiences by affecting my sensory mechanisms (eyes and nose). Hence, perceptions, Per(r), like intentions, Int(r), are also causal engagements that the agents have with the world. However, while Int(r) has M→W direction of causality, Per(r) has W→M direction of causality, in that the world causes the sensory stimuli that we experience as seeing woods and smelling flowers.

Where beliefs and desires importantly figure in all this is that only because I know and have the beliefs that I have about the world do I perceive these objects under the aspect that I do (as trees and as flowers), and because of my desires (as the basis of my values), this perceptual experience takes on its pleasantness/unpleasantness, rightness/wrongness, and so on. Hence, if I held to an immanentist cosmology and squatter ethos, I would also experience these objects as having agentive qualities akin to my own, possibly disclosing or manifesting the spiritual powers of the spirit custodians of the forest and eliciting from me certain intentions-to-act whereby I could satisfy relevant moral concerns, and so on. In precisely the same way, the animals I tracked would be experienced as subjects much like myself, and I would experience my killing as hunting, not poaching, as long as I did the killing according to the deontic rules that constitute the content of my hunting intentions.

All this means that action, practice, activities, interactions, events, and so on, along with perceptions (seeing X, feeling Y), are direct intentional causal engagements that agents have with the world, including with each other. To act is to change the world by way of satisfying intentions, and simultaneously, to see is to be acted upon by the world by way of satisfying the visual perception. This simply means that we cannot act without perceiving the effects we have, and perceiving these effects recursively affects our intentions since, without perceiving veridically, we could never know when our intentions have been satisfied.

INTENTIONALITY AND ARCHAEOLOGICAL INTERPRETATION

All this can be clarified from the perspective that particularly counts for archaeology. When we see a scattering of deer bones and flint flakes that we interpret to be humanly caused, we are claiming to be directly seeing this as the residue of the conditions of satisfaction of the exercise of a complex stream of prehistoric intentions. When we then classify these conditions of satisfaction as deer butchering and the place as a prehistoric deer-butchering site, we are characterizing the patterning in terms of the claimed know-how that made up the representational content (r) of the complex prior intentions (hunting strategy) that the behavior producing this patterning satisfied. This interpretation entails that the butchering was done by means of intentional steps having specific know-how contents, and these implicate the exercise of a substrategy of the hunting strategy, what we can term a butchering strategy. This strategy necessarily implies the satisfaction of the desires/needs that this type of action typically fulfils, for example, the desire/need to eat. All this means that in characterizing the material residue in this way, we are committed to the claim that there must have existed in the understanding of the responsible prehistoric agents the requisite beliefs that made this strategy possible, since only if these existed could the patterning as we have characterized it exist. Of course, in deontic ecological terms, part of the know-how would include the rules of style by which the killing is constituted as the type of hunting act intended, thereby reproducing and possibly enhancing the reputation of the responsible agent as a fine hunter. If so, then we have to lay over this whole interpretation the prescriptive and proscriptive deontics of hunting, and these necessarily presuppose the ethos and its structure of ethical and moral principles that go along with the particular type of beliefs that made it possible to have those deontics.

If we get the first step right, that is to say, if we correctly interpret the material residue that we are examining as among the conditions of satisfaction of a hunting activity, we necessarily implicate a hunting strategy, and the latter necessarily had representational contents, and, therefore, the rest follows. This necessity arises from the nature of intentionality as theorized above; that is, beliefs, desires, perceptions, and intentions are relatively autonomous intentional states and therefore are integrated to constitute a significant part of the agent's total cognitive-normative makeup. Furthermore, according to the warranting model, intentional behaviors presuppose the existence of a human community since the formation of our action intentions necessitates occupying the appropriate social positions and having the standing in the community that endows one with the appropriate deontics—that is, rights and duties—that empower one to act. (In this case, I am differentiating between the power-to-behave and the power-to-act. The former is a physiological capacity; the latter is a socially and culturally constituted capacity.) These rights and duties directly articulate with shared notions of obligations and privileges that can exist only as an integrated part of the collective intentionality, referred to above as a cultural tradition.

Finally, none of this commits us to a deterministic view of action. Neither social positions nor beliefs and desires determine action. They only make it possible for us to perform the actions that we do. As I point out above, we hold all sorts of beliefs and desires about the objects, processes, events, and states of the world without thereby being compelled to act on them. However, if I intend to catch the train on time, I can formulate that intention only if I believe that there are such things as trains "to catch" and if I have the requisite know-how specifying what will count as "catching the train on time"—such as knowing how to read a schedule, knowing how a schedule authoritatively structures time so that I have rights concerning when the train ought to arrive, knowing how to conduct myself so that my behavior will count as "boarding the train," for example, purchasing a ticket—and the whole presuppositional structure of cultural knowledge (belief) and strategic know-how (intention) that makes it possible for me to formulate and exercise my train-catching intentions.

Still, all this knowledge and know-how does not compel me to act. Similarly, I can have all this collective knowledge and even have good deontic reasons to catch the train on time (for example, I have the duty to go to work), yet this desire will not compel me to formulate the intention to catch the train. Finally, I can formulate the intention to catch the train by way of fulfilling the responsibilities I have to my employer, my family, and so on, and even partly implement the intention by leaving my domicile on time to "catch the train," and nevertheless I may end up deciding to go by bus. However, if I actually do "catch the train" on time, then, in retroductive terms, it was necessarily the case that I had and exercised all those states of intentionality (that is, intentions, desires, perceptions, and beliefs), as well as necessarily occupying the social positions of employee, father, husband, and so on, that made this complex structure of intentionality possible to have and exercise.

So, once the action is properly characterized in terms of conditions of satisfaction, the retroductive inferential chain of action→intention→perception→desire→belief + social position/circumstance is logically entailed by this theory of intentionality. However, the reverse deductive-predictive inferential chain of social position/circumstance + belief→ desire→perception→intention→action is not entailed (that is, it is contingent, and therefore it is nondeterministic).[4] In effect, the agent is responsible for the actions she/he actually performs. Hence, I can know the total intentionality plus the social circumstance of a person (or group), and my prediction that she/he/they will perform action X can fail, while, if I have correctly characterized the action nature of the material patterning, then, as the conditions of satisfaction of the intentions it realized, I can retroductively enter into the intentionality plus social situation that must have existed for that action to have occurred.

This has important interpretive implications for archaeology, since it sustains the principle that both our social positions and our intentionality are necessary for action, while emphasizing that this necessity never translates into treating social structure and intentionality as monoliths that determine our actions, in the sense of impelling/compelling us to act. Rather, these are among the enabling and constraining conditions of our activities. If the actions are performed, then the social structures and intentionality that such actions entail must have existed, or else the activities could not have been performed. I can now explicitly relate this theory of intentionality to the components of a cultural tradition, namely, cosmology, ethos, worldview, and ideology.

CULTURAL TRADITIONS AND INTENTIONALITY

While the above analysis articulates the basic structure of intentionality, it is incomplete for my purposes since, as it stands, it could be used to describe how a perfect sociopath would operate, a sociopath being someone who effectively treats social life in zero-sum game terms. A very clever person untouched by deontics, one whose life is dominated by the pursuit of pleasure and avoidance of pain, could have and exercise all the required knowledge and practical know-how simply to ensure the greatest self-satisfying benefits at the least personal costs. Rights and duties would simply be experienced as benefits and costs, and if the costs (for normal subjects, costs would include the deontic dimension, for example, moral duties) required to perform certain actions were greater than the possible benefits (for normal subjects, benefits would include rights and esteem) that could be achieved, the sociopath would not perform them. In a sense, the sociopath is much more predictable than the socially normal human.

Components making up a cultural tradition are shared forms of intentionality that, simultaneously, are reflexive. This does not mean that I am advocating a group mind or a transcendental teleology. If you and I both have the belief "Henry is an honest man," then we each have the same token belief, and my belief is an intentional state of my mind, and your belief is an intentional state of your mind. Beliefs are always held in individual minds because they are embodied properties of the human brain. Therefore, aggregating these two belief tokens does not constitute a collective mental state. As I treat it, what makes a collective belief is that it is reflexive in the sense that part of having the belief (for example, that the world is round) is that those who hold it recognize that it is a shared and largely commonsense knowledge. Giddens (1979, 5, 251–53) uses the term *mutual knowledge* in a somewhat similar manner to my notion of collective belief as reflexive. This means that the collective belief includes as part of its representational content the usually implicit representation that "everyone" holds that belief. Cosmologies are collective world beliefs in this sense.

As complexes of collective beliefs that have the world or cosmos as their object, cosmologies are part of their own condition of satisfaction in that part of what makes them true is that they have as an intrinsic part of their content the representation that "everyone" has these collective beliefs as part of her/his cognitive makeup. This makes cosmologies not objectively but intersubjectively true, since the objective aspect of the content is what specifies the world and its makeup as a given cosmology's condition of satisfaction, and this world can be quite different from what the content specifies, thereby constituting the cosmology as a false belief. Therefore, while cosmologies have this reflexivity, they do not entail conformity and commitment by those who hold them, since these beliefs exist as properties of autonomous agents. Hence, even though she/he knows that the collective beliefs are part of the cognitive makeup of "everyone" (that is, of all "normal" humans), any individual in a group can privately consider these collective beliefs, or some of them, to be false.

This collective consciousness is possible only if the agents have effortless reflexivity, that is, only if they are able to be effortlessly aware of their own consciousness and are able to express their beliefs, either to themselves or to others. Thus, as a complex set of collective world beliefs, a cosmology entails the mental capacity of effortless reflexivity on the part of the social subjects who interact on the largely taken-for-granted practical assumption that everyone has the same knowledge or belief. An important aspect of their cosmologies will be collective beliefs about the social world and the way it "fits" into the cosmos—in effect, a collective sociology.

An ethos is the set of collective values and standards that make up our sense of what objects, processes, states of affairs, activities, and properties (including personal and social) are worthy and honorable and what are despicable and humiliating (Harré 1979, 3–4; Taylor 1985a, 23–24). It is also reflexive, in two ways. As in the case of cosmology, part of the content of this set of values, attitudes, and standards includes the representation that "everyone" has these same values. But it is also reflexive in a second sense. An ethos clearly informs our desires and wants, but these cannot be identified with an ethos, since, as stated above, a sociopath can have desires and wants, dislikes and aversions, while not having any sense of what is worthy or unworthy. Therefore, the second sense in which an ethos is reflexive is that it is constituted of second-order desires, wants, and values, these being standards that specify which first-order wants and desires, Des(r), are worthy and honorable and which are unworthy and dishonorable. Charles Taylor (1985a, 16–21) speaks of such second-order desires and wants as strong evaluations and strong attitudes; he contrasts them with ordinary, nonreflexive, first-order desires and wants. Thus, the standards and principles that underwrite these second-order values constitute the moral structure of a community, and I believe that calling this complex its ethos is appropriate.

However, I must stress that, except that they are reflexive, cosmological beliefs and second-order values/desires are logically structured very much like ordinary beliefs and desires. That is, just as beliefs have mind-to-world direction of fit and desires have world-to-mind direction of fit, so cosmology and ethos also have mind-to-world and world-to-mind direction of fit, respectively. Also like ordinary desires, second-order values/desires lack intentional causality. Therefore, they are not the efficient causes of collective actions, although all collective actions and the strategies that they realize presuppose a community ethos, as well as a structure of cosmology and collective sociology. This means that intervening between cosmology/ethos and collective activity is a set of collective intentions realized as community strategies. These collective intentions are also reflexive; that is, their representational contents are attuned to the ethos as deontic rules and protocols that specify the conditions that those carrying out and performing any given activity must bring about, including the form of the activity itself, for this activity to count as and be the type of activity intended, thereby fulfilling the strategic goals by satisfying the collective intentions. I have chosen to define an ideology in these terms, as a complex of collective prior intentions that make up the core of a group's strategy; the exercise of the latter is the performance of collective practices. Therefore, ideology as a set of collective prior intentions is also reflexive, differentiating it from ordinary prior intentions. The first-order intention to indulge in rich food satisfies an organic appetite. However, reflexive intentions would be deontic in nature as proscriptions and prescriptions (taboos specifying what behaviors must be avoided and imperatives stipulating what behaviors must be done). These ideologies presuppose and draw on strong or second-order values and principles. Therefore, a complex of proscriptions and prescriptions, or taboos and imperatives, constitutes an important part of the deontic content of the collective prior intentions of a community, that is to say, its ideology or set of ideologies that presupposes the community's ethos.[5]

To gain a sense of how this would work, assume that a reflexive agent would tend to be committed to a particular ideology, for example, the dietary rules and protocols of her/his religious group or cult. Therefore, in the appropriate circumstances, she/he would draw on and exercise these know-how dietary rules. Quite often these will proscribe, or make taboo, a range of possible and, indeed, at the first-order level, quite often desirable comestibles specifically to avoid sacred pollution while at the same time satisfying what are taken to be sacred goals by prescribing the consumption of what are defined as higher, second-order comestibles. Thus the dietary practices realize an ideology, and they would be taken to manifest strong values—an ethos. The latter would presuppose a particular cosmology that would make these proscriptions and prescriptions intelligible, including, of course, the range of foods and related conditions that these proscriptions and prescriptions specify. In the appropriate circumstances, those who are seen to follow these ideological rules are perceived by their fellows as worthy and honorable persons. In these terms, to succumb to the pleasure of eating what should not be eaten counts as shameful, and someone who does so and is committed to the dietary rules will feel guilty while others who are committed to these same rules will scorn her/him. Finally, a worldview is also the collective perception that a people have of their world (natural and social), largely in virtue of their cosmology and ethos. Again, it is reflexive in the sense that part of perceiving the world as being immanently sacred—for example, perceiving the mound on which one is standing as embodying the essential properties of the earth, and so on—is that "everyone" who is accompanying one is having the same perceptual experiences.

THE RELATIVE AUTONOMY OF COMPONENTS OF CULTURAL TRADITIONS

Some very important implications for archaeological interpretation and understanding arise from this view of cultural tradition. Because the basic structures constituting a cultural tradition (that is, cosmology, ethos, worldview, and ideology) are collective realizations of the four basic forms of intentionality—beliefs, desires, perceptions, and intentions—and because the latter are relatively autonomous, it follows that the four basic components of cultural traditions are also relatively autonomous. For this reason, two or more peoples having different histories can, however, share the same cosmology and have the same ethos, by virtue of which they have very similar worldviews, while differing significantly in ideologies and the forms of practices that realize these ideologies. For example, assume that both Tribe A and Tribe B occupy the same region and practice the same subsistence technology, as well as share the same immanentist cosmology and the same ethos, and have worldviews that are also largely the same. Thus, each would perceptually experience the world as immanently sacred and, in doing so, equally grapple with resolving the essential contradiction of existence arising from having to hunt and gather regularly to survive, thereby intervening into the sacred-natural order. Therefore, each tribe must continually rectify, justify, and constitute its ecological practices as warranted interventions. Despite sharing all this, however, their separate histories could quite easily lead them to differ in terms of proscriptions and prescriptions constituting the know-how that is the representational contents of the midwifery ritual aspect of their ecological strategies, which then belong to the ideological domain. Therefore, in principle these ideologies can systematically vary between the two tribes.

The most immediately tangible difference might be displayed in style. As I argue in an earlier chapter, styles mediate the symbolic pragmatics of action intentions, and, therefore, the users of tools that bear style are thereby endowed with action-constitutive force. Thus, members of Tribe A may typically use hunting gear that bears styles that contrast with those styles of the functionally equivalent hunting gear used by members of Tribe B. Each considers its tribal tools as appropriate hunting warrants, that is, as effective means to warrant their killing behaviors as appropriate hunting acts in the view of the spirit custodians of the animals and in whom, given their shared cosmology, both tribes believe. However, because of the stylistic differences, the members of these two tribes would perceive each others' tools as infelicitous—certainly not effective action warrants—even though they might concede that in instrumental terms the two sets are nearly equivalent. It is even possible, as in the San case (Weissner 1983, 269), that one group will even assess the hunting gear of the other as superior in terms of killing efficiency, while still eschewing emulating this gear. That is, despite their acknowledging the superior practicality of their neighbors' hunting gear, they would consider that using gear of that style would constitute poaching acts, thereby endangering the viability of the resources in the region that the two groups share.

If the know-how content of the collective intentions of a people as realized in their everyday material lives is part of the broader ideology of this region, then ideology also embraces the notion of ecological strategy, this being the rationalized system of subsistence and settlement strategies that is realized in and mediates their subsistence and settlement practices. Therefore, a subsistence and settlement strategy is part of the ideological sphere of a people, since part of articulating it would require specifying the rules and protocols that make up the representational content of subsistence intentions. Hence, a central, usually taken-for-granted, component of these representational contents will be rules of style. These necessarily presuppose strong values and attitudes, that is, the moral standards that make up the ethos.

INTEGRATED AND FUSED VIEWS OF CULTURAL TRADITIONS

At the beginning of this chapter, I note the tendency for many archaeologists to use only one or two of the terms delineated above to cover the different forms of collective consciousness, favoring, for example, *cosmology* or *ideology* to refer to the totality of a cultural tradition. I suggest that this tendency reveals an inadequate theory of human consciousness, effectively treating it as a largely unstructured domain so that cultural traditions are assumed to be inextricably blended. I will refer to this blending as the fused view of cultural traditions, and it contrasts with the integrated view that I outline above. The claim that a cultural tradition is fused or blended implicates characterizing it is a single "package," and this means that for a community to have a particular world belief (cosmology), it must also have all the strong values and attitudes (ethos), collective perceptions (worldview), and collective intentions (ideology) that go along with that cosmology. This fused view has important implications in understanding variation in the archaeological record, since it suggests that any modifying of the ideological rules entails modifying the whole package of values and beliefs also. In effect, the only way a people can change their fused cultural tradition is to replace the old with a new tradition. If this is the case, then assessing the significance of variation in the archaeological record becomes highly problematic. Precisely what does the emergence of a new ceramic pattern mean? For example, what is the significance of the rather abrupt appearance of Z-twist cordmarked pottery in the later Late Woodland while the preexisting S-twist pottery continued? Does the Z-twist variation count as a cultural innovation or a migration of a people with a different cultural tradition? If the latter is argued, then the fused view implies that this minor cordmarking variation presupposes a radical difference in cosmology and ethos between the two peoples. However, if the Z-twist variation is argued to be an in situ innovation, then, under the fused view, a radical home-grown replacement of the total cultural tradition is suggested.

Of course, the argument could be made that Z-twist/S-twist cordmarking is simply a practical nonsymbolic attribute and therefore is unrelated to cultural traditions, which are always realized in conventional forms.[6] However, invoking practicality does not work when applied to large-scale construction. Archaeologists generally agree that symbolism is strongly realized in the constructing of mounds. Under the fused view, interpreting the apparently abrupt emergence of multiple-mound locales such as Cahokia as the outcome of massive and radical cultural innovation becomes almost unavoidable. Indeed, this is precisely what Thomas Emerson and Timothy Pauketat have argued for in a series of recent publications (Emerson et al. 2003, 179; Emerson and Pauketat 2002, 109; Pauketat 1994, 171–73; 1997, 31–32; Pauketat and Emerson 1997a, 5, 20; 1999, 303–8). In their terms, the building of mounds, woodhenges, and plazas marks an abrupt replacement of the cultural traditions of the pre-Mississippian occupants of the American Bottom, for the most part these being the immediate ancestors of those responsible for the mounds. The religious beliefs are transformed from the earlier period by the claim that some select humans are godlike (Emerson 2003a, 74–75; Pauketat 1994, 34–35), the earthly representatives of the ruling powers of the cosmos, and that those who are ruled have the obligation and sacred duty to follow the edicts of this new set of sacred rulers. This new vision of the world alienates the ordinary people from their own cultural traditions, forcing the latter "underground," while transforming the believers into commoners dependent for guidance on the bestowers of this new fused vision, who thereby enhance their elite power. Mound construction is deemed the most effective mode of relating to the sacred powers of the cosmos, and this must be mediated through the leadership of the new rulers. Thus, symbolic construction is accounted for in these political-ideological terms and a new social world is generated, as radically different in social structure as the newly imposed fused cultural traditions that made all this possible.

I may have done some injustice to Emerson and Pauketat's version of the hierarchical monistic modular polity account of the archaeological record of the American Bottom, since its actual presentation and development by them is much more sophisticated than I have outlined. For example, my approach to ideology does connect with Emerson's when he points out that an essential part of his interpretive approach "is the specific correlation of an idealist cosmological universe with its materialistic expression in the real world through multitudinous material symbols, that is, the material 'containers' of the cosmos" (Emerson 1997a, 191). Since this is stated in the context of interpreting Cahokia, I take him to mean that "the material 'containers' of the cosmos" are the monumental earthworks and woodhenges—their size, makeup, and positioning within the local environment and relative to each other, and so on.

There is a certain ambiguity, however, in the symbolic nature of Cahokian monumentalism as he characterizes it. Above I quote his claim that the "multitudinous material symbols" express this "idealist cosmological universe." The ambiguity is this: Are the monuments as "multitudinous material symbols" used to express the cosmology or to express the cosmos? If they are being characterized as expressing a cosmology per se, then Cahokia was built as a set of "multitudinous material symbols" just so as to refer to the cosmos by way of expressing the collective world beliefs of the builders. If this is the case, then this is an example of the referential fallacy, since it is claiming that monuments are being used as symbols to express the users' concepts and beliefs (cosmology) so as to refer to the objects of the concepts (the cosmos). Speaking of the symbolic usage of monuments in these terms, therefore, fails to make their construction intelligible. After all, why would a people choose monumental construction as a mode of expressing their beliefs so as to refer to the objects of these beliefs, even such important beliefs as the sacred nature of the cosmos, when they could express these same beliefs more precisely and much more cheaply by simply using words?

If, however, Emerson is saying that Cahokia and its monuments were built to express the cosmos as such, then that statement is consistent with the symbolic pragmatic view that I promote in this book, since Emerson would be characterizing the monuments of Cahokia as expressive iconic symbols. As icons of the cosmos, they would be experienced by the builders as expressively participating in the nature of what the mounds represent, the cosmos, or, more correctly, as participating in certain aspectual properties of the cosmos or world. As such, the intelligibility that explains them is pragmatic or action-constitutive. That is, in the collective understanding of the builders, these earthworks were the most effective material media for performing critically important social acts of world renewal; the reason for this is that the monumentalism of Cahokia would be taken to be participating in and thereby presencing the essential powers of those aspects of cosmos that the monuments represent, thereby transforming the collective material behaviors used to build them and also those performed within their context into the complex range of rituals intended. This is the symbolic pragmatic reading. Therefore, if Emerson means by his words "multitudinous material symbols" and "idealist cosmological universe" that Cahokia is a monumental symbol that expresses the cosmos, then I can fully accept that claim, since it is a symbolic pragmatic interpretation (although he does not use that terminology).

However, from this agreement it does not follow that his treatment of ideology and cosmology is any less fused in nature—that is, in Emerson's view (one shared by Pauketat), these new material symbols manifest a radical break with the past, in terms of both cultural traditions and social structures. In contrast, in terms of the integrated view of cultural traditions, while I accept that a new ideological strategy is being manifested, the conclusion does not follow logically that the ethos and cosmology that made formulating this strategy possible changed in any significant way; of course, this applies equally to the social conditions that are presupposed by these earthworks. Indeed, the opposite is the case. The change in ideology that the development of new monumental material symbols maps would likely have occurred only if the cosmology and ethos that they presupposed remained largely unchanged and, along with this, only if the social structures that made this ideological change possible also remained largely unchanged.

Deep and Surface Structures

This raises a very important issue, of course. The integrated view of cultural traditions implicates a surface/deep structuring. As Searle's theory of intentionality emphasizes, the formulation of intentions by responsible agents presupposes holding the beliefs and having the desires that make formulating these intentions possible. Also presupposed in the formulation and exercising of intentions is that the agent occupies the social position(s) that makes it possible for her/him to elicit the requisite recognition from relevant social others that thereby constitutes the agent's behavior as the social activity intended. Hence, all activity presupposes and, of course, reproduces and/or transforms both the social and the cultural structures that enable the agents to perform that activity. The deep cultural structures are postulated here to be the cosmology and ethos, including the collective sociology. This implies that representational contents of ideology and worldview constitute the surface structures of cultural traditions.

In these terms, in general, cosmology and ethos tend to be the most spatio-temporally stable components of a cultural tradition, while ideology and worldview are the components that tend to have the least spatio-temporal stability. This is because, as noted above, any modification of an ideology presupposes a stable cosmology or a cosmology that, while also possibly being modified, retains much of its essential content. Also, since an ideology is realized in actions and their outcomes, recognizing the action nature (or pragmatic nature) of the behaviors is an interpretive exercise that draws on pre-existing beliefs and values and either reproduces or transforms the perceptual experiences of the parties involved. Hence, it is likely that cosmology and ethos will remain largely constant within a region and from generation to generation, while worldviews and ideologies will largely co-vary.

Ideology underwrites and is realized in action; therefore, it is also realized as the most immediate expressive component. If it is the most changeable, then radical changes in material cultural patterning logically can occur without necessarily indexing equivalently radical changes in the cosmology and ethos that made these ideological changes possible. (Only a fused cultural tradition would require such "global" modification.) Also, ideology is never realized abstractly.

It is always exercised and reproduced in behavior since it both governs and is reproduced and/or transformed by these activities. Its nature also means that it is internally variable—that is, there will be competing ideologies, or (as I prefer to say) a community's ideological position always consists of the current status among competing ideological stances or postures. Therefore, a community's ideology is always greater than its current manifestation in material symbols.

Indeed, the reason why a number of ideological stances can coexist in the same community is that their proponents share the same cosmology and ethos. Thus, everyone can agree that the world is immanently sacred, that the sun is a sacred and potent entity that intentionally rises in the east and goes to rest in the west, and that human intervention in the natural order can weaken the essential powers of the sun and therefore it needs to be replenished regularly. What will most likely be disputed is precisely what the conditions of satisfaction are that, if brought about, will ensure that this replenishment is most effectively done. The rules that specify the conditions of satisfaction are not "written in the heavens," although the proponents of a given ideology typically assume that they are. Therefore, disagreement over ritual rules (for example, disagreement over the sacrifice, timing, and the form and size of the ritual facilities) can become quite bitter, with each ideological party believing that its ideological strategy defines the preferred way of doing things—that it is the "true way" while the other ways are always inadequate. Hence, dispute, negotiation, and even agreement, when arrived at, never finally settle the matter. However, they also, largely unwittingly, reproduce the framework of cosmology and ethos that makes the ideological negotiations and disagreements possible.

Because ideology as collective prior intentions or collective strategy is realized in concrete action and its material media, ideological stances are always collective strategies of real groups. These groups prefer performing actions as specified by their ideological stances, since these constitute for them the most authentic conditions of satisfaction of these stances and therefore count in their view as the most felicitous material mode of discharging their sacred duties. Since a community will have a range of ideological stances, while sharing the same cosmology and ethos, there is utility in terming the different parties that bear and promote these different ideologies *ideological factions*. The ideological position of a community or group is manifested in the symbolic pragmatic component of its material culture and the overall patterning, and its variation in time and space maps the shifts in the community's ideological position as the preferences of one faction gain greater expression than those of competing factions. Hence, changes in ideological forms can be used by the archaeologist to assess the shifting balance of power among ideological factions.

Factions are often treated as ephemeral social phenomena. In this sense, they could constitute surface social structures and would presuppose deep social structures of which they are the current expression. Importantly, therefore, since social position is an intrinsic constituent component of action, a parallel deep and surface structuring can be applied to the social system. Deep social structures (such as kinship, class, and ethnicity) can remain stable while the surface structural manifestation of these can vary as part of the ideological variation. I will return to this notion of factions as ideologically constituted groupings later, as it figures importantly in the interpretation of Cahokia and the other associated monumental locales of the American Bottom.

Of course, the claim I make here that archaeologists tend to treat cultural traditions as fused immediately relates to one possible source of the gradualist/rupturalist dispute that Andrew Fortier and Dale McElrath (2002, 174–78) have elucidated. Fortier and McElrath reject the gradualist view and promote the rupturalist view. In effect, they deny that cultural traditions can be modified slowly over time; instead, cultural traditions must be transformed radically, even replaced. Hence, the abrupt appearance of multiple mound sites entails a "profound social upheaval" (Fortier and McElrath 2002, 203). In contrast, the view that I carefully elucidate here—namely, that cultural traditions are integrated as relatively autonomous deep and surface structures—eliminates one of the premises on which this gradualist/rupturalist dispute hinges. Cosmology and ethos, as well as the deep social structures of a social system, tend to remain constant over time and space, while worldview and ideology, as well as the material realization of social structures, can radically modify and fluctuate. Hence, the abrupt emergence of multiple-mound locales can be explained as surface structural ideological and social modifications that simultaneously reproduced the deep structures of cosmology, ethos, and the fundamental social structural axes that made these modifications possible.

Sacred Landscapes

Since the actual material behaviors that Mississippian period peoples in the American Bottom performed in modifying the topography of the environment would be the realization of an ideology presupposing an immanentist cosmology, these peoples would experience their own behavioral interventions as the social activity of cosmos-construction and reconstruction. The constitutive element is located in the intentionality underwriting and realized in this behavior. Therefore, in performing the constructive behavior according to the ideological rules, these peoples transformed their own behavior so that it counted as and, for them, was collective activity by which they endowed Cahokia with the sacredness of that which they took its multiple monumental components to be representing, namely, the essential properties of the multiple aspects of the cosmos (in particular, its sacred powers of creation and procreation). Hence their construction activity was experienced as part of and, for the most part, an enhancement of the sacredness that was immanent in the land itself.

Of course, while a people take the sacredness that they experience to be a property of the world itself, in my construal of cultural traditions, sacredness is a phenomenal property of the collective perceptual experience (that is to say, of the worldview), best characterized as the emotions of awe, reverence, veneration, wonder, and so on, and elicited by both the monuments that they constructed and the ritual(s) that they performed in this monumental context.[7] This is akin to what I stated earlier in defining an icon. A symbol is an icon if it is understood by the users as participating in the essential nature of what it represents. An iconic symbolic pragmatic device, then, is taken by the knowledgeable subjects as deriving its transformative meaning/power by presencing the powers of what it represents. In the realist terms that I outline above, since the experience of sacredness is a property of the experience itself (and not necessarily of the environment that is its object), then this is a reified experience. Of course, if the environment actually is sacred, then this would be an authentic and not a reified experience.

What this means is that while a people's ongoing perceptual experiencing is ontologically separate from the world that is the object of this experiencing, they normally do not experience it this way. The world, of course, has causal impact on a people's perceptual experiences. However, this causality is always mediated by the same representational content that makes up the content of a people's cosmology. Thus, a people will perceptually experience their world as immanently sacred not because the world that is the object of their perception is necessarily sacred but because they have a cosmology from which they formulate the representational contents of their worldview and, therefore, they construe the object of this worldview—the cosmos—in these terms. This explains why two peoples having radically different cosmologies can and will have different worldviews of the very same physical world: that is to say, their perceptual experiencing of this very same world will be different. Thus, instead of claiming that the Mississippian peoples constructed a sacred landscape through the building of great mounds and palisades, one might more realistically say that they constituted their perceptual experience of Cahokia as a sacred landscape through actively constructing its monumental components as icons so that these monuments presenced for them the cosmic properties so desired.

With this delineation of the basic theoretical framework of deontic ecology and the elucidation of cultural traditions and the component notions of cosmology, ethos, worldview, and ideology completed, I can now turn to theorizing the types of social systems that people would constitute in occupying a world that they experienced as immanently sacred. This means picking up the more germane aspects of the hierarchical monistic modular polity and heterarchical polyistic locale-centric accounts, which will act as the general framework for postulating the American Bottom social system and its modification.

4

Deontic Ecology, Cultural Traditions, and Social Systems

I can now elucidate theoretically the type of social system articulation that would be consistent with my outline of deontic ecology and the integrated notion of cultural traditions. This synthesis is of central importance because it forms the foundation of the critical assessment of the hierarchical monistic modular polity and heterarchical polyistic locale-centric accounts of Cahokia and the American Bottom archaeological record that is the core of this book. My discussion of cosmology, ethos, worldview, and ideology in the preceding chapter has an important theoretical point in this regard. Deontic ecology argues that the human-environment relation is as much culturally constructed as it is governed by material imperatives, and to say this is to say that while this relation obviously is grounded on the practical imperatives of biological survival, it is simultaneously constituted in the phenomenological experience of the responsible subjects through the medium of their cultural traditions. The key cultural component in the constitution of this relation is the set of constitutive rules; these would be part of the content of the subsistence and settlement strategy of a people. As such, along with governing the practical outcomes of such practices, this content would also stipulate the expressive forms that must be followed and achieved so that the behavioral interventions count as the type of socioecological activities intended. For example, in an immanently sacred world, a standard deontic component of the ecological strategy would be the proscriptive and prescriptive rules and protocols that make up the midwifery ritual aspect of these practices, thereby constituting ecological practices as having an irreducibly ideological nature, and, largely unwittingly, reproducing the ecological relations. Therefore, according to my elucidation of cultural traditions, since any ideological perspective presupposes a cosmology, this means that instead of archaeologists treating the cognitive-normative aspect expressed through symbol and the material-instrumental aspects of a prehistoric culture as largely independent, they must treat these aspects as intrinsically related.

As I argue in chapter 2, one implication of this claim for understanding settlement and subsistence seems to be clear: different types of cosmology tend to correlate with different types of tenure. In this regard, I correlate proprietorial domain and custodial domain with transcendentalist and immanentist cosmologies, respectively.[1] Since different types of domain entail different ways of constituting the human-environment relation, this dichotomy also implicates different types of settlement systems, and these mediate and reproduce different types of social systems, which I refer to as monistic modular and polyistic locale-centric types, respectively. It is time to elucidate the reasons for correlating exclusive territorialism with monistic modularism and inclusive territorialism with polyistic locale-centrism.

In my discussion of cultural traditions in previous chapters, I use the term *squatter* to characterize the type of ethos associated with an immanentist cosmology. Part of the aptness of this term is that it connotes the core moral imperatives of the ethos, namely, living lightly on the land while exploiting local natural resources only to the degree necessary for survival, thereby minimizing pollution while resanctifying the land and the physical resources. It follows that the reputations of groups will hinge on how well they achieve the ongoing resolution of the essential contradiction of human existence. Since the land and its resources are available to all, all are responsible to exploit the land so that none will suffer and the land will be enhanced. This is the core of the human-land relation termed *custodial tenure*.

Now, as I note in chapter 1, while it would appear logical that a squatter ethos would take agentive equality to be a central value, this is not necessarily the case. The principal value underwriting the squatter ethos would not be equality but autonomy. As I use the term, *autonomy* is the recognition that an agent is entitled to be recognized as having responsibility for her/his own actions. By enshrining autonomy, a squatter ethos necessarily recognizes differences and "inequalities" as grounds for equitable rather than either equal or unequal access to resources. Hence, those guided by a squatter ethos respect differential needs and superior competency, but only if the former are fulfilled and the latter are exercised in terms of the squatter ethos. It follows that even though inequalities are recognized and even respected, they do not translate into dominating social power, since this would contradict the central relational principle of the squatter ethos, namely, agentive autonomy. Therefore, under the inclusive territorialism characteristic of an immanentist cosmology and squatter ethos, all parties have entitlements to those resources required to sustain their status of being autonomous. In these terms, large families necessarily require quantitatively more resources to maintain their autonomy than do small families, and therefore the former are entitled to a proportionally greater access to the available resources than are the latter. This inequality, however, does not translate into the large kin group's having dominance over the small kin group.

Of course, accessibility to natural resources can be constrained by nonsocial factors (for example, seasonality, the nature of the resource itself, being mobile or fixed, and so on), so that the availability of resources often cannot satisfy the aggregate needs. Therefore, some form of rationing of access would not be uncommon. In conformity with a squatter ethos, the principle of the queue would most likely operate. In our society, the queue is, literally, the lineup that usually occurs at bus stops or other areas in which public material and/or service resources are accessed and used. When the needs exceed the immediate supply, they have to be rationed so that everyone receives her/his entitlement. Therefore, when the rush is on for public transportation, everyone understands the squatter principle of "first come--first served," with each taking only the resources needed. Hence, in any given instance in which resource availability and needs do not match, a rank order typically emerges.[2] Expanding the notion of the queue as a fundamental principle of custodial domain would promote quite a different articulation of social structural axes from that characteristic of exclusive territorialism.

As I discuss briefly in chapter 1 when sketching out the heterarchical polyistic locale-centric account, ecological conditions could develop that would promote a disembedding of basic social structural axes on which to generate contrasting kinship and companionship groupings, and these would sustain a form of mutually recognized autonomy. That is, instead of a single structural axis, kinship, constituting a monistic or unitary system, two or more structural axes would come into play, constituting a polyistic system. Although companionship and kinship constitute a duality, each can be further structured (for example, male and female sodalities, as well as patrilineal or matrilineal kinship), thereby constituting a polyistic system. The kin groups would, of course, be based on descent-related generational social structures, constituting family, lineage, and clan relations. Because of the conjunction of male/female and senior/junior generations, the principle of autonomy would create kinship categories that would have complementary rather than dominant/subordinate responsibilities. The active senior generation of women would be responsible for tasks that are clearly defined as separate and different from those of the active senior generation of men, although these would be economically complementary. Nevertheless, the practical nature of the male/female relation would be a constant source of contradiction of the principle of autonomy. This would promote the proliferation of task-oriented taboos and imperatives by which the duties of the two genders are kept distinct, thereby enhancing their respective autonomy, and these would be realized as subsistence and settlement midwifery rituals.

However, the intergenerational kinship relation would also have its contradictions. The practical dependence of the junior generation, particularly as children, on the senior, parenting generation would be a condition that contradicts the principle of agentive autonomy. Since parents and children age together (Giddens 1979, 128–30), as the child matures, parental responsibility and the offspring's growing sense of autonomy might well clash. Therefore, in social systems within which agentive autonomy is a central relational principle, kinship organizations always have to contend with the internal stresses set up by the structural contradictions of the relation between generational responsibilities and individual autonomy.

Such male/female gender and senior/junior intergenerational structural contradictions are much more easily avoided in the formation of companionship-based sodalities. These are typically homogeneous organizations based on the conjunction of same-age and same-gender structures. Homogeneous groups promote relating individuals to each other as autonomous agents having the same range of responsibilities; therefore, social reciprocities of exchanging and sharing become part of everyday interaction. That is, they form as peer-based groups of companions in which mutual recognition of individual autonomy can find its fullest social expression. Indeed, there is no shame in recognizing variability in personal attributes and competencies among same-age/same-gender peers, since these differences become the opportunity to gain reputation and esteem without, however, being able to dominate, although differential personal influence would be prevalent. Thus, the individuals making up an age cohort of young men can relate to each other as autonomous agents, and they can sort out among themselves the actual differences of competencies and capacities according to mutually recognized strengths and limitations. The development of homogeneous groups based on companionship can flourish.

Furthermore, unlike the sodalities of monistic modular societies, the peer-based sodalities that form within the regimes of inclusive territorialism would maintain their mutual autonomy relative to each other and would actively sustain an arm's-length relation with kin groupings, particularly since the kinship positions that the participants in these groups also occupy would require constant negotiation and the maintenance of traditional kinship-based taboos and imperatives that guide their social interaction. That is, overall, the sodalities are social contexts in which the members are comfortable among their peers; the kin groups are social contexts in which stresses and strains are constantly negotiated, avoided, and patched up, where possible.

Since the active generations of a polyistic social system usually belong to both the kinship and the sodality group components that constitute a given system, the autonomy between the groups can never translate into mutual independence. The clan-cult relation, therefore, is akin to the relations structuring intentionality. As I discuss in chapter 3, the component forms of intentionality are relatively autonomous in the sense that each can exist only in relation to the total consciousness. In a similar way, I will speak of the kinship and companionship groups of a polyistic community as being relatively autonomous, and I will characterize the relationship manifesting this relative autonomy as being arm's-length in nature. Given the symbolic pragmatic view, such an arm's-length relation will usually be marked in the range of material cultural features, facilities, and artifacts that are constitutive components of the activities that participants in these two different types of social groupings regularly perform. For example, the kinship groups will be manifested in domestic dwellings and the sodality groups in structures that (since domesticity, as such, would be a peripheral aspect of group life) would emphasize collective activities, such as group-based ritual.

What characterizes the social structure of a polyistic community, therefore, is the relative autonomy of kinship-based and companionship-based sodality groups and the nature of the contradictions characteristic of each. Individuals, of course, typically would belong to both types simultaneously, according to their overall station in life. Both types of groupings would be constituted as custodial corporations, each having its own set of spatially related arm's-length sacred locales, and possibly each would have separate custodial paths linking these locales into ramifying social networks, thereby constituting the locale-centric dimension. However, the practical nature of pathways might require that they be shared between kin and sodality groups in the same region: the kin groups having duties to perform that fit their responsibility, for example, the maintenance of appropriate usage by respecting the relevant subsistence and settlement proscriptions and prescriptions, and so on; and the sodalities having the duties of performing rituals to cleanse the paths of any pollution that their own activities may have produced, as well as performing special world renewal rites by which to rectify the residual pollution that domestic settlement and subsistence inevitably cause. Therefore, sodalities based on same-age/same-gender structural principles would probably have combined religious and economic tasks. Even military duties would logically emerge. However, militarily directed aggression would vary according to how the arm's-length relations between relatively autonomous kin and sodality groups would be articulated in settlement patterns.

Differential Settlement and Subsistence Pattern Articulations

Under certain conditions of ecological stress discussed below, preindustrial social systems based on a settlement strategy that promotes high mobility and extensive foraging would probably reduce mobility and focus subsistence practices along the lines argued by James Brown (1985, 208; 1986, 318; Brown and Vierra 1983, 168). Referring to it as the risk-management model, he argues that the social systems of the Midcontinent during the Early Holocene period had a highly mobile settlement regime focused on exploiting the upland zones. A group of foragers would move often and together, maintaining a rather tight monistic-like integration. This is often referred to as the residential mobility strategy, and it would be a major condition for the formation of small, largely autonomous kinship-based communities.

However, starting circa 6000 B.C., the cool and moist conditions of the Early Holocene gave way to a warming trend associated with upland desiccation and riverine aggradation. This is referred to as the Hypsithermal period. These upland autonomous foraging groups, Brown argues, increasingly converged on the same resource patches. High residential mobility began to enhance rather than minimize survival risks. This enhancement of risk was related not so much to stressing the resource patches, he claims, but to the increasing likelihood that these autonomous groups would converge on the same and increasingly limited resources patches and, therefore, would start to compete aggressively against each other for the diminishing resources. Brown argues that this fear instigated a mutual avoidance strategy, realized by these monistic kinship communities starting to settle down in the bottomlands, which were becoming increasingly attractive because of the aggradation of the rivers and the expansion of the valley and floodplain-type resource base. Hence, a process of reducing mobility occurred, and this was characterized by the gradual extending of seasonal occupation of base camps in the river valleys. Brown claims that this settling down promoted the development of a system of foraging based on special kin-based task groups that would be sent afield to hunt and gather, bringing their foraging products back to the base camps for sharing. This use of task groups for specialized extraction practices is termed the *logistical mobility strategy*.

Therefore, Brown has linked settlement and subsistence changes to both environmental and population dynamics as these would be perceived and strategically structured in the seasonal rounds of the people themselves. In fact, his account can be seen as characterizing the ecological strategy of the Archaic period in proscriptive terms: a way of life based on largely unfettered mobility was transformed by a deliberate avoidance or proscriptive strategy. However, corresponding with his basically monistic perspective, the deontics that he invokes are those characteristic of exclusive territorialism and proprietorial domain. Although the foragers when fully mobile do not need to claim permanent control of land (indeed, doing so is counterproductive to the strategy of high mobility), the individual group is integrated by strong kinship relations. That is, Brown is drawing on a particular range of the anthropological literature of kinship-based foraging groups, and this account therefore presupposes a particular deontic perspective. Adult males are responsible for their offspring and related dependents, and kin cooperate and share tasks in terms of age and gender. Thus, the aggression they manifest toward strangers would be as much the expression of their need to effectively fulfil their duties to their offspring, siblings, and spouses as to fulfil their pursuit of personal need to survive.

Implicated in this would be the sense that a given kin group has a right to prevent strangers from exploiting the foods of the kin group's territory, this right deriving from the responsibilities that members of the kin group have to feed their dependents. Such rights are exclusionary in nature and, effectively if not formally, express and manifest the notion of proprietorship. Therefore, a cosmological perspective is clearly presupposed by Brown's argument. This is the presumption that prehistoric foraging groups will have a transcendalist cosmology that characterizes the world as being divisible into parts that are "ownable"—which means that reconstruing Brown's convergence avoidance account into alternative immanentist cosmological terms, as I do below, does not contrast an objective against a deontic ecological account. Rather, it explores the same archaeological record using an alternative deontic view, namely, an immanentist cosmology–squatter ethos deontic ecological perspective.

Accordingly, as I postulate above, the ecological activities of a foraging people with an immanentist cosmology and the squatter ethos would place a high value on living lightly on the land, admiring those who minimize the disorder their necessary ecological interventions cause to the world by practicing high mobility and a complex of subsistence practices rich in midwifery ritual. Seen in these terms, the value that foragers have for mobility is primary or basic not because it minimizes survival risk but because it is the logical outcome of the squatter ethos. Given the essential contradiction of human existence, as autonomous foraging groups increasingly converge on the same resource patches (as postulated by Brown), the greatest threat that they would perceive would not be mutual aggression arising out of increased competition for limited resources but the increasing sacred pollution caused by their resource-patch convergence. Since the squatter ethos is a widespread cultural tradition, the autonomous groups would resolve this common problem for which they were all responsible by cooperatively negotiating the best way to avoid or minimize disordering (polluting) the sacred natural order. Since under the squatter ethos each party is autonomous, decision making by means of consensus is logically entailed. Therefore, if there is going to be effective multiparty action, it has to be done through negotiated consensus.

Thus, Brown is likely quite correct. Under these conditions, foragers would initiate and collectively negotiate and promote an avoidance strategy involving reducing mobility and intensifying resource use in one area—but for reasons that are the opposite of those put forward in his model. Although intensifying resource use in the valleys could not be avoidable under these objective conditions, it could reduce resource use in the most affected upland areas; therefore, in the assessment of the participating groups, it would result in either an overall reduction or at least a minimizing of exploitation-induced pollution. At the same time, of course, the squatter ethos would sustain a high value on mobility since this is the most effective means of living lightly on the land, and groups would thus be motivated to minimize the reduction of mobility while simultaneously minimizing both the size and the period of aggregation of groups. Therefore, while some large aggregations might occur for rather short and specifically defined periods, in terms of domestic arrangements, this settling down would be characterized by the formation of small, probably nuclear family groups in seasonal camps having the practicably widest possible dispersal. These new circumstances could also promote innovating or modifying traditional midwifery ritual practices, for example, by adopting new raw materials for tool production, such as copper or selected cherts, that are viewed as having more effective warranting properties than traditional raw materials.

As I suggest in chapter 2, in an immanently sacred world, the association between mortuary practices and world renewal ritual makes sense. The exploitation of resources by humans is typically perceived as their participating in the recycling of the spiritual powers of the exploited species and, therefore, as the reproducing and regenerating of the cosmos. I thus will postulate that complementing these new domestic settlement and subsistence arrangements brought about by reduced mobility would be the recruitment of traditional mortuary practices to serve as both funerary and world renewal/thanksgiving ritual, by which resources and land could be publicly and regularly resanctified, thereby reversing the inevitable increase of pollution that the reduced mobility would engender. The recruitment of the spiritual essences of humans at death in order to serve as offerings to the cosmos would simply be an extension of this notion of death as part of the recycling of life (Byers 2004, chapters 7 and 8). Hence, rather impressive-appearing mortuary locales displaying attributes of public mortuary ritual mediating both funerary and world renewal would emerge, while everyday settlement would remain rather dispersed and seasonal.

This raises a significant alternative perspective regarding the nature of the Archaic mortuary record as interpreted by Douglas Charles and Jane Buikstra (1983, 121–24; also see Charles 1985, 223–24; 1995, 78–80, 86; Charles et al. 1986, 458–59, 471), and, more generally, for the way in which the mortuary sphere is treated by many in North American archaeology. As I note in chapter 2, Lynne Goldstein (1980, 7–8; 1981, 53–54; 1995, 116–18) defines a cemetery as a specialized mortuary zone that is likely to demarcate a corporate kin group. Charles and Buikstra accept this notion of the cemetery and thereby reduce all other mortuary locales as secondary, these being sites that include mortuary residue as simply one of several different activity components thereby promoting a rank ordering of mortuary sites into cemeteries and other, or noncemeteries. The latter category of mortuary site, therefore, becomes largely excluded from any serious characterizing of the mortuary sphere of a people. I have more to say about this approach, but for my immediate purposes, I will refer to it here as the cemetery or funerary view, and it distinctly promotes the sense that only cemeteries are legitimate mortuary sites, while all other mortuary sites are, to one degree or another, peripheral or secondary in importance or even in some manner deviant in these social systems.

To reorient our understanding of the mortuary sphere in North American archaeology, I have elsewhere treated all sites that display collective mortuary residue as collective burial locales or CBLs (Byers 2004, 177–201). Cemeteries are clearly one type of CBL. However, they are not the only type, and in the North American archaeological mortuary record, they may not even be the most important type. Indeed, under the polyistic locale-centric account, I postulate that the range of Archaic mortuary sites that Charles and Buikstra have identified (namely, the midden burial sites, the floodplain exchange center sites, and the bluff-top cemeteries) might be more coherently treated as different types of mortuary/world renewal CBLs, as I discuss below.

The above illustrates that two basic deontic ecological accounts can be given of the same archaeological record, each being quite different depending on the type of cosmology that is postulated since, under the integrated view of cultural traditions, along with these different cosmologies are possible differences in ethos, worldview, and ideology. What I need to do now is redescribe the changes in the social systems of the Early to Middle Archaic periods in immanentist deontic ecological strategic terms, thereby preparing the background to extend the same view to the American Bottom pre-Mississippian and Mississippian mortuary records. In this regard, I can say that initially, during the Early Archaic, the squatter ethos was realized in an almost unfettered way as the exploiting populations practiced high mobility by dispersing across the region. Ritual was built into subsistence and settlement primarily as midwifery practices, and mortuary practices also effected minimal modification. This strategy can be characterized as a proscriptive subsistence-settlement/ceremonial regime. That is, all three aspects of the deontic ecological strategy are proscriptive, designed to minimize the degree of permanently induced change brought about by human behavioral intervention in the pursuit of survival and reputation. However, under the emically perceived objective conditions of rising ecological pressure related to the increasing desiccation of the uplands, which motivated the increasing convergence of groups on the same resources patches, and the simultaneous amelioration of lowland resources, the deontic ecological strategy modified to what I term here the *proscriptive subsistence-settlement/prescriptive ceremonial orientation*.

This seems a fair characterization of the Middle Archaic deontic ecological regime, which also extended into the Late Archaic, since even though reducing mobility and shifting away from the uplands to the lowlands while focusing more subsistence in these smaller but more resource-rich territories intensified exploitation and settlement, this new subsistence and settlement posture still constituted overall a complex proscriptive deontic ecological strategy. That is, while this move entailed living less lightly on the land, it also reduced the level of exploitation of the upland resources that would otherwise have borne the brunt of the exploitation stress, while also shifting the burden to lowland resources that were, in fact, ameliorating. Moreover, as suggested above, the logic engendered by the essential contradiction would have provoked a reciprocal or compensating strategy of mortuary-mediated world renewal ritual. Since the latter would have been imperative to reverse the increased levels of pollution under the stress of overall intensifying subsistence and settlement conditions, its occurrence in the form of CBLs in the archaeological record can be characterized as a prescriptive tactical ceremonial move. Thus, the total deontic nature of this ecological strategy can be seen as dually but differentially complementary, as both proscriptive and prescriptive, therefore constituting a proscriptive subsistence-settlement/prescriptive ceremonial regime. I have argued elsewhere that the latter prevails well into the Woodland period and is most fully realized materially in such central Ohio Valley complexes as the Adena, the Ohio, and the Illinois Hopewell (Byers 2004, chapters 8 and 9). In effect, the emergence of specialized mortuary-related ceremonial locales, referred to here as world renewal CBLs, can be understood as a prescriptive deontic ecological strategic move tied to the development of a less mobile lifeway while preserving and realizing the squatter ethos in these new objective circumstances.

According to Brown's risk-management model, the early Holocene systems of the Midcontinent would be characterized as autonomous kinship-based communities forming a monistic social system, using my terms. Because of the high mobility, communities would be widely dispersed and the total community would move, possibly with some seasonal splitting and reassembling along kinship lines. In these circumstances, there would be no opportunity for generational and gender structures to become disembedded from the kinship structure. However, according to this model, with the shift to reduced mobility, exclusive territorialism would emerge. The settling-down process, therefore, also would promote semisedentary seasonal base camps using special logistical task groups.

I can agree with Brown's model that early Holocene foraging communities practicing a residential mobility strategy would tend to form monistic-like social systems. However, under the inclusive territorial perspective, I see a very different long-term scenario developing. As I note above, under certain conditions, a disembedding of social structural axes could occur. I postulate that the initial strategy of reducing mobility by way of avoiding stressing the upland environment would be just such a major condition. This is because, as Brown points out, reduced mobility would promote a logistical strategy requiring special task forces regularly exploiting the upland regions while the rest of the community resided in seasonal valley base camps. In fact, because of the squatter ethos and inclusive territorialism, a logistical subsistence strategy would be ideal since these special task groups could move freely across the land without any fear of being denied access, and, indeed, spacing among them would be strongly promoted, thereby ensuring minimal environmental stressing and maximal "living lightly." However, the same proscriptive principle would promote river valley bottom settlement distribution that would make task-force labor recruitment within any given seasonal base camp group a major problem, since this proscriptive settlement posture would promote small and dispersed seasonal base camps. This would mean that individual base camp groups would generally be unable to sustain autonomous task groups.[3]

On first consideration, this combination would seem to be a problem. However, this would be the case only if, in fact, territories were exclusive. Instead, under the inclusive territorial regime, the conjunction of these conditions—reduced mobility, small dispersed seasonal base camps, and the need to use special-purpose upland-directed mobile task groups—would promote the disembedding of the structural axes of generation and gender and open up the formation of homogeneous companionship-based groups. Given the above conditions, practical logic would lead to the practice across regions for young persons, usually males, from the small dispersed seasonal base camps to regularly meet up with each other in the upland region. Rather than competing, they would be cooperating in what would be initially ad hoc special task groups. They would share their successes and return to their separate domestic base camps. These initial groupings would promote companionship among many junior age-grade males who would be from different families and even different valleys. Within one or two generations, as "settling down" proceeded, these interactions would become entrenched or institutionalized and would constitute same-age/same-gender groupings, that is, companionship-based sodalities.

The regionwide result would be two parallel sets of socially complementary groupings that would be relatively autonomous to each other: one based on kinship, the other on companionship. Since I theorize that the former became extended kin groups and the latter came to extend their midwifery ritual to embrace wider public ritual addressing overall world renewal concerns, thereby taking on cultlike tendencies, I will refer to the two groupings generically as clans and cults. In general, clans would interrelate with each other to constitute a complex regional network of mutually autonomous clans, and cults would interrelate with each other to constitute a parallel network of mutually autonomous cults. More than one type of cult is possible, however; therefore, rather than frame the groupings as two strictly parallel networks of clans and cults, I postulate the existence of one network of clans and two or more networks of cult types, constituting a polyistic network of autonomous groups. Defining the limits of a social system would always be relative to the locale from which it was being "overseen." Hence, regions would constitute ramifying polyistic locale-centric social systems.

BIFURCATED AND INTEGRATED SETTLEMENT ARTICULATION MODES

The question that now arises is how a community system based on relatively autonomous clans and cults would be manifested in the settlement pattern. First, as relatively autonomous groups, the relation between them would be heterarchical in the sense that each would respect the autonomy of the other and, therefore, neither would intervene in the other's internal affairs. In material terms, since each would have ritual as well as practical duties to perform, each would have its own set of practical and sacred structures, and these would be spatially related to manifest the clan-cult arm's-length relation that is characteristic of relatively autonomous groupings. However, because of their mutually recognized relative autonomy, the spatial relations could be highly flexible. In any given region, the spatial patterning of the material features housing the two types of groups could modify radically across time. This process would generate a continuum of different settlement articulation modes. One extreme of this continuum would be characterized by the kin and cult groups of any given community maintaining separate structures in mutually exclusive locales. I will term this the *bifurcated settlement articulation mode*. The other extreme is for the clans and cults of a given community to jointly maintain a single compound locale internally patterned by the simultaneous maintenance of two distinct sets of structures: for example, domestic dwellings and ritual structures. I will term this the *integrated settlement articulation mode*. Between these two extremes would be spatial patternings displaying various degrees of integrated-to-bifurcated settlement articulation, keyed into the proscriptive/prescriptive calculus of minimizing pollution and enhancing sanctification in the context of demographic and environmental changes.[4]

An integrated settlement articulation mode entails the joint occupation and development of a single main settlement locale of a community internally structured into clan and cult spaces and structures. Therefore, the community plan will display both ritual and domestic structures. Since cults and clans occupy the same common spatial locale they would likely share some of the communal facilities, such as ceremonial plazas, ritual "marker posts," sacred pits, and so on. However, their co-existence in the same locale should be manifested by a patterning of the communal component of the settlement that cannot be accounted for in straightforward unitary terms. That is, there will be a complexity apparent in the patterning that can be more coherently accounted for in terms of the type of arm's-length relations that could be expected of relatively autonomous clans and cults rather than in the unitary kinship terms favored by the hierarchical monistic modular polity perspective.

A bifurcated settlement articulation tends strongly toward a pattern in which the two sets of clan and cult locales are spatially exclusive and mutually complementary in the makeup of their associated structures and facilities. Typically, the cult sodality locales will contain the major structures, facilities, and artifacts that mark ritual and ceremony: special buildings, monumental earthworks, and a public ritual life richly expressed in the stylistics of the locales. However, since cult members would typically spend periods of time as transient occupants, there will also be different types of dwellings appropriate to the different categories of cult membership (for example, barracks-like dwellings for young, bachelor-status companions; houselike dwellings for older married members and their dependents). In contrast, the kin-group locales in a bifurcated system will be strongly domestic and mundane in their material makeup. However, because clans would perform rituals appropriate to their needs and interests, some ritual paraphernalia and facilities would probably also be present, although it would make up a somewhat minor aspect of the habitation locales and their contents.

Integrated and bifurcated settlement articulation modes should not be confused with dispersed and nucleated settlements. A heterarchical polyistic locale-centric social system displaying the bifurcated settlement articulation mode could have dispersed kin-group settlement in parallel with nucleated cult locales, as I argue partly characterized the Middle Mississippian settlement pattern of the American Bottom. The reverse could also occur—in which the kin groups were nucleated and the sodality groups were dispersed—although this possibility is less likely. Whether as an integrated or as a bifurcated settlement articulation mode, the legitimacy of both clan and cult groups to their own formation and the building and using of their settlement locales would be based on custodianship warranted by founding myths. The social system could become more complex—not by the development of rank and class, although this is not impossible, but simply by either the clan or the cult groups (or both) becoming more developed. For example, as I comment earlier, the cult groups responsible for world renewal could be specialized into male and female as well as senior and junior cults; alternatively, they could be combined in different ways to form compound cults, while retaining the same basic cultural principle of agentive and intergroup autonomy. It is for this reason that their interactions would tend to generate heterarchical relations (that is, relations based on mutual autonomy, consensus, and recognition of differential but reciprocal and/or complementary responsibilities).

Another important function of cults would be military. However, the military posture of a cult would be quite different under an integrated as compared to a bifurcated settlement articulation mode. Under the latter, since the cult locales are literally separate from the clan locales, there would be a strong tendency for clans and cults to be selective in terms of their types of armed aggression. For example, only other cult locales would be proper military targets by cults. That is, under the special conditions of settlement bifurcation, although not necessarily absolutely the case, part of the logic of the arm's-length relations between clan and cult groups would be mutual neutrality in regard to aggression. Thus, a clan would conduct its own feuds against other clans and, of course, build its own alliances with other clans. Similarly, when required, a cult would be aggressive toward another similar cult and, of course, could build its own cult alliances based on heterarchical structures of mutual cooperation, and if the latter became materially manifested, such an alliance might be realized as a multiple-mound locale such as Cahokia.

Under the bifurcated settlement articulation mode, there would be a strong tendency for a particular cult to draw its members from all the regional clan groups. Therefore, not only would the latter groups tend to avoid hostilities among themselves, but also the cults of a region would tend to avoid mutual hostilities. This means that both interclan and intercult hostilities would tend to be conducted over long distances (this deduction follows from the fact that two neighboring cults would tend not to be mutually aggressive if some of the members of one were kin of some of the members of the other). Everything else being equal, when occurring, intercult aggression would tend to increase with the geographical distances. Indeed, for world renewal cults, part of the reason to carry out formal intercult aggression (that is, warfare) could be directly tied in with lethal human sacrificial strategy, an important point that I explore in more detail later. Thus, cult sodalities would probably have a range of tasks that would be regularly performed and intrinsically tied to the cult's specialized ritual functions, such as military functions to procure sacrificial victims, long-distance resource expeditions to procure exotics for producing key iconic warrants of ritual, vision quests as modes of initiation and promotion of members, and so on.

Under an integrated settlement articulation mode, some of the same rules and practices would apply. This is because if the clans are based on, for example, patrilineality, then their exogamous alliances would mean that the members of the cults of a local region would be the actual or future in-laws of the members of clans in neighboring villages and towns. In the case of matrilineality, it is likely that the members of the male-based cults of a local town would be the brothers of the women living in the neighboring towns. However, under an integrated mode—unlike the selectivity exhibited under a bifurcated mode— aggression over long or even medium distances performed by cult sodalities with a specialized military role to play would not selectively target only other cult sodalities since, of course, under an integrated mode, enemy cult sodalities would be integrated into enemy towns.

As I note above, different types of cults (for example, female-based and male-based world renewal fertility cults) could co-exist. Therefore, any given region would be constituted as multiple parallel networks of autonomous clans (matrilineal and/or patrilineal) and autonomous cults (female and/or male, junior and/or senior generational), thereby constituting what I have called a heterarchical polyistic locale-centric social system. Even though a particular region could have several different types of cult sodalities and even possibly contrasting clan organizations—with one part of the region being based on matrilineal clans, the other on patrilineal clans—structurally this is a dual clan-cult system. Therefore, I will term this perspective the *Dual Clan-Cult model,* and the social systems it postulates are of a heterarchical polyistic locale-centric nature.[5]

The geographical scope of a particular social system would always be relative to the prevailing settlement articulation mode. Under the bifurcated settlement articulation mode, the geographical scope of the two networks—clans and cults—would differ. The interests of the clans would limit the effective reach of the network of clan alliances while, as I suggest above, the interests of the cults would extend their networks in some cases across significantly large stretches and into a variety of geographical zones. Even the qualitative nature of the interaction would be different, since the interests of the clans would focus their efforts on practical and ritual conditions of their own reproduction (instrumental exchange and intermarriage) while that of the cult networks (constituted as alliances and enmities) would focus their interests on the practical and ritual conditions of world renewal practices.[6]

A similar openness and indefiniteness of spatial extension would exist under the integrated settlement articulation mode, albeit more constrained spatially. Each town and village would be mutually recognized as autonomous, and they would be linked as an indefinitely ramifying heterarchical network. However, compared to a bifurcated polyistic locale-centric social system, an integrated one would have a greater practical defining of territory, which would be particularly appropriate for sedentary gardening and agricultural systems that might give the local system the appearance of being "closed," a sort of pseudo- modularism. However, the boundaries would be based not on juridical rights but on practical convenience and local knowledge. There would be no exclusive rights associated with the use of the surrounding resources. Rather, local habitual users would be bound by responsibility to use the resources appropriately. Out of this would emerge certain qualified rights that I defined earlier as custodial usufruct. Custodial usufruct (which would also be associated with a bifurcated system, of course) would require continual negotiations and consensus in the allocating and reallocating of land among the regional towns and villages and, of course, extending these negotiations to any in-migrating groups.

The question raised by the above bifurcated-integrated continuum is what might be the conditions that would promote integrated or bifurcated settlement articulation modal tendencies. As I note in chapter 2, an ecological strategy presupposes emically based assessments. Therefore, under the influence of a squatter ethos, local peoples perceiving that their own pursuit of survival was putting an increasing pressure on the land would promote intensifying ritual, thereby shifting to a greater prescriptive ceremonial regime. That is, the relation between settlement articulation and ecological strategies in the form of subsistence practices is a direct, strategic relation presupposing an immanentist cosmology and squatter ethos. As subsistence intensifies in the context of integrated settlements, the perception of increasing levels of sacred pollution promotes calls for new strategies of rectification and compensation. One strategic approach would be a consensus-based decision to shift to a bifurcated posture, and this would be effected by the clans and cults constituting a community spatially disengaging from their integrated settlement villages, thereby reducing the pollution burden per unit of land caused by sedentary settlement, along with promoting shorter periods of occupation of any given domestic locale. A concomitant and complementary aspect of the disengagement strategy would be the expansion of world renewal ritual through the promotion of larger world renewal cult locales by means of intercult alliances. Thus, while the local cult sites would remain dispersed and rather small scale, the cults would tend to link up with each other through expanding alliances, thereby cooperating in building a few large-scale ritual locales by which to enhance the regionwide renewal ritual outcomes. This above suggestion is the basic premise of what I term the *World Renewal Cult Heterarchy model,* Cahokia being the best-known expression of this type of world renewal cult center. In the next chapter, I develop the mortuary model that is relevant to the heterarchical polyistic locale-centric account. Before I elucidate this model, however, and to conclude this chapter, a concrete analogical example of how a heterarchical polyistic locale-centric social system operates can be very useful.

THE BIFURCATED NYAKYUSA COMMUNITY SETTLEMENT

The Nyakyusa were a people of East Africa whose subsistence was based on mixed savanna-based cattle husbandry and village-based horticulture. Each village was economically dependent on this mixed gardening and cattle grazing. While the land immediately surrounding the village was used for gardens that were prepared and hoed by the men but cultivated by the women, the savanna was common land under inclusive tenure, and so it was open to cattle grazing by all the villages. Therefore, the village was based on zero-dimensional custodial usufruct, and access to pasture land was based on two-dimensional inclusive tenure. However, the structural axis on which the villages were based was not kinship, although the Nyakyusa had patrilineages and, indeed, patrilineal descent groups controlled the many cattle herds. The men who founded a given village were lifelong companions of the same age, within about a five- to eight-year span of each other. They, along with their wives and children, made up the village. Monica Wilson (1963) referred to these as age-set villages. All the age-set villages of the same generation constituted the active age-grade of the Nyakyusa social system. Each age-grade had a generational age span of thirty to thirty-five years. When the men of the active generation retired from village life, they dissolved their age-sets (that is, they dissolved their villages), and each man went to join his male siblings as lineage brothers to share ancestral cult duties by occupying sacred forest locales where the lineage ancestors dwelt. There they carried out rituals directed toward encouraging the ancestors to sustain the lineage's cattle herds.

As Wilson describes the Nyakyusa socialization and life cycle, when sons reached the age of seven or so, their fathers would typically give them responsibility to care for a few cattle. Each boy was encouraged by his parents to tend the cattle in the savanna, well away from the gardens surrounding the villages. During a boy's initial savanna sojourn, he would meet up with other boys of his own approximate age from different, widely dispersed villages. These boys would typically become close companions, thereby constituting an age-set or age cohort sharing the care of the cattle to which each had been entrusted by his father. Because a group of companions would all be within the same five to eight-year age spread, this meant that the oldest and youngest sons of the same men would often end up with different companions. As the groups of young companions entered adolescence, they were encouraged by their parents to form semipermanent camps. Finally, as they matured and married, they formed their own age-cohort village:

> Each age-grade, or generation, covers a span of 30 to 35 years, and each village comprises an age-set with a span of 5 to 8 years. . . . The average age of members in each age-grade varies with the date of the last "coming out" ceremony. Just before the ceremony elders with ritual functions are those over 65 or 70; the mature men of the ruling generation are those between 35 and 65; and the "boys" who have not yet "come out," those between 10 and 35. Just after the ceremony the ruling generation consists of those between about 10 and 35, anyone over 35 being an elder. (Wilson 1963, 32)

In terms of settlement articulation mode, the Nyakyusa would form a bifurcated system based on the separation of the generations with the senior "retired" male members of the patrilineages and their surviving spouses occupying the sacred forest communal ancestor cult locales, and the active adult generation of sons with their spouses and children occupying the nucleated domestic villages dispersed across the savanna. In structural terms, the dual, open-networked Nyakyusa social system of mutually autonomous age-set villages and ancestor cults is much along the lines I postulate for the American Bottom under the Dual Clan-Cult model, except in reverse. While the Nyakyusa domestic village was based on the companionship principle of same-age/same-gender and the Nyakyusa sacred forest cults were ancestor-based and managed by lineage elders, the domestic domain of the American Bottom is postulated as having been based on kinship and the world renewal cults as based on companionship. I argue in the following chapter that, from the beginning, these same-gender/same-age cults would have been autonomous communal cults.

The evolution of the American Bottom, therefore, is largely the evolution of the arm's-length relations between the relatively autonomous cults and clans. In the next chapter I expand on the required mortuary and cult models to complete the theoretical framework required to critically interpret Cahokia and the American Bottom in these terms.

Mortuary Practices, Cults, and Social Systems

In my elucidation of deontic ecology, I point out that Douglas Charles and Jane Buikstra (1983, 120–21) have highlighted the important relation between territorialism, ecological practices, and mortuary practices and that, in parallel with James Brown's view of the evolution of Archaic period settlement practices, their position basically hinges on the claim that exclusive territorialism was the primitive or first form of tenure. Charles and Buikstra see the development of exclusive territories as largely based on the natural tendency of social animals, humans included, to be territorial and aggressive in conditions promoting competition for limited resources:

> Corporate behavior in human societies is actually a form of territorial behavior, which is a near universal in the animal kingdom. Most, if not all, animals that exhibit social behavior regularly occupy and defend a specific area generally referred to as a territory. Territorial behavior is related to the general phenomenon of spacing between individual organisms. … A territory is usually defined as a defended area, but defense of an area may refer to the use of scent glands, visual displays, and vocalizations as well as aggressive behavior. (Charles and Buikstra 1983, 120–21)

With this naturalized view of territorialism, they treat mortuary practices—and, in particular, the material outcome of these practices in the form of prominently placed mounds—as a mode of legitimizing exclusive claims to territories and/or the resources of these territories.

As I note in earlier chapters, within Charles and Buikstra's theory, much hinges on the notion of the cemetery as the symbolic constituent of proprietorial corporate domains. However, I treat the cemetery as simply one type of collective burial locale (CBL). I will call their claim the Cemetery model, and I speak of the theoretical perspective underwriting this model as the funerary paradigm. This is currently the dominant mortuary paradigm in North American prehistoric archaeology; in its most extreme form, its primary attribute is that it defines the mortuary sphere as centrally identified with funerary practices. A more moderate expression of this paradigm may recognize a range of mortuary-related behaviors, such as secondary interment, bundle burial, cremation, and so on. However, even these are usually treated as funerary stages, thereby maintaining the "funeral" as defining the real social nature of the mortuary sphere.

What the Cemetery model adds to the basic funerary paradigm is the exclusive territorial component. Since the model treats the mortuary practices as central to the deontics of proprietorial domain and also expresses the prevailing mortuary paradigm, the fact that the mortuary component of the Mississippian period in the American Bottom is treated in these terms under the various versions of the hierarchical modular polity account is not surprising (Milner 1983, 3, 23–32; 1984, 470–73). Indeed, confirmation of the claim that Cahokia is the center of a hierarchical order is forcefully made by focusing on the elaborate mortuary contents of Mound 72, "proving" indubitably that the two sets of "central" burials and their spatially associated mortuary deposits can best be understood as the outcome of the funerals of major members of the ruling elite of Cahokia.[1] Even the burials recognized as the outcome of lethal acts are subsumed either to being part of the funerary treatment accorded to the deemed-elite deceased or as being dedicated to the memory of these rulers (Fowler et al. 1999, 168, 173–77). Therefore, by extension the Mississippian period mortuary practices of the American Bottom have been largely interpreted in terms of the Cemetery model as functioning to entrench and reproduce ranked property rights and the hierarchical differentiation of the elite and commoners that flows from this ranking.

However, these same mortuary data take on a completely different symbolic pragmatic meaning when viewed in terms of the Dual Clan-Cult model. Picking up on my earlier postulations in chapters 2 and 4 (that in social systems based on immanentist cosmologies, mortuary practices would be coopted to serve both mortuary and world renewal/thanksgiving goals), I argue here that the American Bottom mortuary data can be best treated as the expression of a complex mortuary sphere constituted by an integrated system of mortuary behaviors incorporating both clan-based *funerary* and cult-based *world renewal* rituals. Rather than manifesting hierarchy and dominance, therefore, they manifest autonomy and cooperative clan-based funerary and cult-based world renewal ritual, with the latter having a strong sacrificial pragmatics.

To make this argument, however, I must first elucidate a theory that can be used to interpret the mortuary data in these terms. In accordance with the inclusive territorial view and its associated claim that human-land relations would be based on custodial tenure with the usage being of a custodial usufruct nature, I postulate that the American Bottom mortuary record was the ritual outcome and medium by which both human and world renewal were accomplished simultaneously. Human death would be treated as the first step in human rebirth, and the rituals directed to ensuring this rebirth would be only the first of a series of renewal rituals, each incremental step shifting the focus from renewal of the human to the renewal of the group to the renewal of the cosmos.

MORTUARY PRACTICES AND WORLD RENEWAL

Robert Hall's view on Native American mortuary practices, expressed in numerous publications and symposia, has been very influential on the development of my thought in this area. He has noted that many historically known Native North American cultures had complex mortuary practices involving different, incrementally staged rites—for example, the initial death rites, the rites of the adoption of the name of the dead by a living person, mourning rites, followed by memorial rites, and so on—each rite being mediated either by the deceased, by some selected skeletal component(s) of the deceased, or by some iconic symbolic representation of the deceased that is taken to presence one or more of her/his sacred aspects, that is, the name spirit, the spirit of the flesh, the spirits of the bones, and so on.[2] Adding to the importance of Hall's analysis is the observation he makes that the incrementally ordered mortuary rites also typically constitute renewal practices (Hall 1997, 18–35).

When mortuary practices are seen in this light, trying to subsume the complex material residue of the mortuary rites characteristic of most prehistoric Native North American peoples to the funerary practices characteristic of the Euro-American culture becomes problematic, and to do so probably seriously distorts our understanding of the former. Hence, I argue here that the material residue of prehistoric North American mortuary practices can be more coherently understood as having mediated an incremental series of mortuary rites than a series of mortuary events subsumed under the rubric of funerary ritual and burial. The initial death rite might be roughly equivalent to what participants in the Euro-American culture recognize as a funeral. However, this would be only the first stage of the mortuary process. The "funeral" may be followed several months later by a spirit release rite, which would also be a mourning rite. This rite would require disinterring the deceased, cleaning and bundling the bones (this process being an intrinsic part of the mourning ritual), curation, and, finally, reburial in a new location. Part of the reburial rite might also be a name adoption rite. This would involve ritually invoking and presencing the names of the deceased and transferring them to appropriate recipients, thereby reincarnating the name spirits in the person(s) of the adoptee(s). At the same time, however, the rituals might include a component by which the spirits of the bones of the deceased are released and directed as a gift to the cosmos, and so on. As an example, Hall has noted, "The Feast of the Dead of the Great Lakes Algonquian was . . . an occasion not only for consolidating intertribal relations but also for symbolically reincarnating deceased tribesmen by transferring their names to others, much as the dead founders of the Iroquois League were symbolically reincarnated by transferring their names to their successors during Condolence councils" (Hall 1997, 40).

The bones of the dead were always potent symbolic pragmatic devices for performing ritual by which reproduction was enhanced. Among the historic Oglala-Lakota Sioux of the Western Dakotas, the "soul keepers" were custodians responsible for bone bundles of the deceased. While (literally) bearing/caring for these bones, they worked under a number of prohibitions by which the special powers of the bones were sustained to enhance hunting success: "The soul keeper was free to ride with the hunting parties, but it was his role to sit by himself on a nearby hill with his pipe, praying for the welfare of his people and the success of the hunt. If a buffalo were killed near him he could claim it. He could not himself butcher it because he was restricted from touching knives or blood" (Hall 1997, 27). Hall uses the historic Southeastern societies as his linchpin connecting these mortuary traditions back to the Middle and Early Woodland. He notes, "The analogy may be extended by considering that world renewal ceremonialism may have been an integral part of some, perhaps much, Woodland mound burial, as suggested for the Midwest, just as world renewal ritual and the curation of dead Suns were an integral part of mound-top Mississippian ceremonialism in the Southeast" (Hall 1984, 274).

Treating the dead as symbolic capital for ritually releasing souls to be reborn and/or to renew the society and the world is consistent with cultural traditions that constitute the world as immanently sacred and that promote the attitudes and values of a squatter ethos. Therefore, as societies of this type intensify their ecological practices, they can be expected to evolve a complex mortuary record that, in very important ways, maps out the range of incremental steps that this series of rebirth/renewal rites would require, from extended to flexed burial, to secondary bundle burials, to burials of selected bones, and even cremation. Indeed, from the Middle Archaic into historic times, in general, the mortuary record of the Midcontinent manifests just such a complexity.

The inadequacy of the funerary paradigm to interpret this complexity becomes clear. Typically, archaeologists consider the "funeral" to be the only or the most relevant mortuary rite. Therefore, under the funerary paradigm, accounting for the great variability of the mortuary record becomes a major problem. What could cause this variation? Typically, two factors are invoked: the objective circumstances-of-death factor, and the social complexity factor. The latter is given primary weight to explain the variation, while the former is used to cover variation that seems to those working within the funerary paradigm to compromise the respect that should be accorded the dead. Thus, most (not all) secondary burials are assumed to be the result of the circumstances-of-death factor, with this being that death occurred during winter or when the person was away from home territory—hence, an immediate and "proper" funerary burial would have been impossible. Alternatively, such postmortem manipulation has been argued as possibly registering a lower-status deceased person. This relates to the social complexity factor, which hinges on the notion that the deceased was given mortuary treatment consistent with her/his social standing at the time of death. George Milner expresses this perspective very well in his summary introduction to the Sand Prairie or late Moorehead phase mortuary data of the East St. Louis Stone Quarry cemetery site, asserting that the mortuary "treatment of the dead is influenced by deceased's age, sex, social group affiliation, and status positions held during life. The ritual aspects of funerary proceedings and the location, configuration, and contents of the disposal facilities represent formal means of symbolizing socially significant characteristics of the deceased" (Milner 1983, 3).

In these terms, a highly invariant mortuary record with only a few secondary burials caused by the inconvenient circumstances of death indicates a community that emphasized social equality so that whatever variability in social structure there is, it is given little or no formal recognition in burials. Such redundant treatment is assumed to be characteristic of simple societies, particularly those based on mobile foraging or simple horticulture. As the mortuary treatment becomes more varied, particularly if the society becomes less mobile and more horticulturally developed (thereby reducing the possibility of death occurring while the person is away) the greater variability is assumed to map a progressive complexifying of society in which both rank and functional specialization figure as critical social variables that are marked formally in the funerary patterning. As Milner explains this variability, "Peoples throughout the world tend to symbolize much of the social behavior associated with funerals through the form and organization of various cemetery components. For example, differences can exist in the construction and morphology of graves, in the selection of materials to accompany the dead, in the treatment of corpses, and in the spatial organization of interments within formally defined burial areas" (Milner 1983, 3).

Note that Milner's generalization that peoples tend to "symbolize much of the social behavior associated with funerals through the form and organization of various cemetery components" by varying the form of graves, the artifact associations, the postmortem treatment, and spatial organization seems to be saying that these latter variations encode the "socially significant characteristics of the deceased." If this is the case, then in fact the symbolic dimension that is immanent in the variable treatment is only incidentally mortuary symbolism since it is actually symbolizing the social standing of the deceased in life. In short, this mortuary treatment is a symbolism not of death but of life, and of course it expresses the referential fallacy, reducing the symbolic component to making reference to the social status of the deceased, a status that would typically be known by all the participants in any case and therefore would be redundant. If the symbolism simply refers to the living status of the deceased, then it follows that the only indicator that a mortuary practice occurred is the presence of the deceased, as such, and we could say that this is not symbolic at all.

One of the problems with the funerary paradigm is that not only does it reduce the mortuary sphere to funerary practices, but also there is a strong tendency to naturalize the latter. That is, besides the need to have the deceased present, this view really does not recognize any symbolic pragmatic rules by which to specify what forms of behaviors mediated by the manipulation of the dead count as mortuary acts of the type intended (for example, funerary). Instead, there is the assumption that actions are defined by their objective material appearances and consequences: bodies buried are the results of funerals, and any variation must be the result of factors that are only incidentally related to the mortuary event.[3] This means that the factors displaying variation have been added to the "funeral" by way of symbolically "referring" to the social standing of the person prior to death. Therefore, these factors are only secondary or, as I state above, incidental mortuary symbols. Or, if this is not a tenable claim, then the variation is the result of particular objective circumstances of death, such as having occurred in the winter or far from home. If these two explanations are also not tenable (such as in the case of bundled bone burials occurring in fully sedentary societies located in places where there is no significant winter), then such variation is attributed to the cultural way in which these peoples in prehistory carried out funerals—and this is simply question begging.

However, even the Western cultural mortuary sphere has a rather large number of implicit and explicit pragmatic (that is, action-constitutive) rules that stipulate how the deceased must be treated in order for the event to figure as a felicitous funeral. That is to say, even we as members of the Western culture world have rules that specify the conditions of satisfaction that must be brought about, and much of this treatment would be quite independent of the social standing of the deceased prior to death. In short, there are symbolic pragmatic rules of funerals, as such. Of course, particular instances of this type of event will also be subject to impression management tactics as part of the pervasive pursuit of reputation, so that those whose reputations are tested by the way in which they are seen to treat their deceased may include material symbolic pragmatic elements that might well present the most positive view of the deceased to all the funerary participants. However, none of these symbolic additions is part of the constitution of the event as a funeral. Another way of putting this is to say that none of these additions would be specified by the contents of the funerary ideology as being among the conditions of satisfaction constituting the performance as a funeral. Indeed, care must be taken to ensure that these additions for the sake of the pursuit of reputation do not "push the envelope" and contradict the mortuary-defining symbolic pragmatics of the event, whether funerary or some other mortuary event, or else the additions will be counterproductive in terms of reputation.

Furthermore, a problem with the funerary paradigm is that, even in the Western cultural world, the funeral does not exhaust the mortuary sphere. Mourning and memorial events are significant components. The symbolic pragmatics of these events clearly distinguish them from the funeral. The timing of the events, the place, the participants, and the relationship of the deceased to the event are both similar to and quite distinct from the funeral itself, no matter what social standing the deceased had. Indeed, some of the most important public mortuary events might entail rules that dictate that the felicity of the event depends on the anonymity of the deceased, as in the case of a national memorial performed before the tomb of the Unknown Soldier.

I believe that applying the funerary paradigm to the mortuary sphere of prehistoric Native North American peoples is an error. If the sphere is treated as being relatively autonomous, then, in fact, it subsumes the strategies making up the pursuit of reputation. Thus, even the simplest or least complex of these prehistoric social systems may have quite complex mortuary spheres. This is because even a "simple" social system can embody an immanentist cosmology that postulates humans as possessing multiple souls—the name spirit, the spirit of the flesh, the spirits of the bones, with subclassificatory body-part spirits, and so on—and, as postulated under the Dual Clan-Cult model, we can add to this source of variation the existence of multiple organizations that can vary between integrated and bifurcated settlement articulation and having differential mortuary needs and duties to fulfil toward their deceased. Therefore, we can anticipate a complexly varied mortuary record mapping social systems in which dominance hierarchies may be absent.

The Mourning/World Renewal Mortuary Model

I can now elucidate a mortuary theory that fits the inclusive territorial/custodial domain paradigm and the type of heterarchical polyistic locale-centric social system that it postulates. This alternative will figure importantly in my interpretation of the American Bottom Mississippian period mortuary data. I have termed it the *Mourning/World Renewal Mortuary model* (Byers 2004, chapter 8). Applied to the American Bottom mortuary sphere, this model postulates that it was organized as an incremental series of dual mortuary/world renewal rites. This series of mortuary rites will be termed the *funerary→mourning→spirit release→world renewal ritual process*. It is an incremental process in the sense that each stage, moving from left to right, has its own mortuary character, and the material outcome of that stage serves as the warranting context and medium for generating the ritual of the next stage.

As pointed out above in Milner's quotation, even under the funerary paradigm the deceased are treated as social persons. Social persons are participants in social events, and although typically such participants are living humans, this is not necessarily the case. Spirits, the actual dead, and, in the absence of the dead, symbolic representations of them in the form of dolls, mummies, or some other icon can all be understood as social persons if they are accorded such status in the particular culture (Fowler 2004, 24–35, 45–48). A social person is a participant in an event because she/he/it/they occupy a position constituted by rights, duties, entitlements, and responsibilities, and these define the range of interactions that the person as participant is expected to fulfil with other participants in similar and/or reciprocal positions. These positions can be usefully characterized in terms of the symbolic pragmatic weight they have in determining the social nature of the given event. Focal social positions, for example, determine the social nature of the event itself. Thus, if the person presiding in a collective activity is a judge and is regarded by relevant others as such, then the event is a legal hearing. Without the judge present and actively presiding, the rest of the aggregation of persons cannot activate the positions that they would otherwise occupy as participants. Hence, the behaviors of the occupants of focal positions constitute the key set of actions that constitute the social nature of the event, and the occupants of auxiliary positions typically treat the conduct of the focal participants as the action cues by which they guide themselves in performing their own and reciprocal actions (Harré 1979, 46–60).

As discussed earlier, the styles of clothing, adornments, accessories, and so on, are the symbolic pragmatic devices that mediate behaviors and constitute these as social actions. Social positions are typically constituted through the standard range of such devices, which manifest the action powers that these positions endow their occupants. The key artifactual warranting materials of focal positions, then, can be called focal warrants, and those of auxiliary positions are auxiliary warrants. Ancillary warrants can be those secondary material symbols that can be present and used by participants, as long as they do not contradict the symbolic pragmatic meanings of the focal and auxiliary warrants that they must use (*must* being used in the pragmatic-constitutive rather than the regulatory sense).

Mortuary events are like other social events in that they are also constituted by participants occupying relevant positions and interacting through the mediation of their warranting devices. However, mortuary events are also unique since, according to the above, the deceased are both participants and warrants. The presence of the deceased (or their symbolically mediated presence) is what constitutes the event as mortuary in nature. In any given instance, without the deceased present as participants, either in some bodily forms or some symbolic forms that expressively presence the culturally and socially relevant aspects of the deceased, the behaviors of the other participants cannot be constituted as being the mortuary event of the type intended. At the same time, however, since the deceased are in a state of material existence that makes them akin to other material objects, their material presence is possible only because they were carried to the event, and therefore, along with the casket, crypt, and so on, they are part of the symbolic pragmatic facilities that constitute the event as the type of mortuary ritual intended.

The deceased thus have a unique standing. On the one hand, they are material things much like the artifacts with which they are often associated, and they can therefore be used as symbolic warrants. On the other hand, they are not just like these other things, since, in fact, it is because of the deceased (or their expressive symbolic representation) that the living take themselves to be participating in a mortuary event at all. This raises the question, Should the deceased be treated as participants occupying mortuary social positions or as symbolic warrants, focal or auxiliary, mediating mortuary events? My brief answer to this question is to treat them as both; the weight of relevance of these two roles in any particular case will vary according to the type of mortuary event being performed. I term this the *dual participant–symbolic warranting role*. This dual role accommodates a broad range of mortuary rites, including the funeral or its equivalent.

This participant-warranting ambiguity does not arise with respect to living participants. Their role is marked and constituted by means of the material warrants they wear, carry, and manipulate, and their collective, reflexive awareness of the meaning of these items directs them in their interactions in the presence of the deceased. That is, the living are extrinsically endowed by their symbolic warrants with the social powers of their mortuary positions; their mortuary responsibilities arise from the relationship they hold in that context, particularly in regard to but not limited to the deceased. The deceased, however, are intrinsically endowed by virtue of being in a state of death—in whatever way this state is recognized in different societies. Consequently, the deceased make up highly valued participants in mortuary events, and simultaneously, in some societies, their physicality constitutes a highly valued symbolic pragmatic resource, a form of symbolic capital. This resource—their bodies or body parts—can be manipulated, quite literally, as symbolic pragmatic devices by which the living constitute different types of mortuary events.

This dual participant–symbolic warranting status arises from the recognition in probably all human societies that, while death brings about changes in human agents, it does not eliminate their action capacities. Of course, the deceased as agents cannot behave in the same way as when they were living. However, they typically are still recognized as having action capacities—in many cases, very special capacities—depending on the cultural beliefs (cosmology), values and attitudes (ethos), and mortuary protocols (ideology) of the society. Famously, the death of the Inca ruler of Tawantinsuyu was not seen as eliminating his action powers: if anything, they were enhanced. The position and power of the ruler in his deceased state were embodied in his mummy, which was endowed with all the clothing, furniture, palaces, and estates that the ruler possessed when living. The senior son became the new ruler, while the rest of his male siblings became the collective stewards (custodians?) of their deceased father (and his estates), who continued to exercise his will through his living sons. They performed regular consultative rituals with the royal mummy and translated the signs that they received as the will of the deceased Inca, upon which they were empowered to act (Conrad and Demarest 1984, 113–16).

This simultaneity of the deceased's being both mortuary participant and mortuary warrant means that the systematic postmortem corporeal modification of the deceased can be treated as an important symbolic pragmatic mode of constituting each incremental stage of the mortuary process, from funerary to mourning to memorial rite, and so on, with the deceased in each incremental ritual step manifesting a reduced participant weight and a greater symbolic warranting weight. To illustrate this point, I would have you assume that a given mortuary program has a broad range of postmortem manipulatory practices, as marked empirically by the range of burial forms. In those cases where the deceased are presented in a manner that largely replicates their self-presentation when living, at least as closely as practicably possible, this treatment would constitute them as occupying the primary focal position of the event, being the virtual hosts of these mortuary activities. It makes sense that as hosts or at least honored guests, the deceased would be associated with the range of artifacts and facilities that, as symbolic warrants, defined their social standing in life. This is part of what is meant by being hosts or honored guests, and this type of mortuary event might adequately be characterized as a funeral, understood in the broad sense of initial death-separation rites.

Following the funeral, however, the positions that the deceased subsequently occupy are less as participants and more as symbolic warrants, as marked by each incremental step of postmortem manipulation to which they are subjected—flexed burial, bundle burial, body-parts burial, individually deposited cremation, mass cremation deposit, and so on. In short, each step marks a progressive reduction of their participant powers (from focal to auxiliary to ancillary) and an unfolding of their symbolic warranting powers. Each of these steps also marks a social abstraction of the deceased from their personal identification as father or mother, brother or sister, sodality brother or sister, to a more general socially relevant identification, as senior male lineage member or senior sodality companion, to lineage or sodality member. Paralleling this abstracting process would be the move from the identifiable bodies (funerals) to the named bone bundles (mourning rites) to the unnamed body parts (mortuary offerings), and so on.

This does not mean that such a literal and social "deconstruction" dehumanizes the deceased, for their humanness is what makes sense out of the formal modes of treatment. Rather, the incremental stages of modification progressively expose and release the multiple spiritually enlivened symbolic pragmatic forces that are embodied in the deceased: the name spirit, the spirit of the flesh, the spirit of bones, and so on. Of course, each incremental step counts as a mortuary ritual. It also has a material outcome, namely, the modification of the deceased such that these material transformations can be used as symbolic pragmatic devices for subsequent types of mortuary rituals. In this sense, the multiple states of the deceased count as different types of symbolic capital that can be drawn upon at a later date to mediate the next ritual stage.

A similar and parallel transformation occurs with the mortuary features, facilities, and artifactual associations. From the perspective of the participants, these material things actually take on different symbolic pragmatic meaning with each ritual step. The artifacts associated with the initial mortuary event in which the deceased is the host are the warrants of the deceased as host or honored guest and are present either as personalty or as mortuary gifts. At the next stage, the artifacts might become gifts that the newly released soul gives away to the participants or endows to the institution responsible for the event. These might be curated to be used as media of the next step. This might require the use of the bones of the deceased, or selected skeletal components, to be used as the media of a spirit release rite, which simultaneously is taken to be a world renewal rite since the life-spirit of the bones is given to the cosmos. Any associated artifacts, then, even if they are the same type as those associated with the original funerary rite, become part of the offering act. Thus, while the initial symbolic pragmatic meaning of the burial facility might be as a grave, if it is used in the third rite, it might be more adequately characterized as a world renewal altar, and the mortuary residue (for example, a bundle of bones and a ritually broken pot) becomes the medium and final residue of a world renewal offering.

Importantly, while the funerary→mourning→spirit release→world renewal ritual process applies to the total range of mortuary practices, not all deceased would necessarily be subjected to every step. Several conditions would control the degree to which any given deceased would be processed. First, there would be the minimal pragmatic factor: the basic mortuary strategy that would specify the minimal range of mortuary practices to which any deceased should be subjected. This range of rules would define the relative autonomy of the mortuary sphere. Thus, no matter what the social standing of the deceased at death, qualified by particular circumstances, all deceased could be expected to receive this basic treatment. In addition to this treatment, however, would be the ritual needs and responsibilities of the different social groups that had obligations toward the deceased. As a member of a cult, the deceased would be recruited primarily to mediate renewal ritual. The deceased members and/or their deceased dependents (such as children, spouses, and even elderly parents) could be subjected to mediating a series of renewal rites by this cult, depending largely on the particular renewal needs that the organization was fulfilling and, of course, depending on the standing of the deceased in the cult. Complex rules would govern this process. For example, I can imagine that renewal rituals would be performed at major solar and/or lunar turning points. The significance of these different turning points would be used to gauge the number and mortuary state of the deceased that would be needed. Some renewal rites might need uncremated bones as sacred bundles, while others might require such sacred bone bundles to be cremated.

Along with the needs of cults to perform mortuary/world renewal rites would be the needs of clans to perform mortuary/clan renewal/thanksgiving rites. Thus, following the initial "funerary" rites, negotiations between clans and cults might occur to determine whether a particular deceased would be appropriated to the cult or to the clan for further ritual processing. However, in general, these intervening conditions would not suppress or cancel out any of the basic mortuary treatment, because only if this basic treatment was respected would the deceased serve in their dual participant–symbolic warranting capacity to further the goals and fulfil the responsibilities of either clan or cult. Furthermore, as noted above, just as the ritual process would transform the deceased into different material media of mortuary/renewal rites, so also would the symbolic pragmatic force of the mediating facilities be modified, and this modification process may be only partially or totally irreversible. Therefore, in any given cult CBL, there might come to be a complex patterning of mortuary pits, some containing the residue of what are identified as primary burials, others bundle burials, others with only a few so-called stray bones, while still others lack any overt human residue. Although all the pits appear very similar, this patterning indicates that they were perceived and used as a set of changing and largely irreversibly transforming symbolic pragmatic mortuary devices.

To put this approach into current mortuary interpretive context, I note that James Brown (1995, 392) has recently argued that there are currently two theoretical mortuary approaches, which he terms the *individualist* and the *representationist*. The former "views the dead as *individuals* and their mortuary treatment as somehow representative of some feature, aspect, or attribute they possessed before death . . . [in the sense that] treatment in death is determined by one's former status as a living individual," while the latter argues that the treatment of the deceased is "in accordance to the needs and wishes of the living" (emphasis in the original). He goes on to emphasize that the representationist view interprets this treatment as having "a strongly political aspect, such as the use of the dead to consecrate a monument, or the practice of determining the treatment of the corpse on criteria completely independent of the age, sex, or social standing of the deceased—such as the day on the ritual calendar or the stage of mound development and cemetery use" (Brown 1995, 392).

Clearly, on these criteria, both the Cemetery model and the Mourning/World Renewal Mortuary model can be seen as having a strongly representationist orientation. Where they particularly differ, however, is that the former is committed to the funerary paradigm while the latter model incorporates the funerary aspect as simply a part of the larger mortuary sphere. This broader perspective adds considerably to Brown's characterization of the representationist view. In these broader terms, the deceased have great value as symbolic pragmatic capital by which groups that had responsibility to the deceased could perform felicitous mortuary-based rituals that achieved culturally intelligible goals, thereby enhancing the reputations of the groups responsible. Finally, and most importantly, this perspective significantly expands the possible range of social factors that could be causally responsible for the observed mortuary variation, thereby also enhancing the capacity for archaeology to expand its understanding of the nature of these prehistoric social systems.

Since the Mourning/World Renewal Mortuary model postulates that the deceased or their bodily components served as critical dual participant–symbolic warranting media of this complex incremental process of mortuary/renewal rituals, their use in rituals emphasizing the renewal aspect would suggest that they served as renewal offerings. This notion of an offering immediately implicates a sacrificial paradigm. This is precisely what I intend. Therefore, I postulate that the postmortem manipulatory behavior constitutes the renewal aspects of these incremental mortuary events as postmortem human sacrifice. This term has been coined to contrast with lethal human sacrifice. Lethal human sacrifice is also a mortuary event, of course, but it is unique in that, done under the appropriate symbolic warranting conditions, the intentional killing of a participant is a necessary part of constituting the behavioral process as a mortuary ritual of the type intended, that is, as a social or, more likely, a world renewal sacrificial ritual of the type practiced, for instance, by most, if not all, Classic and Post-Classic Mesoamerican societies (Conrad and Demarest 1984;

Sugiyama 1989; Townsend 1979, 1992; Van Zantwijk 1985).[4] A postmortem human sacrifice, however, is a mortuary ritual in which deliberate human killing does not figure among the conditions of satisfaction of the mortuary intentions. Death is "natural" or caused by some agency or event extrinsic to the subsequent mortuary events. Once death occurs, however, it is "cultivated" by the living treating the deceased as highly valued symbolic pragmatic ritual capital, as discussed above.

This distinction between postmortem and lethal human sacrifice is implicated in Hall's comparative overview of the sacrificial dimension of the mortuary practices as marked by the Dickson Mounds site, Mound 72 of the Cahokia site, and the Aztecan and Toltecan sacrificial fertility practices. Hall observes, "It is my belief that in Aztec practices we are witnessing the final phase of a shift from the ritual use of unscheduled deaths, such as those over the Dickson Mounds four, to the use of the scheduled deaths that we have called sacrifice" (Hall 2000, 250). While Hall does not use the term *postmortem sacrifice* in characterizing the "Dickson Mounds four" as evidence of "the ritual use of unscheduled deaths," he would appear to be expressing the same sense that defines this terminology, in that the agency causing the deaths was extrinsic to the sacrificial ritual.

Finally, I stress that while the notion of the cemetery is valid, going beyond it is important in order to characterize the possible range of CBLs. Later I suggest the criteria for differentiating among cemetery and noncemetery CBLs. However, I simply note here that, as I define it, the term *collective burial locale* (or CBL) refers to any locale that was clearly the context of two or more mortuary events, in that they contain buried—that is, deliberately deposited—human remains, no matter in what state, for example, primary or secondary burials, flexed or bundled bones, cremated deposits, and so on, including facilities that were identical to those containing human residue but which, in this case, had no such residue. Thus, a mound containing mortuary remains deliberately placed would have among its symbolic pragmatic meanings that of being a CBL of one type or another. This also means that a CBL need not be exclusively mortuary in nature. It may well contain evidence that nonmortuary events also occurred. Rather than the presence of nonmortuary remains detracting from the mortuary analysis, however, this simply helps define the type of CBL it was.

Before I directly address the archaeological record of the American Bottom, one more theoretical perspective needs to be elucidated since it is critical to the thesis of this book. The application of this mortuary model to the Mississippian mortuary record of the American Bottom presupposes the cultic aspect postulated under the Dual Clan-Cult model. Therefore, I elucidate below a theory of cults that can be used as the framework of my interpretation not only of the mortuary record but also of much of the monumental and artifactual record of this region.

The Autonomous Cult Model

I have found A. F. C. Wallace's (1966) anthropological theory of religion and religious cults to be extremely useful since it focuses on the organizational parameters of religious practices and beliefs. These organizational parameters are treated by him as cults, and although I draw on his categories of cult organizations, I also must make several critical modifications to his theory. Wallace's theory is well known as recognizing four basic cult types: individualistic, shamanic, communal, and ecclesiastical. The individualistic cult is characterized by a direct social relation between an individual and a spiritual power constituting the individual↔spirit-guardian structure. The shamanic cult has basically the same individual↔spirit structure except that, as a shaman, the individual possesses extraordinary spiritual powers that attract powerful spiritual beings as her/his partners. The shaman also is expected to serve her/his community by performing seances during times of stress. Using her/his powers and specialized know-how, the shaman effects cures for the sick, solicits good hunting for the hungry, and so on.[5]

While both the shamanic and the individualistic cults are largely situation-dependent, emerging only in situations perceived by the relevant parties as unusual, stressful, critical, and so on, in Wallace's theoretical scheme, the communal cult is situation-constitutive, having and acting on a ceremonial schedule. However, in his scheme a communal cult is not an autonomous group but simply the religious posture of an established sodality, either kinship based, such as a lineage or clan, or companionship based, such as a men's military society. These kin and nonkin sodalities normally have formal leadership positions whose occupants are responsible for planning affairs in advance. Since the sodalities also have religious functions to perform, they normally have ritual cycles, often (although not always) tied to the seasonal cycles. Hence, a particular sodality shifts into its cult posture according to the schedule and sometimes in response to emergencies, by the responsible leaders declaring and authorizing the performance of the appropriate ritual activities. This means that the leaders of the sodality simply move into their ritual leadership positions, often by quite literally donning specially designed and appropriate clothing, such as headdresses, masks, cloaks, adornments, and so on. These are their warrants of ritual. When needed, they usually elicit the specialized know-how and skills of local shamans to lead and/or conduct the more esoteric rituals. Note that the shaman is not an officer of the organization. As soon as the ritual or rituals are terminated, this religious specialist in her/his capacity as a shaman has no further call on the sodality, or vice versa, until possibly the next time the sodality calls on her/him/them to provide these specialized skills and competencies.

The most complex cult organization in Wallace's theory is the ecclesiastical cult. This also is situation-constitutive, operating on a ritual schedule, with officers, ranks, specialists, and so on. However, it also exists as a formal congregation. That is, unlike the communal cult, which is simply actualized by the aggregation of the members of the communal sodality shifting into the religious posture, the ecclesiastical cult is typically an autonomous corporate religious group. Since both communal and ecclesiastical cults have officers, ritual schedules, and so on, the critical difference between them largely hinges on the position of the religious specialist. While, as noted above, in communal cults this is a contracted professional, a shaman, in the ecclesiastical cult, it is a priest. That is, the congregation of the ecclesiastical cult is constituted by the clergy/laity structure. This means that, whereas in the communal cult the regular and ritual leaders are the same persons, in the ecclesiastical cult, these constitute two separate leadership positions, laity and clergy, and each often has a hierarchical leadership structure. The result is a special type of dynamism as laity and clergy leadership compete for overall cult power.

Wallace uses the three logical possibilities of relative power distribution between clergy and laity leadership to postulate three subtypes of ecclesiastical cults. When the prevailing power is in the hands of the laity leadership, this constitutes the congregationalist cult. Episcopalian cults are characterized by the opposite, that is, the clergy leadership dominates. Presbyterian cults are characterized by a balancing of power and responsibility between the laity and clergy leadership. Usually this is accomplished by a division of responsibilities, with the laity having greater control of the secular aspect of the organization and the clergy of the religious. However, typically, final authority often resides with the laity.

For Wallace, a scalar combination of these four types of cults constitutes the religious organization of a society. A society with a shamanistic religion has only individualistic and shamanic cults. He claims that the shamanistic religion is typical of foraging societies. Tribal societies form communalistic religious organizations based on individualistic, shamanic, and communal cults, the latter embedded in kin and nonkin sodalities. States and, possibly, complex chiefdoms typically have ecclesiastical cults, and these exist as the core of what he referred to as olympian and/or monotheistic religions. The ecclesiastical cult is usually specialized across the recognized cosmogony of deities. However, the religion also includes the various (and "lesser") communal, shamanistic, and individualistic cults. The latter three would be embedded in the overall social system as the religious postures of clans, lineages, and families, as well as shamans or shamanic colleges.

CRITICAL DISCUSSION OF CULTS AND SOCIAL SYSTEMS

There is a strong, largely taken-for-granted bias in Wallace's theoretical scheme. The clearest expression of this is his use of the terminology of Western Christendom in defining ecclesiastical cults and complex religious organization. However, I actually find these terms to be very useful since they pick out important structural aspects that apply cross-culturally, such as the clergy/laity structure, the competition for leadership this incurs, and so on. However, a more subtle bias is simultaneously piggybacked on the use of this Western Christendom terminology. In using these terms, the theory imports the sociopolitical nature of the social systems that they implicate (namely, monistic modular polities) and imposes it on tribal and band social systems, simultaneously and in a largely matter-of-fact manner treating these as monistic modular polities based on kinship as the dominant social structural axis. At the same time, the theory postulates a major social systems cleavage plane, which is particularly evident in Wallace's distinguishing between communal and ecclesiastical cults in that only the latter, not the former, are autonomous organizations. The implication is that tribal and band social systems based on the dominance of kinship are too simple (not sufficiently complex structurally) to generate or sustain autonomous cults, that is, ecclesiastical cults. Only state societies and borderline or complex chiefdoms are sufficiently complex structurally to do so. Therefore, only at the level of complex chiefdoms and states might specialized and permanent religious congregations emerge, constituting autonomous ecclesiastical cults. Under the monistic modular polity view, then, less complex societies, such as tribes or even simple chiefdoms, can sustain only individualistic, shamanic, and communal cults, and the latter are always simply the religious posture of kin- or non-kin-based sodality groups, with the kin-based sodalities prevailing in the overall structure of authority.

When measured against the Dual Clan-Cult model, Wallace's religious theory needs to be modified. Individualist, shamanic, and communal cults can be treated in precisely the same way as he postulates—with one important modification. We must recognize that the prevalence of the squatter ethos and its core value of agentive autonomy means that tribal and, in some conditions, band social systems can sustain autonomous as well as subsumed cults. Thus, the privileging of kinship as the basis of a tribal society has to be eliminated and the notion of the relative autonomy of kinship and companionship sodalities put forward as primary. Denying kinship as privileged is not to deny its importance. Avoiding the privileging of kinship simply says that kinship does not define the type of social system I am articulating; rather, the complementary or relative autonomy of kinship and companionship groups is what defines social systems. Certainly, in a polyistic locale-centric community, kin sodalities are critically important organizations. However, as argued in earlier chapters (and as illustrated by the Nyakyusa age-set village system), nonkin sodalities can be equally or even more critically important, and both types can and, in this type of social system, must exist as relatively autonomous organizations since individuals belong to both types simultaneously. For this reason I will use the term *Autonomous Cult model* for this characterization of the cultic dimension of the Dual Clan-Cult model.

In this case, while the Autonomous Cult model recognizes that both types of sodalities—kinship based and companionship based—can constitute communal cults, only the former and not the latter exists as a religious posture of the kinship-based sodality, that is, clan and lineage. In contrast, the companionship-based sodality is a constituted cult organization, although, as a communal cult, it is one that lacks the clergy/laity structure. Furthermore, neither the clan-based nor the companionship-based communal cult is privileged over the other, thereby constituting the basic complementary clan-cult type of heterarchical polyistic locale-centric social systems as described in earlier chapters.

This modification has important implications. Because companionship-based communal cults would be relatively autonomous, I postulate that, under special historical-emergent conditions, they could evolve into ecclesiastic-like cults, which I have termed elsewhere *ecclesiastic-communal cults* (Byers 2004, chapter 12). These are characterized by having a congregation dually structured into laity/clergy, with the laity structured into junior/senior generations and even, possibly, male/female sectors. Therefore, the members of this type of cult would typically be caught up in conflicts generated by the contradictions resulting from this complex structuring of clergy/laity, senior/junior generations, and male/female genders.

The Ecclesiastic-Communal Cult

Clearly, the ecclesiastic-communal cult is not part of Wallace's scheme. However, a heterarchical polyistic locale-centric social system presents a completely different set of possibilities from the monistic modular perspective that his theory presupposes. In this case, since clans and cults are relatively autonomous, their historical development can take different paths. In general, since the clan-based communal cult is the religious posture of this organizational type, its stability or change is simply a moment of the reproduction of the clan structure, and structural changes would occur only if the clan structure itself changed. However, this is not the case for the companionship-based communal cult organizational type; under certain conditions it could transform into the more complex ecclesiastic-communal cult type. For example, separate female- and male-based communal cults could act cooperatively in performing ritual, effectively integrating into a compound communal cult having complementary female and male sectors. Alternatively, a region could promote a dual set of mutually autonomous same-sex communal cults structured by junior and senior generations. Under certain conditions these senior and junior age-grade communal cults might pursue cooperation, thereby integrating while still maintaining the mutually recognized autonomy of the senior and junior age-grades. This would constitute a condition promoting further innovation by making the peripatetic shamans into permanent participants and would quite quickly come to constitute the clergy/laity structure, with a junior/senior-structured laity sector. This is the reason that I term this type of emergent organization the *ecclesiastic-communal cult*: it combines the companionship-based communal structure with the clergy/laity structure. Rather than elucidating a separate model to characterize this cult, I will consider it to be simply an extension of the Autonomous Cult model—albeit an important one, since I postulate that this organizational type figured centrally in the transition from the Emergent Mississippian, or Terminal Late Woodland, period to the Mississippian period.[6]

Hierarchy, Labor, and Autonomy

Critically important here is to emphasize the immanentist cosmology and squatter ethos of the cultural traditions of this type of social system. The squatter ethos enshrines the autonomy of the agent, whether this is an individual, an age-set, a gender-set, or a total cult. I suggest in chapter 4 that autonomy is not the same as equality. In a social system sustaining and sustained by a squatter ethos, inequality is taken to be a normal state of affairs. However, this engenders equitability of treatment, not dominance. An individual may be stronger than another or more skilled in certain competencies. A group may be able to mobilize more labor than another and be more senior than another. However, the principle of autonomy and its complement of equitability do not allow this recognized inequality to translate into social dominance or subordination and dependence. Instead, it is translated into differential responsibilities and reputations. If autonomy is the right to exercise responsibilities without being subjected to interference from other parties, then the driving motive for this is to accrue recognition as a worthy and honorable person or group both in one's own eyes and in the eyes of other autonomous persons or groups. In polyistic locale-centric social systems, therefore, the principle of autonomy is pervasive or hegemonic, paralleled by the principle of equitability.

Because autonomy recognizes inequality of powers and capacities, it also can ground hierarchical differences, but this is a principled hierarchy in which these differences are recognized as reasonable by all the parties since it enables them to discharge their responsibilities according to their position and without direction by or interference from other parties. Female-based cults or the female sectors of dual-gendered cults would have distinctly different but complementary responsibilities from those of male-based cults or the male sectors of dual-gendered cults. The male sector of a dual-gendered cult or even a simple male-based cult would expect that the complementary female sector or female-based cult would carry out its responsibilities, and vice versa, since each would require the performance of the ritual actions of the other to make the performance of its own ritual felicitous, thereby each fulfilling its respective duties.

This complementarity would apply to the age-grade ordering, also. As outlined above, an ecclesiastic-communal cult could be centrally constituted by at least two generations—a junior age-grade and a senior age-grade—along with pre-junior and elder age-grades. These would be ranked in order of the principle of seniority. As in the Nyakyusa example, each autonomous age-grade would have its traditional set of responsibilities within the total cult organization. Taking a conservative stance in this regard, instead of the Nyakyusa generational span of thirty to thirty-five years, I postulate that an age-grade would have a generational span of twenty-five to thirty years, and the majority of the membership of a cult, structured by hierarchically related senior and junior age-grades, would collectively cover a fifty-to-sixty-year span, the youngest of the junior age-grade being about fifteen years old and the (few) eldest of the senior age-grade, about sixty-five to seventy-five. Furthermore, each age-grade (junior and senior) would be internally differentiated by age-sets, each having a span of about five to eight years separating the youngest and oldest, that would also be rank-ordered by seniority, constituting each age-grade as internally structured by an age-set hierarchy of three to five levels.[7]

Attached to this dual hierarchy would be substantive, traditionally established entitlements, responsibilities, and duties that would translate into different forms of benefits and tasks, some involving manual labor, some involving skilled labor, and some involving ritual performative labor. In an immanently sacred world, such labor would be assessed according to its perceived effects both on the sanctity of the natural order and on the polluting/sanctifying effect on the responsible agents. Labor, therefore, would be valued along a menial/polluting↔esteemed/sanctifying continuum. Forms of labor that have great direct physical impact would have more polluting than sanctifying import on both the world and the agent and therefore would probably have a heavier menial than an esteemed valuation. Forms of labor having a lesser physical impact component and a greater representational performative impact, such as invoking spiritual powers through ritual, would have more sanctifying than polluting import, again on both the world and the agent, and therefore would probably have a heavier esteemed than a menial valuation.

In general, the traditional distribution of polluting and sanctifying tasks would be allocated across the age-set hierarchy and between the junior and senior age-grade sectors in terms of relative menial-esteemed value of the labor realized in the different tasks. Thus, as age-sets were promoted up the age-grade hierarchy and from the junior to the senior age-grade, they would change the type of labor they performed. For example, while the physical transformations involved in building a sacred platform mound might be warranted by an assessment that it has greater overall sanctifying than polluting impact, it would count as having more agent-polluting than agent-sanctifying benefit to the actual laborer and, therefore, as being more menial than esteemed in nature. In a sense, the laborers as responsible agents take on the pollution burden entailed by deliberately disordering the local topography, a form of self-sacrifice. This labor would be warranted and rectified by being performed under the authoritative declaration of the sanctifiers, the leaders of the senior age-grade, with the declarative performatives being treated as esteemed ritual since they had a greater sanctifying than polluting outcome. Among these sanctifiers would be those who could instruct and lead the young laborers on how to cleanse themselves, for example, by conducting a sweat lodge ritual.

Hence, while the polluters and the sanctifiers were autonomous parties, they were also mutually dependent, performing what they collectively perceived as complementary actions. Therefore, they were mutually dependent autonomous agents, tied together through shared responsibilities. In short, this would be a form of relative autonomy. The sanctifiers could not perform the esteemed task of ritual sacrifice to discharge their duties without the polluters having performed the menial task of ritual construction, and the workers could not have the self-polluting and world-polluting effects of their menial labor rectified and reversed without the sanctifying ritual labor of those performing the esteemed sanctifying representational performative labor.

This general labor distribution by age-set would be crosscut by specialization. For example, some young males or females might be chosen to be trained in specialized ritual because of their perceived ritual competence. They would become apprentices to shamanic-like priests in the clergy sector, and they would be expected to perform labor having greater sanctifying value than would other youths of the same age-set who did not receive this specialized instruction. In the normal course of promotion they would become cult priests and be caught up in the clergy career trajectory, while their companions would remain laity.

Since a cult would be based on the hierarchical age-grade structure, it would be reproduced through promotions. Again, with the Nyakyusa serving as an illustrative guide, these promotions would probably occur synchronously. At a certain point, all the survivors of the senior age-grade would retire, becoming esteemed elders, thereby making way for the junior age-grade to be promoted en masse to the senior age-grade and the preinitiated age-grade sets being indoctrinated and promoted en masse as the new junior age-grade sector, and so on. However, since the cult has a laity/clergy structure, there would be two parallel and partly integrated promotional cycles, one for the laity and one for the clergy. In all probability, the clergy would be responsible for overall training of the ordinary preinitiates and even for some of the ritual training of the junior age-grade members; as stated earlier, they would be in a position to observe any youths who might be interested in and noted as capable of the special training required to become a shamanic priest. This also means that while an age-set would sustain its collective identity through every stage of promotion, some members would be recruited laterally to join the clergy. This, however, would not break the bonds of companionship, so that when a companion became a priest, he or she would probably still have a special relation to his/her age-set companions who continued as laity-sector members.

Hence, the total cult would be hierarchical in terms of age-grade seniority, with an internal differentiation of laity and specialized clergy constituting two parallel leadership hierarchies, and possibly of specialized artisans having a strong shamanic priestlike standing who were responsible for producing the specialized warrants of ritual. However, this hierarchy would not likely become the basis of a fundamental class structure. Even speaking in terms of "elite" and "non-elite" would be problematic because differential position would be strongly age-dependent and, to a significant degree, structured by the age-set system so that in the fullness of time all active participants in the cult would pass through every status level. Also, as dictated by the principle of autonomy, each age-set would select its own peer leaders, who would be accorded public recognition in cultwide initiation and promotion ceremonies. These leaders would move through the leadership hierarchy in tandem with their age-sets. Since each age-set is an autonomous group of companions, it would be represented by its peer-selected leaders in all relevant decision-making arenas. Therefore, cult decisions would always be based on councils, and the members of these councils would be the leaders of each age-set.

Since the guiding principle of interaction would be the relative autonomy of the component parts, only when a council achieved consensus could a declaration be promulgated that would specify the activity to be performed (including the activity's particular form, timing, and so on), by which the cult would discharge its duties. This declaration then would become the main enabling act by which each age-set could collectively exercise its power-to-act so as to fulfil its particular responsibilities in accordance with the consensus-based council declaration, the content of the latter specifying the conditions of satisfaction of the collective prior intention. That is, the declaration of the council is not the exercise of dominance power or "power-over" the hierarchically organized age-set components. The authoritative, consensus-based declaration, through its being uttered according to the recognized mode, simply creates the conditions that would enable age-sets to act in terms of their recognized responsibilities. Cultwide recognition of this condition would be an important part of cult motivational momentum since each group would know that in exercising its responsibilities by performing its traditional tasks in relation to the goals specified by the declaration, it was neither imposing nor being imposed on by the other age-sets. Rather, the exercise of its power-to-act and the expectations of other relatively autonomous age-sets in the hierarchy was the enabling condition by which these others were able to exercise their power-to-act capacities, and vice versa.

Elsewhere I have used the term *stratified egalitarianism* to refer to this form of rank differentiation (Byers 2004, 250–51). However, while age-set peers are formally equal, I believe that the egalitarianism of individual age-sets does not adequately characterize the unique nature of this form of hierarchical differentiation, because age-sets could sustain the structural principle of egalitarianism while being subsumed into dominance hierarchies. Only in systems based on the principle of autonomy could enabling hierarchies be the existing norm, these being hierarchies that integrate mutually or relatively autonomous agents. Therefore, I will term this form of social rank structuring a *stratified autonomy,* and the type of hierarchy that it makes possible I will term an *enabling hierarchy*—in deliberate contrast to a dominance hierarchy. The latter manifests the principles of dominance/subordination, and in my view, it is the kind assumed by those who promote the various versions of the hierarchical monistic modular polity account.

An enabling hierarchy is stratified in all of the normal senses, but its constituent units, as strata, are relatively autonomous. In the case of the enabling hierarchy that is the ecclesiastic-communal cult, each age-set recognizes its members as formally equal. Therefore, all the members of the cult have an equal opportunity to be chosen by their age-set peers for positions of leadership in accordance with the rank level of their age-set. This also means that (1) differences in skills and competencies (that is, actual inequalities) are relevant and recognized as normal, while (2) each individual recognizes the autonomy of her/his peers and is recognized as autonomous by them.

I want to avoid being labeled dogmatic by noting here that an enabling hierarchy also has a certain degree of dominance power embedded in it. Recognizing this accords with Anthony Giddens's (1979, 88) notion of social power as always being realized as a dialectic of dominance and autonomy. As Giddens observes,

Social systems are constituted as regularized practices; power within social systems can thus be treated *as involving reproduced relations of autonomy and dependence in social interaction.* Power relations therefore are always *two-way,* even if the power of one actor or party in a social relation is minimal compared to another. Power relations are relations of autonomy and dependence, but even the most autonomous agent is in some degree dependent, and the most dependent actor or party in a relation retains some autonomy. (Giddens 1979, 93)

However, as I note in chapter 2, Giddens's social theory, as powerful as it is, also presupposes a monistic modular perspective, and this means that the governing ethos principles are exclusivity and dominance. When Giddens's understanding of social power is incorporated into the polyistic locale-centric perspective, since autonomy is the prevailing principle and dominance is distinctly "subordinate" in terms of asymmetries, institutional powers will be predominantly enabling. When they are differentiated and formed into an organizational hierarchy, the latter will still be predominantly an enabling device by which relatively autonomous agents will exercise their power-to-act capacities. Of course, there is no doubt that a dominance hierarchy also has embedded in it an enabling capacity, for example, by being the opportunity-context for those at the same level to display their differential competencies in the competition for promotion.

As I suggest above, the critical differences between an enabling hierarchy and a dominance hierarchy (the former constituting a heterarchy based on recognized differences of one or another type) are the two different ethos principles: autonomy in the former case, thereby encouraging all-level and even centralized consultation and consensus-based decision making almost inescapable; and dominance in the latter, thereby making centralized decision making and a chain-of-command structure inescapable. I suggest in chapter 4 that queues (for example, the waiting lines at bus stops or by those in need in the emergency wards of hospitals) emerge when access to public domain resources exceeds immediate availability. Queues are a form of situational enabling hierarchy since the differentiation that determines the rank ordering is based on the primary rule of "first come–first served." That is, social access to limited resources is determined not by social standing but by objective, differential timing. Literally, the first comers have priority over the later comers. Why this is not a dominance-based priority is because it is based on the consensus immanent in the primary rule, which is itself collective in the sense that part of the know-how includes the assumption that everyone knows the rule. Hence, the queue constitutes a situational enabling hierarchy by which rationing of public resources is effected in a manner that is consistent with the principle of agentive autonomy.

However, the principle of agentive autonomy also allows for overriding rules. Those in a bus queue typically recognize that the disabled and the elderly have the moral priority to "jump the queue" while the first come–first served principle applies to all the others. In a hospital emergency room, of course, while the first come–first served rule applies, its application is always framed by the triage rules that define priority as going to those in most urgent need. Rather than the triage rules transgressing the principle of autonomy, the opposite is true; in this situation, equitability operates to ensure that because of the specially urgent nature of the needs of the agent, she/he is "bumped" over those who may have arrived first. Of course, since an emergency ward is typically treated in North American society as in the public domain, those responsible for its operation constitute the custodians, and their authority arises from the duty they have to ensure that the clients forming the constantly regenerated queue have their needs fulfilled in accordance with the principle of agentive autonomy as embedded in the triage rules.

Applying this notion of the queue to characterize the ecclesiastic-communal cult enabling hierarchy might be helpful, even though this hierarchy is not situational. However, in an important sense, it can be understood as a queue in that the first come–first served principle is structured into the cycling of the generations, which becomes the basis of the seniority principle for the allocation of differentiated responsibilities and social standing. In effect, the first come–first served principle is based on the relative age of the members. Since each age-set moves through every level of the enabling hierarchy, each individual has an equal opportunity to pursue the leadership positions attached to each level. Of course, individual history will certainly count, so that a young person chosen by her/his companion peers to be one of their age-set leaders is likely to be reselected with each promotion. However, because each level has a different set of duties, the required competencies can change and individuals' competencies can develop, so that the peer-chosen leadership might modify with each promotion.

Working within the opposite perspective of the hierarchical monistic modular account, Thomas Emerson (1997c, 14) argues that peer selection of the leaders directing the sacred construction of Cahokia would lead to their becoming identified with the sanctity of these monuments. Clearly, I would argue the opposite, namely, that for several reasons, an enabling hierarchy would be unlikely to promote any inheritance of position or power (although this would not be impossible). For one thing, since the cult was voluntary, adolescent youths would very likely not join the cults to which their parents belonged. Second, since leadership was by peer-based selection, even should a young man join the cult of one of his senior male relatives (even though the latter may have held a high-ranking leadership office), this position would not determine that his companions would choose him as their peer leader. Third, as important as the cult would be in the social life of individuals, it would not monopolize social life. The clan system would be equally important, and it would also be based on the principle of autonomy—although, as discussed earlier, it would have its own type of internal contradictions since the nurturing responsibilities of kinship can conflict with the principle of autonomy as the young grow up. Also, it would require leadership competencies and capacities that would be different in certain ways from those required for cult leadership positions. In short, in this dual clan-cult social system, individuals would pursue dual social careers. This duality can be energizing, endowing social life with a dynamism that opens up great opportunities for the individual.

As a complement to this duality, the social standing that an individual might gain in the cult sphere would have little or no impact on her/his standing in the domestic and clan sphere. Any spillover would be simply a result of the reputation of the individual, not an indication that the cult position she/he held would be a source of power to enhance her/his standing in the clan sphere, or vice versa. Hence, not only does the principle of autonomy as applied to the cult sphere create an enabling hierarchy, but also the principle ensures that the clan and cult spheres would sustain an arm's-length relation in that one would not intervene in the affairs of the other, while each would exist as an enabling condition of the other's activities and, of course, its capacity to reproduce.

Characterizing Heterarchy

All this marks an important theoretical departure from standard views of inequality and social power. Since hierarchy is usually treated as the organizational expression of inequality, heterarchy is usually assumed to be the organizational expression of equality. This may often be the case in a world where exclusive territorialism prevails; but as I suggest above, it usually is not the case in a world of inclusive territorialism. That is, in an immanently sacred world where the squatter ethos with its core value of agentive autonomy prevails, two socially identical groups can be unequal in any number of different ways and still relate to each other as autonomous. What constitutes their heterarchical relation, therefore, is the mutual recognition of their autonomous nature, and the latter makes differential capacities, size, and so on, irrelevant in terms of their social nature. For example, the two groups can be world renewal cults that are unequal in terms of size, skills, capacities, and so on. These differences, however, are irrelevant in terms of constituting their heterarchical relations, while their mutual recognition as world renewal cults is critically relevant. As I define it, therefore, an alliance of ecclesiastic-communal cults based on the principle of mutual autonomy will constitute one form of heterarchy.

Earlier in this chapter, I use the term *relative autonomy* to characterize the type of autonomy expressed in the arm's-length relation of the clans and cults, and above I use the term *mutual autonomy* to characterize the structure of a cult alliance as heterarchical. As I construe it, the difference is fairly straight-forward. Mutual autonomy links parties as autonomous agents—individuals or groups—on the basis of their shared social identities, in which case they constitute a heterarchical grouping based on mutual autonomy. Relative autonomy links autonomous agents on the basis of their complementary social identity (in effect, on what they do not share). A community based on the cult-clan duality, therefore, constitutes a complex grouping based on relative autonomy, as manifested in the arm's-length relation in and by which each recognizes the other's autonomy while reproducing their differences. However, since autonomy is the operative word in characterizing a heterarchy, then it follows that this sort of community must logically also be a type of heterarchy. In this case, since the heterarchy is integrated on the basis of complementary differences, terming it a *complementary heterarchy* (in contrast to the above alliance of cults, which I will term a *mutualistic heterarchy*) might be useful. As I define it, therefore, a heterarchy is based on the principle of agentive autonomy. Two basic types of heterarchies can be distinguished, complementary and mutualistic: the former is based on the principle of relative autonomy, and the latter on the principle of mutual autonomy. Since both can co-exist with recognized inequality of powers and capacities, it follows that both can manifest heterarchical relations ordered as enabling hierarchies.[8]

In sum, the heterarchical polyistic locale-centric account of the American Bottom social system hinges on two different heterarchical models: the Dual Clan-Cult model that characterizes the kinship and companionship organizations as relatively autonomous groups constituting a single community as a complementary heterarchy; and the Autonomous Cult model that characterizes the cults structurally as stratified autonomous organizations based on the principle of seniority and realized as enabling hierarchies. As suggested above, if these autonomous cults allied among themselves, they would likely construct mutualistic heterarchies that I term *world renewal cult heterarchies*; these are identified in the literature as multiple-mound centers.

Communal Class Structure

I see the enabling hierarchical cult organization that I have outlined above as incorporating many of the characteristics of Dean Saitta's (1994, 206–9) Marxian views of the political economy of a communal social system. He prefaces his comments by noting that most types of societies require surplus production since labor is necessary for social reproduction itself. He points out that Marx defined three basic forms of surplus appropriation—communal, tributary, and capitalist—and only the latter two are characterized as the outcome of fundamental class processes that generate classes that relate to each other as exploitative appropriators and exploited producers. Saitta argues that the communal process generates classes that do not relate in this manner, since the surplus production and its appropriation are voluntary (or, as I would say, consensual); therefore, the communal process creates and reproduces reciprocal rather than antagonistic class relations: "In communal societies, primary producers are both appropriators *and* performers of surplus; that is, appropriation is collective in form and producers fill dual class positions.... Communal formations are thus the only ones which lack a class *division*" (Saitta 1994, 207, emphases in original).

I see this view as being consistent with my elucidation of an enabling hierarchy based on the principle of agentive autonomy. The interaction mediated by the allocation of this surplus production in the form of material entitlements is what Saitta terms the "*subsumed* class process ... [which] refers to the distribution of surplus labor *by* the appropriators *to* specific individuals who provide the political, economic, and cultural conditions that allow a particular fundamental process ... to exist" (Saitta 1994, 207, emphases in original). Hence, in a communal system, the producers of this self-appropriated labor (and/or its products) and the recipients stand to each other as subsumed classes. In these terms, age-set cult leaders would be responsible for the entitlement resources they received from higher officers, and in turn, they would distribute these to their companions. These resources would discharge the entitlements that the cult owed the age-sets for their labor as the primary producers of cult ritual. The total cult organized as a enabling hierarchy of primary, secondary, and tertiary producers ranked according to traditional age-set tasks would be internally related through reciprocal gifting that reproduced the autonomy of each level.

This correlates very neatly with the notion of an enabling hierarchy in which autonomous age-sets responsibly constitute their material interventions as the types of menial-to-esteemed labor tasks that were traditional to each level and were performed without imposing demands on others. Instead, as consensually performed activities, the labor and/or labor products of a lower-ranking age-set were the conditions that enabled the higher-ranking age-sets to perform their labor. The labor of the higher-ranking age-sets, then, recursively reciprocated upon the lower-ranking age-set as the condition of its productive activity, and so on.

Clearly, Saitta's view of Cahokia differs markedly from the various versions of the hierarchical modular polity account that I have summarized. He suggests that the archaeological record of the American Bottom does not support the claim that elite-commoner relations constituted a fundamental class division. I agree with him. However, he still treats Cahokia as a hierarchical modular polity, albeit a communal one. Therefore, in all other respects, Cahokia was a dominant power with defended boundaries, and so on. This means that Saitta seems committed to the view that kinship was the basic structural axis on which communal processes could operate and that, should cult sodalities emerge, they would be subsumed to the kinship-based organizations. In contrast, I maintain that his communal political-economic model fits very well with the Dual Clan-Cult model, which stresses the relative autonomy of clans and cults, and the Autonomous Cult model, which allows for an enabling hierarchy of subsumed age-sets. In these terms, the political-economic relations between clans and cults of the American Bottom would also be of a subsumed nature. As relatively autonomous groups, clans in negotiations with the cults would determine whether or not to produce a surplus to support the cults' activities. The transfer of this surplus would be performed under conditions that would emphasize the arm's-length nature of the relation. For example, the surplus would be a gift from the clan to the cult to assist the latter in its performance of world renewal activities, which, of course, would reciprocally rebound to the benefit of the clans as a means of rectifying their polluting actions, thereby enhancing their production levels. In the context of receiving the surplus, the cults might proffer gifts, for example of Ramey-Incised ritual jars containing potent maize seeds to ensure future crops, and so on. That is, the clan would treat the cult as an enabling condition that promoted its own reproduction, and the cult would reciprocally treat the clan as an enabling condition allowing it to discharge its sacred duties to the cosmos, and so on.[9] Indeed, I argue in a later chapter that strains developing in this relation may have been instrumental in bringing about the "collapse" of the American Bottom social system and the abandonment of the region.

This completes the essential part of the theoretical framework that is necessary for interpreting the archaeological record of the American Bottom in terms of the heterarchical polyistic locale-centric account. I will initiate this interpretation by focusing on the Sponemann phase occupation of the Sponemann site, which is located about 4.5 kilometers northeast of Cahokia and is dated as the earliest phase of the Terminal Late Woodland period (Fortier and McElrath 2002, 183). This site study serves as the basis for adding substance to the deontic ecological framework by developing the Sacred Maize model, which postulates that a midwifery subsistence ritual innovation that modified the traditional usage of maize was the primary historical factor that initiated the trajectory of social development that culminated in the Mississippian period. Following the initial demonstration of the Sacred Maize model using the empirical data of the Sponemann site, I summarize the hierarchical monistic modular polity account of the development of the Terminal Late Woodland period using the empirical data of the Range site. This standard view will be critiqued and the alternative heterarchical polyistic locale-centric account will be given by drawing on the Dual Clan-Cult model and the Autonomous Cult model as the theoretical background. The completion of this critique and interpretation will lead directly into the Mississippian period, initiated by an in-depth critical discussion of current interpretations of Cahokia and its social structural nature.

6

The Sacred Maize Model and the Sponemann Site

The Sacred Maize model as applied to the American Bottom postulates that a series of related ideological innovations—essentially midwifery rituals—was successfully implemented and marked the Terminal Late Woodland period and that, largely unwittingly, this implementation instigated a population expansion and further innovation tied into world renewal ritual, culminating in the emergence of Cahokia. Before the Sacred Maize model is elucidated, however, use of the terms *Terminal Late Woodland* and *Emergent Mississippian* needs to be clarified. As noted in chapter 1, according to Andrew Fortier and Dale McElrath (2002, 174, 182–83), the theoretical rationale for speaking of the developments during the one or two centuries prior to emergence of the Cahokia as the Emergent Mississippian period has become problematic. Fortier and McElrath argue that implicit in the term *emergent* is the assumption that the formation of Cahokia was immanent in the operation of objective factors of environmental, economic, and/or demographic change and growth. Therefore, arguing that it biases the interpretation of the data and mischaracterizes the real causes of the emergence of Cahokia, they reject this term and replace it with the term *Terminal Late Woodland*. Following Timothy Pauketat (1997, 30–32, 51; 2002, 150–54) in this regard, they attribute the emergence of Cahokia to the political-ideological strategy of the elite who had risen during the pre-Mississippian times. They agree with Pauketat's assessment that this was a very rapid emergence, a "Big Bang," and they add that it amounted to being a "profound social upheaval" (Fortier and McElrath 2002, 203) of the American Bottom social system.

While I am also a strong advocate of the historical approach to account for the archaeological record, and while I have no problems with the new terminology for this period, I find three problems with the approach that they promote. First, their approach has a strong voluntaristic aspect to it, as if the elites can unproblematically negotiate and change the structural conditions that made their actions possible and successful; that is (again following Pauketat in this regard), Fortier and McElrath assume that the elites can wilfully change the received cosmology and/or ideology as needed to create conditions that would entice the non-elites to perform actions that were detrimental to their own interest. The second problem is that, besides taking the elite/commoner structuring as almost a given, this characterization of the "Big Bang" also presupposes a fused view of cultural traditions in the sense that once an ideological position is changed, the whole cognitive-normative order is transformed. Third, the approach taken by Fortier and McElrath assumes a form of instrumental/symbolic dualism so that the ecological and symbolic spheres are naturally independent and separate. Therefore, no matter what objective environmental or demographic changes occur, these will stimulate only practical ecological modifications that have no direct but only a spillover effect on the symbolic sphere. Hence, they are not sufficient causes of social and cultural change. For Fortier and McElrath, sufficient causes arise from the active agents of society, such as the elites, manipulating the symbolic ideological sphere quite independently of the ecological to generate and implement political strategies beneficial to their interests.

The Sacred Maize model challenges these assumptions, and it does so on the theoretical grounds of deontic ecology and the integrated view of cultural traditions. This denies the dualism separating the material instrumental and symbolic spheres to argue that ecological changes, such as the introduction of maize into the subsistence diet, are as much symbolically as materially constituted innovations and, therefore, that ecological innovations are as much sociopolitical as objective in nature. It also means that the perceptions of the objective changes that promoted the subsistence innovations were necessarily constituted as a result of assessing the implications of these changes within and through the context of the received cultural traditions, making ecological modifications fully social and historical.

Furthermore, although the Sacred Maize model addresses only the way in which deontic ecological innovations initiated further objective changes (for example, economic and demographic) that created conditions leading to the emergence of Cahokia, the ecological condition that it identifies as instigating the innovations was not resolved or dissolved with this emergence because this condition was what I earlier referred to as the essential contradiction of human existence in a world that was experienced as immanently sacred. Since Cahokia is postulated as the long-term outcome of the initial innovations, it follows that by characterizing the deontic ecological conditions and the innovations designed to accommodate to them, the Sacred Maize model also informs us about the social nature of Cahokia and the other multiple-mound sites of the Mississippian period of the American Bottom.

Setting these theoretical issues aside, however, as I state above, I can agree with Fortier and McElrath's proposal for the new terminology. Therefore, I will use their term, the *Terminal Late Woodland period* (and its definition), in referring to those pre-Mississippian times in the American Bottom and its surrounding uplands during which maize emerged as a major subsistence crop. However, I maintain that the central culturally structured dynamic bringing about the changes can be most adequately characterized in deontic ecological terms, and therefore they were symbolically constituted social as well as ecological innovations that were a critical part of the historical development of the American Bottom. Following Fortier and McElrath (2002, 202) in this regard, I will also treat the Sponemann phase occupation of the Sponemann site (Figure 6.1), dated to circa cal A.D. 850–900, as the earliest known site marking the Terminal Late Woodland period (see Figure 1.7).

THE SACRED MAIZE MODEL

As noted above, the Sacred Maize model postulates the innovation and implementation of a series of interrelated midwifery subsistence rituals that initiated the Terminal Late Woodland period and generated a recursive process of population expansion and further innovation, all tied into world renewal ritual. The innovation of world renewal ritual, as discussed earlier, was required to rectify what came to be perceived as the intensifying of sacred pollution generated as the unwitting outcome of the success of the initial midwifery rituals, this outcome being the expanding level of settlement and the intensifying degree of subsistence entailed by demographic packing. The initial midwifery innovation is postulated to have involved recruiting the symbolic pragmatic meaning of maize, traditionally used as a sacred medium of renewal ritual, to enable the expansion of the agricultural base by transforming into a sacred reproductive moment the destructive intervention of opening largely untouched areas and exposing the land. In effect, while opening and exposing the land was experienced as polluting, the transformation of the newly exposed land of these areas into maize gardens was experienced as resanctifying and enhancing the land's sacred powers. The critical factor here is the sacred powers believed to be immanent in the maize itself. In this case, by transforming the newly opened land into maize gardens, the new maize gardens were taken to enhance and reproduce or renew the sacred productive powers of the land.

However, a further significant material innovation was required to ensure the success of this new usage of maize, since expanding production of maize

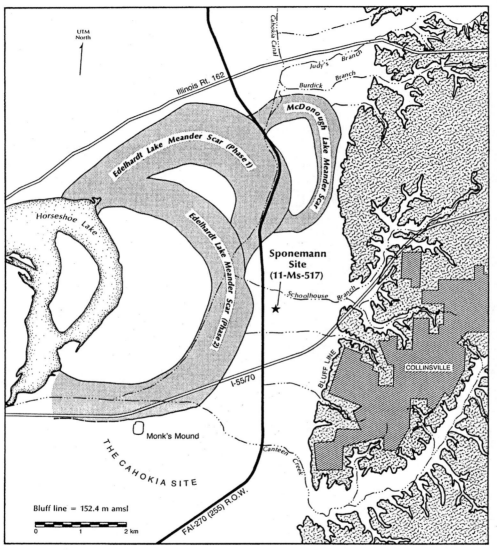

Figure 6.1. Map of Sponemann site location. (Fortier et al. 1991, figure 3.1, p. 12. Courtesy of the Illinois Transportation Archaeological Research Program, University of Illinois.)

beyond the traditional ritual-usage levels in this manner presented the need to avoid wasting this "surplus." Clearly, the simple solution would have been to incorporate maize into the everyday diet of the people; however, few dietary modifications are simple, since they constitute foodways that are themselves structures of rules and protocols underwriting social practices (Johannessen 1993b, 203–5). In particular, since the traditional production and usage of maize was limited to ritual purposes, everyday usage would likely have been seen as endangering its sanctity. I postulate here that the primary source of this danger would have been the mixing of maize with the "ordinary" traditionally cultivated subsistence crops, such as maygrass, chenopodium, little barley, and erect knotweed, as well as possibly the other wild grains that were also exploited. This meant articulating and expanding the application of the traditional rules and protocols for processing maize, by which it was normally kept separate from the everyday foods, so that its purity was ensured while it was being used on a daily basis. Because this meant the modification of the established prescriptive and proscriptive rules by which the mixing of sacred maize with nonmaize seeds during processing, storage, preparation, and consumption was avoided, elaborating and extending these rules in action constituted a new set of midwifery rites, and this means that these new rules were also a form of ideological subsistence innovation. Hence, two strategically related ideological subsistence innovations are postulated by the Sacred Maize model: (1) the application of the traditional ritual cleansing powers of maize to the sanctifying of expanding landscape clearance and land usage; and (2) the elaboration of processing rules that would ensure the avoidance of mixing maize used for everyday consumption with the "ordinary" traditional cultivated and wild crops (and through these rules maintaining the sanctifying powers of maize).

The expansion of the population and settlement that these related innovations generated would probably not have been among the original conditions of satisfaction of those who promoted these strategic innovations. That is, the expansion would have been a necessary but unwitting consequence of the innovations. However, once the polluting consequences arising from expanding demographics and intensifying settlement started to be noted, probably quite rapidly, further rectifying innovations would have been required. These second-level ideological innovations would have occurred primarily in the public realm of world renewal ritual. Therefore, a spiraling of population growth, subsistence intensification, and settlement density would have driven strategically related ceremonial and settlement transformations. These transformations characterized the Terminal Late Woodland period and historically culminated in the Mississippian period.[1] Hence, demonstrating this model in the empirical data is critically necessary before proceeding with the larger elucidation and interpretation of the Mississippian period archaeological record.

The Z-Twist/S-Twist Pattern

The Sacred Maize model purports to address and, at least to some degree, resolve an important puzzle about the history of maize in the Midcontinent: the recognized fact that maize was known and cultivated in the region as a ritual crop for generations before its cultivation was expanded in the Terminal Late Woodland to make it an important part of the subsistence diet (Fritz 1992, 21; Hall 1980; Johannessen 1993a, 74–75, 77; Rindos and Johannessen 1991, 42; Scarry 1993, 90; Wymer 1993, 154). For the most part, it did not replace but simply extended the range of subsistence crops that was cultivated (Johannessen 1993b, 203). However, there is a second archaeological puzzle that I believe the Sacred Maize model can address and resolve. This relates to a rather minor modification to the traditional design of Late Woodland pottery that marked the Terminal Late Woodland period. Late Woodland pottery is recognized as being well made, even though the only outstanding decorative treatment is that, typically, the body surface was heavily cordmarked.[2] Almost inevitably this cordmarking was done with S-twist cordage. When maize emerged as a staple crop across the Midcontinent, Z-twist cordmarked pottery also appeared. Importantly, just as maize did not replace traditional crops, so, in general, Z-twist cordmarking did not replace the more traditional S-twist cordmarking. Instead, the new Z-twist cordmarking was added. Also, the two forms of cordmarking were rarely applied to the same vessel. Instead, typically, assemblages came to be made up of two categories of pots: one having S-twist and the other Z-twist cordmarking (Kelly et al. 1990, 121). If this Z-twist/S-twist difference is ignored, except for some variation in temper and lip decoration, the jars and bowls making up a given Terminal Late Woodland assemblage were essentially undifferentiated (Fortier et al. 1991, 327–28).

The addition of maize to the traditional staple crops and the addition of Z-twist pottery to the traditional S-twist pottery seem to have occurred simultaneously. Rather than treating these two changes as coincidental, the Sacred Maize model postulates a causal linkage, the cause being the perceived need to maintain the sacredness of maize in the new circumstances of its being used as a subsistence crop alongside the traditional crops. As suggested above, a major method of preventing the reduction of the sacredness of maize would be to avoid mixing it with the other subsistence crops. The Z-twist/S-twist duality would be among the ideological innovations that served to accomplish this end. This claim, of course, requires further clarification and objective empirical demonstration, and much of the rest of this chapter will be dedicated to this goal. Before I turn to this task, however, I present and critique other accounts of these two modifications in the archaeological record of the Terminal Late Woodland.

In regard to the introduction of maize as a subsistence crop, the claim has been made that maize was more cost efficient and more storable and could be grown in a wider variety of areas than such traditional indigenous crops as chenopodium, maygrass, erect knotweed, and little barley and, therefore, that maize cultivation allowed greater food production with less labor and more effectively met the needs of an expanding population. However, careful comparative calculations between each of these indigenous crops and maize have been made, and these demonstrate that maize, in general, does not have any greater labor, storage, or nutritional advantages over the traditional crops. One researcher summarizes the results of these calculations:

> Many arguments that stress major differences in yields, nutritional contents, labor costs, and processing losses, with the goal of establishing the economic advantages of maize as opposed to starchy seeds, are not supported by empirical data. Possibly, the reasons why maize supplanted starchy seeds in some regions do not lie in advantageous economic factors, but rather in evolving social and ceremonial factors. Purely nutritional arguments are unfounded, given dietary inadequacies of maize, and the evidence for significant increases in dental and infectious diseases, growth stresses, and cumulative mortality, particularly among children, that were partly if not largely due to increased maize consumption. (Lopinot 1992, 55)

Furthermore, even with an expanding population, the traditional crops could be grown wherever maize could be grown; they were just as productive, equally storable, and probably more nutritious; and they may have been even less labor costly than maize. Seen in these objective terms, the rather abrupt emergence of maize as a staple subsistence crop after many generations of minimal cultivation for ritual purposes still stands as an unresolved puzzle.[3]

With regard to the emergence of the Z-twist/S-twist duality, a particular difficulty in explaining this duality seems apparent. While to the archaeological observer cordmarking is obvious, what is not obvious is whether it is Z-twist or S-twist. Indeed, the dual patterning was first noted only recently, by Patrick

Munson (1971, 10). Therefore, archaeologists have commonly assumed that the development of Z-twist cordmarking and the continuity of a dual Z-twist/S-twist patterning on separate pots in the same ceramic assemblages are probably unrelated to the pottery production intentions of the producers. To put this in terms of intentionality, the Z-twist/S-twist distinction, as such, is generally assumed not to have been among the conditions of satisfaction of the intentions of the potters who produced it. Instead, it is taken to be the unwitting outcome of changes in ceramic production routine. For example, citing Robert Hall's explanation, Steven Ozuk argues that the high incidence of Z-twist pottery in the Terminal Late Woodland period Dohack phase occupation of the Range site may be the result of shifting from producing cord by hand-thigh rolling to producing it by spindle twisting (Kelly et al. 1990, 121). The problem with this explanation has been addressed by Penelope Drooker. In her view, "in vertical twining there may well be a tendency for right-handed crafts people to twine in the S direction, [but] there is no overwhelming physical reason why one twist direction would be preferred over another by a weaver working horizontally" (Drooker 1992, 163). That is to say, even if a spindle technology was innovated or introduced, assuming that the traditional S-twist twining was done by right-handed people, there would be no reason for these individuals not to continue to favor the latter direction in using the spindle. Furthermore, since typically the Z-twist/S-twist patterning is kept distinct in any given assemblage such that pots have only one or the other type of cordmarking, this would mean that the same community would be divided proportionately between one set of potters who preferred Z-twist cordage and another who preferred S-twist cordage. Given the small size of these early Terminal Late Woodland villages and hamlets, this seems highly implausible.

Another suggestion has been to claim major migrations of new populations with the habit of producing Z-twist cordage. Therefore, the appearance of this attribute is claimed to be simply the result of migrating populations continuing their practical routines in new areas. Differential proportions of Z-twist and S-twist and the changes over time would map migration trends. Mark Seeman and William Dancey (2000, 601), however, are "less than enthusiastic" with this explanation, pointing out that, since the emergence of the dual Z-twist/S-twist patterning occurred more or less at the same time throughout the Midcontinent, it seems highly unlikely that it could be caused by immigrant cultural groups. Also, this would require large surrounding areas of the Late Woodland period having exclusively Z-twist cordmarked pottery produced by the ancestors of the Z-twisting immigrants. None of this is indicated in the archaeological record of the early or middle Late Woodland.

One should note that the puzzle arises largely from the assumption that, in practical terms, while cordmarking might have some technical advantages in production and usage, there would seem to be no particular advantage in using one type of cordage twist over the other; moreover, even if somehow this pottery came to be used for some purpose surplus to its more immediate practical uses, how could a Z-twist/S-twist contrast serve as an effective stylistic coding device? After all, since the contrast is not really that noticeable, there would be no apparent symbolic or aesthetic purpose attached to one or the other form of twist. In short, generating and feeding this puzzle is the referential fallacy of material cultural style that assumes that stylistic attributes are used to refer to the social identity of the users and, therefore, must be clearly noticeable to the nonuser of the artifacts: if an attribute is not immediately noticeable to observers, then it is not a useful medium for conveying social or any other information.

Of course, the warranting view of style also emphasizes the communicative moment. However, as discussed in full earlier, this view takes a strong expressive perspective. Style is essentially an expressive medium by which the intentions and social positions of the users are not referred to but manifested to relevant others, thereby simultaneously presencing one or more essential warranting properties of this object. This expressive communicative usage is what makes style a constitutive medium of the action nature of the behavior that it mediates. More importantly with respect to the Z-twist/S-twist contrast, the deontic ecological perspective also expands the range of relevant "others" involved in the action-constitutive communicative moment. In an immanently sacred world, the sacred powers are potent agents. Indeed, according to this view, in such a world, a built-in component of the users' experiences would be the understanding that the iconic nature of style presences these sacred powers.

I will add to this clarification two further cautionary notes. First, while the stylistic patterning may be unnoticeable or noticeable only with difficulty to the archaeologist (possibly requiring up-close visual examination), it might be very noticeable to those expecting it. Second, perception is not limited to vision. Therefore, what will mediate style and how style will be produced can both lie outside the normal range of expectations of the archaeologist. For example, in the case of jars, not only visual but also tactile perception may be significant to the user, particularly since, as practical items are used in domestic contexts, users' vision would often be limited by poor lighting.[4] Working in such cramped and poorly lit quarters, experienced users of pots would probably be able to identify Z-twist from S-twist ceramic cordmarking by touch.[5]

Importantly, it is unlikely that these contrasting forms of cordmarking would make any difference to the objective uses of the pots. Both sets of pots could be used for the same range of purposes—cooking, storage, serving, and so on. However, in terms of the symbolic pragmatics of style, for the users, these ceramic patterns would be part of what was required in order that the behaviors that the pots were habitually used to mediate would count as the fully felicitous subsistence-processing/consumption activities intended. Another way of putting this is to say that if part of the patterning is deliberately varied while the rest of the patterning remains the same, such that no objective differences of use would be likely, as in the case of making effectively identical pottery that contrasts possibly only in terms of Z-twist/S-twist cordmarking, then the cordmarking contrast must be mediating an emically experienced and constituted difference. Therefore, the systematic variation is the product of an ideological production posture. In short, this Z-twist/S-twist cordmarking duality manifests an important constitutive contrast generating two objectively similar but emically contrasting ceramic-usage spheres.

The Deontic Ecological Perspective

As specified above, the Sacred Maize model postulates that the emergence of maize as an important subsistence crop was due to two related midwifery ritual innovations, one being characterized as the recruiting of the special potency of maize so as to warrant the opening of previously untouched areas to allow for the expansion of food production while enhancing the reproductive sanctity of the land, the other being to incorporate this sacred plant in everyday consumption while maintaining its sanctity. With regard to the first claim, Tim Ingold's theory of land is quite relevant. In his view, there is a distinction between landscape and land that is critically important in deontic ecological terms:

> The distinction between *land* and *landscape* is crucial. . . . We can observe soil, rocks, trees, vegetation, hills and valleys, lakes and rivers: together these add up to the landscape, but the land is none of these things. Like the weight of physical bodies, and the value of commodities, land seems to be the common denominator of the natural world, inhering in all its multifarious manifestations but directly visible in none. . . . I suggest that to turn a piece of the landscape into a field is to

remove a covering of *specific things that grow,* leaving *a general potential for growth.* It is to this creative potential that the concept of land refers, and its appropriation is what we mean by land tenure. (Ingold 1987, 153–54)

Therefore, as I suggest above, in an immanently sacred world, exposing the land in this sense would be a major mode of intervening into the sacred natural order, and it would be experienced as requiring major ritual care to ensure the land's sanctity. This view is what underwrites the central claim of the Sacred Maize model, namely, that maize was recruited not primarily for its nutritional but for its sanctifying powers. To support this claim, a useful approach would be to theoretically ground the notion that the type of intervention into the natural order entailed by gardening would have played a significant role in the emergence of maize as a subsistence crop and that this development can be understood more coherently as being the result of the proscriptive attitude toward subsistence interventions characteristic of a squatter ethos rather than being the result of rather limited emic awareness of the economic benefits of cultivation.

Bruce Smith's (1987, 36–38; 1992a, 290–91; 1992b, 110; 1995, 202–4) Floodplain model treats the emergence and domestication of indigenous crops (such as chenopodium, marsh elder, and sunflower) as the unwitting, that is, unintentional, consequence of the settling-down process initiated by the onset of the Hypsithermal. Basic to this model is the claim that the weedy ancestors of these crops were preadapted to be successful invaders of humanly disturbed areas in the valley bottoms. Therefore, as humans routinely occupied the same valley bottom sites on a seasonal basis, they would inevitably remove the undergrowth, distribute garbage, and so on, unwittingly generating ideal conditions for the proliferation of these weeds. Part of this settling-down process would involve a slow expansion in the level of exploitation of these weedy seed-bearing floodplain species. Gathered wild seeds would be routinely returned to the base camps; inevitably there would be spillage of seeds, and they would start to sprout in these ideal conditions, transforming the seasonally occupied locales into "domestilocalities," as Smith terms them. Indeed, according to the Floodplain model, the long, drawn-out nature of the development of indigenous crop production is attributed to its being primarily the unintended and, for a considerable period, an unobserved outcome of this settling-down process. Only somewhat belatedly (largely as a result of not initially noting the incursion of these weeds into their base camps) would the populations start to deliberately cultivate the weedy species; at a later date, they would start to set seed aside specifically for future planting. This final step would serve as the condition for selective cultivation, unwittingly leading to domestication. Therefore, the reason that domestication was such a long, drawn-out process—starting possibly as early as 6000 or 5000 B.C. with the onset of the Hypsithermal and coming to (partial) fruition only around 1000 B.C.—was primarily that it was a series of accidents rather than the result of design.

In contrast, while certainly maintaining that the domestication process was nonteleological in the sense of not being the goal of an ecological strategy, the deontic ecological view expressed by Ingold's distinction between land and landscape justifies the claim that this long, drawn-out process was the outcome of the squatter attitude and the immanentist cosmology that informed the ecological and economic strategies of these same populations. These deep structures of the cultural traditions would promote a proscriptive settlement and subsistence strategic posture that would favor minimizing the amount of landscape disturbance specifically so as to avoid exposing the land, *sensu* Ingold, since this would count as sacred pollution. Deliberately removing any extensive landscape coverage, therefore, would be experienced as a major form of disturbing the sacred natural order and would require a special protective and rectification ritual strategy to make it possible.

This suggests that the circumstances bringing about the type of settlement locales that Smith has dubbed "domestilocalities" were deliberately avoided or minimized for the sake of the sacred natural order. That is to say, as noted earlier, while reducing mobility and intensifying occupation, populations would still minimize settlement nucleation (maximize settlement dispersal) to the degree practicable and would also promote rapid turnover of base camps to minimize the type of environmental disturbance that the Floodplain model postulates. Therefore, under this view, the long, drawn-out nature of the process would be the outcome of a proscriptive everyday settlement and subsistence strategy that—over the long term and in incremental steps—failed, thereby provoking the corresponding incremental innovations of rectifying ritual practices, particularly the recruiting of the mortuary sphere by innovating postmortem sacrifice to resanctify the land. Owing to the continuity of the deep structures of cosmology and ethos, this same reluctance to deliberately disorder nature would have been in place in the Late Woodland populations. Seen in these terms, the claim of the Sacred Maize model seems highly plausible, namely, that the sanctifying powers of maize were recruited at this time to enable the modification of the landscape to a degree that had not been possible earlier, while simultaneously sustaining a perceived viable balance between human resource exploitation and land sanctity. To use maize in this manner, therefore, was not simply to add another food to the everyday diet of the people. In fact, as stated above, the use of maize for everyday sustenance would have presented practical problems of maintaining the ritual purity of maize. Therefore, the real reason for the rather rapid expansion of maize cultivation would have been the result of promoting it as actually enhancing the land while contributing to resolving the essential contradiction of human survival.

At this point, one may appropriately ask what grounds there are to support the claim that maize, in particular, was recruited for this purpose. Indeed, the basic intelligibility of the Sacred Maize model hinges on the claim that, in the cosmology of prehistoric Native Americans, maize held a special sacredness, one that could be used ideologically to innovate a ritual technique that would warrant the systematic exposure of the land through the formation of maize fields. One avenue of support for the model is to seek evidence in the ethnographic literature of historic Native American peoples that maize indeed held a special role in their cultural traditions. Because of the deep structural nature of cosmology, projecting such maize-related beliefs back into prehistory would be rather safe.

In fact, there is ample anthropological evidence to support this likelihood. Many if not all historically known Native American peoples who were dependent on maize treated this plant as having a special status, such that it was almost the duty of people to plant, cultivate, and harvest an annual maize crop. Very strong prescriptions and proscriptions were applied to the handling of maize. The seed could not be treated disrespectfully or mixed with nonmaize seed. Cultivators, usually women, typically acted so that maize kernels were kept separate from other seeds until planting, and they avoided indiscriminate scattering.[6] When the Cheyenne, for example, abandoned their sedentary, maize-based village life in the upper Missouri, apparently to return to mobile foraging (in this case, focusing on hunting bison), the women continued to maintain the tradition of planting maize gardens, primarily to harvest maize for ritual purposes. Their gardens were small squares, and the maize seeds were planted in a quincunx pattern, a few seeds per corner and a few in the center (Will and Hyde 1964, 90). This is a well-known symbolic expression of the quadripartite sectoring of the cosmos with the central position representing the Great Tree that, as the *axis mundi,* supported the Heavens in its branches, passed its trunk through the Middle World, and anchored the Underworld with its roots. As Hall (1996, 121–23) has pointed out, different variations of this pattern were characteristic of the maize gardens of the Zuni, the Tewa, the

Omaha, and the Hopi, among others. Hence, the maize gardens were widely perceived as particularly sacred, embodying the cosmos and presencing its sanctifying powers.

The sacredness of maize was expressed in the following way to George Will and George Hyde by Scattered Corn, an elderly Mandan woman who was the daughter of the last Mandan Corn priest: "[C]orn was always treated with the greatest respect and care; no grains were ever left scattered about and the stalks were never touched with metal knives.[7] The empty corn caches were purified and blessed before the corn was placed in them" (Will and Hyde 1964, 204). Moreover, in Omaha cosmology, corn was "considered . . . to be a 'mother' and one of their myths describes the birth of the corn as well as the buffalo, from Mother Earth . . . [and they had] great reverence . . . for the corn" (Will and Hyde 1964, 204–5). Each step in the production process of maize was strongly ritualized, constituting maize agriculture as a series of rites that marked the seasonal stages. In fact, many if not all of the Native American peoples of the upper Missouri who occupied villages and practiced both (maize) agriculture and (bison) hunting scheduled the latter to follow the second (June) hoeing of the maize fields (Will and Hyde 1964, 77–97).[8]

The Avoidance Argument

While this completes the rationale underwriting the central claim of the Sacred Maize model (namely, that maize emerged as a subsistence crop because its traditional sanctifying powers were recruited to warrant the systematic exposing of the land so that gardening could be expanded, ultimately leading to the development of farm fields), the question to address now is the resolution of the practical problem raised by this expansion of maize cultivation: maintaining the sanctity of maize while it was being used on an everyday subsistence basis side-by-side with the more traditional crops. First, this claim is not as unusual as some might think. The principle of having prohibitions against mixing foods of different emic categories is common to many foodways. For example, the kosher rules in orthodox and conservative Judaism ensure that culturally contrasting categories of food are kept physically separate from each other. This separation is sustained by specific proscriptions against mixing these different foods, and this avoidance will be built into either the total or a partial subsistence process, from garden or field production through harvest, storage, preparation, and, finally, consumption. Disposal in middens could possibly also require proscriptions, although this would probably vary. The point would be to prevent the mixing of food categories from polluting the household. It is not that one category of food is sacred and the other is not; rather, the nature of the sacredness of each is such that mixing across categories would be an unwarranted disturbance of the sacred natural order.

Therefore, as a core part of demonstrating the Sacred Maize model, the radical transformation in the prehistoric diet postulated by the model would be expected to entail the innovation of taboos of food separation of the above sort. Since maize and nonmaize seed crops have very similar objective requirements for effective storage, preparation, and consumption (Smith 1992a, 10–12), the preparatory facilities and equipment would have to be clearly marked to prevent the unwitting mixing of facilities and foods. The rules of separation would involve probably all or most of the stages: gardens, harvesting, process, distribution, collective storage, in-house stocking, cooking, and consuming. Since the entire range of food preparation entails the routines of everyday life, we could expect some consistent contrast, such as the Z-twist/S-twist duality, as a very effective and simple means to serve in the last three stages. A complement to the Z-twist/S-twist duality would be specialized facilities for storage that are clearly set apart in form and/or space, thereby ensuring that storage of one category of food is not inadvertently done in a facility that was used for the contrasting category. Storage pits and storage cribs might do the job. Finally, keeping the two categories spatially separate in harvesting seems plausible.

TESTING THE SACRED MAIZE MODEL

The Ceramic Evidence

The first step in validating the Sacred Maize model in the American Bottom is to test the Z-twist/S-twist dual patterning as a hypothesis. To do so, one must first target a clear example of a site that is generally recognized as the earliest known in the region indisputably manifesting the simultaneous appearance of both the Z-twist/S-twist duality and the subsistence production of maize, while maintaining the continuity of the rest of the Late Woodland cultural practices. Ideal for this purpose is the Sponemann site. In his overview of the Sponemann site report, Andrew Fortier (Fortier et al. 1991, 8) claims that the site is the earliest known in the American Bottom marking the introduction of maize as a subsistence crop, possibly fifty years before its widespread staple subsistence use in the American Bottom (also see Fortier and Jackson 2000, 132). Fortier and his colleagues (1991, 6) call this the Sponemann phase, and they date it to circa cal A.D. 850 or earlier (see Figure 1.7). The key traits that

Fortier enumerates for defining the phase are (1) the appearance of maize in quantities implicating its use as a staple crop, (2) a new set of ceramic traits (see below), and (3) the continuity of the rest of the typical Late Woodland ceramics and residence patternings. Fortier specifies:

> The Emergent Mississippian [Terminal Late Woodland] assemblages can be differentiated from the previous Late Woodland, Early Bluff, Patrick phase traditions mainly by the occurrence in the Emergent Mississippian [Terminal Late Woodland] assemblages of substantial quantities of maize, Z-twist cord decoration, and exterior lip impressing. Shifts in ceramic temper, i.e., grit/grog to limestone in the Pulcher tradition, also characterize this transition. Maize in particular seemed to denote a clear marker, since extensive sampling of Patrick phase features had repeatedly failed to uncover major evidence of maize use. (Fortier et al. 1991, 6)

The new ceramic traits are best represented in what Thomas Maher (Fortier et al. 1991, 217) refers to as the Sponemann jar. This jar is very similar in many respects to the associated Late Woodland grog-tempered Patrick phase jar that is also commonly found on this site. However, the two jars vary systematically on several traits. The typical Sponemann jar has exterior Z-twist cordmarking; it has chert- or other rock-grit temper; it has a rim that often has exterior and/or superior lip plain-dowel or cordwrapped-stick incising; and the rim is sometimes castellated. The typical Patrick jar continues the older Late Woodland tradition of exterior S-twist cordmarking; it has grog temper; its rim has interior lip incising; and it is uncastellated.

Maher specifically identifies the chert tempering and Z-twist cordmarking of the Sponemann jar as related to a similar pottery found farther north: "It appears, therefore, that there is a strong relationship between some of the ceramics found at the Sponemann site and those found further north in the Mississippi River valley and in the lower Missouri Valley" (Fortier et al. 1991, 192 [also see 159–60, 247]). Maher attributes the simultaneous appearance of these ceramic traits and maize at the Sponemann site to groups migrating from this more northern region (also see Fortier and Jackson 2000, 130–32). Maher particularly points out that the distribution of the two jar types across the Sponemann site is very mixed and that this mixing prevents a determination of whether the Sponemann and Patrick jar assemblages at the Sponemann site delineate a chronological development or the shared occupation by two distinct cultural populations, each maintaining its separate ceramic tradition.

While also recognizing the problem of determining whether this distribution delineates a chronological sequence or else co-occupation of migrant and local populations, Fortier (Fortier et al. 1991, 328) is strongly attracted to the latter scenario.

There is a third scenario, of course—that this mixed distribution of two jar types in the same site is consistent with avoidance of mixing maize and nonmaize during crop processing, storage, preparation, and consumption, as postulated by the Sacred Maize model. That is, although one would have difficulty in predicting precisely how this avoidance against mixing would be successfully accomplished, the Z-twist/S-twist duality—complemented by the use of different tempers and, unexpectedly, contrasting lip treatment—would seem an ideal solution to this postulated avoidance problem.

Thus, there are three possible explanations for the Z-twist/S-twist duality ceramic evidence: (1) sequential occupation of the same site first by indigenous Patrick jar–assemblage users and then by immigrant Sponemann jar–assemblage users; (2) co-occupation by both groups of users; and (3) the innovation of a dual assemblage to mediate the taboo against mixing maize and nonmaize grains. Adjudicating among these three would require another line of evidence. If this second line of evidence confirms possibility 3 above, then it can subsume the second possible explanation, since the second and third possibilities are not mutually exclusive. That is, immigrants could have brought in the Z-twist/S-twist dual ceramic assemblage along with maize and then continued to co-occupy the site with the original occupants. Together, these possibilities would eliminate the first. Below I present the second line of evidence, which is based on the distribution of maize and the traditional cultivated species across the cultural features of the Sponemann phase of the Sponemann site.

The Mixing-Prohibition Hypothesis

While the innovation of the Z-twist and the superior and/or exterior lip incising as a contrast to the traditional S-twist/ interior lip incising can be logically tied to the prohibition against mixing maize and nonmaize plant foods, this prohibition would probably apply to all stages in the preparing and processing of these food crops, not only to the stages requiring the use of ceramics. Therefore, the Sacred Maize model can be used to generate the further expectation that I term the *mixing-prohibition hypothesis*. This stipulates that there should be a recognizable patterning across the Sponemann site of cultural features containing the residue of food processing and that this patterning can best be accounted for as a result of a generalized prohibition against mixing together maize and nonmaize subsistence crops during their respective processing, distribution, and consumption.

However, because the model is also claiming that maize became part of the everyday diet, maize would necessarily have been caught up in everyday food processing, and therefore an absolute separation of subsistence residue into exclusively maize and exclusively nonmaize cultural features and pits cannot be expected. Rather, there should be a great deal of overlap, largely paralleling the mixing of Sponemann and Patrick pottery. Nevertheless, analysis of the archaeobotanical contents of features—limited to the identifiable residue of maize and the four traditionally cultivated seed crops, namely, chenopodium, maygrass, erect knotweed, and little barley—should reveal a patterning that can be most coherently accounted for in terms of the mixing-prohibition hypothesis. While demonstrating the hypothesis requires targeting only the five relevant species as listed above, this is not to claim that other species were unimportant. However, the targeted species constitute the bulk of the cultivated materials making up the archaeobotanical remains, and any patterning that they reveal could probably be equally applied to these rarer or less commonly exploited species.

The proportion of features in which the residue of one of the targeted subsistence species is found is assumed to represent its overall contribution to the everyday diet. This is termed the *Ubiquity Index (UI)* of that species, and it is a well-established method for estimating the relative importance of species in the everyday diet. While a given cultural feature will usually have representation of more than one type of cultigen, each species should occupy some features as isolates. The proportion of features in which a targeted species is an isolate will be termed the *Exclusivity Index (EI)* for that species. Overall, such isolates should be rare—but even rarer for those species having lower-end UIs. If randomness is assumed, part of the reason for this is that since the distribution of a species with a higher-end UI will take up a larger proportion of the available cultural features than will a species with a lower-end UI not only will a species with a lower-end UI have a more limited distribution, but also because of the more widespread distribution of the higher-end UI species a disproportionately lower number of features can be expected to be available in which the lower-end UI species could be deposited as isolates. Therefore, the null hypothesis would suggest that the EIs of the five targeted species should vary directly but disproportionately, with the higher-end UI species having EIs that are disproportionately greater than the EIs of the lower-end UI species, or, stated in a reciprocal manner, with the lower-end UI species having EIs that are disproportionately smaller than the EIs of the upper-end UI species. If a comparison of the EI/UI ratios of the targeted botanical species of a given site does not support this disproportionate variation (in that one of the species has an EI that is relatively greater than its UI would support), then clearly some systematic factor or factors were at work that biased the distribution of that species. Alternative possible biasing factors can then be examined against the distribution data, and if these factors can be rejected, the deviant EI/UI ratio supports rejecting the null hypothesis and justifies supporting the mixing-prohibition hypothesis, namely, in this case, that avoiding mixing maize with the seed crops was routinely practiced on the Sponemann site during the Sponemann phase.

I carried out a detailed distributional analysis of the archaeobotanical record of the Sponemann site (Appendix A, Tables A-1 through A-9), limited to the Sponemann phase occupation. Fortunately, the team of archaeologists responsible for excavating and reporting on this site carried out a comprehensive archaeobotanical analysis of the cultural features, an undertaking for which they should be highly commended. They established that 615 features define the Sponemann phase occupation, and the contents of 439 of these features (71 percent, a significantly large sample) were sampled and analyzed (Appendix A, Table A.1).[9] Many of these features were eliminated from this analysis either because they had no significant biotic content or because the identifiable biotic content that they had did not include one or more of the five targeted species. This reduced the total number of features used in the analysis by 69, yielding 370 (Appendix A, Table A.4). Since the UIs displayed in Table 6.1 are based on this reduced sample, they are higher than those calculated by the excavators, who used all the cultural features as their base. However, limiting the number of relevant features in this manner serves my purpose since I am interested only in the EI/UI distribution ratio of the targeted species.

Table 6.1 summarizes the sitewide UIs, EIs, and EI/UI ratios for the five species from the 370 relevant features of the Sponemann phase occupation. Maygrass clearly had the widest distribution: 268 out of the 370 features had identifiable maygrass residue in them (268/370 = 0.72 UI). Among these 268, there were 81 features in which maygrass was exclusive (81/370), constituting a maygrass EI of 0.22 (Appendix A, Table A.5). When the same procedure was followed for each of the other targeted species, the sitewide UIs and EIs were established (Appendix A, Tables A.6–A.9). The claim that the EIs of the targeted botanical species should vary disproportionately and directly with the

Table 6.1. Sitewide UIs and EIs of Targeted Species

Species	Ubiquity Index	Exclusivity Index	EI/UI Ratio
Maygrass	0.72	0.22	0.31
Maize	0.39[a]	0.09	0.23
Chenopodium	0.38	0.04	0.11
Erect Knotweed	0.30	0.04	0.13
Little Barley	0.18	0.02	0.11

a. Fortier and colleagues (1991, 460) report 34% UI for maize, but they are using all analyzed features. I discount those features lacking any residue of the five targeted species.

respective UIs applies almost perfectly to the four traditional seed crops (Table 6.1, column 3 [EI/UI ratios]). Maygrass has the highest UI, the highest EI, and, of course, the highest EI/UI ratio (0.31). Of the seed crops, chenopodium has the second-highest UI but a disproportionately lower EI, as indicated by its EI/UI ratio (0.11). While erect knotweed has a lower UI than chenopodium, it has approximately the same EI, and its EI/UI ratio (0.13) is likewise disproportionately lower than that of maygrass. Notably, however, this is not the case for maize. In fact, the maize EI/UI ratio (0.23) is almost three-quarters that of the maygrass EI/UI ratio (0.31); with a UI only slightly more than half that of maygrass, maize clearly has a higher EI/UI ratio than its UI would lead us to expect. This is particularly highlighted by the fact that chenopodium and maize have almost the same UI (0.38 and 0.39, respectively), while the EI/UI ratio of maize is 2.10 times that of chenopodium. However, all of these calculations are consistent with the Sacred Maize model, since the model suggests that the treatment accorded to maize was special in the sense of reducing the likelihood that maize would be mixed with the seed crops, while apparently little or no such treatment was accorded to the seed crops themselves.

To highlight that this comparative EI/UI ratio pattern indicates special treatment for maize, I calculated a modified EI for each species. The relevance of the modified EI is that it establishes the proportion of isolates of each species in relation to the specific UI of each, thereby neutralizing to some degree the influence of the differential UI variation among species. This calculation allows for a direct comparison of the degree of exclusivity among these species using the modified EI/UI ratios, referred to below as EI(M)/UI ratios.

As listed in Table 6.2, the sitewide EI(M)/UI ratios (indicated in the third column) sort the five targeted species a little differently compared to the unmodified EI/UI ratios in Table 6.1. While the unmodified EI/UI of maize is second highest in comparison to the EI/UI of maygrass (0.23 and 0.31, respec-

Table 6.2. Sitewide UIs and Modified EIs plus EI(M)/UI Ratio of Targeted Species

Species	Ubiquity Index	Exclusivity Index (M)	EI(M)/UI Ratio
Maygrass	0.72	0.30	0.42
Maize	0.39	0.24	0.62
Chenopodium	0.38	0.10	0.26
Erect Knotweed	0.30	0.13	0.43
Little Barley	0.18	0.09	0.50

tively), the EI(M)/UI ratios of these two species are reversed, such that maize has a modified ratio of 0.62, significantly higher than the maygrass modified ratio of 0.42. Even more striking is that the modified ratios of little barley, erect knotweed, and maygrass are fairly equalized (0.50, 0.43, and 0.42, respectively), while chenopodium has the lowest (0.26). The high EI(M)/UI ratio for maize confirms its special nature. That is, compared to all the traditional seed crops, maize has a disproportionately higher rather than a lower EI. In short, this is consistent with the expectations of the mixing-prohibition hypothesis.

However, this finding would give considerably more support to the model if other possible causes of the relatively high EI/UI ratios of maize could be examined and eliminated. For example, Community 3—made up of Cluster 3 (see chapter 7), possibly the longest occupied of the Sponemann phase clusters—displays a patterning of features that warranted Fortier's grouping them into two sectors (Fortier et al. 1991, 139): the northwestern and the southeastern (Figure 6.2, 3b and 3a respectively). Fortier observes that in sector 3a there was a strong representation of nutshell and maize, while in sector 3b there was a strong representation of maygrass:

> The southeast quadrant yielded the highest percentage of maize remains at the site and certainly in this cluster. It is interesting that these pits are generally not very deep and do not contain as much material overall as those in the northwest quadrant. Another significant aspect of this area is the relatively high incidence of nut remains. Whereas only two pits in the northwest quadrant (Features 390 and 404) produced more than 100 nut fragments, eight pits in the southeast quadrant yielded that many fragments, and these others produced between 50 and 100 fragments. (Fortier et al. 1991, 139)

Fortier goes on to argue that this patterning is the result of seasonal occupation, with the inhabitants of Community 3 occupying the northwestern sector

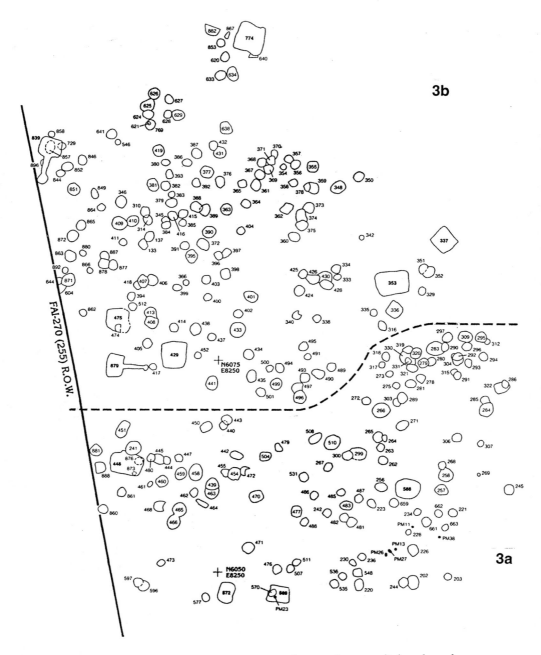

Figure 6.2. Sponemann site, Community 3 plan, southeastern (3a) and northwestern (3b) sectors. (Fortier et al. 1991, fig. 9.56, p. 313. Courtesy of the Illinois Transportation Archaeological Research Program, University of Illinois.)

Table 6.3. Community 3, Clusterwide UIs and EIs of Targeted Species

Species	Ubiquity Index	Exclusivity Index
Maygrass	0.69 (sitewide, 0.72)	0.17 (sitewide, 0.22)
Maize	0.45 (sitewide, 0.39)	0.13 (sitewide, 0.09)
Chenopodium	0.35 (sitewide, 0.38)	0.02 (sitewide, 0.04)
Erect Knotweed	0.32 (sitewide, 0.30)	0.04 (sitewide, 0.04)
Little Barley	0.18 (sitewide, 0.18)	0.03 (sitewide, 0.02)

in the spring (when maygrass was harvested) and, presumably, the same individuals occupying the southeastern sector in the fall: "We could conjecture, therefore, that the southeastern sector may have been occupied to a great extent during the fall months, when both mature maize and nuts could have been harvested and consumed" (Fortier et al. 1991, 139).

The alternative account under the mixing-prohibition hypothesis, however, postulates that this variation in distribution between the two sectors—in particular, the very high maize UI in the southeastern sector—is consistent with the view that (1) both sectors were occupied equivalently during the spring and fall seasons, and (2) the southeastern sector was the locus of collective maize harvesting and, possibly, storage. If this could be verified, the mixing-prohibition hypothesis would be confirmed, the Z-twist/S-twist hypothesis would be reinforced, and, by logical extension, sufficient credibility would be extended to the Sacred Maize model to warrant a reinterpretation of the settlement patterning of the Sponemann phase occupation of this site. Therefore, to verify which is the preferred explanation, I carried out the same type of distribution analysis as I did for the total site but limited the analyzed features to those in Cluster 3 (Table 6.3). Since the same basic pattern of EIs and UIs emerged, no computation of the EI/UI ratios was necessary.

First, I established the (unmodified) UIs and EIs for all five species in this cluster (Appendix B, Tables B.1–B.9). Then, by using the division of the cluster into northwestern (3b) and southeastern (3a) sectors as determined in the site report, I compared these UIs and EIs across the sectors and found that the UIs and EIs for the five targeted species for Cluster 3 largely replicate the sitewide distributions for the same species (Table 6.3). That is, the disproportionately high EI for maize is fully retained and in fact increases significantly, confirming Fortier's comment that maize had its highest density in this cluster. The sitewide UI and EI for maize are 0.39 and 0.09, respectively, while for Cluster 3 they are 0.45 and 0.13, respectively. These ratios are highly significant, especially since the number of cultural features analyzed across the total site was proportionately greater in the Community 3 cluster than in the other clusters. Furthermore, as Fortier suggests (Fortier et al. 1991, 137), the Community 3 cluster was probably occupied for a much longer time than any of the other clusters—possibly two generations. Since this longer occupation would have increased the possibility of random mixing of the contents of features, the increase of the clusterwide EI of maize over the sitewide EI is significant. This would support the claim that a special effort to avoid mixing maize and indigenous seed cultigens was part of the routine processing of these subsistence resources.

I did not discount the possibility that this pattern could be undermined if the northwestern and southeastern sectors of Cluster 3 are compared separately. As noted above, according to Fortier (Fortier et al. 1991, 139), there was a much higher occurrence of features containing maygrass in the northwestern than in the southeastern sector, as well as a larger number of features containing more than fifty nut shells and features containing maize in the southeastern than in the northwestern sector. On these grounds, he suggests the northwestern sector was occupied primarily in the spring months, when maygrass was harvested and processed, and the southeastern sector was occupied primarily in the fall months, when maize and nuts, along with chenopodium and erect knotweed, were harvested.

Table 6.4 confirms that the northwestern- and southeastern-sector UIs of maygrass are weighted in the above manner, but the differences are rather minor. The maygrass UIs of 0.71 in the northwestern sector and 0.67 in the southeastern sector are not significantly different; nor are they significantly different from the sitewide maygrass UI of 0.72. The maygrass EIs for both sectors are 0.17; I consider these ratios to be significantly lower than the sitewide maygrass EI of 0.22, suggesting the effect of the longer-term occupation of this cluster in comparison to those of the other clusters. While according to Fortier features with more than fifty nut shell fragments and features containing remains of maize are both more common in the southeastern than in the northwestern sector, both nut shells and maize are well represented in the latter sector. Of course, the maize UIs and EIs for the two sectors are quite distinctly different: the northwestern sector yielded a maize UI of 0.33 and an EI of 0.12; in the southeastern sector, the UI is an extraordinarily high 0.55, with the EI of 0.14 being the highest maize EI in the site. I address this wide variation below. In any case, when taken together, these factors suggest that both sectors of Cluster 3 were occupied almost equally in the spring during the maygrass harvest and, no doubt, also in the fall, although something was going on in the southeastern

Table 6.4. Community 3, UIs and EIs of Targeted Species by Sector

	Ubiquity Index		Exclusivity Index	
Species	Northwest—3b	Southeast—3a	Northwest—3b	Southeast—3a
Maygrass	0.71	0.67 (site wide 0.72)	0.17	0.17 (site wide 0.22)
Maize	0.33	0.55 (site wide 0.39)	0.12	0.14 (site wide 0.09)
Chenopodium	0.42	0.29 (site wide 0.38)	0.02	0.02 (site wide 0.04)
Erect Knotweed	0.37	0.28 (site wide 0.30)	0.04	0.04 (site wide 0.04)
Little Barley	0.24	0.13 (site wide 0.18)	0.02	0.03 (site wide 0.02)

sector that accounts for the maize UI of 0.55 compared to the significantly lower maize UI of 0.33 in the northwestern sector.

What this difference in the maize patterning suggests is a very real difference not in terms of seasonal occupation but in terms of the harvesting and processing of crops. The greater UI and EI for maize in the southeastern sector and its much more limited UI but still disproportionately high EI in the northwestern sector suggest that the southeastern sector was the focus of fall-time collective harvesting and storage, while the reduced UI in the northwestern sector may have been the result of individual domestic consumption. The fact that, despite the lower UI (0.33) in the northwestern sector, this area still retained a higher EI (0.12) than the sitewide maize EI (0.09) simply reinforces the care with which the postulated proscription against mixing was carried out in the context of domestic consumption.

The conclusion of this analysis strongly supports equivalent occupation of both the northwestern and the southeastern sector of Cluster 3 from spring to fall, with a collective fall harvest of maize likely occurring in the southeastern sector. Finally, the patterning of the maize distribution across the site strongly supports the claim that maize had a higher EI than can be accounted for by the randomness that such collective fall harvesting and everyday subsistence processing should generate. It follows that there was a factor at work, both everyday and during harvesting season, that enhanced the exclusivity of maize. This conclusion allows rejecting the null hypothesis, and it is consistent with the expectations of the mixing-prohibition hypothesis, which in turn reinforces the Z-twist/S-twist hypothesis. The latter suggests that this dichotomy emerged as a midwifery subsistence ritual innovation by which to ensure that maize and nonmaize seed crops would be kept separate during everyday processing. That is, there would be two parallel sets of pottery: one used for maize and one for nonmaize seed crops. Since the ritual innovation prohibiting the mixing of maize and nonmaize seed crops is consistent with the core claim of the Sacred Maize model, namely, that the sacred symbolic pragmatic meaning of maize was recruited to enable more intensive cultivation while minimizing pollution, this analysis lends considerable empirical support to this model.

Finally, an assessment of the possible significance to the development of the American Bottom social system of the innovative cultural traits disclosed in the material patterning of the Sponemann site is included in a recent discussion of the Late Woodland Patrick phase by Andrew Fortier and Douglas Jackson (2000, 132). They note that very little diffusion or historical continuity of the Sponemann phase traits seems to have occurred. For example, no Sponemann occupation has been noted south of Cahokia, and, as they emphasize, "*with the exception of Z-twist cordage,* Sponemann ceramic traits such as castellation and chert tempering were not adopted and used in later assemblages" (emphasis added). They conclude by suggesting, "What is clear is that the Sponemann phase populations, *with the notable exception of maize use,* do not seem to have had a lasting effect on other local populations" (emphasis added). However, they also comment that, at least at the Sponemann site itself, the occupants seemed to have been ahead of their time in that "Sponemann ceramic assemblages . . . contain a number of early Emergent Mississippian [Terminal Late Woodland] traits, such as predominant use of Z-twist cord decoration and exterior lip treatment."

While Fortier and Jackson appear to be correct in that a number of traits did not persist, I must disagree with their overall conclusion, because the very traits relevant to empirically grounding the Sacred Maize model did persist: specifically, the Z-twist/S-twist duality and the use of maize as a staple crop. Since the Sacred Maize model argues that the addition of subsistence use to the traditional sacred ritual use of maize was what initiated the demographic expansion and the perceived intensification of sacred pollution leading to the emergence of the Mississippian period, far from having little or merely ephemeral impact on the American Bottom development, the postulated prohibition against mixing maize and nonmaize grain crops and the ceramic innovations that these populations introduced would seem to have had a profound impact. With this conclusion I proceed in the next chapter to interpret the Sponemann settlement pattern in developmental terms, as the working out over time of shifting proscriptive-prescriptive deontics arising from intensified cultivation and settlement as predicated under the Sacred Maize model.

The Early Terminal Late Woodland Period Sponemann Community Development

Andrew Fortier and his colleagues (1991, 57) note that the Sponemann phase occupation of this site was made up of thirty-one rectangular single-post structures, six single-post features commonly referred to in the literature as keyhole structures, and associated pits and related features (plus one small circular single-post structure). These formed at least six spatial clusterings. As can be seen in Figure 7.1, the keyhole structures were distributed across the northern half of the site. Three of these—the most northern structure (Feature 685) and the two more southern keyhole structures (Features 730 and 762) connected by a "shared" ramp, along with their spatially associated pit features—form the northernmost sector of the site and were labeled as Cluster 6 by the excavators. The rest of the structures with associated pits were initially treated sequentially from south to north as Clusters 1 through 5. As a result of further analysis of this patterning, the initial Clusters 4 and 5 were combined into a single Cluster 4/5. These five clusters—Clusters 1, 2, 3, 4/5, and 6—were then interpreted as forming four chronologically sequential community occupations, numbered south to north as Communities 1, 2, 3, and 4 (Figure 7.1).

Interestingly, the six keyhole structures were lumped together as the cold-season dwellings of Community 4. Therefore, according to the excavators, Community 4 displays the most complex community plan, since its rectangular structures and associated pits (Cluster 4/5) have been interpreted as the warm-season dwellings and the linear cluster of six keyhole structures as the cold-season dwellings of the same community: "It is conjectured that this configuration of keyholes may represent a winter seasonal encampment. It is not clear which community is associated with this settlement, but it is argued here that Community 4 may be the best candidate" (Fortier et al. 1991, 155). This claim was supported by the observations that (1) both the Cluster 4/5 rectangular structures and the keyhole structures were in the northern sector of the site, (2) the average floor area of both keyhole and rectangular structures was the same (about 4.3 square meters to 4.6 square meters), and (3) tobacco seeds

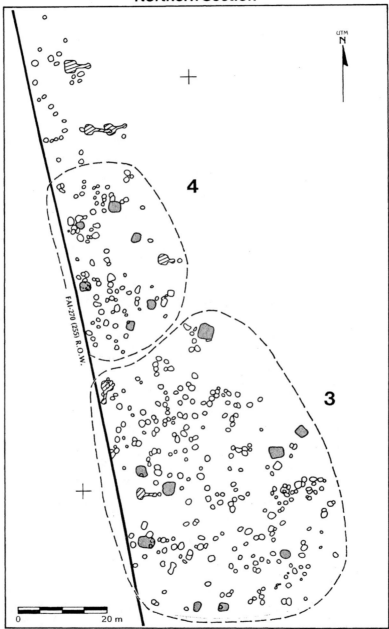

Figure 7.1. Communities 1–4 of the Sponemann site. (Fortier et al. 1991, fig. 8.27, p. 149; Figure 8.28, p. 150. Courtesy of the Illinois Transportation Archaeological Research Program, University of Illinois.)

Southern Section

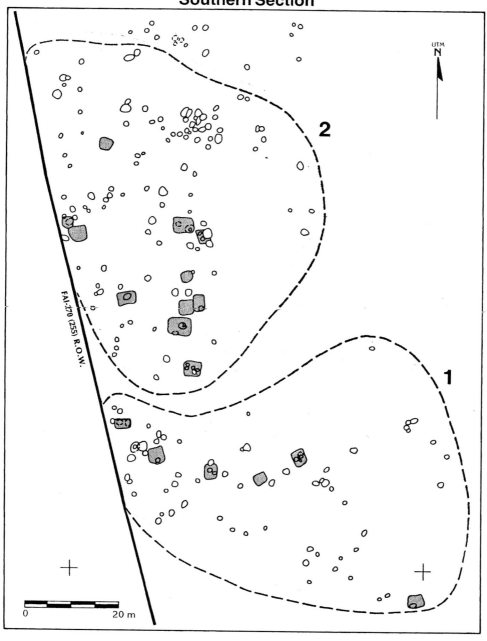

FAI-270 (255) R.O.W.

UTM
N

2

1

0   20 m

and other rare items were found in some of the structures of both clusters. I say more about this claim later.

Sorting these clusters in terms of relative chronology is quite important. As noted in chapter 6, the Sponemann and Patrick ceramic assemblages are not useful for this purpose, since they are quite thoroughly mixed across the site.[1] Since ceramics cannot be used for fine chronological ordering, the most useful attributes for this purpose might be the variable range of the average size of the structures. This is the approach that Fortier uses (Fortier et al. 1991, 133). He notes that the average size of the structures in the southern sector exceeds the average size of known Late Woodland Patrick phase structures of the American Bottom and concludes that these "Sponemann phase structures . . . appear somewhat anomalous in comparison with other structures from this period. This might add some credence to the view that this assemblage was intrusive into the American Bottom" (Fortier et al. 1991, 78). He uses the change in relative sizes of these structures as a rough relative chronology, reasoning that if the Sponemann jar and maize indicate a migrant population from upstream in the Mississippi drainage, then the migrants may also have brought with them the practice of building houses much larger than the Patrick phase norm of the Late Woodland period of the American Bottom: "Is it possible that those unusual structures represent facilities built by the initial Sponemann phase settlers of the American Bottom, or at least of this site?" (Fortier et al. 1991, 133).

In these terms, moving from the southern to the northern clusters, Fortier noted a distinct difference in the number of rectangular structures and associated pits, the average floor area size, and the relative areal size of the four communities (Fortier et al. 1991, 151). Community 1 had six rectangular structures averaging 6.8 square meters and also had seventy-one pits (Fortier et al. 1991, 131, 151), well above the average for other known Patrick phase structures in the American Bottom. These six relatively large structures were arranged (Figure 7.1) in a shallow northwest-southeast semicircular band about 80 meters long, and each was about 15 meters from its neighbors. The floor basins displayed little wall slumpage and had superimposed pits, indicating rapid abandonment, filling, and then postabandonment use, possibly as earth ovens. Presumably, this means that occupants of later structures—for example, those immediately to the north constituting Community 2—used the abandoned house basins of Cluster 1 as earth ovens (Fortier et al. 1991, 131). Community 1 also displayed the lowest maize ubiquity index (UI) of all the clusters.

Community 2 covered a larger area than Community 1 and formed an oval measuring about 70 meters north–south by 50 meters east–west (Figure 7.1).

It had almost double the number of rectangular structures—eleven compared to the six of Community 1, immediately south—and many more storage pits, about 122, although proportionally this is lower than the seventy-one pits of Community 1. However, the pits of Community 2 were generally larger and the average size of these rectangular structures was 8.85 square meters, distinctly larger even than the structures of Community 1 (Fortier et al. 1991, 151). As for Community 1, the maize UI for Community 2 was also relatively low.

Community 3 (see Figure 6.1) occupied the center portion of the total site, forming an oval 60 meters north–south and 50 meters east–west and covering an area about 50 square meters smaller than the area of Community 2. There were eleven rectangular structures, the same as in Community 2. However, these averaged 5.33 square meters (smaller than the rectangular structures of the latter community), and several of these appeared to be paired. Associated with these eleven structures were 274 pits, more than double the number that was associated with the eleven much larger rectangular structures of Community 2. As I comment in chapter 6, Fortier considers Cluster 3/Community 3 to have been occupied for a longer period than any of the other clusters. Interestingly, in support of this claim are the facts that the maize UI, as Fortier and his colleagues calculated it, was twice that of Community 2 and that Community 3 had three times the amount of limestone, which is generally recognized as important in the processing of maize.[2]

The structures of Community 4 were arranged roughly in a semicircle with its open side facing east. It was the smallest of the four, having six rectangular structures with 104 pits making up the compound Cluster 4/5. However, as noted above, according to the excavators the inhabitants of this community also occupied all of the keyhole structures during the cold season, although only a single keyhole structure, Feature 773 (Fortier et al. 1991, 142) was spatially located in Cluster 4/5. The average size of the six rectangular structures was about 4.3 square meters. Fortier notes that along with having the smallest average size of rectangular structures, Community 4 was also spatially the most dense (Fortier et al. 1991, 155).

In sum, four separate community plans are recognized as making up the Sponemann phase occupation of this site. Fortier suggests that the two southern clusters may be the earliest, basing this suggestion on the assumptions mentioned above, namely, that maize and the Z-twist, chert-tempered pottery were brought in by migrants from the upstream Mississippi Valley, where the Late Woodland period residential structures are thought to have been larger than those typical in the American Bottom. He reinforces this chronology by not-

ing that these two southern communities had the lowest maize UI of the Sponemann site, which is consistent with the suggestion that these communities
would constitute the earliest known use of maize as a staple subsistence crop
in the American Bottom. Community 3 would have then followed, and the
more northern Community 4 would mark the terminal Sponemann phase occupation, with the six keyhole structures featuring as the winter or cold-season
quarters of this occupation.

PROSCRIPTIVE/PRESCRIPTIVE SETTLEMENT
AND SUBSISTENCE DYNAMICS

The chronological scheme of Communities 1 through 4, as summarized above,
seems quite consistent with the predictions that flow from the Sacred Maize
model. The contents of the Community 1 cluster display all the indications of
the earliest occupation. Its houses had the second-largest average floor area. The
lowest number and sizes of pits along with the lack of interior fire sources are
the clearest indication of this cluster's having been occupied for only part of the
year, primarily from early spring to late fall. The size of these large rectangular
structures suggests that they could have been occupied by extended families.
With the coming of winter, the community would likely have dispersed, with
each extended family possibly remaining together. This can be expected for a
community that is initially intensifying its subsistence regime, that is, the expansion of maize as a staple crop. Warm-season occupation with winter abandonment would count as a proscriptive tactic to reduce settlement-induced pollution. Community 1 also had the lowest maize UI, which would be consistent
if it marks the initial introduction of maize as an important subsistence crop.
Finally, the fact that the house basins were used as earth ovens after being abandoned suggests that Community 2, occupying the cluster immediately north,
was responsible for this recycling, making that cluster second in the sequential
occupation of this site.

The attributes of the Community 2 cluster seem to fit it best as the occupation following Community 1. Extended families seem to have been retained
and enlarged, as the eleven rectangular structures have the largest average floor
areas of the Sponemann phase occupation of the site. Simultaneously, its maize
UI is not that much greater than that of Community 1, but the number of pits
is greater, as is their size, suggesting that overall the proportion of food production is greater for this occupation than the preceding one. Also, if the earth-oven
pits found superimposed in the basins of the Community 1 structures were pro-

duced by Community 2, then these would have to be added to the total number of Cluster 2 pit features. The expansion of the size of the extended family, as indicated by the greater average floor area, the greater size of the pits, and the use of earlier house basins as earth ovens all indicate population expansion, as suggested under the Sacred Maize model. At this time, land was probably not felt to be at a premium—at least not when the community was initially laid out, since it covers a relatively expansive area. Keeping the individual structures well spaced could be a proscriptive settlement strategy, minimizing the pollution load per unit area. Occupation appears to have still occurred during only part of the year since there are no interior sources of heat in the dwellings and, as stated above, the major cooking was done outdoors by using the floor basins of the abandoned structures of Community 1 as earth ovens (Fortier et al. 1991, 136). Therefore, I would assess Community 2 as manifesting a proscriptive settlement and moderately less proscriptive subsistence regime (I discuss the ritual component below) since, in settlement terms, it sustained the part-year occupancy posture of Community 1 while the larger and greater number of pits suggests a development toward a less proscriptive subsistence orientation.

The layout of Community 3 may be expressing an emerging premium on gardening plots. It has the same number of rectangular structures as Community 2, but they are significantly smaller in floor area and the overall size of the distribution area is significantly smaller than is covered by the cluster of dwellings of Community 2. Furthermore, according to the excavators, it was probably occupied for a longer period than any of the other clusters. With the absence of internal sources of heating, Community 3 would appear to have sustained the pattern of cold-season abandonment with reoccupation in the warm season. As I suggest in the previous chapter, the focus on maize processing in the southeastern sector of Community 3 may reflect collective and spatially separated processing of this seasonally distinct and specially sacred crop.

A pairing of structures may also have occurred at that time, and with the smaller overall size of each structure, this might indicate a splitting of the extended families into smaller, possibly nuclear units. The pairing of structures, the longer period of overall occupation, and the suggestion of a premium on land imply that neighbors might have begun to occupy nearby ridges that had previously been available for gardening and, therefore, that the region surrounding Community 3 may have been experiencing an expansion of population, as would be anticipated under the Sacred Maize model.

These are the signs of a deontic ecological strategy under rising stress as the subsistence practices start to move away from the proscriptive and toward the prescriptive pole. Therefore, the patterning of the rectangular structures making up Community 4 suggests a significant modification from the settlement patterning of Community 3. The Community 4 cluster is smaller in both the number of residential structures and the area incorporated, indicating a smaller overall warm-season population. Furthermore, the distinctly smaller average floor space and the possibility that this pattern continues to display the practice of cold-season abandonment suggest that the land premium was developing more intensely. What may have happened, therefore, was the beginning of the expansion and dispersion of settlement in hamlets across the landscape (away from the more favorable higher land bordering the eastern bluffs) and, at the same time, the spreading of maize agriculture. If this later Sponemann phase occupation is any indication of general settlement tendencies in this sector of the American Bottom at this time, then smaller communities had emerged, and they had sustained a dual cold-season/warm-season settlement posture, suggesting proscriptive ideological tactics with regard to settlement, coupled with an escalating move away from the proscriptive and toward the prescriptive subsistence strategic posture, since much more land was being used for cultivation. These changes would probably have been carried over into later phases, as I discuss in the following chapter.

However, the cold-season/warm-season settlement posture claim raises an important issue that clearly sets me at odds with the interpretation by Fortier and his colleagues, which, as I comment earlier, treats the Sponemann phase of this site as a year-round settlement. Fortier and Jackson (2000, 134), for example, assert that during the Patrick phase—and this would include the Sponemann phase of the Terminal Late Woodland period—intensively occupied villages had "permanent, year-round occupation." However, I am inclined toward Brad Koldehoff's (2002, 4) view in this regard. In Koldehoff's recent analysis of the Woodland Ridge site, a bluff-top site overlooking the southern sector of the northern American Bottom, he raises the significant possibility that the degree of mobility practiced by Late Woodland American Bottom populations was greater than is generally assumed. The Sponemann phase populations of the northern sector of the American Bottom very likely had basically the same settlement practices as those responsible for the Woodland Ridge site, even though this southern-sector Patrick phase site had no maize or other Sponemann-related materials (although Koldehoff found one example of a Z-twist cordmarked bowl). In Koldehoff's estimation, this bluff-top site, and possibly the Patrick phase occupations of the Dohack and Stemler Bluff sites (the latter being less than one kilometer from the Woodland Ridge site), were seasonal, subseasonal, or short-term aggregation sites used primarily for activities mediated by feasting (Koldehoff 2002, 160–61, 164). The groups would have been small, in the nuclear family size (or, in my view, within the size range of an age-set of companions accompanied by their families), possibly only a few aggregating at a time. This claim would be consistent with the premise I have suggested that the floodplain village sites may have been occupied only during the warm season and that even during this period, small groups, such as age-sets of local cults, would have periodically met in the uplands at such sites as Woodland Ridge and Stemler Bluff.

THE SPONEMANN SITE RITUAL/CEREMONIAL SPHERE

This possibility not only raises the issue of seasonal compared to year-round occupation, but also raises the question that must now be addressed, namely, the nature of the ritual or ceremonial sphere at the Sponemann site. This means addressing the question of the settlement articulation mode as manifested in this site. The Dual Clan-Cult model characterizes the prehistoric social systems of the Eastern Woodlands as, for the most part, being based on relatively autonomous kinship-based and non-kinship-based groups, generically treated as clan and cult sodalities, respectively. As discussed earlier, these two relatively autonomous groupings would have maintained an arm's-length relation with each other. The manner by which this relation was sustained would have underwritten the settlement articulation mode. As noted under the Dual Clan-Cult model, clan ritual would be directed toward kinship concerns, such as midwifery subsistence and settlement rituals, marriage alliance, kin-based life-crisis cycles, and the like, while public, world-renewal/thanksgiving type ceremonies would be the primary concern of the age-grade cults.

In these terms, therefore, I postulate that the ritual sphere of the Late Woodland and Terminal Late Woodland periods would be divided into two subspheres: one clan related and the other cult related. Since clan-related features would be in the majority, being basically embedded in the spatial relations of the residential dwelling structures, it is likely that cult-based ritual features would be in a distinct minority. The cult custodial duties would require conducting world renewal ritual on behalf of the whole community, and the structures that cult members would use would be built to serve this special purpose. Therefore, they would probably be distinctly different in form from everyday dwellings. This distinction is not arbitrary but is based on the special symbolic pragmatic requirements related to the felicitous performance of ritual that they would mediate. Not only would their form serve this need, but they also should display artifactual and featural patterns that cannot be accounted for in terms of everyday domestic needs, even when midwifery ritual is intrinsic to the domestic routine.

Combining an ideological solution to enhancing the outcome of the ritual with a practical solution to maintaining the clan-cult arm's-length relation in such small and probably seasonally occupied clusters as described above would promote a spatial peripheralization of the cult features from the domestic dwellings. This would reinforce the relative autonomy of the clan and cult as well as ensure a separation of the sanctity of these special ritual structures from the pollution of everyday domestic life. Accordingly, I postulate that the form, the content, and the patterned distribution of the keyhole structures are consistent with these expectations.

Keyhole Structures

Keyhole structures are ubiquitous across the Midwest in the later Late Woodland; in general, their disappearance from the archaeological record marks the end of the Late Woodland period.[3] As noted above, there are six recognized keyhole structures at the Sponemann site (Figure 7.1). However, all of these are found in the northern portion. Two are located within the Community 3 precinct, one is in the precinct of Community 4, and three make up Cluster 6, the northernmost part of the site. They were rectilinear to square semisubterranean buildings with single-post wall construction and had an average area of 4.61 square meters (Fortier et al. 1991, 155). Each had a shallow ramp or channel about 2 meters long and 43 to 70 centimeters wide, extending from the center of (usually but not always) the long side of the structure and usually terminated at the distal end by a shallow circular or semicircular basin that was 9–20 centimeters deep (Fortier et al. 1991, 78, 80–81, 151). For five out of the six structures at the Sponemann site, these ramps were oriented eastward. In some cases, several of these keyhole structures are "chained" by the ramp of one linking it to the floor basin of its proximal neighbor and the ramp of the latter linking it to its proximal neighbor, and so on, but only two keyhole structures (Features 730 and 762 in Cluster 6) were linked in this way at the Sponemann site.

Fortier and colleagues (1991, 147–48, 155) point out that none of the keyhole structures had an interior fireplace (and also stress that essentially none of the structures of this occupation, rectangular or keyhole, had interior fire features). They also comment on the low level of debris typically found on the floors or mixed in the fill of the keyhole structures. However, some interesting materials were found. For example, there were only eighty-eight tobacco seeds found in the Sponemann phase occupation. Eighty-three of these were found in Feature 730, one of the northern keyhole structures (Fortier et al. 1991, 417). Also found were discoids, pipe fragments, and maize. Typically the ramp displays no packing that would have been caused if it had been used as a passage entryway. In fact, Fortier and colleagues point out that, in several cases, there were post molds in the middle of the ramp where it connected to the floor basin, indicating that there was no doorway at that point. The distal basin was also typically shallow and had little or no debris associated with it or its fill.[4]

Fortier and his colleagues explore several possible functions of the keyhole structure. They dismiss the possibility that it was a sweat lodge, since all these structures lacked interior hearths. Only one keyhole structure had an exterior pit immediately adjacent to a wall that showed signs of burning. Keyhole Feature 730 "also contained the remains of . . . tropical cultigens, maize and cucurbits, but none of the feature-associated materials except for the large number of tobacco seeds suggests possible ceremonial or ritual activities in or near the structure" (Fortier et al. 1991, 414). Fortier also points out that similar materials were found at the Range site and interpreted as indicating ritual activity. In any case, as pointed out above, Fortier concludes that the keyhole structure must have been a specialized cold-season residence, while the rectangular structures without ramps were used as summer or warm-season residences.

This is contradictory to my above postulate, which is that the keyhole structure embodied the cult-based ceremonial sphere of the Sponemann phase occupation. In my view, the reasons for making this assertion seem fairly obvious. The associated materials—tobacco, discoids, and pipes, as well as the very "clean" nature of their contents—strongly implicate ritual practices. Furthermore, the distinctive ramp–distal basin complex feature was clearly never used in a practical sense, nor could it have been, since there was probably no related doorway. Instead, where a door entrance would be expected, posts were inserted, suggesting that the "ramps" might mark a "spirit" entrance and/or exit. A similar, apparently deliberate blocking of free entry into a specialized structure was recognized by Robert Bell (1972, 163) at the Mississippian Harlan site in Oklahoma. He interpreted this blocking as marking a mortuary structure, an interpretation concurred with by James Brown (1975, 5).

In their report on the Fish Lake site, Fortier and colleagues (1984, 21–36, 48–52, 75–81) note that all but two of the nine structure features they revealed at this important Patrick phase site were keyhole structures, and at least three of the latter (Features 32, 34, 81) had posts placed in such a manner as to seriously impede access and/or egress through the presumed eastern "entrance" at the point where the ramp and basins joined. In most cases these were freestanding posts. Also, in at least two cases there was clear indication of either a single or a dual line of posts directly associated with the ramp that would have made access into the structure basin through the ramp effectively impossible. As a result, Fortier and colleagues (1984, 80) conclude, "The narrow Fish Lake keyhole ramps and the presence of posts in the ramps would have effectively blocked access to anyone attempting to utilize these passageways as crawlways."

In sum, while Fortier and his colleagues (1984, 1991) treat the keyhole structures as domiciles and claim that ramps and distal pits were heating components, in my view, the clear impediments to access reinforces the notion that the ramp/basin juncture might be better treated as a spirit entrance. In my reading, therefore, the keyhole structures are special-purpose ceremonial facilities demarcating the cult-based ritual sphere, or an important part of it, and the rectangular structures in general mark and constitute the domestic sphere.

Keyhole Structures and the Dual Clan-Cult Model Critique

Part of the problem with this claim, however, is the distribution of the keyhole structures. For example, Communities 1 and 2, the southernmost and apparently the earliest, have no spatially associated keyhole structures. This would suggest that these two communities had no special-purpose ritual features, even though, according to the Sacred Maize model, they were undergoing the type of ecological stress that would promote the development of the world renewal ritual sphere. The centrally located and possibly longest occupied of the clusters, Community 3, has only two. Indeed, the largest concentration of keyhole structures is north of Community 4, the northernmost of the identified communities. That is, there seems to be considerable disparity between the distribution of the keyhole structures and the ritual needs of the sequential communities.

However, as suggested above, one tactic in conditions of rising settlement-induced sacred pollution that could be anticipated is to spatially distance the domestic and cult structures while maintaining a single, integrated settlement. Since the keyhole structure is postulated to be the primary ritual cult locale, finding that it is located apart from the residential structures would be consistent with the model and, in fact, would realize the arm's-length relation that clans and cults maintained as part of respecting their relative autonomy while also maintaining the sanctity of the ritual locale. Therefore, it is notable that the southernmost keyhole structure, Feature 879, is located on the boundary between the rectilinear structures making up the northwestern and southeastern sectors of Community 3. This location suggests that this keyhole structure existed before Community 3 and that it was the first keyhole structure. If this is the case, then it would probably have been constructed by the cult sector of Community 1, the earliest occupation to the south. The position of Feature 879 at that time would have placed it north and away from the residential structures, thereby manifesting the arm's-length relation postulated above. When the community abandoned Cluster 1 and moved north to occupy Cluster 2, since the keyhole structure Feature 879 was still north of the new community layout, it was maintained. However, a second cult may have then formed, in this case constructing the keyhole structure Feature 839 north of the older keyhole structure and in the place that defined the (future) northwestern corner of Cluster 3. This also was the only one of the six keyhole structures that had its ramp oriented in a southwesterly instead of an easterly direction.

This expansion of the expression of the ritual sphere would be consistent with the intensification of the subsistence regime discussed above. This dual cult pattern could also be manifesting a dual ritual structuring, for example, based on male/female or junior/senior age-grade structuring, or a combination. As I discuss earlier under the Autonomous Cult model, generational and/or gender structuring can be anticipated. This duality may be why these two keyhole structures were distant from each other and had their ramps oriented in different directions. Therefore, it is possible that the expression of a second communal cult emerged in Community 2, with one cult sustaining the use of the original keyhole structure, Feature 879, and the new cult responsible for building and using Feature 839 as its ritual structure.

With the community abandoning Cluster 2 and moving northward to construct the layout of Cluster 3, the expression of the dual cult system could have been retained. However, to respect the clan-cult autonomy, since Community 3 would have surrounded the original ritual keyhole structures, these would have been abandoned and two new ones built away from Community 3. This would account for Features 773 and 762, built to the north of this residential precinct. Even with the subsequent move of the community northward again, so that it occupied Cluster 4/5, Feature 762 would still have been north of the new community layout. Since Feature 773 would have been in the center of the new community layout, it would have needed to be abandoned. This would account for the construction of Feature 685, the northernmost structure of the site. Since Feature 762 would have been quite old, having been built when Community 3 was founded, it may also have been replaced, in this case, by Feature 730. This latter keyhole structure was actually connected to Feature 762 by having its distal basin pit dug into the fill of the latter's floor basin, which suggests that a direct historical continuity of cult was being manifested.

THE SPONEMANN PHASE OCCUPATION: SUMMARY

In sum, the above interpretation of the Sponemann phase occupation is consistent with the Sacred Maize model in that it shows that the incorporation of maize as a major subsistence crop is correlated with the expansion of population, the elaboration of world renewal ritual through the construction of a sequential series of keyhole structures, and the modification of the deontic ecological posture from a strongly proscriptive toward a less proscriptive settlement orientation correlated with an intensifying prescriptive subsistence ceremonial orientation. In effect, the total Sponemann phase occupation of this site manifests a particular type of integrated settlement articulation mode in response to the earliest effects of expanding population and intensifying land usage. I term this the *peripheral-integrated settlement articulation modal pattern,* and it is correlated with an emerging proscriptive settlement–prescriptive subsistence/ceremonial ecological strategy.

I call this a peripheral-integrated settlement articulation mode because of the reliance on the localized separation in space of the residential and specialized ritual locales, partly constituting and maintaining the relatively autonomous arm's-length relation of clan and cult and constituting this settlement as a complementary heterarchy. I characterize its ecological strategy in the above manner because the community was becoming fully reliant on a mixed maize/nonmaize cultivation regime (prescriptive subsistence orientation) and was maintaining the distal spacing of the residential dwellings while seasonally fallowing the settlement area by abandoning it in the cold season, before fully abandoning it after an extensive series of reoccupations (proscriptive settlement orientation). In ceremonial sphere terms, the settlement was definitely leaning toward a prescriptive orientation, as marked by the specialized nature of the keyhole structures and their distal spacing from the domestic dwellings, as well as the possibility that significant portions of off-season periods may have been devoted by the cults to upland-based ritual at such sites as Woodland Ridge and Stemler Bluff. All this suggests that, if the integrated settlement articulation mode is to be sustained under increasing ecological stress (for example, should permanent, year-round occupation occur as a result of increasing demands on land), then a different variant of domestic clan and ritual cult integrated settlement articulation should develop. This would clearly entail a greater material presence of the cult since this type of occupation would signal greater settlement- and subsistence-related pollution, calling for more intensive, prescriptive-oriented world renewal ritual.

To strengthen the validity of the Sacred Maize model, I postulate that the clan-cult duality, initially manifested in the peripheral-integrated manner described above, further developed during the Terminal Late Woodland period, while remaining largely within the integrated settlement articulation mode. This development, therefore, should manifest changing patternings that can be more coherently accounted for in terms of the clan-cult duality postulated under the heterarchical polyistic locale-centric account than in terms of unitary clan kinship postulated under the hierarchical monistic modular polity account. Identifying these patterns requires assessing the Terminal Late Woodland settlement data following the Sponemann phase. I turn to this task in the next chapter by examining the Range site. I summarize the current interpretations of that site's community plans, critique them, and then offer the alternative, thereby establishing the interpretive background framework for addressing the Mississippian period, with special attention on the role of Cahokia within the regional system of the American Bottom.

The Development of Terminal Late Woodland Period American Bottom Settlement

The Range Site

Most proponents of the hierarchical monistic modular polity view accept that the postulated Mississippian period dominance-based hierarchical social system of complex chiefdoms emerged rather suddenly from a system of simple chiefdoms that developed during the Terminal Late Woodland period (Pauketat 1994, 23–34). John Kelly's (1990a, 1990b) interpretation of the Range site is an important foundation of this view. He explicitly comments that an "underlying premise of the Range site problem orientation was that a shift from a relatively egalitarian Late Woodland society to a more hierarchical Mississippian sociopolitical structure took place within the context of a number of socioeconomic transformations, including the intensification of agricultural systems and the appearance of sedentary communities that were participating in a larger scale hierarchical settlement system" (Kelly 1990a, 71; also see Kelly et al. 1984, 157).

Because of the reliance of the hierarchical monistic modular polity account on the prior existence of a simple ranked social system from which the postulated paramountcy of Cahokia could emerge (Pauketat and Emerson 1997a, 20), it is critical that I give the alternative view of the Terminal Late Woodland period. This can be succinctly stated. The social system of this period can be understood as the ongoing material development of clan and cult arm's-length relations within the context and through the medium of a modifying integrated settlement articulation mode. Under the Sacred Maize model, a driving force of this developing relation would have been the escalating population growth, itself encouraged by the expansion of agriculture initiated by the midwifery ritual innovations allowing the use of maize as a subsistence crop. This trajectory would come to be characterized by ongoing elaboration of public ritual directed toward two mutually related goals—rectification and enhancement of world sanctity and renewal and, as a consequence, the enhancement of community reputation. The traditional responsibilities of the clan, of course, would be focused on community renewal, and that of the cults, on world renewal. However, there would be close cooperation between clans and cults to enhance the collective reputation of the community, especially since, with the increasing level of sacred pollution that this population growth was perceived to generate, the peripheral-integrated settlement articulation mode might come to be seen as inadequate for the task. Instead, a new form of integrated settlement articulation mode might develop based on the clans and cults cooperating in building and sharing ritual facilities, while maintaining a formal dichotomy expressing and reconstituting their traditional arm's-length relationship.

This particular combination is most clearly manifested in the formation of the central "square" or plaza with related ritual features, partly surrounded by residential structures while being internally structured into complementary sacred spaces. These could be specialized cult spaces and structures or, alternatively, a shared central space with separate but complementary clan and cult ritual structures. Furthermore, the older peripheral-integrated modal posture would not be totally abandoned. Instead, it would be continued in a modified form so that both a central ceremonial plaza and a more distally spaced set of cult-related ritual features could be expected, with the domestic sphere of residences sandwiched in between. I term this the *plaza-periphery integrated settlement articulation mode.* As postulated, this plaza-periphery mode would express the cooperative interaction between the leadership of clans and cults while each grouping maintained its relative autonomy. Therefore, we would expect the formation of complex formal and spatial patterns. Clan leaders would have their larger residences since, of course, they would be expected to host ritual events presided over by the clans; cults would have their specialized structures, probably maintaining the older tradition of placing these in a position peripheral to the settlement cluster. With these possibilities in mind, I initiate this analysis with a summary description of the Range site starting with the Late Woodland Patrick phase, followed by the occupations recognized for the southern American Bottom Terminal Late Woodland period: the Dohack, Range, George Reeves, and Lindeman phases.

A few words concerning dating and terminology are first required. As noted earlier, the term *Terminal Late Woodland* is now used by most American Bottom archaeologists to refer to what was termed the *Emergent Mississippian* period. This latter term was introduced by John Kelly (1982, 224), and his chronology for this period and the preceding Patrick phase of the Late Woodland period and the succeeding Lohmann/Lindhorst phase of the Mississippian period was based on a combination of uncalibrated radiocarbon dates and seriation of formal variation in features, feature distribution, and artifacts, in particular, ceramics. He dated the Emergent Mississippian period between (uncalibrated) circa A.D. 750/800 and 1000. The preceding Patrick phase was dated (uncalibrated) circa A.D. 600–750, and the Lohmann/Lindhorst phase was dated (uncalibrated) circa A.D. 1000–1050 (see Figure 1.5; see also Kelly 1990b, 117, fig. 49). Applying a calibrated chronology, Andrew Fortier and colleagues (Fortier and Jackson 2000, 123; Fortier and McElrath 2002, 174) have made adjustments to these dates, forwarding the Patrick phase to circa cal A.D. 650 and extending the absolute time span to A.D. 900 so that its current dating is circa cal A.D. 650–900 and possibly later (see Figure 1.7). Their reluctance to extend the phase to circa cal A.D. 950–1000, despite some radiocarbon dates that would support this later date, is based on the unreliability of these dates and the fact that it would reduce the temporal scope of the Terminal Late Woodland period to a mere fifty years—circa cal A.D. 1000–1050. They opt for the more conservative terminal Patrick phase date of circa cal A.D. 900. As Fortier and Jackson comment, "We would argue . . . that radiometric dating techniques, calibrated or not, simply cannot provide the kind of resolution needed to establish absolute sequential parameters in an area such as the American Bottom, which exhibits so much cultural diversity in so short a time frame" (Fortier and Jackson 2000, 124).

What all this highlights is the very problematic nature of the claimed emergence of simple chiefdoms during the Terminal Late Woodland, a point that Fortier and McElrath (2002, 203) stress and that I also address in detail below. However, one should note that while a certain reduction of the span of the Terminal Late Woodland period phases may be necessary, Fortier and McElrath (2002, 200) affirm that the relative chronology of the phases that Kelly originally suggested using seriation are supported by the data; therefore, this order of the phases and their definitions remain unchanged.

I now turn to a summary description and critique of the interpretation of the continuities and changes displayed at the Range site. For the Patrick and the early Terminal Late Woodland Dohack and Range phases, their respective descriptions will be followed by a summary of the current hierarchical monistic modular polity account interpretations, which are then critiqued and followed by the alternative heterarchical polyistic locale-centric account interpretations. For the later Terminal Late Woodland George Reeves phase and Lindeman phase occupations, I will shift to giving short descriptions of the community plans along with a critical comparative presentation of the hierarchical and heterarchical interpretive accounts.

THE PERIPHERAL-INTEGRATED SETTLEMENT ARTICULATION MODE PERIOD OF THE RANGE SITE

The Range site is located in the lower sector of the northern expanse of the American Bottom, about four kilometers northeast of the Lunsford-Pulcher multiple-mound locale (see Figure 1.1). Typical of most floodplain sites, it is located on a low ridge. Its eastern edge borders the Prairie Lake marsh and lake zone; the eastern margin of this zone abuts the bluffs overlooking the American Bottom. More than 5,500 cultural features were exposed at this site, the majority dating to the later Late Woodland and the Terminal Late Woodland periods (Kelly 1990a, 71). As noted above, using the uncalibrated system, Kelly dated the Patrick phase at the Range site circa A.D. 600–750 (cal A.D. 650–900) and the following Dohack phase at circa A.D. 750–850 (cal A.D. 900–940).[1] In fact, he argues that only the later half of the Dohack phase is represented at the Range site, and he dates these occupations to between circa A.D. 800 and 850 (cal A.D. 920–940). This leaves an estimated uncalibrated fifty-year (circa A.D. 750–800) or a calibrated twenty-year (circa cal A.D.900–920) occupational hiatus at the Range site prior to the earliest Dohack phase occupation. Kelly's reasoning in this regard is that the radical changes between the settlement clusters and contents of the Dohack phase occupations and those of the preceding Patrick phase occupations must be the result of such an occupational hiatus: "Abundant evidence for this intervening time period, and a smoother and more gradual transition in material culture and subsistence between the Patrick and Dohack phases, is present at the recently excavated Sponemann site to the north" (Kelly 1990a, 88). That is, because there appears to be a smoother Late Woodland–Terminal Late Woodland transition revealed at the Sponemann site, and this is not the case at the Range site, Kelly concludes that there is no occupational period at the Range site that maps this transition. Therefore, the transition must have occurred elsewhere in this zone. Two of those radical changes marking the Dohack phase were the sudden appearance of the Z-twist/S-twist duality and the use of maize as a subsistence crop (its ubiquity index, or UI, being about 50), indicating that the same dual changes that had occurred probably earlier at the Sponemann site also occurred at the Range site.

Based on my analysis of the Sponemann site in the two previous chapters, rather than marking a hiatus in settlement occupation, these abrupt changes at the Range site mark the rather rapid adoption of the midwifery ritual postulated under the Sacred Maize model. Since this is a surface structural ideological and not a deep structural cosmological transformation, it can occur quite rapidly. Therefore, the population of the Range site could have maintained ongoing occupation while rapidly embracing the Z-twist/S-twist duality, so much so that, according to Stephen Ozuk, about 87.2 percent of the Dohack phase ceramics had Z-twist cordmarking (Kelly et al. 1990, 121), correlated with over 50 percent ubiquity for maize (Kelly 1990b, 126).

Therefore, by setting aside the hiatus claim, the dating of the Range site can be broadly summarized as the Patrick phase occurring circa cal A.D. 650–900 and the Dohack phase, circa cal A.D. 900–940, marking the opening of the Terminal Late Woodland period at the Range site. Certainly, when calibrated, the range of radiocarbon dates that Kelly procured would appear to be consistent with this dating (Kelly 1990a, 73, table 8). Furthermore, it is clear that the Patrick phase occupation at the Range site is much more extensive than the Sponemann phase occupation at the Sponemann site. The latter may have covered only four or five decades (circa cal A.D. 850–900), which would correspond to only the last fifth of the Patrick phase occupation of the Range site, while the Patrick phase occupation of the Range site could be at least five times that time span, thereby accounting for the multiple Patrick phase community plans, as described below.

The Patrick Phase Occupations

Kelly recognizes nine separate Patrick phase occupation areas, which he labels as Occupation Areas P-1 through P-9 (Kelly 1990a, 74–75, 79–89, 108; 1990b, 119–24; Kelly et al. 1987, 136–38). Occupation Areas P-1 and P-2 were the two northernmost loci. These had no structures, and given "the low density of debris and limited diversity of tool types" (Kelly 1990a, 79), he estimates that they were short-term occupations. Occupation Areas P-8 and P-9 were the southernmost loci. Although they had structures, since they abutted the west side of the highway right-of-way, he suggests that they represent only the small eastern edge of larger communities that are probably located off the right-of-way (Kelly et al. 1987, 141). Notably, the four structures making up Occupation Area P-8 were all keyhole structures, and they had only a scattering of spatially associated pit features. According to Kelly's figure 21c (Kelly 1990a, 80), all of these pit features were somewhat distant from the keyhole structures, "suggesting that the settlement extended further west" (Kelly et al. 1987, 224), where there was a significant amount of surface material.

Kelly focuses on Occupation Areas P-3 through P-7, identifying Occupation Area P-3 as a homestead with three structures and a widespread cluster of pit features. All three of these were keyhole structures, and two were linked in the same manner as the two discussed in the previous chapter at the Sponemann site. Occupation Area P-3 had a very large scattering of pit features located fairly well east of the keyhole structures. This extensive set of features had a linear northeast-southwest orientation. On the basis of the high pit-to-structure ratio (93:1), Kelly estimates a rather lengthy occupation by at least two households (Kelly 1990a, 79). Occupation Areas P-4, P-5, P-6, and P-7 made up the largest clusters. Kelly treated Occupation Area P-4 as a hamlet; given the sizes of Occupation Areas P-5, P-6, and P-7, he designated these as villages. The structures of Occupation Area P-6 (Figure 8.1) formed a semicircular cluster with the open side facing west. There were at least sixteen (possibly seventeen) basin structures with a fair amount of superpositioning (Kelly et al. 1987, 216). Seven of these were keyhole structures, and four or five of these keyhole structures had pits and/or structures superimposed on them. Kelly and colleagues (1987, 216) comment that this cluster, Occupation Area P-6, probably represents a dual occupation and that, as was the case for P-8 and P-9, it was probably simply the eastern sector of a larger grouping that extends west of the right-of-way, presumably where the majority of the rest of the postulated village would be found if excavations were conducted there. They also note that, as in Occupation Area P-5, the earth ovens "were located near structures . . . , thus reinforcing the idea that these features were part of a large, planned community" (Kelly et al. 1987, 221).[2]

Occupation Area P-7 (Figure 8.2) was treated by Kelly as the smallest and, possibly, the last of the Patrick phase villages at the Range site. It was a semicircular cluster of at least fourteen structures, three or four of which were keyhole structures. Because it was both the smallest of the occupations he termed villages and possibly the last, he suggests that it was the result of "the fissioning of a larger-village community" (Kelly 1990a, 86). Presumably, this larger community would have been Occupation Area P-5. The latter was the largest Patrick phase occupation (Figures 8.3 and 8.4). It was made up of thirty-three structures. Of these thirty-three, possibly sixteen were keyhole structures, comprising almost half of the total recognized number of Occupation Area P-5 structures! At least twelve of these keyhole structures had their ramps oriented in an easterly to southeasterly direction. One of the three having ramps ori-

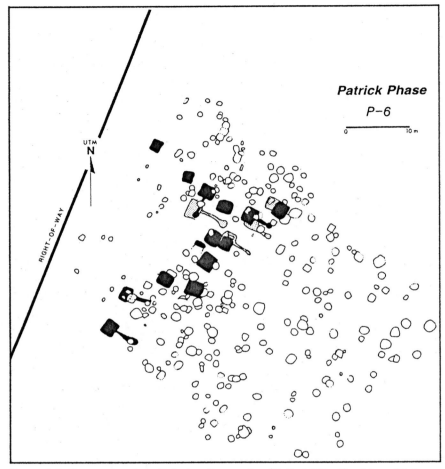

Figure 8.1. Occupation Area P-6 plan, Range site. (Kelly 1990a, fig. 26, p. 85. From "Range Site Community Patterns and the Mississippian Emergence," by John E. Kelly, in *The Mississippian Emergence*, Bruce D. Smith, ed., Smithsonian Institution Press. Reprinted by permission of publisher.)

ented south had its distal pit overlapping the basin of a keyhole structure that had its ramp oriented in an easterly direction. There was one large single-post structure in the northwest corner of the cluster. The remaining fifteen or sixteen structures of Occupation Area P-5 were regular rectangular, single-post structures. Excluding the large northwest single-post structure, and making no distinction between rectangular and keyhole structures, Kelly grouped all of these structures into several separate smaller clusters, each associated with

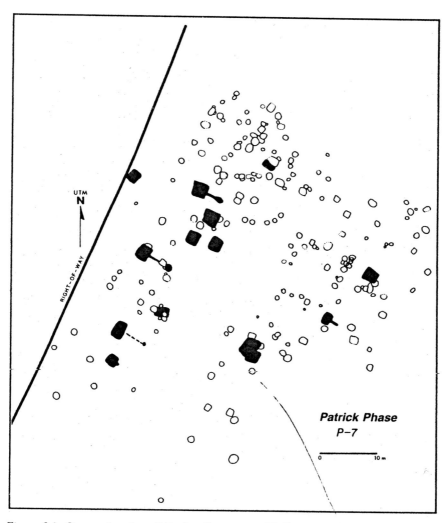

Figure 8.2. Occupation Area P-7 plan, Range site. (Kelly 1990a, fig. 27, p. 86. From "Range Site Community Patterns and the Mississippian Emergence," by John E. Kelly, in *The Mississippian Emergence,* Bruce D. Smith, ed., Smithsonian Institution Press. Reprinted by permission of publisher.)

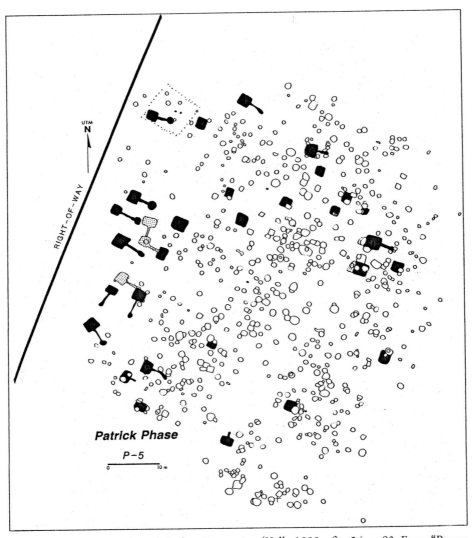

Figure 8.3. Occupation Area P-5 plan, Range site. (Kelly 1990a, fig. 24, p. 83. From "Range Site Community Patterns and the Mississippian Emergence," by John E. Kelly, in *The Mississippian Emergence,* Bruce D. Smith, ed., Smithsonian Institution Press. Reprinted by permission of publisher.)

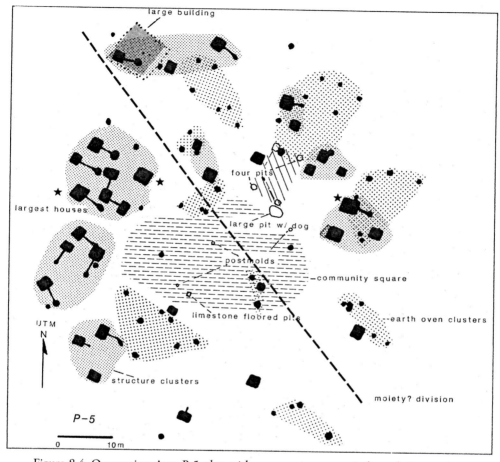

Figure 8.4. Occupation Area P-5 plan with community square indicated, Range site. (Kelly 1990a, fig. 25, p. 84. From "Range Site Community Patterns and the Mississippian Emergence," by John E. Kelly, in *The Mississippian Emergence,* Bruce D. Smith, ed., Smithsonian Institution Press. Reprinted by permission of publisher.)

earth-oven pits. He interprets these structure/oven pit clusters as delineating nuclear family households and, in some cases, possibly extended kin groups. Most of the clusters, he argues, were arranged in a semicircle around an open area that he terms a *community square.* This area is indicated in Figure 8.4.

Kelly comments that this square had a large post in its approximate center. (However, Figure 8.4 seems to show at least three posts differentially located in this square.) He also describes the square as containing six limestone-paved pits. On the northeast side of the square there were four rectangular pits with limestone bases organized in a roughly symmetrical, rectilinear pattern, "reminiscent of the four-fold division of the world so well documented for historic Indian groups of the Southeast" (Kelly 1990a, 85). Just south of the southeast corner of this quadripartite pattern was a fifth pit, the largest in Occupation Area P-5. It contained the skeleton of a dog with "several puppies in her birth canal" (Kelly 1990a, 85).[3] On the southwest side of the square opposite these pits, there was another pit with a limestone base. Finally, Kelly suggests that the arrangement of the clusters of structures around this square (Figure 8.4) indicates a possible division of the community into "two segments that may reflect a larger moiety division of the community. . . . Each of these 'moiety' segments contained a large basin house that, on the basis of structure size and association, may mark the location of certain 'moiety' leaders" (Kelly 1990a, 85). To reinforce the claimed ritual nature of this square and its associated pits and posts, he marshals considerable evidence, including concentrations of pipes, disks, and discoidals distributed around the periphery of the square, to conclude that the domestic residences/square pattern of the village displays a distinction between domestic and ritual zones.

Just north of this large P-5 village is the Occupation Area P-4 hamlet (Figure 8.5). P-4 was made up of seven basin structures and two large single-post structures. Again, on the basis of the distribution of pipes and discoidals, Kelly suggests that "P-4 may have filled a specialized role in a larger settlement system" (Kelly 1990a, 84). He emphasizes this by pointing out that "A large number of earth ovens were [sic] concentrated just to the west of the southernmost single-post structure, and these earth ovens contained an unusually high frequency of bowl rims. . . . [In sum, Occupation Area P-4 was] centered around activities involving games and the preparation and serving of food. In certain respects it is strongly reminiscent of nodal communities . . . of the later Mississippian period" (Kelly 1990a, 84). He concludes that the domestic residence/ritual square pattern displays a social system that manifested some type of dual-like kinship-based organization with nuclear or possibly extended family units.

Critique

Kelly and his colleagues (Kelly 1990a; Kelly et al. 1984; 1987) have raised a number of important points that relate to possible types of settlements, such as hamlets and villages, and the importance of recognizing the role that ritual plays in these communities. For example, in regard to Occupation Area P-5, the community square and its associated features were an important manifestation of community ritual. Kelly in particular also suggests that the control of

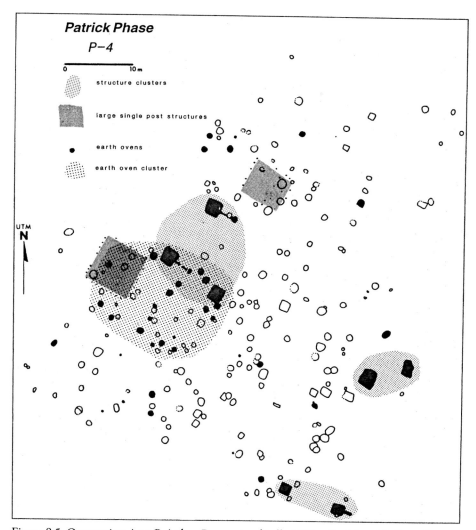

Figure 8.5. Occupation Area P-4 plan, Range site. (Kelly 1990a, fig. 23, p. 82. From "Range Site Community Patterns and the Mississippian Emergence," by John E. Kelly, in *The Mississippian Emergence,* Bruce D. Smith, ed., Smithsonian Institution Press. Reprinted by permission of publisher.)

this ritual area was not distributed equally across the community but was predominantly embodied in those community members located in the northeast sector. His claim is based on the distribution of formal components: for example, the quadripartite set of pits, the large "dog-pit," and the "central" posts are located on that side of the square (Kelly 1990a, 85). He also emphasizes the distribution of concentrations of pipes and discoids around the periphery of the square and the contrast between the large single-post structure and the smaller basin structures.

Despite attending to these important formal variations and asymmetries of distribution demarcating ritual and domestic zones, and while he certainly noted the contrast between the rectangular and keyhole structures, Kelly does not attempt to account for these formal differences. Indeed, he gives the impression that the differences are not really relevant to understanding the community layouts. One possible reason for this is that, unlike the Sponemann phase where keyhole structures form a distinct minority, in those parts of the Patrick phase occupations of the Range site that were exposed, keyhole structures are just short of being in the majority and, in this sense, apparently part of the "ordinary" dwelling structures. Even so, given Kelly's care to discriminate formal differences among artifacts and features, the fact that he does not seriously address these outstanding formal differences seems strange; as is fully discussed in the previous two chapters, Fortier does address these and concludes that the formal differences mark the keyhole structures as winter residences. However, Kelly denies this possibility, arguing that, although the ramp and distal pit unit may have served as a means of channeling heat from the east-rising sun into the main basin of the keyhole structure, this would not have given any advantage to those occupants who might use the structure in the winter. For Kelly, the structure basin, with or without a ramp, is what would have served as an important mode of heat control: "These extended entryways may have been constructed to regulate the flow of heat into the structures. . . . The entryway tunnels, in conjunction with the end pits, would have then functioned to warm the structure interiors. . . . However, there was no evidence at the Range site to preclude their use during other times of the year. The same is true of the small rectilinear structures. House basins would have maintained heat during the winter and cooled structures during the summer" (Kelly et al. 1987, 168).

In contrast, I have claimed that keyhole structures embodied an important component of the cult ritual sphere. I will extend this interpretation to the Patrick phase keyhole structures of the Range site. There are a number of grounds for doing this that are independent of the formal properties identifying these features at both the Sponemann and the Range site. In the case of the Sponemann site keyhole structures, I point out in the preceding chapter the particular "neatness" of their basin floors. Also, it is notable that discoids, pipes, and other related artifacts (including the residue of tobacco), all associated with ceremony, were found concentrated in the keyhole structure area. These same characteristics were also found in relation to the keyhole structures of the Range site. Besides these attributes, in chapter 7 I particularly emphasize the contrast between the linear distribution of the Sponemann keyhole structures and the clustering arrangement of the rectangular structures, arguing that the two types of structures, when contemporary, would have been spatially separated as a result of the arm's-length clan-cult relation. Hence, a sort of musical-chairs chronological development occurred. At the Sponemann site, this means that the keyhole and rectangular structures that are spatially proximal to each other were not contemporary.

Is there some justification to apply to the Range site this notion of the non-contemporaneity of proximally related keyhole and rectangular structures? A closer examination of Occupation Area P-6 (Figure 8.1) would suggest that there is. As noted above, Kelly and his colleagues (1987, 219) point out that in the Patrick phase occupation, this area had the highest frequency of overlapping features. Many pit features were superimposed, particularly in the northern sector, although some of these may have been associated with the southern sector of Occupation Area P-5, immediately north of P-6. Notably, 26 percent of the structures in the western sector of Occupation Area P-6 were superimposed; indeed, Kelly and his colleagues (1987, 216) discerned two crosscutting sets of structures, one forming a southwest-northeast line and the other forming a semicircular set of structures facing west. Kelly and colleagues conclude, "In fact, Occupation Area P-6 probably extended not only to the north into Occupation Area P-5, but also to the west, outside the right-of-way limits. Several structures in Occupation Area P-6 formed a line that may have also included structures in the southern and western position of Occupation Area P-5." Furthermore, there are at least ten keyhole structures in the southern and western sector of Occupation Area P-5 (Figures 8.3 and 8.4), and they effectively form a linear extension of the keyhole structures in the northwestern sector of Occupation Area P-6 (Figure 8.1) to the immediate south of P-5. Kelly and colleagues also comment that the earth ovens in Occupation Area P-6 were, as "in

Occupation Area P-5, . . . located near structures . . . , thus reinforcing the idea that these features were part of a large, planned community" (Kelly et al. 1987, 221). They also note that there must have been two sequential occupations.

Why all this is interesting is because a careful examination of Figure 8.1 clearly shows that the keyhole and rectangular structures of Occupation Area P-6 can be analytically separated into two groupings, with the keyhole structures forming a linear arrangement running southwest-northeast and the rectangular structures forming a semicircular cluster. The semicircular cluster of P-6 would be the eastern end of "a large, planned community" most of which, as pointed out above, was probably west of the highway right-of-way. If this is the case, then the keyhole structures and the small rectangular structures were likely sequential, probably with the latter following the former, since, if Kelly and colleagues are correct, the rectangular structures formed a semicircular cluster facing west, suggesting that it is simply the eastern half of the larger western-located community plan. This also means that there are probably many more rectangular structures that are unaccounted for in this western sector, suggesting that we need to consider the possibility that, in total, there are more rectangular than keyhole structures, despite the current data.

To reinforce this suggestion, a similar patterning may be discerned in Occupation Area P-5, immediately north of Occupation Area P-6 (as pointed out above, the northern sector of P-6 may have overlapped with the southern sector of P-5). First, the large single-post structure in the northwest corner of Occupation Area P-5 seems to be superimposed over the smaller keyhole structure, suggesting that the former postdates the latter. However, this ocerlap is only suggestive, since Kelly and colleagues (1987, 213) point out that which structure was first could not be determined: "A keyhole structure was located within this structure; however, it was not possible to determine the relative positioning of the structures. The large, rectilinear structure may be associated with the other large, rectilinear structures in Occupation Area P-4 to the north."[4] In this regard, it is notable that the keyhole structures and the small rectangular structures also seem to sort out in a manner similar to the above analysis of Occupation Area P-6. In fact, with one or possibly two exceptions, all of the keyhole structures in Occupation Area P-5 are located on the northwestern side of the occupation area. Not only do they make a linear arrangement similar to the keyhole structures in Occupation Area P-6 to their south, but also the two sets are effectively in the same line. Even more interesting is the fact that the distribution of earth ovens and associated rectangular structures of Occupation Area P-5 encircle the community square and are, in general, to the east of the keyhole structures (Figures 8.3 and 8.4). If this community square is treated as if it had only the rectangular structures, it might be the type of community plan to which Kelly and colleagues suggest the semicircular set of rectangular structures of Occupation Area P-6 belonged. If so, then Occupation Area P-5 may also incorporate at least two subphases, the first possibly defined by the keyhole structures and the second by the large, single-post building and the rectangular basin structures.

The "keyhole phase" would seem to be quite extensive since not only are there at least sixteen keyhole structures, but also there may be two paired sets, one in the southwest sector and the other in the northeast sector. The latter would suggest a direct historical continuity. Furthermore, not only do the majority of keyhole structures of these two sets align with the keyhole structures of Occupation Area P-6, when the total set of Patrick phase occupations is looked at, a very distinct linear pattern of keyhole structures is clearly discernible, similar to although more extensive than the linear arrangement of the six Sponemann phase keyhole structures. That is, almost all the keyhole structures run parallel to the ridge orientation, and almost all of the ramps are oriented easterly, suggesting that there is a sequential chronological continuity linking the Patrick phase keyhole structures of the Range site together.

In the preceding chapter I argue that in the case of the Sponemann site, this linear arrangement of keyhole structures was the result of the same cult (or two cults) systematically abandoning their old keyhole structures and building a new set to the north as the more southerly residential community also moved north. The fact that there are many more keyhole structures at the Range site than at the Sponemann site may simply be a matter of temporal depth. As commented above, the Sponemann phase occupation of the Sponemann site may have lasted for only four or five decades, while the Patrick phase occupations of the Range site probably incorporate the total Patrick phase, about 250 or more years. Furthermore, if the keyhole structures are analytically removed from Occupation Area P-5, leaving behind only the rectangular structures and associated pits and earth ovens, the number of structures of this occupation area is reduced considerably, to a somewhat skimpy distribution of about fifteen. The patterning of these structures maintains the central square and, interestingly, becomes much more similar to the patterning of Cluster 3 rectangular structures at the Sponemann site. In the latter case, Andrew Fortier comments that this configuration of nine rectangular structures may delineate a courtyard: "It is possible that an actual courtyard exists in the central area, but the numerous pits there obscure any definable limits. In addition, a central marker post . . .

could not be found" (Fortier et al. 1991, 137). When the two keyhole structures of this Cluster 3 are analytically removed, the similarities become even clearer. It is notable, also, that both the possible courtyard delineated by the Cluster 3 rectangular structures of the Sponemann site and the community square incorporated into Occupation Area P-5 of the Range site were heavily pockmarked by pits (compare Figures 6.1 and 8.3).

It has already been noted that Kelly estimates that Occupation Area P-6 was only the eastern sector of a larger village, the rest being west of the right-of-way. He argues that the same would be the case for Occupation Areas P-7, P-8, and P-9. Even Occupation Area P-5 (the largest Patrick phase occupation cluster), abuts this western extreme of the right-of-way, and, as Kelly and his colleagues (1987, 216) comment, the limits of this area "were somewhat arbitrary, and additional features belonging to this area may have extended beyond the boundaries delineated." That is, many more structures might be lying to the west of the known ones. Of course, this is negative evidence. However, as I mention above, it is notable that the known keyhole structures of the Patrick phase occupation of the Range site are linearly arranged along the higher portion of the ridge and almost abutting the western margin of the right-of-way, leaving sufficient space on the western side of the ridge to accommodate numerous rectangular structures. If this is the case, the spacing between these hypothetical western structures and the known keyhole structures would probably be sufficient to count as realizing the postulated arm's-length relation between clans and cults. That is, the keyhole structures would represent the cults and the rectangular structures, the kin groups.

Alternative Account

There are three large single-post structures related to the Patrick phase. Occupation Area P-4 has two, and each of these is paired with a keyhole structure (Figure 8.5). This cluster is immediately north of Occupation Area P-5, which has one large single-post structure located on its northwest periphery. Kelly interprets Occupation Area P-4 as a hamlet. In fact, he clearly separates these single-post buildings from the village ritual sphere. With regard to the Occupation Area P-5 patterning, he comments that the "four pits are probably involved in ceremonies associated with the community square, while the peripherally located structure was probably restricted in use to certain segments of the community" (Kelly 1990a, 108). This suggests that he is recognizing two ritual spheres, one embodied by the community square, with its quadripartite pits-and-post complex, and one marked by the single-post rectangular structures. I concur with his analysis in terms of defining two distinct ritual spheres. However, he considers these two spheres to be ranked. He interprets the separation of the large structures from the square and, in particular, the separation of Occupation Area P-4 from Occupation Area P-5 as marking a specialized relation, probably based on dominance, since, for him, Occupation Area P-4 was unusual in that it "may have filled a specialized role in a larger settlement system," which he suggests would be similar to that of the nodal communities of the following Mississippian period (Kelly 1990a, 84). Thomas Emerson (1992, 206) claims that these nodal communities were occupied by ritual and political rural leaders who were, in turn, subordinate to Cahokia. By saying that this occupation area had "a specialized role in a larger settlement system," therefore, Kelly seems to be claiming that this locale was, in fact, akin to the "nodal communities" of the Mississippian period, which is to say that he is treating it as a locale of a socially ranking and possibly dominant specialized group.

However, the above patterning can easily be accommodated to a very different view, namely, that the occupation area represents an early expression of the patterning that I have characterized as the plaza-periphery integrated settlement articulation mode. It is important to remember that, according to Kelly, Occupation Areas P-4, P-5, and P-6 (organized from north to south) were occupied during the later part of the Patrick phase and, therefore, could be displaying an important modification in the settlement articulation mode, namely, the postulated shift from the peripheral-integrated to the plaza-periphery integrated mode. Furthermore, cults and clans would have been very localized so that, in most cases, the cult members would also have been members of the kin groups, either consanguineal or affinal. Therefore, the two organizations could be expected to cooperate while, precisely because of the dual kin and cult membership, the cults would maintain separate locales for their own specialized ritual. The patterning of the Occupation Area P-5 layout can easily be interpreted as having this nature. The large single-post building is on the periphery of the community cluster. It also appears to superimpose upon a keyhole structure, and if the latter was an earlier expression of the cult ritual sphere, then a direct developmental continuity is indicated here.

According to this account, therefore, partway through the Patrick phase an important and complex ritual innovation was introduced, manifested by the replacement of the keyhole ritual structure with the large, single-post rectangular structure without the traditional basin floor or ramp. This innovation would also mark the shift from the peripheral-integrated settlement articulation mode, manifested by the spatial distancing of keyhole and rectangular structures, to the plaza-periphery integrated settlement articulation mode.

Kelly's interpretation of these Patrick phase occupations entails accepting a transformation of the deep social structures, namely, the introduction of differentiating kinship-related groups by means of hierarchical ranking, thereby manifesting a form of exclusivity that, if not strongly apparent in the Patrick phase, certainly is claimed to lead to a dominance hierarchy in the Terminal Late Woodland period, as I note shortly. The alternative I am suggesting entails simply an ideological, surface structural change, one that was deliberately innovated and that brought about a shift from a peripheral-integrated to a plaza-periphery integrated articulation posture while sustaining the same deep social structuring of clan and cult. This claim can be supported by focusing analysis on the rectangular structures. If we allow for the fact that Occupation Area P-5 has about half again the number of structures in Cluster 3 in the Sponemann site, then settlement and subsistence practices seem to have been intensifying at the Range site, and this would have promoted the innovation of compensating forms of world renewal ritual, even though, and possibly because, maize was not a factor at the Range site during the Patrick phase. That is, the expansion of gardening area was occurring without the midwifery ritual mediation of sacred maize to warrant this land opening and to at least partly rectify rising settlement- and subsistence-related pollution.

In sum, the settlement data that Kelly has interpreted as marking the first tentative move toward a hierarchical social system can be recharacterized and reinterpreted. The emergence of the large single-post structures, the community square, and the quadripartite pits-and-post complex—which Kelly interprets in ritual fertility terms—can all be accounted for as ideological innovations indicating a leaning away from a proscriptive and toward a prescriptive ceremonial strategic orientation, probably in response to an escalating (that is, prescriptive) subsistence regime. I now turn to summarizing the Dohack phase data, representing the earliest phase of the Terminal Late Woodland period, and Kelly's interpretation of these data, followed by my critique and alternative interpretation.

THE DOHACK PHASE OCCUPATIONS

As I comment above, while Kelly dates the temporal scope of the Dohack phase to circa A.D. 750–850 (cal A.D. 900–940), in order to account for the abrupt appearance of the Terminal Late Woodland traits of maize and Z-twist/S-twist ceramics, he argues for a settlement hiatus during the first half of the Dohack phase at the Range site. Therefore, he claims that the Dohack phase occupation at the Range site actually started circa A.D. 800 (cal A.D. 920). I suggest above that this rather abrupt appearance simply represents the rapid breakdown of the initial resistance to these subsistence innovations postulated under the Sacred Maize model and first manifested at the Sponemann site circa cal A.D. 850 or earlier, followed by their being rapidly accepted across the American Bottom. Therefore, no settlement hiatus needs to be postulated for the Range site, suggesting that the emergence of the Dohack phase of the Terminal Late Woodland period occurred at this and other sites across the region circa cal A.D. 900.

Description

One of the key characteristics of this phase is the disappearance of the keyhole structures. This phase is characterized by the formalization of the community square into a quadripartite pits-and-post/plaza complex. The plaza was delineated by clusters of single-post rectangular basin structures. Also, often a set of larger structures, pits, and other features was present but located on the edge or periphery of the occupation. This patterning is interpreted by Kelly in hierarchical ranking terms. While the general absence of interior hearths suggests that Dohack phase settlements at the Range site are still keyed to the warm season, there was a tendency to reuse the same structures for a longer period of time than during the Patrick phase, as indicated by reconstruction of major features. In Occupation Area D-2 (Figure 8.6), the largest of the Dohack phase occupation clusters, the "four central rectangular pits marking the center of the community appear to have undergone a single episode of renewal and rebuilding, as reflected by the presence of two central postmolds and two pairs of pits at the northern corners of the central complex of pits. . . . The pits defining the southern corners of this central complex were apparently rebuilt or renewed in the same location" (Kelly 1990a, 89–90). Furthermore, there is another indicator of an expanding population compared to the Patrick phase: the Dohack phase community was formed in some depth around the central plaza. In Occupation Area D-2, there were two concentric circles of clusters of domestic courtyard structures (Figure 8.6). As Kelly observes,

> The innermost ring is composed of nine structures. . . . Except for the two paired structures that are located on the northern edge of the community square, these houses are spatially separated from each other. Eight of the

structures in this inner ring form a semicircle about the four central pits along the south, west, and north sides of the community square. Located on the east edge of the community square and aligned with the central pit features, the final structure of this inner ring is the second largest structure in the village. (Kelly 1990a, 90)

The second or outer ring of structures formed seven residential clusters of two to four houses each, and six of these clusters were spatially associated with six of the nine inner ring structures. In addition, Kelly writes, "The only two structures with internal hearths . . . are located across the community square from each other, on its southern and northern sides, with the southern hearth structure the largest house in the village" (Kelly 1990a, 90–91).

Interestingly, two keyhole structures are indicated in Figure 8.6, one each in the two northernmost clusters. Kelly also notes the presence of one or two more

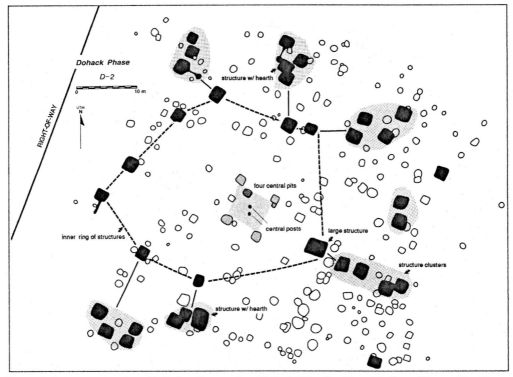

Figure 8.6. Occupation Area D-2 plan, Range site. (Kelly 1990a, fig. 30, p. 90. From "Range Site Community Patterns and the Mississippian Emergence," by John E. Kelly, in *The Mississippian Emergence*, Bruce D. Smith, ed., Smithsonian Institution Press. Reprinted by permission of publisher.)

keyhole structures incorporated into other Dohack phase clusters. Given that these structures form almost the majority in the preceding Patrick phase and are recognized as key markers of the Patrick phase (Fortier and Jackson 2000, 138), it is quite likely that they are more correctly treated as Patrick phase features. The two that are incorporated into Occupation Area D-2 would neatly fit into the northern set of keyhole structures of Occupation Area P-5, since Occupation Areas D-2 and P-5 are almost isomorphic (see Figure 8.4).

Occupation Area D-5 (Figure 8.7) is treated by Kelly as following D-2. Occupation Areas D-1 and D-3 have large, single-post wall buildings located

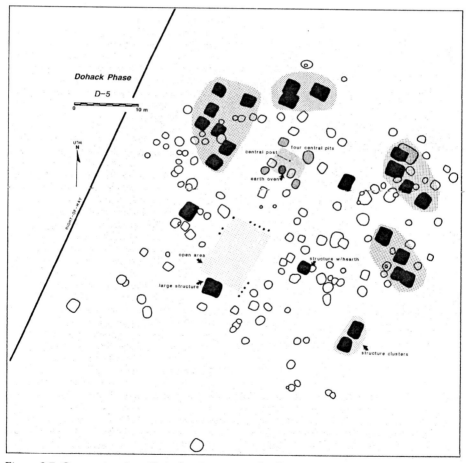

Figure 8.7. Occupation Area D-5 plan, Range site. (Kelly 1990a, fig. 31, p. 91. From "Range Site Community Patterns and the Mississippian Emergence," by John E. Kelly, in *The Mississippian Emergence,* Bruce D. Smith, ed., Smithsonian Institution Press. Reprinted by permission of publisher.)

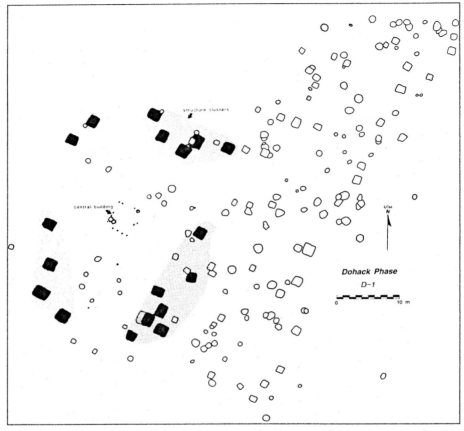

Figure 8.8. Occupation Area D-1 plan, Range site. (Kelly 1990a, fig. 33, p. 93. From "Range Site Community Patterns and the Mississippian Emergence," by John E. Kelly, in *The Mississippian Emergence*, Bruce D. Smith, ed., Smithsonian Institution Press. Reprinted by permission of publisher.)

in their plazas, or *central community squares,* as he now terms them (Figures 8.8 and 8.9, respectively). The area of both buildings is about 16 square meters (about 4 meters by 4 meters in dimension), and neither has a hearth. The clusters of residential houses are grouped around the square with considerable space between them. Kelly assesses the internal settlement patterning of the Dohack phase occupations as clearly indicating a more coherent centralization of the community plan in that phase compared to the preceding Patrick phase. He views the combination of quadripartite pits-and-post/plaza complex and large rectangular structures as manifesting a commitment to community ritual

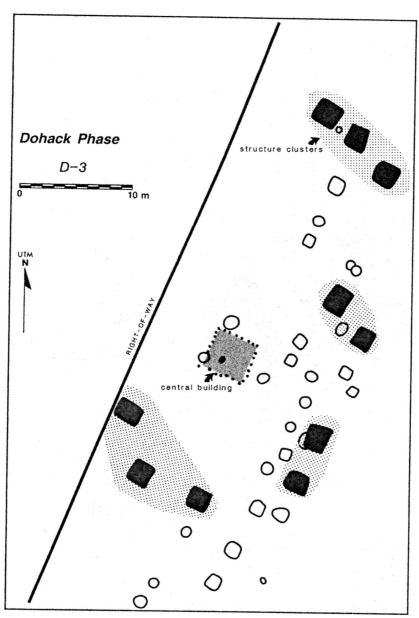

Dohack Phase

D-3

0   10 m

UTM
N

RIGHT-OF-WAY

structure clusters

central building

Figure 8.9. Occupation Area D-3 plan, Range site. (Kelly 1990a, fig. 32, p. 92. From "Range Site Community Patterns and the Mississippian Emergence," by John E. Kelly, in *The Mississippian Emergence,* Bruce D. Smith, ed., Smithsonian Institution Press. Reprinted by permission of publisher.)

oriented around fertility. In fact, in his view, the large rectangular structures with hearths were "the precursor of temples or elite structures . . . [of the] 'fire-sun-deity' complex. . . . [In addition,] the two different types of central facilities—below-ground storage pits and above-ground structures—may reflect the duality of the upperworld and underworld" (Kelly 1990a, 92), which represent for him a fertility complex. Although "only dimly reflected in the archaeological record, these newly emergent symbolic elements were likely integrated with concerns and ceremonies centered on agricultural success and fertility, and functioned within a developing belief system that operated to bind and stabilize such agricultural communities" (Kelly 1990a, 92–93).

These ritual components are directly related by him to village leadership. He suggests that the "larger houses may be those of community leaders, while those having internal hearths may have been either residences of ceremonial practitioners or structures with specialized functions" (Kelly 1990a, 92). This is an important comment. With regard to Occupation Area D-2 (Figure 8.6), the larger structures, the structures with internal hearths, and the quadripartite pits-and-post complex were located within the central plaza with the cluster of residential structures delineating the northeastern, southeastern, and southwestern sides. The two paired sets of individual structures formed the northwestern side of the plaza. Occupation Area D-5 (Figure 8.7), although the smaller, was even more complex. Rather than the four pits being centered, they were located north of the center and defined "the northeast end of a corridor or community square that was essentially devoid of features" (Kelly 1990a, 91). Kelly points out that one of the largest structures of D-5 is situated at the southwestern end of this area. A line drawn from this large structure to the four pits would form a southwest-northeast axis across the plaza. Furthermore, a series of screens delineates "portions of its northwest, northeast, and southeast sides," and Kelly adds that "two spatially isolated structures are situated on the northwest and southeast boundaries of this central feature-free area on a 90 degree axis with, and balancing, the cluster of four pit features and the large structure just described. The remaining structures of this D-5 village were distributed in a semicircular pattern of five household clusters" (Kelly 1990a, 92).

In short, there would appear to be two crosscutting axes defining the ritual sphere of this settlement: the long northeast-southwest axis linking the northeastern pit features to the southwestern structure, and the northwest-southeast axis linking the two isolated structures (one with an interior hearth) at the southerly end. This clearly implicates the view that the ritual sphere of Dohack phase communities was dually structured, with one aspect possibly under the responsibility of the lineage leaders and the other under the responsibility of ritual specialists—or, as Kelly puts it, those structures "having internal hearths may have been either residences of ceremonial practitioners or structures with specialized functions" (Kelly 1990a, 92).

Critique and Alternative Account

Kelly's claim that the Dohack phase occupations appear to reflect a more coherent community plan can be restated as manifesting a definitive shift from a peripheral-integrated to a plaza-periphery integrated settlement articulation mode. That is, rather than a greater coherence it is a different coherence that is being manifested. The Patrick phase "squares" were somewhat messy, being pockmarked by pit features, while the peripherally located keyhole structures had little in the way of nearby pit features. If the latter structures embodied an important part of the cult ritual sphere, then the formation of the Dohack phase plaza with its carefully placed pits and posts and its absence of scattered storage pits is simply the expression of clan and cult ritual practices sharing the same plaza area. Reinforcing this claim is the observation that the clusters of domestic structures of Occupation Area D-5 formed a semicircle around the quadripartite pits-and-post complex at the northeast end of the village plaza (Figure 8.7). The largest structure at the opposite or southwest end of the plaza was partly separated from the northeast end by screens. This means that this large structure and the two structures forming the crosscutting 90° northwest-southeast axis were effectively separated from the domestic sector. Hence, the plaza has complementary and crosscutting axes, reinforcing the possibility of a cult-clan division of the village and suggesting the plaza-periphery integrated settlement articulation mode. In this case, the southeast-northwest axis sectors the northeast and southwest ends into (domestic) clan and (world renewal) cult spheres, respectively, and the northeast-southwest axis probably bifurcates the clans, possibly as moieties, and the cult sphere, possibly by male and female gender or, possibly, senior and junior generation.

This plaza-periphery settlement articulation mode does not deny that hierarchy can come into play. Hierarchy will probably be marked by differentially sized residences, as Kelly suggests. However, under the squatter ethos and immanentist cosmology, this would be an enabling hierarchy constituted of autonomous agents, and the two organizations as manifested in this patterning would relate to constitute the village as a complementary heterarchy, with each organizational sector (clan and cult) respecting the sphere of responsibility of the other and, of course, cooperating in the care and use of the common facilities, such as the plaza, pits, and posts, and so on. Hence, this community plan layout can be comfortably accounted for in terms of the clan-cult duality manifesting a plaza-periphery integrated settlement articulation mode. In this mode, the two parallel social organizations of clan and cult leadership would not transform their positions into dominance over their followers or over each other. The leaders would be expected to pursue consensus, and from this consensus, the collective actions would flow. On the basis of my earlier theoretical elucidation of organizations based on the principle of agentive autonomy, I interpret this community plan as disclosing a complementary heterarchy characterized by a clan-cult arm's-length structuring based on relative autonomy, with the cult being organized as an enabling hierarchy. That is, while Kelly interprets the plaza with its specialized structures and quadripartite pits-and-post complex in terms of a hierarchical monistic modular polity type of social system, the very same patterning can be seen as the expression of the plaza-periphery integrated settlement articulation mode consistent with a type of social system postulated under the heterarchical polyistic locale-centric account.

THE RANGE PHASE OCCUPATIONS

This dual ritual sectoring was carried over into the Range phase occupations of the Range site and would be dated circa cal A.D. 940–980 (uncal A.D. 850–900). The variation in size among the communities continued with the formation of hamlets and villages, although Kelly and his colleagues (1990, 548) particularly note that, in general, the Range phase occupations tend to be smaller than the preceding Dohack phase occupations. This might be indicative of population expansion provoking a more proscriptive settlement strategy. Still, these investigators claim that, with the exception of the disappearance of the central structures in the plaza, the same range of symbolic elements as those of the Dohack phase continued and, possibly, became more entrenched, given the apparently greater propensity for rebuilding peripheral structures and hearths.

Description

The R-1 Range phase village (Figure 8.10), which Kelly treats as the penultimate Range phase occupation, displays the earlier Dohack phase semicircle pattern of tightly clustered domestic structures "suggestive of extended family households" (Kelly 1990a, 96). The northwest-facing side of the semicircle was partly blocked by "three tightly grouped structures" (Kelly 1990a, 96). Oppo-

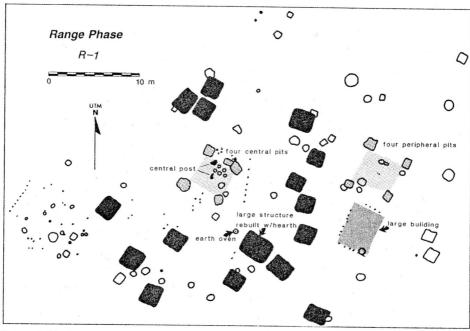

Figure 8.10. Occupation Area R-1 plan, Range site. (Kelly 1990a, fig. 38, p. 97. From "Range Site Community Patterns and the Mississippian Emergence," by John E. Kelly, in *The Mississippian Emergence*, Bruce D. Smith, ed., Smithsonian Institution Press. Reprinted by permission of publisher.)

site them on the southeast side of the square was a large structure with internal hearths that had been rebuilt at least once. The quadripartite pits-and-post complex was located centrally in the plaza, northwest of the large structure with an internal hearth. The large pits had been rebuilt at least twice, and the post had been replaced at least once. There was a second post that had been erected within the rectangle formed by the surrounding pits. The largest structure of this R-1 village was also associated with a quadripartite pits-and-post complex. It is notable, however, that this structure is located on the eastern periphery of the village. This is an interesting positioning for a structure that must have had some special function, since it suggests an activity zone that had some deliberately determined degree of physical isolation and separation from the major public activity zone, the latter being demarcated by the central square. Therefore, despite the apparently closer integrating of the ritual and domestic zone around the larger central square, this large, peripherally set

building with a large quadripartite pits- and-post complex suggests a continuing arm's-length relation between ritual spheres, which first became apparent
in the Patrick phase village clustering, carried over into the Dohack phase occupations of the Terminal Late Woodland, and became much more formalized
in the Range phase.

Critique

While stressing the continuity between the Dohack and Range phases, Kelly,
quite correctly I believe, points out that only in the Range phase did the total
range of expressive patterning come together into a single complex of "large
structures, internal hearths, evidence of rebuilding, central or apical location"
(Kelly 1990a, 96–97). He goes on, however, to argue that

> the coalescing of these elements within Range phase communities may
> reflect the consolidation of political authority and the sanctification of
> this authority through the presence of fire and the rebuilding and renewal
> of these structures. The evidence for the reexcavation of the four central
> pits of the R-1 village may also reflect ritual, busklike renewal. If this is
> the case, the large focal structures and central pit features might represent
> a significant forerunner of the plaza–platform mound configuration as-
> sociated with the Mississippian towns. (Kelly 1990a, 97)

I think he is right to stress the continuity between the ritual components
of the Range phase villages and the equivalent ritual components of the Mississippian. However, it does not follow that the "coalescing" of these ritual
component features of the Terminal Late Woodland communities reflects "the
consolidation of political authority and the sanctification of this authority."[5]
Instead, I suggest that this coalescence is the development and modifying of
the material conditions of satisfaction of the dual clan-cult arm's-length relation. However, rather than reiterate this point now, I will complete this summary of the Terminal Late Woodland period occupations of the Range site by
focusing on the two last phases (the George Reeves and Lindeman phases),
since the occupational patterning of these two phases manifests this development particularly well.

The George Reeves Phase Occupations

The George Reeves phase (circa cal A.D. 980–1020) and Lindeman phase (circa
cal A.D. 1020–1050) are very important. If we can generalize from the Range

site data to the American Bottom, they mark the final community plan developments prior to the emergence of the Mississippian period, and thus they deserve careful analysis.

Description

Kelly notes that the George Reeves phase community structures (Figure 8.11) are distributed over 1.7 hectares. Several of these structures, however, constitute components that were out of chronological phase with each other. Using ceramic stylistic variation, he sectors them into separate groupings that display three levels of settlement types: farmsteads, hamlets, and villages. Within the total layout of the George Reeves phase occupational component, the major central sector, G-2, constitutes what he calls the large village. This is made up of 151 domestic structures (specialized structures are not included in the count) covering an areal extent of 175 meters northeast-southwest and 94 meters northwest-southeast (Kelly 1990a, table 9, 89). Kelly treats the most southerly (G-3) cluster of structures (Figure 8.11) as an isolated farmstead and the most northerly (G-1) cluster of seven structures as a hamlet. This hamlet seems to be comprised of all residential structures. As noted above, these were not contemporaneous with the G-2 sector, which forms the bulk of the George Reeves phase occupation. Kelly notes the two western flanking clusters, G-2a to the northwest and G-2b to the southwest, and admits finding these "difficult to interpret" (Kelly 1990a, 97). While he suggests that they might be hamlets, he prefers to treat them as outliers of the main G-2 cluster, on which he then focuses.

He divides the G-2 cluster into subdivisions, G-2a through G-2k, moving from north to south. There appear to be three major squares, or plazas, as he labels them—G-2c, G-2d, and G-2h—each delineated by linearly arranged structures that enclose them, and each with associated central quadripartite pits-and-post complexes. In a number of cases, these display distinct indications of rebuilding, which he interprets as marking considerable time depth for this large settlement (Kelly 1990a, 98). He labels G-2h as the "central plaza." G-2d is north of the latter. They are separated by two smaller plazas, G-2f and G-2g, the former to the west of the latter, with both having the typical four pits. G-2c, the major northern cluster, and G-2h, the major southern cluster, each has the full complement of four pits and central post. However, G-2d, the cluster that intervenes between them, appears to have only limestone-floored pits and lacks the quadripartite pits-and-post complex. Kelly labels it a "secondary plaza." South of G-2h there are three more clusters: G-2i, G-2j, and

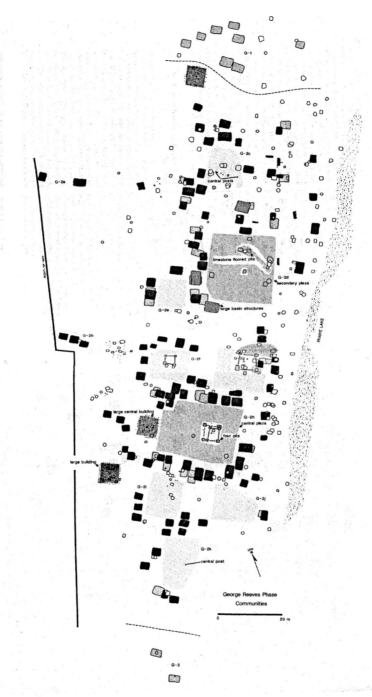

Figure 8.11. George Reeves phase village plan, Range site. (Kelly 1990a, fig. 40, pp. 100–101. From "Range Site Community Patterns and the Mississippian Emergence," by John E. Kelly, in *The Mississippian Emergence*, Bruce D. Smith, ed., Smithsonian Institution Press. Reprinted by permission of publisher.)

G-2k. The latter is the southernmost plaza, having a central post but lacking the four pits. G-2i has a north-south linear arrangement of three structures and a large building northwest of them. No pits or posts are indicated. G-2j is a set of three structures apparently arranged around a square, and it is immediately southeast of G-2h. "In addition to the symmetrical arrangement of courtyard groups," Kelly notes, "a dichotomy is evident between those to the north of the southern plaza [G-2f and G-2g] versus those on the south [G-2l and G-2j]. The northern courtyard centers are highlighted by the quadripartite set of pits with a central post while those groups to the south exhibit only a central post. These two courtyard group patterns can be traced back into the early Emergent Mississippian [Terminal Late Woodland]" (Kelly 1996, 105).

Kelly elaborates his discussion of the George Reeves phase occupation by focusing on G-2h, the "central plaza." He notes that the plaza axis is delineated by the quadripartite pits-and-post complex on the east side and the "large central building" opposite this on the west side. The house structures are linearly arranged east-west, primarily on the north and south sides of the plaza. He particularly notes that the central plaza is "symmetrically flanked by a series of additional courtyards" (Kelly 1990a, 99), these being G-2f and G-2g at the northwest and northeast corners of the central plaza, respectively, and G-2i and G-2j at the southwest and southeast corners, respectively. He also notes that there were two large buildings, both positioned in a manner suggesting that they were peripheral to the rest of the community. These are the "large building" southwest of the central plaza, G-2h, and another large rectangular building northwest of the G-2c plaza, at the northern end of the occupation zone. This latter building, he notes, was initially 32 square meters and then was expanded to 42 square meters, and rebuilt again during the subsequent Lindeman phase occupation. He recognizes that these two structures were physically separated, but he treats them as equivalent socially, both being similar in "overall size, peripheral location, and presumed specialized use by certain segments of the community" (Kelly 1990a, 99).

He interprets the G-2h central plaza and its four flanking courtyards as manifesting a major social development out of the Range phase. While the quadripartite pits-and-post/plaza complex and the large structures represent the continuity of ritual traditions, he interprets the four flanking courtyards and their domestic structures as marking the "the amalgamation of a number of different kinship groups at a single location" and the central plaza around which the courtyards are located as reflecting "the spatial distribution of a series of ranked social groups . . . [and this] represents the best evidence currently available for the initial emergence . . . [by cal A.D. 980–1020] of a *ranked form of sociopolitical organization* in the American Bottom region" (Kelly 1990a, 99, emphasis added). Kelly continues by noting that although "no mound construction is present, the large structure at the one end of the central courtyard is perhaps the chief's house" (Kelly 1990a, 99). In short, he postulates that this patterning represents a deep structural transformation of the social system of the earlier phases of the Terminal Late Woodland period while the ritual cultural structures remain constant: "The four pits and central post located at the opposite end of the community plaza undoubtedly played the same ceremonial and symbolic role" (Kelly 1990a, 99) as they had in the preceding Dohack and Range phases. From this he logically interprets the "northernmost and secondary plaza and courtyard . . . as a separate and subordinate social group" (Kelly 1990a, 99).

Critique and Alternative Account

If one is already committed to the notion that formal differentiation equates with ranking, then it is logical to treat this G-2 patterning as representing "the best evidence currently available for the initial emergence . . . of a ranked form of sociopolitical organization." However, this formal-difference-equals-ranking view leaves out too much. For example, it does not assimilate the peripheral components of the site: the two large buildings mentioned above, one near the extreme northwest corner of the G-2c cluster and the other near the extreme southwest corner of G-2h. Also, G-2a and G-2b, the two isolated western clusters, are not explained, except as "difficult to interpret," seemingly residential in nature and yet outlying structures. Similarly, the two large buildings are explained simply as having been special, used only by "certain segments of the community." To extend the logic of a ranked society, then, one could argue that these segments must have been part of the upper hierarchy. However, this does not fit very well with Kelly's claim that the community chief (the senior ranking position) occupied the large structure anchoring the western end of the ritual axis of the G-2h central plaza. How would those individuals associated with the two so-called high-ranking peripheral structures relate to those associated with the chiefly structure?

Again, given the hierarchical assumption, Kelly interprets the four courtyards flanking the central plaza as subordinate in rank to the central plaza. However, as he has pointed out more recently, these four flanking plazas and their central facilities seem to manifest complementary rather than ranking kinship components: "Symmetrically arranged within the various courtyards and plazas of the [George Reeves phase] Range site community, these elements and their arrangements embodied and reified certain symbolic meanings associated with particular segments of the society, such as clans or phratries. For example, a central post is associated with courtyards south of the main plaza and is in opposition to the four pits associated with the northern courtyards" (Kelly 2000, 169–72). While the fact that these flanking courtyards lack the total ritual complement that the central plaza has can be interpreted as marking the courtyards as lower ranked, when this patterning is looked at in terms of the heterarchical polyistic locale-central account (and given Kelly's claim that the two northern and southern sets stand in a complementary oppositional nature to each other), the courtyards could represent corporate kinship groups performing only part of the ritual cycle that is performed in the central plaza. Therefore, the four flanking courtyards might be quite adequately interpreted as manifesting four related but mutually autonomous kin groups. Each kin group would be responsible for its own courtyard and its associated ritual; however, they would be collectively responsible for building and maintaining the central plaza, as well as, in cooperation with the cult sodalities, collectively performing the total ritual cycle associated with this central plaza. This would mean that the social principle underwriting the amalgamation of the groups would be a mutual autonomy and not a dominance hierarchy.

Furthermore, if all the structures recorded are assumed to have been more or less contemporary, then the northern G-2c and G-2d plazas—the latter (marked by Kelly as a "secondary plaza") mediating between G-2c and the central plaza, G-2h—would represent two more sectors of the total town. Indeed, Kelly (2000, 169) has made a modification to his earlier interpretation, namely, that the village can be understood as constituted by two distinct segments: G-2h and the two northern plazas, G-2c and G-2d. However, G-2d, the plaza between G-2h and G-2c, lacks the post, while being marked by a unique set of rectangular pits with limestone floors. This suggests that G-2d was different in ritual character from both G-2c and G-2h. While flanked to the north and south by these latter two plazas, G-2d was peripheral in terms of its ritual nature, suggesting that it might actually be more akin to those groups associated with the two large rectangular buildings to the north and south of it, as well as the outlying G-2a and G-2b clusters.

In short, this alternative account of the complex patterning of the George Reeves phase occupation sees it as a developed form of the plaza-periphery integrated settlement articulation mode. This account does not rely on postulating a radical transformation in the deep social structures of the Terminal

Late Woodland social system, since the peripheral and plaza components represent the traditional cult and clan structures, respectively. With relatively autonomous groupings occupying the same overall locale in which active adults held joint membership in both a particular cult sodality and one of the clan or lineage components, the ritual aspect of the settlement could be expected to have been separated as much as practicably possible to realize the arm's-length relation that relative autonomy would entail.

Furthermore, if we assume again that all or most components of this extensive G-2 occupation are contemporary, there may be at least three major cultic focal locales (the two large peripheral northwest and southwest buildings, and the central G-2d or "secondary plaza," which could actually be the joint responsibility of the groups responsible for the large peripheral structures), thereby reducing a triple patterning to a dual patterning. Add to this multiplicity of cultic locales the peripheral western clusters G-2a and G-2b, and a complexity of cults is suggested. That is, what may be manifested here for the first time is an alliance of cults forming a mutualistic world renewal cult heterarchy that emerged out of or even promoted the coalescence of several mutually autonomous villages of the Range phase type into this complex settlement. At this point it would be very hard to say that G-2 was either a compound clan village with crosscutting cult sodalities or a compound mutualistic cult heterarchy with crosscutting clan residential courtyards. In fact, I suggest that, individually, both would be mischaracterizations. Therefore, it is safer to combine the two descriptions and say that this was a complex heterarchical polyistic locale-centric community displaying the compound plaza-periphery integrated settlement articulation mode, in which an alliance of mutually autonomous cults and an alliance of mutually autonomous clans were complementary components.

Hence, rather than portray the complicated community plan of the George Reeves phase occupation as constituting a complex village of ranked clans/lineages, I postulate that it represents a community manifesting what I here term a *compound plaza-periphery integrated articulation mode*. In heterarchical terms, it seems to combine both complementary and mutualistic forms of heterarchy. The relative autonomy of the dual clan-cult arm's-length relation and the mutual autonomy of both the allied cults and the allied clans are simultaneously manifested in the combined multiple plazas and the associated peripheral ritual structures. This is why I refer to it as the compound plaza-periphery mode.

Both interpretations (the hierarchically ranked clan village and dual clan-cult heterarchical village) implicate a complex social system capable of transforming into an even more complex system. Which account should be favored? In terms of the hermeneutic spiral method, the models are tested by means of comparing their explanatory power. The model that can account for the same data in the most coherent and logical manner with the fewest unexplained anomalies is contingently accepted as the best approximation of the past social system. Since it is only contingently the best approximation, however, its contingent acceptance does not terminate the debate. This is only a step in the process. Therefore, the favored model stands only until a better approximation is presented, one that is demonstrated as fitting more closely the social reality manifested or disclosed in the archaeological record than alternative models that challenge it. The next step in this descriptive summary and critique is to examine the development of G-2 and its transition in the Lindeman phase occupation.

THE LINDEMAN PHASE OCCUPATIONS

The George Reeves–Lindeman transition, as Kelly terms it, witnesses the original G-2 occupation being displaced slightly northward (Figure 8.12). The structures south of G-2h (the central plaza) were abandoned, including the large southwestern building that complements the large northwestern building (which remains), and several new structures were constructed to extend the east side of G-2c slightly north. The central plaza, G-2h, was modified in a manner that Kelly describes as "splitting." The structures on the southern and northern sides of this original plaza are significantly reduced in number, "with a rectangular basin structure and internal hearth placed on the north edge equidistant from the large square building to the southwest and the quadripartite pit arrangement to the southeast" (Kelly 1990a, 99). I am not sure why he characterizes this as splitting the original plaza into two courtyards. It could as easily be described as an elongated east-west courtyard defined by the large, single-post building on the west side, the quadripartite pits-and-post complex on the east side, and the large structure with an internal hearth defining the north-south axis.

To the north, the G-2f and G-2g flanking courtyards remain. However, they are reduced in terms of complexity of pits and numbers of structures. North of these courtyards, the G-2d locale with the large, limestone-floored pits (earlier termed the secondary plaza) is relabelled by Kelly as the new "central plaza," marked by a deep rectangular pit constructed at its center. This pit had white sand spread just above its base, which Kelly suggests "may represent ritual pu-

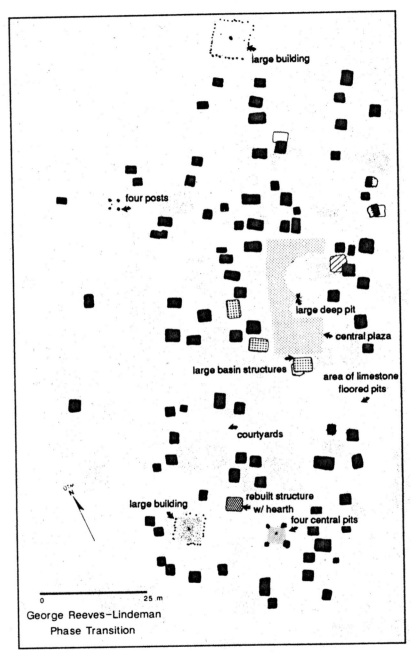

large building

four posts

large deep pit

central plaza

large basin structures

area of limestone
floored pits

courtyards

rebuilt structure
w/ hearth

large building

four central pits

UTM
N

0   25 m

George Reeves–Lindeman
Phase Transition

Figure 8.12. George Reeves–Lindeman phase transition, Range site. (Kelly 1990a, fig. 41, p. 99. From "Range Site Community Patterns and the Mississippian Emergence," by John E. Kelly, in *The Mississippian Emergence,* Bruce D. Smith, ed., Smithsonian Institution Press. Reprinted by permission of publisher.)

rification" (Kelly 1990a, 99). Other ritual components in the form of more limestone-floored pits, a large basin structure, and so on, were added. Again, northwestern and northeastern flanking courtyards with associated residential structures were built around this new central plaza. Interestingly, Kelly notes what would appear to be a second ritual locus, a large post set up in the peripheral "northeast" area of the village. He considers these changes to simply replicate the earlier hierarchically generated complexity: "Like the earlier G-2 village, the various courtyards of the new community configuration represent a number of different social groups. The central courtyard or plaza, with its larger bordering structures, undoubtedly represents the ranking lineage. In marked contrast to the earlier George Reeves and Range communities, however, the expected symbolic elements are not as obvious and are more difficult to interpret" (Kelly 1990a, 104).

Out of this configuration emerged the Lindeman phase occupation of the Range site (circa cal A.D. 1020–1050), displaying "a number of dramatic changes in the existing community plan" (Kelly 1990a, 104). The community layout (Figure 8.13) continued to be displaced northward, or more specifically, northwestward, with more of the southeastern quadrant being abandoned. Kelly sees the settlement as taking on a semicircular pattern facing east toward Prairie Lake. However, this is not a hollow semicircle, since the eastern side of the village is defined by a roughly linear series of structures. From Kelly's description, there seem to be two major ritual locales spatially related. Based on the combination of a large rectangular structure and a quadripartite pits-and-post complex, what he labels as the "central plaza (later)" is located near the lake, with the majority of the courtyards to the north and a smaller number to the south. This plaza, oriented about 20° east of north, is quite extensive, with the northern end having a large pit and, about two-thirds of the length of the plaza from the large pit, a "large basin structure." South of this basin structure there is a large quadripartite pits complex. About halfway between this complex and the large northern pit there are two post pits, one on the southeast side and the other on the northwest side of this long plaza. A line connecting these two posts would divide the plaza, and if extended, it would bisect a unique building on the northwest periphery of the village. As Kelly comments, this rectangular building is unusual not only because it has the lowest width-to-length ratio (0.52) of any building in the community and was symmetrically positioned "at the western apex of the community," but also because its floor was unique, being "highest in the center and sloped markedly toward a series of irregular,

Figure 8.13. Lindeman phase settlement plan, Range site. (Kelly 1990a, fig. 42, pp. 102–3. From "Range Site Community Patterns and the Mississippian Emergence," by John E. Kelly, in *The Mississippian Emergence,* Bruce D. Smith, ed., Smithsonian Institution Press. Reprinted by permission of publisher.)

broad, shallow wall trenches" (Kelly 1990a, 104). It also had a high incidence of Monks Mound Red ceramic bowls, as well as several other unique features.

To the immediate northeast of this unusual structure there was a large arc of structures delineating a complexly structured courtyard having two interrelated sets of pits formed in the traditional quadripartite pattern (one with the full complement of four pits, the other having three pits and using one of the pits of the former set to complete its quadripartite pattern).[6] Both had internally associated patterns of posts (one centered, the other formed in a semicircle).

On the basis of ceramic evidence, Kelly suggests that the central plaza predated the courtyard but that "both [were] undoubtedly contemporary at some point" (Kelly 1990a, 104). Several other peripheral courtyards had single quadripartite pit complexes. Kelly suggests that these different pit complexes did not play a community-wide ritual role but were more related to the ritual practices of each courtyard group. Ceramic evidence suggests that they were built at different times during the village's occupation. They do not display any rebuilding, suggesting that they were used only briefly, possibly to mediate the performance of some form of dedicatory ritual. It is even possible that they were built one at a time, although Kelly admits that this is speculative.

Over time, the village actually diminished in size (Figure 8.14). It formed into a broad semicircular linear set of residential structures with the open area having a circular single-post structure at its center. On the northern periphery of the community there was a quadripartite pit unit without a central post. Kelly suggests that this diminished size toward the end of the Lindeman phase presumably was the result of "the former inhabitants and descendants . . . [being] incorporated within the [nearby] Pulcher mound center community, or . . . [being] established [in] a new settlement at another location" (Kelly 1990a, 105). What he is alluding to here is the rather rapid Terminal Late Woodland–Mississippian transition. Although the transition is thought to have been rapid, he is suggesting that there was a period of organizational reduction marked by the shift away from the central plaza to the individualized courtyards and even that the northern and southern sectors of the village may have been divided into two smaller villages. In his view, this last period would have been characterized by out-migration as part of this process of settlement articulation change, and as he suggests, some of the population may have moved southwest to nearby Lunsford-Pulcher, swelling this community and helping to transform it into a multiple-mound locale, bringing in the first stages of the Mississippian period.

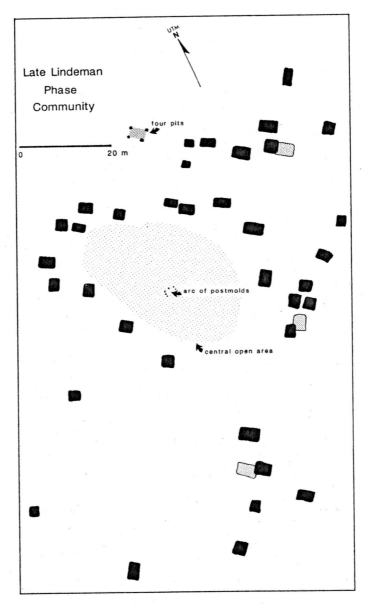

Figure 8.14. Later Lindeman phase settlement plan, Range site. (Kelly 1990a, fig. 43, p. 105. From "Range Site Community Patterns and the Mississippian Emergence," by John E. Kelly, in *The Mississippian Emergence*, Bruce D. Smith, ed., Smithsonian Institution Press. Reprinted by permission of publisher.)

Critique and Alternative Account

Kelly's interpretation of the Lindeman phase occupation as displaying an advanced hierarchical or simple chiefdom type of social system can be reinterpreted as manifesting the maximum development of a compound plaza-periphery integrated settlement articulation mode, essentially reaching the limits of this modal type. Figure 8.13 shows the central plaza as having two almost contradictory tendencies. The plaza is extremely elongated, and the major residential population seems to cluster at its northern end. In fact, much of this clustering distances many of these structures from the plaza itself. Crosscutting the plaza is almost a virtual plaza, as defined by the east-west axis constituted by the two quadripartite pits-and-post complexes and the "specialized building." As Kelly points out, this building seems to have an ancillary plaza with the two interlocking quadripartite pits-and-post complexes. Then there is the large building at the north end, as peripheral in its positioning as the specialized western building is.

I suggest that this patterning indicates that the arm's-length relation manifesting the relatively autonomous clan-cult duality within a compound plaza-periphery integrated settlement was undergoing extreme stress. The "specialized building," its associated northeast courtyards with the unique interlocked quadripartite pits, the northernmost large single-post building, the tendency for most of the residential structures to be located along the eastern side of the village and in the northeastern quarter, and the dual axes of the central plaza (the southwest-northeast axis paralleling the spatial positioning of the residential structures, and the southeast-northwest crosscutting axis targeting the "specialized building") all indicate a maximal stressing of the integrated settlement articulation mode. The multiplication of cult-based facilities and plazas could be expected if, in fact, as postulated above, this is a compound plaza-periphery community based on a cult alliance in parallel with a clan alliance, each being mutually autonomous alliances (mutualistic heterarchies) while the two sets of alliances—clans and cults—related to each other as relatively autonomous components constituting the overall village as an overarching complementary heterarchy.

If this patterning indicates that the arm's-length relation of clans and cults within a single integrated community layout was not only undergoing extreme stress but had maximized, this would be a condition that would promote the alliance of the resident autonomous cults, or certain factions in the cults constituting the alliance, to argue for a more radical form of material mediation of world renewal ritual, a form that could not be developed within the confines of the traditional integrated community. The notion of renewing the world through the construction and reconstruction of earthen platforms by which the earth could be regularly "regrown" and renewed would be an ideological innovation that, as I argue, could not be fully realized in this integrated village context. While an integrated settlement articulation mode might promote ritual, it also intensifies pollution as the community becomes more sedentary. Indeed, a fully prescriptive ceremonial sphere might be contingent on more fully spatially disengaging and distancing the cult-based ritual locales from the pollution of everyday settlement life than can be permitted in the constraints of the integrated settlement articulation mode. The result would be not a disintegration of the social system but a disengaging of the clan and cult alliances and a bifurcation of settlement into specialized and complementary clan and cult settlement modes.

The probability that this is what happened and that it is manifested in the Range site data can be demonstrated by reexamining the closing stage of the Lindeman phase occupation. Kelly suggests that the reduction in structures was a result of some of the clans moving to the Lunsford-Pulcher locale. In terms of the hierarchical modular polity account, these would be high-ranking clans, possibly accompanied by low-ranking and related "client or servant" clans. Indeed, this is how Kelly explains the obvious reduction in complexity of patterning of this final occupation stage. As indicated in Figure 8.14, all the large structures are effectively gone, and there are no peripheral structures. The ritual complexes are reduced to one set of quadripartite pits and a few post pit molds; the settlement, as he suggests, may actually have split into two.

I perceive a problem here, however. Why should a move of high-ranking families with attached lesser-ranking families be allowed to dismantle the social structure of the Lindeman phase occupation? Surely, under such a move, the ranking families would retain their position in the "rural" area. Of course, the overall population level might fall. However, to the degree that ritual patterning is treated as the medium through which the ranking families control the majority (a basic premise shared to one degree or another by the different versions of the hierarchical monistic modular polity account), the basic pattern of the community should remain constant. There should be a central plaza, smaller but with all the requisite warrants of ritual. Presumably the specialists attached to the ranking lineages and occupying the peripheral structures would still do so, although possibly in fewer and smaller structures. However, this is precisely what does not happen. The dual patterning that Kelly has recognized as emergent at least by the Dohack phase—and, if the keyhole structures are accepted as ritual facilities, even by the preceding Patrick phase—essentially disappears. The hierarchical modular monistic polity account does not explain this disappearance. Not only does it have difficulty accounting for the perceived duality that evolved, but also it cannot account for the apparent disappearance of the expression of this duality at the Range site, a duality that had been a constant theme throughout the Terminal Late Woodland and possibly earlier.

CLAN-CULT DISENGAGEMENT

Above, I conclude that the George Reeves phase occupation, G-2, exemplifies a compound plaza-periphery integrated settlement articulation mode that manifested probably two mutualistic heterarchies of clans and cults linked to constitute the community as a complementary clan-cult heterarchy. What could we expect if this compound plaza-periphery integrated village transformed as part of a regionwide bifurcated settlement articulation mode? The bifurcated settlement articulation is characterized by the clans and cults occupying distally separate and formally different locales. This bifurcation means that the clans and cults would spatially disengage. If the plaza was the result of these two mutualistic alliances (one based on kinship and the other on a dual expression of same-gender/same-age companionship) maintaining the traditional arm's-length relation by cooperative interaction, then the disengaging of these two groups would result in two different locale types. The kinship-based locale would focus on subsistence and clan reproduction; the cult locale would focus on world renewal ritual. We could anticipate that the former would be strongly domestic in orientation, with some local-level integrative institution constituting a domestic-like household with ceremonial elements. This domestic orientation would be manifested by the absence of complex plazas and world renewal ritual paraphernalia, in effect resulting in a simple clan-based village having some minimal differentiation, the latter expressing the enabling hierarchy of clan leadership.

Since the rationale for the bifurcation would arise partly from the cults' pursuit of the enhancing of world renewal ritual, then the cults might retain their mutualistic heterarchical alliances while generating locales that emphasize the plaza and its related ritual facilities. Released from the presence of domestic, agricultural-based settlements and focusing their labor on world renewal ritual, the cult alliances would probably expand the plazas and innovate new forms for mediating world renewal, such as platform mounds and temples. Therefore,

I postulate that mounds and plazas most clearly exemplify the cult locales; since these would require larger labor forces than any typical Lindeman phase occupation could mobilize, these would be the manifestation of compound cult alliances—what might be referred to as affiliations of cult alliances or mutualistic heterarchies or, more simply, world renewal cult heterarchies.

In sum, seen in the above terms, rather than the coalescence of settlements forming the complex villages of the later Terminal Late Woodland manifesting hierarchical social systems, such as simple chiefdoms, such coalescence actually mediated and manifested the initial complementary cult and clan alliances constituting complex heterarchically organized villages in the compound plaza-periphery integrated settlement articulation mode. The development of the above tendencies would also have been the condition for the transformation of the traditional communal cults into a growing set of ecclesiastic-communal cults. With these articulated by the Lindeman phase, the stage would be set for dynamic interaction among cults and within the different sectors of the cults (in particular, the laity/clergy and senior/junior age-grade structured sectors). Within this structural framework, plaza–platform mound ritual innovations would be hatched and implemented through promoting the spatial disengagement of the clans and cults.

This completes the theoretical, interpretive, and empirical background necessary to proceed with the description and interpretation of the Middle Mississippian culture of the Mississippian period of the American Bottom. I initiate the latter in the next chapter with the elucidation of the World Renewal Cult Heterarchy model. This model is specifically designed to articulate the type of social system manifested in Cahokia and the other mound locales that would be consistent with the principles of immanent sacredness, squatter ethos, inclusive territorialism, custodial domain, agentive autonomy, enabling hierarchy, and so on, these being the basic concepts underwriting the heterarchical polyistic locale-centric account of Cahokia and its associated mound locales.

9

Cahokia as a World Renewal Cult Heterarchy

As I discuss in detail in chapter 1 and subsequent chapters, the prevailing general characterization of the American Bottom social system during the Mississippian period treats Cahokia as the political seat of a dominance-based hierarchical monistic modular polity. This polity has been construed in a broad range of terms, from being an urban "Teotihuacan-on-the-Mississippi" with a four-tiered settlement hierarchy that was politically and economically dominant over a major portion of the central Mississippi Valley—if not the Midcontinent (Fowler 1997, 10; O'Brien 1989, 285–86; Porter 1969, 159; Winters 1974, 43–45), including the upper Mississippi Valley (Kelly 1982, 165–87)—to being, in more constrained regional terms, a pre-state urbanlike paramount chiefdom dominant over the American Bottom and, possibly, the more immediate surrounding region (Pauketat 1994, 183–84; Pauketat and Emerson 1997a, 19–20). In this regard, the most restrained view has been to treat Cahokia as a major player in an unstable and fluctuating system of competing floodplain-based simple and complex chiefdoms having little if any impact beyond the American Bottom proper (Milner 1990, 20–21; 1998, 12–14; 2003, 136).

While these different versions of the hierarchical monistic modular polity account recognize that religion played a role in Cahokia and other multiple-mound locales, they give it secondary relevance in characterizing the social nature of these locales, essentially subsuming the religious to the political-economic aspect. For example, while Thomas Emerson (1997a, 228; 1997c, 39) and Timothy Pauketat (1997, 31) treat cosmology and ideology as dynamic components of the development of Cahokia, they do not characterize the social organizational nature of Cahokia in these terms. In general, for them, cosmology and ideology are treated as simply important cultural conditions—the religious tools—that were manipulated by the political elite to enhance their collective and personal interests, largely at the cost of the interests of the commoners.

While Pauketat and Emerson are the most adept in their treatment of the religious dimension as a political tool, effectively all versions of the hierarchical monistic modular polity account decenter and sideline the religious dimension in characterizing the social nature of Cahokia itself, subsuming the religious to the political and economic. I consider this to be a profound mistake, because the most important step required to explain a social phenomenon is to establish its essential social nature, followed by delineating the conditions that made its emergence, reproduction, and transformation possible (Bhaskar 1978, 163–73). Therefore, if Cahokia was a locale that had religious meaning and purpose for its builders and occupants, as most archaeologists concede that it was, then the social system it manifests may be least adequately characterized in primarily political and/or economic terms. Rather, the latter dimensions must be seen as aspects of an essentially religious social system. Hence, I will reverse the privileging by treating the religious dimension of Cahokia as primary in characterizing this social system. In keeping with the deontic ecological approach favored in this book, I will here treat Cahokia as a cooperative and very active religious center of a complex mutualistic world renewal cult heterarchy, an affiliation of autonomous world renewal cult alliances that emerged out of the disengaging of complementary clan-cult heterarchical communities of the later Terminal Late Woodland period, as described in the preceding chapter.

Characterizing Cahokia and such sites as mutualistic heterarchies constructed of multiple autonomous world renewal cults dispersed across the American Bottom and, to some degree, in the surrounding uplands is certainly not to say that the political and economic dimensions are unimportant. In fact, this view recognizes these aspects to be critical to the material transformations that occurred during Cahokian history. However, in the approach I take here, the political and economic dimensions must be framed and subsumed within the religious dimension since this is the one that constituted the real social nature of the locale and therefore constituted the framework of purposes by which ideological strategies and political decisions concerning economic allocations were made possible and intelligible.

To put this in the socio-intentionalist terms discussed fully earlier, in tandem with its mound-based neighbors, Cahokia, its historical reproduction/transformation in the form of multiple mounds and their contents, the structures built on them, the plazas and their associated structures, the great palisade, the woodhenges, and the spatial distribution and directional orientation of all these monumental features would be the material conditions of satisfaction of complex, constantly changing collective prior intentions or ideological strategies. The representational contents of these ideological strategies (often opposed and competing) would have specified how all these material components must be in order for the collective behaviors they mediated to count as the types of ritual activities intended and by which the duties of the responsible groups would be regularly discharged, thereby realizing in an ongoing manner the essential raison d'être of Cahokia: namely, world renewal. That is, I claim here that Cahokia was a monumental iconic warrant of world renewal. Therefore, the political and economic strategies of its participating groups would be subsumed to and made possible only when serving and being seen to serve tactically in achieving this central, ongoing, religiously inspired and directed purpose. In short, only through characterization of a locale exhibiting the material complexity displayed by Cahokia in terms that would reflect the probable nature and meaning that it had for the groups that constructed and occupied it, can the structuring and exercising of political and economic powers of this type of social system become clear.

Of course, another social dimension must be recognized. This is the problem of reputation. I argue in an earlier chapter that reputation, both individual and collective, is a powerful motivating factor that strongly encourages responsible, autonomous human agents to act in ways that would appear to be irrational if reputation is not taken into account. Actions are the basis on which reputations are constructed. Since the assessments of actions are the basis on which character is perceived and recognized, there will be a continual and taken-for-granted collective awareness by the responsible groups that their behaviors must be performed such that these behaviors will be experienced by themselves and perceived by relevant others as proper and even outstanding conduct of the type intended. These assessments, then, constitute the reputation of the actors and their social groups.

THE WORLD RENEWAL CULT HETERARCHY MODEL

Look at the layout of a large American shopping mall. This is certainly an impressive, even monumental locale, and it certainly has a political dimension to it. However, the latter does not explain its existence and form. The economic dimension does this; therefore, the relevant defining social power that characterizes the mall and the interactions that occur there—as well as making its existence and material layout possible and intelligible—arises from its commercial nature. Furthermore, the administrative group supervising the operations of the mall, per se, does not define either its social nature or its political scope. Rather, framed by the mall's commercial economic raison d'être, the local administration can be seen as serving the economic goals of the corporate proprietors of the shopping mall via serving the economic needs of the commercial units that have tenancy rights on specific commercial outlets and, therefore, stand to the proprietors in a legal contractual relation.

What about these commercial outlets? How are they organized, and how do they relate to each other, if at all? A large shopping mall is made up of a broad range of retail establishments, specialists to generalists. Some are single, self-contained firms in the sense that the owning corporations (often family based but legal and autonomous corporate proprietors) are also located in the shopping mall, and, indeed, often the owners of these stores manage and work in them. At the other extreme, there are the dominant anchor establishments: outlets of such large firms as J. C. Penney and Sears. Still, as impressive as some of these outlets can be, any normal participant in the larger society knows that the J. C. Penney, Sears, and other large retail outlets at a major but local mall are only part of large autonomous corporations that have similar outlets in many other shopping malls.

The question to ask then is fairly straightforward. In a proprietorial system, since ownership is the basis of social powers, where do the powers actually reside that are manifested in a large and impressive shopping mall? For example, say one of the major stores is a Sears outlet. The economic authoritative power that this commercial outlet discloses in its impressive size and the rich variety of commodities certainly does not reside in either the outlet or the shopping mall. It is located in the head offices of Sears, Inc., and ultimately it is embodied in the shareholders that own it, who, for the most part, probably never actually go to any of the shopping malls where the store outlets are located. Generalizing from this, one can see that the economic power and authority manifested in shopping malls distributed across the (mostly) American landscape actually reside in the head offices of the firms that own the major outlets—and this also includes the firms that own the malls. In these terms, thinking of the local administrators of a typical shopping mall or the managers of any of the retail outlets as the "chiefs" or leaders of the entities represented at the malls becomes superficial and misleading. In social organizational terms, of course, the shopping mall is an economic heterarchy in that the participating firms are mutually autonomous, albeit, of course, ranked in terms of relative commercial wealth, power, and prestige.

If this analogy is developed further, one can clearly see that the layout of the shopping mall is governed not by political regulatory or even social status concerns but by the rationale of the merchandising strategies that are intrinsic to the social nature of this type of locale. The shopping mall is a marketing outlet of merchandising firms, and the rules of the competitive marketing game apply (among which are the relevant governmental regulatory rules, of course). The layout of the mall and its geographical location must be made sense of in these terms. For example, its geographical position is determined by a profit-directed marketing strategy that aims to maximize the number of consumer clients in terms of their spending capacity. Therefore, population size, consuming capacity, purchasing power, commuting accessibility, and so on, figure as important strategic factors. The layout of the mall can be made sense of in related marketing terms. For example, the relative position and size of the different outlets might be correlated with the marketing principle that the largest outlets serving the broadest range of consumer needs attract the largest relative number and the most diverse range of shoppers. Therefore, someone familiar with this merchandising world might anticipate that the largest and most generalized outlets will be located at opposite ends of a long corridor lined by more specialized outlets. Hence, the layout manifests a strategy by which autonomous economic outlets can share the same locale in such a way as to maximize the draw and enhance the cycling of clients. Of course, relative status rank plays an important role here. However, it is constructed on and fits the same marketing principles that govern the overall layout of the mall, in that the anchor outlets are the most prestigious and the other outlets are often literally ranked largely in terms of their spatial relations with the latter.

Even as competitors, outlets selling the same type of products can benefit from being in the same shopping mall since this strategy entails the tactical understanding that potential shoppers will know that the choice will be wider and prices will be governed by the "hidden hand" of economic competition. At least that would appear to be the dominant ethos underwriting the economic activity of buying and selling in a capitalist, "free market" society. However, there is another "hidden hand," this being the rules governing the pursuit of reputation, which is critically important to any free-market marketing strategy. Therefore, the forms, sizes, and layouts of the individual outlets will be partly determined in these same commercial-marketing terms, thereby reinforcing the reputation of the firms that are represented in the different malls.

In the shopping mall context, however, there is a third, more concrete "hidden hand," one that is usually deliberately tucked away out of public sight. This is the local administration of the shopping mall. Its presence is made known in the persons of service personnel, security officers, cleaners, and so on. However, if a shopper wants to talk to the administrative "powers," for example, the mall manager, most would be at a loss to know exactly where to go. The administrative offices are generally assumed to be on the premises, somewhere, but the administrators might prefer to be rather invisible to most shopping clients while, of course, also avoiding using space that could be more profitably used for commercial outlets. Seen in terms of the particular nature of the shopping mall, this tendency toward being publicly invisible is not at all puzzling, even though the administration has and exercises real if limited political power within the confines of the shopping mall and the system of contracts that it implements and manages.

Furthermore, while most shoppers would have no problem agreeing on the relative commercial rank of the different outlets in the shopping mall, only the employees in each case are really concerned about the chain of command that governs the operations of the individual stores and outlets. Even the largest outlet has no or at least very limited regulatory power with regard to the shoppers. Its power with regard to the administration of the shopping mall may be largely a function of the economic standing of the firm that owns it. When the manager of the local outlet of a national department store complains to the mall manager that the level of cleanliness and neatness of the public corridors is deteriorating, any rational shopping mall manager will take this seriously, and so on.

Now imagine the multiple mounds making up Cahokia, including Monks Mound (the single largest pre-Columbian construction north of Mexico), as being a multiple set of "outlets" of mutualistic alliances of autonomous world renewal cults distributed across the American Bottom. Rather than constituting an economic mutualistic heterarchy, of course, Cahokia would constitute a religious mutualistic heterarchy of autonomous world renewal cults, themselves organized into alliances. Therefore, each cult may have its "head office" in its own district, which, in fact, may be quite distant from the locale of the cult alliance to which it belongs. Indeed, a cult may be in alliance with a number of other cults in other districts of a region, and a given alliance might act as a collective custodian of a lesser mound locale, such as the single-mound Lohmann site. Several such cult alliances in this sector of the American Bottom might have historically cooperated in building and acting as the collective custodians of the Lunsford-Pulcher site, a more southern multiple-mound site. Other affiliations of alliances in the upper sector of the northern expanse of the American Bottom might have cooperated in a similar manner, with one affiliation of alliances building Mitchell, another building East St. Louis, and so on. In short, Lunsford-Pulcher, Mitchell, St. Louis, and East St. Louis might also be thought of as world renewal cult heterarchies constructed by separate mutualistic affiliations of regional alliances of individual autonomous cults. If this is the case, then the social power that was responsible for the building and using of each of these district single-mound and regional or sectoral multiple-mound sites would have actually been distributed across the landscape and located in the multiple autonomous cults of the region, the latter being the basic constituent components of this extensive system of mutualistic heterarchies. Indeed, individually, these autonomous cults might be rather archaeologically invisible, occupying small nonmound sites that nevertheless displayed the requisite features, facilities, and artifactual residue required for their own local ritual practices.

The shopping mall and Cahokia share an important social property in that both are mutualistic heterarchies in the sense that the constituent components of each relate as autonomous organizations having and recognizing each other as having the same nature: retail outlets and world renewal cults, respectively. While the term *mall* might be appropriate in referring to the shopping center, it becomes inappropriate in application to cult alliances (for example, by referring to the complex aggregation of cults as a world renewal cult "mall"). I thought of using the term *acropolis* or, more simply, *cult center,* except that immediately this terminology contradicts the structural nature that the shopping mall analogy is intended to highlight, namely, that the real power manifested in Cahokia and the other multiple-mound locales resides not in these massive locales but in the cult locales distributed in the countryside.[1] Lacking a better term, I have chosen to speak of these multiple-mound locales as world renewal cult heterarchies, emphasizing the mutually autonomous nature of the basic constituent cults. Another difference that is important to underline between the shopping mall and the affiliation of cult alliances is that while the relations among the constituent units of both are heterarchical in nature, in most cases the individual components of the shopping mall are internally organized as dominance hierarchies while the cult alliances are internally organized as enabling hierarchies, as postulated under the Autonomous Cult model.

The value of the shopping mall analogy, therefore, is not in drawing parallels to the substantive or essential social nature of Cahokia but in showing how a complex monumental locale can manifest and be the material outcome of a power structure that does not reside in that locale but instead resides in the constituent autonomous groups—in this case, autonomous cults distributed across the American Bottom landscape and, in all likelihood, in the nearby uplands. This distribution would characterize these locales as constituting essentially a heterarchical social system in which agentive autonomy would be the ruling ethos-value and consensus would be the governing decision-making mechanism.

This analogy makes it possible to think of several cult alliances being affiliated with the express purpose of building and using monumental earthworks, such as Monks Mound, for collective world renewal ritual purpose, while the constituent units of these alliances—the individual autonomous cults—actually have their own locales distributed across the countryside. To carry out this religious activity requiring the symbolic pragmatic mediation of monumental iconic warrants, the constituent autonomous cults would constitute a recognized alliance and pool their resources to set up and maintain a local Cahokian "outlet," if you will. This would be one of the lesser sets of Cahokian mounds with associated plazas, ritual structures, and residential quarters (such as the Kunnemann Group, the Merrell Group, the Powell Group, and other such groups described in the next chapter) and presided over by local "managers" drawn from the different cults making up the alliances and mandated by their respective alliances to represent their interests by managing activities that conform to these interests. Therefore, they would be responsible to administer their alliances' affairs at Cahokia (or East St. Louis, St. Louis, and so on). Each would make sure the precinct quarters of his/her alliance were properly maintained, the cyclic world renewal rituals were performed, the training of initiates was carried out, and the required labor resources as provided by its constituent autonomous cults were allocated according to consensual decisions. They might be responsible to supervise the alliance's local farm fields in or around the precincts of Cahokia, constructing and repairing the alliance's quarters that would be occupied by members in transient residence, organizing the long-distance expeditions to procure the required ritual resources (such as shells from the gulf area, galena from the Ozarks, copper from northern Michigan), administering to the special needs of the alliance's skilled, probably shamanic-like artisans, and so on. All this would be carried out in cooperation with other cult alliances that together would constitute an affiliation of alliances as the responsible custodians of world renewal cult heterarchies such as Cahokia or East St. Louis, and so on.

Of course, the resident administrators would very likely not work alone. Rather, they would be working participants of councils made up of peer-chosen representatives from every constituent level of the cult structure, including senior to junior age-sets, as well as the shamanic clergy and their constituent units organized by seniority and specialization. Therefore, the work of the councils at any given heterarchy would be continuous, and a critical part of this work would be ensuring the smooth cycling of members of the autonomous cults from their different base locales in the countryside to the "outlets" in Cahokia, supervising the training, initiation, and promotion of members, as well as ensuring the discharging of all the economic duties of the cult alliance—in particular, ensuring that the entitlements in terms of food, residential quarters, specialized clothing in the form of ritual garments, masks, weaponry, and so on, were both produced and/or exchanged and then distributed to each member participant according to her/his standing in the cult.[2] Among the resources that would be collected and then distributed according to entitlements would be selected cuts of deer and elk. It is well recognized that this type of food was consumed in the multiple-mound locales while being essentially absent from the diets of those in the countryside (L. Kelly 1997, 86–88). This distinction is often cited as evidence in support of the hierarchical monistic modular polity account, claiming that only the elites of Cahokia had access to such select forms of high-protein food. However, in terms of the World Renewal Cult Heterarchy model, such a diet would be characteristic of young men who, as transients residing for the duration of their duty schedules in the bachelor quarters of their respective cult alliances at Cahokia, would be expected—possibly as part of their cult training—to conduct hunting expeditions in the uplands to acquire foods of this type by which the cults could ensure that both the hunters and their Cahokian-bound companions—male and female, junior and senior—received the appropriate subsistence entitlements. This deer and elk meat would not be a sign of privilege, as such, but would serve as the basis of ritual feasts, and some of these feasts might have prescriptions stipulating that only such meats were appropriate for these particular rites. In short, the administrating councils of the different cult alliances working in affiliation with each other at Cahokia would cooperate to ensure that the large-scale ritual that required collective cooperation could be properly performed.

In this regard, Pauketat (2002, 157) has recently reported on the excavations he supervised of the large sub–Mound 51 borrow pit, commenting on the massive amount of debris indicating the residue of ritual feasts:

Aside from some possible domestic refuse, the pit contains a rich, dense assortment of broken pots, finely made items and production debris, pigments, crystals, shell beads, tobacco seeds, red cedar branchlets, chippage from red cedar and bald cyprus woodworking, oak and hickory firewood, numerous fruit, squash, and starchy seed, and a narrow range of the meaty portions of deer, swans without wings, large fish, prairie chicken, and the like. Our conclusion is that this pit contains feasting debris. . . . Extrapolating from the analyzed samples to estimate a total zone volume produces insights into the scale of feasting. There are portions of between several hundred to 2,000 deer and pieces of between hundreds to thousands of broken ceramic pots in each of three discrete single-event zones! The tobacco seeds possibly number in the millions.

He uses these data as grounds for his claim that Cahokia was a hierarchical paramount chiefdom. In contrast, the very same data can be equally or even more coherently accounted for as the outcome of the type of large-scale collective ritual that cooperating cult alliances of a world renewal cult heterarchy would produce. Of course, by choosing the phrasing "equally or even more coherently," I am suggesting that adjudicating between these alternatives will require additional empirical evidence, which I present in subsequent chapters.

Analogies are limited and, if pushed too far, can be misleading. For example, usually a shopping mall is owned by a firm that is separate from the firms that rent the retail outlets. In effect, there is a landlord-tenant relation at the core of the shopping mall. This would not be the case for Cahokia and other multiple-mound locales. As postulated above, the affiliation of cult alliances would be the collective custodians, and each alliance would be represented by its in situ councillors. That is, the administrating councillors of each of the constituent mound-plaza complexes, while answering to their respective cult alliances, would locally (and as part of the affiliation of cult alliances) cooperate together to oversee those aspects of Cahokia that were of central and common interest. There would probably be three major foci of cooperative operation: (1) the overall layout of Cahokia, particularly agreeing on the procedure by which each alliance selected the location of its facilities, mounds, plazas, and so on, in relation to the total site; (2) the central precinct, including Monks Mound, the Grand Plaza, the associated mounds, and the palisade; and (3) the woodhenge complexes. This means that the political-administrative structure of Cahokia would be a rather direct expression of the structure of alliances that participated in it.

However, there is the possibility that some of these local Cahokian officials could achieve some relative autonomy from the alliances and the autonomous cults that constituted them. In particular, while much of the construction, use, and operation of Cahokia would manifest a form of cultural knowledge and know-how that all the cults would be expected to have, some of the knowledge and know-how would be esoteric, requiring membership in a specialized sodality. I am here thinking in particular of the special nature of the ritual know-how most probably associated with celestial cycles (for example, the solar cycle, the lunar cycle, the mapping of the movement of special "stars," possibly even the oscillation of the Milky Way, and so on), as well as the myths associated with them. All this esoteric information would require intense and planned training to make sure that this knowledge and know-how was maintained from one generation to the next. A group of specialists of this sort would be particularly responsible for the material constructions that were perceived as iconic representations of these celestial phenomena, such as the sacred central plaza posts and, in particular, the great woodhenges. Because of their special symbolic pragmatic know-how in this critically important domain, this group might have constituted a relatively exclusive sodality able to leverage special autonomy for itself and use this autonomy to expand its influence in Cahokia, actually challenging and constraining the autonomy of the constituent cults. This possibility, along with the empirical evidence to support it, is discussed in some detail later in the book.

What all this means is that we cannot use the relative sizes of the mound locales as a measure of rank or standing of the constituent groups that were responsible. This is not to claim that, for example, participating in the largest multiple-mound locale—Cahokia—was not important in determining the standing and reputation of a cult in the American Bottom. Clearly, it would be, and all cults could be expected (and most would want) to participate in Cahokia through one or another alliance. However, we can assess the overall standing of an autonomous cult only if we can identify its base locale and compare this base to similar locales. I suggest above that these base locales would not be marked by mounds. I assume that those nonmound cult locales that are the most impressive in terms of number and variety of structures, ritual artifacts, and so on, probably had high standing in the American Bottom. This assumption is logical because the reputation of a given cult would be based on the effectiveness of its world renewal ritual, which would in turn be contingent on having the required material resources as symbolic pragmatic devices. Therefore, a basic minimum of the latter would be necessary. Building reputation, however, would have required reaching beyond local world renewal ritual and actively cooperating in regionwide ritual practices. This is why cults would typically cooperate in alliances. Therefore, an autonomous cult that had a greater-than-average quantity in the range of symbolic pragmatic devices constituting its base locale (such as large communal structures, more than the normal number of storage facilities, sweat lodges, ritual ceramics, exotics in the form of galena, hematite, and so on, all of which are critically important for constituting ritual) clearly would have this "surplus" only if it had already discharged its alliance responsibilities. To do the latter would have required investing adequate labor and material resources in the ritual operations of its alliance at the world renewal cult heterarchy or heterarchies in which it participated. Since it was maintaining a respectable presence in one or more of the cult heterarchies where cooperative ritual had its greatest renewal impact and, therefore, had its greatest payoff in reputation for its responsible cult, having a base cult locale that was larger and more complex than average would confirm its overall standing and reputation.

What this means is that the largest multiple-mound locale, Cahokia, was probably the most important for determining the reputation of autonomous cults. However, those who resided there and managed it cooperatively would not occupy the highest-ranking positions of their cults, because the local administrative councillors would be selected by their peers, and they would therefore come from across the status levels of their respective ecclesiastic-communal cults. Of course, their work at Cahokia would probably be an important part of their cult careers by which their personal reputations were constructed. Because of the transient nature of residence, however, a small and probably more senior grouping of these administrative councillors would probably come to be rather permanent residents, thereby acting as the primary source of cultic continuity in a social environment that was constantly changing as most participating members cycled between their cult heterarchies, their individual cult locales, and their domestic clan locales. However, these senior permanent administrators would probably be rather middle ranking in overall cult position since the primary decision making of a cult would be made in its own locale in the countryside.

In sum, in archaeological terms, to find the source of the social power that was manifested in Monks Mound, the Grand Plaza, and the multiple mound/plazas that were widely clustered around them, we have to look away from Cahokia and search the countryside of the American Bottom (and possibly of the uplands), where the responsible autonomous cults would be distributed in their base locales. As suggested above, the multiple-mound locales as heterarchies may have been ranked in terms of relative prestige, but with respect to each other, they would have been mutually autonomous, being of the same social nature. Therefore, while Cahokia was probably the most prestigious of the multiple-mound locales, it had no authority over the others. In these terms, I am postulating that East St. Louis, St. Louis, Lunsford-Pulcher, Mitchell, and Cahokia were competing world renewal cult heterarchies, and what they were competing for was reputation as the places where the most effective and important world renewal rituals were performed. At the same time, however, at a deeper level, seen as a network of world renewal cult heterarchies, they were also cooperating in a common and universal endeavor, this being to perform world renewal ritual that would collectively enhance the cosmos.

OVERVIEW OF THE AMERICAN BOTTOM MISSISSIPPIAN PERIOD SYSTEM

To complement the World Renewal Cult Heterarchy model and round out this discussion, I should add the overall characterization of the American Bottom heterarchical social system as postulated under the Dual Clan-Cult model. Since the cults and cult alliances that were responsible for Cahokia and its neighboring multiple-mound locales were mutualistic heterarchies with respect to each other but relatively autonomous organizations with respect to the parallel clan organizations, they would sustain an arm's-length relation with the latter networks of mutualistic kinship alliances that were distributed across the American Bottom in their dispersed villages. This means that even though there would be a great deal of membership overlap, the clans were not answerable to the cults, and vice versa. Of course, the clans and lineages would have their own ritual sphere to maintain, focusing on all the practices by which to ensure their continuity, marriage alliance ritual, funerary practices, birth rites, and initiations, not to mention the rich repertoire of midwifery ritual embedded in hunting, fishing, and agricultural practices. No doubt there would be ongoing gifting of material contributions by the clans to the cults to reciprocate for the world renewal rituals that the latter performed. Related to these contributions would be negotiations concerning the financing that clans would undertake to have the local cults, male- and female-based, accept their youths for initiation and training. In general, the clan-cult negotiations that mediated these economic relations would be strongly qualified by the fact that the negotiators were members in both organizations.

I noted earlier under the Dual Clan-Cult model and the Autonomous Cult model that these negotiations would be required as a result of a group of young companions (that is, same-age/same-gender youths) selecting a cult to join. Once accepted by a cult, a group of youths would embark as an age-set on the process of training, involving ordeals, sacred quests, and so on. This process would take the group of companions through a series of steps, from the lowest as initiates, to the senior adolescent age-grade rank, to the junior adult age-grade rank, and finally, after possibly a total of twenty to twenty-five years, into the senior age-grade rank. At this point, rather than remaining in the cult, many of the members who had survived to this age (forty to forty-five years old) would probably retire from active service, possibly participating only in major ritual cycles. There would usually be several in a given age-set who stayed active as senior leaders of the cult, thereby ensuring that the next generation was properly inculcated. All these years of cult participation would be paralleled by full participation in their clans as sons, daughters, husbands, wives, senior generation fathers and mothers, grandparents, and so on. Those companions who retired from their cults on reaching the senior age-grade level would, of course, devote much of their time and efforts on clan, lineage, and family duties, using their old companions who remained active in the cults as contacts to encourage acceptance of their own sons or daughters, grandsons or granddaughters (as the case might be), as new members.

In effect, this division of labor between clan and cult would mean a constant moving of persons back and forth between cult and clan locales. This movement would be staggered across the landscape so that, except at special ritual events, there would be essentially a constant, although punctuated, occupation of both domestic and cult locales. I elaborate on this cult structuring and the impact it would have had on settlement later, but it entails a form of mobile sedentism in which cult locales would typically be occupied by transient occupying members. Pauketat (2002, 153–54; 2003, 42–43, 48) has argued, particularly focusing on Cahokia, that we should expand the range of groups that could have participated in the mound locales of the American Bottom. He suggests that migrant populations established themselves in the nearby uplands and, while residing there, contributed their labor and resources to the upkeep and development of Cahokia. I am quite amenable to this suggestion. I can even accept the possibility that these communities set themselves up in integrated villages, such as at the Halliday site or the Hal Smith site, while those living there who constituted upland autonomous cults allocated their ritual energies between local upland-based and American Bottom–based ritual locales.[3] Later I examine the new data on these Lohmann and Stirling phase upland mortuary and nonmortuary sites and the relation that the occupants of these sites may have had with the world renewal cult heterarchies of the American Bottom floodplain.

In sum, under the World Renewal Cult Heterarchy model, the major monumental components of Cahokia represent an aggregation or, more adequately conceptualized, an affiliation of alliances of autonomous ecclesiastic-communal cults. In this regard, I have suggested that the so-called second-order or second-tier centers—St. Louis, East St. Louis, Lunsford-Pulcher, and Mitchell—were recognized as having the same social nature as Cahokia. Therefore, rather than being subordinated to Cahokia, all were cooperating in the collective world renewal task while, of course, they were competing with each other, striving to ensure that the ritual performed in each of their contexts was seen as equally felicitous as (or even more felicitous than) that being performed at Cahokia. The competition was in pursuit of reputation and not of political power or economic wealth per se. The participant cults of each world renewal cult heterarchy would perceive the total set of such locales as a network of *axes mundi* mediating human-cosmos interaction, and the self-identified duty of each cult would be to fulfil its custodial responsibilities by performing its world renewal ritual in a manner that all would see to be felicitous. As I suggest in an earlier chapter under the Mourning/World Renewal Mortuary model, this would include postmortem and even, possibly, lethal human sacrifice.

If a cult at one heterarchy perceived the cults at neighboring heterarchies as slackening, it might decide to shift some of its resources to one of these neighbors, either through assisting in the ritual construction of one of the established cult alliances or initiating a new construction program after negotiating with the alliances that were already there. These negotiations might not simply be a matter of organizing the provision of labor. A cult might claim that it could introduce a new form of ritual that would enhance the world renewal outcome. That is, these would be essentially ideological negotiations with factional disputes occurring within cults, across cult alliances, and among the affiliation of cult alliances that constituted a world renewal cult heterarchy. Although the individual autonomous cults located in a district would probably not require mounds as the bases of their ritual structures, if they allied, it is likely (although this would not necessarily be the case) that the alliance would construct at least one mound as part of serving the raison d'être of the alliance, this being to enlarge the beneficial impact of ritual on the sanctity of the surrounding landscape.

In this world, since direct material intervention in the natural order would count as direct intervention into the sacred structures of the world, the magnitude of warranted construction (that is, construction having a controlled and desired sanctifying effect) would be part of the strategy to enhance the beneficial impact that humans could have. However, even this would have ideological implications since mound construction itself entails a major form of intervention into the natural order. Although this would be warranted as sacred construction, there would be ongoing differences of opinion fueling arguments concerning the layout, spacing, and even magnitude of these earthworks and related constructions. This ongoing ideological debate over the appropriateness of the architectural design would be couched in contrasts, each contrast being the basis for polarizing particular ideological positions and the rallying of opposing factions, requiring factional negotiations to resolve. I develop the factional aspect of the World Renewal Cult Heterarchy model in chapter 16, referring to it as the Ideological Cult Faction model.

CONCLUSION

The World Renewal Cult Heterarchy model constitutes a major deconstruction of the current views about the nature of Cahokia and similar multiple-mound sites and a reordering based on recognizing their essential social nature as world renewal cult heterarchies sustaining active interrelations across the American Bottom and even in the nearby uplands. Such deconstruction requires considerable empirical grounding, which I initiate in the following chapter, first by giving a summary description of Cahokia as it is currently known, relying particularly on the work of Melvin Fowler. However, his work also sets the theoretical basis of the hierarchical monistic modular polity account. Therefore, this summary description will be used to initiate a comprehensive critique of this account, starting with his interpretation of Cahokia as a structure of kinship-based subcommunities organized hierarchically. This chapter will be followed by a chapter summarizing the interpretation of the so-called rural settlement pattern of the Mississippian period recently proposed by Thomas Emerson (1997b, 174–75; 1997c, 73–79, 148–78), in which he clearly characterizes the countryside settlement pattern as a "rural" extension subordinated to the paramount chief seated at Cahokia. Following my critique, I recharacterize the social nature of these same data in terms that reinforce the World Renewal Cult Heterarchy model, arguing that, for the most part, these make up the locales of the individual autonomous cults that constitute the world renewal cult heterarchies. I then turn to a summary and critique of the interpretation of the American Bottom Mississippian mortuary record. The mortuary record is of such special importance, however, that it will require several chapters, one giving an overview, another dedicated to summarizing Mound 72 and its associated contents and context (Woodhenge 72), and a third addressing the upland mortuary data, showing how the heterarchical polyistic locale-centric account can more effectively assimilate and interpret these data than can the alternative hierarchical monistic modular polity account. With the critical grounding of the World Renewal Cult Heterarchy model completed, I will return to the task I initiated at the end of chapter 8, namely, characterizing the nature of the Terminal Late Woodland period–Mississippian period transition, referred to by Pauketat (1997, 31; 2002, 152) as the "Big Bang" in the American Bottom.

Cahokia as a Hierarchical Monistic Modular Polity

A Critical View

The term *downtown* is used by most American Bottom archaeologists to refer to the "core" of Cahokia, which consists of both the central precinct of Cahokia and the set of mound-plaza complexes that immediately frame it on the north, east, and west sides (Pauketat 1998, 1). The central precinct, as such, consists of Monks Mound, the very large central space to its immediate south now generally called the Grand Plaza, and the large ancillary mounds that frame the latter on the east, south, and west sides (Figure 1.4). In the late Stirling phase, the central precinct with its great mounds and the Grand Plaza was framed by a large timber curtain wall (often called the palisade) built along the east, south, and west sides (Figure 10.1). Although there is no direct evidence that the palisade actually was extended along the northern base line of Monks Mound, thereby closing off access to the central precinct from the Cahokian floodplain, many archaeologists assume or argue that it was; indeed, in Figure 10.1, the timber curtain wall is indicated as if it actually had been built. Melvin Fowler is quite frank about the lack of evidence: "*There is no evidence to date of a palisade along the north side of Monks Mound*, but it is probable that such a north wall did exist. Thus proposed, the palisade enclosed an area of approximately 83 hectares (205 acres) with 18 mounds inside the wall. In the north-central portion of this enclosed area was Monks Mound" (1997, 189–90, emphasis added). Given the size and extent of this timber curtain wall, and the fact that it had a series of regularly spaced timber structures attached to it (usually referred to as "bastions" or "watchtowers"), many if not most archaeologists accept that this monumental feature served a defensive function. Fowler, for example, states, "It is obvious from the bastions, or watchtowers, that the palisade was for defensive purposes, but it also defined or delimited the central precinct" (Fowler 1997, 193).[1] He goes on to specify that he prefers to treat only the central precinct, that is, the area that the palisade actually incorporates, as the "downtown" of Cahokia, which he clearly considers to be a city: "The area within the palisade undoubtedly was not only the seat of

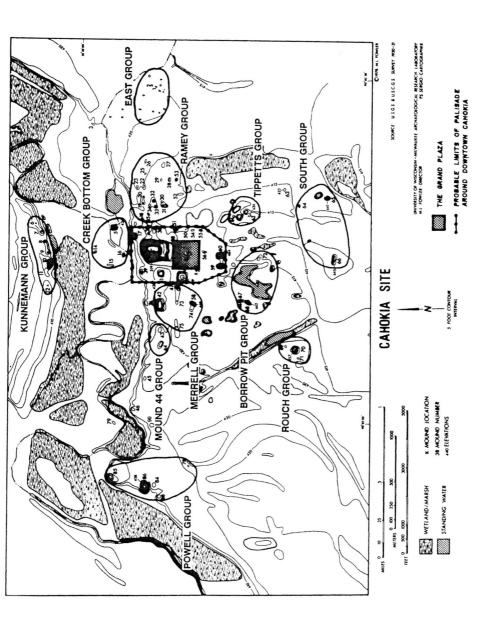

Figure 10.1. Cahokia plaza-mound groups. (Fowler 1997, fig. 10.1, p. 194. Courtesy of the Illinois Transportation Archaeological Research Program, University of Illinois.)

power but also the residential area for Cahokia's elite. This area has often been referred to by archaeologists working in the region as 'downtown' Cahokia. ... I prefer to retain this term only for the palisaded portion of Cahokia proper. It was also the central city in the sense of being the focus of community activities" (Fowler 1997, 193).

Accordingly, the central precinct consists of at least four categories of monumental features: the great mounds that define it, including Monks Mound; the great timber structures that were built and often rebuilt on top of the platform mounds in tandem with the construction of new mantling strata; the Grand Plaza; and the curtain wall, also called the palisade. There is no doubt that the Grand Plaza was itself the outcome of a major construction project (Dalan 1997, 93, 96–97; Holly et al. 1997, 233). This is because it is probable that the first terrace of Monks Mound was constructed using fill that was taken from the zone to its south. This created a large borrow pit. The construction of the plaza, therefore, entailed refilling this borrow pit. This was done starting with midden earth and then using sterile earth, probably procured from more distant parts of the site, thereby completing the upper surface area. The timber curtain wall was also the outcome of a major construction project, repeated several times. Assuming that the curtain wall actually was four-sided, William Iseminger and colleagues (1990, 35) have estimated that it and its associated bastions would have required at least twenty thousand mature trees. Many of these would have been procured from the upland zone, brought to the site, prepared, and then placed in the deep wall-trench that was the foundation of the wall. Initially constructed in the late Stirling phase, the feature was rebuilt and/or extended at least three times, the second construction occurring in terminal Stirling–early Moorehead time, and the third and fourth reconstructions in the Moorehead phase (Iseminger et al. 1990, 31, 148).

Such terms as *downtown, central city, palisade, central precinct, elite residences,* and so on, are not socially neutral. They presuppose a particular characterization of Cahokia as a unitary settlement with an internal rank-ordering of the constituent communities, or subcommunities, in terms of the position of their mound-plaza groups relative to the privileged central precinct. Indeed, this is precisely how Fowler proceeds, interpreting the spatial patterning of the mound-plaza groupings outside the central precinct as a concentric series of satellite communities constituting the subcommunities of Cahokia. The outer satellite ring of subcommunities is composed of five clusters, which he numbers I through V, and the inner satellite ring of subcommunities is composed of six clusters, VI through XI (Figure 10.1). Group I is the North Group, or, as it is more often termed, the Kunnemann Group. This is a linear cluster of eight mounds on the north bank of Cahokia Creek, directly opposite Monks Mound on the south bank. Group II is the East Group, composed of Mounds 1 and 2 and other lesser features. It constitutes what is generally recognized as the eastern extreme of Cahokia. The South Group, or Group III—directly south of Monks Mound and anchored by Mounds 64, 65, and 66—is conventionally recognized as delineating the southern extreme of Cahokia. It is subdivided by Fowler into eastern and western subgroups: the former consists of Mounds 64 and 65, along with associated lesser mounds; the latter consists of Mound 66, or Rattlesnake Mound, with associated Mounds 82 and 83, which are small conical mounds. Rattlesnake Mound is the largest ridge-top mound earthwork of Cahokia. It is oriented east-west. The two small associated conical mounds, 82 and 83, Fowler suggests, were perhaps the locales of sacrificial rites dedicated to high-status burials in the Rattlesnake Mound, although, according to Fowler's report of excavations by Warren K. Moorehead, no burials were actually noted in these small conical mounds.[2] Fowler notes, "Rattlesnake Mound, and its associated dedicatory mounds, is such an unusual feature of the site due to its shape and positioning that it must be considered a special-function area. It may be a marker mound for the north-south axis of the site" (Fowler 1997, 197). The rest of the mounds of this group—the most distinctive being Mound 64 and Mound 65 (paired ridge-top and platform mounds)—are east and slightly north of Rattlesnake Mound (Mound 66), along with nearby Mounds 63, 80, and 81.

Southwest of Monks Mound and more than one kilometer north and west of the South Group is the Rouch Group, or Group IV. Mound 70, one of the largest mounds in Cahokia, is a well-defined platform mound. Mounds 69 and 71 (north and west of Mound 70, respectively) are small mounds of indistinct form. Well over one kilometer northwest of Group IV is Group V, also termed the Powell or West Group. This group is conventionally treated as the western limiting marker of the Cahokia site. The Powell Mound (Mound 86) is the most prominent feature of this cluster. It is a large east-west ridge-top mound. The Jondro Mound (Mound 78) is about five hundred meters southeast of the Powell Mound. Although Fowler includes Mound 78 as part of the Powell Group, he also suggests that Mounds 78 and 85 are so far from the Powell Mound that they might be isolates.

The clusters forming the inner satellite ring of subcommunities are, of course, closer to "downtown" Cahokia. John Kelly (1996, 101–6; 1997, 146–47) argues that each of the clusters immediately bordering the east, west, and north sides of the central precinct has a central plaza. On the north side is the Creek Bottom Group, or Group VI, made up of Mounds 5, 13, 14, 15, and 16. On the immediate east side and outside the palisade is the Ramey Group, or Group VII. It is the largest cluster, made up of at least twenty-one mounds (including many platforms and conicals, some in association), and, in total, surrounding a four-hectare open area that also is probably a plaza. The Tippetts Group (Group VIII) is southeast of the palisade. It consists of Mounds 61 (platform), 62 (conical), and 95 (ridge top). These are located beside the large Borrow Pit 5-2 and make an inverted L-shape. Mounds 61 and 62 are placed in a north-south alignment and are connected by a causeway, and Mound 95 is due east of 61. As Fowler (1997, 198) observes,

> Extending northeast from Mound 62 is a peninsula into the borrow pit. This tongue of higher ground terminates in a square area with the sides oriented to the cardinal points. The square is about 35 meters ... on a side. The center of this square is at the geometrical center of the Tippetts group. This peninsula is a deliberately constructed feature and served as the plaza for the Tippetts group. Both Moorehead and recent surveys suggest that there is extensive habitation to the north of the Tippetts group.

The Borrow Pit Group, or Group IX, is made up of five mounds on the edge of the largest borrow pit, Borrow Pit 5-1. There is no evidence of a community, or a clustering of structures, associated with this group, but according to Fowler, "because of the special characteristics of some of the mounds in this group, it is possible that the area around the borrow pit and south of the stockade may have been a special-use area rather than a community per se. In this regard it might be compared to the Mortuary Precinct inside the palisade" (Fowler 1997, 199). Fowler divides the Borrow Pit Group into two subgroups: Group IXa and Group IXb. Group IXa consists of Mounds 72 and 96. He has established by excavation that—besides the fact that Mound 72 contains the most complex of the known Cahokian mortuary deposits, including over 260 burials—the two mounds are part of what is possibly the earliest of the Cahokian woodhenges. Fowler (1991, 6–9; 1996, 40–45; Fowler et al. 1999, 141–55) refers to this as Woodhenge 72.[3] Associated with these two mounds is the small Mound 94, about 250 meters north. Group IXb is a set of three mounds west of Borrow Pit 5-1. These are Mounds 67, 68, and 93. The first two are a paired set (a conical and a platform mound, respectively):

These two mounds are on a north-south axis and appear to have been built on a connecting platform. They are nearly identical to but smaller than Fox (60) and Round Top (59) . . . [and] are also probably representative of a charnel-house and burial-mound complex. . . . [Two] hundred meters . . . west of Mound 67 is Mound 93. The contours defining this mound are irregular but suggest that it may have been oriented with its long axis northeast–southwest. The relationship of Mound 93 to Mounds 67 and 68 and Borrow Pit 5-1 is very similar to the arrangement of mounds and borrow pit in the Tippetts group (VIII). This includes being built around a borrow pit. (Fowler 1997, 199)

The Mound 44 Group, or Group X, is located on what is called Tract 15A. It consists of Mounds 43, 44, 91, and 92. These are situated so as to make up a small seventy-square-meter plaza west of Monks Mound. This is the smallest known plaza-mound cluster, but it is among the best defined of these subcommunities. Mound 44, the largest of the group, is a rectangular platform mound. Fowler comments that the others are small and poorly defined in form. The plaza area was systematically surface collected and indicated little debris. In contrast, the area east of Mound 43 had a rich residue of domestic materials. Here, Fowler comments that, according to Moorehead's report, this indicated a "village." Excavations west of Mound 44 also revealed an extensive residential area. This was occupied probably in the early Mississippian period (Lohmann phase), and then it was transformed in the Stirling phase into the plaza for most of the well-known woodhenges of Cahokia. Fowler notes, "However, some of the Woodhenges may have been contemporary with the Mound 44 group. Thus, Group X includes four mounds around a plaza, a habitation around this mound grouping, and sun calendars or Woodhenges" (Fowler 1997, 199).

Finally, the last of the inner satellite ring of clusters is the Merrell Group, Group XI, immediately west of the palisade. This is anchored by the Merrell Mound (Mound 42), which is a large rectangular platform with its long axis oriented east–west. It has a second or higher platform on its southwest corner. The other mounds associated with this group are Mounds 47, 58, 73, 74, 75, and 76. About 150 meters south of the Merrell Mound is Mound 58, which is a large conical mound. Associated with it is Mound 74, a smaller conical mound (Fowler suggests that Mound 74 is probably a western platform extension of Mound 58). An east-west axis bisecting the north-south line connecting Mounds 58 and 42 cuts Mounds 75 and 47. Mound 73 is located near the center of this area. Mound 76 is a small earthwork north of the Merrell Mound and is aligned with Mounds 42, 73, and 58.

DISCUSSION

In a number of cases, these mound groups are associated with a central plaza or, in some cases, central bodies or associated bodies of water, some of them being manmade borrow pits. Fowler also points out that most of these plaza/mound complexes are associated with residential structures located to one side or surrounding them. This plaza/mound/residential association is interpreted by Fowler as a subcommunity of the larger Cahokian community. The implication is clear: those who occupied the central precinct with the dominant Monks Mound, the Grand Plaza, and the surrounding palisade constituted the political, religious, and social apex of Cahokia. Of course, since Cahokia is the largest settlement of the American Bottom, this precinct and its monumental mounds and associated mound-top structures also constituted the political and social center of the total region. Fowler states this point directly: "Any consideration of the community organization at ancient Cahokia must take heed of this fact. Monks Mound and the area around it were the center of the community and undoubtedly the seat of control. Surrounding it were points of lesser focus, the residences of lesser functionaries, and the satellite communities they controlled. . . . The area within the palisade undoubtedly was not only the seat of power but also the residential area for Cahokia's elite" (Fowler 1997, 193). This means that, in Fowler's interpretation, the social relations linking the eleven groups to the central precinct constituted a political, social, and religious hierarchy, with the leading resident of the central precinct dominating in the affairs of the total region.

Fowler also notes a chain of rather isolated and distantly spaced mounds west of the Powell Group along the south bank of Cahokia Creek. These "fill the gap" between Cahokia and East St. Louis. However, they are too widely spaced from each other to make up a cluster, and yet they are not sufficiently isolated so as to allow a reasonable division to be made that would count as a boundary between Cahokia and East St. Louis. Fowler (1997, 200) observes,

> The location of these mounds (76, 45, 46, 90, and 85) at regular intervals along the south bank of Cahokia Creek is very similar to the situation mapped by Patrick between the Powell group at the western edge of the Cahokia site and the 40 or more mounds reported by Brackenridge in East St. Louis. The highest ridge of ground in the region is along the south bank of Cahokia Creek. This was undoubtedly the major pedestrian traffic route as Cahokia Creek was the most important water route.

These isolated mounds may have served as monitoring points or way stations along these avenues leading to downtown Cahokia.[4]

Therefore, he suggests lumping Cahokia, the string of isolated mounds, and East St. Louis into a single complex. Indeed, he suggests that the northern terminus of this complex was at Mitchell, several kilometers northwest of Cahokia, and that its western terminus was actually the large multiple-mound St. Louis site on the west bank of the Mississippi River.

This suggestion picks up the same point that Timothy Pauketat has made in referring to this total, strung-out set of mound constructions with the Cahokian cluster at the center as the "sprawling Central Political-Administrative Complex" of the "sacral paramount chiefdom" of Cahokia (Pauketat 1994, 4; 1998, 1; Pauketat and Emerson 1997a, 8). This characterization is fully supported by David Anderson (1997, 250–51). However, George Milner (1990, 20–21; 1998, 13–14; 2003, 134–37) has expressed strong reservations. While Milner agrees that the mounds that archaeologists conventionally take as constituting the Cahokia site actually defined a paramount chiefdom, he sees this widespread distribution of mound complexes—such as St. Louis, East St. Louis, Lunsford-Pulcher, and the well-spaced single-mound locales forming a rough north-south chain more or less defining the linear extent of the American Bottom, and so on—as representing a complexly related and evolving set of so-called quasi-autonomous chiefdoms competing for power against each other. Some centers might have waxed while neighboring centers were waning, so that the focus of power was rarely unitary. In Milner's view, even though Cahokia was obviously the largest of these mound clusters, it may actually have dominated actively for only a rather brief period, while experiencing a long period of declining power requiring careful balancing of one upstart chiefdom off against another: "In the American Bottom, an extended period of population increase and the development of more-or-less equivalent polities culminated in the early Mississippian establishment of Cahokia as the paramount center of a regional system. Cahokia's florescence was followed by a protracted period of declining influence coupled with system decomposition" (Milner 1990, 27).

CRITIQUE

The above summary of Cahokia reinforces my earlier comments that there is a common core of all the versions of the hierarchical monistic modular polity account, whether they fall into the gradualist or the "Big Bang" rupturist category: this commonality is the notion that Cahokia was a political center with associated economic, social, military, and even religious aspects and that these aspects were not simply incidentally related but were functionally subsumed to the political. Given this view, it seems reasonable that competing simple and even complex chiefdoms would require defined boundaries. Without boundaries, how is a chief to know that his neighbors may be invading his territory? Furthermore, this political center would require a palisade, if for no other reason than to allow the chiefdom time to rally its forces should a preemptive attack by an enemy chiefdom be launched. An important mode of defense would be to treat this boundary as a frontier and set up a series of small fortified towns, each under an appointed subchief. These towns could serve as advanced surveillance stations against neighboring chiefdoms while simultaneously presencing the chief's authority among her/his people on the frontier. Therefore, we would expect a series of small, fortified towns (single mounds plus residential structures) strategically spaced from the center and in the surrounding region.

Of course, such a center/periphery modular polity could exist only in the context of other like modules. Therefore, the American Bottom should have a typical central-place patterning, which, as it evolved politically, would create several larger centers, each with its circle of lesser frontier towns. If one single political seat emerged, therefore, it should be at the center, with lesser centers regularly spaced between it and the frontier fortresses. Each of these secondary towns would also have lesser communities dispersed around it. In effect, this would be Fowler's multitiered model. In fact, while reducing the four tiers to three tiers, this is the type of pattern that Pauketat and Emerson (1997a, 8) claim is the case for the American Bottom. Emerson (1991, 236) argues that this patterning emerged in the later stages of the Terminal Late Woodland period, claiming that it characterizes the American Bottom social process for at least fifty years prior to the Lohmann phase. That is, Cahokia is the primal center, with Mitchell to the northwest, Lunsford-Pulcher to the south, and East St. Louis to the west with, possibly, an extension across the Mississippi to St. Louis. There is no second-tier center east of Cahokia.

The problem with this claim is in drawing the actual boundaries. Most archaeologists recognize (as noted above) that there seems to be no clear spacing of these mound groups, at least in the upper sector of the northern expanse, that would allow a reasonable drawing of the boundaries.[5] Indeed, as I point out above, Pauketat actually speaks of Cahokia as simply the core of the sprawling "political-administrative complex," a position that is supported by Fowler

(1997, 200–201), as well as many others. Furthermore, the secondary centers of East St. Louis, St. Louis, Mitchell, and Lunsford-Pulcher (not to mention the more southern string of centers, such as Washaussen, Maeys, and so on) do not seem to constitute the type of defensive posture that outlying political-religious-military subcenters should have. This political-administrative sprawl, in fact, is recognized by a number of archaeologists to be unique in terms of what we could expect a paramount chiefdom to look like. David Anderson (1997, 249), speaking from the perspective of the historically known paramount chiefdoms of the Southeast, notes that the total area covered by this sprawling "political-administrative center" conforms approximately to the average size of a single complex historical chiefdom in the Southeast, while also noting that such a chiefdom might have only one, or possibly two, communities with two to four mounds, at the most. Despite this disparity between the "typical" Southeastern chiefdoms with one-, two-, or three-mound central communities in territories equivalent in size to the northern expanse of the American Bottom with its more than two hundred mounds, he does not question that both had the same political, mortuary, and settlement systems. All that is different is the scale. That is, the two-hundred-plus mounds making up the central political-administrative complex of Cahokia "clearly indicate that it is the scale of Cahokia that is different not the basic political structures, which conform to that of chiefdom society, in which leadership positions were kin-based and hereditary, with ruling elites drawn from ranked classes and lineages" (Anderson 1997, 249).

As archaeologists we have to respect the archaeological data as the basis for confirming our models. If the settlement pattern data of a prehistoric social system (namely, Cahokia and the American Bottom) are uniquely different from the settlement pattern data of a known, or assumed-to-be-known, social system (that is to say, the historical Southeastern paramount chiefdoms), then how can a direct analogy between the two differing systems be made? What warrant does the archaeologist have to claim that it is merely the scale of the societies and not the social structures that are different?[6] Moreover, how can social systems having the same social structures and being based on the same subsistence technologies in equivalent environments differ so radically in scale? This is very puzzling.

In the conclusion of their analysis of the material record of the well-known historic Coosa paramount chiefdom, David Hally and colleagues (1990, 133–34) make a very important observation: "If paramount chiefdoms such as Coosa involved primarily personal relationships between chiefs and subordinate chiefs and these were largely of a symbolic nature, if paramount chiefs made few demands . . . of subordinate chiefs and their provinces, and if paramount chiefdoms were rather unstable and short-lived . . . [then] archaeological evidence of them may be virtually nonexistent." In short, this type of system (that is, a paramount chiefdom of the Coosa type, the same type that Cahokia is claimed to be) could very well be invisible archaeologically. Anderson is very aware of this study, since he cites the same paper: "The various chiefdoms making up the sixteenth-century province of Coosa located in northern Georgia and eastern Tennessee, for example, had distinctive ceramic assemblages, and the paramountcy cross-cut two major ceramic traditions, Dallas and Lamar. . . . All but invisible archaeologically, the recognition of Coosa relies as much on ethnological analysis as on archaeology" (Anderson 1997, 256–57).

Therefore, I find it puzzling that, while recognizing the radical difference between the settlement pattern of Cahokia and those of the Southeastern chiefdoms, and while recognizing that the Coosa paramount chiefdom, as such, was "[a]ll but invisible archaeologically," Anderson does not question but only reiterates that "the basic political structures" of Cahokia and these historically known Southeastern social systems were the same in that they "conform to that of a chiefdom society, in which leadership positions were kin-based and hereditary, with ruling elites drawn from ranked classes and lineages." I can only conclude that what is exhibited here is the tyranny of the hierarchical monistic modular polity account.

Setting aside this question for the moment, we can turn to what is visible archaeologically at Cahokia. With the possible exception of the Grand Plaza and its surrounding palisade, Cahokia, as such, seems to be poorly designed and laid out for its purported role of a political capital having a strong military aspect. The subcommunities that Fowler describes are spaced hundreds of meters and even in some cases more than a kilometer apart. If they were closer together, not only would they be in a better situation to give each other military support should they be attacked, but also the different groups would be able to display and claim their relative ranks more effectively by having their mounds within clearer comparative viewing distance of each other. Furthermore, while defense is important, equally or even more important is the need for internal surveillance in a centralized paramount chiefdom. A chiefdom hierarchy is constituted by positions occupied by those who share the same substantive authority as the paramount chief. Thus, lower chiefs often perceive themselves as having the same powers as higher chiefs, the only difference being their lower rank-position. For this reason, a paramount chief typically maintains a careful and ongoing surveillance of the activities of the lesser-ranking chiefs. The most efficient way of doing this is to require the residences of the subchiefs in the paramount's capital to be close to the paramount chief's residence, from which the latter can keep an eye on their comings and goings to ensure that no plots are being hatched. When the subchiefs are not in residence at the capital, they are often required to leave close kin in the paramount's capital, effectively as hostages to their good conduct.

As an extension of this line of argument, Jon Muller's (1997, 275–76) view is noteworthy. In his opinion, one of the several primary functions of these multiple-mound sites was to incorporate mortuary facilities for the housing of the bones of the ancestors of the paramount chief. Drawing on the funerary view, which I have commented is widely used by proponents of the hierarchical monistic modular polity account, Muller notes that the point of these charnel structures was for the ruling chief to use the bones of his/her chiefly ancestors to validate his/her authority. Indeed, Muller claims that this is such a critical function that a ruling chief would normally prevent lesser chiefs from building similar facilities in the paramount center:

> Since there was such importance to mortuary remains as validation of power, probably even to targeting the rival's ancestors in his or her 'temple' for destruction, it would be surprising to me if the ruling chief would encourage or even allow the construction of (mortuary-related) mounds at locations under his or her authority ... [and] because of the clear threat of rival claims by the subordinate 'chiefs' ... there would seem little reason for the paramount or central chief to have assisted the local personage in making the assertion to authority that a mound usually, and nearly universally, represents. (Muller 1997, 275–76)[7]

Certainly, under the logic of the hierarchical monistic modular polity account, this is a reasonable argument. A number of the mound-plaza subcommunities of Cahokia did indeed have mortuary components. Therefore, under this account, one can quite legitimately anticipate that, as the seat of a paramount chief, Cahokia should have a mortuary sphere that is strongly spatially constrained. To the degree that the postulated paramount chief could not prevent the construction of such facilities, it would be politically strategic that he or she would ensure that their siting allowed for close surveillance and tight control of their use, so that the proper priority of mortuary ritual was accorded to his/her own ancestors' remains. Hence, I can add the necessity of monitoring and controlling the rank-order of the mortuary ritual by the paramount chief to the above political-surveillance function to reinforce the claim that these sub-communities should be tightly focused spatially, as much as possible within the central precinct, rather than being dispersed over a fourteen-square-kilometer area.

Finally, this brings me to the large and complex timber curtain wall and bastions that effectively defined the boundary of the central precinct. I have already commented that the plaza and curtain wall were monumental features in their own right. The timbers of the wall were placed in a wall trench and spaced fairly closely together. They averaged about 30 centimeters in diameter and must have extended at least twelve feet aboveground, if not more. The bastion timber posts were similar in size. Also, extralarge posts were set at strategic points in the bastions, probably as extra support for upper floors. A similar tactic was used along the curtain wall, although there the larger posts were more widely spaced; it is likely that these were simply to reinforce the wall itself. Iseminger and colleagues (1990, 31–32) comment that the bastions were spaced regularly, probably about 20 meters apart. They were relatively small and circular (3.5 meters in diameter) in the initial Stirling phase construction. In the subsequent reconstructions, the bastions were rectangular and larger. The first rectangular bastions were attached to the timber wall, forming closed gorges, probably having small passageways as entrances from the plaza side. The later bastions had open gorges, that is, they were open on the inner side of the wall facing into the plaza. Less regularly spaced than the bastions, apparently, were L-shaped or screened gates that gave direct access into the central precinct. As noted above, several findings—the bastions, the L-shaped defendable entrances, the extent of the wall, and the presence of arrow points near the location of the curtain wall with damage of the type characteristically caused by hitting wood or bone—have led to the conclusion that the primary purpose of this construction was defensive, although, as Pauketat argues in Iseminger et al. (1990, 148), it would also have been touted as a major expression of the concern of the paramount chief for the well-being of his people, since they would be permitted to take refuge in it during military attacks.

When Fowler proposed that this extensive timber curtain wall probably fully enclosed the central precinct, the only direct evidence of its existence was a series of excavations demonstrating the eastern and southeastern extension of this wall. Therefore, he had to postulate that, in fact, there were western and northern walls, while admitting that at that time no concrete evidence existed to support this claim. As he essentially noted, the latter claim rests largely on (1) the logic implicated in characterizing the known curtain wall with bastions as a defensive feature and (2) some aerial photographs that showed soil markings on the west and north sides that may have indicated the buried remains of similar timber curtain walls (Fowler 1997, 190). More recently, however, Mary Beth Trubitt (2003, 155) has reported on excavations that clearly indicate the existence of the proposed western wall (see note 1). Therefore, while Fowler's postulate of a northern wall has not been confirmed, his claim that there would be a symmetrical western wall balancing the eastern wall has been confirmed.

As I note earlier, the absence of concrete evidence of a northern east-west curtain wall is generally recognized. Iseminger and colleagues (1990, 29) also point out that some archaeologists have suggested that such evidence will not be found, owing to the erosion of the ridge overlooking Cahokia Creek. They also comment that others have suggested that no wall will be found because it was never necessary, since the fall-off into the Cahokia Creek floodplain would have been an adequate northern boundary. I do not find either claim to be convincing. James Anderson (1969, 93–95) summarized the excavations that he made in an attempt to trace a northern curtain wall. In the aerial photos mentioned above, a distinct line that looked promising was shown to run along the base of the north side of Monks Mound. However, Anderson pointed out that this was a former farm road. Furthermore, he actually traced the eastern curtain wall to its northeastern extremity, "where it turned slightly to the west and terminated. Excavation to the north and west produced several features including east/west wall trenches. A test pit . . . midway between Monks Mound and Unit B did not reveal a continuation of this trench" (Anderson 1969, 94–95). Furthermore, while Trubitt has reported on the recent excavations that revealed the west wall, she also commented that part of the total ongoing project was to locate evidence of the north wall (Trubitt 2003, 155). While reporting on finding residue of the west wall, she does not comment on whether any excavations actually were made to find the north wall. Presumably this will be attempted later. In any case, it is clear that at the time of her report, there was still no evidence publicly available of a curtain wall closing off the north side of Monks Mound from the Cahokia Creek bottom that it overlooks.

In the light of both Trubitt's report and, especially, James Anderson's excavation, the claim that erosion of the ridge eliminated evidence of the wall is not convincing. If erosion had occurred, such that the residue of an east-west northern curtain wall had been destroyed, this erosion would also have encroached on the residue of the northern terminus of the eastern curtain wall so that this residue would abut the fall-off edge of the ridge. Thus, there would be no bending "slightly to the west," nor would there be any land "north and west" of the "east/west wall trenches" revealed by Anderson's excavation. In short, not only was Anderson unable to find any indicators of a former curtain wall along the northern base of Monks Mound, but also what he did find suggests that, in fact, no such wall ever existed.

If we look farther afield to other Mississippian sites that display the residue of curtain walls with bastions, a similar three-sided open pattern is evident. For example, Lynne Goldstein and John Richards (1991, 197) have provided nineteenth-century plan maps of the layout of Aztalan in the upper Mississippi Valley. This is a well-known site that is contemporaneous with Cahokia. According to their illustrations, the Aztalan curtain wall forms a large C-shape with the open side overlooking the river bottom. It also has regularly spaced bastions, and, as in the Cahokian case, the Aztalan palisade was expansively rebuilt. Similarly, in a review of the history of the archaeological investigations of the Linn-Heilig site on the Mississippi floodplain in Union County in southwestern Illinois, Charles Cobb (1991, 57–59; also 1989, 86) comments on the illustration of this site he derived from Thomas Perrine's 1873 report for the Bureau of Ethnology. Perrine pointed out that the site had an extensive embankment earthwork that partly surrounded it. The earthwork was about four feet high at that time. Cobb adds the comment that this earthwork was probably simply the foundation of a "palisade wall." He also notes, however, that there was no embankment in the northeastern corner of the earthwork overlooking the local Clear Creek, but he added that this creek "likely served similar defensive purposes" (Cobb 1991, 57) as the embankment and postulated curtain wall and bastions. As mentioned above, Aztalan also had bastions (probably similar to those on the palisade around the central precinct of Cahokia), and the Linn-Heilig embankment had regularly spaced short extensions almost mimicking bastions. If Cobb is correct and this embankment was the foundation for a timber wall construction, then these embankment projections could have been the foundations for bastions.

One should also note that the same open-sided curtain-wall-with-bastion pattern has been recognized at the Angel site (Black 1967, 54–55; Green and Munson 1978, 313, 322), at the Kincaid site (Muller 1978, 282), at the major Southeastern Moundville site (Knight and Steponaitis 1998, 4–5), and at Etowah (King 2003, 78–79). In all cases, the open side overlooks the river or floodplain. In short, there seems to be a distinct pattern here—namely, when a curtain wall exists, it is three-sided, and the open side overlooks the local creek bottom. In one case, Moundville, an argument can be made that the drop-off from the plaza to the river bottom (about seventeen meters, according to

Knight and Steponaitis 1998, 2) is sufficiently high and precipitous to have served as a natural defensive wall. In none of the others, however, can this argument be convincingly made, since the drop-off either is only a few meters or is absent because the site is at the river level (for example, the Angel site and Etowah). The apparent absence of a northern curtain wall along the base of Monks Mound, therefore, is not only not unique, it seems to be typical.

Since there is no current evidence that there was a fourth side to the Cahokian palisade (despite active attempts to establish its existence), whereas there is abundant precedence for the absence of a fourth side in other major Mississippian sites, I conclude that in all probability there never was a northern wall at Cahokia. In fact, the enclosed palisade proposal largely arises from the logic of the hierarchical monistic modular polity account and the expectations generated by this account; that is, modular polities based on exclusive territories often must defend their capitals since the seizure of the political center counts as the conquest of the surrounding land. Therefore, palisades, stockades, or fortresses built around their main centers and/or at strategic points on the boundaries or frontiers are part of what is usually required for such defense.

I want to stress here that none of this critique should be construed as a claim that polyistic locale-centric social systems lack a coercive aggressive posture. This is certainly not the case. However, when this posture generates military institutions, their organization and expression will be consistent with the range of needs of the groups occupying the locales, such as Cahokia. Under the World Renewal Cult Heterarchy model, since these groups are postulated to be cult sodalities, they do not, in general, have any need to defend territory. That is to say, even should a locale be seized by an enemy, this would have no impact on the deontics of the usage of the surrounding land. Therefore, as I comment below and elaborate in later chapters, one can logically postulate that the warfare conducted by world renewal cults would be geared to their ritual needs, namely, procuring resources that, as perceived under a sacrificial ideology, were required to mediate this ritual; very possibly, a leading resource would be the procuring of victims for lethal sacrificial offerings. Indeed, I argue in more detail later and empirically ground the claim that lethal sacrifice was part of the Middle Mississippian way of life.

This postulation of the ritual basis for warfare—combined with the size of the wall, its ongoing repair and reconstruction, the presence of projectile points indicating hostile use, the regularly spaced bastions, the defendable entry gates, and so on—means that, despite my claim that there probably was no northern wall, I have no problem accepting that one of the functions of this elaborate curtain wall was military defense. However, because this elaborate and costly construction had one open side, it probably had more than military functions to fulfill. Indeed, assuming that it served the military needs of a world renewal cult heterarchy, the other and probably more central function of this monumental feature would be ritual in nature, and this would account for the absence of the northern wall. If so, then the imperatives presupposed by this ritual function would have a strong effect on qualifying the forms of aggressive behaviors that both attackers and defenders would be required to carry out in order for these to be constituted as the type of military conduct that the two parties took themselves to be performing. Another way of putting this is to treat the absence of empirical data for a northern curtain wall and the presence of the rest of the wall and its associated features and artifacts (for example, bastions, defended entries, and spent projectiles) as the opportunity to explore the symbolic pragmatics that must have been realized in a C-shaped or U-shaped curtain wall such that, despite the absence of a northern wall, it could serve as both a military and a ritual medium.

The open-sided nature of the palisade directly overlooking swampy bottomland replicates a type of embankment earthwork form in Ohio Hopewell that I have elsewhere referred to as the C-form earthwork (Byers 1987, 60–62; 2004, 24–29). The eponymous Hopewell site in Ross County, Ohio, is an excellent example of this type. The C-form is a large embankment with the two ends terminating at the terrace edge overlooking the bottomland of the North Fork.[8] This embankment surrounded most of the numerous mounds of this site. I believe that the C-form, however, is older than Middle Woodland and is found in several examples in the lower Mississippi and tributary drainages. It is also found as the primary embankment associated with the Toltec Mounds site, although this is clearly a Late Woodland period site (Sherrod and Rolingson 1987, 37). The parallels between the orientation of the C-form embankment earthwork and the large timber curtain wall are striking: both have open sides overlooking the nearby bottomland, and both incorporate major mounds. I have argued that the Ohio Hopewell embankment earthworks were monumental iconic symbols of the cosmos under the solar aspect. In effect, the earthworks were taken to embody the sacred powers immanent in the vertically structured framework of the cosmos. On the grounds of the stability of the deep structures of Native American cosmology, I propose to extend the general sense of this interpretation to the great timber feature of Cahokia, which, for the moment, I will assume was an open timber C-form.

In principle, treating the great timber curtain wall with bastions as a sacred

C-form palisade that was both an iconic representation of the cosmic frame and a military feature is not contradictory. The Aztecs built a massive wall around the central sacred precinct of Tenochtitlan. This wall, termed the Serpent Wall, encircled the pyramid-platform temples that were the residences of the major Mesoamerican deities, especially the Templo Mayor, the great pyramid that supported the dual temples of Huitzilopochtli (the patron deity of Tenochtitlan) and Tezcatlipoca (one of the twin sons of the creator gods, Ome Tecuhtli and Ome Cihuatl). The plaza encircled by this wall also contained the pyramid-platform temples of a number of the other important deities, including the circular pyramid-platform of Quetzalcoatl, the twin brother of Tezcatlipoca. These were carefully arranged with respect to each other and important horizon celestial turning points. The great Serpent Wall that encircled this central plaza was understood by the Aztecs to embody the sacred powers immanent in the framework of the cosmos, the Cipactli beast that the twin sons of the creator gods tore asunder, throwing one half up to create the heavens and the other half down to create the underworld. Thus, the great Serpent Wall transformed the central plaza and the pyramid-platforms it contained into a monumental icon of the cosmos (Townsend 1992, 116–22; Van Zantwijk 1985, 198–206).

Of course, while the Serpent Wall had important symbolic pragmatic value as an essential monumental icon for transforming the central precinct of Tenochtitlan into the cosmic stage so that collective behavioral repertoires, such as the infamous massive lethal human sacrifices, would count as the type of collective world renewal rituals intended, it could also serve as a military defense wall. However, this defensive function was probably not its primary symbolic pragmatic point for the Aztecs. Although we can never witness Cahokian ritual, the combination of great mounds, Grand Plaza, and monumental C-form timber wall with bastions is very reminiscent of the great Serpent Wall of Tenochtitlan and its associated pyramid-platform-temple complexes. To extend the parallel, not only would the wall have served as a critical symbolic pragmatic device of world renewal ritual, including the bastions as both ritual stations and military posts, the mounds and plaza that it partially surrounded may also have been under the custodial care of different and autonomous cults or, more likely, cult alliances, each specializing in sacrificial ritual performed to enhance the powers of one or another sacred aspect of the cosmos associated with the particular mound.

However, all analogies have their limits. In this case, the very scale of Monks Mound suggests that it was unique among the other mounds within this postulated sacred C-form palisade. While the other mounds may have been under the custodial care of separate and autonomous cult alliances, the singular nature of Monks Mound would have made it the custodial responsibility of all the affiliated cult alliances that were responsible for constructing and occupying Cahokia. That is, I postulate that no single cult or cult alliance was responsible for Monks Mound, the Grand Plaza, and the great sacred C-form palisade. Their magnitude, centrality, and complexity recommend treating them as the collective responsibility of all the affiliated cult alliances that participated in Cahokia, as postulated under the World Renewal Cult Heterarchy model. The logic of this proposal arises from the model itself. It also suggests looking at the total layout of the mound clusters of Cahokia in these terms, as I do later in chapters 16 and 17.

This discussion illustrates the importance of how we characterize the social nature of a locale. For example, if Cahokia is characterized primarily in political terms, then the curtain wall becomes a palisade that is missing a fourth wall, thereby creating an anomaly. As I point out above, attempts to dissolve the anomaly rely on claims that the natural ridge would have substituted for a timber wall (which is certainly a questionable proposition) or that the wall had been built but that unfortunately its residue was destroyed by erosion (an equally questionable proposition, given known excavation results). However, if we characterize Cahokia primarily in religious terms, not only can the anomaly be dissolved quite easily, but also doing so gives us new insight into this cultural world since, if Cahokia is treated as a major world renewal cult heterarchy, the C-form timber wall can be accounted for in ritual as well as military terms and the former will also define what type of aggressive behavior will count as felicitous military acts.

This means that the curtain wall's fundamental meaning was of the same symbolic pragmatic order as the mounds and plaza that it (almost) surrounded, namely, as a monumental icon of the cosmos. Hence, the absence of the northern wall was deliberate, implicating the conclusion that leaving the northern side overlooking the floodplain unblocked was among the conditions of satisfaction for the curtain wall to count as the sacred C-form palisade that it was intended to be. A monumental ritual icon also having a military function, then, implicates a military posture directed toward achieving religiously defined goals by military means that are themselves ideologically defined. If it is accepted that the world renewal ritual was mediated by both postmortem and lethal forms of human sacrifice as postulated under the Mourning/World Renewal Mortuary model (and demonstrated in detail later), then it follows that procuring lethal sacrificial victims and preventing one's own from becoming lethal sacrificial victims of the enemy may have been the primary purposes of the military activities.

This also means that the aggression committed to procure such victims and prevent one's own members from being procured as future victims must itself be subsumed to and be a part of the ritual sacrificial process. Hence, the sacred C-form palisade implicates a highly ritualized warfare, having built-in proscriptions and prescriptions defining what forms of aggression would count as felicitous military conduct. In all likelihood, the primary rule would be that any aggressive behavior by an enemy force that engaged the defending forces of Cahokia through the "open" side of the wall would not count as a felicitous procuring of lethal sacrificial victims. Although objectively the enemy might succeed to capture, kill, and/or damage persons and/or damage property by attacking through the undefended northern "rear," the aggressive behavioral interventions would fail to achieve the primary purpose since the attackers would be flouting the constitutive rules of sacrificial warfare. Therefore, any aggressive attacks in this manner causing damage or destruction would not be perceived as felicitous religiously rule-governed military activities. Instead, such attacks would be perceived by relevant others as unworthy and dishonorable activities that were wasteful of lives and polluting to the cosmos. This interpretation not only dissolves the anomaly of the "missing" wall, but also opens up a perspective on the nature of Mississippian social life, one that is developed in more detail in later chapters.

CONCLUSION

A social system of the type postulated under the hierarchical monistic modular polity account should generate a regional settlement pattern in which there is a well-defined spatial separation between the center and its subcenters, in which each subcenter, acting as both a frontier military post and the presencing of the central authority, should have its military as well as religious structures, and where the central community should not only be the largest and most impressive, but also should be fortified in its own right and be rather compact. Indeed, the fortification should take in most if not all of the major constructions of an elite residential, religious, and political nature. I submit that none of this is the case for Cahokia and the other regional mound locales. The palisade, as impressive as it is, is too small for this defensive purpose since it does not incorporate the majority of major mounds and plazas. The great mounds of Cahokia, as impressive as they are, are too dispersed. The other mound locales (such as East

St. Louis, Mitchell, and so on), while each being impressively large in itself, are also too dispersed; moreover, although Kelly (1997, 165–66) has noted some "fencing," it seems quite inadequate to constitute the type of fortification that these mound locales should have as defensive frontier outposts. In short, if Cahokia was the center of a powerful polity of the type postulated under the hierarchical monistic modular polity account, its patterning fails to live up to the expectations that we could reasonably deduce from this account.

In accordance with the hermeneutic spiral method, the validity of the hierarchical monistic modular polity account can be further questioned by critically examining other aspects of the archaeological record that have been interpreted in terms supportive of this account and then showing how auxiliary models under the heterarchical polyistic locale-centric account can interpret these same aspects more coherently. Two of these aspects that have been thoroughly analyzed are the countryside settlement pattern and the mortuary pattern. In the next chapter I review and critique Thomas Emerson's interpretation of the countryside settlement pattern, which he claims supports the view that Cahokia was the dominant centralized power. I then interpret these same data in terms of the heterarchical polyistic locale-centric account. Subsequently, I summarize the mortuary aspect of this archaeological record (primarily drawing on the work by George Milner, Melvin Fowler, Thomas Emerson, and supporting researchers), critique the funerary paradigm interpretations that they give, and then present the alternative Mourning/World Renewal Mortuary model. These two analyses, combined with the above critique, justify my presenting the alternative heterarchical polyistic locale-centric account of the Terminal Late Woodland–Mississippian transition as the outcome of a rapid shift from a compound plaza-periphery integrated settlement articulation mode, as illustrated in the closing phases of the Range site (chapter 8), to a radically bifurcated settlement articulation mode, as most fully illustrated by Cahokia itself.

The "Rural" Settlement Pattern

The countryside settlement pattern of the American Bottom Mississippian period, this being the settlement component separate from the multiple-mound
sites themselves, has been thoroughly analyzed and interpreted by Thomas
Emerson (1992, 202–6; 1997a, 221–27; 1997b, 174–84; 1997c, 38–41, 62,
148). He refers to this countryside settlement sector as the rural component
of the American Bottom social system, and this is perfectly in keeping with
the view that Cahokia was the urban center of a dominant paramount chiefdom. In brief, his argument is that the Mississippian period population in the
countryside was organized under a dispersed village system. The dispersed village comprised a set of kin-related commoners in their individual farmsteads,
which were fairly widely spaced across the landscape in a local region and
linked together through a complex of integrative institutions located in what
he characterizes as household, civic, and ceremonial nodal sites. The household
nodal sites were the residences of the local kin-group leaders, while the ceremonial nodal sites and the civic nodal sites were the locales of rural mortuary and
fertility cults, and the local rural elite leaders, respectively. He interprets the
fertility cults as initially having their cultural roots in the communities of the
preceding Terminal Late Woodland period, while progressively coming under the dominance of the central ruling power in Cahokia. In effect, he treats
both civic and ceremonial nodal locales as the essential ideological tools by
which this paramount chiefdom came to fully subordinate and dominate the
dispersed village population of the countryside during the Stirling phase.

In contrast, I will demonstrate that the very same settlement data can be
more coherently interpreted in terms of the World Renewal Cult Heterarchy
model. As elucidated fully in chapter 9, this model characterizes Cahokia and
similar multiple-mound sites as world renewal cult heterarchies that were cooperatively constructed by affiliated alliances of mutually autonomous cults.
These multiple-mound locales served as monumental iconic media by which
the cults could collectively discharge their sacred duties. This means that the
social power manifested in these complex multiple-mound locales did not reside there but, instead, inhered in the locales of the autonomous cults, and

these were dispersed across the American Bottom and, possibly, in the nearby upland zone.

When the conditions postulated by the World Renewal Cult Heterarchy model are coupled with the conditions postulated by the Dual Clan-Cult model, we can expect to find a range of ceremonial sites acting as the base locales of autonomous cults and clearly distinguishable from the clan-based sites of everyday domestic life, in terms of both spatial separation and material cultural content. Furthermore, as autonomous cults caught up in the competitive pursuit of reputation, differential scales in the complexity and variety of these base locales can be expected, these being a measure of their relative standing among their cult peers. Therefore, I argue that the sites Emerson characterizes as ceremonial and civic nodal locales can be more coherently understood in these autonomous cult terms than in the dispersed village terms that he postulates. However, I retain the use of the term, dispersed villages, while redefining these as the local networks of household nodal and regular household sites constituting and embodying the clan system. That is to say, I argue that the nodal household sites constituted the highest level of the dispersed clan network and, further, that the spatial separation of the nodal household and nodal cult sites is perfectly consistent with the radical bifurcated settlement articulation mode postulated as generated by the disengaging of the clans and cults, as briefly outlined in the summary of chapter 8. Hence, the ceremonial nodal sites were occupied by local autonomous world renewal cults that participated in alliances that affiliated to form the world renewal cult heterarchies. This means that the nodal domestic-like households and their surrounding regular households constituted the local dispersed village occupied by the network of clans.

THE SEQUENTIAL SETTLEMENT ARTICULATION MODE

The best way to outline the relevant data is to summarize Emerson's presentation and interpretation of the "rural" archaeological record. The use of quotation marks around "rural" is deliberate on my part since this term is not social structurally neutral. A rural sector exists only in complementary opposition to an urban sector. Entailed by the urban-rural polarity, of course, is a complex social, political, economic, and cultural relationship that in general can be characterized as dominance-subordination, center-periphery, specialized-generalized, ruling elite–subordinated peasantry, and so on. This sort of polarization is what Emerson means, of course, since the data as he presents them are taken to register the imposition of political, economic, and specialized ritual (ideological) institutions on the countryside by the urban elite to govern and regulate a concomitant mass of rural commoners. Although the regulation of the commoners was presumably effected by Cahokian-derived religious and civic-ceremonial institutions imposing sacred duties on the rural sector, the real point of this subordination was to ensure a constant flow of corvée labor and tribute to the political center at Cahokia. The factual, almost axiomatic status that Emerson endows on this hierarchical monistic modular polity view is well expressed by him in the following: "I believe that the hierarchical nature of the Cahokia polity can be accepted as a *given,* based on the existing evidence of the archaeological record. Consequently, I assume that, in keeping with the known attributes of such societies and forms of government, the Cahokian chiefly elite emphasized centripetal control of surpluses, labor, religion, and trade" (Emerson 1997c, 188, emphasis added).

Using the new data derived from the extensive excavations of the FAI-270 Archaeological Mitigation Project, Emerson is able to modify Fowler's well-known four-tier hierarchical model. This model characterizes countryside or nonmound sites as being the lowest and undifferentiated fourth-level rural homesteads linked in subordinate relations with third-level single-mound centers, which in turn were linked to the nearby district second-level multiple-mound center, which had direct subordinate links to the paramountcy of Cahokia. Emerson terms this type of hierarchical pattern the *direct settlement articulation mode* (Emerson 1997c, 71). It treats the settlement hierarchy as constituted by two or more levels related by dominance rank and, usually, differentiated in terms of function. However, all the units of each level are homogeneous. The homesteads constitute the lowest or fourth level. The single-mound sites constitute third-level local administrative towns. The smaller multiple-mound centers constitute the regional administrative towns, with these being themselves directly subordinate to the largest first-level multiple-mound center, Cahokia.

Using the new settlement data, Emerson proposes an alternative view, which he terms the *sequential settlement articulation mode* (1997b, 174; 1997c, 71–77; see Figure 11.1). The significant difference between the direct and the sequential articulation mode, he argues, is the sectoring of the lower, nonmound level of the hierarchy into specialized political, religious, and economic loci. The economic loci consist of the primary self-supporting farming households that, although physically isolated from each other, are socially integrated into dispersed village settlements through, probably, the direct linkage with a lineage-

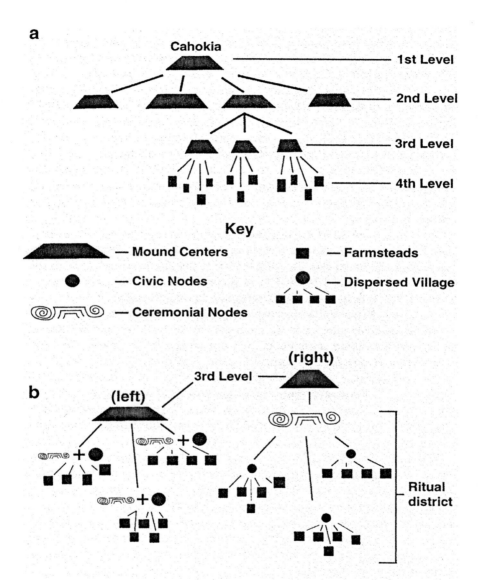

Figure 11.1. Direct (a) and sequential (b) settlement articulation modes. (Emerson 1997c, fig. 4.1, p. 72. Used with permission of the University of Alabama Press.)

or clan-type commoner leader who is resident at the local nodal household (Emerson 1992, 206; 1997b, 174–75; 1997c, 73). These sites in a local district are linked into what he terms a civic node, acting as the primary political-communal node of a district. The civic node would be under the leadership of a low-ranking elite individual appointed or at least recognized by Cahokia as the local leader. This civic node would be closely related to but distinct functionally from neighboring religious ceremonial nodes that might themselves serve to integrate a number of civic and household nodal groupings of a local district with a local regional single-mound town site. Emerson notes, "It is possible that those nodal centers may have been linked through ceremonial nodes to form a ritual district . . . of multiple dispersed villages. It was those dispersed villages that articulated with the mound center. Such systems are thought to have been operational in the Black Bottom, the American Bottom, and for the earlier settlements in the Central Illinois River Valley" (Emerson 1997c, 73).

In Emerson's model, while these religious ceremonial cult nodal locales were generally concerned with Green Corn fertility ritual, they were further specialized into temple-based mortuary-fertility cult ritual (1997b, 177). The Green Corn ceremonial nodal cult locales were in close cooperation with the civic (non-cult) nodal sites, whereas the temple-based mortuary-fertility cult nodal locales were more specialized and apparently became even more spatially and socially isolated from the local dispersed villages during the Stirling phase. According to Emerson, this growing isolation from the grass roots signified the growing centralization of Cahokian power and authority:

> One of the difficult tasks facing us is deriving some measure of the power relationships between the hierarchical levels in Mississippian society. Here I will argue that the relative strength of these cults as illustrated in the rural areas is one such subjective measure. Specifically, the ability of the elite to control the fertility symbolism and rituals at rural centers is a direct measure of their control of the rural population, and that expropriation of the fertility cult by the elite was most marked in Stirling times. (Emerson 1997a, 217–18)

In sum, this structured complex of ordinary households, household nodes, and elite-governed civic and religious-ceremonial nodes constitutes the lowest structural level of the settlement system, and Emerson refers to it as the dispersed village system of a district. He notes, "I think that the basic definition of community for a Mississippian rural family was a group of households integrated via nodal sites with their community meeting houses, sweat houses, storage structures, local leaders, and temple-mortuary complexes. This dispersed village pattern can be seen as the basic integrative unit of political/ social/religious activities" (Emerson 1997c, 184).

Ceremonial and Civic Nodal Site Analyses

Emerson specifies that while the household nodal site type would have one or two standard dwelling structures essentially similar to those of the ordinary household site, it would be differentiated from the latter by having facilities and artifacts that clearly mark it as a place for local feasting and other forms of interaction not associated with the everyday life of the typical farmstead. He uses the Julien site (Figure 11.2) to delineate the archaeological indicators of the household nodal site during the Lohmann phase, suggesting that, at least during this early phase of the Mississippian period, the household nodal site would probably have been the residence of the local kin-group leader (Emerson 1997c, 85). The Julien site had a single residential building with two adjacent limestone-floored circular buildings that may have been used for ceremonial and/or storage purposes. It had a "marker post," apparently a carryover from the Terminal Late Woodland village plaza, as well as caches of tools, exotic items, and, in particular, a relatively large number of bowls.

Emerson uses the Lohmann phase occupation data of the Range site to delineate the organizational level above the household nodal site, this being composed of two different nodal site types: civic and ceremonial, illustrated by Range ML-1 and Range ML-2 nodal sites (Figure 11.3 and Figure 11.4), respectively. These were two spatially close but, he claims, socially separate although possibly complementary sites that were aligned on a north-south axis. He interprets the southern Range ML-2 site as the religious-ceremonial nodal site and the northern Range ML-1 site as the civic nodal site. Although the latter had little debris, it had a "massive 60-square-meter, square, single-post, open-sided, roofed, communal building containing benches and cooking facilities" (Emerson 1997b, 177). Emerson suggests that large structures such as these might be "men's houses." Since his assumption is that kinship was the primary structural axis in the rural area, the implication is that these would have been used by the males of the rural lineages in the region.[1] In contrast, he interprets the Range ML-2 nodal site immediately south of the latter as serving a fertility-ritual function (Figure 11.4). This site had two rectangular structures: one in the normal residential size range and a second smaller structure that possibly had served a special ceremonial purpose. There was a "massive" rectangular pit associated with these two structures. Both the smaller structure and

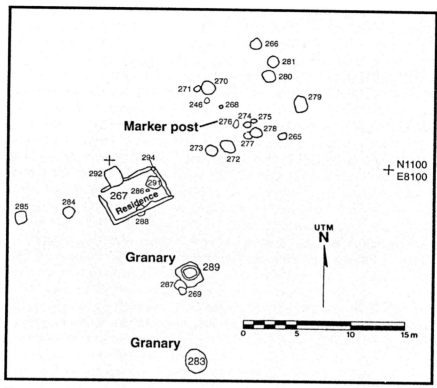

Figure 11.2. Lohmann phase Julien nodal household site. (Emerson 1997c, fig. 5.1, p. 84. Used with permission of the University of Alabama Press.)

the pit contained a large quantity and a varied range of debris that, Emerson says, reinforces the likelihood of the ritual nature of this site: exotic minerals, more than seventy vessels (some ritually broken), beads, a stone discoidal, and, in particular, remains of red cedar and tobacco. He specifically interprets the data of the Range ML-2 site as "extensive evidence of some form of religious renewal ceremony. Traditionally, such renewal ceremonies have been linked to Green Corn or Busk ceremonialism" (Emerson 1997b, 177).

Emerson goes on to stress that these two nodal sites not only had a strong communal flavor, but also seemed to be related in a complementary manner. Besides being spatially close, although socially distinct (civic and religious), the large, open-sided structure in Range ML-1 had little debris, while the structures and features of Range ML-2 had a great deal. He suggests, therefore, that "ML-2 represents the ceremonial—and religious—activity area balanced

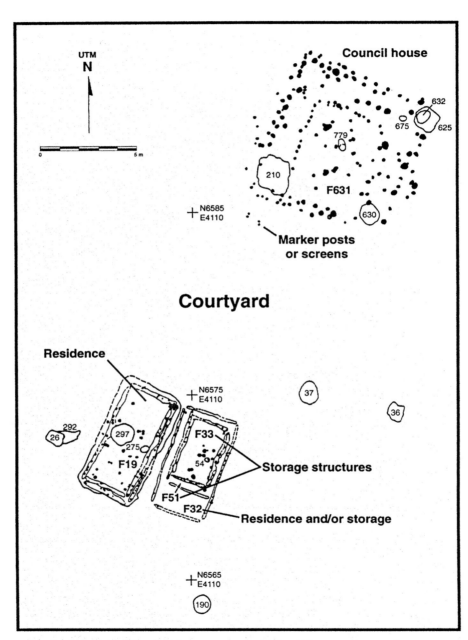

Figure 11.3. Lohmann phase Range ML-1 civic nodal site. (Emerson 1997c, fig. 5.2, p. 89. Used with permission of the University of Alabama Press.)

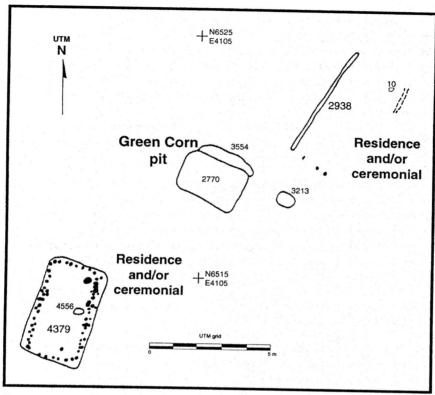

Figure 11.4. Lohmann phase Range ML-2 ceremonial nodal site. (Emerson 1997c, fig. 5.3, p. 90. Used with permission of the University of Alabama Press.)

against the civic nature of ML-1 to create a unified complex" (Emerson 1997b, 177). He concludes that Range ML-2 displays "the first clear demonstration of elite controlled ceremonial construction in the rural countryside" (Emerson 1997a, 218). He claims that these elites, although subordinate to the Cahokian authorities, were not specialists, either religious or political. Instead, they were "drawn from the local, dispersed-village civic leadership" (Emerson 1997a, 221). He stresses this point because he argues that religious and political specializations were imposed by Cahokia only at the end of the Lohmann and into the Stirling phase, as I point out below.

There is another type of ceremonial nodal site in the Lohmann phase that, while displaying similarities to Range ML-1 and Range ML-2, is also different since it has a mortuary component, a dimension that is absent from the former two. The Lohmann phase occupation of the BBB Motor site (Figure 11.5) rep-

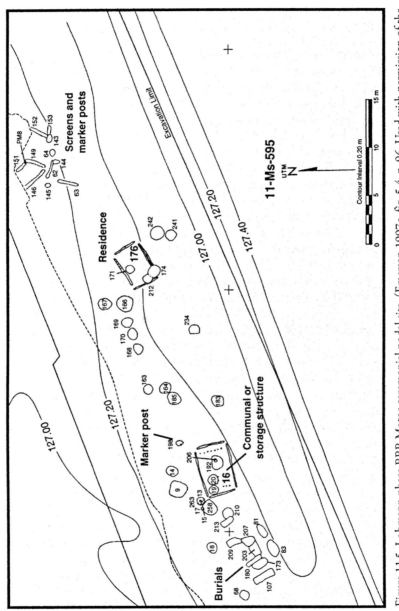

Figure 11.5. Lohmann phase BBB Motor ceremonial nodal site. (Emerson 1997c, fig. 5.4, p. 96. Used with permission of the University of Alabama Press.)

resents this type (Emerson 1997a, 221; 1997c, 79). In fact, Emerson suggests that the personal domicile of the local guardian of the mortuary locus may have been in the associated rectangular structure. Another nearby rectangular structure had internal benches, marking it for communal use, possibly related to mortuary ritual. Emerson points out that the eight or more deceased, most of them indicated only by a few teeth and some surviving long bones, have no distinctive artifactual associations. Nevertheless, because of its overall isolation and because there were both adult and infant remains in the burial locus, he concludes that this was a rural cemetery of a low-level elite lineage.

He claims that a close relation of the elites to the residents of the local dispersed villages is characteristic during the Lohmann phase, and he concludes his assessment of these Lohmann phase civic and ceremonial-fertility and/or mortuary temple–fertility nodal sites as being the primary social organizations by which the integration of the rural population into the power structure of Cahokia was effected. However, in his view, this communal orientation simply served as the basis for ushering in the greater dominance of Cahokia over the countryside in the Stirling phase. That is, he argues that the Stirling phase civic nodal locales became the seats of political (civic) elite specialists, drawing their authority directly from the Cahokian paramountcy. In parallel, the leadership of the ceremonial nodes became professional priests, drawing their authority from the monopolization of ritual artifacts (in my terminology, iconic warrants), such as the Missouri fire-clay figurines depicting the Earth Mother found at the early Stirling phase BBB Motor nodal site (Figure 11.6). The rural-elite ritual practitioners were further specialized into fertility (for example, the Sponemann nodal site) and mortuary cults (for example, the BBB Motor nodal site) with their resident priests and attendants. In Emerson's judgment,

> the Stirling component at BBB Motor indicates the existence of a full-time, organized mortuary priesthood, probably in residence at the temple. The developing complexity of the ritual paraphernalia, hallucinogenic medicines, mortuary ceremonialism (as evidenced by the grave house and corpse manipulations), and the elaborate organizational pattern of the site indicate such activities were in the hands of trained specialists. The isolated site location, size, and layout also indicates that these ceremonies were not communally oriented, or at least not for public participation. An additional argument for the presence of a specialized priesthood at this time is the recovery of shaman figurines and depictions from the graves of individuals who may have been priests. (Emerson 1997a, 223–25)

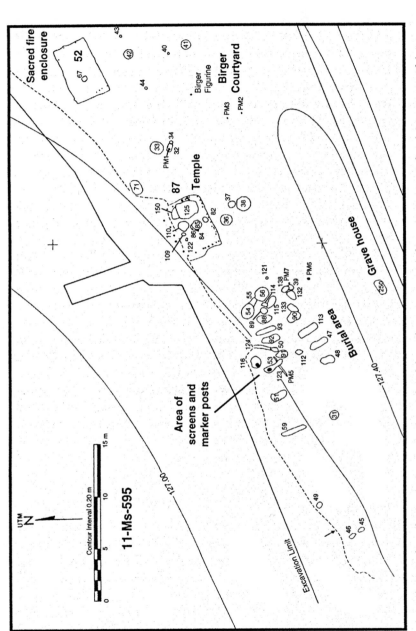

Figure 11.6. Stirling phase BBB Motor ceremonial nodal site. (Emerson 1997c, fig. 5.9, p. 116. Used with permission of the University of Alabama Press.)

Emerson also argues that the monopolization of mortuary with fertility ritual at the Stirling phase BBB Motor site indicates that the burials represented possibly a local "lineage segment of the ruling elite at Cahokia" (Emerson 1997a, 225).

Despite the fact that the Sponemann site is only 1 kilometer north of the BBB Motor site (and 4.5 kilometers from Cahokia), Emerson particularly treats the late Stirling phase occupation of the Sponemann site as support for strong and direct ties between this rural ceremonial center and Cahokia, ties that were promoted by the layout of this site, which, for him, indicates the exclusion of the local rural population from the sacred activities that occupied its priestly residents (Figure 11.7). He characterizes this site as "a large fertility cult complex complete with multiple specialized buildings, including a temple structure, storage buildings, ritual activity buildings, sacred fire enclosures, 'world renewal dumps,' benches, isolated wall trenches, and, perhaps, a large accompanying set of high-status residences" (Emerson 1997a, 225). He points out, however, that (in marked contrast to the early Stirling phase occupation of the nearby BBB Motor nodal site) the late Stirling phase nodal occupation of the Sponemann site had no associated mortuary complex.

This absence of mortuary residue from the Sponemann nodal site is interesting since Emerson argues that both mortuary and fertility rites were performed at the BBB Motor site, while the specialized fertility ritual of the Sponemann site was not mortuary related. It is important to note here that these two sites are not only spatially close, but also chronologically sequential. A resolution of this puzzle may be the simple suggestion made by Douglas Jackson and colleagues that the group occupying the late Stirling phase Sponemann nodal site may simply have moved from the early Stirling phase BBB Motor site: "A movement of such small ceremonial centers through time in this locality is evident" (Jackson et al. 1992, 215). This claim is reinforced by noting the many parallels between the two sites, including the ritual breakage and burial of flint-clay Earth Mother figurines. If this is the case, then logically we could conclude that, in fact, the BBB Motor site was not fully abandoned when the group moved to its new Sponemann site quarters. While performing some of the ritual processes at the Sponemann site, they continued to use the BBB Motor site to serve the mortuary component of their rituals.[2]

As mentioned earlier, Emerson claims that the Stirling phase civic nodal centers display only specialized political power and that this is derived from Cahokia. He cites three sites to represent the spectrum of Stirling phase civic nodes: the Labras Lake site (Figure 11.8), the Julien site (Figure 11.9), and the

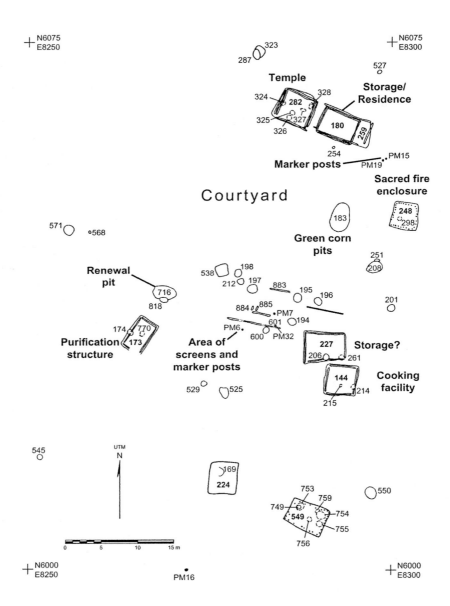

Figure 11.7. Stirling phase Sponemann ceremonial nodal site. (Emerson 1997c, fig. 5.11, p. 125. Courtesy of the Illinois Transportation Archaeological Research Program, University of Illinois.)

Range site (Figure 11.10). As he stresses, what particularly marks the Stirling phase civic nodal site is the circular sweat house. Labras Lake, the smallest and least complex of the three sites, had two sweat houses associated with three rectangular wall-trench structures organized around a courtyard with marker posts. The debris found at the site contained a Ramey knife, beakers, effigy ceramics, Ramey-Incised ceramics, a red-filmed water bottle, and some exotic minerals. All these, Emerson claims, mark it as elite based but lacking any material indication that specialized fertility rituals or mortuary rituals were performed there. Therefore, it had no ritual function, as such, and would probably have served only a political or civic function. He states, "The Stirling civic nodal sites, with a virtual absence of cult paraphernalia or symbolism, indicate the emergence of local political leadership with a political rather than cult basis" (Emerson 1997a, 225).

The Stirling phase occupation of the Julien civic nodal site (Figure 11.9) was similar to but "slightly more complex" (Emerson 1997b, 182) than the Labras Lake site, having five rectangular structures (two superimposed) and one sweat house arranged in complementary clusters on the southeast and northwest sides of the central courtyard. Again the same range of features and artifacts was found here as at Labras Lake, except with more variety: marker posts, Ramey-Incised ceramics, exotic materials, and so on.

The most complex of these Stirling phase civic nodes was Range MS-1 (Figure 11.10), which had two clusters of three rectangular structures, each oriented on a north-south axis of the central courtyard in a manner similar to the earlier Lohmann phase Range ML-1 and Range ML-2 nodal sites. The northern Range MS-1 cluster had four sweat houses. One of the rectangular wall-trench structures was very large, with a significant amount of food debris. The typical range of artifacts was found, but what Emerson considers material media of fertility and busk-related ceremonialism were absent.

All three of these sites, he claims, were clearly civic nodal centers (being politically and not religiously oriented integrative locales), whereas the BBB Motor and Sponemann nodal sites were apolitical but religiously oriented, the latter possibly having only fertility ritual functions and the former having both fertility and mortuary ritual functions (Emerson and Jackson 1984, 342). In particular, Emerson notes that, in contrast to the civic nodal sites, the religious-ceremonial nodal sites (such as the Stirling phase BBB Motor site) were isolated from the surrounding homestead sites. He writes, "It is not self-evident how such ceremonial sites articulated with the surrounding settlements,

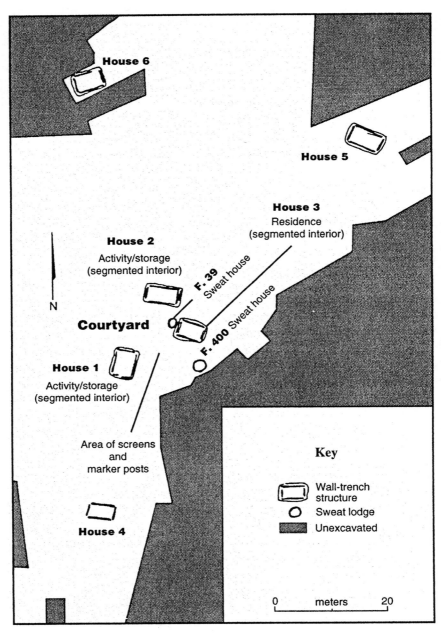

Figure 11.8. Stirling phase Labras Lake civic nodal site. (Emerson 1997c, fig. 5.6, p. 103. Used with permission of the University of Alabama Press.)

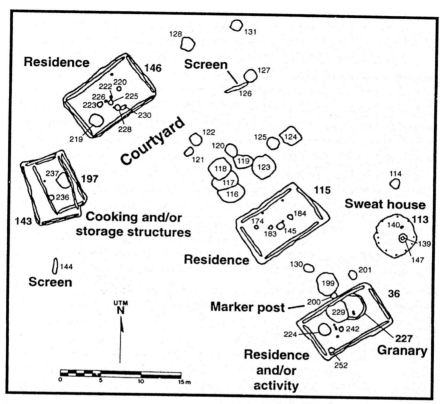

Figure 11.9. Stirling phase Julien civic nodal site. (Emerson 1997c, fig. 5.8, p. 112. Used with permission of the University of Alabama Press.)

... [but] this ceremonial node may have served as the local religious center and charnel house for more dispersed villages" (Emerson 1997c, 79).

What he considers to be the core of his model is the strong contrast between the patternings of the Lohmann phase and the Stirling phase nodal sites. He treats the contrasting elements as indicating the progressive subordination of the rural dispersed villages to the centralizing power of Cahokia. He particularly identifies the communal components of the civic and ceremonial nodal centers of the Lohmann phase as manifesting "a division between civic or cult leaders operating from a communal or cult base" (Emerson 1997a, 225), and he sees this division as having some continuity from the more communal-oriented village and town structuring of the preceding later Terminal Late Woodland period. In contrast, he claims that the Stirling phase marked a strong separation of civic and ceremonial responsibilities from the communal base, with the

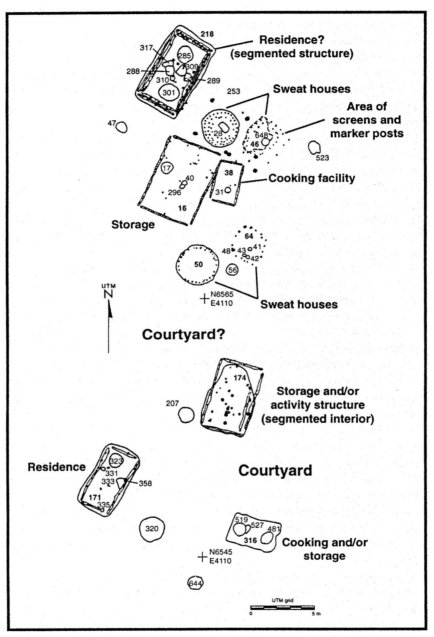

Figure 11.10. Stirling phase Range civic nodal site (MS-1). (Emerson 1997c, fig. 5.7, p. 108. Used with permission of the University of Alabama Press.)

ceremonial nodal centers displaying all the marks of a specialized, Cahokia-derived priestly cult: "The expropriation of the fertility cult [such as the BBB Motor site] as part of the dominant ideology by the Cahokian elite during the Lohmann-Stirling transition was a major ideological tool in creating and sanctifying elite sacredness and consolidating elite *power over.* The manipulation of fertility cosmology through a system of 'rites of intensification' and associated symbols of authority served to naturalize the inherent social inequality that was a major hallmark of Stirling life" (Emerson 1997a, 228, emphasis in original).

Critique

This is a complex interpretation of the "rural" social structure that manages to fit the data into the hierarchical monistic modular polity account in a manner that, to my knowledge, no one else has done. However, is it a valid characterization of the settlement patterning that could be anticipated of a hierarchical monistic modular polity? I do not think so. As I argue in the previous chapter, the paramount center of such a social system should display a rather tight settlement layout since the paramount chief would be concerned with maintaining close surveillance of the comings and goings of the lesser chiefs in the community. This concern for surveillance would be extended as a central component in the strategy to control the countryside. The paramount chief would not want the rural elites to be dispersed, and where some dispersal was necessary, he would want local centers, or nodes, to be laid out so as to be able to keep tight control on the scattered homesteads through aggregating kin-based leaders within and close to these nodal centers. Furthermore, the perspective of the community leaders of the rural commoners should not be ignored. It would be to their advantage to be physically positioned so as to have access to the local elite leaders, since these would be the patrons whom they could approach and with whom they could negotiate benefits for their kin dependents. Therefore, not only should the rural religious and political structures of the chiefdom be spatially related, but also they should be complemented by a clustering of the domestic residences of these local leaders of the commoner kin groups. This would be advantageous to the local political and ritual elite specialists since, as the surveillance arm of the paramount chief, they would be well positioned to maintain effective control over the countryside through the medium of the rural leadership occupying neighboring housing.

Emerson actually recognizes an apparent misfit between the political and social integrative needs of a paramount chiefdom and the actual physical spacing and orientation of these nodal locales, since he expresses some puzzlement that the religious-cult nodal sites, in particular, were physically and socially isolated. For example, the BBB Motor and Sponemann nodal sites "do not seem to have been communally oriented as one might predict in the case of fertility cults but instead were restricted in accessibility. This suggests that ritual access may have been limited to the rural elite—*certainly a seemingly inappropriate role for cults that characteristically act to integrate a dispersed community*" (Emerson 1997a, 227, emphasis added). He attempts to resolve this puzzle by suggesting that this restricted accessibility "is in keeping with the suggestion that many of the Stirling phase symbols (e.g., Ramey-Incised ceramics) served as much to naturalize the dominance of the elite as to integrate the social classes. . . . I suggest that this phenomenon is the result of the elite expropriation of the fertility cult as part of their centralization of power and their increased consolidation of the ritual population" (Emerson 1997a, 227).

I find this a questionable resolution, since Emerson is suggesting two separate and alternative functions for these cults. On the one hand, he comments that they served "to integrate the social classes," and on the other, that they served "to naturalize the dominance of the elite." However, surely these are not alternative or different functions? Rather, they are strategically related means and ends. The use of symbols "to naturalize the dominance of the elite" was the method to achieve and sustain the goal "to integrate the social classes." If so, then this means that the goal can be achieved only if the commoners are regularly involved in the process, namely, fertility ritual in the cult context. Of course, this returns me to the expectation under the hierarchical monistic modular polity account that, in fact, these cult locales should not have restricted accessibility, nor should the household nodal sites be spatially separate from the civic nodal sites that are deemed political.

In short, a paramount chiefdom should opt for something more akin to what Emerson refers to as the direct settlement articulation mode, even though this still allows for an overly dispersed patterning of the farming residences. Instead, Emerson argues that, during the Stirling phase, at the height of the claimed era of centralized control from Cahokia, the nodes were politically and religiously specialized and spatially separated from each other and, in particular, from the rural populations that they were supposed to be integrating. In short, the major ideological lever that the rulers of Cahokia are postulated to have been using to control the countryside—namely, the fertility cult system that the paramountcy is claimed to have expropriated from local communal control—was at the same time socially and physically isolated from the commoners.

I also find unconvincing the claim that two separate types of elite-controlled nodal locales would maintain mutual separation. It seems counterintuitive in terms of the ideological paradigm Emerson is using. Why would the Cahokia rulers benefit from separating the religious cults in their ceremonial nodal locales from the political elites in their civic nodal locales? Indeed, as noted above, Emerson alludes to his claim that the Cahokian elite-controlled distribution of Ramey-Incised ceramics was a major means of dominating the countryside since these ceramics bore cosmogonic symbols relating the rulers to fertility ritual (Emerson 1997a, 214, 216; also see Pauketat 1992, 38; 1994, 162). Each of the civic nodes displays these ceramics. The sweat houses, which he argues are particular marks of these civic centers, are generally recognized as important ritual purification facilities. Therefore, in terms of ceramics and sweat houses, not to mention the array of artifactual materials, these "civic" nodal locales are as much religious as they might be political! Importantly, Emerson fully endorses (1997a, 228; 1997c, 41, 63) Timothy Pauketat's (1994, 184) claims that the Stirling phase was characterized by an entrenching and sacralizing of the Cahokian paramount chief and chiefdom. Therefore, instead of splitting and separating the Lohmann phase Range ML-1/ML-2 complex, a dominance-hierarchical social system of the type claimed by Emerson for Cahokia should have imposed a closer cooperation of the rural civic and religious authorities so that they would support each other and reinforce the authority of the socially and spatially distant Cahokian paramount chief, thereby enhancing the control over the dispersed villages of the rural commoners.

The nature of the Stirling phase Range MS-1 complex makes the existence of the type of mortuary practices at the Lohmann phase and Stirling phase BBB Motor ceremonial nodal site particularly difficult to fit into this model. If the latter was a ceremonial-type organization similar as the one at the Range MS-1 site, as Emerson claims, why was the mortuary aspect present at the Lohmann and Stirling phase BBB Motor nodal complex and absent from the Range MS-1 complex? Mortuary practices would seem to be an excellent medium of religiously mediated social, cultural, and political dominance. We know that these practices constituted major ritual events in Cahokia at this time, and their extension to all the nodal sites would seem to be the very type of strategic move that a dominance-pursuing Cahokia would make.

There is one more puzzle that this account does not resolve: the permeability of the boundary separating the commoner domestic household sites from the elite nodal sites. Emerson, in fact, directly recognizes but does not explain this anomaly. He partly expresses his awareness of this permeability in noting the presence of domestic debris in what he recognizes to be the civic and ceremonial nodal locales. Of course, this type of debris could be explained as the result of the need to have service personnel (commoners) on duty in the elite locales. However, the social boundary supposedly separating commoners and elites becomes more problematic and puzzling in noting that exotica—such as galena, mica, hematite, select cherts, sometimes fine trinotched projectile points, shell beads, rock crystals, and so on—are found in almost every ordinary rural farmstead (although when found in these rural farmsteads, these materials always make up a very minor component). Nevertheless, as Emerson notes, "[I]t is obvious that the residents of farmstead sites had access to these materials, although the social, political, or religious mechanisms that provided them are not clear" (Emerson 1997c, 160). Despite this recognition, however, he goes on to assert that the "presence of such items . . . should not deter us from distinguishing, in the Mississippian countryside, between such small family residences and the large multibuilding, nodal and religious centers. . . . While there was variation among farmsteads, none of them reached the size or complexity of the nodal centers described here" (Emerson 1997c, 160). This is a valid comment, of course. But it avoids the problem and, in fact, simply highlights the anomalous nature of the distribution of rural exotica under this dominance-type hierarchical monistic modular polity social system. Given that the nodal sites are distinctly separated from the ordinary farmsteads, under the hierarchical view, we could legitimately expect a rather impermeable social boundary marked by a distinct absence of elite exotica from the residential sites of the rural commoners.

While I endorse Emerson's claim that these data and their patterning very effectively delineate two general categories of "rural" sites in the American Bottom of the Mississippian period—the ordinary farmstead sites and the nodal sites—the resulting interpretation is an excessively convoluted and problematic characterization of the countryside settlement articulation. Emerson postulates four nodal types for the Lohmann phase: (1) the household nodal site (the Julien site), (2) the civic nodal site (the Range ML-1 site), (3) the nonmortuary ceremonial nodal site (the Range ML-2 site), and (4) the mortuary temple ceremonial nodal site (the Lohmann phase BBB Motor site). However, he equivocates over whether the Range ML-1 civic nodal site might not be better termed a civic-ceremonial site on the grounds that it is spatially close to the Range ML-2 ceremonial nodal site, while maintaining that, in fact, they were separate types of nodal sites (Emerson 1997b, 177). For the Stirling phase, there is no more equivocating on his part: the civic and ceremonial nodal sites are distinctly different and unrelated, with one being a type of specialized political-civic and the other a type of specialized ceremonial-religious nodal site. However, the ceremonial-religious nodal sites become problematic. He divides these into two types: priestly temple–fertility (Sponemann site) and mortuary temple–fertility (BBB Motor site) ceremonial nodal sites. Furthermore, identifying the political-civic nodal sites becomes problematic since the appearance of "sweat houses" becomes central in this regard. However, Emerson admits that these facilities are widely recognized in the literature as manifesting strong ritual meaning, clearly implicating a religious dimension, while the two presumably ceremonial nodal site types, as represented by the Sponemann and BBB Motor sites, effectively differ from each other only in terms of the presence or absence of mortuary residue.

This elaborate characterization is accomplished by highlighting differences while downplaying similarities across the archaeological record of these nodal sites. Thus, differences that may constitute rather minor variants at the symbolic pragmatic level are taken by Emerson to manifest contrast at the deep cosmological and social structural level. In chapter 3 I elucidate the notion of the integrated cultural tradition, based on Searle's well-formed theory of intentionality (1983, 26–140). I have argued that the notion of integrated cultural traditions can be used to claim that quite radical, ideologically related changes in material culture can occur without entailing deep cosmological and/or deep social structural changes. Of course, such deep structural changes may arise over the long term as an unwittingly generated series of consequences of the initial surface structural changes (ideological), as is argued under the Sacred Maize model with respect to the rather sudden, widespread appearance of the dual Z-twist/S-twist cordmarking attribute. In any case, seen in these terms, rather than sweat houses or sweat lodges and Ramey-Incised pottery marking changes in the deep cosmological structures of the American Bottom cultural tradition and/or a correspondingly deep social structural change constituting the intensification of dominance over the "rural" communities, these material cultural variations over time that Emerson has delineated could simply be ideological in nature. Therefore, while certainly marking a dynamic process, these changes can be reinterpreted as simply part of reproducing and reentrenching the deep cultural and social structures of the Lohmann phase. Indeed, in chapter 17 I interpret the data in these terms.

The above claim that there can be radical material cultural changes that, as surface structural transformations, actually preserve and largely reproduce the deep cultural traditions and social structures that made them possible is particularly supported when these changes are situated within the intraphase and interphase invariances that mark this archaeological record. For example, take Emerson's treatment of the Stirling phase Sponemann and BBB Motor nodal sites. He notes that they shared the same range of figurines having the same substantive representational cosmogonic themes and that these figurines were subjected to the same type of ritual breakage and deposition. He also notes that the two sites had the same range of rectilinear structures and the same range of artifactual materials (for example, red cedar, tobacco, Ramey-Incised ceramics, crystals, galena, and other ritual-related materials). However, he treats the two sites as having different socioritual characters, on the grounds that the former lacks and the latter has clear mortuary associations. The result is that he splits what are categorically the same nodal site types into two different types of cult organizations—a priestly temple cult and a mortuary temple cult.

The claimed isolation of nodal sites from the surrounding "rural" population, the presence of mortuary components at some ceremonial nodal sites and their absence at others that would appear to be of the same order, the distribution of exotica and other "elite"-related elements across what should be an impermeable non-nodal/nodal site boundary, and the convoluted typology of nodal sites based on emphasizing differences over similarities in the archaeological record so as to map a claimed process of centralization and specialization of political, mortuary, and fertility practices make this account of "rural" social organization incompatible with what could be legitimately expected of a centralized paramount chiefdom of the type postulated under the hierarchical monistic modular polity account. I could expand on the above critique. However, the hermeneutic spiral method advocates that the best way to complete a critique is with an alternative account that resolves the puzzles and anomalies that alternative accounts raise and do not resolve. In this way, instead of simply rejecting an account and producing a knowledge stand-off or vacuum, we can make a rational choice between the different accounts, and not only is the knowledge stand-off or vacuum avoided but also knowledge is advanced.

THE BIFURCATED SETTLEMENT ARTICULATION MODE ACCOUNT

The heterarchical polyistic locale-centric account uses the very same data summarized above to generate a quite different interpretive reconstruction of the countryside social system. It accepts one central claim of the above account—namely, that there were four basic types of sites in the countryside, the regular domestic farmstead site and three nodal site types—and it accepts splitting these latter nodal sites into the household nodal site type and two nonhousehold nodal site types. However, it characterizes these nodal sites and the relations among them quite differently from the sequential settlement articulation modal treatment. These sites are treated as the manifestation in the countryside of a bifurcated settlement articulation mode based on a strong notion of relative autonomy of clans and cults such that the structure of relations constitutes the countryside settlement complex in heterarchical terms. As such, the four site types must be recharacterized as clan and cult locales, and this means that their spatial distribution manifests the traditional clan-cult arm's-length relation (as a consequence, generating the countryside aspect of the bifurcated settlement articulation mode in the American Bottom). In bifurcated settlement articulation modal terms, therefore, I draw the line between the household nodal and the nonhousehold nodal sites and treat these relatively autonomous locales constituting the countryside settlement pattern as a complementary heterarchical system. The dispersed village, if you wish, is "truncated" at the level of the region's household nodal sites and their associated regular household sites. The other, nonhousehold nodal sites in a region constitute the autonomous cult sphere.

This description is perfectly consistent with my earlier discussion of the termination of the Lindeman phase occupation of the Range site. The disengaging of the cults and clans was a key component of the process that generated the bifurcated settlement articulation mode characterized by the dispersal of the kinship residences and the formation of the mound-plaza locales. Under the World Renewal Cult Heterarchy model, I argue that the multiple-mound locales were mutualistic heterarchies formed by affiliations of autonomous cult alliances and that the social power manifested at these complex multiple-mound locales would actually have inhered in the base locales of autonomous cults dispersed across the countryside. Therefore, there should be nonmound locales that can be unequivocally identifiable as autonomous cult locales embodying a ritual sphere, and these sites should also be clearly spatially and socially separate from sites that can be unequivocally identified as embodying the clan-based domestic sphere, along with its ritual aspect. Thus, in the former sites, elements of the ritual sphere should dominate over the ordinary domestic elements, marking these as companionship-based cult sodality locales, and in the latter sites, elements of the domestic sphere should dominate over the ritual elements, marking these as kinship-based clan-type locales.

I believe that this type of distinction has been eminently well outlined empirically by Emerson's detailed description of the settlement patterning of the Lohmann and Stirling phase countryside. In these terms, instead of the nonhousehold nodal types being civic-, mortuary-, and fertility-type ceremonial nodes, they resolve into a dually structured world renewal cult system. The household nodal site that Emerson postulates as the lowest-level "commoner" integrative site, then, must be reconstrued as the highest-level kinship-based site. The nodal household sites in a local region no doubt mediated the linkages that made up the dispersed villages of a district to constitute the network of mutually autonomous clans.

Whereas Emerson's account stresses hierarchy and subordination of the ordinary and household nodal site types to the different ceremonial- and civic-type nodal sites, the key presupposition of the bifurcated settlement articulation modal account stresses the relative autonomy of clan and cult site types. This follows from the premise that autonomy is the central value of a cultural world that has a squatter ethos and an immanentist cosmology as the core deep structural components of the cultural traditions. Therefore, for cults in their nodal site locales to impose themselves in the affairs of the clans and their dispersed villages (and vice versa) would be inconceivable. Hence, the sites Emerson speaks of as civic and ceremonial nodal sites are reconstrued here as the sacred locales of autonomous cults. As noted above, these would be the basic constituent components of the cult alliances that are manifested in the spatially separated and distinct plaza-mound clusters that collectively make up world renewal cult heterarchies. Under the Dual Clan-Cult model, the population in any given district, and probably in a region, would participate in both networks. Hence, individuals would be constantly passing back and forth from one locale type to the other as their cult and clan responsibilities required. Several men might occupy neighboring households as fathers and sons, while dispersing for extensive periods, possibly several weeks or more, to different cult locales, bringing back to their clan-based home dwellings some exotic minerals or ritual ceramics for use in clan-based ritual events. Seen in these terms, the Lohmann phase occupation of the Julien nodal household site (Figure 11.2) would represent a typical local lineage nodal household, and the set of ordinary household sites dispersed along the ridges around it would be occupied by the families, either nuclear or extended, making up the local lineage. A local region's set of dispersed household nodal sites would constitute the local clan network, possibly made up of several intermarrying clans. At this point, more precise theorizing of the nature of this kinship system will not be pursued, although unilineal descent structures would be most probable. Indeed, although I speak above in terms of male lineage leaders, the lineages could be either matrilineal or patrilineal. However, I will not pursue that matter here, leaving it for future research.

In these terms, therefore, the Range ML-1 and Range ML-2 nodal sites of the Lohmann phase occupation of the Range site (Figures 11.3 and 11.4) do not constitute separate or even separate but cooperating civic and ceremonial nodal groups. Instead, the paired sites with marker posts, a "Green Corn pit," large structures with multiple single-post walls, a courtyard, communal storage pits, and residential structures (as well as multiple ceramic vessels, exotic minerals, and so on) embody a unitary social entity, an autonomous ecclesiastic-communal world renewal cult, having a world renewal lodge, the young men's quarters, the senior men's quarters (or, possibly, the resident priest's quarters), and so on. In such an arrangement, we would expect domestic debris, as the result of regular but transient residency. In some cases, selected cult members would probably occupy the locale for quite extended periods while preparing for world renewal rituals to be held at this locale, at the single-mound locale of the cult's alliance, or at the world renewal cult heterarchy with which the cult's alliance was affiliated. Other cult members would attend for shorter periods, both to participate in the rituals and, possibly, remaining for several weeks to discharge domestic duties, such as planting, weeding, and harvesting to produce food to support transient members at the alliance's world renewal cult heterarchy. A continual cycling of members would occur such that there would be constant but fluctuating occupation.

The Lohmann phase BBB Motor site (Figure 11.5) with its mortuary component would also constitute an autonomous ecclesiastic-communal world renewal cult or even, possibly, a cult alliance. It would also probably be based on companionship, with a dual age-grade structure crosscut by the laity/clergy structure. However, I will postulate that rather than male based it would probably be female based. This seems to be reasonable since, as Emerson clearly specifies, the early Stirling phase occupation of this site is rich in Earth Mother symbolism, as is the nearby late Stirling phase Sponemann site (Figure 11.7; Jackson et al. 1992, 65, 302–5). If the Lohmann phase Range ML-1/ML-2 complex nodal site and the Lohmann phase BBB Motor nodal site are taken to represent two basic types of mutually autonomous world renewal cults structured in complementary opposition by gender, then Emerson's claim that these would be specialized in the nature of their ritual is correct. However, the nature of this specialization would be different from the one that he posits. For him, the Range ML-2 nodal site was a ceremonial site in which traditional, rural-based, and (presumably) female-related green corn ceremonialism played an important role, while the cult of the BBB Motor nodal site was specialized in mortuary ritual. In contrast, I posit that the male-female complementary opposition is fundamental in characterizing these two as different types of mutually autonomous ecclesiastic-communal world renewal cults. Hence, given the mortuary component and the rich association with Earth Mother symbolism, the BBB Motor nodal type would be responsible for postmortem sacrificial world renewal ritual directed toward renewing the sacred female powers of world reproduction. As the complementary opposite to the female-fertility powers of this type of cult, the Range ML-1/ML-2 complex nodal type is posited to be responsible for ritual directed toward renewing the sacred male powers of world reproduction.

I will generically term these complementary attributes the powers of (female) fecundity and (male) fertility, respectively. These two terms, *fecundity* and *fertility,* have closely related meanings, of course. However, while fertility can refer to either male or female reproductive powers, fecundity is distinctly female related. Since the cults are postulated to be world renewal organizations, it follows that the immanentist cosmology entailed by these types of cult locales would treat the world as a complementary duality of male/female powers of reproduction. These powers would be understood as being distributed as immanently sacred properties of the different sectors of the cosmos, with one sector possessing the power of fecundity (in the sense of the capacity to become or be made pregnant) and the other possessing the complementary capacity of fertility (in the sense of the capacity to make pregnant). Therefore, the world would be divided into complementary oppositions of heavens/underworld, water/earth, north/south, east/west, and so on. Each half possesses the powers that are complementary to the powers of the other half, and the ritual union of both is required for the reproduction and renewal of the cosmos to occur and be sustained. Hence the cult system would be in parallel with the structuring of the cosmos, and the relations between the two cult types would be treated as replicating the relations that the participants understood constituted the world as a totality.

If the Lohmann phase nodal sites can be sorted into mutually autonomous cults structured by the complementary male fertility and female fecundity contrast, then the Stirling phase nodal sites can be recharacterized in similar terms.[3] Therefore, the Labras Lake (Figure 11.8), Julien (Figure 11.9), and Range (Figure 11.10) nodal sites can be treated as autonomous male-based ecclesiastic-communal cults sustaining continuity from their Lohmann phase roots. In similar terms, if the elaborate earlier Stirling phase BBB Motor nodal site is, in fact, an autonomous female-based ecclesiastic-communal cult, then so is its northern near-neighbor, the later Stirling phase Sponemann nodal site. As I point out above, part of the Stirling phase mortuary component of the BBB Motor site could actually be the residue of postmortem sacrifice initially performed at the Sponemann nodal site, just to the north, and then terminated with appropriate rituals of postmortem manipulation and burial at the BBB Motor site. In fact, Emerson and Jackson (1984, 218) report clear evidence that at least some of the deceased were subjected to defleshing before being buried. In terms of the Mourning/World Renewal Mortuary model, this is a strong sign that the mortuary practices were forms of postmortem human sacrifice, and this is fully consistent with the view that the BBB Motor nodal site was an autonomous world renewal cult locale. Furthermore, the mortuary component is itself dually structured. This could be the result of intergenerational continuity, with the late Stirling phase usage of the mortuary-related components having been kept separate from the early Stirling phase components.[4]

Resolving Anomalies

Emerson argues that through the medium of its periphery—the rural countryside—the "waxing and waning . . . [of] Cahokia's political and ideological power will be most starkly manifested" (Emerson 1997c, 36). Therefore, he accounts for the Stirling phase expansion and elaboration of these nonmound ceremonial nodal sites as the result of the specialization of political and religious institutions that, in turn, recursively expanded the power of the paramount chief in Cahokia by enhancing the elite's control over the rural producers. (I critique this claim above.) The alternative heterarchical account of this elaboration reverses the direction of power. In terms consistent with the World Renewal Cult Heterarchy model, Cahokia expanded in the Stirling phase as a result of a widespread shift in factional power within the mutually autonomous constituent cults. As I argue in detail later in chapters 16 and 17, a chronic aspect of the cult heterarchies of the Mississippian period of the American Bottom would be cult factionalism. I term these the proscriptive-autonomist

and prescriptive-centralist factions. In these terms, the Stirling phase is characterized as a period of growing dominance of the autonomist factions by their
gaining more from than they had to give up to the centralist factions. Part of
what the former had to surrender in order to enhance their cult autonomy was
to favor an expansion and elaboration of key monumental aspects of the world
renewal cult heterarchies at the cost of other aspects. In fact, with regard to
Cahokia, I argue in chapter 17 that a major focus of contention involved the
relations between those who promoted the woodhenges (in my view, representing the centralist orientation) and those who promoted the central precinct (representing the autonomist orientation). Much hinged on how these
components could be integrated so as to most effectively presence the essential
powers of the cosmos, conceptualized in terms of the reproductive powers of
male fertility and female fecundity.

In any case, I argue that the expansion of mounds and plazas, the building of
the palisade, the razing of the Lohmann phase plaza and ritual structures and
residential quarters on Tract 15A and the Dunham Tract, the abandoning of
Woodhenge 72, and the building of later woodhenges are all marks of competing autonomist and centralist factions of the mutually autonomous cults making up the heterarchical affiliation of cult alliances. While the autonomist factions prevailed, not all the changes were gains for them. Emerson (1997c, 181)
recognizes that, during the Stirling phase, the quantity and range of exotics
was reduced from the level that had been characteristic of the Lohmann phase.
Pauketat (1994, 163) also comments on "the absence or extreme low density
of copper, exotic cherts, and nonlocal minerals in [early Stirling] features" in
Tract 15A and the Dunham Tract and notes that this scarcity is corroborated
by "the similar patterns recognized in other Stirling phase assemblages associated with the Kunnemann Mound, outlying rural sites, and even [late Stirling]
15A-DT remains"; he speculates that this "may reflect a regionwide pattern of
decreased exotica diversity" (Pauketat 1994, 163–65).

Emerson resolves this anomaly by postulating that reduced amounts and
constrained distribution of such elite power-constitutive artifactual material
marks the enhancement rather than the diminution of Cahokia's centralized
power. For him, this reduction must have been the result of the elites in Cahokia imposing the need for this material to be processed by their own client-artisans. Only then could it count as having "true symbolic value." Hence,
in the Stirling phase, the reduced level of the materials from which the "artifacts of power," as he terms them (Emerson 1997c, 4), were produced comes
to define the expansion of centralized power since "the limited presence of

exotics during the Stirling phase indicates the firm control by the elite on resource distribution or, at least, on their sanctification" (Emerson 1997c, 182).
However, Emerson takes the opposite position concerning the significance of
the rather sudden widespread, effectively ubiquitous distribution of Ramey-
Incised pottery. For him, the ubiquity of these Stirling phase ceramics marks
the dominance of the Cahokian elite over the countryside. As in the case for
exotica, he claims that the power of this pottery derived from elite control
of both the client-artisans who produced it and the ritual processes through
which it was distributed. Summarizing the interpretation that he and Pauketat
gave of the substantive content meaning and the distribution of Ramey-Incised
pottery, he says that it served to mediate rites of intensification associated with
green corn (or busk) ceremonialism, "evidence for whose existence is plentiful
in Cahokia-Mississippian culture . . . [and that during] such festivals, elite distribution would result in the widespread distribution of both these vessels and
their message—a message that we argued reinforced and naturalized political
centralization and elite supremacy" (Pauketat 1997a, 214; also see Pauketat
1994, 185).

These two views concerning the distribution of "artifacts of power" seem
to contradict each other. On the one hand, both the large quantity and the
widespread distribution of elite-mediated and centrally controlled and produced Ramey-Incised pottery are claimed to mark and be the medium of the
subordination of the countryside to the dominant Cahokian elite; and on the
other, both the significantly reduced quantity and the constrained distribution
of elite-mediated and centrally controlled and produced exotica are claimed to
mark and be the medium of the same subordination. In contrast, in terms of
the World Renewal Cult Heterarchy model and the Dual Clan-Cult model,
both the reduced distribution of exotica and the widespread distribution of
Ramey-Incised pottery during the Stirling phase can be explained in mutually
supportive and parallel ideological factional terms. I detail these explanations
later in chapter 17, but, briefly stated, in the former case, the reduced level of
exotica during the Stirling phase would probably be the result of reduced levels
of long-distance procurement and exchange related to a shift of power favoring
the autonomist factions over the centralist factions at Cahokia. This would
generate a greater emphasis on a defensive over an earlier offensive posture with
regard to long-distance warfare related to world renewal sacrificial ritual. In
the case of the appearance, quantity, and distribution of Ramey-Incised ceramics, the same factional competition would promote the innovation and centralization of the production and distribution of this pottery as the expression

and constitution of cult autonomy. Why the latter would be the case is that the arm's-length clan-cult relation was characterized by a deeply inculcated view that the cults had the sacred duty to work hard to rectify subsistence- and settlement-caused sacred pollution. This meant that they had the obligation to enhance clan-based rituals that would promote local sanctification of the land, and the clans were entitled to receive the products and services from the local autonomous cults to this end. Therefore, Emerson and Pauketat are quite correct in claiming that the appearance and widespread distribution of Ramey-Incised pottery map an important Stirling phase ideological innovation. However, rather than marking subordination, the appearance and widespread distribution of Ramey-Incised ceramics and reduced distribution of exotica in the Stirling phase material cultural change mark the enhancement of the autonomy of cults and the respect that clans and cults had for each other's autonomy and mutual duties.

This argument can also be extended to explain why reduced variation among local material cultural traditions became the developing characteristic of the Mississippian period. In addition to the above changes, Emerson and Pauketat note that shell-tempered pottery, in particular—as well as wall-trench construction, internal storage, sweat lodges, and so on—are the result of a dominant center. The bifurcated settlement articulation modal account argues that, in fact, this standardization is consistent with the World Renewal Cult Heterarchy model. In these terms, in order for autonomous cults from different sectors of the American Bottom, and also probably in the surrounding uplands, to work together in these contexts, they would have to standardize the forms and makeup of their material culture since the latter constituted the critical symbolic warrants of their ritual. Only by negotiating standardized symbolic pragmatic rules as the content of a shared generalized ideology by which ritual action was constituted could alliances develop and be sustained. John Kelly (1982, 35, 175; 1990a, 77; 1990b, 124–28; 1992, 175) has demonstrated the parallel continuity of the (northern) Late Bluff and (southern) Pulcher ceramic traditions as largely defining the Terminal Late Woodland period. These two traditions sustained their autonomy despite considerable interaction among the users and continued to do so into the early Mississippian period. However, as fully discussed earlier in chapter 8, the later stages of these pre-Mississippian times were characterized by the compound plaza-periphery integrated settlement articulation mode so that the cult and clan alliances were closely linked and localized by sharing the same settlement locales. Even when cults started to interact across the American Bottom, as indicated by some mixing of the two ceramic traditions, local cults were primarily participants in regional villages, and cult and clan complementary alliances operated as the core of the larger compound plaza-periphery integrated Lindeman/Edelhardt phase villages. Hence, they would have promoted the maintenance rather than the dissolution of the two traditions.

Even so, Monks Mound Red ceramics of the Pulcher tradition are found to have emerged and become widespread during the later phases of the Terminal Late Woodland, almost presaging the distribution of Stirling phase Ramey-Incised ceramics. As Pauketat points out (1994, 55–57), the distribution of Monks Mound Red ceramics is largely independent of the standard ware of the two traditions, suggesting that the cults of these two traditions, although still relatively well integrated into the towns and villages, had already negotiated and established a neutral ceramic medium by which to cooperate in ritual practices. This is also the time when Lunsford-Pulcher, Cahokia, East St. Louis, and so on, may have started to be the focus of cult alliances from across the American Bottom. Therefore, the standardization of certain elements of material culture may have been initially cult stimulated and may have simply escalated with the rather abrupt shift from the integrated to the bifurcated settlement articulation modal orientation. Shell-tempered pottery and then Ramey-Incised ceramics are probably among the media and the results of this process, initiated through consensus-oriented negotiations promoting innovation and standardization that chooses a third way. In this case, rather than choosing limestone-tempered Pulcher pottery over grit-and-grog-tempered Late Bluff pottery, or vice versa, the peoples of the American Bottom almost universally favored shell-tempered ceramics, a choice no doubt underwritten by an innovative ideological rationale. Much more can be said on these topics, and thus I return to these in chapter 17.

Conclusion

Thus, in this bifurcated settlement articulation modal account of the country-side settlement pattern, the two parallel networks of nodal locales are postulated to have maintained a strong continuity of relatively autonomous clans and cults across the Lohmann and Stirling phases while manifesting an ongoing and developing consensus-orientated compromise among ideological factional orientations. In this case, the cult system is seen as constituted by at least two parallel networks of mutually autonomous but, in terms of substantive ritual, complementary cult types. As I suggest above, the female-based world renew-al fecundity cult is represented by the BBB Motor site (Lohmann and early

Stirling phases) and the Sponemann site (late Stirling). The male-based world renewal fertility cult system is represented in the Lohmann phase by Range ML-1/ML-2 (treated here as a single complex nodal locale) and in the Stirling phase by the Labras Lake nodal site, the complex Range MS-1 nodal site, and the Julien nodal site. What clearly changes and marks these two phases is the development of formal Stirling phase symbolic pragmatic warranting features, facilities, and artifacts, such as the "sweat houses," the Ramey-Incised ceramics, and the Earth Mother figurines, these being the outcome of consensus-oriented ideological negotiation and emulation. What do not change, in this view, are the deep structural nature of the two cult organizations, their mutual autonomy, their participation in mutualistic heterarchies, and their arm's-length relative autonomy with the parallel network of clan alliances. Therefore, whereas Emerson's sequential settlement articulation modal account has to argue for a radical expropriation of traditional mortuary-fertility cult practices of the Lohmann phase BBB Motor nodal site by Cahokian-based religious specialists in the Stirling phase, the bifurcated settlement articulation modal account stresses the continuity of traditional organizational structures mediated by innovation at the ideological and surface social structural level, while simultaneously, although largely unwittingly, serving to sustain deep structures of cultural tradition and the deep clan-cult social structures.

Admittedly, the data to support this female fecundity and male fertility cult duality are quite skimpy since there may be only two known sites that would represent the female fecundity cult type (the BBB Motor site in the Lohmann and early Stirling phases, and the later Stirling phase Sponemann site) and only three known nodal sites representing the male fertility cult type (the Lohmann and Stirling phase Range site, and the Stirling phase Julien and Labras Lake sites). But these are the same data that Emerson has used to support his more radical claim for the development of a rather complex political and ideological expansion of Cahokia. However, what could be expected under the bifurcated account is a replication of this fertility/fecundity complementary duality in the multiple-mound world renewal cult heterarchies. It is interesting, therefore, that a number of dualities found in Cahokia could be related in this way. Pauketat (1993, 146), for example, has argued that the paired rectangular platform and circular conical mounds may be serving not as a paired charnel-house platform and burial mound, as widely thought (for example, Fowler 1997, 199), but as paired (rectangular and circular) platforms for the support of rectangular and circular timber structures. He suggests that the former would be a temple and the latter, a communal meeting house. However, an alternative could be that both structures were renewal lodges (that is, temples), with the rectangular structure being the renewal lodge of the male-based fertility cult and the circular being the renewal lodge of the complementary female-based fecundity cult, or vice versa. An even clearer example of male-female structuring is the well-known mortuary contents of Mound 72. I am particularly speaking of the two sets of burials marking the termination of what would appear to be two related lethal human sacrificial ritual offering events: the four young males with their heads and hands removed, and more than fifty young females. As I argue in a later chapter in considerable detail, rather than treating these as sacrifices to memorialize Burial 13—the upper burial on the "bed of beads" (Fowler 1991, 3, 10; Fowler et al. 1999, 176–77)—we might better interpret them as the lethal sacrificial offering media of a major form of world renewal ritual related to Woodhenge 72.

In sum, as autonomous fertility and fecundity world renewal cults, how would these countryside nodal cult sites relate to the mound-plaza locales, such as East St. Louis, St. Louis, Mitchell, Lunsford-Pulcher, and even Cahokia? As postulated under the World Renewal Cult Heterarchy model, the social power that was manifested in these multiple-mound locales was not vested there. Rather, it resided in these multiple complex nodal sites, and these were built, maintained, and under the custodial care and control of the many autonomous cults distributed across the landscape. From these locales, the autonomous cults pooled their labor among themselves by forming mutualistic heterarchical cult alliances to enable all to pursue their essential and common collective goal, namely, the maintenance of cosmic harmony from the vantage point of a special part of the world named by its modern occupants the American Bottom.

12

Cahokian Mortuary Practices

The Media of World Renewal Ritual

The mortuary data of the Mississippian period of the American Bottom have been used by almost all the proponents of the hierarchical monistic modular polity account as primary evidence for validating the central notions of rank and dominance as characterizing the Middle Mississippian social system. Here I want to use the same data as evidence in support of the heterarchical polyistic locale-centric account, in general, and of the World Renewal Cult Heterarchy model, in particular.

George Milner has undertaken a comprehensive analysis of the mortuary data to reconstruct the general level of health of the prehistoric populations of the American Bottom. He takes as a given that the "Mississippian cultural systems" were stratified, and from this he deduces that the "skeletal collections representing . . . [elite and non-elite] should display evidence of somewhat differing levels of health" (Milner 1982, 231). His findings in this regard are quite germane, since his conclusions in this and subsequent cases do not support these expectations. Indeed, he observes, "The data presented in this study of the American Bottom collections indicate a relatively high level of community health during the Mississippian period. These results seem to reflect access to a nutritionally complete diet, which included storable foodstuffs, and a low or moderate disease load" (Milner 1982, 242). He qualifies his general conclusions by pointing out that there was an apparently high infant mortality rate (Milner 1982, 227). However, he attributes this not to the differential social standing of "elite" and "commoner" parents, although he maintains that such a social stratification existed, but to the widespread use of maize gruel as a food for infant weaning. Lacking two essential amino acids, unless supplemented with other foods, such a diet would expose infants to nutritional stress. He estimates a regional systemwide infant mortality rate of about 50 percent (Milner 1982, 233–35, 254).

Dean Saitta has also picked up on this same mismatch between the equitable distribution of the level of health of these populations and the claim that the mortuary data represent a dominance-based hierarchical social system. As he critically comments, "perhaps most significantly, health data on Mississippian skeletal populations from major mound centers do not suggest a significant nutritional separation between 'elites' and 'commoners'" (Saitta 1994, 211–12). Thomas Emerson, however, downplays Saitta's observations: "Saitta's assumption that elite exploitation (more accurately read *power over* here) must have been reflected in the material deprivation of the commoners seems overdrawn. Cahokian elite were able to commit the labor of their fellow citizens to massive public works . . . [and] to differentiate themselves in elaborate mortuary displays that subsumed extensive wealth and took the lives of many of their citizens for sacrifice" (Emerson 1997c, 187, emphasis in original).

Precisely what are these "elaborate mortuary displays" to which Emerson is referring? According to Milner, who up to that time had reviewed the whole known range of Mississippian period mortuary data associated with the American Bottom, including the Kane (mortuary) Mounds site on the bluffs overlooking Cahokia, there is a "strong communal emphasis in the burial of people in virtually all of these mortuary features. Single features containing numerous skeletons or piles of disarticulated bones were found in the St. Louis Big Mound, the East St. Louis Cemetery Mound, the Mitchell burial mound, the Cahokia Powell and Rattlesnake mounds, and the Wilson Mound" (Milner 1998, 132). Clearly, the elaborate burials that Emerson cites cannot be a reference to the above, since all of the burials are described as having "a strong communal emphasis" and all are treated similarly—as bundle burials. Therefore, the displays of elaborate mortuary residue to which Emerson is alluding seem to basically consist of Mound 72 and its contents.

Mound 72 is a rather small ridge-top mound about 930 meters due south of Monks Mound (Figure 1.4). Its contents are certainly impressive, consisting of between 260 and 267 burials, the majority being mass burial deposits, as well as several large deposits of artifacts, large collective mortuary deposit pits, and so on, all of which are examined in detail in the next chapter. However, these particular mortuary data are certainly not the ones to which Saitta is making reference in his criticism. Rather, he is making reference to Milner's broad data-based analysis of the mortuary record, which, as pointed out above, both he and Milner assess as quite strongly communal in nature. Therefore, Emerson's invoking "elaborate mortuary displays that subsumed extensive wealth and took the lives of many of their citizens for sacrifice"—namely, the contents of Mound 72—seems to be a very selective use of the mortuary data on his part. When the rest of the known mortuary data found in association with mounds in Cahokia, St. Louis, and East St. Louis, as well as supposedly "commoner" mortuary data in "rural" cemeteries, and so on, is considered (as was Saitta's intention), Saitta's assessment is definitely not "overdrawn." Therefore, I will second Saitta in this regard and add to his point by arguing that the mortuary data not only contradict the expectations that several proponents of the hierarchical monistic modular polity account predict, but also strongly point to the operations of mortuary-mediated world renewal ritual. Therefore, I postulate here that much of these mortuary data can be more coherently interpreted as the medium and outcome of postmortem human sacrifice rather than as the funerary outcome of an hierarchical elite-commoner society.

Importantly, the Mourning/World Renewal Mortuary model (which is the theoretical framework I have developed for interpreting the mortuary data in a manner relevant to the heterarchical polyistic locale-centric account) and the Cemetery model (which is the basic theoretical framework used by Milner and other proponents of the various versions of the hierarchical monistic modular account) clearly allow for postulating contrasting empirical expectations. These expectations relate to the range of types of collective burial locales (CBLs) and the range of contents associated with each type. Therefore, it is quite appropriate to ask what type of CBLs could be expected under the Cemetery model as opposed to those expected under the Mourning/World Renewal Mortuary model; it is equally appropriate to ask what the contents of the former CBLs would be like, as compared to the contents of the latter CBLs, and then assess the American Bottom data under these alternative views.

In terms of the Cemetery model, the CBLs should be isolated from each other, since, of course, they are the symbolic constituents of a corporate group's exclusive control over the surrounding territory (Charles and Buikstra 1983, 121). Also, since the point of recruiting the deceased for this purpose is to constitute them as the ancestors in virtue of whom their living descendants inherit exclusive rights to the surrounding territory, the descendants have reason to maintain the bodily integrity of the deceased, who then become the embodiment of the powerful ancestors of the descent group. Therefore, funerals terminated by primary burials in the CBLs would be expected to prevail, and the building of mutually exclusive cemetery CBLs to mark sacred burial spots would be expected. This means that we would expect a very limited range of CBL types, effectively all being cemeteries (as the mortuary residences of the ancestors of the different modular polities), and these would be more or less regularly spaced from each other. The only variation in these burial locales would be size, and the larger CBLs would of course be internally structured according to the type and number of discrete kinship units recognized and the way they related (for example, via rank or specialization, or both).

The Cemetery model certainly allows for variation in the treatment of the individual deceased in terms of the variety of symbolic warranting devices but less so in terms of postmortem manipulation. Low levels and variation in artifact accompaniments and low levels and variation in labor investment in mortuary facilities would mark a simple society. The reverse would mark a complex society. Since the assumption of the proprietorial domain perspective is that these are kinship-based societies, then complexity would characteristically reflect ranked kinship groups, such as lineages and clans, associated with ascribed leadership and specialization of esteem-endowing roles favoring the higher- over the lower-ranking groups (Milner 1982, 83–86; 1983, 3). Variation in postmortem bodily manipulation of the deceased would be anticipated only in the case of fairly to highly mobile social systems, since under the Cemetery model, the primary systematic cause of this variation relates to the inconvenience factor. In general, only mobile communities should have many instances of bone bundles. In the case of sedentary societies, therefore, given a proprietorial domain regime, there should be a moderately to very low incidence of postmortem manipulation. The great majority of the deceased would be primary extended interments marking the termination of funerals. Flexed and/or bundle burials might mark the fewer instances of those who died in winter or when on distant expeditions.

Because the Mourning/World Renewal Mortuary model recognizes the total funerary→mourning→spirit release→world renewal process, it can embrace the mortuary spheres of both monistic modular and polyistic locale-centric social systems. Since the latter types of social systems are characterized by at least two major social organizational types (clans and cults), this model can postulate two contrasting ways in which these relatively autonomous organizations would relate to each other through the treatment of the deceased to which both types of groups owed responsibility. On the one hand, a competitive posture is possible, and on the other, a cooperative posture. The competitive posture would occur when clans might perceive that if the cults appropriated too many of the clan's deceased members as postmortem sacrificial victims, this would diminish the clan's ability to achieve its own mortuary goals of constituting potent ancestors; simultaneously, the cults would perceive that if the clans appropriated too many of the cult's deceased members and/or deceased dependents of their living members, this would diminish the cult's capacity to discharge its world renewal duties. In these circumstances, ongoing negotiations between clans and cults over the appropriation of the deceased to which both had entitlements and responsibilities would be chronic. The mortuary result would be a dual mortuary record generating two contrasting sets of CBLs, one representing the clans and the other the cults. Since clans emphasized the focal participant role, their CBLs would be characterized by a high degree of extended burials with very little in the way of bone bundles and/or postmortem manipulation. In contrast, the cult CBLs would display strong and richly varied evidence of postfunerary mortuary practices realizing the whole range of postmortem manipulation: some primary burials, bundle burials, burials of separate body parts, and even cremation, all of these mediating different types of renewal ritual or different stages in the complex incremental series of mortuary rituals constituting the mortuary sphere. Correlated with the clan/cult CBL duality would be a strong emphasis on ceremonialism in the cult CBLs (to a degree that would be superfluous to funerary rites), including significant variation in artifacts and facilities, since these would be the outcome of different renewal rituals mediated by deceased who had achieved different levels in the enabling hierarchies of the cults. In contrast, since kinship stresses unity through suppressing differences, there would be a minimal amount of postmortem-related variation in clan CBLs.

The cooperative clan-cult posture would tend to emerge in circumstances in which the intensity of settlement and subsistence was broadly perceived to have reached such a critically high level that everyone recognized the impossibility of avoiding the generation of high levels of sacred pollution. In these conditions, the cults would be perceived as primary institutions specialized to rectify and reverse the sacred pollution caused largely by sedentary settlement and the intensive subsistence practices of the clans. Therefore, the clans' concern over the degree of pollution that everyday domestic life was necessarily producing would promote harmonizing their mortuary practices with the cults' focus on the use of the deceased as sacrificial media.

The ongoing survival and reproduction of the population and the sanctity of the local region, therefore, would require a cooperative entente between clans and cults in terms of mortuary goals, and this ongoing entente would generate a very different mortuary record from that generated by the above competitive posture. In this case, while clans and cults would maintain separate and autonomous mortuary spheres, the CBLs would be primarily cult-based locales directly linked into the world renewal ceremonialism of the mound-plaza sites or of the nodal cult sites. To put it slightly differently, while the clans would still be responsible for funerary rituals, these latter mortuary practices would be largely invisible archaeologically, since the termination of the funerary ritual would be marked by the post-funerary transfer of the bodies to the care of the cults to use as world renewal postmortem sacrificial media. Hence, we might only be able to infer indirectly that funerary rites had been carried out by clans. That is, following the clan-directed funerary rites (possibly ensuring the release of the name spirit and some other spiritual components that would be believed to be directly reborn in the new clan members), the bodies of the deceased, in whole or in bundled parts, would be passed on to the cults, where they would be subjected to further postmortem treatment in which their spiritual essences would be released as sacrificial offerings to the cosmos. The tangible end product of the complex mortuary process would be manifested primarily in the absence of funerary CBLs and the prevalence of large, collective cult CBLs displaying a strong emphasis on postmortem manipulation marking the more extreme symbolic warranting pole of the participant-symbolic warranting duality. A consequence of this sharing of mortuary duties might be the finding of stray human bones in domestic locales where the deceased had been temporarily curated after the funerals.

In sum, under a hierarchical monistic modular polity system based on proprietary corporate clans, a unitary CBL system should exist, with a strong emphasis on primary burial and with variation in artifact and burial facilities correlated with the presence or absence of ranked clans and specialization. These CBLs should be distant from each other, since they would demarcate exclusive territories of which they were the spiritual, civic, and, often, geographical centers. Under a heterarchical polyistic locale-centric system based on custodial clans and cults, either a dual CBL system based on a moderately antagonistic mortuary-mediated clan/cult arm's-length relation would exist or else a harmonized CBL system would prevail. The former case would generate distinctly different clan and cult CBLs. The clan CBLs would have strong funerary characteristics but with a low variation of artifacts and burial facilities, emphasizing the unity of the clan, and the cult CBLs would be characterized by the whole gamut of participant↔symbolic warranting criteria, along with a high variation of artifacts and burial facilities, the latter displaying evidence of re-use and cycling, thereby recognizing the differential positioning of the deceased on the cultic enabling hierarchy as well as the different types of mortuary-mediated world renewal sacrificial rituals that would be performed. In the harmonized CBL case, the funerary, clan-based component of the mortuary sphere would be largely invisible archaeologically, and pretty well only the cult-based world renewal component would be strongly manifested; the latter would display a range of communal-like postmortem treatments as the outcome of world re-newal ritual.

Discussion

It is clear that the nature of the clan-cult relation in a polyistic-type social sys-tem is a function of the relative degree of polluting that everyday settlement and subsistence practices are perceived to be generating. It must be noted, also, that the same types of immanentist cosmology and squatter ethos are being manifested in these contrasting cases, despite the different material outcomes. That is, participants in a social system would normally maintain the integrity of their traditional cosmology and ethos while changing and transforming the ideological strategies generating their mortuary practices, shifting from an antagonistic dual clan-cult CBL system to a harmonized dual clan-cult sys-tem promoting the cult-based CBL network, or vice versa. Therefore, under conditions of perceived maximum settlement- and subsistence-generated sa-cred pollution, as I suggest above, the clan and cult mortuary spheres would be harmonized, and, while clan-based mortuary practices would definitely oc-cur, these would be rather invisible archaeologically while producing primarily cult-based CBLs displaying the end product of a series of world renewal rites mediated by escalating stages of postmortem manipulation.

Moreover, cult CBLs under a harmonized mortuary regime would often be marked by monumental construction. This monumentalism plays a particularly important role, since these large constructions would count as iconic symbolic pragmatic devices expressively representing and presencing the relevant essen-tial sacred properties of the cosmos. Mound platforms, for example, might be viewed as icons of the earth and sky, while plazas and large water-filled borrow pits might be icons of the middle world and underworld. Under the symbolic pragmatic perspective, for the mortuary events to count as postmortem sacri-ficial world renewal rituals, they would have to be performed in these contexts; we would therefore also expect cosmological congruency patterns to emerge (for example, alignments with critical solar, lunar, and/or other celestial turn-ing points or mythically important directional orientations), by which the es-sential powers of the cosmos would be experienced by the participants as being presenced in the earthworks themselves. We could also expect potent symbolic pragmatic devices such as posts and "palisades," representing the framework of the cosmos and/or the *axis mundi* that linked the heavens/middle world/ underworld into a single vertically ordered cosmic structure. Since postmortem sacrifice would play a central role, some whole bodies but predominantly flexed or bundled burials or body-part burials that would be understood as particularly associated with the nature of the mound or post might be deposited as critical constitutive symbolic pragmatic devices of foundation rites or as rites for renewing the potency of these major iconic constructions.

Thus we could expect a range of treatments making up the monumental cult CBLs: from potent artifacts and facilities to large, collective mortuary burials. The latter could result from the repetitive nature of renewal rites tied to the seasonal and/or celestial cycles. They could also be tied into the cult reproductive cycles. Since the cults would be based on the generational cycle, initiates would become junior age-grade members and junior age-grade members would be promoted through the age-set enabling hierarchy, becoming senior age-grade members and, finally, elders. This process would be institutionalized as cultwide rites of passage, and each major promotion might involve the closing of the mortuary depository of those companions who had died and had been processed as postmortem sacrificial offerings during the prior period.

Before proceeding with the demonstration of which model the mortuary record best supports, I will note that until the emergence of the Mississippian period in the American Bottom, the mortuary sphere in the floodplain was almost invisible archaeologically. This was the case for the Late Woodland period as well as the Terminal Late Woodland period. For example, Andrew Fortier and colleagues (1991) report no Sponemann phase mortuary remains at the Sponemann site. Milner (in Kelly et al. 1987, 403) reports some scattered human remains at the Range site during the Patrick phase but even fewer during the Dohack and Range phases of the Terminal Late Woodland (also see Kelly et al. 1990, 267). Milner characterizes most of these as the unintended or incidental by-products of mortuary practices, and he comments that the archaeological context of the remains "indicates that recovered bones were, for the most part, adventitious inclusions in the fills of nonmortuary features . . . [probably the result of being] placed initially on scaffolds or in trees near Late Woodland communities" (in Kelly et al. 1987, 403).

Since these communities constructed permanent villages, even though they may have occupied these villages only during the warm seasons, this mortuary treatment would not mark the type we could expect of a highly sedentary people. Instead, it appears to mark the first steps in a longer mortuary process, for example, the funerary and (possibly) the mourning steps only. Thus, according to this interpretive framework, these scattered human remains caught up in the fill of cultural pits and house basins may have been the result of bones being misplaced when the exposed bodies were bundled and removed to be buried elsewhere. Indeed, the absence of mortuary remains from Late Woodland and Terminal Late Woodland period settlement in the American Bottom is generally acknowledged by archaeologists to be one of the puzzles of this archaeological record. This suggests that we should look to the bluffs and the nearby uplands in search for the requisite CBLs.[1]

DESCRIPTION, ANALYSIS, AND INITIAL CONCLUSION

I initiate this analysis by focusing on four American Bottom mortuary sites that have been excavated and/or analyzed using modern archaeological standards: the East St. Louis Stone Quarry site, the Kane Mounds site (a site on the eastern bluffs overlooking the floodplain), the Wilson Mound, and Mound 72. The first three are summarized and interpreted below, and Mound 72 is described, analyzed, and interpreted in detail in the following chapter. In this case, I will reverse the temporal order, moving from the later Mississippian period backward to the early Mississippian period.

The East St. Louis Stone Quarry Cemetery Site

Despite its name, this site is not part of the East St. Louis multiple-mound site. Rather, it is a small mortuary locale near the Range site in the southern sector of the northern expanse of the American Bottom (Figure 12.1). This CBL represents the Sand Prairie phase, the last phase of the Mississippian period, or—if recent claims by Thomas Emerson and Eva Hargrave (2000, 5–7; also reported in Hedman and Hargrave 1999, ix, 87–89) are accepted—the terminal Moorehead/early Sand Prairie transition. In any case, this CBL marks the later Mississippian mortuary developments in this southern region. The fact that the site was thoroughly excavated and analyzed by George Milner using modern field and laboratory techniques makes it invaluable.

Milner (1983, 1, 23) points out that the site can be logically treated as having two related components: what he calls the charnel structure and the grave burials (Figure 12.2). In fact, as will become clear in this discussion, this dual structuring is probably pervasive in the mortuary patterning of the Mississippian period of the American Bottom. Milner describes the charnel structure as a building having a limestone-paved floor, which he labels Feature 72, and four corner posts that presumably supported the roof. I will call this building the Feature 72 structure to distinguish it from Feature 72 (which is the limestone floor itself). This structure was built with its walls oriented to the

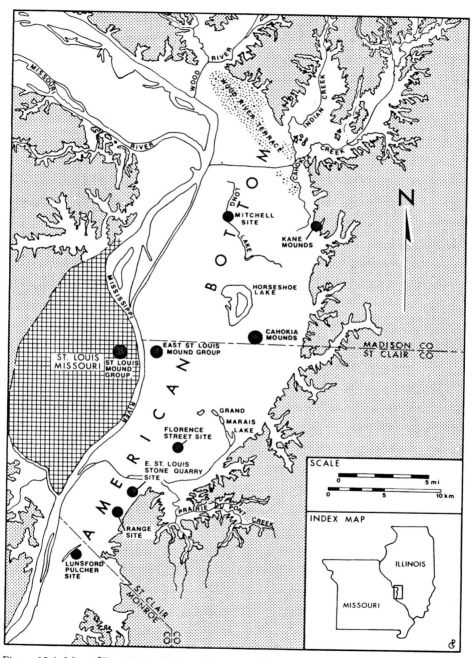

Figure 12.1. Map of East St. Louis Stone Quarry site location. (Milner 1983, fig. 1, p. 2. Courtesy of the Illinois Transportation Archaeological Research Program, University of Illinois.)

cardinal points. Flanking its sides were four stone-lined pits, one parallel to each wall (Features 66, 71, 74, and 75). Several meters to the southwest of the structure there was an isolated posthole, which Milner interprets as a marker pole. Surrounding the Feature 72 structure and its four stone-lined pits, forming a roughly concentric series of circles, were very similar multiple stone-box pit features. Most of these were large enough to contain a fully extended body and in some cases were larger than would be necessary for this purpose. There were some extended or slightly flexed burials. Many contained one or more sets of human remains: often bone bundles and/or isolated body parts and often only dental remains. Since many of the bundle burials and/or small deposits of isolated remains were in stone-box features that were the same size as those that contained extended burials, these stone-box features likely were typically re-used to mediate a range of postmortem behaviors, from initial extended burial to flexed burial, to bundle burial, to partial remains burial. Indeed, as Milner observes, "Compelling archeological evidence exists for the prehistoric reuse of the East St. Louis Stone Quarry mortuary pits. Partitions that subdivided the graves, the removal of limestone slabs, and the disposition of human bones in several graves indicate that many features were used on more than one occasion" (Milner 1983, 32).

Milner also notes that many if not all of these stone-box pits were put in place after the Feature 72 structure and its four associated stone-lined pits and limestone floor had been abandoned and closed with a shallow covering of earth fill:

> The charnel structure and its four flanking mortuary pits had apparently been abandoned and covered with a layer of fill by the time many of the peripherally located graves were in use. Only one pit feature (Feature 67) superimposed the limestone slab platform; however, the four flanking mortuary pits were superimposed by numerous features. Certainly, the structure must have been dismantled by the time Feature 67, a stone-box grave, was constructed. This grave superimposed a post feature (Feature 34) where one of the structure's four corner supports had been located. (Milner 1983, 23)

Apparently, then, either shortly before or after the Feature 72 structure was dismantled and the limestone floor (Feature 72) with its piles of long bones was covered with a fifteen-centimeter layer of earth, no further charnel-type mortuary activity occurred directly on this area. However, the immediate surrounding area seemed not only appropriate but also necessary for continuing

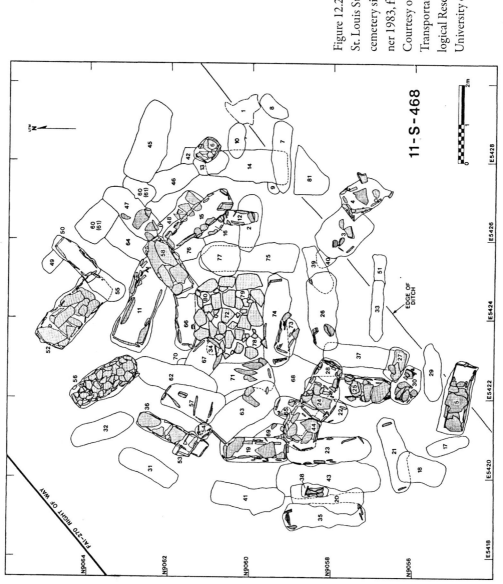

Figure 12.2. Plan of East St. Louis Stone Quarry cemetery site. (Milner 1983, fig. 8, p. 27. Courtesy of the Illinois Transportation Archaeological Research Program, University of Illinois.)

mortuary use. As Milner argues, the oldest stone-box pits and their mortuary contents were those that were closest to the Feature 72 structure, and, in general, while many of these were built so as to "overlap the four flanking mortuary pits," only one of these overlapped the stone-paved floor, indicating that this floor and its structure had been abandoned. As the space immediately encircling Feature 72 became overly crowded, new stone-box pits were built on the perimeter of the earlier pits.

This is an interesting mortuary pattern since it reveals a chronology of usage that raises the question of the precise symbolic pragmatic nature of this Feature 72 structure—stone-box mortuary pit spatial relation. I will term the Feature 72 structure, the four stone-box features that flanked its walls, and its floor the *Feature 72 complex*. I will term the stone-box mortuary pits surrounding this complex the *peripheral stone-box mortuary pits*. Since the latter were apparently placed there after the Feature 72 complex had been closed, then what role, if any, could the latter have played in the mortuary processes leading up to the burials found in the peripheral stone-box mortuary pits surrounding it? In contrast, if it had no relevant role to play, then why was this Feature 72 complex clearly the focus around which these peripheral stone-box pits were placed? The answers to these questions will have to remain hypothetical for now. However, they highlight the type of empirical data that future research could be directed to retrieving.

Milner points out that stone-box pits with a similar mix of burial treatments formed in the same concentric series of circles were found in the nearby Sand Prairie phase components of the Florence Street site and the Range site (alternatively, if Emerson et al. [1983, 289] and Hedman and Hargrave [1999, 67–69] are correct, these components would also be dated to the late Moorehead–early Sand Prairie transition). These two sites, however, lacked a central charnel complex equivalent to the Feature 72 complex, although the Florence Street site burial locale had what Milner calls a "charnel area" in its center, this being an area where initial mortuary processing may have occurred. If we assume that the peripheral stone-box pits of the East St. Louis Stone Quarry and the similar formation of stone-box pits of the Florence Street and Range sites realized equivalent symbolic pragmatic meaning (that is, mediating equivalent mortuary rites), then we can deduce that the initial mortuary processing of the deceased found within the peripheral stone-box pit features of the East St. Louis Stone Quarry site had been done elsewhere, in one or more sites having mortuary facilities that were the equivalent of the Feature 72 complex, which had been abandoned by the time its associated peripheral stone-box pit features were being used. Similarly, because of the lack of an equivalent Feature 72 complex at the Florence Street and Range sites, the deceased found at these sites must also have been given their initial processing in an extrasite facility that was the equivalent of the Feature 72 complex. Indeed, this processing might have been at the Feature 72 complex of the East St. Louis Stone Quarry site.

There appears to be a distinct pattern here. The charnel structure at one locale (for example, the Feature 72 complex of the East St. Louis Stone Quarry) may have been used as the first step in the processing of the deceased that were buried in a peripheral mortuary pit area at other nearby sites (for example, the Florence Street and Range sites). When the Feature 72 charnel structure was closed, a new charnel complex may have been constructed at a nearby but currently unknown locale. The requisite initial mortuary processing of the sort carried out in the then closed Feature 72 complex may have been performed there, and some of the deceased from this locale may have been buried in stone-box pits placed around the former Feature 72 structure complex at the East St. Louis Stone Quarry site, and so on.

There is another possibility, of course, this being that all the peripheral stone-box pit features found at the three sites are later than the East St. Louis Stone Quarry Feature 72 complex. This would mean that the latter not only predates the peripheral stone-box pits that surround it, but also predates the stone-box pits of the Florence Street and Range sites. If so, then the stone-box pits were innovated as individual crypts substituting for the function of the Feature 72 complex. However, I find this highly unlikely. Milner makes very clear that the four flanking stone-box pits were built as intrinsic structural elements of the Feature 72 structure itself, one each on the north, south, east, and west sides. These four pits also contained mortuary contents similar to the contents found in the encircling pits (Figure 12.2). Furthermore, the stone-paved floor of the Feature 72 charnel structure served as a mortuary depository in its own right; several carefully aligned sets of human long bones had been set on it before the floor was covered. Milner estimates that they represent at least thirteen individuals—adults, subadults, and children. Therefore, it is clear that the Feature 72 complex was used as an important facility for only part of the total mortuary process, which was continued and finally terminated with burial elsewhere. Since, according to Milner's analysis, the closest and oldest of peripheral stone-box pits were actually on top of the stone-box pits that flanked Structure 72, the conclusion, as suggested above, is that the deceased processed through these flanking pits were buried elsewhere—for example, in stone-box pit CBLs without charnel structures, such as the Florence Street and Range sites, as noted in the first scenario above.

If this analysis is correct, it has the following interesting implication. The mortuary activities mediated by peripheral stone-box pits without charnel structures, on the one hand, and, on the other, the mortuary activities performed in charnel structures that may have been several kilometers away were related as part of a single, complex mortuary process. This means that the usage of a given charnel-structure complex, such as the Feature 72 complex, would be linked to the usage of one or more peripheral stone-box pit CBLs that could be several kilometers separate from it. Seen from the opposite direction, a given peripheral stone-box pit CBL without a charnel structure would have had its deceased initially processed in different charnel complexes, such as the Feature 72 complex of the East St. Louis Stone Quarry site. What all this means is that there is only partial and possibly very little congruency between charnel-structure CBL complexes, peripheral stone-box pit CBLs, and communities.[2] Another way of putting this is to say that during this period there were two types of spatially separated but contemporaneously used and interlinked CBLs: the charnel-house complex CBL and the peripheral stone-box pit CBL. The former was used to mediate the performance of the first portion of the total mortuary process; the latter was used for the second and terminal portion. Thus, with the completion of the appropriate part of the process at the charnel-structure complex, the deceased would have been bundled and transported to the appropriate peripheral stone-box pit CBL. When, for reasons currently unknown, a charnel-house complex CBL was abandoned and dismantled, the same site was then used to mediate the second portion of the total process, as illustrated by the temporal-spatial sectoring of the mortuary data of the East St. Louis Stone Quarry site, and a new charnel-structure complex opened nearby.

While the funerary view would have great difficulty in accommodating all of these aspects, none of them is difficult for the mortuary perspective articulated by the Mourning/World Renewal Mortuary model to accommodate. While funerary rites would be part of the mortuary process, the subsequent multiple mortuary ritual stages postulated above would ensure that the end product of the process would have very little funerary relevance and a great deal of social and world renewal relevance. If the domestic community is considered to be the primary context of funerary and related mortuary rites, then these initial steps could have been performed by the responsible communities even prior to the use of the charnel-structure complex. Thus, the immediate families and lineages of the deceased would have the opportunity to treat the deceased as "hosts" of their own funerary events. Then the deceased could have been carried, possibly in a pole-litter, to the charnel-structure complex CBL of the responsible cult or cult alliance, where the body would be placed in one of the flanking stone-box pits. There mourning and various related rites involving the releasing of the different spiritual essences of the deceased could be performed. The body could then be removed and carried to a "laying-in" crypt altar, that is, a peripheral stone-box pit CBL without a charnel structure, where it would be temporarily buried. Several months later, it could be disinterred and the bones could be cleaned and carried either to the previous charnel structure or to another, where further spirit release rites having a strong postmortem sacrificial component could be performed. The bones could then be bundled with those of other deceased individuals and deposited in another peripheral stone-box mortuary pit CBL.

Each incremental step would depersonalize and further abstract the deceased as postmortem sacrificial offerings to the cosmos. Not all the deceased would necessarily be put through all the stages, since each stage would be keyed to a ritual schedule. Thus, traditional rules might exist regulating the conditions under which a stone-box pit in a local cult CBL could or could not be opened and reused. For example, if the roof of a stone box broke, its deceased (even if still in the extended burial state) might have had to be left in place and another stone box built over it. Also, as suggested in chapter 5, the symbolic pragmatic nature of a given stone-box pit could be modified with incremental usage, first acting as a "laying-in" crypt, then as a mourning/spirit release sacrificial altar, and, possibly, finally as a terminal collective memorial offering altar. This shifting meaning may have been largely irreversible so that while a stone-box pit used as "laying-in" crypt could be reused as a sacrificial altar, the reverse would be prohibited. That is, once used as a sacrificial altar, it could not be reused as a "laying-in" crypt. Hence, we could anticipate some cases of stone-box pits being abandoned and empty, not being reusable as an earlier type and not needed as a later type. The overall processual result would be a broad mix of mortuary treatments, none or few of which could be attributed to the social standing of the deceased at the time of death. Rather, this complex treatment would result from the incremental unfolding of the symbolic pragmatic rules of postmortem sacrificial ritual, and these rules would make the treatment of the deceased largely independent of their particular social standings at the time of death, particularly as each incremental step was performed.

In summary, based on the somewhat limited empirical data available, the Sand Prairie phase (or terminal Moorehead–early Sand Prairie phase) mortuary sphere in the southern sector may have been structured into a rather open network of charnel-structure complex CBLs and peripheral stone-box "laying-in" crypt CBLs that was laced across the region. Although there would be practical limitations imposed on the distribution of the deceased across this network, this distribution would not be congruent with kinship communities. This suggests that the charnel structure/"laying-in" crypt/collective memorial altar crypt network would largely be under the responsibility of world renewal cults. However, these cults would work closely with local clans, which suggests a strong tendency toward the formation of a dual clan-cult integrated settlement articulation mode, even though the later Mississippian period continued to have dispersed farmsteads as the primary domestic settlement pattern. Since we know that some cult activity still occurred at the major mound-plaza locales during at least the terminal Moorehead–early Sand Prairie transition, especially at Cahokia, the cults and clans (despite their closer integration) apparently still maintained considerable arm's-length relations.[3] However, the local flavor of the charnel structure/"laying-in" crypt/spirit release altar/collective memorial altar CBL network suggests that much of the world renewal ritual sphere was no longer sustained at these cult heterarchy locales in the way that it had been in earlier Mississippian phases (see below). Thus, in this southern sector of the northern expanse, the affiliations of cult alliances were probably largely a distant memory at this time. Even what evidence there is of a Sand Prairie phase occupation at Cahokia suggests that this occupation was almost certainly more ad hoc in nature. In effect, at least in the southern sector of the northern expanse, the charnel structure/"laying-in" crypt CBL system had replaced the more centralized world renewal cult heterarchy CBL system that dominated during Cahokia's heyday, clearly indicating a dismantling of the strongly bifurcated settlement articulation mode of the preceding era and the reemergence of a social system with a tendency toward a local clan-cult integrated settlement articulation mode, although not yet fully realized.

The Kane Mounds Site

Still working more or less backward in time, I will summarize and interpret the Moorehead phase Kane Mounds mortuary complex. I say "more or less" since, according to Emerson and Hargrave (2000, 5–7), it is likely that the Kane Mounds site has both early and late Moorehead phase components, the latter probably being roughly contemporary with the above East St. Louis Stone Quarry and related sites. In any case, there is an immediate and somewhat outstanding difference between the Moorehead phase Kane Mounds mortuary patterning and the East St. Louis Stone Quarry pattern as exemplified in the above discussion: the absence of the stone-box pit feature and the charnel structure (although Milner [1984, 482] argues that there is a charnel area—and in his dissertation [1982, 299], written earlier, he suggests that there was a mortuary structure). While the stone-box pit feature has been assumed to mark the Sand Prairie phrase, Emerson and Hargrave suggest that this assumption may be a mistake. Instead of this complex being diffused from the "Middle Cumberland of Tennessee sometime after A.D. 1300," as assumed up till now, they assert that the evidence "now suggests that American Bottom stone graves appear nearly as early as those in the Midsouth and southern Illinois" (Emerson and Hargrave 2000, 5).

Besides the absence of the stone-box pit features in the Kane Mounds site, there is a second difference. Milner's descriptions clearly indicate that although extended, flexed, and disarticulated mortuary deposits were common in both the East St. Louis Stone Quarry site and the Kane Mounds site, they differed in the presence of cremation at the latter site (Emerson and Hargrave 2000, 12; Melbye 1963, 23) and its apparent absence at the former.[4] Of course, the settings of the two mortuary contexts were also quite different. While the East St. Louis Stone Quarry site is in the floodplain near the base of the eastern bluffs, the Kane Mounds site is in the northern sector and directly on the bluffs overlooking the American Bottom (Melbye 1963, 1). In fact, from this site, two major world renewal cult heterarchies in the floodplain could be easily seen: the Mitchell site about 6.4 kilometers due west, and Cahokia, about 12 kilometers to the southwest. It is particularly notable that, with respect to the extended burials (there were equally as many bone bundles), F. Jerome Melbye (1963, 9) discerned two populations according to the directional orientation of the bodies: one set was oriented due west toward the Mitchell site; the other, toward Cahokia. Melbye suggests that each of the two populations was related to the mound locale toward which the deceased were oriented.

This is an interesting comment. Why would those using the same mortuary locale orient their deceased toward two different multiple-mound locales? Few have seen this pattern as a puzzle, possibly because they identify these two locales—Cahokia and Mitchell—not as delineating separate social entities (that is, world renewal cult heterarchies) but as components of the same social entity, a paramount chiefdom, that were related in hierarchical terms, with Cahokia being dominant over Mitchell. This notion is clearly part of Milner's thinking since, on the basis of relative artifact association, he suggests that the two different groups may be distinguished in terms of relative rank with the Mitchell-oriented group having higher status than the Cahokia-oriented group. Indeed, he observes, "At the Kane Mounds site, mortuary features oriented towards the Mitchell site seemed to contain more artifacts than features oriented toward the Cahokia site" (Milner 1984, 477). In contrast, under the World Renewal Cult Heterarchy model, it was postulated that a cult alliance might participate in more than one world renewal cult heterarchy. Indeed, such participation would be a major means of maximizing the reputation of a cult alliance. Seen in these terms, the Kane Mounds site could be reinterpreted as the CBL of a cult alliance, and this division of the burials into two mortuary populations—one oriented toward Cahokia and one toward Mitchell—could be interpreted as marking and constituting this cult alliance's budgeting of its symbolic capital so as to maximize the effect of such symbolic capital, both in terms of world renewal ritual and, of course, in terms of alliance reputation.

This raises an important question, of course. If Cahokia and Mitchell were major affiliations of world renewal cult alliances, why would the Kane Mounds CBL exist? Surely the cult alliance would want to terminate the world renewal process in the two main cult heterarchies. It is quite possible that, indeed, the Kane Mounds CBL was not designed to mediate the final step of mortuary process. That is, the mixture of bone bundles and extended burials suggests that only some of the mourning/world renewal mortuary treatments of only some of the deceased were terminated with final burial at the Kane Mounds (these possibly being the bundle burials). This explanation would suggest that the two groups of extended burials were only partway through their respective mortuary processing. Those oriented toward Cahokia, therefore, would normally have been disinterred at the proper time, bundled, and taken to Cahokia to be used as symbolic pragmatic media of terminal postmortem sacrificial world renewal rituals (see below). Similarly, those oriented toward Mitchell would be marked for the same range of terminal rituals at that site. The Kane Mounds site, therefore, may have served both as a terminating CBL and as a staging CBL. Many of the deceased that were found, particularly the extended burials, may have simply been those that, for reasons not known now, had not been disinterred for use in the next and possibly terminal ritual stages at Cahokia or Mitchell. The Kane Mounds CBL mortuary complex, therefore, serves as evidence in support of two earlier suggestions. Under the Mourning/World Renewal Mortuary model, cults were postulated to have treated their deceased as symbolic capital by which they could effectively participate in world renewal rituals. Under the World Renewal Cult Heterarchy model, a cult alliance was postulated to have participated in more than one world renewal cult heterarchy.

However, there is another possibility. It is also important to note that the Kane Mounds CBL is a Moorehead phase site, and this phase saw considerable reduction in population and activity at Cahokia and the other world renewal cult heterarchies. The contrast between the Stirling and Moorehead phase cult alliance mound-plaza complexes of Cahokia (for example, the so-called subcommunities) may be related to the recognition in the Moorehead phase that the investment of world renewal ritual labor in Cahokia had reached the point of diminishing returns, and any continued occupation during this phase may thus represent a period of "boot-camp" training of the junior age-sets of the cult alliances that were still active in this locale. In contrast, the previous Stirling phase marked the highest degree of participation and the greatest level of labor investment. During this phase, most of the mound-plaza complexes expanded even while huge amounts of labor were cooperatively invested in the creation and expansion of the central precinct—including expanding Monks Mound to its maximum, building the largest temple structure on its highest terrace, and building the great palisade, including rebuilding it possibly at least three times, the last rebuildings being done in the Moorehead phase.

The Moorehead phase, however, is marked by the abandonment of many of the mound-plaza complexes, or at least the abandonment of the buildings that framed these plazas, and their replacement with fewer but larger buildings fairly widely separated from each other. These could have been the expression of junior age-sets who built and occupied them more as barracks than as domestic residences. That is, these would have been excellent group residences for young bachelors who lived as transients in Cahokia as part of their cults' "boot-camp" training periods. This explanation would be consistent with the claim that Cahokia was then at the point at which iconic construction was perceived as having less sanctifying benefit than similar labor investment in other locales. Indeed, many of the major mounds at Cahokia (and also possibly at Mitchell) were closed by that time, this closure being marked by the placement of major mantles of black gumbo with no subsequent construction of a structure, suggesting that the black gumbo was a crucial part of ritually sealing the mound and terminating its use (Pauketat 1993, 146–47; Smith 1969, 87).

If this is the case, then many of the CBL mounds of Cahokia and Mitchell may have been closed by the time that the Kane Mounds CBL was operating. The responsible cult alliance, however, would have continued to invoke the

WILSON MOUND

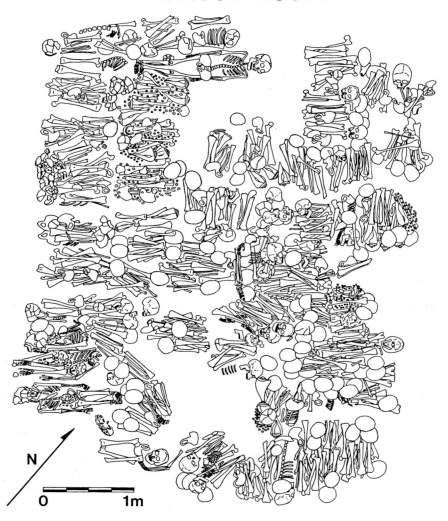

Figure 12.3. The charnel area of the Wilson Mound. (Milner 1984, fig. 5, p. 481. Reproduced by permission of the Society for American Archaeology from *American Antiquity* 49(3), 1984.)

sacred powers embodied in Cahokia and Mitchell as *axes mundi* to perform felicitous world renewal ritual. In this case, they would have invoked these sacred powers of Cahokia and Mitchell by long-distance interaction, relocating their CBL on a prominent position along the bluff line where they could align their deceased with these major world renewal cult heterarchies. Hence, in keeping with the general notion that world renewal cult heterarchies embodied the essential powers of the cosmos that they represented, the Kane Mounds CBL, situated on the eastern bluffs, would be able to invoke and participate in these powers even though it was spatially distant from both Cahokia and Mitchell.

In sum, the mortuary practices and CBLs of the later Mississippian period in the American Bottom clearly do not conform to what would be expected under the funerary view, while they are quite consistent with the Mourning/World Renewal Mortuary model, particularly the harmonized clan-cult version that would be expected in a heterarchical polyistic locale-centric social system experiencing highly intensified levels of subsistence and settlement. I will now move further back in time to the Stirling phase, considered by many archaeologists to be the high point of the Mississippian period of the American Bottom. The structure and contents of the Wilson Mound (Figure 12.3) can probably represent the whole set of known mounds of this type, such as the Powell Mound, the large Mitchell site burial mound, the East St. Louis burial mound, and the Great Mound of St. Louis. Milner considers all of these to be elite mounds—that is, he treats all these mounds as containing elite deceased, although different mounds may have had different degrees of "eliteness" (Milner 1998, 132).

The Wilson Mound Site

The Wilson Mound is considered by Milner to be one of the lesser elite CBLs of the Stirling phase floodplain region. This status assignment is based on both the rich but unvaried nature of the mortuary artifacts and the mound's rather isolated position with respect to the main body of Cahokian earthworks:

> What distinguished the Wilson Mound artifact assemblage from those associated with the non-elite cemeteries was the sheer quantity of beads and, especially, the presence of many whelk shells. While the large number of shell artifacts buried with the Wilson Mound skeletons probably indicated membership in the elite social stratum, the relative position of these individuals within that social structure apparently did not warrant the inclusion of artifacts restricted to the highest level of the elite hierarchy. The location of the Wilson Mound on the outskirts of the Cahokia

site reinforces this interpretation, since the mound was situated far from the central walled precinct, presumably the most important part of the Cahokia site. Geographic and social distances were perhaps congruent, at least in this case. (Milner 1984, 482–83)

The primary mortuary feature of the mound was located on the platform under the upper level of the mound. It was rectangular and a little larger than 4 meters by 5 meters (Figure 12.3). Milner specifies that most of the burials were "disarticulated and grouped to form distinct bundles containing the remains of several different individuals" (Milner 1984, 480). Associated with these burials were large quantities of whelk shells, both worked and unworked, and whelk shell beads displaying the whole qualitative range, from quite roughly made beads to the finest beads (Milner 1998, 131–32). Also, many bundle burials had completed whelk beads accompanying them.

Critical Discussion

Even though having multiple bundle burials, thereby displaying a distinct communal-like (commoner) pattern, the Wilson Mound is interpreted by Milner as an elite cemetery, although a distinctly "lesser elite" cemetery. He comes to this conclusion on the basis of several criteria. First, it is materially rich. Its richness, however, is *only* in whelk shells and beads. That is, one reason the mound funerary burials count as only among lesser elite is that they lack the variety of exotica that he claims one would expect of elite treatment. Furthermore, according to Milner, while "entire whelk shells and derived artifacts evidently were valued by the Mississippian Indians of the American Bottom" it turns out that "all segments of this society had at least limited access to such items" (1984, 482), confirming my earlier comment in the previous chapter that the boundary between "elite" and "commoner" seemed to be unusually permeable for a class-structured or even a ranked chiefdom society. Second, and possible equally or even more telling, the deceased of the Wilson Mound are lesser elite because the mound is located west of the Powell Mound, which is itself treated as conventionally marking the western boundary of Cahokia. For him, these burials must count as only lesser elite. According to his criteria, a burial population is "elite" only if it is found in a mound having rich artifactual residue (the more varied and exotic the more elitist) and if it is associated with one of the multiple-mound sites (if it is found in a mound that is isolated, such as the Kane Mounds site, then it does not count as an elite but as a commoner mound). That its relative position marks its "eliteness" is clear since if it is located, as in the Wilson Mound case, so as to be neither completely isolated nor clearly a closely related part of a multiple-mound locale, then it hovers socially in-between.

While appearing straightforward, the criteria Milner uses to define the categories of "elite" and "commoner" CBLs become a bit convoluted and circular in application. As mentioned above, he has two primary criteria for a CBL to count as an elite mortuary feature: (1) it must be a materially rich mound; and (2) the mound must be in association with others, constituting a multiple-mound site. That is to say, if mortuary remains are found in a mound that can pass as one making up what I refer to as a world renewal cult heterarchy site, then they are elite CBLs and the mortuary contents are, ipso facto, elite burials. If similar remains are found in a mound that is not part of a cult heterarchy, such as the Kane Mounds, then they are non-elite. This means that if a mortuary mound is on the margin of a multiple-mound site, as in the case of the Wilson Mound, it can pass as elite but is distinctly not among those that have high elite status. Similarly, of course, if mortuary remains are found within the precincts of a multiple-mound site but not in a mound (for example, the Fingerhut site in Cahokia), then these qualify as non-elite, presumably being the retainers of the elites found in the nearby mounds.[5] However, this assessment of non-eliteness is gained at some cost to overall coherence. For example, with regard to outlying cemeteries, the absence of a mound at the BBB Motor site requires Milner's identifying this as a non-elite cemetery, despite the presence of the rich Stirling phase figurines and other indicators of ritual, including a possible temple and/or priestly residential structure, as recognized by Emerson (1997b, 178, 184). Therefore, I detect some equivocation on Milner's part when he comments that perhaps "the BBB Motor site structures, which did not contain bones, were temples or buildings used by mortuary attendants. Yet the BBB Motor site pairing of structures and burials is reminiscent of the charnel structure and burial mound found at large Mississippian town-and-mound centers throughout the Southeast and Midwest, including Cahokia" (Milner 1984, 473).

Clearly Milner has contradictory criteria underwriting his interpretive treatment of the mortuary record. He is reliant on the funerary view, of course, and he is also committed to the hierarchical monistic modular polity account and the assumption that differential mortuary treatment marks differential rank. Given these premises, he concludes that mound burial treatment equals elite rank, as long as the mounds are in "centers" and are not isolated, and that nonmound burials equal commoner rank, unless they are situated in isolated, nonmound locales that have structures and facilities that can be interpreted as nondomestic and, even better, religious in nature. However, there are also mounds that are non-elite because, although clearly having nondomestic and (probably) religious structures, they are very isolated on the bluffs overlooking the floodplain.

According to the funerary view, however, status does not depend on only the mortuary context. The material content and facilities of the burial components must also be appropriate to the rank of the deceased. In these terms, high-ranking individuals should be marked by special artifacts, exclusive post-mortem treatment, excessive labor investment in their mortuary facilities (for example, graves), and so on. Since Mississippian settlement is sedentary, there should be minimal bone bundle burials. However, in the American Bottom Mississippian period, bone bundles are equally common in "commoner" and "elite" CBLs. Exotic artifacts, often associated with "elite" burial, are found in "rural" (that is, "commoner") contexts, while being absent in some "elite" burial mounds (a point that Milner stresses [2003, 137]). As I point out above, Milner recognizes the Wilson Mound as marginally elite because of its peripheral association with the other Cahokian mounds but notes that, except for quantities of shell (both bead artifacts and unmodified shell material), the other types of exotic artifacts that one could expect to find in an elite CBL, such as copper sheets, mica blocks, crystals, exotic chert artifacts, and so on, are absent.

In sum, the convoluted nature of Milner's mortuary criteria results in a conclusion that, in my view, is internally contradictory. He observes, "The communal treatment of the dead, which included burial in large mortuary features, is characteristic of the American Bottom elite burial areas. An emphasis on communal mortuary behavior perhaps reflected the structuring of American Bottom society" (Milner 1984, 482). While I can agree with Milner that an "emphasis on communal mortuary behavior perhaps reflected the structuring of American Bottom society," this would not be consistent with a dominance hierarchical structuring. Indeed, recently Milner has taken particular note of the difficulties with his argument by claiming that, at least in the early stages of ranked societies, the privileging of the elite does not translate into depriving the commoner of either adequate nutrition or, for that matter, some access to wealth (Milner 2003, 137). According to Milner's reasoning, during the early stages of hierarchical formation, the elite rulers (the "chiefs") do not have any special privileges that would ensure their having an average higher level of health than those they subordinate. As he puts it, "rather obvious examples of fine artifacts, special architecture, and elaborate mortuary practices indicating the existence of social hierarchies precede the capacity of leaders to martial sufficient resources to have much of an effect on their health" and, therefore, since skeletal "indicators of diet and disease provide a mixed picture of status-related differences in the physical well-being of members of Mississippian societies, . . . it is by no means clear that important people ate much better or were any healthier than everybody else" (Milner 2003, 137).

Interestingly, he does not provide any theoretical support or empirical grounding for this assertion other than the American Bottom mortuary record. For example, even if we accept that the etiquette of chiefly rule may stipulate that elites must eat and live much like commoners (even to the point of suffering nutritional deprivation in common with their followers when necessary), we need not deduce from this generality that the dependents of the elites would need to be subjected to the same constraints as the dependents of the commoners, especially the infants and children. In periods of nutritional hardship, for example, although the adult elites, caught up in the spirit of noblesse oblige, might join their followers in mutual suffering, they very likely would buffer their own infants from the same nutritional deprivation. Since such relatively short periods of deprivation impact mostly on infants and children, then, under such a chiefly regime, not only should infant and child mortality rates be lower for the offspring of the elites (since the young dependents of the elites would not suffer the type of nutritional deprivation causing, for example, a high incidence of linear enamel hyperplasia, noted by Milner as a major indicator of short-term infant and childhood nutritional stress), but also the absence of evidence of childhood nutritional deprivation should quickly come to characterize adult elite burials.

The problem is that this absence of linear enamel hyperplasia is precisely what does not occur in the supposed elite cemeteries that Milner studies. Instead, there is an equitable distribution of health and disease across the adult mortuary population. Indeed, as I note earlier, in Milner's in-depth study of the American Bottom mortuary record, he concludes that the mortuary "collections indicate a relatively high level of community health during the Mississippian period. . . . [This reflects] access to a nutritionally complete diet, which included storable foodstuffs, and a low or moderate disease load" (Milner 1982, 242). While he did not expect this finding, it is fully consistent with the heterarchical polyistic locale-centric account. The latter recognizes that disparities will exist but that these are embodied in enabling hierarchical structures, and these are based on agentive autonomy. Hence, when rationing is required the queue-principle goes into effect and resources are distributed equitably according to need: all families and their young dependents, without discrimination or bias, will have access to the same proportional quantity and quality of resources so that all will be subject to the same nutritional and other materially based stresses.

Alternative Account

The alternative interpretation, of course, is to treat the mortuary record of the Stirling phase as the outcome of cult alliance CBLs. In this way many of the inconsistencies outlined above are dissolved. First, the aspects of this record that support its communal attribution are fully consistent with this model. As specified in detail earlier in this chapter, the mortuary data mediating a world renewal cult heterarchy would be expected to display the outcome of major and systematic postmortem manipulation. Each incremental step in the postmortem manipulation process would see the individualism of the deceased being suppressed as the relevance of the deceased's participant mortuary role is reduced and that of the symbolic warranting role is forefronted. This is also consistent with finding artifacts in deposits that cannot be associated with any particular individual. Milner's description of the Wilson Mound mortuary deposit fits what we could expect of such postmortem manipulation:

> Only a few of these bones were articulated, most were disarticulated and grouped to form distinct bundles containing the remains of several different individuals. . . . Many of the disarticulated bones displayed multiple cut marks where ligaments and tendons had once been inserted and several long bones had cut marks distributed along the lengths of their diaphyses. These cut marks indicate that the bones had been separated from one another and cleaned of adhering soft tissue. The varied degrees of articulation as well as the location and extent of cutting suggest that the skeletons were at different stages of decomposition before the bones were separated, cleaned, and, finally, buried in the Wilson Mound feature. (Milner 1984, 480)

There are two particularly notable components to the patterning described above: (1) the bone bundles of groups of individuals were deposited as discrete sets; and (2) the individuals making up a grouping were at different stages of bodily decomposition when all the deceased were gathered (Figure 12.3). Under the mourning/world renewal mortuary view, the deceased constitute an important treasury of the symbolic pragmatic capital enabling the cult to perform world renewal rituals mediated by postmortem human sacrificial offerings. Therefore, the deceased would be curated in anticipation of important rituals (for example, temporarily deposited in mortuary pits so as to hasten flesh decomposition or stored on scaffolding). Each cult making up an alliance would be expected to contribute an appropriate sacrificial offering at the time of a world renewal rite. Consistent with the above in the Wilson Mound are the bone bundles composed of a collection of different individuals who were at different stages of decomposition, some requiring flesh removal and others not requiring this. Cults would have to dip into their mortuary capital treasury according to seasonally or other objectively determined scheduling and not according to convenience of death of their members and their dependents. Furthermore, if their mortuary treasuries were a bit low, they could apparently supplement or substitute postmortem offerings with ocean shell beads and/or raw material of ocean shell.

That these deposits were discrete sets of several individuals bundled together and separated from other like sets is also completely consistent with the claim of the World Renewal Cult Heterarchy model, namely, that several autonomous cults would constitute a mutualistic alliance. It is likely, therefore, that these discrete deposits (as indicated in Figure 12.3) demarcate the contributions of particular autonomous cults making up a given alliance. That is, the discrete sets of several individual bundles of bones would be consistent with the mortuary contributions of each cult being separated within the total collection so that each cult could be recognized as fulfilling its obligations and thereby sustaining its reputation. Furthermore, as part of the world renewal process, neighboring cult alliances would be invited to participate, and they would also be expected to contribute bone bundles of their own deceased or their symbolic pragmatic equivalent (for example, marine shells, either as beads or worked and unworked shell pieces). Again, these would be kept together as a discrete group offering so that all the participating cults could be given public recognition of their contributions.

In short, the Wilson Mound and its contents would be consistent with the notion that the separate communities making up Cahokia and its precincts were not individual kinship-based communities but instead were cult alliances that affiliated into a world renewal cult heterarchy. Since the contents of the Wilson Mound (that is, dual mortuary area/charnel house, large and discrete sets of bone bundles, large and usually discrete sets of exotic artifact deposits separate from the burial deposits as such, and so on) are replicated in other known large mounds, this conclusion can be generalized to the latter mounds, thereby reinforcing the World Renewal Cult Heterarchy model.

PROVISIONAL CONCLUSION

This overview of the mortuary record for the Stirling, Moorehead, and (possibly) Sand Prairie phases prepares the grounds for stepping back to the opening of the Mississippian period, the Lohmann phase. In one sense, some of the best mortuary data available relate to this phase. In another sense, however, the data are also very limited since they are almost exclusively based on two mortuary locales: Mound 72 in Cahokia and the Lohmann phase occupation of the BBB Motor site, about four kilometers northeast of "downtown" Cahokia.[6] Both of these locales have been intensely studied, and the excavators (in both cases) have assessed them as elite burial locales, with Mound 72 being characterized as possibly containing the Lohmann phase chiefs of an important subcommunity of Cahokia, or their immediate relatives, along with retainers (Fowler et al. 1999, 187–89), and the Lohmann phase occupation of the BBB Motor site being assessed as the rural nodal site of a low-ranking elite lineage (Emerson 1997a, 221).

In the preceding chapter I address the latter site and argue that it probably manifests the operations of an autonomous female-based fecundity world renewal cult or cult alliance. Instead of repeating that argument here, I will focus on Mound 72. This is a very important and complex feature, and, as I comment at the beginning of this chapter, it has been used by proponents of all the different versions of the hierarchical monistic modular polity account to demonstrate that Cahokia could be nothing else but a dominance-based, rank-ordered society, the seat of one or more powerful rulers. To do justice to this important feature and the interpretations that have been made of it, therefore, I devote the following chapter to a description of the mound and its associated material features and contents, a summary description of its larger context (Woodhenge 72), and a critique of the hierarchical account of this major feature. This overview is followed by the detailed presentation of the alternative account, namely, that Mound 72 was the CBL of a specialized collegial-priestly cult, which I term the *Woodhenge 72 cult,* which means that the complex mortuary contents should be interpreted as the material medium, context, and outcome of a history of both postmortem and lethal human sacrifice by which the cosmos was sustained.

13

Mound 72

Funerary Monument or World Renewal Icon?

Mound 72 takes us back to the Lohmann phase (or earlier), which has been deemed the opening scene of the Mississippian period in the American Bottom. As I note in an earlier chapter, many proponents of the hierarchical monistic modular polity account point or allude to Mound 72 as being among the strongest supporting evidence for this view.[1] Although Mound 72 has many bundle burials, it also has a large number of extended burials. In fact, the latter make up the majority of mortuary deposits. Therefore, on first appearance numerous indicators would suggest that this was a cemetery manifesting hierarchy and differential status. However, the supposition that Mound 72 is a cemetery or even marks a chiefdom-type social system does not logically follow from this burial pattern, since, under the Autonomous Cult model (and especially the ecclesiastic-communal cult version), hierarchy generated by social differentiation based on specialization (laity/clergy) and age-set seniority is recognized as part of this type of cult. At the same time, however, we must remember that under this model the hierarchy is characterized as an enabling and not a dominance hierarchy. Autonomy is the operative value of the squatter ethos. This means that the hierarchy is built on the authority of obligations, duties, responsibilities, and entitlements, and not on rights and privileges; furthermore, it also means that decisions are made by consensus among all the parties that must implement the decisions.

I first describe the most relevant components and associations of Mound 72. This is followed by the hierarchical monistic modular polity interpretation, which, of course, takes a strong funerary perspective with regard to the mortuary data and a symbolic referential perspective with regard to the monumental aspect of this mound and its archaeological context—in particular, what Melvin Fowler refers to as Woodhenge 72 (Fowler 1991, 6–9; 1996, 49–55; Fowler et al. 1999, 1–11). Following a critique of the funerary and symbolic referential interpretations of these mortuary data and their immediate material context, I reinterpret the same data in the framework of the Mourning/World Renewal

Mortuary model and the symbolic pragmatic perspective. When Woodhenge 72 and its associated feature, Mound 72, are in total shown to be interpreted more coherently in these rather than the former terms, the World Renewal Cult Heterarchy model is strongly supported.

The Monumental Component

As noted in the previous chapter, Mound 72 is a rather small ridge-top mound that is about 930 meters due south of Monks Mound or, more specifically, due south of a large post pit that was found on the southwestern corner of the first terrace of Monks Mound (Fowler 1991, 3). There are a number of other ridge-top mounds in Cahokia, such as Rattlesnake Mound (Mound 66), which is the largest ridge-top mound, Powell Mound (Mound 86), and Mound 95 of the Tippetts Group. Not only are all of these larger than Mound 72, but also they are oriented due east-west, while Mound 72, which is only about fifty meters long, is oriented to azimuth 120° (an orientation that reciprocally marks the southeastern winter solstice sunrise and the northwestern summer solstice sunset). Furthermore, Fowler has established that the southeast end of Mound 72 covers a large post pit and that a line joining this post pit and the post pit on the southwest corner of the first terrace of Monks Mound would define a north-south axis. He also established that there is a second, matching post pit under the northwest end of Mound 72. He calls the southeast feature Post Pit 1 (PP1 or Feature 1) and the northwest feature Post Pit 2 (PP2 or Feature 204; Figure 13.1).

PP1 and PP2 are effectively identical to the post pits characteristic of the large woodhenges in Tract 15A due west of Monks Mound and northwest of Mound 72. Four—or possibly five or more—woodhenge circles or partial circles were sequentially constructed on Tract 15A. Most had or shared a large observation post at the epicenter. Aligning the center post of the Tract 15A woodhenges with different perimeter posts, an observer could note the equinoctial and the summer and winter solstitial sunrises on the eastern horizon. In fact, the east-west axis through the center post was aligned through the large post pit on the southwest corner of the first terrace of Monks Mound, and the same post pit was aligned north-to-south with PP1 of Mound 72. We now know that these Tract 15A woodhenges were built and used after Mound 72 was abandoned.

Fowler has identified Mound 96, a small mound 125 meters southwest of Mound 72. He has noted that a line drawn from PP1 to the center of Mound

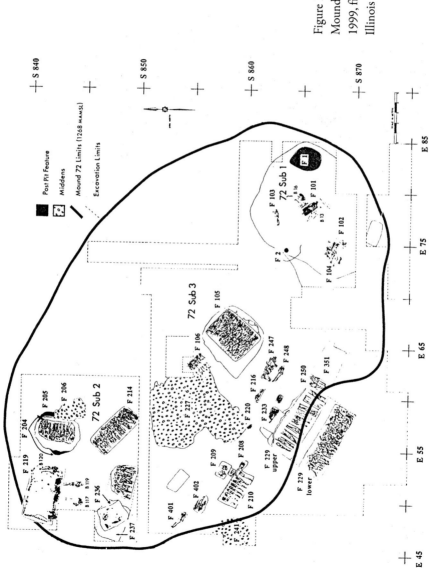

Figure 13.1. Plan map of Mound 72. (Fowler et al. 1999, fig. 1.6, p. 7. Courtesy Illinois State Museum.)

96 would delineate the reciprocal summer solstice rising and winter solstice setting points on the horizon (Fowler 1991, 3). He postulated that PP1, PP2, and the possible post pit under Mound 96 were major components of a woodhenge monument. To confirm this hypothesis, he undertook a series of geomagnetic surveys combined with coring to locate undersurface anomalies that could be excavated to confirm whether they were post pits and thereby demonstrate the residue of a woodhenge circle (Figure 13.2). Indeed, in this way he was able to establish three more post pits, all in the eastern arc. He notes, "This confirmation of three more post pits along the eastern arc, including such significant positions as the winter solstice and equinox loci, greatly strengthens the hypothesis of the existence of Woodhenge 72" (Fowler et al. 1999, 151; also see Fowler 1996, 36–40).

Woodhenge 72 is about 125 meters in diameter and is postulated to have had forty-eight perimeter posts averaging 40 to 50 centimeters in diameter and set in post pits up to 3 meters deep. Radiocarbon dating suggests that it may actually predate the Lohmann phase of the Mississippian period (Fowler et al. 1999, 59–60). Of course, as mentioned earlier, a line drawn due north from PP1 to the post pit on the southwest corner of the terrace of Monks Mound defines a north-south axis. Thus, just as the woodhenges of Tract 15A relate to Monks Mound, in this case, by means of the east-west equinoctial axis, the earlier Woodhenge 72 was equivalently linked to Monks Mound, in this case, by PP1 being part of the north-south axis through the southwest corner post of Monks Mound as well as being part of the configuration delineating the summer solstice sunrise.

As an earthen construction, Mound 72 is internally complex (Figure 13.1). It consists of three primary mounds covered by the construction of a major mantle of earth. Fowler refers to these primary mounds as 72Sub1, 72Sub2, and 72Sub3. PP1 (Feature 1) and PP2 (Feature 204) are covered by 72Sub1 and 72Sub2, respectively. Primary mound 72Sub3 is, roughly speaking, midway between PP1 and PP2. Primary mound 72Sub1 started as a low rectangular mound, which covered a set of burials placed on the ground in its western sector, and it also incorporated into its eastern sector the posts that were sequentially set in PP1. Subsequently, 72Sub1 was modified with the addition of a ramp oriented due west and another oriented due east. At least three and possibly four post insertion-and-extraction cycles were carried out during the history of usage of PP1, two prior to the construction of 72Sub1 and one or possibly two after.

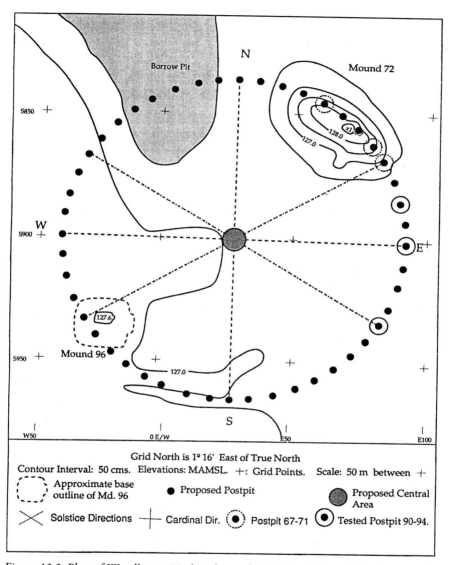

Figure 13.2. Plan of Woodhenge 72. (Fowler et al. 1999, fig. 11.1, p. 142. Courtesy Illinois State Museum.)

The complementary northeastern primary mound 72Sub2 also started as a low rectangular platform, in this case covering the remains of a wall-trench structure that is interpreted by Fowler as a charnel house. His interpretation is based on the presence of a series of deceased (both bone bundle burials and extended burials) placed on a low platform immediately covering the charnel structure and then covered with more earth. In a manner similar to the incorporation of PP1 by 72Sub1, 72Sub2 incorporated PP2 into its northeast corner. In both cases, perimeter posts were inserted and extracted from these pits prior to the construction of their respective primary mounds. Using radiocarbon dating of a midden in PP2 and of log cribbing in PP1, Fowler concludes that these two post pits were probably used contemporaneously and that they may very well have been initially constructed in the later Terminal Late Woodland period. If he is correct, this means that Woodhenge 72 would predate the Mississippian period.

What all this suggests is that not only did the activities related to Woodhenge 72 predate the timing of the mortuary events that these two primary mounds cover, but also Woodhenge 72 and these primary mounds continued to be used well after they were constructed. That is, as important as the mortuary events may have been, these primary mounds were not cemeteries as such, since they were used as mound platforms on which to conduct ongoing Woodhenge 72–related ritual activities, including the performance of post extraction-insertion rituals, and more mortuary rites. This point raises a question about the nature of the mortuary events themselves. While archaeologists have generally recognized that a number of the burials under 72Sub1 and those incorporated into 72Sub2 were the material residue of the funerals of ranking elites of Cahokia, if these two primary mounds were actively used for rituals well after these particular mortuary events had been completed, then they certainly would not count as cemeteries in the sense that cemeteries are specialized CBLs generated by a series of terminal funerary events, as defined by the Cemetery model.

In any case, a series of construction additions made to 72Sub2—tightly related to mortuary events of a very important nature (described below)—resulted in the formation of a third primary mound, 72Sub3, bracketed by 72Sub2 to the northwest and 72Sub1 to the southeast. Ultimately, with further modifications, primary mound 72Sub3 was expanded northwest to cover and incorporate most of 72Sub2, and it was extended southeast to just short of primary mound 72Sub1. Indeed, sometimes Fowler speaks of 72Sub3 as simply the extension of 72Sub2 (Fowler 1996, 45). Following a series of important mortuary events performed along the southwestern sector of this expanded primary mound, all three were covered by an earth mantle topped by a ridging formation, thereby constituting Mound 72.[2] After a number of further intrusive mortuary deposits were made, Mound 72 was abandoned; this probably also marked the abandonment of Woodhenge 72 and the opening of a new woodhenge to the northwest in Tract 15-A. These changes also are usually taken to mark the end of the Lohmann phase and the opening of the Stirling phase.

The Mortuary Component

As noted above, several mortuary deposits were made on the original ground surface and subsequently covered by the building of primary mound 72Sub1 (Figure 13.1 and Figure 13.3; Rose 1999, 64). The most important was the well-known Beaded Burial, which actually consisted of two adult male burials, Burials 13 and 14, placed five meters west of PP1, with Burial 13 being positioned on top of Burial 14. Most archaeologists have treated these as terminal funerary burials. Spatially associated with them were four other deceased, and these together constitute what is referred to as Feature 101 (Figure 13.3). Burial 13 is treated by many as the remains of an individual who occupied a high-ranking position in the political hierarchy of Cahokia. Indeed, although specifically denied by Fowler (Fowler et al. 1999, 188), the suggestion has been made that the Burial 13 deceased may have been one of the ruling paramount chiefs (see, for example, Emerson and Pauketat 2002, 114).

As noted above, Burial 13 is on top of Burial 14. The two were separated by a woven textile richly decorated with about twenty thousand marine-shell beads (Fowler et al. 1999, 132). While Jerome Rose refers to this artifact as a beaded cape (Rose 1999, 76), Fowler has termed it a platform of beads. He has also noted that it is apparently in the form of a raptor, probably a falcon.[3] Burial 13 is in a supine position on top of the cape and with head facing southeast, and Burial 14 is in a prone position under the cape, and this individual is oriented in the reverse, head to the northwest (Fowler et al. 1999, 167). Fowler also notes that at least "20 bone-disc beads were recovered around the 'Beaded Burial' . . . [indicating that] the burials were bound before placement in this burial context" (Fowler et al. 1999, 132). Finally, although the post in PP1 (Woodhenge 72 Locus V-NE, Figure 13.2) was only about 4.5–5 meters immediately east of this dual burial, the 145° burial axis orients on Locus III-NE, which is two posts to the southeast of PP1.[4] The Locus III-NE post apparently played a very significant role in terms of the total mortuary program

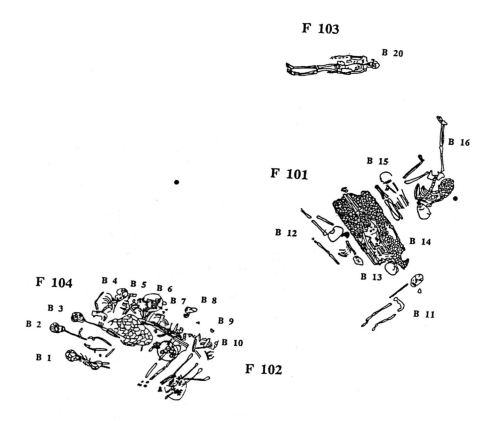

Figure 13.3. The Beaded Burials. (Fowler et al. 1999, fig. 6.1, p. 64. Courtesy Illinois State Museum.)

associated with Mound 72 since, as I describe in detail shortly, at least four other major burial events—Features 214, 105, 106, and 229—were also oriented on this locus (Figure 13.4). However, these latter features and the events that generated them occurred much later than the mortuary deposits under 72Sub1.

Since in this perspective Burials 13 and 14 are interpreted as the result of funerary rites performed for two of the ruling elites (or "chiefs") of one or more of the subcommunities making up Cahokia, they might logically be interpreted as determining the standing of the four other associated Feature 101 burials (Figure 13.3). In this case, drawing analogically on the mortuary rites of the historic Natchez for the paramount chief (their Great Sun, as reported in Swanton 1911, 138–40), most Cahokian archaeologists treat these other buri-

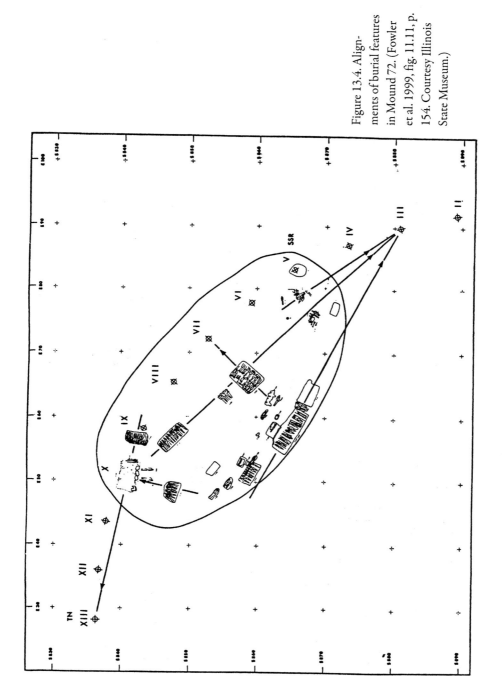

Figure 13.4. Alignments of burial features in Mound 72. (Fowler et al. 1999, fig. 11.11, p. 154. Courtesy Illinois State Museum.)

als as auxiliary components of Burials 13 and 14 and refer to these deceased as "retainers." Of these burials, only three—Burials 11, 12, and 16—are primary burials. Burial 15 is clearly a bundle burial. Interpreting these individuals as sacrificed retainers is supported by the fact that Burial 16 is in a prone position with one leg flexed. Rose suggests that this positioning may be the result of the individual's having been "thrown down or not completely dead [sic] when positioned" (Rose 1999, 64), an interpretation that is supported by Fowler (Fowler et al. 1999, 168). By extension, the individuals in the other two primary burials, Burial 11 and Burial 12, may also have been killed as lethal sacrifices. Fowler includes Burial 20 (Feature 103) within this group of retainers.

Feature 102 is a set of seven burials about seven meters southwest of Feature 101 and also on the ground beneath the primary mound 72Sub1 (Burials 4–10, Figure 13.3).[5] Fowler (Fowler et al. 1999, 168) describes these as secondary burials, being partially disarticulated. This implies that, after a period of exposure, possibly in a charnel structure, they were buried. Rose notes that five were young adults and that the ages of the other two were indeterminable; in addition, while their sex could not be specified, "two exhibit gracile characteristics of females" (Rose 1999, 64). Associated with these burials was the largest and most impressive deposit of artifacts found in the American Bottom mortuary context, including, according to Steven Ahler, two separate deposits of projectile points, organized as bundles: cache 1550 (332 points) being associated with Burial 10, and cache 1551 (413 points) being associated with Burial 6 (Ahler 1999, 102–3). There were fifteen chunkey stones organized in two piles. Fowler notes that ten "stones were just below the hips and over the upper right leg of Burial 8, and a second group of five stones was lying against the upper left leg of Burial 7" (Fowler et al. 1999, 137); in addition, there were three conjoined rolls of copper sheeting (referred to as a "staff" by Fowler), a large deposit of unworked mica sheets (deteriorated into fragments), and a large cache of two or three thousand beads associated with the possible residue of a leather bag (Fowler et al. 1999, 136). Features 101, 102, and 103 are treated by Fowler as contemporaneous, probably the outcome of a complex mortuary event that was terminated by the placement of a meter-thick covering of sediments constituting the first stage of primary mound 72Sub1, probably with its third post insertion:

> With the deposit of all these burials and accompanying goods, the burial ceremonies were completed. The burials were then covered by a well-constructed platform mound just over 1m in height, Mound 72Sub1. . . . The primary sediment utilized was a very dark gumbo clay intermixed with

some sediments of lighter color. The overall appearance was of a blue-black mound. Once the mound achieved the desired form and height, ... it was capped with a specially prepared mix of sand and clay, which gave the entire surface an almost white color. This 10-centimeter-thick surface was very durable and resistant to weathering. (Fowler et al. 1999, 170)

As noted above, the northwestern primary mound, 72Sub2, was also associated with a complex set of mortuary features. As described by Fowler, it is a low, two-tiered or stepped rectangular platform "oriented to the cardinal points with the lower platform or terrace on the east. In form, 72Sub2 was roughly the same as the earlier 72Sub1 without the apron over the post pit area" (Fowler et al. 1999, 28). Excavation to the base of the western half of this mound revealed the residue of a wall-trench structure with a shallow basin (Feature 225). Its eastern screened wall was about seven meters west of PP2 (Figures 13.1). After this structure had been removed and its basin filled, a low platform mound was built over it, about thirty centimeters high. PP2 (Locus IX-NE) and possibly the post in Locus X-NE to its northwest are assumed to have been maintained as intrinsic components of this low platform (Figure 13.4). According to Fowler, this "low platform was apparently built for the purpose of displaying a series of human remains. Some of these were remains of persons whose bodies had been stored for some time, as they were deposited as bundles of bones" (Fowler et al. 1999, 175).

The bundle burials and the extended burials placed on the platform covering the charnel structure (Feature 225) are referred to as Feature 219 (Figure 13.5). The bundle burials were located on the area defined as covering the south wall trench of the charnel structure. The area covering the east wall trench had two extended burials (Burials 119 and 120), and immediately south of the central part of the south wall-trench there were two more (Burials 117 and 118). Rose (1999, 65) divides the bundle burials into two categories: bone pile burials (Burials 121 and 122) and bundle burials proper. The bone pile was placed in the region covering the central portion of the south wall-trench, and it contained an estimated thirteen individuals. The bones were organized into three piles by category: long bones, flat bones, and skulls (with small bones). The flat bones (presumably ribs, scapulas, innominates, and so on) were in the center; the long bones, to the east of them; and the skulls and small bones, to the west. At the west end of this south wall-trench area were four bundle burials with their skulls placed to the south.

The two extended burials (Burials 119 and 120), positioned just above the east end of the charnel structure, were aligned north-south with heads to the

F 219

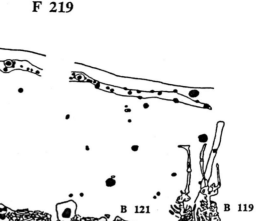

Figure 13.5. Feature 225 (charnel structure) and Feature 219, the associated burials. (Fowler et al. 1999, fig. 6.2, p. 65. Courtesy Illinois State Museum.)

south. According to Fowler, these were probably the ranking burials of this feature: "These were both males positioned with the dorsal side up. The eastern most of these burials (Burial 119) had his head facing west" (Fowler et al. 1999, 175). Fowler specifically draws a parallel between these two adult male burials and Burials 13 and 14 under 72Sub1 on the basis of dual patterning, both being associated with primary mounds and post pits and having associated deceased. He notes that Burials 13 and 14 were organized so that the former was on top of the latter, but he considers this largely a variant of Burials 120 and 119, which were side by side. Hence, he suggests that these latter two burials were probably the "primary personages" of Feature 219 and, therefore, that the associated burials would have been "offerings to these two" (Fowler et al. 1999, 176). These offerings would include not only the bundle and pile burials but also Burials 117 and 118—the two extended, heads-to-south burials southwest of these "central personages."

According to Rose (1999, 66), Burial 117 was probably the remains of a young (25–35) female, oriented with her head south. She was in a supine position "[b]oth arms were flexed with the hands placed with the palm-side up near the neck." She wore a beaded choker around her neck, as was found for Burial 118, east of her. This person was a young (25–35) male in a prone position, head to the south and facing west, also with arms flexed and the hands near the neck. Rose goes on to comment that the prone position "with hands near the face or neck is not unique and has been found elsewhere, but its significance is unknown" (Rose 1999, 66). In this regard, he comments that Burial 119, the male burial at the east end of the charnel structure, had the "right arm . . . flexed with the digits passing beneath the cervical vertebrae. What appears to be a hair piece made of shell beads was located 3 to 4 cm east of the neck" (Rose 1999, 66).

There are many more individual and small-group burial deposits in Mound 72, about half being extended and half being bundle burials. These are not described here except when needed. Instead, I now shift the focus to the other major Mound 72 mortuary deposits, these being a set of large pits containing mass burial deposits. Features 205 and 237 appear to have been the first of this type. Feature 205 is found due east of Feature 219, described above, and Feature 237 is found southwest of Feature 219 (Figure 13.1). Feature 237 consists of a large pit dug into the southern slope of 72Sub2, with its sides oriented almost to the cardinal directions and its long axis being a few degrees south of east. It contained nineteen extended individual burials laid in two layers. Once the pit was dug, the bottom was lined with sand and then with matting. The first or bottom layer of mortuary deposits consisted of ten extended burials. They were covered with another woven matting. Nine burials were placed on top, and another matting was laid down. All were oriented slightly east of north with heads toward the north. The pit was then filled. Rose estimates that the deceased were females and that the age span was between fifteen and twenty-five years old. As he suggests, the "limited sex and age range of this mass burial suggests sacrifice rather than an epidemic" (Rose 1999, 68).

A considerable period later, another pit was dug into the top of Feature 237, without penetrating to the burial level. This is referred to as Feature 236, and it contained the second large deposit of artifacts in Mound 72, including the largest cache of beads (estimated to be about thirty-six thousand), a large pile of chert projectile points, several broken ceramic vessels, many bone points, and so on. Feature 236 was slightly smaller than the underlying Feature 237, and its long axis was oriented parallel to the axis of Mound 72. Ahler (1999, 105) estimates that the "excavation and filling of this cache pit was evidently the last set of activities carried out in the northwest section of the mound. The change in orientation of the cache pit marked the beginning of activities that were associated with Mound 72Sub3 construction."

Feature 205 was very similar to Feature 237 except that it was a mortuary pit dug into the western insertion/extraction ramp of PP2 (Feature 204). Like Feature 237, its east-west axis was aligned a few degrees south of east, and its base was lined with fine sand and covered with matting. The mortuary deposit of twenty-two individual extended bodies was also in two layers, with the bodies oriented east-west (heads to the west), in contrast to the north-south orientation of the bodies in Feature 237. Again, the lower and upper layers were separated by matting, and the upper layer was also covered with matting, and then the pit was filled. Rose (1999, 66) estimates that these deceased also were younger females, ranging from twenty to thirty years of age.

These two mortuary features were directly associated with the primary mound 72Sub2 during its early phase. Marking a new phase was the formation of both Feature 236 with its large cache of artifacts, described above, and Feature 214, another mass mortuary pit deposit (Figure 13.1). This pit was dug into a ramp that had been built projecting from the southeast corner of 72Sub2, effectively reorienting this mound about 30° south of east, the same orientation as Feature 236. Unlike the two earlier mortuary pits, this one did not appear to have a sand-lined base, although it did have some form of bottom covering (probably matting). Twenty-four extended burials were laid in two layers, heads to the northeast, with matting covering and separating the lower layer from the upper layer, and another matting material covering the upper layer. Again, Rose estimates that all these were young females, "indicating sacrificial burial" (1999, 69). The pit was filled and shaped into a ramp with a trench on three sides and the northwest end incorporated into the summit of 72Sub2.[6]

The space between the southeast ramp extension of 72Sub2 and 72Sub1 came to be the location of two, probably complementary, mortuary deposits oriented along this new 135° axis: Features 105 and 106 (Figure 13.1 and Figure 13.6). Feature 106 consisted of four decapitated and handless males laid parallel on the original ground surface with torsos to the northeast. There were clear marks in the neck area indicating repeated "cutting with a small sharp instrument" (Rose 1999, 69). The deceased were young to middle-aged males, and the mortuary deposits were covered by a low mound. Feature 105 was a large

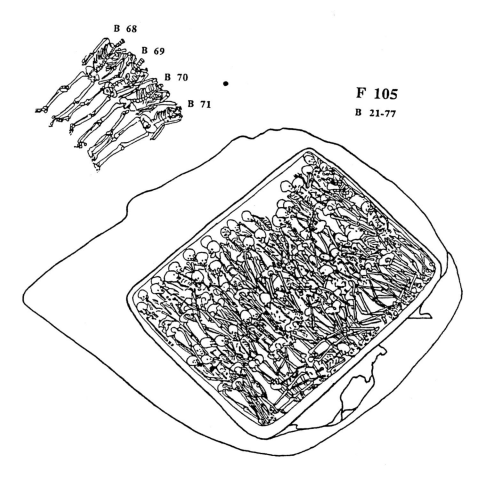

Figure 13.6. Features 105 and 106. (Fowler et al. 1999, fig. 6.6, p. 69. Courtesy Illinois State Museum.)

mortuary pit, very similar to the ones described above, except built to take fifty-three young females in two layers. The bodies in both the lower and upper layers were formed as two southwest-northeast oriented rows of extended burials with heads to the northwest. In the bottom layer, the feet of those making up the northwest row were by the heads of the bodies of those making up the southeast row. The same dual patterning was repeated for the upper layer of burials. Again, as in Features 205, 237, and 214, these were young females.

However, only a small sand patch, rather than a stratum, was reported on the bottom of the pit, while there were, apparently, the usual three layers of matting—one below, one separating the bottom from the upper layer, and one over the upper layer. Rose comments that the focus on young females and the "similarities to the other mass graves . . . substantiate the hypothesis that these were sacrificial burials" (Rose 1999, 70). It is likely that Features 105 and 106 were very close in time, since, according to Fowler, "some spillage of sediments from that mound construction [over Feature 106] can be seen in the west wall of the [Feature 105] pit. The females in Feature 105 were a dedicatory offering at the foot of the mound for the beheaded and behanded burials. The bodies of these young women and the portions of the mound over Feature 106 were covered over by a conical mound about 2 m high. The highest point of this mound . . . marked the central point of this area between 72Sub1 and 72Sub2" (Fowler et al. 1999, 177). Subsequently, this whole area, including most of 72Sub2, was covered by a single mound that Fowler refers to as 72Sub3. It stops short of the northwestern edge of 72Sub1.

Sometime before the final construction of Mound 72 by means of adding a covering mantle across all three primary mounds, what might be considered the most interesting mass mortuary deposit was made on the southwest side of 72Sub3. This is Feature 229, a long pit with its axis oriented northwest-southeast, effectively parallel to the axis on which Features 105 and 106 were oriented (Figure 13.7). As with most of the others, the floor of the pit was covered with white sand. The deceased were placed in two layers, more or less oriented on a perpendicular to the northwest-southeast axis. The lower layer consisted of twenty-nine adults, mostly males, ranging from quite young (15–20) to middle-aged (35–45). There is considerable evidence that most if not all of these individuals were violently killed in situ. There was abundant indication of violent blows to the back of the necks of several and at least three cases of decapitation, and most of the bodies were found prone, as if they had stood facing into the pit and along its southwest edge and then were hit from behind, causing them to collapse forward into the pit. The bodies were apparently left largely as they fell, since there was considerable disarray in their limbs. The mandible of one deceased had been fractured, and the heads of some of the others, although still attached to the bodies, were effectively partially removed (Rose 1999, 70; see also Fowler et al. 1999, 181). This lower stratum of burials was then covered by possibly a double layer of matting.

In strong contrast to the disarray of the lower stratum, the upper stratum of deceased consisted of ten neatly placed burial units consisting of a total of

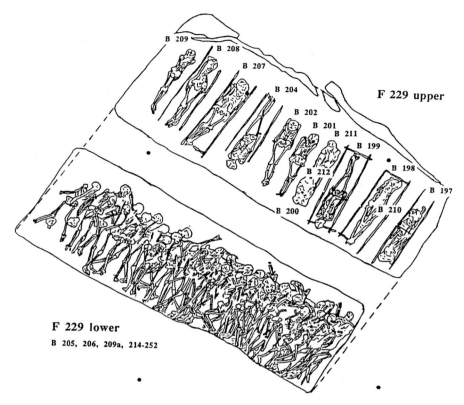

Figure 13.7. Feature 229. (Fowler et al. 1999, fig. 6.7, p. 71. Courtesy Illinois State Museum.)

fifteen individuals, all apparently curated, having been placed on litters and brought to this pit. They were placed in a northwest-southeast row, but their bodies were oriented northeast-southwest, with some heads to the southwest and some to the northeast, indicating that the deceased had probably been wrapped when brought on the litters. Although residue of only six cedar pole litters survived, likely all of the deceased had been on litters, since in one case there were pole impressions left in the matrix but no wood residues. Therefore, some of the litter poles may have been made of wood that was less rot resistant than cedar. All the deceased showed clear indications of extended postmortem exposure. Although most of the remains displayed a fair degree of bodily integrity, several were distinct bundle burials. All the bodies had been tightly bound, as indicated by bone tie beads being present in almost every case; even where these were not present, indications were clear of tight constriction to the body, usually at the upper chest/neck area, the elbows, and the feet. A number of the extended burials had the head significantly displaced from the normal position, usually by being pushed into the thorax region, and some had the upper vertebrae dislodged or missing. For example, the skull of Burial 202, placed about the middle of the row, "had been displaced onto the upper thorax region. As the axis was missing and the cervical vertebra was disturbed, decapitation before burial is suggested. The elbows were again severely constricted. This in conjunction with tie beads suggests binding" (Rose 1999, 72). The same was the case for Burial 207: "The dislocation of the skull and constriction at the elbows indicated binding" (Rose 1999, 72). Again, the constriction of Burial 209 (15–20 years of age, of indeterminable sex) "was severe and the head pushed down onto the chest lacks cervical vertebrae. This again suggests partial decomposition prior to preparation for burial" (Rose 1999, 72).

While both Rose and Fowler consider that the deceased making up the lower and upper strata of the first three mass mortuary deposits that I summarize above were lethal sacrifices, they agree that only the deceased making up the bottom of the two strata of Feature 229 had been subjected to lethal sacrifice.[7] In fact, Rose makes very clear that the contrast of the deceased in the lower and the upper strata—the former being sacrificial and the latter being funerary burial—means that the deceased in the upper stratum would have been from quite high ranking segments of the community while those in the lower stratum would have been from the very lowest stratum. In this regard, Rose suggests that some of them may have been war captives, particularly those found with embedded projectile points and/or with severe blows to the necks. For these reasons, he assessed all of the Feature 229–Lower burials as "the lowest social rank in the mound" (Rose 1999, 76). Indeed, partly because of their being deemed to have the lowest rank, Rose justified assigning high rank to the burials of the upper layer.

Probably not too long after its completion, Feature 229 and the associated primary mounds were covered by a mantle of sediments that generated Mound 72. A few other mortuary deposits were made into this mantle, but, as I comment above, the completion of this mound probably marked the abandonment of Woodhenge 72 and the opening of the first of a sequential series of woodhenges in Tract 15A.

I hope that I have done justice to the amazing and in-depth contribution that Fowler's extensive archaeological work has made. This is a permanent contribution to American Bottom archaeology. Of course, much more could be said about the layout of Woodhenge 72, the developmental history of the ritual locale that became what is called Mound 72, and the relations between the two. Some of this is discussed below. I have also left out a number of other "mass" mortuary deposits, as well as a good number of single or dual mortuary deposits, both extended and bone bundles. However, the above should be sufficient to indicate the range of mortuary events that occurred—these are quite adequate, I believe, to serve as the basis for summarizing and critiquing the interpretive treatment that I have claimed is characteristic of the hierarchical monistic modular polity account. In keeping with the hermeneutic spiral method, this interpretation and critique are followed by the alternative heterarchical polyistic locale-centric account in terms of the Mourning/World Renewal Mortuary model.

THE SYMBOLIC REFERENTIAL VIEW OF WOODHENGE 72

The interpretation that Fowler (Fowler et al. 1999, 167–89) presents of Woodhenge 72 and its associated Mound 72 is comprehensive. I will first summarize and critique his interpretation of Woodhenge 72 and Mound 72 as monuments and then I will examine his funerary interpretation of the mortuary contents of the latter. His characterization of Woodhenge 72 as a monumental expression of the cosmology is linked with the claim that the social system responsible for this monumental feature was itself organized to be congruent with this belief system. He draws his inspiration from the cosmology and social structure of historically known Native North American peoples, particularly using the culture and society of the historic Osage of the lower Missouri drainage as his analogical framework. He stresses that this is only for heuristic purposes, since making claims of direct connections between Cahokia and the Osage cannot be established definitively, even though in the 1700s and 1800s the Osage occupied the Osage River drainage in south-central Missouri, not too distant from the American Bottom. However, he asserts that the analogy is useful since the basic cultural themes and fundamental social structures of the Osage are variations of cultural and social structures that are widespread across the eastern and midcontinental regions (Fowler et al. 1999, 183; also see Kelly 1996, 97, 107).

According to Osage cosmology, the world is structured vertically into the Sky World and the Earth World, mediated by the Middle World (or *ho'-e-ga*), which is occupied by humans and all visible life-forms (Bailey 1995, 29–31). The world is also divided horizontally into east and west sectors. These vertical and horizontal sectors are related in a complementary oppositional manner, with the east representing the sacred powers of life associated with daylight, redness, maleness, and so on, and the west representing the sacred powers of death associated with night, blackness, femaleness, and so on. The Sky World is the world of life; the Earth World, the place of death. The immanentist cosmology of the Osage characterizes the Sun as a living, intentional sacred agent who is reborn each day by rising in the east from its "grave" below the earth, passing through the Sky World, and dying in the west by setting back into the earth (Fowler et al. 1999, 185; Kelly 1996, 106–9).

Fowler then correlates the dual structuring of the cosmos as expressed by the Osage cosmology with the dual structuring of the Osage society, pointing out that the historic Osage communities were divided into Sky and Earth moieties. In their traditional historic village settlements, the community was physically divided, with the lodges or houses of the Sky moiety clans located in the northern sector and those of the Earth moiety clans in the southern sector. The east-west axis of the village community was perceived as the pathway of the Sun. As Fowler notes, "Each half of the Osage town had a leader. The houses of these leaders were situated near the central path or divide—the Sky Chief to the north and Earth Chief to the south. These houses were on an east-to-west alignment with doors at either end. Both these leaders had equal power in the community and were considered the highest authorities. There was dual leadership with both major divisions of the cosmos represented" (Fowler et al. 1999, 185). In sum, Fowler claims that the social structure and the cosmology are simultaneously expressed in the community's settlement pattern. He then uses this cosmological and settlement-ideological summary to give a referential interpretation of Woodhenge 72, warranting this move by noting that the perimeter post circle was laid out in such a manner as to incorporate the major solar rising and setting turning points, that is, the solstices and equinoxes: "Consider the idea that the Woodhenge circle is a monumental representation of this same type of cosmology. The east-to-west axis (equinox sunrise to equinox sunset) divides the circle into an upper (north?) half, representing the Sky World, and a lower (south?) half, representing the Earth World" (Fowler et al. 1999, 183).

In chapter 10 I outline Fowler's interpretation of the patterning of Cahokia and his claim that it manifests a compound set of subcommunities related to each other in rank order, with the postulated community responsible for Monks Mound and the central precinct being probably the ranking community. Possibly realizing that this patterning cannot be neatly analyzed in the simpler dual terms of the Osage cultural and social kinship structures, he suggests, however, that the individual subcommunities might be amenable to this dualism and that Woodhenge 72 and the associated primary earthwork mounds (72Sub1 and 72Sub2) might therefore be the monumental expression of a dual structuring similar to the type expressed in Osage cosmology and underwriting the layout of their villages. Thus, the two primary mounds may represent the two moiety chiefs of one of the higher-ranking subcommunities of Cahokia, and the central personages buried in each—probably Burial 13 (the upper Beaded Burial) at the base of 72Sub1, and Burial 120, the deceased associated with Burial 119 and positioned atop the eastern wall-trench of the charnel house associated with 72Sub2—might be the dual chiefs of this subcommunity. In this regard, as I note earlier in this chapter, he does not agree with some claims that characterize the central burials of Mound 72 as the actual paramount chief or chiefs of Cahokia. Instead, he says, that these burials

were probably leaders of only one of the many communities of early Cahokia. The location of Woodhenge 3 in the western portion of Cahokia, for example, may represent another. Early Cahokia was probably made up of groups of chiefdoms whose headquarters were at Cahokia but whose power and wealth lay, perhaps, in the hinterlands in the American Bottom and beyond. It was the binding of these chiefdoms into a single political entity dominated by Monks Mound, and the leader headquartered there, that made Cahokia the center of the four quarters of the universe in its time. Mound 72 hints at this, but the final answers must be found elsewhere. (Fowler et al. 1999, 188–89)

Critique

The foregoing assessment is an exemplary expression of the hierarchical monistic modular polity view of the overall organization of the American Bottom social system. It highlights the two major attributes of this account by claiming, first, that Cahokia was a complex paramount chiefdom having ranked subchiefdoms, and second, that these subchiefdoms were headquartered in Cahokia while their sources of "power and wealth" were located (as exclusive territories?) "perhaps, in the hinterlands in the American Bottom and beyond." As we would expect, the funerary paradigm is applied to the mortuary record to reinforce this interpretation. Of course, there is a fundamental intelligibility to the view that Woodhenge 72, its directional alignments with the turning points defining the solar cycle, and its spatial relations with other monuments, such as Monks Mound, can be interpreted in terms of the cultural traditions they implicate. My support of this orientation should be clear, given my theoretical discussion of cultural traditions and their serving as the representational content of the symbolic aspect of material cultural features and artifacts. However, Fowler assumes a direct expressive relation between cosmology and settlement patterning. Note here that cosmology is a system of collective world beliefs. As such, what it is about is the cosmos, so that if the cosmos is the way that the representational content of the cosmology depicts it to be, then the cosmology is true. Therefore, by my saying that Fowler assumes a direct expressive relation between cosmology and settlement, I am saying that he is claiming that the settlement layout is an expression of a system of collective world beliefs, not an expression of what these beliefs are about, and presumably, the settlement is laid out in this way in order to refer to or designate the cosmos (or targeted aspects of the cosmos).

I have great difficulty with this claim since it commits the referential fallacy. As I note in chapter 3, typically the symbolic aspect of material culture is not used to make reference. Instead, it is used to exercise and manifest symbolic pragmatic force, namely, the warranting power to constitute the behavior it mediates as the type of activity intended. As I argue in this earlier chapter, constituting the action nature of behavior entails the doer expressing the appropriate intentions and manifesting the appropriate social position she/he occupies. Since both intentions and social positions are intangibles that must be expressed or disclosed to be known to relevant others, the stylistic aspect of material culture is critically important. It is the stylistics by which these intangible properties are manifested in the perception/understanding of all relevant parties. I also add in this earlier discussion that, typically, the symbolism of material cultural features, facilities, and artifacts are experienced as reified by their users. This means that they are experienced as icons—symbols that are taken to be participating in the very nature of what they represent. For a symbol to be part of what it represents means that it is used expressively, not referentially. To be used expressively means that it is used to address, invoke, manifest, or presence the relevant properties of the phenomenon that it represents (Taylor 1985b, 266–73).[8]

If this is the case, then a reassessment of the aspect of the Osage cultural tradition or collective intentionality directly underwriting and governing their settlement patterning has to be made. Certainly, this settlement patterning manifests their cultural tradition, but the aspect it is realizing in a direct manner would not be their cosmology (that is, their collective beliefs), but would instead be their ideology (that is, their collective settlement strategy). The contents of this W→M direction of fit strategy would be the range of rules and protocols that specified the patterned way that the settlement layout must be to satisfy the collective prior intentions. Thus, the division of the settlement into northern and southern sectors, and so on, manifests these rules and protocols; therefore, these rules would be ideological surface structures having considerable historical contingency. Where the cosmology figures in this is as the background of collective beliefs of the people, and while these would not be expressed or manifested in the settlement pattern, they would be presupposed by this pattern since the cosmology would be among the deep structures of the Osage cultural traditions that would make the settlement ideology intelligible and possible. As noted in chapter 3, by virtue of the relative autonomy of the basic collective intentional states of belief (cosmology), desire (ethos), perception (worldview), and intention (ideology), the ideologies of different peoples can significantly differ while their cosmologies can be significantly similar.

Therefore, although I am comfortable with Fowler's claim that the cosmology of the Osage, the Omaha, the Pawnee, or any of a number of potentially relevant historic Native American people would be a good model for the cosmology presupposed by Woodhenge 72, the logic of the view that cultural traditions are integrated and not fused does not permit the assumption that the Osage village layout and the Woodhenge 72 layout manifest similar ideologies—unless, of course, the group responsible for Woodhenge 72 was of the same social nature as he claimed for the Osage settlement, namely, a residential clan-based community divided into moieties. However, in fact, Fowler's own comments clearly deny that the Woodhenge 72 group could have been a community of this type, since he specifically notes the absence of any domestic settlement debris or residue in or around Woodhenge 72:

> In the Mound 72 area this ancient landscape was little modified. Of all the surface surveys, aerial photograph examination, soil coring, excavation, and mapping, not one has ever produced any evidence—potsherds, bones, or other artifacts—indicative of human utilization or modification of the area. . . . The stratigraphy of the mound and surrounding area indicates that the first intensive use of the area was the construction of Woodhenge 72. There may have been earlier, light human use of the area for gardens or wetland exploitation but nothing similar to that recorded a hundred or so meters to the north. (Fowler et al. 1999, 159)

Hence, unlike the other subcommunities constituted as mound-plaza-residential compiexes that Fowler claims make up most of Cahokia, Woodhenge 72 was a distinct isolate. This suggests that the social nature of the group responsible for Woodhenge 72 was not the type that he ascribes for the Osage and, for that matter, that the group itself was not quite like the groups responsible for the "standard" mound-plaza-residential complexes.

In sum, while I can accept that the Osage community layout and Woodhenge 72 might well presuppose a similar cosmology, the premise that they manifest similar ideological structures does not logically follow. The Osage village layout may be best treated as manifesting a settlement-subsistence or midwifery-type ideology, while, of course, the layout of Woodhenge 72 and (as I discuss below) its association with the mortuary contents of Mound 72 make it more likely to manifest a world renewal ideology that served the needs of the world renewal cult sphere.

Furthermore, Fowler himself may be somewhat skeptical about his referentialism as adequately accounting for the construction and layout of Woodhenge 72, since he invokes other functions and purposes of major constructions, possibly to add greater gravity to the role of monuments. Citing Richard Bradley, Fowler suggests that Woodhenge 72 may also have served as a collective memory device, but Fowler emphasizes that the object of this collective memory device "is not a past of people and deeds, rather it is a past represented by the endless movement of heavenly bodies in a cycle that transcends time" (Fowler at al. 1999, 157). Remembering is a form of believing, of course; therefore, treating Woodhenge 72 as a monumental memory device is another expression of the referential fallacy—making the claim, in this case, that monuments may have been built to refer to collective memories. However, Fowler supplements the importance of innovative monumental expression of cosmological origin beliefs by suggesting that in building these monuments, humans alter their perception; moreover, "by linking the operations of great monuments to the unchanging world of nature their builders were putting the significance of these constructions beyond any kind of challenge" (Fowler et al. 1999, 157, quoting Richard Bradley 1993, 62).

Certainly, I have no problem with part of this claim since, of course, by saying that "great monuments" are linked to "an unchanging world of nature," Fowler is giving an iconic characterization of monuments. But there are two problems with his construal. First, since the monuments are linked to "an unchanging world of nature," he assumes that the relation linking humans to the sacred is intransitive in that whatever humans do in building monuments, since the world of nature is unchanging, this construction has no impact on its essential, that is, sacred, nature. That is, this claim presupposes a transcendental cosmology. Therefore, since human intervention makes no essential difference to the "unchanging world of nature," it reduces the production of monuments as symbols to a somewhat pointless exercise of merely referencing this sacred order of nature. Hence, some other purpose must be postulated that would make these massive labor expenditures intelligible. What could be more important than modifying collective consciousness? But this raises the second problem. Asserting that monumentalism modifies perception cannot be itself a condition motivating the practice. In terms of the theory of intentionality, the monument, as such, is always the condition of satisfaction of prior motives and not of unknown future consequences. That is, as presented, this claim presupposes the existence of the very sort of human collective consciousness that the building of monuments is supposed to bring about. Therefore, while he may be correct in asserting that monumentalism modifies human consciousness, the latter can only occur after and not before the development of the practice. Hence, the claim does not explain monumentalism, the labor required, or the organization mobilized to achieve it.

Alternative Interpretation

The building of monuments having the cosmos as their objects can be made intelligible if Fowler's insight into the iconic nature of monuments is treated in symbolic pragmatic terms. As such, the point of the builders' "linking the operations of great monuments to the unchanging world of nature" was not an exercise to put "the significance of these constructions beyond any kind of challenge" but was instead a means of quite literally presencing the creative powers that were experienced by the builders as being immanent in the cosmos. Hence, as expressive icons participating in the nature of what they represented, the relation of monuments to the cosmos was already part of the ideological know-how as well as part of the background cosmology of the builders, so that not only were the monuments experienced by their users as manifesting and presencing the essential nature of what they were about, but also the very activity of construction was experienced as world renewing in nature. Of course, as a reified usage this presencing existed only in the collective experiencing of those who were caught up in the symbolic pragmatic usage of monuments and settlement layouts. However, this presencing, combined with the notion of action as symbolically constituted, explains why monuments (and community layouts) are critically important to a people possessing immanentist cosmologies and why considerable effort and labor can be invested in their production. In sum, in the understanding of builders and users, as a monumental icon participating in the essential nature of those aspects of the cosmos that it was taken to be representing, Woodhenge 72 transformed the behaviors performed in its context into the type of ritual activity intended, and this transformation occurred in the instance of the behavioral performance.[9]

In sum, as I note above, although the symbolic pragmatic meaning of Woodhenge 72 certainly entails the relevant cosmological beliefs and principles, in these same terms, the point of constructing monuments was not to express or refer to these beliefs and principles or, of course, to refer to the objects of these beliefs. Rather, the cosmology has the important role of being the deep structural framework of beliefs that make the existence of Woodhenge 72 possible. In short, expressing the cosmology, as such, would not have been among the conditions of satisfaction of the intentions of the builders—but Woodhenge 72 could not have been built without this cultural background. In symbolic pragmatic terms, what Woodhenge 72 made possible and, therefore, why it was built, was to express and presence the essential powers of the relevant aspect(s) of the cosmos, as these were presupposed in the cosmology-as-known by the builders/users, so that the latter could collectively manifest their ritual intentions and relevant social standing and thereby constitute their behavioral interventions performed in its context as the type of ritual activities they intended. In terms of the World Renewal Cult Heterarchy and the Mourning/World Renewal Mortuary models, these would be world renewal rituals. In counterfactual terms, in the absence of Woodhenge 72 or other such equivalent material features, the behaviors would not and could not count as world renewal rituals.

THE MOUND 72 BURIAL CONTENTS

This brings me to the mortuary interpretation of Mound 72. The funerary paradigm is an essential tool of the hierarchical monistic modular polity approach; therefore, variation and complexity in mortuary patterning is taken to be largely a function of differential rank and hierarchy. Thus, effectively all mortuary patterning is subsumed to the funerary perspective, even when a significant proportion of the mortuary events is recognized to be most coherently interpreted as lethal sacrifice.[10]

Interpretation of Mound 72 Burials

Rose specifically states that his method is directed toward sorting out the mortuary events in terms of the ranking of the individual burials and group burials.

Thus, his analytical goal is to pinpoint those individual and group burials that display properties—such as artifact associations, physical positioning in the mound relative to significant loci (for example, post pits), burial treatment, and so on—that would warrant treating them as being high-ranking funerary burials and then sorting out all the others into lesser ranks according to the assumed relations with these high-ranking burials. Basing his analysis on spatial association with PP1 and PP2, combined with primary burial treatment, association with others treated as possible sacrificial victims, and so on, he targets Burial 13 and Burial 120 and/or Burial 119 as the remains of ranking personages. That is, he agrees with Fowler's interpretation in this regard. Rose then notes all those extended and secondary burials that do not seem to be candidates of lethal sacrifice, primarily because they are not part of the series of mass burials described and summarized above and also because they are focused in the southwest sector of Mound 72 (which he interprets as high-status ground because of its propinquity to Burial 13) and concludes that these are midranking burials.[11]

This assignment of rank raises the question of the relative status of the litter burials associated with the mass lethal sacrifice of the individuals making up Feature 229–Lower. However, Rose has little difficulty in making this determination, since the litter burials were all secondary burials, while many of the lethally sacrificed deceased were clearly killed by a heavy blow to the nape of the neck, probably when standing by the side of the burial pit. Thus, just as Burial 13 is marked as high status because of both the sacrificial treatment of the associated retainers and the large deposit of mortuary goods, so the individuals of Feature 229–Upper are deemed to be high-ranking members of the community because of being associated with lethal sacrificial victims formed as a platform under them. Of course, these individuals are not as high ranking as the Burial 13 personage. They are also not as low as the midrank burials, since the latter were not directly associated with lethal sacrificial victims. Rose then classifies all the lethal sacrificial victims described above as forming two low-ranking groupings. Because the female victims—such as those in Feature 237, Feature 214, and Feature 105—were neatly laid in rows and displayed no overt signs of violent deaths, he ranks these above the deceased of Feature 229–Lower, the latter probably being war captives. Although differing over the details, Fowler largely agrees with this assessment (Fowler et al. 1999, 158).

Critique

One central problem with the funerary approach is that it does not adequately account for the total range of mortuary treatments (Brown 2003, 82). Rose notes that all those he assesses as the highest-ranking deceased are primary extended burials and that these are associated with lethal human sacrifices (such as the retainers associated directly with the Beaded Burials and the fifty-three young female lethal sacrificial victims of Feature 105, also deemed to be dedicated to the memory of the Beaded Burials). From this pattern he concludes that high rank is marked by extended burial. This conclusion raises a problem, however, since not only are all or most of those deceased that are deemed to be low-ranking lethal sacrifices also primary extended burials, but also about half of the midranking burials deemed funerary are not extended burials. Instead, these midranking burials display considerable postmortem manipulation, including bone bundling, possibly bone piling, and even body-part burials. How can this contradiction be explained while maintaining that primary extended burial treatment is the mark of rank?

Rose resolves the problem in a very interesting manner—by postulating that the funerary burial events recorded in Mound 72 constitute "two distinct mortuary programs" (Rose 1999, 78): high elite and mid- and/or subelite. Thus he treats the primary extended burials of the individuals presumed to be the highest in rank—Burials 13/14 and (probably) Burials 119/120—as the outcome of terminal high-elite funerary rites and treats the lethal sacrificial burials, which are also primary extended burials, simply as non-elite sacrificial adjuncts to these latter highest-ranking burials. However, the rest of the burials (making up almost 40 percent of the mortuary events and displaying a broad range of postmortem treatment, from rather immediate burial—lacking any signs of extended postmortem exposure—to clear signs of postmortem exposure, to bundle burials, to piles of bones, albeit distinctly ordered piles, such as in Feature 219) are explained as the product of a second and distinctly separate mortuary program that was attuned to "a concern with the sun's yearly cycle or calendar . . . [as] indicated by the contemporaneous sun circles, or 'Woodhenges,' found at Cahokia" (Rose 1999, 78). Thus, Rose explains this broad range of treatments as marking those deceased of the mid- and/or subelite who had been curated with their terminal funerary burials being performed collectively and in tune with the solar cycle:

> If deaths were random and burial dates fixed (occurring about three or four times a year), then the proportion of completely decayed to partially decayed bodies would be about equal. This is similar to the distribution of primary and bundle burials in Mound 72. In addition if all those who were destined to be interred in Mound 72 were buried together at each burial date, the combination of primary and bundle burials that we have

found would be explained. This hypothesis is further supported by the seven partially articulated skeletons. In these cases the interval between death and burial was not sufficient to complete decomposition. (Rose 1999, 78)[12]

There are several problems with this solution, however. First (while I certainly can agree that these burials were very likely organized in terms of the solar cycle), other than recognizing the possibility that there was "a concern with the sun's yearly cycle or calendar," Rose gives no theoretical account of how this concern would figure in governing the patterning of mortuary practices. Second, and possibly related to an inadequate mortuary theory, his hypothesis does not explain why the highest-ranking burials would be excluded from the same solar-regulated process. If performing a terminal funerary rite in accordance with the turning points of the solar cycle would count as a primary condition of satisfaction of the funerary intentions that, if exercised in action, would fulfill the duties that the living held toward the dead (although he does not say why this would be the case), why would this not also be the case for the highest-ranking individuals and their sacrificial victims? The third problem, implicated by his ignoring the most directly available evidence that would give some empirical support to this claim (namely, Woodhenge 72 itself), is the disconnection between the "two distinct mortuary programs," on the one hand, and the monumental constructions, on the other. That is, while Rose treats the midrank funerary deposits as expressing "a concern with the sun's yearly cycle or calendar," he treats the major and visible indicators of ritual—the large lethal sacrificial deposits—as largely unrelated or only incidentally related to the monumental constructions that are the material context of these practices. Instead, the large artifactual and the lethal sacrificial mortuary deposits are treated as dedicated to the central personages.

I find all this reasoning problematic. First, the fact is that many if not all of the mass lethal sacrifice features occurred well after the "central personages" (Burials 13/14 and Burials 119/120) had been deposited. Second, following these burials, both associated primary mounds (72Sub1 and 72Sub2) were actively used, added to, and modified as intrinsic material components of Woodhenge 72—for example, the post in PP1 was replaced at least once, and possibly twice, after the mortuary deposits of Burials 13 and 14 and "retainers" had been made and after the first stage of primary mound 72Sub1 had been completed. This ongoing post-burial usage applies also for primary mound 72Sub2. Therefore, this extensive history of woodhenge-related ritual between the initial burials and the performance of the series of mass sacrificial burials suggests that, in fact, the latter burials were more directly part of the subsequent woodhenge ritual than they were part of the much earlier burials. However, Fowler claims that all the activities following these post-72Sub1 primary mound mortuary rites were carried out as dedicatory rites to the latter. Indeed, in these terms, the construction of 72Sub3 was done in the manner that it was precisely so as to commemorate Burials 13 and 14. As Fowler observes, "The center of this mound (72Sub3), both its platform and terrace, aimed at the center of 72Sub1, or the point directly over the beaded burial. The fact that 72Sub1 was not included in the creation of 72Sub3 indicates that this latter mound and its contents were all offerings of dedication and commemoration to the former mound and its status contents" (Fowler et al. 1999, 177; see also Figure 13.4). This claim of a continual directing of sacrifice to Burial 13 is specifically expressed by Fowler when, in summarizing his rank ordering of the mortuary data, he comments on the lethal victims: "The third category includes those burials described above as sacrifice burials. These groups of burials are located in portions of the mound to indicate their relationship, in terms of burial ritual, to the other groups. The burials are placed in specially prepared pits as offerings or dedications of the central individuals" (Fowler et al. 1999, 158).

THE ALTERNATIVE MOURNING/WORLD RENEWAL MORTUARY MODEL ACCOUNT

The solution to these problems relies upon two approaches: first, to replace the claim that "two distinct mortuary programs" were practiced in the locale of Mound 72 with the claim that only one was practiced (this being the type postulated under the Mourning/World Renewal Mortuary model); second, to replace the interpretation that the lethal sacrifices were dedicated to the "central personages" with the claim that these were woodhenge-related lethal sacrificial world renewal rituals. In the former case, in fact, the range of postmortem treatments that Rose specifies is precisely what would be expected under the Mourning/World Renewal Mortuary model. That is, a program concerned "with the sun's yearly cycle or calendar" would have been realized as a postfunerary→mourning→spirit release→world renewal process. In these terms, the bone bundles and the burials displaying signs of extended exposure would manifest different and later stages of this process and therefore would be forms of postmortem human sacrifice. The extended burials that are interpreted as individuals who had been killed as part of the mortuary process would also, of course, be sacrifices, but lethal and not postmortem sacrificial offerings. Does this mean that the "ranking" extended burials showing little or no signs of exposure, such as Burials 13 and 14, would mark the latter as terminal funerary ritual? This is quite possible and would be accounted for in terms not that different from Fowler's, except that whereas he treats them as subcommunity chiefs, I would treat them as custodial priests of the Woodhenge 72 cult. (I modify this position considerably shortly.)

Therefore, there is no necessity to postulate a dual mortuary program, as Rose does. Furthermore, this interpretation reconnects the mortuary ritual with the Woodhenge 72 and Mound 72 monumental programs. Indeed, in terms of symbolic pragmatics, the primary reason these mortuary behaviors were performed in the context of these monuments was so that they would be constituted as the required lethal and postmortem sacrificial world renewal rituals by which the Woodhenge cult was able to discharge its sacred cosmic duties of renewal and thanks. The concern that Rose postulates was central to Cahokia mortuary practices, therefore, can be amplified by treating these mortuary events as crucial human sacrifices that were directed to the renewal of the cosmos under the solar aspect. This claim is reinforced by the fact that the submound features of Mound 72 were constructed the way they were to be expressive iconic symbols of the cosmos under the solar aspect; as such, they were taken to act as symbolic pragmatic devices by which the mortuary behaviors, performed according to events making up the solar cycle, were constituted as world renewal rituals mediated by postmortem sacrificial offerings. As Fowler makes very clear, the axes of these major mortuary pit deposits—in particular, Features 229, 214, 105, and 106—were deliberately constructed to orient with the marker post at Locus III-NE (Figures 13.2 and 13.4). Even the "Beaded Burial" was oriented in this direction.[13] This orientation pattern suggests that the burials were performed the way they were because the deceased were taken to be mediating different forms of sacrificial spirit release rites that were intended to participate in the renewal of the cosmos through the medium of the post in Locus III-NE, an integral part of the larger Woodhenge 72. If this interpretation is accepted, then, in fact, instead of our treating Woodhenge 72 and the mortuary components of Mound 72 as only contingently related through the notion that some of the mortuary events were the outcome of high-ranking funerals that subsumed the major lethal sacrificial events while only a minority of the mortuary events were, in some vague manner, "solar related," we should understand these two bodies of data as being systematically and intrinsically linked as the ongoing outcome of a single comprehensive and historically developing strategic program of world renewal cult ritual.

Critique

However, given the recognized level of lethal human sacrifice (about 60 percent of the 260 to 272 estimated burials), lethal human sacrifice may have played an even greater role than either Fowler or Rose recognize or than I recognize in the world renewal account that I have just given. Is it possible that some or possibly all of the mortuary events that are deemed under the funerary account to be associated with midranking to quite high ranking deceased are also lethal human sacrificial rites? An initial answer to this question can be made by examining the primary indicators that I (along with Fowler, Rose, and many others) accept as signs of lethal sacrifice and see if these indicators can be extended to other primary extended burials that are not treated above as lethal sacrifices.

It is generally agreed that the large mortuary pits containing multiple deceased—usually of the same sex (usually female) and of junior age-grade rank—mark lethal human sacrifice.[14] In two of these cases (Features 205 and 237), the pits and burials were oriented to the cardinal directions. In the other cases (for example, Features 105, 106, and 229–Lower), the mortuary pits were oriented to the important marker post at Locus III-NE (Figure 13.4). In almost all cases, the pits were lined with sand and the deceased were laid in place in two layers, with the lower layer of burials placed on matting that covered the floors of the mortuary pits, this lower layer of burials being covered with more matting on which the upper layer of burials was laid, and the upper layer of burials also being covered with matting, followed by the pits being filled with earth. Hence, five lethal sacrifice criteria are common: all the deceased are primary extended burials; they are usually young and usually female; all the pits are carefully prepared and are oriented to selected directions; there is a dual layering of burials; and each layer is separated top and bottom by matting. A sixth criterion can be added as applying to most of the above cases. Since—with the exception of a number of the burials in Feature 229–Lower and the four young headless and handless males of Feature 106—the deceased show no overt signs of death caused by violence, they were likely rapidly strangled, a practice that is attested to by historical reports of Natchez lethal mortuary practices (Swanton 1911, 139).

Feature 229 is an exception to the above in several ways (Figure 13.7). Although it displays a dual layering of deceased, only the lower layer is recognized as displaying the outcome of lethal human sacrifice. Also, the lower stratum consists of both males and females; as noted above, unlike the absence of overt signs of killing in the other collective features, many of the deceased display multiple signs of violent in situ death. In contrast, the upper layer was composed of the ten litter burials of fifteen individuals. As I note above, Rose treats them as ranking just below the highest-ranking personages, largely because of the presence of the litters and, of course, the lower stratum of lethal human sacrifices. Under the Mourning/World Renewal Mortuary model, however, these could be interpreted as postmortem sacrifices mediating world renewal ritual. In fact, this was my original interpretation. However, it seems illogical that out of all of the known mass mortuary pit deposits, this is the only stratum of burials that would count as postmortem sacrifices, that is, as persons who died naturally and then were used as symbolic pragmatic media to constitute a mass postmortem sacrificial world renewal offering. Since all the other mass deposits treated the lower and upper strata of burials equally as mass lethal sacrificial offerings—which Feature 229–Lower clearly is—then the curated deceased of Feature 229–Upper should also be interpreted as lethal human sacrifices, albeit—noting Lynne Goldstein's suggestion that lethal acts could be committed elsewhere (note 14)—these ritual acts would have been performed much earlier, with the remains then being subjected to curation and, in some cases, postmortem modification before being finally added as the upper layer of Feature 229.

The logical possibility that the burials of Feature 229–Upper were curated lethal sacrifices suggests the need to reassess their empirical patterning in these terms. Although Rose does not give precise details, he provides a good summary of the patterning and variation of each of the fifteen Feature 229–Upper burials (Rose 1999, 71–72). He notes that several of the ten burial units consisting of fifteen deceased were compound burials (Figure 13.7). Burial 197, the southernmost burial unit in the upper row, was composed of the disarticulated bones of three individuals between the ages of fifteen and twenty-five (one female, one male, and one of indeterminable sex). The bones were wrapped securely, as indicated by seven bone tie beads. Immediately to the northwest of Burial 197 was another compound burial unit—Burials 198 and 210, consisting of one adult and one child. Apparently, these were extended burials but displayed indications of extensive exposure. Six bone tie beads were found in association, apparently with the adult burial: of these, two "beads were just below the head and four just below the pelvis" (Rose 1999, 71).

The next unit northwest contained a single extended individual, Burial 199, a female between twenty-five and thirty-five years old with one bone tie bead lying west of the skull. To her northwest there was another compound unit of three burials: Burials 200 and 212 were both children; lying on top of the children was Burial 211, a female between twenty and twenty-five years old. Apparently, all of these were also extended burials. However, the "constriction of the skeletons and locations of bone tie beads suggest that the burials were bound at each end and the middle. There was no evidence of a litter" (Rose 1999, 71). All of the six remaining units were individual extended burial deposits, and all showed indicators of extensive preburial exposure, with some showing clear indication of postmortem manipulation, including bodily distortion and severe binding. For example, the head of Burial 201, an adult female, "was pushed down onto the chest and the elbows were drawn in. The presence of tie beads and the constriction of the arms again suggest that the skeleton was bound at the shoulders, pelvis, and ankles." Her immediate neighbor to the northwest had been subjected to a very similar treatment: "The skull had been displaced onto the upper thorax region. As the axis was missing and the cervical vertebra was disturbed, decapitation before burial is suggested. The elbows were again severely constricted. This, in conjunction with tie beads, suggests binding" (Rose 1999, 72).

The next unit, Burial 204, probably a female between twenty and twenty-five years old, also displayed signs of binding—presumably the presence of bone tie beads, although Rose does not specify. The last three at the northwestern end of the row also showed severe postmortem manipulation. Burial 207, an adult of indeterminable sex, had the skull dislocated, and "constriction at the elbows indicated binding" (Rose 1999, 72). Burial 208 was fifteen to twenty years old and of indeterminable sex. Rose observed, "The extreme dislocation of the skull and constriction of the elbows could only have resulted from binding a partially decomposed corpse" (Rose 1999, 72). Finally, there was Burial 209, for which "[c]onstriction was severe and the head pushed down onto the chest lacks cervical vertebrae. This again suggests partial decomposition prior to preparation for burial" (Rose 1999, 72).

Rose clearly recognizes that these individuals of Feature 229–Upper—all being young, some being children, and the majority being female (or of indeterminable sex)—had been dead for a considerable period before the terminal litter burial rituals. Indeed, he identifies the tight binding at the head, elbows/pelvis, and leg areas and the presence of bone tie beads as clear indications of lengthy postmortem exposure and, therefore, the need to carry the remains on litters. Still, he defines these deceased as ranking just below the top-ranking personages in Burials 13, 14, 119, and 120. As stated above, I initially considered this upper layer to be fully consistent with postmortem human sacrifice. I still consider this to be likely. However, the postmortem sacrificial mortuary treatment of these individuals could have been in addition to the initial mode of death. That is to say, their being deposited as the upper layer of burials over the lower thirty-nine lethal sacrificial deposits in a material feature that was traditionally used for the ritual deposition of a dual layer of lethal sacrifices suggests that, in fact, those who deposited the deceased in this manner knew at the time of burial that they had also been subjected to lethal sacrifice, although their remains were then curated. If so, then under the World Renewal Cult Heterarchy model, this curation would have been done largely as part of building the "treasuries" of symbolic pragmatic capital of the cult alliances responsible for the postulated lethal sacrifice, possibly just so that they could participate in the major sacrificial event that generated Feature 229. That is, instead of the normal form of postmortem sacrifice arising from "natural" death, some or possibly all of the individuals constituting the upper layer of Feature 229— particularly those displaying major displacement of the heads, binding, and bone displacement—may have been initially subjected to lethal sacrifice and then curated.

In terms of support for the mourning/world renewal mortuary interpretation, nothing actually hinges on this alternative explanation, since the important point is that the upper-layer deposits are sacrificial, whether postmortem, lethal, or both. The less tendentious view would be to claim that they were a series of "normal" postmortem sacrifices. This would be consistent with the major postmortem manipulation to which they were all subjected, in accordance with the mourning/world renewal view. However, if the solely postmortem sacrificial claim is preferred, then Feature 229 must be accepted as being radically anomalous in comparison to the other mass burials in that it would be the only one composed of both lethal and postmortem sacrifices. If we address the intelligibility of this dual-layered mortuary deposit in terms of the theory of intentionality that I elucidate in chapter 3, such an anomaly is highly improbable. In these terms, systematic patterning of the sort displayed by these mass burial features would be critical material conditions of satisfaction of the collective prior intentions of the groups whose behaviors were responsible for producing the mass burials. That is, for the collective prior intentions to be satisfied, the groups would have to use the same behavioral intervention (killing) to bring about the type of patterning that we have identified in these features. When the ideological content of these collective prior intentions is adequately identified (that is, when the content of the ritual strategies that were realized in the collective behaviors generating these burials is correctly identified), then we can also identify the collective motives and purposes that the performance of these ritual actions would discharge (such as sacred communal duties), since the collective prior intentions presuppose the duties (that is, collective second-order desires), and these duties would entail a rather limited range of cosmological notions and ethos principles in order for the activities to have been performed.

The shared properties of these mass features clearly manifest rules—for example, prepared floors, selected alignments, the systematic use of matting, and so on. In particular, the dual layering is distinctive. If we can logically establish that these shared attributes (in particular, this type of layering) are not explicable in practical terms, then we can fairly conclusively determine that the patterning is stylistic in nature. That is to say, it is the outcome of the symbolic pragmatics that guided the way in which the behaviors that generated these material features had to be performed in order for these to be constituted as the type of social activity intended. If the overall empirical properties of the material context of these monumental features—in this case, Woodhenge 72—can be interpreted in terms that ground a specific type of cosmology and its content, then we have a pretty good handle on the intelligibility of the behaviors that produced these mass burials.

Clearly, several attributes of the mass mortuary pits are symbolic-pragmatic in nature—in particular, the prepared floor, the directional orientations, and the matting—since if all that was needed to deposit the dead was a pit, then none of those attributes would be required. The same could be said for the dual layering. Is dual layering simply the outcome of a practical means of saving labor? I think not. Feature 229 was in a location that would allow easy extension so that there was no practical requirement for placing the litter burials on top of a lower level of burials. Simply digging one larger shallow pit might be less laborious than digging a smaller and deeper pit. This assessment equally applies to Feature 105, which was located between 72Sub1 and 72Sub2 (Figures 13.1 and 13.6). This feature, which included fifty-three females, was similarly organized into two layers. The pit floor was lined with fine sand, covered by matting. Then, to make up the lower layer, about half of the victims were neatly laid in, forming two parallel southwest-northeast rows with heads to the northwest and the feet of the northwest row by the heads of the southeast row. These remains were covered by more matting, and the same pattern was repeated to make up the upper layer. This dual feet-to-head patterning would have required those who were placing the bodies to step down into the pit and, for the second layer, to walk over the matting covering the dead in the lower layer. This could have easily been avoided by extending the pit laterally southeast to allow for a single layer of four southwest-northeast rows. The fact that such an extension was not done suggests that this arrangement was meaningful in its own right, that is, a dual layering was prescribed by the ideological rules forming part of the content of the ritual strategy governing this labor. Add to this the care with which each layer was placed—the floor pit prepared with sand, the matting over this, the second matting over the first layer, and the third matting over the second layer—and dual layering would apparently not be a result of labor economizing. Hence, it can be reasonably concluded that the pattern was based on ideological rules and their related rationale specifying what forms of collective behaviors and their material outcome would count as a mass lethal sacrificial offering by which to fulfill the sacred duties of the groups that were responsible.

A sacrifice always entails an object, process, or state of affairs that is the beneficial recipient. Under the funerary paradigm, the recipient targets of these mass lethal sacrifices are assumed to have been the ranking burials, in particular, Burial 13 and (possibly) Burial 14. However, if we instead accept that the Woodhenge structure was viewed as a monumental icon of the cosmos under the solar aspect presencing the essential nature of the sun as it rises in the east into the heavens and sets back into the underworld in the west, then we can reasonably suggest that the solar-associated powers of the cosmos are what would have been the targeted recipient of the lethal sacrifices. Drawing on the Osage cosmology (as commented above), Fowler postulates that the cosmos was experienced by the builders as vertically structured into the Sky World and the Earth World, and between these two components of the cosmos was the Middle World—the surface occupied by all living things, humans included. Woodhenge 72, therefore, presupposes just such a cosmology.

Thus, in symbolic pragmatic terms, if Woodhenge 72 was a primary monumental iconic symbol by which humans could directly intervene into and enhance the cycling of the sun as it was reborn from the underworld and reexpired in the west as it set back into the underworld, then we can easily understand the possible intelligibility of the dual layering of the lethal sacrifices. This suggests a dual, complementary sacrifice by which to renew the sun in both its heavenly and underworld phases: the spiritual essences of the upper layer of the deceased would be directed to the former; those of the lower layer, to the latter. In these terms, the variation in the dual layering of Feature 229—the lower being in situ lethal sacrifices situated in a prone position and the upper being the curated outcome of probably lethal sacrifices—may be understood as recognizing the differential needs of the sun in both its underworld and its heavenly phases.

Besides dissolving the anomalous nature of Feature 229 by invoking a symmetry of lethal sacrifices differentiated only by in situ/secondary burial terms, can we apply any further empirical evidence in support of this interpretation? Above, I review the evidence for the lower layer, including signs of major blows to the back of the neck, decapitation, breakage of mandibles, and even the presence of two arrow points. However, as discussed above, several deceased (in fact, effectively all of the upper layer of extended burials) display significant modifications to bodily integrity. As I describe above, the heads in Burials 209, 208, 207, 204, 202, and 201 were severely dislocated, in some cases being pushed into the thorax region. In particular, Rose (1999, 72) suggests preburial decapitation and binding for Burial 202. The constriction of the elbows is noted as occurring in almost every case, and effectively every burial unit was associated with bone tie beads, which were probably used in conjunction with leather thongs to carry out this constriction. These bone tie beads/thongs are assumed to have been used either to tie the bodies so that they would not fall apart (or fall off the litters) or to tie the wrappings around them. This is quite possible. But Rose comments on the degree of constriction of the bodies that they caused, and rather than binding around a prepared hide or textile covering this suggests direct bodily-contact binding.

As I comment above, the manner of killing the selected victims of Natchez lethal sacrifice is described as strangulation using specially prepared and knotted cords:

> The death cry was uttered. The pellets of tobacco were given to [the fourteen selected victims] . . . and a little water to drink . . . after each [victim's] head was covered with a skin on which the cord was placed around the neck, two men held it in order that it should not be dragged away [to one side] by the stronger party, and the cord, which had a running knot, was held at each end by three men, who drew with all their strength from the two opposite sides. They are so skillful in this operation that it is impossible to describe it as promptly as it is done. (Swanton 1911, 149)

The evidence described above for the mass burials in Feature 229–Upper indicates a similar form of killing. In contrast to the apparent violent blow to the neck that killed individuals composing the lower layer (in the context of Woodhenge 72, by which the essential creative powers of the sun were presenced, thereby transforming the killings into lethal sacrifices), strangulation would be a similar although different form of death meted out to those constituting the upper layer (in contexts that, to those who carried out the killing behavior, counted as equivalent forms of lethal sacrifice). These contexts would likely have been the mound-plaza locales of the different postulated cult alliances affiliated to constitute Cahokia. Instead of the victims of strangulation having their arms and legs held by attending sacrificers, however, they may have been tied so as to prevent struggle; these ties and the bone tie beads found with the deceased of Feature 229–Upper may have been left as essential material conditions of satisfaction of the lethal sacrificial intentions. The victims would also have been curated in the appropriate facilities of each alliance (for example, the charnel house/temple/renewal lodge of an alliance), thereby building up the treasury of symbolic pragmatic capital required so that each alliance could cooperatively participate in major world renewal rituals such as the one identified here as Feature 229.

Feature 219—the charnel house under 72Sub2 (Feature 225)—and some of its associated mortuary deposits placed on the first stage of the platform mound might also have been the outcome of a similar form of lethal sacrifice by strangulation, except performed in situ (Figure 13.5). Burials 117, 118, 119, and 120 made up the extended mortuary component of this feature. Fowler describes these four in the following way (1999, 175):

> Over the area that had been the east end or screened wall of Structure 225, two extended primary burials were positioned. These were both males positioned with the dorsal side up. The eastern most of these burials (Burial 119) had his head facing west. These two burials were oriented on a north-south axis with the heads to the south.
>
> To the south of the Feature 225 area were two extended burials, a male on the east (Burial 118) and a female on the west (Burial 117). The male was positioned dorsal-side-up with face to the west, and the female was ventral-side-up. Both these individuals were oriented north-south with the heads to the south. Both of these individuals had strings of beads in the neck area, and the female had a ceramic vessel of lower Mississippi valley affiliation near her left elbow.

While giving essentially the same description, Rose makes several interesting additions concerning the placement of hands and arms: as pointed out earlier, the young female in Burial 117 was laid ventral side up (supine) and had both arms flexed, with hands near her neck; the deceased male in Burial 118 was prone and had his right hand near his neck; and the prone deceased in Burial 119 had his right hand under his neck (Rose 1999, 66). Unfortunately, Rose gives no description of the arms of Burial 120, lying parallel to and east of Burial 119, nor does Fowler comment on the positioning of the arms, only that, as for Burial 119, the deceased was in a prone position.

If Burial 120 is set aside for lack of evidence, the positioning of the hands in the three other burials could be symptomatic of death by strangulation. Notably, neither Rose nor Fowler comments on the presence of bone tie beads, and since both note the many other instances when these are present, I must assume that no bone tie beads were found with these burials, suggesting that no binding, as such, was carried out. Because of the close association of these burials with Feature 225 (a probable charnel/renewal lodge oriented on PP2), the possibility that these individuals were subjected to lethal sacrifice by strangulation while in an unbound state cannot be dismissed. If a similar possibility can be empirically grounded for the mortuary deposit that is recognized as complementary to Feature 219—namely, Feature 101, the central feature found on the ground directly under 72Sub1 and in association with PP1—this would certainly strengthen the probability that the extended burials of the former feature also display and realize the conditions of satisfaction of lethal human sacrificial collective intentions.

Of the deceased directly associated with the Beaded Burials of Feature 101, at least one (Burial 16) is also usually treated as a lethal sacrificial victim (Figure 13.3). As I note earlier, both Rose and Fowler comment that the position of this person indicates that he may not have been dead at the time of burial and that his positioning—prone, with his right leg flexed—was probably the result of a violent blow (Fowler et al. 1999, 168; Rose 1999, 64). What is not recognized or discussed is the possibility that Burials 13 and 14 were also subjected to lethal sacrifice but by strangulation. This may be heretical to suggest, since, of course, following Fowler's interpretation, most—although not all, as I discuss shortly—archaeologists of the American Bottom treat these two deceased as among the ranking personages of Cahokia.

As I mention above, under the World Renewal Cult Heterarchy model, Woodhenge 72 would be under the custodial responsibility of the specialized Woodhenge cult. Therefore, my first inclination was to treat Burials 13 and 14 as ranking priestly officers of this custodial cult who, because of their position, were considered more valuable serving in the same capacity in their afterlife than as postmortem sacrifices. This would account for the absence of body and/or body-part manipulation that would be indicative of their being postmortem sacrificial offerings in the later stages of mourning/world renewal ritual. However, since the above discussion demonstrates the possibility that lethal human sacrifice may have been much more prevalent than currently believed, the Beaded Burials could be interpreted as lethal human sacrificial victims, and a considerable amount of data could be comfortably construed as evidence in this regard.

First, taken as a set, these two burials do replicate the dual layering of the mass lethal sacrificial features discussed above (although the sand-lined mortuary pit is absent). In this case, they are separated not by ordinary matting but by an elaborate beaded cape. Burial 13, with head oriented southeast, constitutes the upper stratum and is placed in a supine position on top of the beaded cape, which Fowler interprets as an icon of the powers of the sky, being in a form that Fowler perceives to be a raptor (probably a falcon); Burial 14, with head northwest, constitutes the lower stratum and is placed in the prone, or face-down, position. There is also very strong circumstantial evidence that both were subjected to binding. In this case, Fowler notes that there "were a number of disc beads made of bone. The bone beads were found near the bones of the burials indicating that the burials were bound before placement in this burial context. At least 20 bone-disc beads were recovered around the 'Beaded Burial'" (Fowler et al. 1999, 132). These are primary extended burials. Therefore, under Fowler's funerary view, there would seem to be no reason for such binding, since, as noted in the case of the ten burial units of Feature 229–Upper, the funerary perspective attributes this practice and the use of bone tie beads to the curating period and the need to keep the bodies and/or bone bundles in order while being carried on the litters, even though, as commented above, Rose noted that this binding seemed to be very (possibly excessively) constricting.

To reinforce his funerary interpretation, Fowler goes on to emphasize cultural themes that, while proposed as evidence in support of his claim that Burial 13 was the result of a funerary burial of a high-ranking chief, could be very easily reinterpreted in the same lethal sacrificial terms that I apply to the Feature 219 extended burials. The primary cultural theme he notes is the parallel between the raptorial theme of the beaded cape with the body of Burial 13 lying on it and the copper repoussé plaques from Spiro and Etowah displaying the same bird-human theme (Figure 13.8):

The configuration of the individual on top of the bird outline is very familiar to the many representations of associations between humans and raptors in Mississippian art, such as the bird-man effigy tablet found on the east side of Monks Mound. . . . Particularly striking is the similarity of this bird-effigy-and-human burial with a repoussé copper plate from the Spiro Mound. This plate shows a supine individual over a falcon. The way the eyes and other characteristics of the human body are represented indicates a corpse. . . . Thus, the same bird-human relationship is shown in both these contexts—one in an actual interment and the other on a copper plaque. (Fowler et al. 1999, 157)

Although Fowler interprets this parallel as marking Burial 13 as being associated with the Sky World in the deceased's possible capacity as a Sky World chief, one should note that this same plaque can be interpreted as the sacrifice of a "god-pretender," with this "god-pretender" as presented in the raptorial guise having strong heaven-related relevance.[15] Thus, Burial 13 may be the remains of an actual "god-pretender" who was bound with thongs or cords and

Figure 13.8. Copper repoussé plates from Spiro (left) and Etowah (right). (Fowler et al. 1999, fig. 14.2, p. 169. Courtesy Illinois State Museum.)

bone tie beads to prevent movement while being sacrificed by strangulation to the sacred solar powers under the heavenly aspect of the cosmos. Burial 14 can be interpreted in the same way except that, being prone and under the raptorial cape, this individual may have been a sacrificial offering to the same solar-related sacred powers, but under the underworld aspect.

This claim is reinforced by the observation that Fowler quite rightly emphasizes the context of these burials, noting that they are oriented to the marker post at Locus III-NE, which is the same locus to which the axes of the later Feature 214, Feature 106 (the four headless/handless males), Feature 105, and Feature 229 were oriented during mortuary events performed well after Feature 101 was produced and buried (Figure 13.4). While Fowler attributes the convergence of these latter features to their being dedicated to the memory of the Beaded Burials, thereby reinforcing his claim that these were deceased chiefs of an important subcommunity of Cahokia, we might more logically and reasonably treat this common orientation of a series of mortuary deposits performed at very different times as the result of all five features being nearly identical conditions of satisfaction of the same historically developing sacrificial strategy, namely, renewing the reproductive powers of the cosmos under the dual heaven/underworld solar aspect through the warranting medium of the same post at Locus III-NE. Seen in these terms, then, the point of the dual layering of Burials 13 and 14 effectively is to replicate the point of the dual layering of the mass mortuary deposits.

It is again notable that Fowler draws parallels between the Beaded Burials and the retainers, on the one hand, and Burials 119 and 120 of Feature 219, on the other:

> There are some interesting similarities in the two burial programs. Both have central figures representing personages of high status. In 72Sub2, it is not clear who the important personages were. It seems probable to me that the two males in Burials 119 and 120, positioned over the east end of the charnel house, are the primary personages in this complex. The other burials, bundles and extended, are offerings to these two. An intriguing parallel in these two mounds is that each of the central burials is of two males buried side by side or one atop the other. These paired individuals may represent shared power in the political structure of Cahokia. Another similarity in these two burial programs is that both central personages are accompanied by remains of several other individuals, including bundle, extended, and secondary burials. (Fowler et al. 1999, 176)

If Feature 101 and Burials 13 and 14 are sacrifices to the heaven/underworld duality under the solar aspect, then the same might well be the case for the 72Sub2 set of extended burials. However, whether Burials 119 and 120 of the latter would be the equivalent of Burials 13 and 14 is debatable. Both Burials 119 and 120 are prone, while Burial 13 is supine and Burial 14 is prone. In this regard, Burials 117 and 118 display closer parallels to Burials 13 and 14 than do Burials 119 and 120. While the pairs of deceased in both Burials 119/120 and Burials 117/118 are side by side instead of one atop the other, Burial 117 is that of a female in a supine position (similar to Burial 13) and Burial 118 is that of a male in a prone position (similar to Burial 14). Hence, Burials 117/118 could be treated as constituting a dual complementary heaven/underworld lethal sacrifice with the female a lethal sacrifice directed to the heavens, and the male, to the underworld. Furthermore, these two burials lack bone ties while displaying the hand-to-neck pattern, suggesting what happens when unbound persons are strangled. The associated extended deceased in Burials 119 and 120, therefore, may be similar to those associated with the Beaded Burials, namely, supplementary lethal sacrifices.

If the data that I have presented are taken as insufficient to support this lethal sacrifice reading, I am quite prepared to argue the less radical position that Burials 13/14 and Burials 117/118, along with their respective associated deceased, were postmortem sacrifices of ranking custodial priests of Woodhenge 72. However, because of their estimated ages (25–35) and the age-dependency of occupying esteemed positions in an enabling hierarchy structured by seniority, this latter explanation seems the less likely and the former the more likely scenario.

Discussion

According to the hermeneutic spiral method, alternative readings are assessed in terms of the coherence that they attribute to the same body of data, and whichever interpretation endows the data with the greatest coherence is contingently accepted over the others. Therefore, I was particularly pleased that one of the reviewers of this book suggested that I read Brown's recent interpretation of the burials under primary mound 72Sub1 (which I did). I was pleased because I find that Brown's interpretation is fully consistent with my own, while adding considerable substantive content to what I rather abstractly describe above. Therefore, it can be added to enrich and reinforce our understanding of this unique record.

Although Brown (2003, 82) does not identify the Beaded Burials as lethal human sacrifices as such, importantly he characterizes the total set of 72Sub1 burial features as the the outcome of a complex and profoundly important performative ritual act of world renewal in which lethal sacrifice as well as postmortem sacrifice figured centrally (note, however, that Brown does not use these terms, as such). His main argument as I read it is that the primary extended burials—these being Burials 13 and 14 (the Beaded Burials) along with the nearby Burial 20 (Feature 103, Figure 13.3)—manifest the termination of the funerals of these three but that the funerary aspect was subsumed to the world renewal performance itself, constituting these as special forms of postmortem human sacrifice. That is, at their deaths, these deceased were recruited to be principal participants in a major world renewal ritual realized as the reenactment of a battle between culture heros and the powers of the cosmos. This battle was manifested as a sacred game of chunkey, in which some of the participants possibly became literal lethal sacrifices. Brown's summation is worth quoting: "In recapitulation, the original hero team of four game against the anti-hero (Burial 13) and they ultimately lose with their lives. . . . The successor hero (Burial 14) avenges the original team death by defeating the anti-hero, thereby assuming a central role in the performance. He personifies the savior of the collectivity" (Brown 2003, 96).

In this case, the "successor hero" is the upper Beaded Burial, which Brown mistakenly refers to as Burial 14 instead of Burial 13. But the sense is clear. For Brown, the upper burial (Burial 13) is central not because of his status in life but because he was recruited in death to occupy this critical role in the performance of a world renewal ritual realized by the reenactment of this world creation myth. The core of Brown's thesis is that all the burial components at the base of primary mound 72Sub1 must be seen as filling critical roles in a major world renewal performative ritual. In terms that I have already outlined, this ritual would have been taken to presence and reproduce the very forces responsible for the creation events that were the object of the creation myth. Brown goes on to describe the burial components (Figure 13.3):

The original hero team is disposed on three sides of the central burial [Burials 13 and 14]. . . . Burial 15 lies parallel to the central burial on the east, Burial 12 similarly to the west; Burial 11 lies perpendicularly on the south. The leader in two manifestations (Burials 16 and 20) is singled out for special treatment. The seven burials of Feature 102 can be regarded as sacrifices, in a symbolic act that was repeated by the three burials in a later pit (F 104) let down on Feature 102. (Brown 2003, 96)

In short, the only primary incongruency between this account and my above account is the different interpretation of the Beaded Burials. Whereas both Brown and I treat the deceased as role performers in crucial world renewal ritual, he sees them as funerary (postmortem) and not lethal sacrificial participants. Therefore, the reader will have to judge. My own position is clear, of course, and I think that, in fact, it addresses a central anomaly of Brown's model, namely, that he acknowledges lethal sacrifice as highly likely for the majority of the deceased making up the 72Sub1 burial features—linking them directly to the events narrated in the origin myth—while maintaining that only some and not all of the physically central burials were lethal sacrifices. For example (in Brown's terms), the upper Beaded Burial (Burial 13) was the successor culture hero and represented the original culture hero (Burial 16), who in the myth was overcome and killed by the anti-hero (Burial 14), the lower Beaded Burial. Of these three, as I note above, only Burial 16 is treated by Brown as a lethal human sacrifice, while Burials 13 and 14 are treated as funerary participants recruited postmortem to fill these crucial performative roles. In contrast, given the empirical evidence that I have marshalled as criteria of lethal sacrifice—in particular, the dual layering, the bone tie beads, and the likely association of the latter with strangulation—and given the conjunction of Brown's theoretical view with my own, I believe that the more coherent explanation is to consider Burials 13 and 14, as well as all the participants in this performative ritual, as sacrificial offerings constituting, as Brown emphasizes, the enactment of "a public ceremony for a collective, community-wide purpose" (Brown 2003, 97). I will simply add to this excellent interpretation my claim that the community involved was a world renewal cult heterarchy and, of course, that the nature of the ceremony was world renewal in purpose. Seen in these terms, my general interpretation of Burials 13 and 14 as lethal human sacrifices to the heavens and the underworld, respectively, becomes more fully fleshed out with Burial 13 as the god- or hero-pretender whose death revitalizes the hero who, in the creation myth, entered the heavens and with Burial 14 as the complementary god- or anti-hero-pretender whose death revitalizes the underworld so that the total tableau constitutes the literal reaffirmation of the cosmic structure.

CONCLUSION

The polyistic locale-centric heterarchical account explains both the monumental and mortuary data within an integrated theoretical framework. In symbolic pragmatic terms, Woodhenge 72 can be treated as the material outcome of an ideological strategy, in this case, as being a monumental icon of the cosmos presencing its creative and procreative powers, particularly under the solar aspect. This strategy presupposes a cosmology (exemplified in terms of the Osage cosmology) that characterizes the cosmos as vertically structured into the heavens and the underworld, mediated by the middle world, and horizontally structured into (probably) four sacred quarters. Because cosmology and ideology are relatively autonomous forms of collective intentionality, that is, of a cultural tradition, and because ideology, when it is realized, is always realized in action, Woodhenge 72 and the associated mortuary facilities can quite easily be treated as the monumental material conditions of satisfaction of this strategy, one that is historically emergent from a preexisting ideological strategy. Both the preexisting ideology and the ideology that is realized in the Woodhenge 72/Mound 72 complex, although different, presuppose the same cosmology and ethos, the latter being the deep structures largely common to the cultural traditions of the peoples occupying the American Bottom and its upland region.

This perspective directly connects to the World Renewal Cult Heterarchy model—specifically, a heterarchical polyistic locale-centric perspective designed to address Cahokia during the Mississippian period, thereby treating Woodhenge 72 as being under the custodianship of a specialized cult. Hence, the associated primary mounds of Woodhenge 72 (72Sub1, 72Sub2, and 72Sub3, as well as, probably, Mound 96) can be reasonably interpreted as being among the CBLs of this cult. These CBLs would have been the medium and the reproduced outcome of the postfunerary aspect of the funerary→mourning→spirit release→world renewal ritual process, as postulated under the Mourning/World Renewal Mortuary model. In this case, the mortuary record associated with Mound 72 manifests lethal human sacrifice as the primary condition of satisfaction of this postulated cult's ritual strategy, with a lesser emphasis being placed on postmortem human sacrifice. This emphasis placed on lethal sacrifice raises important issues since it indicates a significant difference between the mortuary records of the Lohmann phase and the subsequent Stirling and late Mississippian period CBLs (as discussed in the previous chapter). While postmortem human sacrifice seems to prevail in these later phases, if Mound

72 can be used as a valid measure of ritual priorities, the mortuary sphere of the Lohmann phase would seem to have placed relatively much greater weight on lethal compared to postmortem human sacrifice while the reverse occurred in post-Lohmann phase. I address this issue in later chapters dealing with the cult dynamics of the Cahokian heterarchy.

Before turning to that subject, however, I will complete this mortuary study by examining in more detail the recently published mortuary data relating to the nearby uplands. This will serve to ground my preference for the World Renewal Cult Heterarchy model over the alternative hierarchical monistic modular polity accounts. I will follow the discussion of the upland mortuary data by a critical comparison of alternative accounts of the Terminal Late Woodland–Mississippian transition, first summarizing and critiquing the hierarchical monistic modular account of this transition (which I term the *nucleated-to-sequential settlement articulation account*) and then presenting and empirically grounding the alternative heterarchical polyistic locale-centric account (which I term the *integrated-to-bifurcated settlement articulation account*). The greater coherence of the latter clears the way for a full account of the dynamics of Cahokia, with these characterized as the outcome of an ongoing competition among ideologically based cult factions. This factionalism is elucidated under what I term the *Ideological Cult Faction model* of Cahokia.

Integrating the Floodplain
and Upland Mortuary Records

Recently, several reports and analyses have been published that summarize and interpret new mortuary data found in upland sites representing, possibly, the later Terminal Late Woodland period and most of the Mississippian period. For example, Donald Booth has reported on and interpreted the Center Grove site, which he characterizes as a cemetery that has some parallels to the Lohmann and Stirling phase BBB Motor site (Booth 2001, 53). In addition to summarizing Booth's report on the Center Grove site, Thomas Emerson and colleagues (2003) have summarized the mortuary data of three other upland sites: the Halliday site, the Knoebel South site, and the Stemler Bluff site (Figure 14.1). Included in this report is the Knoebel site, a small village site associated with the mortuary site of Knoebel South (Alt 2001). Kristin Hedman and Eva Hargrave (2003) have summarized and reassessed the mortuary content of the Hill Prairie Mounds site. As I note in chapter 12, a recent reassessment that is possibly most central in the interpretation of these data is Emerson and Hargrave's (2000) analysis of the Kane Mounds site. In this case, they specifically compared its contents to the mortuary components of sites to the north in the Illinois River and upper Mississippi River valleys and also to mortuary components of sites in the lower sector of the northern expanse (namely, the East St. Louis Stone Quarry site and the Florence Street and Range sites) with the point being to demonstrate the claim that immigration and/or the (re)emergent development of ethnic groups occurred in the later Mississippian period in reaction to the reduction in the hegemonic influence of Cahokia in its declining years. Emerson and Hargrave note that "as the Cahokian chiefdom became less unified politically after the mid-thirteenth century, we may see the 'reemergence' of earlier diversity. The decline of centralized power in the American Bottom would have encouraged increased activity by ever-present political factions, but probably would have also allowed many incipient or previously suppressed ethnic factions to reemerge" (Emerson and Hargrave 2000, 18).

Without a doubt both the new data and the interpretations made of them are of great interest and importance to American Bottom archaeology. In this

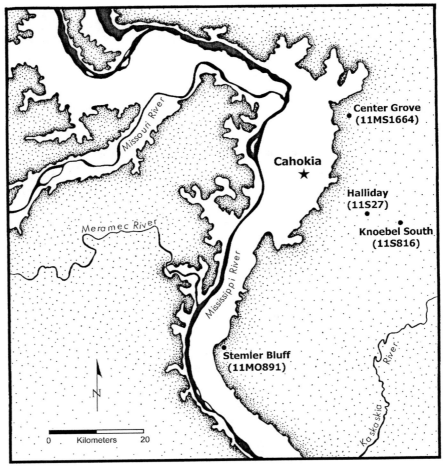

Figure 14.1. Early Mississippian upland mortuary sites. (Booth 2001, fig. 1, p. 39. Courtesy of the Illinois Transportation Archaeological Research Program, University of Illinois.)

chapter I plan to use these data to reassess my earlier mortuary discussions (chapters 12 and 13), which were primarily based on the mortuary data available prior to these new materials. In contrast to the hierarchical monistic modular polity account to which Booth's, Emerson's, Hargrave's, and Hedman's materials relate, it is the heterarchical polyistic locale-centric account (under the World Renewal Cult Heterarchy model) for which I use these data to reinforce and effectively confirm. Starting with the early Mississippian period record and then the later Mississippian period record, I apply the hermeneutic spiral method by first summarizing these new data and their hierarchical monistic modular polity account interpretations. I follow this with a critique of the latter. Then, while making the necessary modification in my earlier interpretation that these new data allow and require—particularly the changes in dating—I show that these same data can be more coherently understood when viewed in terms of the set of models I have already presented in previous chapters.

EARLY MISSISSIPPIAN PERIOD UPLAND MORTUARY SITES

The Center Grove Site

This upland site is situated about 15 kilometers northeast of Cahokia and about 4.5 kilometers east of the bluffs overlooking the American Bottom (Figure 14.1). It is interpreted by its excavator, Donald Booth (2001, 36), to be an early Mississippian period mortuary locale (a cemetery CBL, in my terms) that was probably occupied during the late Lohmann and early Stirling phases. Although there are currently no settlement data that would demonstrate nearby residential habitation structures making up a dispersed village, Booth does not dismiss the possibility (2001, 52–53). Still, the nearest known residential habitation is the Park site, and this is located 2 kilometers west of Center Grove. In effect, this site seems to be quite isolated from any other early Mississippian period settlement. Furthermore, it was largely empty of any habitation debris of its own.

In common with some other known early Mississippian CBL sites in the upland region that I summarize below, the Center Grove site is characterized by having a very limited quantity of human mortuary residue. In fact, of the seventeen features identified as mortuary pits by Booth, only one, Feature 1, had associated human remains (Figure 14.2). This pit feature contained the partial and very fragile residue of the left and right legs and hips of a deceased. The other sixteen mortuary pit features, referred to by him generally as graves, were not only bereft of any observable human remains, but also essentially empty of any cultural artifactual remains. In contrast, there was a limited amount of cultural debris found in the fill of Feature 1—probably the result of incidental addition, according to Booth. As he points out, while all but one of the other sixteen identified mortuary pits were clustered at the northern end of the site, Feature 1 was located relatively near to the permanent structures in the southern sector of this site. He suggests that debris related to the activities associated with these structures was likely caught up in the burial fill of Feature 1.

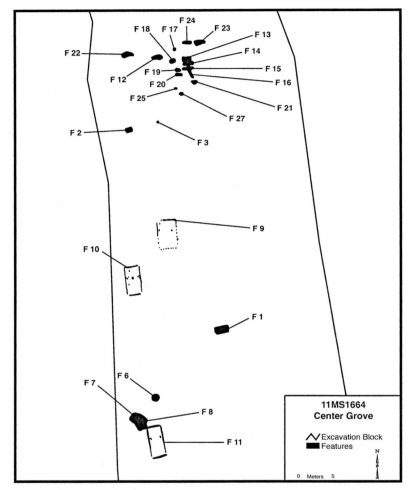

Figure 14.2. Center Grove site. (Booth 2001, fig. 4, p. 43. Courtesy of the Illinois Transportation Archaeological Research Program, University of Illinois.)

As noted above, all but one of the recognized mortuary pit features were clustered at the northern end of the site. With one exception, these were oriented east-west. The exception, Feature 16, was oriented north-south, and it superimposed two of the east-west features (Features 14 and 15). The Feature 14 mortuary pit was also superimposed on the Feature 13 mortuary pit. All this indicates, as Booth notes, "that there were several episodes of interments, with the nonaligned Feature 16 being one of the later" (2001, 47). The southern half of the site contained three rectangular structures in a roughly north-south linear pattern with their long axes also in a north-south direction (Figure 14.2). Feature 9, the northernmost structure, displayed both single-pole and wall-trench construction, while the two southern structures, Features 10 and 11, displayed only wall-trench construction. There were several pits associated with these three structures, the most interesting being a large post pit with associated insertion and extraction ramps immediately north of Feature 11, the southernmost of these three structures. Interestingly, Feature 1, the single mortuary pit with human remains, was situated east of these structures and about equidistant from all three.

Booth notes that these structures were clearly not residential but mortuary in nature, since a similar arrangement of internal nonwall posts was at the north end of each. Citing the mortuary practices of the Southeast as a historical analogy, he suggests that these were the support posts for interior scaffolds on which "corpses were placed in order to desiccate the flesh prior to burial" (Booth 2001, 53). He also notes that the Knoebel South site (see below) had a similar arrangement of trusslike posts, although these were associated with a structure that also had considerable habitational debris. In this case, he argues that the structure was the residence of a local caretaker. In effect, while Center Grove had strong similarities with other upland sites deemed to be mortuary in nature, it was also different; indeed, Booth suggests that it was more akin to the BBB Motor site on the American Bottom because of both its mortuary features and the marker post. However, he also stresses that there was an absence at this site of any clear artifactual indicators of the type of ritual that Emerson identified at the BBB Motor site (Emerson et al. 2003, 175), and he concludes, therefore, that "some of the differences observed between these two sites may be the result of the status and size of the groups utilizing the two mortuary complexes, in other words, an issue of urban versus rural context" (Booth 2001, 53).

The Halliday Site

This site is on the headwaters of Richland Creek, only about fifteen kilometers southeast of Cahokia (Figure 14.1) and a few kilometers northwest of the Knoebel South site, discussed below. It was reported by Timothy Pauketat (2002, 154–59) as part of what he terms the Richland Complex. According to Emerson and colleagues (2003, 166–69), the Halliday site is among the most complex of these known upland sites, having at least seventy single-post rectangular structures organized into courtyard patterns reminiscent of Terminal Late Woodland settlements. Even so, the size of the nearby mortuary zone is the basis for the suggestion that this zone "may contain interments of deceased residents from many of the various Lohmann phase settlements that were present within a mile radius of Halliday" (Emerson et al. 2003, 168). The actual mortuary zone is bilobed, and it is laid out on a ridge slope overlooking the Richland Creek drainage. Forty-seven of these features in total were excavated. Forty-four of these were treated as mortuary pits, and they contained poorly preserved human remains of thirty-two individuals. Apparently all ages and both sexes were represented, and there were no obvious grave goods except possibly two red-slipped bowl fragments found in two of the mortuary pits and a "limestone pipe from the only recovered bundle burial" (Emerson et al. 2003, 169). These features formed seven burial clusters, each with at least three or more burial pit features. Each set of clusters had a similar orientation except Cluster 5, which was formed in a circle around a central post. Two other clusters (Clusters 1 and 2) also formed circular areas with a central post for each. The range of burial forms included some extended and flexed burials and one bundle burial. However, several of the mortuary pit features showed signs of multiple usage, this being indicated by isolated bones. In fact, there were also some isolated bone fragments showing cut marks found in the village area. Emerson and colleagues state, "We infer from this that the inhabitants of the Halliday village practiced an extended mortuary program, with at least some part of the mortuary ritual taking place within the habitation area" (Emerson et al. 2003, 169).

The Knoebel South and Knoebel Sites

These related sites are situated in the uplands adjacent to Silver Creek, a few kilometers southeast of Halliday and about twenty-three kilometers southeast of Cahokia (Figure 14.1). The Knoebel South site forms a single cluster of "elliptical features, some of which are oriented in a circular formation and others in rows" (Emerson et al. 2003, 165). These features were identified by the excavators as graves. However, while at least one of the mortuary pit features at the Center Grove site contained human remains, there were no human remains in the equivalent features at the Knoebel South site. Still, one of the features included an unburnt bark lining. Emerson and colleagues (2003, 165) note that the nearby Knoebel site is judged to be a pre-Mississippian or possibly early Mississippian period site, although they admit that the precise temporal and social relations of these two sites are not currently known.

Identifying the Knoebel South site as having a mortuary nature close to that of the Center Grove site, however, was strengthened by the presence at the nearby Knoebel site of a structure having associated post supports similar to those noted in the above summary of the Center Grove site. Emerson and his colleagues interpreted these as part of a mortuary scaffolding. According to Susan Alt (2001, 148), the Knoebel site is a small village site that, while similar to the Halliday site discussed above, has a different historical span and a number of material differences. While the Halliday site seems largely limited to the Lohmann phase (although it might also extend into the early Stirling phase), she notes that the Knoebel site, in parallel with its associated Knoebel South mortuary site, has pre-Mississippian as well as Lohmann and Stirling phase occupational residue. Also, while the pre-Mississippian basin structures of the Knoebel site displayed the typical single-post wall construction, they were unusually large, with a mean floor area of 11.23 square meters. Alt comments in parentheses that this was "much greater than the size of contemporaneous [pre-Mississippian] structures on the Bottom" (Alt 2001, 148). In fact, the mean size of the subsequent Lohmann phase structures was only slightly larger at 12.06 square meters. However, this falls within the same size range as the house structures of the nearby Lohmann phase Halliday site. Where these differ is that while the Knoebel site displays about the same proportion of wall-trench to single-post construction that is found on the floodplain sites such as Cahokia (55 percent) the Lohmann phase Halliday site, as she stresses, retained the single-post structures characteristic of the American Bottom Terminal Late Woodland period (Alt 2001, 148–49). Also notable, in my view, is that the overall layout of the Knoebel site is different from that of the Halliday site. While the latter has its house structures rather symmetrically clustered around open areas forming courtyards with center posts—very reminiscent of the Terminal Late Woodland village sites, and, as noted above, the nearby mortuary component of the Halliday site was similarly organized into clustered components—the structures of the Knoebel site form two clusters, each organized in a linear manner and separated from each other by an elongated southwest-northeast open area with a central post pit displaying insertion pits (Alt 2001, 147, fig. 9.2).

The Stemler Bluff Site

This site is about 33 kilometers south of Cahokia, making it the most distant of these reported early Mississippian upland mortuary sites (Figure 14.1). It is a multicomponent site having two distinctly different zones, one each on opposite sides of a large sinkhole. The eastern sector constituted a residential area of twenty-two single-post structures and three wall-trench structures. About 110 meters west of the latter, on the other side of the sinkhole, there was a mortuary complex. Emerson and colleagues comment that "the relationship of the two areas is uncertain, although it seems likely that at least some of the burials represent inhabitants from the adjacent settlement" (Emerson et al. 2003, 170). However, on the basis of radiocarbon dates and ceramics, they judge the twenty-two single-post structures of the eastern residential sector to be predominantly Terminal Late Woodland "with little evidence of any strong Mississippian occupation or utilization" (Emerson et al. 2003, 170). Therefore, they suggest that the three wall-trench structures represent a Stirling phase Mississippian hamlet that was probably part of a dispersed village of the local area. This more or less accords with the conclusions of the excavators, who also note the possible significance of this dual structuring by suggesting that Stemler Bluff served as an upland "nodal" site, integrating the upland and lowland communities (Walz et al. 1997, 248).

However, in Emerson and colleagues' (2003, 172) interpretation, the presence of both Terminal Late Woodland–type and (probably) Stirling phase Mississippian-type residential structures makes the cultural assignment of the western mortuary sector quite problematic: "If the cemetery is early Mississippian in date it must represent the burial area for a widely dispersed population. If it is associated with the slightly earlier but much larger Stemler Bluff Terminal Late Woodland, then it is truly unique and would represent the only known cemetery from that time period" (Emerson et al. 2003, 172). While expressing these two possibilities, the authors favor the early Mississippian date for the mortuary component. They note, "The absence of feature superpositioning and the similarity in grave construction would suggest a relatively short period of use as a centralized cemetery, perhaps by the inhabitants of widely scattered villages" (Emerson et al. 2003, 170).

In any case, the western mortuary component of the Stemler Bluff site had fifty-one identified burial features. The distribution of these mortuary pit features suggests three possible circular clusters of pits. The pits were oval to rectangular in plan form and flat bottomed; eight had limestone or timber linings, and there was even one stone-box "grave" (Feature 188), having limestone slabs as the floor, top, and walls and containing partially disarticulated human remains. There were two features with charred timber walls. The remains of twenty-two individuals, poorly preserved, were identified in twenty of these fifty-one features. These included seven primary interments (both extended and loosely flexed), one bundle burial, three with only partial remains, and a number of isolated body parts and skeletal fragments that were caught up in the earth fill of several mortuary pit features. Also, some isolated human skeletal parts were found in the habitation area. All ages and both sexes were represented, but very little in the way of associated cultural remains was found, the most distinctive being some hematite fragments from four mortuary features. The other thirty-one features had no human remains. Of course, with the exception of the Halliday site mortuary component, this absence of human remains from features deemed to be Mississippian mortuary pits is typical in all these cases.

Funerary Interpretation

In each of the above cases, there is a strong, taken-for-granted commitment to the funerary perspective, as clearly indicated by the continual reference to the mortuary pit features as "graves," even when they are empty, and to the clustering of these pits as "cemeteries." However, there is some puzzlement that goes along with this commitment, since a thread of concern is continually expressed over where the communities were that provided the observed grave burials. In this regard, with the possible exception of the Halliday site, archaeologists generally admit that the known distribution of Mississippian habitation in the immediate area of each site was much too limited to warrant such concentrated cemeteries. As noted above, Booth (2001, 52–53) specifically comments on the absence of any known early Mississippian residential habitations within a two-kilometer radius of the Center Grove site. Furthermore, he particularly stresses the paucity—almost the absence—of any domestic debris in the site itself. He concludes that perhaps "this mortuary area served a dispersed population," specifically citing Emerson and colleagues (2003, 170) that the Stemler Bluff site also served a widely dispersed community. Booth thus expresses here what is, for the most part, generally agreed, namely, that these upland cemeteries must have served dispersed communities.

Not only are these generally agreed to have been cemeteries of dispersed communities, but Emerson and colleagues (2003) argue that these cemeteries represent an important mortuary innovation in that the preceding Terminal Late Woodland period of the region was characterized by the nonburial of deceased. Indeed, they note,

> Perhaps the most striking and least discussed changes that we can identify between circa A.D. 1000–1100 in the mortuary practices of the American Bottom are the appearance of bounded cemeteries and in-ground interments. This must have been a tremendous ideological shift for Terminal Late Woodland people. As far as we can surmise, Terminal Late Woodland people likely practiced mortuary rituals that focused on the exposure and natural deterioration of corpses. This appears to be a long-standing pattern in the American Bottom. (Emerson et al. 2003, 177)

Hence, the "sudden" appearance in the uplands during the early Mississippian period of "grave" clusterings constituting "cemeteries" was something that had to be explained. As Emerson and colleagues put it, "[I]f we look at the historical trajectory of late pre-Mississippian and early Mississippian society we do not see a gradualist scenario played out in the archaeological world. In fact, we recognize the abrupt appearance of new and different practices in the Lohmann phase early Mississippian mortuary ritual that seem to reflect the active creation of a polarized society" (Emerson et al. 2003, 179).[1]

Their conclusion is that, for the most part, these dispersed upland communities of the early Mississippian period were attempting through mortuary practices to constitute ancestors by which to carve out their own social identities in the face of hegemonic cultural pressure from the politically and socially dominant polity of Cahokia. This pressure, combined with in-migrating groups, promoted the "reification and personification of ancestral ties through mortuary ritual [providing] stability for the living in a changing world" (Emerson et al. 2003, 179–80). As seen below, a similar invoking of immigration combined with the notion of ethnogenesis is used by Emerson and Hargrave (2000, 2–3, 17–19) to account for the late Mississippian period upland mortuary record, particularly as displayed in the later Moorehead phase component of the Kane Mounds site.

Critique

While making the claim that new mortuary practices emerged as a form of social identification and resistance in the face of Cahokian cultural hegemony (Emerson et al. 2003, 178–80), Emerson and colleagues do not actually explain why so many of these mortuary pits display no human residue. What they do describe is the complex nature of the Mississippian mortuary process, in which postmortem manipulation figures centrally, and they suggest that, for some unknown reason, this postmortem redistribution process was sometimes avoided: "[W]e infer that initially the dead were interred in isolated cemetery plots, and at a later date were exhumed, the bones defleshed and cleaned, and either reburied or redistributed in some manner to the living. We know that this process may sometimes have been modified or interrupted, either deliberately or accidentally, since we have recognized extended, primary burials in some cemeteries" (Emerson et al. 2003, 178). Emerson and colleagues then go on to summarize the widespread nature of this complex process:

> [T]here is an interesting uniformity of practices across the Cahokian community—it entails the recognition, demarcation, and manipula-

tion of mortuary ritual. It takes form first in the creation and then later elaboration of special mortuary spaces (be they rural family plots, isolated charnel houses, or Mound 72) and in the complex manipulation of the physical remains of the dead (i.e., the practices of interment, disinterment, exposure, etc.) and included, perhaps, the occasional retention of the bones of the dead in nonmortuary contexts both at Cahokia and outlying sites. (Emerson et al. 2003, 179)

Tacked on at the end, then, is their explanation of why some human remains are found in nonmortuary contexts, such as storage pits, house basins, and so on. However, this still leaves unexplained the lack of mortuary remains from many of these early Mississippian period upland graves. This is not to claim that there is an explanatory vacuum. Thomas Emerson and Douglas Jackson (1984, 214–15), for example, point out that while many of the mortuary pits at the BBB Motor site also were empty, those that had residue actually showed indication of reuse. Therefore, these pits are recognized to have been typically reused. However, excavators also usually comment that what residue remained was in a state of very poor preservation. The implication, then, is that the absence of mortuary residue from many of these mortuary pit features resulted from the combination of the systematic removal of bodies to be buried elsewhere (usually in the form of bundle burials), the deterioration of the body or bundle burial caused by soil factors, the disinterment of even these remains, and, finally, the distribution of the odd body parts among kin. As Emerson and colleagues point out, the puzzle that remains is not that so many of the pits were devoid of human remains but that some of them had any remains at all in them, particularly full skeletons. As noted above, "We know that this process may sometimes have been modified or interrupted, either deliberately or accidentally, since we have recognized extended, primary burials in some cemeteries" (Emerson et al. 2003, 178).

However, little of this complex postmortem processing accords with Emerson and colleagues' claim that these early practices were promoted by the need for peripheral communities to establish the new tradition of ancestor cults by which they could resist and/or carve themselves a social niche in the dynamic, hegemonic, and dominance-based hierarchical culture and society of Cahokia. In fact, such an explanation seems counterintuitive. After all, the primary premise of the funerary perspective is that a cemetery CBL has the symbolic legitimizing force necessary by which the responsible community carves out its place in a competitive social world. Therefore, rather than displaying empty graves, major reuse, stray bones, and so on, these cemeteries should be well populated with extended burials displaying little in the way of postmortem manipulation.

The Heterarchical Polyistic Locale-Centric Account

This contradiction between the absence of mortuary residue in many cases and the claimed social identifying purposes can be dissolved by the heterarchical polyistic locale-centric account. Indeed, for the most part, the patterning of the early Mississippian period upland mortuary sites as summarized above conforms very neatly with the expectations of the World Renewal Cult Heterarchy and the Mourning/World Renewal Mortuary models. For example, the former model claims that autonomous cults combined into mutualistic alliances and affiliations of alliances for the purpose of performing enhanced mortuary-mediated world renewal ritual, the type postulated under the Mourning/World Renewal Mortuary model. Thus, we could expect different types of collective burial locales (CBLs) corresponding to the organizational levels of autonomous cults, cult alliances, and alliance affiliations. These CBLs would be differentiated in terms of the primary aspect of the funerary→mourning→spirit release→world renewal process that was typically performed at each. Probably, much of the terminal mortuary ritual would be focused in the CBLs of the cult alliances located in the world renewal cult heterarchies, such as Cahokia. Indeed, the performance of a world renewal ritual mediated by lethal human sacrifice would likely occur only in the precincts of the cult heterarchies, as is fully discussed in the previous chapter.

However, there could be several different CBLs for the performance of the intermediate steps in the postmortem sacrificial process, and these would be systematically related. For any given deceased, this process would be initiated by immediate death-separation rites (probably including mourning and terminal funerary rites) and possibly even some clan renewal rites (such as name adoption rituals), thereby drawing in close kin and companions. In the case of a harmonized system as postulated under the World Renewal Cult Heterarchy model, after these rites, the body would be transferred to the cult most closely associated with the deceased. If the deceased was a child or infant, one or the other parent or other close relative would probably be a member of the selected cult. The cult would then treat the deceased as symbolic capital by which to mediate the remaining incremental series of mourning→spirit release→renewal rites. This would probably require the initial wrapping of the body and "storage" on truss-trench scaffolds or the equivalent.[2] The body might be removed and used to mediate further mourning and memorial rites, drawing in a widening range of companions and kin. At a certain point in the ritual cycle, the body would be deposited in a mortuary pit feature in the CBL of the cult, where its flesh would be allowed to deteriorate. This would be followed by disinterment and bone cleaning and bundling in preparation for removal as a sacred bone bundle to the ritual center of the cult's alliance, possibly in one of the mound-plaza complexes of Cahokia. Here it would be combined with the mortuary contributions of the other cults of the alliance, with the total set being deposited collectively as an essential part of a major world renewal ceremony, either in the charnel house of the alliance in its terminal mortuary deposit (such as in the Wilson Mound) or possibly contributed as part of a multialliance participation in the major world renewal ritual (such as in Mound 72).

With this process outlined, what kind of mortuary patterning would be expected? At Cahokia, we should find the alliance CBL type, including two or more cult CBLs. Thus, the two clusters of mortuary pits making up the Fingerhut site, 2.4 kilometers west of Monks Mound (Witty 1993, 425), would probably be the CBL of an alliance, and it may have been used largely to prepare the body for ritual bone cleaning, first through temporary burial and then disinterment, at which point the bones would be cleaned and then bundled and curated in the charnel temple of the cult alliance. Charles Witty determined that the Fingerhut site was constituted of two clusters of mortuary pit features. This suggests the possibility that two autonomous cults in the same alliance acted as the primary custodians. Another alternative is Witty's suggestion that these clusters define separate Lohmann and Stirling phase mortuary events: "The Fingerhut cemetery represents two separate burial areas that encompass a relative short period of time, 150 years during the Lohmann and Stirling phases. . . . Observance of solar phenomena associated with the construction of Woodhenge apparently played an important role in the alignment of the Fingerhut burials" (Witty 1993, 432).

In any case, these burials would be regularly replaced with new deceased, both as extended burials terminating mourning rites in the local charnel structure of the cult alliance and as bone bundles being brought in from the more distant cult CBLs, as illustrated by the Center Grove site. That is, the Center Grove site along with the Knoebel/Knoebel South site and the Mississippian component of the Stemler Bluff site might be best interpreted as auxiliary CBLs of autonomous cults or even, possibly, of cult alliances that, in fact, had their "home" cult locale(s) elsewhere, possibly or probably on the American Bottom.[3] These floodplain cult locales would be represented by the Lohmann phase and Stirling phase Range nodal site and by the Stirling phase Labras Lake and Julien nodal sites (discussed in detail in chapter 11). All these sites are characterized by having a rich residue of ritual materials but lacking mortuary data. This suggests that while initial mourning- and spirit release–type sacrificial mortuary practices may have been performed at these sites, they would generally not involve the scaffold curating or burial of the deceased. Instead, these initial mortuary rites would probably be terminated by a ritual procession carrying the deceased to the cult's auxiliary CBL, possibly located in the uplands, such as the Center Grove or Knoebel/Knoebel South sites, where the remains would be placed on scaffolding. Following the appropriate scaffolding period, they would be buried in a nearby mortuary pit as part of a postmortem sacrificial rite—thus constituting the mortuary pits as sacrificial crypt altars—and when needed by the cult, they would be disinterred, with the bones cleaned, bundled, and carried in sacred procession to the cult's alliance CBL at Cahokia, such as the Fingerhut CBL, or some other cult heterarchy, and so on.

In short, these upland sites would nicely fill the absence of mortuary data in the postulated autonomous male-based fertility cult sites on the floodplain. The upland location of these sites also suggests that this region was not simply a convenient place to "store" the deceased, since, of course, bearing them to these sites and performing further postmortem sacrificial rites (including burial, disinterring, cleaning, and bundling) at these sites would constitute incrementally ordered mourning→memorial→spirit release→world renewal rites. Seen in these terms, the uplands may have had a special meaning for these world renewal fertility cults, and this probably relates to the pre-Mississippian period. Below I discuss the evidence, skimpy as it is, in support of my claim that the mortuary process described above is the continuity of the pre-Mississippian period practices. That is, these upland CBLs are not a radical innovation along the lines argued by Emerson and colleagues (2003, 177) when they state that only with the Lohmann phase did mortuary burials occur and that this innovation occurred suddenly, with the "appearance of bounded cemeteries and in-ground interments," indicating that this "must have been a tremendous ideological shift for Terminal Late Woodland populations." Instead, for the most part, these upland mortuary sites should be viewed not as cemetery CBLs but as auxiliary CBLs of autonomous world renewal cults or cult alliances. Therefore, they would be simply the expression and result of a modification of the same mortuary process that had its roots in the Late Woodland and Terminal Late Woodland. What changed was that, while in the pre-Mississippian period these upland locales may have witnessed the terminal world renewal rites (Wittry et al. 1994, 139), in the Mississippian period they were used for mediating mortuary rites only partway through the total process. If this is the case, then the innovation that occurred to bring about the Mississippian period was the decision to shift most of the terminal postmortem aspect of these world renewal rituals from the upland CBLs to the floodplain. This strategic innovation, therefore, would have been part of the broader strategy resulting in the construction of the world renewal cult heterarchies. The modification of the traditional mortuary process, therefore, would be the addition of the final ritual procession of the deceased, usually in the form of bundle burials, from the upland CBLs to the CBLs of the floodplain world renewal cult heterarchies.

As outlined above, this process would easily account for the multiple mortuary pit features in the upland mortuary locales that were devoid of any human remains. With the exception of the Halliday site, which I address in the next chapter, most of the pit features at the other three sites discussed above—the Central Grove site, the Knoebel South site, and the western component of the Stemler Bluff site—were identified as mortuary pits on the grounds of "looking like" mortuary pits, since most of them contained no direct evidence that they had been used for mortuary purposes. However, the context and the few clear indicators of human residue clearly point to the conclusion that they should be considered mortuary features. Therefore, it is highly likely that, in fact, they had been used to mediate much of the intermediate aspect of the mortuary process and that their being empty was the result of being used for a final mortuary ritual that made their reuse impossible. As I note in chapter 12, the incremental use of these mortuary features modifies their symbolic pragmatic meaning (for example, from being "laying-in" crypts mediating funerary and mourning rites, to being spirit release crypt altars mediating sacrificial rites). The latter ritual would probably prohibit reusing the same pit as a "laying-in" crypt. Hence, with the removal of the final postmortem sacrificial offering, the pit would need to be abandoned.

This process would appear to be well illustrated at the Center Grove site, in which only one mortuary pit had human residue and all the others were empty. In fact, as noted above, Booth comments in several cases that an empty and abandoned mortuary pit was superimposed by another. This observation suggests that two imperatives were operating: in the first case, the proscription against reusing a mortuary pit, as outlined above; and in the second case, the view that the sacrificial ritual supercharged the immediate space with sacredness so that building a new mortuary crypt beside or on top of a previous sacred space was desirable. In time, reuse of the locale by adding earth to the immediate area would allow for the digging of new pits so that these superimposed the older abandoned but still sacredly charged pits.

Therefore, the Center Grove site (and probably the Stemler Bluff and Knoebel sites), both the mortuary and the nonmortuary components, would have come about as a result of a rather minor ritual mortuary innovation involving a shifting of terminal world renewal postmortem sacrificial rites from the upland region to the floodplain. This shift would explain the similarities and differences between the Center Grove site, for example, and the BBB Motor site. Booth observes that the BBB Motor site was rich in ritual materials while the Center Grove site had none, even though the structures at both sites were similar in form and internal organization, and he notes "that Feature 16 at BBB Motor exhibits a variation in the internal post feature noted at Center Grove. In addition, the BBB Motor site Lohmann/Stirling phase mortuary complex, unlike Center Grove, exhibited elaborate ceremonialism, some of which was not directly related to mortuary behavior, for example, green corn ceremonialism" (Booth 2001, 53). However, he also notes that the Center Grove structures average only 9.57 square meters in area and the BBB Motor site structures average 14.4 square meters. He concludes that the variations can be explained in terms of "rural/urban" social differences, suggesting that the BBB Motor site was the larger and more complex of the two because it was the locale of an "urban" community, while the Grove Center site was merely the locale of a "rural" community (Booth 2001, 53). Emerson and colleagues elaborate on this same point:

> At Center Grove the use of the complex is focused solely on mortuary practices. The differences in density of debris, ceremonial focus, and elaboration may relate to the differential status and size of the groups using the two burial areas: BBB Motor is virtually situated in downtown Cahokia, while Center Grove is located on the outskirts of Greater Cahokia. One would expect to find greater ceremonial elaboration, wealth, and population size at sites nearer the Cahokian center than on the fringes. (Emerson et al. 2003, 175)

In contrast, the differences can be as easily or even more easily and reasonably accounted for by noting my postulate in chapter 11—namely, that the BBB Motor site incorporates the CBL component of an autonomous female-based fecundity world renewal cult (or, possibly, a cult alliance), no doubt closely related to the underworld and to Earth Mother powers. This premise suggests that the upland sites are the auxiliary CBLs of the complementary male-based fertility world renewal cults, and this explanation accounts for the absence of mortuary data both in the male-based autonomous cult locales of the flood-plain, such as those at the Range and Labras Lake sites, and at the type of up-land CBL site represented by the Center Grove site. The major ritual parapher-nalia would not be kept at an auxiliary male-based fertility cult CBL but at the alliance cult CBL in Cahokia or Mitchell, and so on. This floodplain-female-underworld : upland-male-heavens complementary relation claim is particu-larly reinforced by my analysis of Woodhenge 72 and the dual stratification of the lethal mortuary deposits of Mound 72 (in particular, the complementary Beaded Burials [Burials 13/14] of Feature 101 and Burials 117/118 of Feature 219). Again, however, the absence of human remains in the majority of the mortuary pit features of the BBB Motor site also suggests that, in a manner similar to that of the cult(s) that were responsible for the Fingerhut CBL, this cult also participated in terminal world renewal ritual at Cahokia. Hence the differences and similarities of the Center Grove and BBB Motor sites, both displaying major marker poles and mortuary-related features, are accounted for comfortably under a combination of the World Renewal Cult Heterar-chy model, the Bifurcated Settlement Articulation Modal account, and the Mourning/World Renewal Mortuary model.

As I comment above, it is highly likely that this complex mourning→spirit release→world renewal mortuary process is not new but a modification of the same process that had its roots in the Late Woodland and Terminal Late Wood-land. This claim is quite the opposite to that made by Emerson and colleagues: "Given the lack of any recognized Terminal Late Woodland cemeteries in the American Bottom we assume that these peoples' mortuary program may have involved the exposure of corpses. *One of the significant changes with the advent of the Mississippian period was the appearance of formal, bounded cemeteries and in-ground interments*" (Emerson et al. 2003, 164, emphasis added). Emerson and colleagues complement this claim by noting that one of the major charac-teristics of the Lohmann phase was the emergence of what they refer to as the cemeteries of "ruling elite of Cahokia" and what I have defined as the CBLs of world renewal cult heterarchies. They specifically claim that this shift mani-fests a deep structural change: "[N]ative cemeteries are virtually absent for at last a millennium prior to making their appearance in the Mississippian era. . . . Such a shift is one more indication of the social, political, and religious trans-formation that accompanied the appearance of the new Mississippian order"

(Emerson et al. 2003, 177). In contrast, the alternative account of these early Mississippian period upland CBLs would argue that they manifest a strong continuity of the preexisting Terminal Late Woodland period mortuary practices and that these also express a continuity of a very ancient tradition of bluff-top world renewal burial ritual.

Interestingly, although the data to support this claim are currently limited, comments by Emerson and colleagues (2003, 188n3) directly relate to this issue. In an extensive note, they state that recent excavations at the Late Woodland ridge-top Lillie site (11MS662) in the northern uplands of the American Bottom has revealed multiple "[i]solated human remains, some burned and then redeposited, representing multiple individuals." In situ partial cremation of a disarticulated child was noted in another feature, and this feature also contained disarticulated "clustered elements of perhaps additional adult individuals." This particular feature may have served multiple crematory events, since it displayed "intense burning, as indicated by red oxidized soil and a thick black charcoal lens . . . in and around the child skeleton." Citing a personal communication with Megan Jost, they comment that similar, although less extensive, mortuary remains were found at the Dugan site, and they conclude, "The fragmentary condition of the remains and evidence of incidental burning suggest that they represent the cleaning out of a mortuary processing area" (Emerson et al. 2003, 181).

There are some more very important data that, even though limited, allow me to push the probable performance of upland mortuary practices even further back in time, possibly into the Patrick phase. The Meyer Cave site is in a small bluff-side cave located in the middle reaches of the American Bottom. Brad Koldehoff and colleagues (2002, 12–13) excavated an accumulation of human bones and Late Woodland cordmarked pottery sherds there. They argue that the cave is too small for it to have attracted human occupation; instead, they conclude, the cave deposits were the result of woodrats (commonly called packrats) gathering the residue of mortuary practices that had involved the exposure of human deceased in nearby trees, on scaffolds, and/or on nearby bluff cliff ledges. All indicators (in particular, the ceramics) point to this as being a Patrick phase accumulation, although Koldehoff and colleagues also comment that the exact dating cannot be confirmed:

> The temporal affiliation of the human remains has not been conclusively established. The presence of Late Woodland charcoal and pottery sherds supports the notion that the human remains are Late Woodland. The co-occurrence of 21 well-preserved fragments of human bone and 32 well-

preserved fragments of Late Woodland pottery is difficult to explain as mere coincidence; they are more likely to have been carried into the cave by woodrats from the surrounding area. Additional support for this conclusion can be drawn from the routine use of bluff-base fans by Late Woodland groups in the vicinity of Meyer Cave, as well as along the entire American Bottom. (Koldehoff et al. 2002, 12–13)[4]

Koldehoff and colleagues suggest that this site may go some way toward accounting for the lack of mortuary data in the known Late Woodland sites on the floodplain, such as the Sponemann phase occupation of the Sponemann site and the Patrick phase and Terminal Late Woodland period occupations of the Range site. In effect, systematic exposure of the dead on or near the bluffs with natural processes accounting for the final dispersal would account for this absence from the settlements.

While this conclusion would accord with the claim by Emerson and colleagues (2003, 177) that pre-Mississippian mortuary practices were characterized by "mortuary rituals that focused on the exposure and natural deterioration of corpses," these remains from the Meyer Cave site may better indicate only the midpoint of the total mortuary process, which was probably completed for any given deceased by final burial on the bluff top or in the vicinity. This claim is made on the basis of the particular nature of the data. As Koldehoff and colleagues (2002, 5) note, the typical woodrat forages within an average of less than 30 meters from its den. Within this range it can move items that do not "exceed about 3 cm in diameter or edge thickness" or exceed about 80 or 90 grams. As stated in the above quotation, the human bones and the pottery sherds were well preserved, which means that they had not been significantly exposed to weathering. For this reason, Koldehoff and colleagues claim that there was a rather rapid removal of this material into the cave. Also of note is that all the sherds and human bones were small. In the former case, of the thirty-two sherds, only "10 measure greater than 3.4 cm in length and . . . the largest, thickest sherd weighs 36.7 g, is 6.8 cm long, and is 0.9 cm thick"; in the latter case, of the twenty-one skeletal elements, none "exceeds 11 cm in length or 3 cm in thickness . . . and [they had] a mean weight of 4.0 g" (Koldehoff et al. 2002, 11). That is, the ceramic and skeletal residue are all well below the maximum and even the average capacity of the woodrats to move within a radius of 30 meters of their nests. This suggests that by the time these rodents were able to tackle the deceased and their associated pottery, all of the larger bones and ceramic pieces had already been removed.

While some of this material, particularly the human remains, could have been taken by other animal scavengers, such a possibility does not explain the absence of larger pot sherds. The only scavengers, other than humans, that might take such materials would be the woodrats, and, of course, the humans would not be scavenging in picking up the larger pieces—they would be performing a mortuary activity. All of this suggests, therefore, that in all probability, the absence of larger skeletal remains and the absence of larger pottery sherds in the woodrat den was primarily the result of these having been collected by kin and companions and removed for final deposit elsewhere, probably as bundle burials, thereby leaving only the very small bones and bone fragments and the smallest pottery sherds for the woodrats to gather. In short, on the one hand, the presence of the human mortuary residue and pottery in the Meyer Cave would fit the claim that the natural tendency of the woodrat to gather nesting material was the causal factor. On the other, the underrepresentation of ceramic and human remains fitting the average capacity of the woodrat to collect would argue against the woodrat as the only causal factor. What is required is the conjunction of two processes: the natural tendencies of woodrats and a type of humanly conducted mourning→spirit release→world renewal process as postulated under the Mourning/World Renewal Mortuary model. While the latter model would not by itself promote a prediction about woodrats caching mortuary remains, postulating woodrats alone as the causal agency does not produce a good fit. Together these two processes do. That is, the patterning of the Meyer Cave woodrat cache is fully consistent with what we could expect given the conjunction of these two agencies.[5]

Although these are limited data, they must be seen within the context of the settlement patterning of the Late and Terminal Late Woodland periods of the American Bottom. As discussed earlier (in chapters 6, 7, and 8), essentially no deliberately deposited human mortuary remains were found in the excavated floodplain sites of these periods, despite the large-scale excavations that were carried out under the FAI-270 Archaeological Mitigation program. Instead, what was found were a few isolated remains of skeletal parts and fragments in pit and basin features, which the excavators suggest were the incidental result of exposing the deceased in scaffolds or trees near the hamlets and villages before removing them. The findings of the Meyer Cave site reinforce this claim.

As noted earlier, Emerson and colleagues (2003, 164, 176–79) explain the absence of pre-Mississippian period mortuary residue in sites on the American Bottom floodplain as a result of complete exposure of the deceased away from the settlement. However, as I point out above, in the same article they recognize in an extensive note that there are upland-based mortuary data that, while limited in quantity, certainly suggest the strong possibility that a rich pre-Mississippian mortuary system existed. This is indeed a strange spatial juxtaposition in that these pre-Mississippian upland and floodplain populations—living within a few kilometers of each other, sharing the same Early and Late Bluff ceramic traditions, having the same range of settlement features (both rectangular single-post and keyhole basin structures) and the same ecological practices, and so on—should seem to differ so radically in mortuary practices. Indeed, it is now recognized that the Late Woodland populations of the upland regions of the American Bottom migrated into the floodplain in the early Late Woodland and expanded this migration in the later Late Woodland (constituting the Late Bluff ceramic tradition), while a similar migration penetrated the southern American Bottom from the Ozark upland regions on the western side of the Mississippi (constituting the Pulcher ceramic tradition) (Kelly 1990b, 117). Therefore, the most reasonable explanation for the absence of any significant bottomland mortuary residue in the pre-Mississippian period of the American Bottom would seem to be that populations migrating into the American Bottom floodplain continued the earlier practice of bluff-top CBLs, a tradition that reaches back in this region to the Middle Archaic, if not earlier (Charles and Buikstra 1983, 124).

In my discussion of the Late Woodland and Terminal Late Woodland integrated settlement articulation mode (chapters 6, 7, and 8), I suggest the possibility that the absence of mortuary data on the floodplain during this period may relate to the locating of terminal mortuary ritual in the uplands. This explanation is perfectly consistent with the premise that the integrated settlement articulation mode manifested the arm's-length relation between the relatively autonomous clan and cult organizations that constituted this integrated dual settlement system. I also argue (in chapters 7 and 8) that the typical Late Woodland community plan displayed this clan-cult arm's-length relation in a combination of spatial separation, layout, and formal differences of the clan-based single-post rectangular and the cult-based keyhole structures and, furthermore, that this same arm's-length relation was continued into the Terminal Late Woodland period, manifested by the combination of ritual plazas encircled by domestic habitation courtyard groups and specialized, peripherally located ritual structures. I termed the former pattern the *periphery-integrated settlement articulation mode* and the latter the *plaza-periphery integrated settlement articulation mode*.

In the light of the above CBL data and, of course, the Meyer Cave site, my initial characterization of the development of the integrated settlement articulation mode now has to be supplemented. Apparently, with the migration of settlers into the American Bottom from the uplands during the Late Woodland period, the series of mortuary-mediated rituals making up the funerary→ mourning→spirit release→world renewal process under the joint responsibility of the clans and cults came to be specialized and separated into two zones. The funerary and related aspects of the process would be located in hamlets and villages displaying the integrated clan-cult articulation mode, and the latter part of the world renewal postmortem sacrificial ritual process would continue to be performed, probably by the cults, in the upland CBLs.[6]

This dual-zone explanation suggests reassessing the Stemler Bluff site along these lines. According to Emerson and colleagues (2003, 170), the Stemler Bluff site is an early Mississippian period cemetery, even though only three of the twenty-five structures in the nonmortuary component of this site east of the sinkhole had wall-trench structures. Because of the disparity between the size of the mortuary component and the paucity of Mississippian structures, they suggest that as a Mississippian cemetery it served a widely dispersed community. However, they also recognize that the twenty-two other nonmortuary structures display the single-pole construction characteristic of the Terminal Late Woodland period. If those responsible for the single-post rectangular structures were also responsible for the majority of the mortuary features in the cemetery, then it "is truly unique and would represent the only known cemetery from that time period" (Emerson et al. 2003, 172).

In contrast, given the perspective of the Mourning/World Renewal Mortuary model and the context of the above discussion, we might reasonably treat the patterning of the Stemler Bluff site as, in fact, displaying a dual-component cult CBL. The twenty-two single-pole structures east of the sinkhole and an unknown proportion of the mortuary pits west of the sinkhole with the associated marker poles could represent a Terminal Late Woodland period CBL under the custodianship of a cult alliance postulated as being a major axis of the compound plaza-periphery integrated village type of the sort represented by the George Reeves and Lindeman phase occupations of the Range site. With the emergence of the early Mississippian period and the world renewal cult heterarchies, the Terminal Late Woodland cult alliance CBLs, like those postulated for Stemler Bluff, would be transformed into auxiliary CBLs of the type suggested above. Certainly, the archaeobotanical assemblage reported for this site would be consistent with this interpretation.

On the basis of the dual mortuary and dwelling components straddling the central sinkhole, Gregory Walz and colleagues (1997, 197–99) characterize this as a nodal site. They also comment on the below-average ubiquity and very low density of starchy seeds and maize.[7] Although they suggest that these results may be "artifacts of sampling and preservation rather than . . . indicators of differing plant procurement and production strategies" (Walz et al. 1997, 197), the results would also be quite consistent with the type of occupation that could be expected of auxiliary cult CBLs, one that would have a high transiency with significant stores carried in rather than cultivated in the locale. Furthermore, this analytical sectoring of the Stemler Bluff site highlights the parallels between this site and the Center Grove site. In this case, the postulated Terminal Late Woodland period patterning of the Stemler Bluff site can easily be interpreted as the transient-type occupation of a cult alliance CBL. The single-pole structures east of the sinkhole would have been used by the transient members carrying out cult mortuary-related duties in the large mortuary component with its marker poles west of the sinkhole. Analytically sectoring out this component leaves an early Mississippian auxiliary cult alliance CBL with its three wall-trench structures used as quarters for transient members on mortuary duty, carrying out ritual practices in the mortuary area west of the sinkhole. The similarities between the latter patterning and the patterning of the Center Grove site thus become striking: they have the same number of wall-trench structures, the same spatial separation between the wall-trench structures and the mortuary component, and the presence of marker poles. Finally, of the fifty-one mortuary pits in the Stemler Bluff mortuary component, thirty-one had no human remains. Although in the remaining pits there were the poorly preserved remains of twenty-two individuals, many of these could be Terminal Late Woodland burials. This means that the majority of the thirty-one pits with no remains would represent the same pattern as found at the Center Grove site—postulated ritual crypts that were emptied of final human remains and abandoned.

Interpreting these upland mortuary sites in this way also means, of course, that I have to expand the characterization of the compound plaza-periphery integrated settlement articulation mode to include the postulated upland cult alliance CBLs. But this is not as radical as it sounds, since it means that if Late Woodland mortuary practices of autonomous cults of individual villages were located on the bluff tops and in the nearby uplands, then the Terminal Late Woodland CBLs would simply be a continuity of these mortuary practices but under the custodial responsibility of emergent autonomous cult alliances. Therefore, rather than treating the Mississippian period emergence as entailing radical deep cultural and social structural innovations, we might instead see it as requiring a rather minor ideological innovation—namely, the moving of ele-ments of the preexisting mortuary ritual performed in these larger upland cult alliance CBLs, such as the postulated Terminal Late Woodland component of Stemler Bluff site, down to the floodplain. This would be the result of and part of the process of the formation of world renewal cult heterarchies. Along with this shift, of course, would be the demotion of the upland CBLs from being the principal cult alliance CBLs to being the upland auxiliary CBLs either of autonomous cults or, more likely, of cult alliances, such as the Center Grove site, the early Mississippian period component of the Stemler Bluff site, and also, possibly of the Knoebel/Knoebel South site.

Indeed, since the average 11.23 square meter size of the Knoebel site sin-gle-post rectangular structures was well above the average floor size of the same Terminal Late Woodland structures making up the floodplain villages, this would suggest that this site was a cult alliance CBL from the beginning. Therefore, this would also require that we sector the mortuary features of the nearby Knoebel South site into two components, one dated to the Terminal Late Woodland and the other to the early Mississippian period. Therefore, of the four early Mississippian upland sites with associated mortuary components noted at the beginning of this chapter, only the Halliday site is left unaccount-ed for in this manner. However, it has some unique attributes that, as I noted earlier, require special discussion and I address this site in the next chapter.

LATE MISSISSIPPIAN PERIOD UPLAND MORTUARY SITES

As noted earlier, two late Mississippian period upland mortuary sites—the Hill Prairie Mounds site and the Kane Mounds site—have also been recently reported. In chapter 12, I note that Emerson and Hargrave (2000, 6) made an important reassessment of the Kane Mounds site, in terms of both its mortuary content and its chronological relations to late Mississippian period floodplain sites (in particular, the Florence Street and East St. Louis Stone Quarry sites). A similar comparison has been made by Hedman and Hargrave (1999) for the Hill Prairie site (Figure 14.3). The Hill Prairie Mounds site is located directly on the bluff overlooking the American Bottom and only about 0.5 kilometers south of the Kane Mounds site. Hill Prairie has been dated to the extreme end of the Moorehead phase, possibly the early Sand Prairie phase (Hedman and Hargrave 1999). In contrast, the Kane Mounds site is considered to have had a longer occupancy period, possibly spanning the Moorehead phase, with its terminal occupancy period probably overlapping the Hill Prairie Mounds site

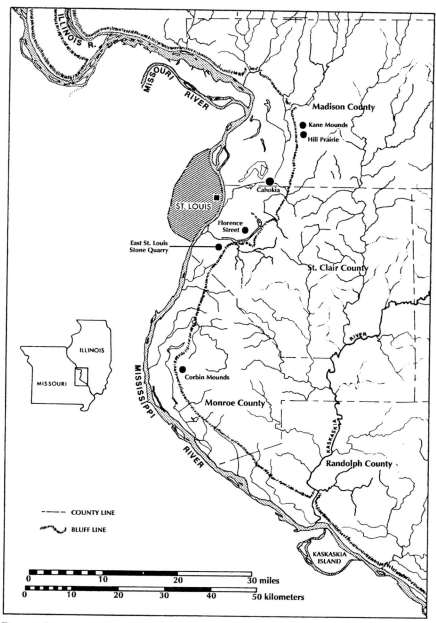

Figure 14.3. Late Mississippian upland and American Bottom mortuary sites. (Hedman and Hargrave 1999, fig. 1.1, p. 2. Courtesy of the Illinois Transportation Archaeological Research Program, University of Illinois.)

(Emerson and Hargrave 2000). In terms of the latter site, the same combination of extended, bundle, and ossuary area burials as at the Kane Mounds site is found. Where these mortuary patterns differ is that there are no signs of cremation at the Hill Prairie Mounds site, an important difference that Emerson and Hargrave note (2000, 12, Table 3). I will not discuss the Hill Prairie Mounds site here but will focus on Emerson and Hargrave's reassessment of the Kane Mounds site and their explanation for it, since the crux of their interpretation of these late Mississippian period upland sites hinges on the analysis of the latter site.

First, Emerson and Hargrave note a very interesting bifurcation of the late Mississippian period mortuary practices in this region. This claim arises from their reassigning the floodplain mortuary sites—such as the stone-box mortuary components of the Florence Street, the Range, and the East St. Louis Stone Quarry sites—from the Sand Prairie phase to the late Moorehead phase (specifically, circa A.D. 1250–1275). They observe that "during the second half of the thirteenth century two local rural mortuary patterns coexisted about Cahokia, characterized by the use of well-defined cemeteries (often the stone box type) with charnel structures and large ossuaries" (Emerson and Hargrave 2000, 6). Emerson and Hargrave note that the Kane Mounds mortuary data display patterning that is quite distinct from that of the largely contemporary floodplain sites, at least those identified in the lower sector of the northern expanse of the American Bottom. In particular, they note that the stone-box mortuary features characteristic of this sector were rare at the Kane Mounds site and, most interestingly, that the use of cremation or fire at the latter site was absent from the floodplain sites. They also point out that fire usage is associated at a number of the mortuary sites in the upper Mississippi and Illinois valleys. The Kane Mounds site also shared the use of shell spoons and burial vessels with these northern sites. On these and several other grounds, Emerson and Hargrave postulate that the Kane Mounds site might be the cemetery of communities that either were attracted by and migrated to the late Mississippian Cahokian world from the north or had migrated south in the early Mississippian period, suppressed their ethnic practices and identities at that time, and only started to reassert their ethnicity in the later Mississippian period.

Emerson and Hargrave particularly note "the many single and multiple burials scattered across the blufftop" and the use of a charnel area "similar to those of northern Mississippian peoples." They conclude,

We think they represent members of emerging (or, perhaps more appropriately, reemerging) subcommunities on the fringes of Cahokia. We must also consider the importance and meaning of non–American Bottom burial practices that cross-cut the Kane Mounds mortuary. The cultural, social, and economic context of these activities suggests some broad possibilities: that diverse hinterland groups might have been present on the fringes of Cahokia, whether as visitors, as residents, or for some other purpose. The asymmetrical relations between these groups and the "Cahokians" led to an increased emphasis of distinctive "ethnic identities." (Emerson and Hargrave 2000, 17–18)[8]

In the terms of this funerary perspective, therefore, late Mississippian period upland and floodplain mortuary sites would have been the cemeteries of at least two constellations of ethnic communities: the descendants of the resident groups who occupied the floodplain from pre-Mississippian times and into Mississippian times, and the (possibly) immigrant upland groups described above. These two constellations would maintain an arm's-length relation through developing contrasting mortuary practices, among other material differences.

Critique

One difficulty that this model of the late Mississippian period upland mortuary sites shares with the account of the early Mississippian upland mortuary sites is the lack of localized communities that can be associated with mortuary sites. If the mortuary practices being performed in these cemetery CBLs had been innovated, borrowed, or diffused to be among the important expressive media of ethnic identity and exclusivity in a social system in a process of decentralization, as Emerson and Hargrave claim, then we could legitimately expect a shift from dispersed villages to nucleated villages, the latter being ethnic based, and having as their major symbolic claim to the local territory a clearly delineated cemetery. Therefore, the absence of a nucleated settlement pattern is the most puzzling part of Emerson and Hargrave's late Mississippian period account of these upland CBLs.

However, Emerson and Hargrave seem to be right when they argue that there were significant incongruencies between the mortuary practices on the floodplain and in the upland region during the later Mississippian period. These incongruencies might definitely indicate a greater arm's-length relationship developing between these two regions, possibly marking a process of disaffiliation of the heterarchies. Furthermore, the claim made by Emerson and Hargrave that strong influences from the northern regions are being manifested in the mortuary patterning of the Kane Mounds site seems to be well grounded. However, the apparent continuity of the dispersed village system would argue against the claim that these processes of ethnogenesis and/or migration, while important, were the primary causal factors. Instead, they may have been an effect of ideological disputes and negotiations that led to interalliance disaffiliation and the active recruiting of new and more distant peoples as sources of cult participation, as I discuss below.

The Heterarchical Polyistic Locale-Centric Account

I argue in chapter 12 that the patterning of the later Mississippian period stone-box CBLs in the southern sector of the northern expanse clearly suggests localized cult alliances. In keeping with Emerson and Hargrave's (2000, 5–7) new dating of these sites, it would appear that Cahokia experienced an even more rapid decline than Emerson and Pauketat (Emerson 1997c, 60; Pauketat and Emerson, 1997a, 22–28; 1997b, 277–78) had earlier argued.[9] Under the World Renewal Cult Heterarchy model, this rapid decline would be partly explained as the result of the developing disaffiliation of the cult alliances in the southern sector of the northern expanse of the American Bottom from the cult heterarchies in the northern sector, especially Cahokia. At the same time, the alliances in the upper sector of the northern expanse, reinforced possibly by emergent autonomous cult alliances in the upland regions, continued to sustain Cahokia as a world renewal cult heterarchy. In short, the northern-derived mortuary traits that Emerson and Hargrave have noted at the Moorehead phase Kane Mounds site might be quite adequately explained as the outcome of recruitment of autonomous cults from the lower and central Illinois Valley, and this recruiting would have involved the newly joining cults introducing their mortuary rites into the American Bottom. Of course, these mortuary practices would be mourning/world renewal postmortem sacrificial rites, and therefore their introduction would occur only after contentious ideological negotiations. This might partly account for the distancing of the relations between the northern and southern sectors of the northern expanse that is indicated by the differences between, for example, the Kane Mounds site mortuary rites and those at the East St. Louis Stone Quarry site. However, we must also note that many other elements of the Kane Mounds site mortuary program, as well as the later program displayed at the Corbin and Hill Prairie Mounds sites, retain the range of postmortem treatments that we would expect under the Mourning/World Renewal Mortuary model.

As elucidated under the Autonomous Cult model, ecclesiastic-communal cults would be open to recruitment, drawing their members from a broad geographic area. Hence, in a developing situation of a postulated disaffiliation of the southern sector alliances, when labor would become scarce in the heterarchies, competition would open cults to innovative ritual, particularly if this would encourage a new source of cult recruitment to replace the disaffiliating cult alliances. These new cults, of course, would be attracted from an area that had already developed the bifurcated settlement articulation mode, and members of the young male age-sets would therefore be free to travel quite some distances. Hence, we would expect the retention of the dispersed village that was part of the bifurcated settlement articulation mode. However, since more long-distance travel would be required for members drawn from the Illinois Valley and parts north, they could very well require larger residences dedicated to the needs of these long-distance "ethnics" to be built at the world renewal cult heterarchies. This would explain the prevalence at Cahokia in the Moorehead phase of large barracklike structures spaced apart from each other, thereby expressing ethnic distancing, while still sharing the same mound-plaza complex.

Hence, in one sense, my account agrees with Emerson and Hargrave's account (2000, 1–3). A form of ethnogenesis would emerge. However, this would not be the exclusive ethnicity of residential, clan-based communities but rather the more open, diverse ethnicity of age-sets of companions drawn from a broad region; therefore, it would be an "inclusive" ethnicity, a plurality of ethnicity coalescing under the umbrella of world renewal cult heterarchies. Ironically and unwittingly, however, it would also be a form of exclusionary ethnicity in that these new ethnic groupings with their atypical mortuary rites might have simply intensified the disaffiliation of the autonomous cults and cult alliances based in the southern sector of the northern expanse of the American Bottom, and this disaffiliation process could be characterized by some bitterness. Therefore, while this infusion of new membership might promote closer ethnic relations among young men and women from the more northern regions, it might also promote more distant relations between the descendants of the original founding cults of Cahokia and the other heterarchies (those that traced their ethnic affiliations to the Late Woodland and Terminal Late Woodland northern sector Late Bluff and southern sector Pulcher traditions, respectively). This disaffiliation might even have been manifested by a growing intraregional militancy during the Moorehead phase, promoting the reconstructing of the sacred C-form palisade with its ritual stations/bastions.

CONCLUSION

The heterarchical polyistic locale-centric has treated these upland mortuary sites as auxiliary cult or cult alliance CBLs (excluding the Halliday site, which I address specifically in the next chapter), thereby eliminating the various anomalies that the hierarchical monistic modular polity account has generated while quite comfortably incorporating these new data and expanding our understanding of the American Bottom. This account has suggested that, rather than the initial Mississippian period mortuary practices of the American Bottom and uplands being an abrupt innovation out of preceding non-CBL practices, they express the continuity of a deep tradition of mortuary-based world renewal CBLs. In this case, I have argued that these practices may have been performed on the bluff tops overlooking the river valleys of the central Mississippian region from possibly the Middle Archaic period, or even earlier. The Mississippian period innovation that occurred in the American Bottom, therefore, lay in shifting to the floodplain the performance of the terminal aspects of these traditional practices as part of the generating of the multiple-mound world renewal cult heterarchies, while continuing to maintain cult and/or cult alliance CBLs in the upland region as auxiliaries of the major alliance CBLs at the floodplain world renewal cult heterarchies.

Hence, the deep structural changes that are implicated by the hierarchical account are not needed in the heterarchical explanatory framework. Instead, these new data can be seen as the result of a rather small innovation in the mortuary ideology that had a large effect on the settlement patterning while maintaining the continuity of the deep cultural traditions of cosmology and ethos and basic social structures of autonomous cults and clans. With this analysis completed, I can now turn to the critical examination of the nature of the processes that generated the Terminal Late Woodland–Mississippian transition. I will follow the hermeneutic spiral method by first summarizing and critiquing the hierarchical monistic modular polity account of this transition and then presenting the alternative heterarchical polyistic locale-centric account.

The Terminal Late Woodland–
Mississippian Transition

Alternative Accounts

Using the theoretical framework and its empirical grounding that I have developed to this point, I can now complete what I initially outlined at the end of chapter 8, namely, the heterarchical polyistic locale-centric account of the Terminal Late Woodland–Mississippian transition. I present this as an alternative to the different versions of the current hierarchical monistic modular polity account of this same transition. Following the hermeneutic spiral method, I first summarize and then critique the latter accounts. For this purpose, I integrate Thomas Emerson's and Timothy Pauketat's versions as the most influential of these. For the sake of convenience, I term this the *Nucleated-Sequential Settlement Articulation* model of the Terminal Late Woodland–Mississippian transition. I then present the alternative heterarchical polyistic locale-centric view, which I term the *Integrated-to-Bifurcated Settlement Articulation* model of the transition.

THE NUCLEATED-SEQUENTIAL SETTLEMENT ARTICULATION MODEL

Emerson treats the Mississippian period "rural" social system as the outcome of a Cahokian-based elite-directed ideological strategy of resettlement. He claims that this strategy was motivated by the large numbers of the rural population that abandoned the multiple hamlets and larger villages of the countryside and moved into the nucleated multiple-mound locales—in particular, Cahokia. According to his model, this rather abrupt implosion of population imposed great strains on the carrying capacity of the Cahokian catchment area. Therefore, to enhance the production of staple products, a resettlement strategy was developed by the American Bottom elite residing in Cahokia and other multiple-mound locales that would generate rural nodal locales. As discussed in depth in chapter 11, these locales, which he refers to as civic and ceremonial nodal sites, effectively presenced the Cahokian political and religious authority in the countryside. The second part of this strategy was the encouraging of the dispersal of the commoners in small farmsteads across the landscape and integrated through central nodal household sites, thereby ensuring the continuing dominance of the rural sector by the urban-based elite. Emerson explains,

> As we now understand the archaeological record, *a population consolidation at centers occurred during the Lohmann phase in conjunction with a subsequent elite-organized dispersion of rural population.* Both the nucleation of population and concurrent reorganization and dispersal of immediate rural populations were in the hands of Cahokian elite. This patterned rural dispersal can be related to an increasing elite need for efficient and intensified use of floodplain topography . . . for agricultural production in response to demands by a centralized political elite. . . . [The] dispersal did not bring into play a direct articulation system of settlement . . . but rather a sequential articulation mode . . . as one might reasonably expect in a complex hierarchical society. The Cahokia elite did not leave the organization of their rural food producers to chance but created a specific, centrally controlled political and religious organization to ensure that foodstuffs were produced and transmitted to Cahokia in an orderly manner. (Emerson 1997c, 255–56)

It seems clear that Emerson is postulating opposing but related population processes as characterizing the Lohmann phase: on the one hand, population was nucleated (that is, "a population consolidation at centers"), and on the other, it was dispersed by the elite (that is, "in conjunction with a subsequent elite-organized dispersion of rural population"). I find characterizing the population process in this way slightly confusing in that the nucleation of population would seem to have to occur first, followed by the development and implementation of elite-organized population dispersal into the sequential distribution discussed in chapter 11. In fact, this is implied in his use of the term *subsequent.* However, he also stresses that the nucleation and the dispersal were performed "in conjunction," which I take to mean that they were concurrent.

This inconsistency may be only apparent, in that he specifies that the "concurrent reorganization" refers to the "dispersal of immediate rural populations" by the Cahokian elite, and this would presumably be the rural population immediately prior to the resettlement process. That is, Emerson may be postulating a two-way shift in the "rural" population of the Terminal Late Woodland American Bottom hamlets and nucleated villages of the sort that John Kelly (1990a, 105) argues may have been responsible for the depopulation of the later Lindeman phase at the Range site. Kelly suggests that the decrease in overall size of the village prior to the Lohmann phase was probably the result of many of the occupants moving to the nearby Lunsford-Pulcher site or to "a new settlement at another location" (Kelly 1990a, 105). I take this to mean that some of the population moved to Lunsford-Pulcher, participating in the nucleation-through-implosion process, while others dispersed into single farmsteads and small hamlets.

However, I am not sure that this is precisely what Emerson means, since Kelly's view seems to be that the nucleation and dispersal were part of the same process, while Emerson juxtaposes in the same statement the two descriptions "in conjunction with" and "a subsequent elite-organized dispersion." Normally, these terms delineate, respectively, simultaneous and sequential timing. While "in conjunction with" seems to be precisely what Kelly is claiming, "subsequent . . . dispersion" would suggest that the latter dispersal occurred sometime after the initial and rapid nucleation marking the early Lohmann phase. In any case, the important point that Emerson seems to be adding to this dual population process of centralizing-nucleation and rural populations dispersing into the sequential settlement articulation mode is that the elites managed it (or at least managed the dispersal aspect of it). However, if his claim is that from the beginning the dispersal was part of the Lohmann phase, then there must have been a pre–Lohmann phase process of population centralizing-nucleation that was not itself part of a discursive elite strategy.

Therefore, as I am going to interpret the above quotation, it is saying that the formation of the mound-plaza locales was initiated in the later Terminal Late Woodland and that this formation would have been among the conditions that motivated the elite strategy that brought about the dispersed village system that was the rural aspect of the Lohmann phase settlement articulation. Therefore, the formation of this dispersed village system following the initial nucleation of the late Terminal Late Woodland period is what marks the rural aspect of the Lohmann phase, which is the conventionally accepted commencement of the Mississippian period.[1]

That this interpretation must be close to Emerson's claim is indicated by his characterization of the later Terminal Late Woodland period settlement from which this resettlement process emerged. He observes, "Just when it appeared that there was a steadily increasing consolidation of multiple Emergent Mississippian [Terminal Late Woodland] villages with their plaza complexes, the transition was in many places apparently 'short-circuited'—this 'short-circuiting' was undoubtedly caused by the pre-emption of local power created by the emergence of nearby simple chiefdoms" (Emerson 1997c, 255). He then goes on to describe the "short-circuiting" preemptive process as outlined in the preceding long quotation.

Two implications concerning Emerson's view of the nature of the Terminal Late Woodland period follow from this. First, it is clear that he is committed to Kelly's general claim that this period witnessed the emergence of small or simple chiefdoms based on the plaza-complex villages. Second, since the "new" power of these dominance-ranked chiefdoms is what was responsible for the "pre-emption of local power" that brought about the sequential settlement articulation mode, and since the latter was simply the "rural" component of the consolidation of hierarchical power in Cahokia and the other major multiple-mound locales, then this whole process clearly would have to have been both abrupt and ruptural in the sense that it would have been a social upheaval (Fortier and McElrath 2002, 203).

Most American Bottom archaeologists concede that the initiation of the population reorganization generating what we now recognize as Lunsford-Pulcher, East St. Louis, Cahokia, and so on, probably started prior to the Lohmann phase.[2] The emergence of the latter phase, then, is marked by a rather sudden "implosion" of population apparently settling at and around Cahokia. Notably, according to this nucleated-sequential view the implosion formed a permanently nucleated population through a radical upheaval of traditional settlement practices. This implosion, bringing about a permanent (or nontransient) population nucleation, has been characterized by Pauketat as the "Big Bang" of the American Bottom: "[A]bout A.D. 1050, the American Bottom experienced the political and economic equivalent of the Big Bang. I have identified this Big Bang in the Bottom as a consequence of the rapid consolidation of political power or regional control presumably by some subset of the high-ranking Emergent Mississippian [that is, Terminal Late Woodland] population. . . . The event brought about the abrupt and large scale transformation of community order, the physical landscape of Cahokia, and the entire northern expanse of the American Bottom floodplain" (Pauketat 1997, 31–32; also see Pauketat 2002, 152). Therefore, in terms of my interpretation of this Emerson-Pauketat view, concurrent with or certainly shortly into this "Big Bang" population nucleation, there would be the formation and implementation of the elite strategy that brought about the sequential settlement articulation mode of dispersed village systems integrated by the elite nodal sites that is comprehensively discussed and critiqued in chapter 11.

For Pauketat, the claimed socially disruptive nature of this "Big Bang" played an important part in the initial ideological strategy of the elite:

> Presumably, the surging numbers of people immigrating to Cahokia from the surrounding countryside would have facilitated this dissolution [of Lindeman/Edelhardt plaza-complex towns]. . . . Whether or not it was entirely intentional, the elimination of an element of the social fabric, perhaps the basal social organizational units of pre-Mississippian society, would have been quite a political feat, casting off as it would have the means by which social resistance might have been mobilized against political consolidation. (Pauketat 1997, 32)

For him, this urbanization may have served to break the grip of what he sees as traditional commonsense kinship-based commitments so that the elite ideology could more effectively take hold of the consciousness of the commoners, thereby ensuring the dominance of the former and the alienation of the latter from their own (commonsense) cultural traditions (Pauketat 1994, 14–16, 23–24). Thus, in harmony with Emerson's view of the Terminal Late Woodland–Mississippian transition, Pauketat sees this population implosion as the termination of a two-step process: first, both small villages and large villages with their plaza complex, probably simple chiefdoms, were abandoned as the majority of their occupants moved into the preexisting and elite-selected towns (probably the seats of dominance-based complex chiefdoms, such as Cahokia and Lunsford-Pulcher, which were thereby transformed into even more complex chiefdoms); and second, the rapid consolidation of these latter chiefdoms (the "Big Bang") to form a sprawling Cahokia under the rule of the paramount chief and his supporting elite of lesser chiefs.

More recently, Pauketat (2000, 32–33) has added an important dimension to the elite-inspired strategy of resettlement, arguing that the paramountcy at Cahokia entrenched the dependency of the rural communities by divesting them of any sense of community autonomy through monopolizing the production and use of cultural symbols, such as woodhenges, mounds, specialized ritual ceramic and lithic assemblages, and so on. He speaks of this as the "politicization" of the pre-Mississippian communities, characterized by Cahokia becoming the central component that tied the dispersed villages into a hegemonic society having its identity delineated and sustained by elite-directed, -controlled, and -centralized symbolism. He also postulates this politically generated rupture bringing about the "Mississippianization" of the American

Bottom as being largely replicated in other parts of the central Mississippi Valley and the Yazoo Basin. That is, he proposes this elite-commoner top-down "Big Bang" politicization of floodplain zones with their adjacent uplands through the centralized-elite's monopolization of community symbols as a general theory to both characterize and explain the Mississippianization of the Southeast. He concludes, "Nucleation and dispersal, even as abrupt as the American Bottom and Yazoo cases, were probably only components of a drawn-out diachronic negotiation of power and tradition. It is plausible that the replacement of a pre-Mississippian settlement landscape, visible at the village level, was a conscious political tactic of certain interest groups" (Pauketat 2000, 34).

Discussion

This complex account of the transition relies on several assumptions, at least three of which I want to address. First, the primary attraction of these selected pre–Lohmann phase locales would be that they were already important political centers, that is, preselected by an emerging dominance-based political elite. Second, this account assumes that these locales were initially simple chiefdoms having a basic hierarchical orientation and that, through competing and allying with each other, some were able to expand their power bases at the cost of the others, with a rather abrupt consolidation occurring circa A.D. 1050 marked by the rapid growth of Cahokia. Third, as noted earlier, the populations of the multiple-mound locales are assumed to have taken up permanent sedentary occupation. That is, in most cases, the occupants of the expanding urban centers treated their residency as permanent, and those who did move back into the rural area did so only under the urging of the elite-directed sequential resettlement strategy as postulated by Emerson.

The first assumption is expressed in the literature by the claim that mound construction at such sites as Lunsford-Pulcher, Cahokia, and so on, probably was initiated during the latter part of the Lindeman/Edelhardt phase (although, when this assumption is expressed, it is always accompanied by the caveat that there is little in the way of supporting evidence for it). The second assumption is drawn largely from the interpretation of the countryside settlement data revealed by the FAI-270 Archaeological Mitigation program, which overwhelmingly characterizes the changes in the settlement pattern as mapping the emergence and development of a hierarchical social system with an attached ritual component, as I fully discuss and critique in chapter 8.

Emerson's account is particularly reliant on these two assumptions since he argues that the emergence of an elite independent of traditional communal and kinship commitments required the initial construction of monuments under the generalized motivation of *communitas* (Emerson 1997c, 13–14). The community of equals, or nominal equals, would willingly cooperate in this sacred endeavor—not realizing that, once the construction was initiated, the managerial group that was initially selected by these nominal equals, their peers, to direct this collective labor would come to be uniquely identified by these same peers with the sacredness of these earthworks and temples. The result would be the alienation of these managers from the peers who selected them and their mutual transformation into self-reproducing "sacred elite" and "commoner" groups.

According to Pauketat (1994, 23–24), these elites, originally dispersed across different chiefdoms, started to intermarry laterally, forming alliances that were entrenched by endogamic marriages, and they also generated a new ideology that would serve their emerging sectoral interests. Apparently, it was this self-perpetuating elite class (developing out of these initial pre–Lohmann phase construction programs and cross-cutting local elite kinship groups) that would be in place and responsible for generating the politically motivated and ideologically guided complex chiefdoms. As part of this "Big Bang" nucleation, they would develop and implement the concurrent rural resettlement strategy, redistributing the remainder of the in situ rural population by forming the dispersed villages of the sequential settlement articulation mode. As Pauketat argues,

> The net effect of dispersal, marriage alliances, and the engagement by high-ranking subgroups in prestige-related warfare would have been the emergence of a shared interregional elite identity . . . [which] could have engendered elite endogamy. . . . [Moreover,] the expansion of one high-ranking core would have entailed the expansion of the other core groups with which it interacted. . . . The regional development of cores . . . would have amounted to the increased peripheralization of low-ranking subgroups. (Pauketat 1994, 23–24)

In Pauketat's version of the transition, since the "Big Bang" was most strongly manifested along the southern bank of Cahokia Creek, and particularly around Monks Mound (about which the claim is made that it must have been initiated during this brief pre-Lohmann phase), the centralization at Cahokia must have occurred largely at the expense of the other nascent paramount chiefdoms. Indeed, these apparently never fully achieved the status as paramounts and, instead, either continued to squabble among themselves and sporadically against the paramountcy at Cahokia (Milner 1990, 21–23; 1998, 13–14), or simply joined as subordinate chiefdoms within the growing hegemony of the central paramountcy of Cahokia. On the basis of my reading of Emerson's and Pauketat's work, I believe that they would support the latter view since, with this centralizing success, the elite of Cahokia would have been able to implement a new stage of social engineering that transformed the more locally and traditionally oriented dispersed villages into the Cahokian-centered sequential settlement articulation mode characterized by specialized political, fertility, and mortuary nodal locales. This marked the Stirling phase, according to Emerson. It is at this point that the real "Leviathan" emerges as the sacralized paramountcy of Cahokia ruled from the sanctity of Monks Mound and the central precinct. By analogy Pauketat argues, "As in Polynesia, Africa, or southeastern North America, the paramount might have been elevated to the status of a local god, with the nonreligious, aggressive, or warrior functions becoming the task of young elite individuals or junior lines of descent" (Pauketat 1994, 35).

The third assumption noted above (namely, that Cahokia and the other multiple-mound locales had permanent sedentary populations) actually is more an axiomatic-like presupposition of this model of the transition rather than a specifically articulated hypothesis. Hence, when the nature of residential occupancy is relevant to any discussion, it is effectively taken for granted as having been (for the most part) permanent. Thus, the major focus of the discussion becomes the numbers of residents involved. Differences in population estimates hinge not on whether a sedentary or a transient population occupied the well-made dwellinglike structures of Cahokia and the other multiple-mound locales but on what the actual density of this permanent population might have been, given the size of the excavated structures, the durability of these structures, the probable number of people per unit structure area, the relative status of the occupants in terms of large or small dwellings, the degree to which the known distribution of structures is a good sample of the total number, the estimated length of the phases, and so on (Milner 1998, 123–26; Pauketat 2002, 154, 162n5; Pauketat and Lopinot 1997, 106–8).

Presuming permanent residency is strange since almost all archaeologists recognize that some form of corvée labor would be involved and that, given the sheer amount of labor required to build the monuments, much of this would logically have to have been regularly drawn in from the "rural" sector (Mehrer 1995, 123, 144–46). Therefore, even under the hierarchical monistic modular polity account, a certain proportion of the estimated aggregation of housing floor space should be reserved for transient labor—and, of course, this estimated number should not be added to the total estimates for either the "permanent" population of these multiple-mound locales or the "rural" population estimates. In any case, if the validity of this permanent occupancy presupposition can be seriously questioned, as it is under the World Renewal Cult Heterarchy model, then not only do the current population estimates have to be reduced, as I discuss shortly, but also the whole question of the simultaneity of population dispersal and population nucleation becomes otiose since, under this model, the vast majority of the occupants of Cahokia and the other heterarchies would be transients who regularly cycled between their dispersed village homes and their cult locale quarters.

Critique

I first want to comment on the characterization of the "Big Bang" as the outcome of an elite ideological strategy that simultaneously nucleated and sequentially dispersed rural populations. As noted above, normally a dispersed population or a population dispersed in larger village centers needs to be aggregated before they can be dispersed. But in this characterization, the aggregation and sequential dispersal are both "concomitant with" and "subsequent to" each other. As Emerson puts it, "a population consolidation at centers occurred during the Lohmann phase in conjunction with a subsequent elite-organized dispersion of rural population" (Emerson 1997c, 255). According to this view, the expansion of the populations of Lohmann phase Cahokia and the other multiple-mound locales and the formation of the sequential dispersed village systems with their network of ceremonial temple, mortuary, and fertility locales, as well as civic nodal locales, would appear to have occurred concurrently, with the maximization of the Cahokian population occurring at the end of the phase. However, this contradicts Emerson's elite strategy model. According to him, the large inflow of population into the urban centers was itself the problem that motivated the elite-based strategy for redistributing the population across the countryside, precisely in order to maximize surplus production: "This patterned rural dispersal can be related to an increasing elite need for efficient and intensified use of floodplain topography . . . for agricultural production in response to demands by a centralized political elite" (Emerson 1997c, 255).

Although the needs he is speaking of are those of the "centralized political elite" in Cahokia, the other multiple-mound locales are also assumed to have aggregated in them similarly but overall smaller populations of commoners to serve their everyday urban-based needs. All of this suggests that the nucleation of population was the causal condition of the sequential dispersal strategy. However, if the sequential dispersal occurred simultaneously ("concurrently") with the nucleation, this elite-strategy account can logically be taken to postulate the formation of the sequential dispersed village system as both the effect of the nucleation forming Cahokia and the other multiple mound locales and a parallel condition of this same nucleation. If it were parallel (that is, contemporaneous), then the nature of the emergence of Cahokia and the other multiple-mound locales would have to be recharacterized, since while they could possibly have been in an ongoing state of having many occupants, they could not have been permanently occupied urbanlike communities, since the sequential dispersal would have simultaneously depopulated them. If this is the case, then it raises doubts that there ever was an elite strategy of population dispersal responsible for the transition.

There seems to be a further inconsistency between the claim that there was an elite strategy for dispersing the population and the evidence concerning the actual nature of the population nucleation. Pauketat and Neal Lopinot claim that the flow of population into Cahokia was abruptly initiated in or around A.D. 1050 and that this was largely the direct result of a depopulation of the countryside: "A reduction in the rural population density seems to have occurred. This reduction may have occurred as a general abandonment of some Emergent Mississippian [Terminal Late Woodland] villages around A.D. 1050. . . . Such abandonment and rural depopulation in general may correspond to the regional centralization of population at Lohmann-phase Cahokia" (Pauketat and Lopinot 1997, 119–20). Note that Pauketat and Lopinot draw a direct link between "rural depopulation" and "regional centralization of population at Lohmann-phase Cahokia." I return to this claim shortly. However, I want to point out that, although this "rural depopulation" appears to have occurred at the commencement of the Lohmann phase, according to Pauketat and Lopinot's population estimates, it was late, and not early, in the Lohmann phase that Cahokia maximized its population size, between 10,200 and 15,300 persons, which then dropped during the Stirling phase to between 5,200 and 7,200 (Pauketat and Lopinot 1997, 115–16).[3] Therefore, their claimed depopulation of the countryside and nucleation at Cahokia apparently continued well after the dispersed village system was in place. Of course, some rural population could be expected to continue to "flow in." However, the point of the elite-directed resettlement strategy, according to Emerson, was to maximize or at least optimize the outflow and minimize any return inflow since the greater the concentration of population in Cahokia and other multiple-mound locales, the lower the efficiency and overall production of rural resources. This would suggest that Emerson's claim of an elite strategy to disperse the population either did not work or else, as noted above, that there was no such strategy.

Besides the above contradiction in population movement what apparently characterizes the Lohmann phase from the beginning (as discussed in chapter 11) is the rather abrupt disappearance of the Terminal Late Woodland period villages, correlated with the equally abrupt appearance of both the dispersed villages and the multiple-mound locales. However, how can the "rural" population be nucleated to form the multiple-mound locales and also be distributed to form the widespread dispersed village system? I suspect that this is at the heart of the above problem of juxtaposing contradictory population distributions. Can Kelly's characterization of the population movements resolve the subsequent/concurrent nucleation/sequential dispersal problem? He saw a sort of selective division of the Terminal Late Woodland period population, with one sector remaining in the countryside by abandoning the old villages and forming the dispersed village system, and one sector aggregating in and being part of the nucleation process generating multiple-mound locales. While such a dual-sector division would certainly dissolve the contradictions implicit in claiming simultaneous/subsequent nucleation and dispersal, it would also mean that no elite strategy would be needed to resettle the countryside and, of course, would also suggest a much lower degree and intensity of nucleation. Therefore, this explanation would not account for the apparent rapidity and magnitude of the expansion of Cahokia and the emergence of the central political administrative complex that Pauketat's "Big Bang" model sees as being at the core of the transition process (Pauketat 1994, 81; 1998, 1; also see Pauketat and Emerson, 1997a, 8). Moreover, as I suggest in chapter 8, the actual dismantling of such Terminal Late Woodland villages as those at the Range site seems to mark the dismantling of the hierarchical power structure that Kelly postulates. This would seem to contradict the very nature of dominance hierarchies. If ranking families and their more immediate retainers moved into the emerging political centers, such as Lunsford-Pulcher and Cahokia, why would they not leave in place the minimal material culture required to sustain their "country seats"? That is, as much as I prefer Kelly's accounting over Emerson and Pauketat's, it would not account for the magnitude of expansion at the multiple-mound sites, nor would it explain the disappearance (in the countryside) of the claimed markers of the hierarchical structure.

The second problem I want to address is the critical nature of the role that the elites play in this Nucleated-Sequential Settlement Articulation model of the Terminal Late Woodland–Mississippian transition. I find Emerson's characterization of the emergence of elites as an unintended historical consequence of *communitas* voluntarism to be lacking an important component. I comment above that he notes that the peer-selected leaders of the groups carrying out the collective activity of monument construction would come to be identified with the special sanctity of these earthworks and, therefore, the positions that they occupied would, quite unwittingly, come to be identified with this same sanctity:

> Evolution of the elite in the promotion of community prosperity increasingly distances those elevated from the community. This distance is created by the ongoing association of the elite with the symbols of the cosmos and sacred universe. The correlation of eliteness with sacredness removes the elites from the communitas even as they are promoted by it. Elite alienation is the product of communal efforts. The elite become inhabitants of a sacred landscape and a cosmic society at the virtual insistence and for the communal good of their society. At the point of alienation one can speak with authority of the institutionalization of inequality—a point that may only be manifested with the emergence of the state. Consequently it is more appropriate to speak of hierarchies as resulting from communal activities and the elite as being the recipients of a consensual power rather than expropriators of such power. (Emerson 1997c, 14)

I think there is some truth in his claim that a certain social "distance is created by the ongoing association of the elite with the symbols of the cosmos and sacred universe," but invoking an "ongoing association of the elite" with these symbols of sacredness is not sufficient to claim that such an association "removes the elites from the communitas" itself. Since the selecting of individuals to occupy the position of leadership of sacred construction occurred within the overall general collective framework of *communitas,* the latter context would necessarily emphasize the principles of being "unsegmented, homogeneous, and unstructured" (Emerson 1997c, 13) so that each generation of elite would also be selected in the same manner. That is, the ongoing, generation-to-generation association of the leaders with the sacred positions would not necessarily form an elite/commoner class structure but simply reproduce the enabling hierarchy based on age-grade seniority that I outline in an earlier chapter under the Autonomous Cult model, explaining how cults would be structured by seniority into enabling hierarchies of age-sets.

Of course, this is not the type of hierarchy Emerson is postulating for Cahokia. For him, the hierarchies are based on the premise of dominance and power-over. This concept of power-over raises the critical difference between the hierarchical account and the heterarchical account of Cahokia and the Middle Mississippian social system. This difference does not hinge on the presence or absence of hierarchy, as such. As I argue under the Autonomous Cult model, both communal and ecclesiastic-communal cults can be and usually are hierarchically structured. The difference is that while Emerson recognizes only one type of hierarchy, defining it as the systematic exercise of dominance generating a rank-order among parties that self-perpetuates, I argue that there can be two different types of hierarchies, one in which dominance is preponderant and one in which enablement is preponderant. What makes the difference is which core ethos principle prevails: dominance or autonomy. As Emerson makes clear, a dominance hierarchy entails the recognition and exercise of power-over as prevailing, while, as I discuss in earlier chapters, an enabling hierarchy entails the recognition and exercise of power-to as prevailing.

I note in an earlier chapter that Elizabeth Brumfiel (1995, 127) has cautioned archaeologists about using the notion of heterarchy, saying that "the study of heterarchy in socioeconomics will benefit from . . . a more explicit terminology. . . . While this terminological imprecision is probably useful for heuristic purposes, it gets in the way of critical understanding." However, as I also note earlier, the problem that she has identified may be one not of nuancing terminology but of clarifying the concept through adequately pinpointing the basic nature of heterarchy. I have argued that the recognition and exercise of the ethos value of agentive autonomy is the defining characteristic of a heterarchical organization. Since autonomous agents recognize the legitimacy of differences and inequalities among themselves, they can also easily accommodate to ranking. Therefore, the notion of a ranked heterarchy is not an oxymoron. When heterarchy manifests ranking, this is constituted as an enabling hierarchy, and this entails decision making based on negotiated consensus among all mutually autonomous or relatively autonomous parties. This is why I speak of Cahokia as a mutualistic heterarchy. Indeed, not only does the World Renewal Cult Heterarchy model postulate Cahokia as a mutualistic heterarchy based on the affiliation of mutually autonomous cult alliances, with the latter being constituted of individual autonomous cults, but also the model argues that the cults are internally organized as enabling hierarchies of age-sets ranked by seniority. Furthermore, the enabling hierarchy that can characterize an autonomous cult can also form a fixed rank order. Typically, however, the occupants of this order are regularly replaced by means of age-set promotion and leadership is reproduced by peer-based selection so that the emergence of an inherited elite is discouraged and, in fact, may be impossible.

The third problem that I want to address that the Nucleated-Sequential Settlement Articulation account raises in my view is the nature of the Terminal Late Woodland–Mississippian "Big Bang" transition that it postulates. The "Big Bang" proponents do not simply claim that this transition occurred rapidly. They also claim generally that this was a "profound social upheaval," as Andrew Fortier and Dale McElrath (2002, 203) express it. For them it was revolutionary rather than evolutionary in nature. This is a strong statement, and I assume that this is partly because of the new calibrated radiocarbon dates for the Terminal Late Woodland. That is, these data require compressing the previous "Emergent Mississippian" period estimate of 200–250 years to a minimum of 100–150 years (Fortier and McElrath 2002, 178).

This narrower time frame certainly presents a problem for the hierarchical monistic modular polity account, since all its versions have recognized that the communities of the pre-Terminal Late Woodland period (that is, the Late Woodland period) and the communities of the post-Terminal Late Woodland period (that is, the Mississippian period) were radically opposite in social nature, with the former being characterized as generally small, egalitarian, triballike communities and the latter as large, complex (and perhaps even paramount) chiefdoms. Since the transition from the former to the latter state had to proceed through the intervening Terminal Late Woodland period, the degree of credibility of the claim that such a radical transition was possible is enhanced as the available time span is increased. Indeed, some might think that even 200–250 years might be insufficient. Therefore, when the radiocarbon data clearly indicate that this span is excessive and that the time span must be reduced to 100 or possibly 150 years, either a modification has to be made in our perception of the nature of the American Bottom social system or else a modification has to be made in our perception of the nature of the American Bottom social change.

If the former is chosen, this requires questioning the basic assumptions of this social systems model, namely, the possibility that there was no transformation from an egalitarian-communal social system to a paramount chiefdom—

which is the point I argue below. If we choose to modify our explanation of the nature of social change, then (since the transition is still treated as the transformation of an egalitarian into a non-egalitarian hierarchical social system), gradualism logically becomes an irrational claim and the only alternative is a radical, abrupt, bite-the-bullet, socially disruptive deep structural transformation. This, of course, is precisely the claim of the "Big Bang" thesis at the heart of the Nucleated-Sequential Settlement Articulation modelling of this transition. It is almost as if the theoretical characterization of the transition has been modelled to fit the presuppositions of the hierarchical monistic modular polity model, namely, that since that model claims that the Late Woodland and Mississippian social formations are fundamentally different and the time span available for the transition is quite short, the transition must have been abrupt, rough, and revolutionary.[4]

One reason all this is problematic is that, as presented, the "Big Bang" also relies on a fused view of cultural traditions. That is, in this thesis, cosmology, ethos, worldview, and ideology are not treated as relatively autonomous components of a cultural tradition. Instead, cultural traditions and ideology are treated as substantively the same, differing only in terms of level of awareness at which the collective consciousness resides. For Pauketat, cultural traditions are just like ideologies except that the former reside at the practical, pre-articulated, commonsense level of the agent's awareness while ideologies reside at the discursive level, thereby always being available to the agents' discursive awareness to be unproblematically drawn on and used strategically. As Pauketat puts it, "We may speak of *ideologies within traditions as the mode of articulation between tradition and the consciousness of individuals.* More precisely, ideologies are the means by which 'interest groups' or sub-collectivities . . . acquire consciousness of themselves, as these subgroups constitute nodes of social interaction within the larger social formation" (Pauketat 1994, 14, emphasis added). Presumably, this discursive awareness of their own traditions is what gives the elite the advantage in negotiations with the commoners, who operate only with commonsense cultural traditions. Since, in Pauketat's terms, these traditional (and fused) beliefs, values, and attitudes reside at the practical level of consciousness, they are not effortlessly available to the discursive consciousness of their possessors. Hence, the commoners cannot draw upon and use their commonsense to critique and resist the action proposals promoted by the discursively aware (that is, ideologically informed) elite. This distinctly advantages the latter in negotiations so that they are able to rather easily subordinate the commoners by proposing and defending activities that benefit elite political and social interests at the cost of the political and social interests of the bewildered commoners (Pauketat 1994, 17–18).

There are two problems here. The first is treating ideology and common-sense traditions as having the same substantive makeup while differing only in terms of level of consciousness and then identifying the elite as having an ideology and the commoners as having only a commonsense tradition, itself a fusion of traditional beliefs, values, and attitudes. This appears to be a very elitist view of prehistory. That is, "commoners" are where they are because they lack the capacity, for whatever reason, to have an ideology, that is, to be able to reflect effortlessly on their own cultural traditions. In contrast, "elites" are where they are because they have this effortless reflexivity. In strong opposition to this view, I have argued that ideology must not be identified with cultural traditions. Rather, it is only one of the four relatively autonomous forms of collective consciousness that make up a cultural tradition. I have qualified it as having the nature of a surface structure in that its existence and exercise presupposes the deep structures of cosmology and ethos of a given cultural tradition. Hence, an ideology can be shaped and changed while actually reproducing and entrenching the cosmology and ethos that make this modification possible. The integrated nature of the cultural traditions presupposes effortless reflexivity as a basic mental property of the populations that bear them. As a result, it is safe to say that neither elites nor commoners in the American Bottom would have had a monopoly on reflexivity and the ideological perspectives that this enables; thus, in general, those occupying either social category have the same capacity to operate discursively. If this is the case, then neither social group would have a psychological advantage over the other that would account for the social structural transformations that are postulated by this dominance hierarchical account.

There is a logical connection between treating the "Big Bang" as necessarily socially disruptive and treating ideology and/or cultural traditions as fused or monolithic in nature. As I fully discuss in chapter 3, this view presumes that the set of beliefs constituting a cultural tradition embraces and incorporates the values and attitudes and, presumably, the know-how rules and protocols that go along with the collective beliefs. In effect, they form a single intrinsic, monolithic, or fused package. Defined in these terms, any modification of ideology (or cultural tradition) would necessarily entail deep cultural and social changes. Using the term *negotiation* to speak of the social processes that would bring about these deep changes cannot help but be misleading. Instead, they would be better characterized as, in effect, cosmological-ideological replacement. That is to say, this whole approach essentially forces its promoters to take a rupturalist approach since (1) the time factor is very limited, (2) the approach allows for little in the way of small-scale modification of cultural traditions, and (3) it promotes interpreting modification in the material culture as registering replacement of the traditional basic social and cultural structures with new and quite different basic social and cultural structures. This underlying premise thus dictates that the type of social change postulated under the Nucleated-Sequential Settlement Articulation model not only has to be a "Big Bang," in the sense of being abrupt, but also, as I note above, must also be in the nature of a major social upheaval.

I am not claiming here that the "Big Bang" thesis in the sense of a social transformation occurring rapidly is invalid—to the contrary. As I discuss below, I agree that this transition was abrupt. However, the integrated notion of cultural traditions characterizes the nature of this abrupt transformation as being considerably different. Cosmology and ethos are deep cultural structures, in the sense that to have collective perceptions (a worldview) and act collectively (in accordance with a given ideological strategy), agents must share a cosmology and ethos within which the worldview and ideology are constituted as intelligible. Therefore, it follows that ideologies and worldviews can and typically do modify and vary according to changing social, environmental, and demographic conditions and, of course, can do so abruptly, that is, creating a "Big Bang," without, however, entailing any significant change in the cosmology or ethos or, for that matter, in core social structures.

THE INTEGRATED-TO-BIFURCATED SETTLEMENT ARTICULATION MODEL

As I briefly outline at the end of chapter 8, the alternative Integrated-to-Bifurcated Settlement Articulation model postulates that the compound plaza-periphery integrated settlement articulation mode of the Terminal Late Woodland heterarchical polyistic locale-centric social system of the American Bottom transformed into a radically bifurcated settlement articulation mode. As suggested in chapter 14, this settlement pattern transformation was probably the outcome of a series of rather minor ideological innovations, particularly related to mortuary/world renewal practices, that left the deep cultural structures constituting the traditional cosmology and ethos and the deep social structures of clan and cult and their relative autonomy largely unchanged. Despite the radical material differences marking the transition, by speaking of it in surface structural terms, it could be expected to be rather rapid. Therefore, this model has no problem accepting the transition as being a rather abrupt "Big Bang" occurrence. However, for the same reason, the claim that this transition was in the form of "social upheaval" should be rejected, because it would have been initiated through the foundational constituent social units making up the compound plaza-periphery integrated villages—that is, the clans and cults—strategically and consensually negotiating a modification of how their traditional arm's-length relations would be best materially realized in the context of intensifying subsistence and settlement.

The result of these negotiations would be a settlement innovation based on a logical inversion of the integrated articulation mode. This would have entailed two important and largely simultaneous modifications. The first would require the physical disengaging of the clan and cult facilities and the redeployment of these into specialized clan-based residential groups or villages (in most cases realized in the dispersed village mode) and specialized cult-based ritual locales. The latter would come to be complexly realized as countryside locales constituting a network of ceremonial nodal sites and, as these autonomous cults formulated cult alliances and alliance affiliations, developing the nucleated multiple-mound sites or, as I have termed them, the *world renewal cult heterarchies*. The second modification would entail the regularization of a form of transiency, with cult members regularly traveling to their cult locales for temporary occupation, after which they would routinely return to their dispersed village homes.

In fact, this transiency may not have been particularly new. In earlier chapters, I trace the historical development of this arm's-length relation using the Late Woodland and Terminal Late Woodland period archaeological records of the Sponemann and Range sites. This relation and its materially mediated development underwrote the shift from the initial Sponemann and Patrick phase peripheral-integrated settlement articulation mode (anchored by the dual patterning of single-post rectangular domestic structures and the keyhole ritual structures) into the Dohack and Range phase plaza-periphery integrated settlement articulation mode, and then the fullest developmental expression of this integrated settlement mode, this being the compound plaza-periphery integrated settlement articulation mode as realized in the George Reeves and Lindeman phase occupations. Much of the developing complexity of the settlement pattern of the American Bottom can be understood in these terms, assuming that the Range site data can be generalized.

However, in the preceding chapter, I further qualify this Terminal Late Woodland account by outlining and interpreting the record of the upland CBLs. If my conclusions in that chapter are correct—namely, that while the funerary aspect of the mortuary practices of the Late Woodland and Terminal Late Woodland periods may have been performed in the floodplain zone, most of the postfunerary→mourning→spirit release→world renewal ritual process was carried out in the upland CBLs—then the logical inference is that, indeed, as radical as the Terminal Late Woodland–Mississippian transition was (particularly in the appearance of the floodplain multiple-mound CBLs), it actually occurred in a context of partial settlement bifurcation in any case. That is, prior to the emergence of the floodplain world renewal cult heterarchies, the separation of the upland CBLs and their associated floodplain compound plaza-periphery alliance villages would have involved travel for cult members, with transient occupation in the upland cult CBLs. If so, then (in accordance with the conclusions arrived at in chapter 14) the mortuary practices of the Late Woodland and Terminal Late Woodland periods would typically have terminated at upland CBLs. Initially, these CBLs likely would have been under the custodianship of the autonomous cults of individual, small, Late Woodland floodplain villages (such as the Sponemann and Range sites)—which probably were occupied only during the warm season, in any case—and then, as population expanded during the Terminal Late Woodland period, the autonomous cults of nearby floodplain settlements may have formed alliances to expand their collective world renewal ritual.[5] Therefore, the Terminal Late Woodland–Mississippian transition (characterized as the outcome of the postulated disengagement of the clan and cult networks in these floodplain compound plaza-periphery integrated villages) was probably effected by a rather minor ideological shift of the traditional mortuary/world renewal practices, motivated, however, by the need to carry out a rather radical shift in the deontic posture of the settlement strategy. This was essentially an abrupt reversing of the gradually intensifying prescriptive settlement posture that was initiated by demographic changes unwittingly generated by the series of midwifery ritual innovations postulated under the Sacred Maize model in chapters 6 and 7; this intensifying settlement posture is mapped by the increasing complexity of the integrated settlement articulation modes of the Terminal Late Woodland period and was manifested in the growth in size and number of integrated towns, as exemplified at the Range site and clearly indicated in the Edelhardt phase occupation of Cahokia (Pauketat 1998, 135).

The reversal or inversion was probably initiated by clan and cult negotiations, with the clans promoting a radically proscriptive settlement strategy, fully realized in the Mississippian period as clan-based dispersed villages integrated through farmstead/household nodal locales, as exemplified by the Lohmann phase Julien site (Emerson 1997c, 85), while preserving the prescriptive subsistence regime of maize agriculture. Simultaneously, the cults would have promoted a nucleation of the mortuary practices, this being effected by moving the terminal phases of the traditional mortuary/world renewal rituals from the uplands to the floodplain. Largely unwittingly, however, this nucleation of alliances of autonomous cults on the floodplain, initially marked by single- or possibly dual-mound constructions with associated CBLs, would have become the condition for escalating cooperative interaction by promoting the affiliation of cult alliances, thereby generating a radically prescriptive ceremonial strategy that came rapidly to be fully realized in the multiple-mound world renewal cult heterarchies. This patterning would characterize the early Mississippian period deontic ecological regime of the American Bottom as manifesting the widespread development and realization of a proscriptive settlement–prescriptive subsistence/ceremonial strategy.

All of this resolves the "concomitant"/"subsequent" problem that I address above as being the central paradox of the Nucleated-Sequential Settlement Articulation model. It would also resolve the problem at the core of Kelly's dual population process. By postulating transient occupancy of the multiple-mound locales under the World Renewal Cult Heterarchy model, the disengagement of clans and cults would allow for simultaneity of dispersed village/multiple-mound locales without any major and rapid population increase being required—and, of course, this can easily account for the overall expansion of structural floor space at the multiple-mound locales without having to postulate a radical, permanent, population nucleation. Simply stated, most of the latter floor space would be occupied by transient cult members who also had countryside clan-based dwellings.

This disengaging process also eliminates the problem of the disappearance of ritual facilities at the large Terminal Late Woodland villages. For example, as Kelly notes, the later Lindeman phase occupation of the Range site lacked most of the ritual facilities and features that had been characteristic in both the George Reeves phase and the early-to-middle Lindeman phase. According to Pauketat (2000, 32–33), this was the result of politicization of community symbols. As he argues, "It is plausible that the replacement of a pre-Mississippian settlement landscape, visible at the village level, was a conscious political tactic of certain interest groups" (Pauketat 2000, 34). Instead, as I see it under this model, this "replacement" was simply the necessary outcome of the negotiated disengagement of clans and cults. That is, by the later stages of the Lindeman phase, the cult alliances that were probably primarily responsible for the complex layout of this and similar villages had already disengaged from the villages, possibly setting up small single-mound CBLs in a given region. Quite quickly, however, the alliances responsible for these initial small mound CBLs would promote affiliations of cult alliances focusing on a mutually selected locale, such as the Lunsford-Pulcher site in the southern sector or Cahokia in the northern sector. This process would become widespread because it would have had a strong moral fervor feeding it. Hence, cult alliances would have been caught up in promoting this new prescriptive ritual stance as an effective and worthy means of reversing the escalating of settlement-based pollution generated under the older prescriptive settlement-subsistence/proscriptive ceremonial strategic regime.

This emerging prescriptive ceremonial strategy would respect the squatter ethos through transient residency; therefore, it would become the standard for determining what would count as reputation enhancing. Cooperating in this endeavor, the clans would have largely willingly dispersed themselves across the landscape, while the cults would have pursued selecting and setting up or transforming earlier integrated villages into world renewal cult heterarchies, dismantling the old residences, expanding plazas by linking up former courtyards, and, probably, innovating mound construction (with mounds perceived as monumental icons of the cosmos) as part of the prescriptive-motivated enhancing of the traditional world renewal ritual that they had been performing.

As argued above, these rapidly emerging cult heterarchies would be occupied by the comings and goings of the cult members making up the alliances, continually supplementing the sets of local administrators of the participating alliances, who constituted probably the major part of the rather small "permanent" residential group. Because many cult members at any time would be moving back and forth between clan and cult locales as their dual responsibilities required, permanent residential quarters and associated facilities would be required for housing transient members organized as age-sets, with the age-sets of bachelor companions occupying the larger barracklike quarters and the more senior and therefore married age-sets of companions with their dependents occupying clusters of smaller "family" dwellings and so on. Residency for a given age-set might vary between a few weeks to six months to a year at a time, depending on the relative position of the age-set in the enabling hierarchy of the cult and the range of tasks that its members were traditionally called upon to perform for their cults.

This settlement articulation mode transition, characterized in tangible terms as the physico-spatial disengaging of clan and cult facilities from the compound plaza-periphery villages of the Terminal Late Woodland period (and in structural terms as the ideological transformation of a prescriptive subsistence-settlement/proscriptive ceremonial regime into a proscriptive settlement–prescriptive subsistence/ceremonial regime) would simultaneously reproduce the traditional deep social structures of relatively autonomous clans and cults and their arm's-length relations, and the deep structures of an immanentist cosmology and a squatter ethos. Accordingly, in terms of the World Renewal Cult Heterarchy model, cults participating in these multiple-mound CBLs would preserve their autonomy by being represented in alliance and affiliation councils that would have quite strict operating procedures, arriving at agreements on the basis of consensus. Thus, the active formation of separate cult locales—both the primary floodplain locales and the auxiliary upland CBLs, as well as the multiple-mound heterarchies with their major temples and CBLs—would have been complemented by the formation of dispersed clan villages.

However, as rapidly and smoothly as this might occur, there probably would have been a time lag. For example, the cult alliances may have first disengaged from the late Lindeman/Edelhardt phase villages, coalescing in selected locales forming the initial single mound-plaza complexes. The clans may have remained in the villages, which would be largely stripped of the plaza-periphery ceremonial features. After a few years, these clan-based nucleated villages, such as the late Lindeman phase occupation of the Range site, would have disaggregated and reformulated as the dispersed villages described above. At the same time, the constituent cults making up the cult alliances would have continued in their alliances but would also have started individually to reestablish separate cult locales. This dual process would have constituted the two parallel networks: one of dispersed villages integrated through the household nodal sites and the other being the dispersed network of complementary male-based fertility and female-based fecundity cult nodal sites, as represented by the Lohmann phase Range ML1-ML2 nodal site and the Lohmann phase BBB Motor nodal site respectively. Added to these would be the transformation of upland cult and cult alliance CBLs into auxiliary world renewal CBLs, as discussed in the previous chapter.

This process would have been partially promoted by the intensifying of pollution associated with expanding field agriculture, in this case being compensated for both by the wider dispersal of maize agriculture (acting as an extensifying form of subsistence production that, as a midwifery subsistence ritual, simultaneously acted, in part, to reverse the consequential pollution) and by the wider dispersal of the farmsteads of the agricultural clan-based producers (reducing the settlement-generated pollution load per unit area of land). At the same time, by concentrating world renewal ceremonialism in specially built monumental iconic warranting contexts, the cults were able to magnify and enhance the sanctifying effects of their more elaborate world renewal rituals, while continuing to maintain auxiliary upland CBLs to supplement traditional renewal rites in this region, as well as to assist in the formation and curation of the deceased as symbolic pragmatic capital that they would draw upon in discharging their alliance duties at the world renewal cult heterarchies. Such a dual process, motivated by a perceived expansion of settlement- and subsistence-induced pollution, may have served as a primary condition for promoting the innovation of lethal human sacrifice in the Lohmann phase that I discuss in chapter 13. Indeed, this innovation may have fed the process promoting the expansion of Cahokia, as is discussed in the following chapter under the Ideological Cult Faction model.

What is missing from this Integrated-to-Bifurcated Settlement Articulation model is the possible substantive contents of the prescriptive ceremonial strategy that would have promoted this bifurcation and helped bring about the transition. As I discuss in some detail in chapter 13, the mortuary residue typical of the world renewal cult heterarchies was the outcome of intensive, probably astronomically and seasonally scheduled world renewal ritual that was mediated by both postmortem and lethal human sacrifice. Therefore, as I argue in the preceding chapter, the sudden appearance of a rich and complex mortuary residue in the American Bottom may be a more important criterion of the transition than the appearance of the great earthworks, as such. As important as these monumental structures were, the sudden appearance of this densely concentrated mortuary residue is what gives us a key to understanding the prescriptive ceremonial strategy that generated this bifurcated settlement pattern.

Simply put, the core of this strategy was to extend the mortuary ritual traditionally performed in the (probably) dispersed pre-Mississippian-era mortuary CBLs of the uplands and bluffs by resituating important components of the ritual onto the floodplain itself. If we accept that the mortuary sphere was constituted of a funerary through to world renewal ritual process, then a good argument can be made that in the collective understanding of the American Bottom peoples (given the immanentist cosmology), the sanctifying outcome of such world renewal ritual could be significantly enhanced if cult alliances pooled their symbolic capital, particularly in the form of war captives and collective deceased, but also by constructing enhanced collective mortuary ritual locales in the form of monumental iconic mounds and plazas—namely, the multiple-mound locales that I claim were the material contexts of these world renewal cult heterarchies.

Hence, charnel structures and associated CBLs would be expected to proliferate at alliance locales and at cult heterarchies. Even individual cult nodal locales would take on an enhanced appearance of ritual features. The latter would be an important indication of the cult's autonomy. As I argue in chapter 11 (with regard to the ritual nodal sites in the countryside) and in chapter 13 (with regard to the Mound 72 mortuary data), the cult network might indeed have been a dual network of male-based fertility and female-based fecundity cults. As suggested in chapter 14, the former may have curated their deceased in auxiliary upland CBLs and then pooled the residue of the deceased as bundle burials in major floodplain world renewal cult heterarchies to enhance their mortuary-mediated world renewal rites. The female-based fecundity cults would possibly have performed mortuary-mediated rites in both the floodplain cult nodal CBLs (such as the Lohmann and Stirling phase occupations of the BBB Motor site) and in the world renewal cult heterarchies. The late Stirling phase Sponemann site, as I argue in chapter 11, probably continued to use the mortuary facilities at the nearby BBB Motor site to terminate at least some of the postmortem sacrificial fecundity renewal rites, enhanced through the mediation of the Earth Mother figurines.

The harmonization of the mortuary goals of clans and cults would mean that one of the most important forms of symbolic capital for a cult would be having custodial responsibility for the postmortem care and use of the deceased. This responsibility would be a primary basis for sustaining cult-clan interaction. Such responsibility does not mean that a cult would dominate a clan, however, since relative autonomy would be respected and the individual clan could select from a number of cults the one or ones to which they would mandate the responsibility for processing many of their deceased members. This is because any given dispersed village could have its clan members distributed among several autonomous cults. Although a cult would have a morally strong claim on one of its own deceased members, under the right circumstances, the clan of the husband of a deceased female belonging to a local fecundity world renewal cult might determine that his fertility cult had greater ritual need of his deceased wife than did her own fecundity cult. In any case, ongoing negotiations among clans and cults would be chronic.

Responsibility for postmortem care and use of the deceased also does not require that cults would have a monopoly on mortuary practices. Under the postulated harmonization of the clan and cult mortuary programs, the funerary rites would probably be the responsibility of kin. These rites would likely not be terminated by burial but by placement of the deceased, wrapped in skins or some other textiles, on high platforms, as postulated by Guy Prentice and Mark Mehrer (1981, 37) with regard to the Lab Woofie site.[6] Subsequently, when a request would be made by the responsible cult, the deceased would be transported to either the cult's auxiliary upland CBL or its cult heterarchy headquarters, whichever was the agreed-upon site where they were to be curated, and ultimately used as postmortem sacrificial offerings in world renewal rituals.

Demonstration

In terms of the hermeneutic spiral, the model that gives the most coherent and fullest account of the same body of data is rationally the one that should be accepted as the best current approximation of the nature of the responsible social system. Accordingly, if the Integrated-to-Bifurcated Settlement Articulation model is adequate, then it should be able to account for more aspects of the archaeological record in a more coherent manner than is done by the Nucleated-Sequential Settlement Articulation model. A good test of this is to contrast basic components of the two models and show how each can be used to account for the same data. In these cases the two models contrast in three important ways: type of residency; type of mortuary practices; and type of social structure. The Integrated-to-Bifurcated Settlement Articulation model characterizes the multiple-mound locales as having transient occupation of the majority of structures with a small "permanent" core of administrators of the autonomous cult alliances. It also postulates a mortuary/world renewal perspective characterizing the mortuary component as cult CBLs. Finally, it postulates a dual settlement posture based on the disengaging of clans and cults. In contrast, the Nucleated-Sequential Settlement Articulation model presupposes permanent sedentary populations, funerary mortuary practices (variation in which is contingent on the social status of the deceased during her/his lifetime), and a hierarchical monistic social structure of elites occupying the multiple-mound centers and commoners occupying dispersed villages. These models can be neatly tested by examining three interesting empirical puzzles related respectively to each of the above: (1) the appearance of a bimodal set of structures in Cahokia and other single- and multiple-mound locales; (2) the distribution of apparently stray human remains in archaeological contexts that do not suggest mortuary interventions of the normal sort, given our understanding of the mortuary record of Cahokia; and (3) the recently observed depopulation of the countryside around Cahokia.

The Bimodal Building Size Puzzle

Pauketat observed a bimodal variation in what he considers to be domestic housing found across the American Bottom from the Lohmann phase on, and particularly focused in Cahokia:

> There is Lohmann-phase evidence of two size modes of domestic buildings, a primary mode with average floor areas of around 10 to 13 m^2 . . . and a large mode of buildings with floor areas between 17 and 27 m^2. The former are associated with segments of Cahokia, smaller administrative centers, and all rural sites (that is, homesteads and farmsteads). The big structures are found only at Cahokia and another small administrative center, the Lohmann site, . . . where they appear to have been segregated from the smaller structures at the level of the community. (Pauketat 1992, 36; also see Pauketat 1998, 112–14)

Furthermore, not only was this bimodal variation carried over into the Stirling phase, it also was accompanied by an overall increase in residence size. As Pauketat describes it,

> The mean floor-area value for ordinary (nonelite) Stirling-phase structures at Cahokia is 16 m^2; . . . the late Stirling-phase structures have average floor areas between 20–25 m^2. . . . These possible nonelite residences are distributed throughout the American Bottom region much like their Lohmann-phase counterparts. The larger-size Stirling-phase structures have been found only at Cahokia. Although sampling problems beset the Stirling-phase data from Cahokia, it does seem that the largest Stirling-phase (residential?) buildings were much larger than the largest Lohmann-phase domiciles. One extraordinarily-large Tract-15A Stirling-phase building (H3) had a floor area of 229 m^2 . . . [and in the Stirling-phase Powell Tract four houses] . . . were 50 m^2 to 60 m^2 in size and one was 178 m^2—all much larger than the rural houses. (Pauketat 1992, 36–37; also see Pauketat 1998, 114)

As noted in the above quotations, the Lohmann phase Tract 15A and Dunham Tract patterning of structures displays this bimodal pattern very well. First, the distribution of the rectangular and circular structures delineates a plaza with large post pits and several pits, one with human remains, the latter likely being associated with one of the Stirling phase woodhenges (Wittry 1996, 30). The southern side of the plaza has only rectangular structures that fit within the smaller mode described above, and all the large rectangular and circular structures are on the northern side—although there are also a number of smaller rectangular structures on the northern side. The eastern side of the plaza, nearest Monks Mound, is demarcated by a large T-form structure, and the western side is demarcated by a large rectangular structure with an adjacent large circular structure. Pauketat suggests that the plaza incorporates at least two of the courtyards of the preceding Terminal Late Woodland Edelhardt phase occupation. Interestingly, these courtyard patterns are similar to the equivalent Lindeman phase occupation at the Range site, those that made up the flanking squares of the central precinct (Kelly 1990a, 99–104). Finally, there is a long trench to the southeast of the plaza, which Pauketat suggests may have been built as a ditch for draining the plaza area. As is typical of the Cahokia site, there is swaling from north to south.

Pauketat presents a highly qualified account of this dual modality. This may be because he wants to emphasize that it has been overlooked, primarily, he suggests, because of the tendency for excavators to average the floor sizes of structures for each phase. He criticizes the averaging approach by noting that "univariate summaries of building floor trends failed to take the effects of, among other things, *differential social status* into account, especially the kind of *differential social status we assume existed at Cahokia*" (Pauketat 1998, 136, emphases added). Here it becomes quite clear that he accounts for this dual size mode primarily in his postulated elite/commoner terms characteristic of the hierarchical monistic modular polity account and its auxiliary, the Nucleated-Sequential Settlement Articulation model. Although he is cautious by adding that other factors (such as the differential needs of Cahokian compared to non-Cahokian locales) should also be taken into account, clearly these differences are likewise largely correlated with differential rank position. Indeed, as he argues, "There may be a significant relationship between household size and structure size through time in the American Bottom region, but this relationship also involves changing corporate group integration, reorganization, building function, community segregation, and status both within Cahokia and between Cahokia and other portions of the American Bottom" (Pauketat

1998, 136). Accordingly, rather limited use by specialists is invoked to account for some of the variability. For example, the variable distribution of the manufacturing residue of exotica at several of the major mound-plaza complexes is accounted for by Pauketat's claiming that high-ranking elites sustained specialized artisans as clients. Across Cahokia, "a plethora of exotic lithic, mineral, and mollusc-shell raw materials" has been found, and such "exotic raw materials were transformed into Cahokian symbols—weapons, tools, figurines, and ornaments—by primary producers and artisans attached to elite American-Bottom patrons" (Pauketat and Emerson 1997a, 18).

In contrast to the foregoing elite/commoner explanation, the bimodal patterning of structures, particularly the separation of these structures into two areas bracketing the Lohmann phase Tract 15A plaza, is fully consistent with the heterarchical polyistic locale-centric account. As I suggest above, differential residence size in this case could be anticipated under the World Renewal Heterarchy Cult model, since marital status rather than rank differences would be relevant. That is, although ranking would be related to marital status, the different needs of the constituent junior and senior age-sets—with the former being for the most part bachelors and the latter, married members—are what might best account for this dual size modality. If we consider the differential needs of these two age-grade categories, the fact that the large rectangular and circular structures are found on the northern side of the Tract 15A Lohmann plaza would suggest that these are the barracks set up for individuals in the transient bachelor age-sets who would occupy such quarters during those periods when they were actively involved in cult affairs. The circular/rectangular division might be demarcating the separation of the genders, although this could also be constituting a distinction between residential quarters, as such, and ritual contexts. In fact, Pauketat suggests that the circular structures were sweat lodges (although only in the Stirling phase did these become common in the countryside cult nodal sites). The small rectangular structures on the southern side of the plaza, basically household dwellings, would be the housing quarters used by transient married cult members and their dependents.

Treating these large and small structures as barracks (or barracklike structures) and houses for different categories of cult members would account for the high incidence of domestic-related debris associated with both. The fact that this dual modality remained constant from phase to phase with an overall enlargement does not measure the growing separation of elite and commoner but, more likely, the general increase in the period of transient occupation as the intensity in cult-performed mortuary/world renewal rites grew. This explanation is particularly indicated with the expansion in nonresidential features, both the timber structures and the mounds. For example, the large T-form building at the eastern end of the plaza and the large rectangular structure with an adjacent large circular structure at the western end could neatly fit the ritual and organizational needs of the cult alliance, with the former possibly serving as its local temple and the large rectangular and circular structures possibly serving as the residences of the shamanic priests (with their associated novices) and the ranking in-house laity cult leaders. The size of the equivalent ritual structures on Tract 15A increased significantly in the Stirling phase, as illustrated by the large House 3, only second in size to the fourth-terrace structure on Monks Mound, the largest known Cahokia facility of this type (Pauketat 1996, 74). In sum, this dual residential structuring can be just as, and possibly more, coherently understood as manifesting the overall ecclesiastic-communal cult structural framework rather than an elite/commoner structure.

Finally, the finding of the residue of crafted exotica in many of these similar plaza-residential complexes is fully consistent with the typical cult alliance structure. Under the Autonomous Cult model, cults would be expected to ensure much of their own ritual artifactual production. Therefore, we could expect such specialization to have been associated with most of the alliance complexes. In each case, some members who showed skills and competencies in this direction would have been recruited to pursue their particular craft expertise, probably being recognized as having strong ritual artisan status and possibly having shamanic-like recognition since typically producing ritual items entails both practical material skills and sacred ritual skills. However, such status would not mark them as having any special privileges, and their residencies would be no less transient than that of their companions. That is, they would typically divide their time between clan and cult, with their craft practices being performed in terms of the cult's needs during the normal period of occupancy.

The Stray Human Remains Puzzle

A number of archaeologists have commented on finding "stray" human remains, often in abandoned structure basins and sometimes in midden pits. Explanations under the hierarchical monistic modular polity accounts usually treat these as the expression of a thoughtless absence of normal mortuary intentions, implying minimal or even no respect expressed toward the deceased. For example, Pauketat comments that Features D5 and D8 pits and Feature 427 in Tract 15A and the Dunham Tract contained fifteen human bones "mixed with faunal refuse. . . . In these cases, human bone is lighter in color and more severely weathered than associated deer bones . . . [and was, therefore,] . . . exposed to the elements for a relatively longer period of time than the animal bones" (Pauketat 1998, 337). In D5, Pauketat observed, these remains came "from several different excavation lots, suggesting that the bones were fairly dispersed within the feature." He suggests rather cavalier practices may have brought about this scattered deposition:

> The human remains appear to have been incidentally kicked into trash pits, or may reflect floor sweepings from buildings or other activity areas. There are no indications that anything approaching complete bodies were deposited in these contexts. Rather, these findings appear to represent the odd bone or two from an individual. Furthermore, the bones may have been highly fragmented prior to deposition. Although the femur and fibula from D5 may have been deposited as intact bones that were later fragmented, the cranial fragments probably entered the pit as fragments rather than as parts of a complete skull. If not, where are the molar teeth, the petrous bones, and other bits of the skull that are solid and resistant to destruction? There are no indications that these remains received special treatment of any kind. The two parietal fragments from D5 are very different in thickness, suggesting that two individuals are represented. The proximal femur fragment is from a small-sized femur and may be from a female. (Pauketat 1998, 337–38)

Pauketat concludes that this treatment clearly indicates the absence of the sort of respect for the dead that might be expected under the Cemetery model: "I am not convinced that the human remains indicate any sort of mortuary behavior beyond taking out the trash" (Pauketat 1998, 338). However, he also notes that since the human bones were caught up in domestic "trash," this clearly indicates that they "were collected and saved in residential structures or other buildings" (Pauketat 1998, 338). He distinguishes, however, between this "trashing" of human bones and more formal treatment. There is currently only a sketchy report on the Burial 1 Feature, which consisted of several femurs belonging to three different deceased. Apparently, this was a formal deposit found associated with a post pit, suggesting a ritually linked relationship (also noted in Wittry 1996, 30).

Of course, in Western culture, the term *trash* or *midden* is identified negatively. It is that which is worthless, even polluting, and must be removed from "civil" society. By defining *midden* in this negative way, we unproblematically extend the same assessment to anything associated with it, so that, as Pauketat implies, no "mortuary behavior" at all is indicated by these stray human bones. From this negative connotation the inference is drawn that the human remains must have been valueless (that is, commoners). Instead of judging these human remains in terms of how we value the midden (as trash), however, we might more logically assess the value of the midden in terms of the associated human and even faunal content that constitutes it. Certainly, the empirically based knowledge of the importance that the deceased played in Mississippian society would suggest this to be a rational interpretive strategy. Therefore, while a midden can be recognized as the material residue of everyday life, the term would not necessarily have had the same connotation for the people of the American Bottom that it does for us of the Western culture. In an immanently sacred world, the success of the hunter hinges on the spirit-guardians making a sacrificial gift to the hunters of the animals in their care, and the hunters must treat the bodies of the animals with respect.[7] This attitude of avoidance and rectification is implicated in the warranting style of the hunter's gear and in the midwifery ritual etiquette governing the careful treatment that the body of the animal would typically be accorded. The bones and other (presumably) nonusable (waste?) components of the animal must be disposed of respectfully.

All such treatment of unusable components of plants and animals generates midden. Indeed, the most common feature in archaeological sites is the midden pit or surface deposit. It may be time to reconsider the meaning we have attributed to these pits, both in cosmological-ethos and in symbolic pragmatic-ideological terms. In the taken-for-granted understanding of those who were responsible for filling them, they may not have been garbage pits in our sense, but special types of burial pits. Seen in these terms, the finding of human bones in midden pits, as unusual as this was (since it was very rare) could very well mark a respectful deposition. That is, in certain circumstances, the only possible proper treatment of some human remains in Cahokia might have been to deposit the bones in a midden, thereby according the same type of respect to these human remains as was accorded to the remains of animals and plants. In this regard, Pauketat's comments on finding these scattered human remains in midden pits, indicating that human remains were typically "collected and saved in residential structures or other buildings," (Pauketat 1998, 338) are notable. Indeed, such deposition of human remains in midden pits is consistent with the view that the deceased were subjected to an incremental series of rites in which they served as postmortem world renewal sacrificial offerings. Therefore, this conclusion helps to confirm the Integrated-to-Bifurcated Settlement Articulation model of the Terminal Late Woodland–Mississippian transition since, as I comment above, this model implicates the Mourning/World Renewal Mortuary model. Certainly, the femurs of three different individuals making up Burial 1 in association with (possibly) a woodhenge post is consistent with this view, suggesting that many rituals required specific parts rather than the whole skeleton of individuals. In these cases, they may be the sacrificial media of a post-setting ritual. "The only human bones found at Tract 15A were three adult legs and one adult arm, all from different individuals and found in one pit" (Wittry 1996, 30).

What is not expected under this model, however, is this type of midden deposition or "scattered burial" of human bones. As I argue in earlier chapters, the deceased were an important form of symbolic capital that had to be economically used to meet a cult's multiple ritual obligations. Hence, in Robert Hall's terms (1997, 27), the Soul Keeper would be an important and recognized position. Under what conditions could bones go astray if curated by a Soul Keeper in transient residential quarters? We know that often the bones of selected body components were cached in pits dug beside the interior wall of a structure (Esarey and Pauketat 1992, 52, 152–53). No doubt in the normal course of events these bodies, or selected components of them, would be retrieved by the responsible Soul Keeper to serve as ritual warranting media (for example, serving to mediate a marker-post foundation rite).

In the above cases, when "stray" bones were found in the "trash," their presence there may simply have been the result of the cached human remains being left behind by the Soul Keeper when her/his residency period was completed. In this rare case, while originally expecting to return, this person did not. This possibility is consistent with the World Renewal Cult Heterarchy model.[8] But such an occurrence should not be surprising, given the cycling of cult members postulated above. Even though at any given time the majority of the occupants of Cahokia would have been transients, they would also have anticipated returning to the same residences that they normally occupied when in Cahokia. However, all plans can go awry. A Soul Keeper might have been promoted and, instead of returning to Cahokia, might have been called on to reside in the cult locale (for example, the Lohmann phase Range MS-1/MS-2 nodal site or the Labras Lake nodal site) or even in the auxiliary CBL of the cult in the uplands (such as the Center Grove site). Responsibility for the human bones he/she had left stored for future ritual use in the interior pit of the transient residency in Cahokia might be transferred to his/her replacement. However, once the direct contact between a Soul Keeper and the human remains was broken, intervening events could unwittingly efface the connection.

An additional explanation is the possibility that, since often only selected components of the temporarily buried (that is, curated) deceased were needed, partial disinterment may have occurred. Partial disinterment could easily result in the unwitting removal and scattering of lesser components, such as finger or toe/ankle bones, in the dim recesses of the structures. Subsequently, possibly during a repair of the structure, the stray bones might be noted. Depending on their state, they might not be usable in the normal manner. As Pauketat notes, all the human bones found in the midden had been significantly weathered. In these postulated circumstances—a type that would not be uncommon under the conditions postulated by the World Renewal Cult Heterarchy model—the most respectful treatment of such bones when found might have been to redeposit them within the sacredly charged midden.

This supposition may be rejected on the grounds that it is merely speculative. However, the alternative "trashing" view is no less speculative; furthermore, it requires ascribing to the occupants of Cahokia and the American Bottom attitudes toward the deceased that contradict the bulk of the mortuary record, as such. Clearly, this record indicates that there were quite explicit rules governing treatment of the dead, whether these rules are construed in narrow funerary terms or in broader mourning/world renewal mortuary terms. If we generally accept that human remains were curated and cycled, then (assuming as postulated under the hierarchical monistic modular polity account that permanent residency of elites and commoners was the practice) there should be no stray human remains. To invoke lowly social status to account for this "trashing" is not convincing since (also under this hierarchical account) the commoners lived in families and the families would therefore be responsible for curating their dead until final burial. Hence, kinship relations and not class relations would govern this curating treatment. In contrast, finding these stray bones is fully consistent with the funerary→mourning→spirit release→world renewal ritual process as postulated under the Mourning/World Renewal Mortuary model and is likewise consistent with the World Renewal Cult Heterarchy model, with its claim that the majority of the occupants of these multiple-mound centers were transients.

The Depopulation Puzzle

The dependence of the Nucleated-Sequential Settlement Articulation model on the permanent-occupation assumption has played an important role in my critique of this view. However, one benefit that this assumption has played for the nucleated-sequential view is to make the depopulation of the zone encircling Cahokia unproblematic. Indeed, the permanent-occupation assumption was used by Pauketat and Lopinot (1997, 119–20) as a major empirical fact to support their claim, as quoted earlier in this chapter, that the rural population abandoned their villages in the immediate area and aggregated en masse to form Cahokia, or at least a major part of it. Emerson and Pauketat (2002, 109) also specifically link the depopulation of the area to a local demographic implosion forming Cahokia:

> One remarkable event that preceded or accompanied the early Lohmann phase flashpoint was a demonstrable depopulation of some rural areas surrounding Cahokia and related lesser centers. This pattern is evident in large aerial surface surveys . . . and in similar findings from excavated samples . . . that show the abandonment and/or marked decrease in rural villages, hamlet, and farmstead occupations between the pre-Mississippian and early Cahokian phases. Evidently, these villagers moved to Cahokia and smaller nucleated centers, producing if only by default a reorganized ritual landscape in the floodplain around Cahokia.

In effect, while the depopulation claim is not a problem for the Nucleated-Sequential Settlement Articulation model, it is a problem for the Integrated-to-Bifurcated Settlement Articulation model since, as argued above, although Cahokia and the other multiple-mound locales would be constantly occupied, the large majority of residents at any one time would be transients. Therefore, what this model could predict is that the zones surrounding the multiple-mound locales would have the same dispersed village patterning as found in the rest of the countryside. In one sense, in fact, this is the case, in that both the BBB Motor and Sponemann nodal sites are in this zone. However, under the Integrated-to-Bifurcated model, these are not part of the dispersed village system but are instead part of the dispersed autonomous cult system. Therefore (according to Pauketat and Lopinot and reiterated by Emerson and Pauketat, above), with the emergence of the Lohmann phase, neither traditional nor dispersed villages appear to have occurred in this zone.

All this depopulation in the zone around Cahokia constitutes a critical problem for—and therefore a challenge of—the Integrated-to-Bifurcated Settlement Articulation model and must be addressed. The way to address it is to re-examine the theoretical framework of the Integrated-to-Bifurcated Settlement Articulation model in order to explore and determine whether this framework can warrant any possible special conditions that would account for this vacant zone and that could also be confirmed by empirical data. In fact, the first step is rather easy. The second step is harder, but I tackle it also. First, recall that I have postulated that part of the rationale for the bifurcation process would be to distance the cult locales from the polluting effect of domestic-based sub-sistence and settlement practices. Hence, villages in and around those locales selected to become world renewal cult heterarchies might plausibly choose to abandon these zones entirely. Claiming this to be a voluntary abandonment would be quite consistent with the heterarchical polyistic locale-centric ac-count in that, as relatively autonomous components, the clans could not be co-erced by the cults to abandon custodial usufruct—nor would the cults attempt such a strategy. Rather, negotiations and consensus would operate. But volun-tary abandonment of villages raises a further problem. Clearly, the bifurcation strategy presupposes a particularly pressing condition that makes breaking up the integrated villages desirable. This would be the perceived intensifying of sa-cred pollution grounded in the rising demographics; therefore, there would be a premium on agricultural land. The question this raises is the following. If the village populations that were to displace themselves from their traditional cus-todial usufruct lands did not move into the multiple-mound locales (a position claimed by the Integrated-to-Bifurcated Settlement Articulation model), then where would they go? The logical answer is that, while no doubt some would find floodplain land that was still available, the majority would move off the floodplain and into the upland zone that, apparently, had been largely unused for agricultural settlement during the Terminal Late Woodland period.

If this is the case, then what could be expected is a rather sudden appearance of dispersed villages in the upland zone that displayed material cultural traits that linked them to the Lohmann phase settlement in the American Bottom. Indeed, there seems to be quite abundant empirical support for this effect, this being the Richland Complex. In fact, Emerson and Pauketat (2002, 110) even comment that the new and sudden occupation of this region at this time may have been partly promoted by the prior absence of agricultural village oc-cupation. However, they also say that these new populations were probably foreign groups from outside the Cahokian region: "Foreign individuals, small groups, or perhaps even whole populations may have been drawn into the Cahokian sphere during these times . . . probably [leading] to the establishment of numerous, possibly distinctive subcommunities within the larger Cahokia community" (Emerson and Pauketat 2002, 109). That Emerson and Pauketat both identify the Richland Complex as being in "the Cahokian sphere during these times" and that the emergent settlement was constituted of these foreign populations becomes clear when they go on to say that "we surmise that the Richland populations represent physically displaced groups. These villagers retained characteristics that, even during the Lohmann phase, bespeak their everyday resistance to becoming fully integrated within the Cahokian realm. The resistance is particularly evident at the Halliday site, located at the headwaters of Richland Creek about 15 km southeast of Cahokia" (Emerson and Pauketat 2002, 110). This conclusion is confirmed by Pauketat, who specifically states that "the surge in Cahokia's population during the eleventh century derived in part from some immigration from outside the American Bottom" (Pauketat 2002, 154–55).

Of course, I discuss these same sites in chapter 14 (namely, the Center Grove site, the Halliday site, the Knoebel/Knoebel South site, and the Stemler Bluff site), and I argue there that, excluding the Halliday site, the others are more likely to have been auxiliary CBLs of autonomous cults or cult alliances that had their major nodal bases located on the floodplain than they are to have been agricultural villages; therefore, they would have been built and used by American Bottom world renewal cults and cult alliances, not by clans. I specifically exclude the Halliday site—and, by extension, other sites similar to Halliday, such as the nearby Hal Smith site (Alt 2001, 146–49)—from this set of sites because the Halliday and other similar sites do not display patterning that would support the claim that they were cult CBLs. Indeed, the patterning that they do display presents an interesting puzzle for American Bottom archaeology because, as Susan Alt has stressed, they embody a combination of architecture, site layout, ceramics, and even lithics that is both similar to and out of phase with the equivalent combination in sites on the floodplain. I noted several of these incongruities earlier, such as the courtyard layout with the center post characteristic of the Terminal Late Woodland period. Indeed, in this regard the Halliday site is very similar to, although smaller than, the late Lindeman phase village of the Range site. The majority of the Halliday houses display the single-post wall attribute. Some of them, however, include what Alt refers to as the hybrid wall attribute: "When viewed in plan, these structures appear to be of wall-trench construction. Upon the excavation of only a few centimeters of soil from the trenches, however, these 'wall trenches' resolve into the typical Halliday (and pre-Mississippian) pattern of post holes. This pattern is also very clearly seen at the nearby Hal Smith site . . . an early Stirling phase (A.D. 1100–1150) village containing several houses with hybrid walls" (Alt 2001, 149). The surface treatment of the ceramics is also very similar to the American Bottom Lohmann phase ceramics, and, in fact, there is a higher proportion of shell tempering at the Halliday site than at contemporary Cahokia. The jars and bowls are also distinctly larger.

Of these attributes, in my view the most striking difference is the courtyard layout and the quite complex mortuary component of this site, although Alt does not address the latter. These are primary puzzles for both accounts of the transition, since both agree that key markers of the Mississippian settlement pattern are the transformation of the nucleated village of the Terminal Late Woodland period into the dispersed village and the appearance of a mortuary component. However, the mortuary component is even more of a puzzle for the integrated-to-bifurcated account since, for the most part, the upland mortuary sites such as Center Grove were not village cemeteries but auxiliary cult CBLs. Thus, if Halliday is typical of many other sites in this upland Mississippian Richland Complex zone, it presents a pressing problem for the Integrated-to-Bifurcated Settlement Articulation model of the transition in that it clearly does not fit into a dispersed village pattern, and, furthermore, it has an associated mortuary component.

My solution to this problem is to present two key postulates and empirically ground them. First, I postulate that the Halliday site and similar sites in the upland region, such as the nearby Hal Smith site, are probably best characterized as nucleated villages. Emerson and Pauketat are probably quite right in inferring that these villages were occupied by displaced peoples. However, whereas Emerson and Pauketat argue that the mix of material cultural similarities and differences listed summarily above is the result of the occupants of upland villages being "foreigners" who were resisting Cahokian hegemony, I postulate that they were the populations of the Terminal Late Woodland villages displaced from the floodplain. In their capacity as members of clans and clan alliances, they had removed themselves from the zone around the emerging Cahokia and possibly from the zones around other emerging multiple-mound sites. For the sake of ease of reference, I will term these two postulates the *Upland Nucleated Village* thesis, and the latter stands as an auxiliary to the Integrated-to-Bifurcated Settlement Articulation model of the transition.

Discussion and Empirical Grounding

In discussing the bifurcated-integrated settlement articulation modal continuum in chapter 4, I emphasize that identifying the integrated mode with nucleated settlement and the bifurcated mode with dispersed settlement (or vice versa) would be a mistake. For example, while the Lindeman phase compound plaza-periphery integrated village of the Range site clearly manifested a nucleation of the population of the local zone, there were also dispersed hamlet settlements in the vicinity. Similarly, while the Mississippian period bifurcated settlement articulation mode was realized in the countryside as dispersed villages (that is, small regular homestead and homestead nodal sites dispersed across the landscape), the Cahokian and the other multiple-mound sites were complex nucleated locales. The difference between the two modes, therefore, is defined not in terms of nucleation/dispersion of population but in terms of the nature of the spatial expression of the clan-cult arm's-length relation. In these terms I note that the bifurcated mode is expressed by the disengagement of the clans and cults and that this disengagement of clan and cult is spatially expressed by the existence of two recognizably different types of locales. This dualism of the locale types is most clearly expressed in the Mississippian period American Bottom countryside by the dispersed village and the network of individually isolated cult nodal locales discussed in chapter 11. However, the bifurcated settlement articulation mode could also be expressed by a nucleated village system paralleled by isolated, dispersed, and rather small cult nodal locales. The nucleated village system would be indicated by the appearance of domestic-based settlements consisting of a number of house clusters having little in the way of the standard ritual facilities and features that are identified with the cult sphere.

I also argue above that the Terminal Late Woodland–Mississippian transition was effected by the clan and cult alliances making up the late Lindeman/Edelhardt phase villages negotiating their disengagement and that this would largely have been effected with little mutual hostility, leading to the formation of the dispersed village system. However, while the disengagement of clans and cults would have become widespread, quite possibly not all clan alliances would have chosen to shift into the dispersed village pattern. Indeed, as I suggest in chapter 4, the latter pattern has important ideological strategic relevance, counting as a proscriptive settlement move by which clans could actively reduce the polluting levels that were perceived as arising from the nucleated pattern of the compound plaza-periphery villages. If this is the case, then an alternative strategy that could be easily innovated would be to retain the clan-alliance component of the village so that the clans would aggregate into nuclear villages having only those ritual components relevant to clan-directed ceremonialism. However, correlated with this strategy would be the abandonment of traditional custodial usufruct lands and a migration to new, previously unused, and therefore relatively unpolluted lands. The most conveniently situated lands of this sort, of course, would be in the upland zone.

These alternative clan-based strategies—the dispersed floodplain clan-based villages and the nucleated upland clan-based villages—however, may not have been equal alternatives. The special material conditions promoting one or the other might have been unequally distributed. That is, the clan components of the traditional villages occupying the zones around the locales selected for development into multiple-mound sites might perceive the special ritual needs of these zones to sustain a high degree of pollution-free sanctity. Sensitive to these needs, the clan components might opt for the strategy of abandonment. That is, as postulated under the Upland Nucleated Village thesis, settlements such as the Halliday site may be the result of clan alliances choosing to displace themselves from their traditional custodial usufruct lands because these lands were too close to the villages that were selected to become multiple-mound locales. As also pointed out, since the disengagement of clans and cults would be partly in response to rising pollution levels caused by nucleated settlement, it follows that the clan components of these villages would most likely migrate to the nearest available zone having the least preexisting pollution burden. All indications would point to the rolling uplands adjacent to the American Bottom. Because this zone would have had little prior pollution burden, the clan components could move into this zone and choose to maintain their traditional courtyard clusters as nucleated villages (minus the cult-sphere material components, of course, since these would have agreed to disengage spatially from the clan components). In contrast, those clan alliances that maintained occupation in the floodplain would exercise the tactic of dispersing farming settlement to minimize pollution.

What could be expected, therefore, is the rather sudden appearance of nucleated villages in the uplands correlated with the emergence of multiple-mound locales on the floodplains. These villages would display the traditional domestic architecture of the American Bottom clan sphere along with the typical kinship-based ritual component (such as traditional post pits) but would lack the rich range of symbolic pragmatics associated with the world renewal cult sphere (such as large communal dwellings with the stone-floored quadripartite pits, large posts with extraction pits, large plazas, chunkey stones, pipes, tobacco, ritual ceramics, and so on).

As I note above, the Halliday site (Alt 2001, 146–50) is a nucleated village site that fits the above expectations, even to the point that the early Lohmann phase dwellings of this site retain the single-post basin structures that were characteristic of the Terminal Late Woodland. As I also note above, Alt indicates that these structures actually combine Lohmann phase Cahokian and Terminal Late Woodland housing traits in that they typically were constructed with single-post walls, clustered around a courtyard with central posts, while a number of houses had what she refers to as hybrid wall-trenches. While these single-post structures, being on the average 12.5 square meters, were larger than the average 7.7-square-meter pre-Mississippian structures, they were actually a little larger than the average of 12.1 square meters at Cahokia (Alt 2001, 146–48; Pauketat 1992, 36; also see Pauketat 1998, 112–14), and they maintained the pre-Mississippian courtyard with central posts (apparently without insertion pits). As I also note above, Alt indicates an equivalent similarity and out-of-phaseness in the floodplain/upland ceramics. In this case, while the basic forms in terms of jars and bowls were the same (including the same surface treatment), the average size of the jars and, in particular, the bowls was considerably greater in these upland villages than in the floodplain sites.

Alt quite reasonably attributes all this to the expansion of the size of the kinship group in the upland Mississippian sites and the need for more communal meals. She also notes the fact that while the shell-tempering hallmark of the Mississippian period was common in the ceramics of both zones, the proportion of shell-tempered pottery in the upland sites exceeded that in the floodplain: "At Halliday, shell temper is used in 87 percent of all vessels. At [nearby] Knoebel, this figure is 73 percent . . . [and], for the same period of time, only 58 percent of Cahokian vessels and 67 percent of the Lohmann site vessels were shell tempered" (Alt 2001, 151). She concludes that shell-tempered pottery was more enthusiastically adopted in the upland zone than in the floodplain and comments that this is quite strange since the rate of breakage, their poor quality, and other defects in the upland ceramics clearly indicated that shell tempering was not suitable for the upland clay. Following Pauketat and Emerson (2002, 110) in this regard, she considers this mixture—the retention of pre-Mississippian traits and, in contrast, the enthusiastic adoption of some Mississippian traits prevalent at Cahokia—to be the mark of upland-village cultural resistance (Alt 2001, 155). She makes no comment on whether these populations were immigrant or developed in situ. Rather, her claim focuses on these upland villages being participants in the upland-floodplain interaction while maintaining an arm's-length (almost a love-hate) relation with Cahokia. She observes, "In other words, upland people appear to have been willing to adopt—or perhaps it would be more correct to suggest that they actively sought—those changes that maintained an affiliation with the currents of change at Cahokia, while they resisted those that would have altered social life. The upland peoples apparently rejected the sociopolitical authority of Cahokia and retained more traditional patterns of living and doing" (Alt 2001, 155).

However, as I note above, Emerson and Pauketat (2002, 110) specifically argue that the Richland Complex villages were probably occupied by outside migrants who moved into the American Bottom zone and indeed claim that as "physically displaced groups," the Richland populations resisted "becoming fully integrated within the Cahokian realm" (also see Emerson et al. 2003, 164). Of course, I suggest that this combination of retaining traditional traits while embracing new ones also found on the floodplain sites fits quite closely what could be expected of the selected and voluntary abandonment of traditional custodial usufruct land by clans as postulated by the Upland Nucleated Village thesis.

In confirmation of all this there is one trait adopted by these populations in resettling as the postulated nucleated clan villages of the uplands that was not manifested in the pre-Mississippian floodplain compound plaza-periphery integrated villages: the appearance of tangible evidence of the mortuary sphere. As I note above, the appearance of a mortuary component at the Halliday site would appear to argue against the Upland Nucleated Village thesis. However, the particular patterning of the mortuary record actually reinforces this thesis. As noted earlier, Emerson and colleagues (2003, 168–69, 179–80) argue that the appearance of the "cemetery" at Halliday and other sites, such as Knoebel and Stemler Bluff, marks the arrival of displaced people who adopted funerary practices to resist the expanding cultural hegemony of Cahokia. Of the sites described and discussed by them, the mortuary component of the Halliday site would come closest to fitting what could be expected of a cemetery CBL, in that the layout of the mortuary pits almost replicates the village courtyard clustering, suggesting that a close structural relation is being manifested. However, the mortuary contents of this component also displays significant postmortem manipulation. Thus, although Alt does not include the mortuary sphere, I would add it to her list of similarities and dissimilarities in that, while the clustering of the mortuary pits suggests a cemetery CBL layout, the range of postmortem manipulation is more typical of the funerary→mourning→spirit release→world renewal process pattern already identified at Cahokia.

How can this patterning be explained? As I argue in chapter 12, the clan-cult relations mediated through the mortuary sphere can manifest one of two possible clan-cult reciprocal postures: a moderately antagonistic relatively autonomous clan-cult arm's-length relation or else a harmonized relation. In the latter, which I argue is strongly manifested in the mortuary record of the floodplain sites, following the initial death-separation rites (such as the "funeral" and the initial mourning rites conducted by the clans), the deceased would be passed on by them to the cults for further postmortem processing, and this would take on a strong postmortem human sacrificial symbolic pragmatic meaning. While the Halliday pattern manifests considerable postmortem manipulation, I see it as fitting more closely the moderately antagonistic than the harmonized clan-cult arm's-length posture. This is not to claim that the Halliday CBL is simply a cemetery. Rather, I observe that, while its layout and close spatial relation with the residential sector of the site suggest that it served primarily the funerary and initial mourning ritual needs of the village, the degree of postmortem manipulation suggests that it was also mediating a fairly strong renewal component. In these terms, although the focus of the village mortuary sphere was on funerary and mourning ritual, the residents of the village would probably release most of their deceased to the custodial care of the cults to which they and their sons and daughters belonged for terminal world renewal ritual usage.

This assessment is supported by the density of usage indicated in the Halliday mortuary sphere. As I discuss in chapter 14, the upland mortuary-component sites that I defined as auxiliary cult CBLs—Center Grove, Stemler Bluff, and Knoebel/Knoebel South—are characterized by having empty mortuary pits prevailing. Indeed, only the form, clustering, association with a major post pit, and common orientation of these features allow them to be identified as mortuary in nature, since the vast majority contained no human residue at all. In strong contrast, most of the mortuary features at the Halliday site had human residue—as bundle burials or isolated body parts—and clear indicators of reuse with scattered human bones. What this contrast between the mortuary patterning of the former sites and the Halliday site suggests is that although the mortuary pits at the Halliday site were regularly reused, they did not reach a stage of symbolic pragmatic nonusability. In contrast, at the Center Grove site and the Knoebel South site, almost all of the pits were devoid of any human or other remains, and at the Center Grove site, many were superimposed by later empty mortuary pits.

What is the significance of this pattern? As I note in chapter 12 while discussing the East St. Louis Quarry site and nearby sites, the appearance of empty mortuary pits probably relates to the irreversible nature of the symbolic pragmatic meaning that is endowed on them by being used for an incremental series of differentiated mortuary rituals. For example, individual stone-lined pits may have been initially used several times as laying-in crypts, then several times as spirit release/mourning crypts, and, finally, as world renewal sacrificial altar crypts. Once used for the latter purpose, because of the special sanctity endowed on them as altar crypts, they could not be reused as laying-in or mourning crypts. This is probably why the Center Grove site mortuary pits were empty. That is, these pits were empty because they had been used for a series of rituals similar to the above, and after having been used to mediate the terminal sacrificial rituals at this site, they could not be reused as laying-in or mourning crypts.

This practice would be characteristic of cult CBLs. But this appears not to have been the case at the Halliday CBL, since thirty-two poorly preserved remains of individuals were found in the forty-four shallow mortuary pits, a number of which clearly showed reuse (Emerson et al. 2003, 167–69). Since apparently all of the mortuary pits were reused and few of them were empty, the rituals that they mediated were rather limited in nature and similar such that their symbolic pragmatic meaning remained effectively the same, allowing regular reusage. This usage was probably as laying-in and mourning crypts, with the latter having possible clan-oriented renewal purpose. In short, these rituals did not extend to postmortem human sacrifice as mediated, for example, at the Knoebel South, Stemler Bluff, and Center Grove sites. This presumption of usage restricted to only the funerary and initial mourning ritual part of the full funerary→mourning→spirit release→renewal process is reinforced by the observation that even though the Knoebel site appears to be a nucleated village like the Halliday site, it has stronger similarities to the Center Grove site. Its mortuary pits in the associated Knoebel South component are all empty; it has center post pits with extraction pits, and the majority of its structures display the wall-trench attribute—some even display both wall-trench and single-post walls, as is the case for one of the three structures at the Center Grove site.

How does the rest of the patterning of the Halliday site fit the Upland Nucleated Village thesis? It is important to note that the overall village layout of the Halliday site is reminiscent of the terminal pre-Mississippian layout of the Range site village, as discussed in chapter 8. In the latter case, as at the Halliday site, there is also an absence of the large plaza with the associated quadripartite post-pit complex, while there are courtyard clusters with post pits. That is, except for the absence of the mortuary sphere, the final stages of the Lindeman phase Range village are very similar to the Halliday site, except that the latter is smaller. In my earlier discussion, I point out that this pattern probably manifests the first stages of the clan-cult disengaging, quickly followed by this nucleated community shifting into the dispersed village pattern. One can easily imagine that if the dispersal had not occurred at the late Lindeman phase Range site, this nucleated village would have come to be made up of the same overall patterning as the Halliday site, also probably with the larger housing and even, possibly, the retention of the single-post wall trait as the expression of the kinship sphere. Since the clans would be sharing the same village, they would tend to have a fairly rich interaction mediated by feasting, and, while adopting ceramic traits marking the Mississippian period (for example, shell tempering and so on), they might also very well develop larger jars and bowls.

However, none of this happened, probably because of the perceived need to disperse these late Lindeman phase nucleated villages to reduce pollution levels. As I argue above, under the Upland Nucleated Village thesis, this need to disperse would not be the case for those clans that opted to move to the uplands since this was rather underused landscape in this regard, and, therefore, they could legitimately retain the nucleated pattern while disengaging with their cults. As I note earlier in chapter 12, one of the conditions that promotes a harmonized mortuary sphere is the intensity of settlement- and subsistence-related pollution. Without that condition, clan negotiations with their disengaged cults would lead to the former retaining more control of the mortuary sphere than would the clans constituting the dispersed villages. In sum, if this interpretation of the Halliday site can be generalized for the Lohmann phase upland villages, then their architectural attributes displaying single-post structures, courtyards, center posts (without extraction pits), mortuary components having a strong funerary-mourning related aspect and absence of the terminal world renewal sacrificial aspect of the upland cult CBLs (marked by the prevalence of empty mortuary pits), ceramics showing close interaction with the floodplain sites, and so on, constitute significant empirical evidence in support of the Upland Nucleated Village thesis.

Much more research is required in this regard, of course. For example, while there are clear linkages tying both the postulated upland cult CBL sites and the nucleated village sites to the American Bottom, what is their relation to the nearby Silver Creek drainage multiple-mound Emerald site or the other multiple-mound Copper and Pfeffer sites (Koldehoff et al. 1993, 337–39)? These would seem to be closely related if not intrinsic components of this Richland Complex. However, as it stands now, the Halliday site and the Hal Smith site (as representing nucleated villages) and the Center Grove site, the Knoebel/Knoebel South site, and the Stemler Bluff site (as representing auxiliary CBL sites) seem to be pointing in the direction postulated by the Upland Nucleated Village thesis. If further research supports this claim, then we can infer that the rapid abandonment of the zones around the emerging multiple-mound locales during the initial Lohmann phase and the coterminous emergence of these nucleated village sites in the upland region would be directly linked with the population in the latter having voluntarily abandoned their traditional custodial usufruct domains and displacing themselves to the uplands. Simultaneously the cults of these latter villages may have been among the founders of the multiple-mound locales that became world renewal cult heterarchies such as Cahokia and East St. Louis.

Conclusion

Respecting the hermeneutic spiral method, in this chapter I have given alternative models accounting for the Terminal Late Woodland–Mississippian transition. I have confirmed the greater adequacy of the Integrated-to-Bifurcated Settlement Articulation model compared to the Nucleated-Sequential Settlement Articulation model of the archaeological record marking the emergence of the Mississippian period by showing how the former can give a more coherent account for a number of apparently unrelated patternings compared to their explanation under the latter. This leaves me with one more major question. How comprehensively can the World Renewal Cult Heterarchy model and its associated models initiate addressing the layout and modifications of Cahokia compared to the alternative Hierarchical Monistic Modular Polity model? In the next chapter I first present one version of this account of the dynamics underwriting the layout of the plaza-mound complexes making up Cahokia. Of course, the basic premise of this account is that size, layout, and relative positioning of these complexes were governed largely by the relative rank and power of the elites who resided in them. George Milner has applied this logic to account for both the siting of the mound locales and the internal layout of multiple-mound locales. After a critique of this approach, I then apply the World Renewal Cult Heterarchy model to the same problem, first by elucidating the Ideological Cult Faction model (an auxiliary of the World Renewal Cult Heterarchy and the Autonomous Cult models) and then by using this model to interpret certain key aspects of Cahokia as being the outcome of ongoing competition among ideological factions of the constituent autonomous cult components that, ultimately, led to their abandoning this and similar world renewal cult heterarchies.

The Organizational Principles
of Multiple-Mound Locales

George Milner (1998, 167–70) has applied an objective-materialist approach to account for the siting of mound locales, effectively arguing that while the setting of the mound locale may have been chosen by its occupants (in particular, the ranking "chiefly lineage"), the chiefdom "town-and-mound center" (Milner 1990, 18) was selected by the setting in that, as chiefdoms waxed and waned in political and economic strength, ultimately their success or failure was determined by the natural capacity of the setting to support a competitively large population. Milner argues, "No chiefly lineage was successful over the long run in a suboptimal setting. The people in such places who strove to better their social standing were destined to fail, and they did so fairly regularly judging from the sites with small mounds in areas with an inadequate mix of dry ground, deep wetlands, and regularly inundated low-lying land" (Milner 1998, 119). In these terms, Milner notes that the successful chiefly lineages had their mound locales situated on the foremost ridges overlooking the most extensive areas of wetland and backed by an abundant well-drained land area that could support a sizeable agricultural population. Because Cahokia was situated in the center of the largest and, in these terms, most productive sector of the American Bottom, its presumed chiefs became the most successful of these chiefly lineages.

Having stressed the objective criteria for the siting of both single- and multiple-mound locales, however, Milner then accounts for the layout, spacing, and relative positioning of mounds within "town-and-mound complexes" (Milner 1984, 476) in terms that are only indirectly related to objective criteria. They are indirect because he does not treat mound construction and placement within these sites as intrinsic to the subsistence regime. Rather, with respect to large multiple-mound locales, he suggests that the size, number, and positioning of mound-plaza subcommunities would be largely a function of the competition among elites for rank. The rank of the subcommunity would be determined relative to the dominant focal community. Typical of the proponents of the hierarchical account, Milner argues that at Cahokia the ranking elite of the focal community resided in the central precinct and, therefore, that tracts of land nearest to this core would be highly valued real estate for the esteem-endowing capacity that they would have:

> The placement and extent of the central precinct, coupled with the large sizes of several mounds, underscored the social distance the succession of paramount chiefs and their close kin were trying to put between themselves and lesser members of this society. . . . Later mounds and associated clusters of houses were distributed for the most part relative to either the swamp or the central precinct, the latter a result of wanting to be near the principal chief. The use of prime areas—the central precinct and the bank crest bordering the swamp—was a prerogative of important social groups. When a shortage of good land developed near the central precinct, people settled wherever they could, as shown by a few mounds near Monks Mound that were built in otherwise undesirable low-lying ground. (Milner 1998, 157)

It is notable that Milner recognizes there are multiple-mound sites—and mound-plaza groups within such sites—that do not fit his objective and social-ranking account of the siting and layout of mound locales; he explains these by saying that social imperatives could intervene and promote decisions that were counterintuitive in terms of practical material imperatives.[1] For example, he notes that the twenty-five or so mounds of the St. Louis site were positioned on high ground overlooking the Mississippi River, thereby actually being disconnected from the type of land- and water-based resources that his materialist stance would predict. However, as he emphasizes,

> It is the only major mound group in this stretch of the valley whose location does not conform to the wetlands and dry ground floodplain settings considered optimal for settlement. Perhaps here, and only here, can it be said that the dictates of the social environment outweighed the constraints imposed by the natural landscape. This mound group was located at the western end of a scatter of mounds, in some places heavier than others, that extended through East St. Louis to Monks Mound and beyond, almost reaching the Illinois bluffs. Unfortunately, little is known about the St. Louis group because it was destroyed by the mid-nineteenth century. (Milner 1998, 120)

In short, only in exceptional circumstances would or could social imperatives overrule the practicality of materialist imperatives in governing site selection.

This inversion of social over material imperatives, he claims, is also exemplified, although rarely, in the case of the relative positioning of mound-plaza groups within a large multiple-mound site. In the above quotation, Milner notes that at Cahokia some latecomers chose impractical locations that were nevertheless rank-constitutive. The Creek Bottom Group at Cahokia, which apparently is the group he alludes to in the first quotation above, was a set of five mounds, probably with an associated plaza, that was actually built in the least favorable location in terms of practical needs: the swampy floodplain of Cahokia Creek immediately north of Monks Mound (Figure 10.1). Milner accounts for this physically impractical positioning as the result of a late-arriving chiefly lineage choosing to build in the floodplain where its mounds could be right next to the central precinct, thereby ensuring it a ranking social position, instead of building in the more distant "suburbs," which would mark it as having a relatively low social standing, which he claims was the case for those responsible for the Wilson Mound (discussed in chapter 12). As Milner describes the rationale, "Here it is clear that priority was placed on proximity to important places rather than on common sense: the heady experience of being close to Monks Mound won out over wet feet. Nowhere besides Cahokia were mounds encompassed by GLO-defined wetlands" (Milner 1998, 113).

CRITIQUE

Clearly, while recognizing the odd case of social overriding material imperatives, Milner prefers the objective ecological account since, as he sees it, the overall positioning of the mound locales is firmly grounded on practical objective ecological factors. Indeed, it is because the settings of the St. Louis site and the Creek Bottom Group do not fit the expectations of his materialist model that, as he notes, they are anomalous (Milner 1998, 120). But can these simply be dismissed as unimportant exceptions to the materialist imperatives? I think not. Indeed, Milner's recognition that the positioning of the St. Louis town-and-mound complex was anomalous is a significant test of his objective materialist account in that, first, the St. Louis site is not simply the seat of a chief that failed to "make it," as he claims was the case for the many single-mound sites, the latter being invoked by him to support his materialist claim. In his terms, it is precisely because these many single-mound sites were located in productively less-favored zones that the founding chiefly lineages failed to expand their power. However, the St. Louis multiple-mound locale is third in size only to Cahokia—and fourth in size when compared with all known Southeastern multiple-mound sites (Emerson 2002, 129). Despite lacking the resources that

Milner claims would have been the deciding factor in determining the success of the chiefdom, it was quite able to develop to third ranking in the American Bottom, clearly a contradiction of his theoretical posture.

Milner invokes the social imperative factor, apparently to save his materialist argument, by claiming that "perhaps here, and only here, can it be said that the dictates of the social environment outweighed the constraints imposed by the natural landscape" (Milner 1998, 120). The implication here is that social environments have the potential of promoting materially irrational behaviors; hence, choices made in respect to these behaviors have to be explained by highlighting the uniqueness of the social environment. Therefore, Milner goes on to point out that St. Louis was "the western end of a scatter of mounds, in some places heavier than others, that extended through East St. Louis to Monks Mound and beyond, almost reaching the Illinois bluffs" (Milner 1998, 120). However, this uniqueness of the social environment does not help very much since, according to his general sociopolitical interpretation of the town-and-mound complexes, these were the seats of quasi-autonomous districts that were "self-sufficient in terms of the basic resources needed to sustain life, at least in all but the worst of times" (Milner 1998, 13). Since the positioning of the St. Louis complex, combined with its size, would appear to prevent it from being self-sufficient even in the best of times, the hierarchical monistic modular polity premises of his approach would lead us to infer that it must have been simply the dependent western extension of this "scatter of mounds" that extended to "Monks Mound and beyond." This suggests that Milner's view is dependent on Timothy Pauketat's interpretation of this extensive grouping as the sprawling political-administrative complex of the sacralized paramount chiefdom of Cahokia.

While this might account for the anomalous nature of the siting of the St. Louis site, the problem with this is that Milner explicitly rejects this view. For him, even when Cahokia became dominant, the other chiefdoms continued to be largely independent, quasi-autonomous, and economically self-sufficient. Therefore, Milner's account of the siting of St. Louis is not convincing, and, rather than this anomalous positioning of the St. Louis site simply being the exception that proves the general rule (that is, that social imperatives can promote the rare irrational choice whereby material imperatives are overridden), I would suggest that it quite undermines the validity of his objectivist ecological account.

His account of the siting of the Creek Bottom Group simply reinforces this conclusion. In fact, it aptly illustrates the fact that even when an objectivist account is preferred, the motives of a prehistoric population and the cultural traditions and social structures that make them possible must still be recognized, since these intangibles were part of what constituted the behavioral streams that produced the material patterns to be the type of social activity that the archaeologist claims it was. In this regard, given Milner's objectivist ecological account, what type of cultural traditions must these prehistoric populations have had? Quite simply, if the argument is made that objective material imperatives determined the positioning of sites and mounds, then those who were responsible for making the decisions had to have been guided by the same type of objectivist cultural traditions as are presupposed by Milner's materialist theory. In short, for the objective materialist approach to work, the assumption must be made that those who were responsible for the material cultural patterning were themselves informed by a cultural tradition that largely replicated the objectivist theoretical perspective of the archaeologist or at least replicated the central principles of this perspective.[2] Hence, the intentions and motives with which the responsible prehistoric agents acted would have entailed a cosmology characterizing the world in objective terms, as simply so much inert matter to be manipulated as efficiently as possible to satisfy the objective imperatives of survival. Of course, in terms of their ethos, it also follows that they recognized exclusive territories as legitimate forms of domain. In short, unless we wish to deny that prehistoric peoples were motivated by wants and desires structured by collective notions of the nature of the world, for them to be able to make decisions on the use of land similar to those assumed by Milner's objectivist account, then they must have had notions about exclusive territories and subordination within a dominance hierarchy.

This is certainly possible. However, a major problem with attributing objectivist cultural traditions to the responsible prehistoric population is that, since the members of this group would embody and act upon this type of objectivist cosmology and proprietorial ethos, they would attribute little or no value to building mounds on a stretch of land that could not support the requisite population (St. Louis) or, for that matter, on a floodplain that would be subject to major flooding, possibly every spring at the commencement of the growing season. Indeed, for that matter, this objectivist cosmology and proprietorial ethos would attribute no value at all to any large-scale construction that could not be demonstrated as enhancing objective needs, for example, as defensive structures. Therefore, far from viewing mound construction as a mode of reputation enhancement, a population drawing on an objectivist perspective would view such construction activities as profoundly irrational, a waste of energy and resources, and bound to lead the group into ecological and political failure. Those who promoted such activities would become the targets of scorn and derision rather than being the recipients of esteem and honor by which to recruit many followers. Hence, in such a social world, any potential leader who attempted to attract followers by promoting mound construction at all, much less on a regularly inundated floodplain, would be assiduously avoided.

In short, there is an internal contradiction in Milner's account (and by extension, im most if not all versions of the modular polity view), since his claim that monumental construction was carried out to accrue rank and esteem for its builders is at odds with the cosmology and ethos that this objectivist account necessarily presupposes for these same builders. Therefore, for us to understand the dynamics of mound siting, building, and layout, we must first characterize the earthworks in terms that would make sense within the social milieu that was responsible. Such a characterization requires postulating a set of cultural traditions and social structures that would endow such material practices and their outcomes with intelligibility. This task, as I hope I have demonstrated, is not as difficult to accomplish as it would appear. After all, the interpretation of these mounds is not done in either a theoretical or a material cultural vacuum. Woodhenge 72, Mound 72, the range of CBLs and their mortuary data, the associated artifacts, facilities, and so on, clearly implicate a religious perspective. The theoretical structure that has been presented and empirically grounded gives good reasons to interpret the mounds primarily in terms of their religious rather than their political meaning—and it is the former, not the latter, that would be the basis of their symbolic pragmatic meaning, thereby constituting any construction strategy directed to such monumentalism as socially valued and prestigious.

In short, as I argue when elucidating the World Renewal Cult Heterarchy model, treating the religious dimension as central in characterizing these mound locales (and doing this in historical terms) would give credible grounds for postulating the possible range of environmental factors that would have counted in the understanding of the responsible social groupings as relevant and important for situating these mound features where they are found, along with the relative arrangement of their constituent mound-plaza complexes. In these terms, clearly such constructions would have been reputation enhancing because they were seen and used as monumental iconic warrants by which the collective tasks involved in constructing and reconstructing them were central components of major world renewal rituals by which the pursuit of community and world survival was enhanced.

The anomalies of setting identified by Milner, then, become an opportunity to enhance the precise nature of this world renewal ritual. The case of the three-sided palisade leads to the retroductive question, What type of military practices must have existed in order to account for this defensive construction? The answer, of course, required characterizing these practices as part of the religious world renewal ritual strategy. In a similar way, we can ask the retroductive question, What sort of religious practices must have existed in order to account for the existence of these anomalous sitings? The answer that most effectively dissolves these anomalies and turns them into conditions of satisfaction of religious practices can then be accepted as a better approximation of the actual choices that were made than the one given by Milner's alternative materialist view. It will stand until challenged and replaced by a better approximation. By using this perspective—namely, by treating the religious aspect as setting priorities in determining the criteria for both the general siting of multiple-mound sites and the layout of mound-plaza complexes within these sites—I will address and attempt to resolve/dissolve the first anomaly mentioned above, the positioning of the St. Louis Mound group, and this will lead into resolving/dissolving the second anomaly, the positioning of the Creek Bottom Group within Cahokia.

THE ALTERNATIVE MOUND-SITING ACCOUNT

To understand the setting of St. Louis, I can draw on my earlier conclusions, namely, that mound building was part of the ritual process of world renewal and that the positioning of multiple-mound locales in terms of their natural surroundings and relations to each other (in particular, St. Louis and East St. Louis) would be critically important to their effectiveness as iconic warrants of the intended ritual activity. East St. Louis, the larger of the two, and St. Louis, second in size to it, were separated by the Mississippi River (Figure 1.1). Is this pattern of paired mound groupings separated by water repeated? In fact, Cahokia displays the same pattern. The main body of mounds of Cahokia is positioned on the southern bank of Cahokia Creek, and on the far opposite, northern bank there is the smaller Kunnemann Group (see Figure 10.1). This dual patterning is structurally similar to the East St. Louis–St. Louis patterning except that the latter brackets the Mississippi River while the former brackets the much smaller Cahokia Creek. However, Cahokia Creek serves as the major drainage system of the northern expanse of the American Bottom, receiving most of its water from the neighboring eastern and northeastern uplands. In an important respect, therefore, it is a smaller-scale version of the Mississippi.

The question can now be asked, How would this dual patterning serve the ritual needs of the occupants of these sites? To answer this question I must first postulate a cosmological perspective that this patterning might be reasonably treated as presupposing. In terms of the theory of integrated cultural traditions that I have presented, cosmology and ethos are deep structures having great temporal and spatial stability. Therefore, as I discuss in chapter 13, drawing on the deep structural cultural traditions of historically known Native American peoples is quite legitimate. In these terms, the sky, the earth, and the under-ground—redescribed as the heavens or upper world, the middle world, and the underworld(s)—figure as important components of the cosmos, with water as the medium that links all three together. Water is associated with the heavens in the form of clouds and rain; with the earth or the middle world in the form of lakes, swamps, and rivers; and it pervades the underworld in the form of underground caves, pools, and streams.

The well-known Earth Diver myth of the Eastern Woodlands Native American peoples characterizes the world in the beginning as a great inverted bowl of the heavens suspended on the World Rim that encircled the primordial sea (Hall 1997, 18–30). The creator god sends an amphibious animal (an otter, beaver, frog, or duck—the identity of the creature varies with the different versions) to swim to the bottom of the primordial sea to bring up mud in its beak, paws, mouth, and so on. The creator god takes this mud and rubs it to create the earth, and the earth is set floating on the sea, constituting the middle world between the heavens and the underworld. The cycling of water from the heavens as rain onto the middle world, where it forms and reforms lakes and rivers and flows under the earth in the caves of the underworld constitutes the continual reproduction of the life of the cosmos.

Several archaeologists (Emerson 1992, 208; Milner 1998, 126–27) have pointed out that, over the long term, the level of the American Bottom ground-water was steadily rising and reducing the amount of available agricultural land. Milner also stresses that, in objective terms, the hydrological system of the American Bottom was critical to the occupying populations. He has noted the extreme fluctuation in the hydrological system that could and no doubt did occur from year to year. Although the seasonal floods were expected, the height and extent that they might take were always unknown but would be a matter of major concern: too high, and huge areas of land would be flooded and crops destroyed; too low, and drought would set in. Then there was the continual danger of out-of-season flash floods that could transform the anticipated good crop year into a disaster. In Milner's opinion, "The overall picture would have been nothing other than gloomy during much of the Mississippian period, despite the richness of the valley. The inhabitants of the valley were perched on the cusp between success and failure, and a series of bad years would have been disastrous for them. Problems experienced in reducing the worst effects of harvest failures were a direct consequence of the comparatively large numbers of people who lived in the valley during Mississippian times" (Milner 1998, 78). While I think that Milner is being excessive in his assessment of the degree of uncertainty to which the population would be reduced, there is little question that the American Bottom occupation would be carefully attuned to the variation in the hydrological system. In a world experienced as immanently sacred, this system would be conceived of (cosmology) and perceptually experienced as (worldview) a living process. Water and its flowing and cycling would be clearly a target-object of world renewal ritual. Indeed, ensuring its renewal and constancy may have been a primary focus of American Bottom world renewal ritual.

With this perspective as the framework, we can quite plausibly theorize that flood season would be a critical period that was perceived as reproducing the essential nature of the primordial sea. Significant aspects of world renewal ritual could be directed toward re-creating the world in the original manner by transforming the "mud" derived from the bottom of this "sea," represented by the cresting of the floods, into the middle world. This might be appropriately termed the *regrowing-of-the-earth ritual*. Therefore, one possible and very important criterion for siting a world renewal cult heterarchy setting would be to select an area by which the cyclic transformations of the local topography caused by the seasonal (and even nonseasonal) floods could be patently perceived as recapitulating the event of world creation and all the insecurities that this implied. In this view, the Cahokia Creek floodplain and the Mississippi River would be variations on the same world-creation recapitulation theme, and both the flooding of the Cahokia Creek lowlands and the swelling of the Mississippi River would represent and presence the powers of the primordial sea rising across and submerging the land.

Treated in these terms, which characterize the possible perspective of the American Bottom people in ways that are totally consistent with their (postulated) immanentist cosmology and squatter ethos, the positioning of the St.

Louis and East St. Louis mound sites, on the one hand, and the Kunnemann Mound group and Monks Mound with its associated mound groups, on the other, were equivalent—each possibly being an iconic representation of the World Rim encircling the "primordial sea," that is, the Mississippi and Cahokia Creek at full flood. Therefore, these two bodies of water at the flood would both represent and embody the powers of the primordial sea, and the rising of the seasonal and out-of-season floods would represent world destruction by inundation; the performance of world renewal ritual timed with the swelling and/or the receding of the flood would represent and participate in the world's re-creation.

Cahokia Creek would be particularly desirable as a setting for constructing an *axis mundi* since it would allow for the innovation of building mounds and performing ritual directly on the floodplain in full flood, something that would not be possible in the middle of the Mississippi River. Hence, the innovation of building the Creek Bottom Group in the floodplain would realize and serve as a major iconic component of a world renewal ritual strategy. The positioning of these mounds, as a critical part of the ritual strategy, would ensure that they would become partly if not fully covered by the rising flood waters, thereby representing the land as it was in the beginning, namely, below the primordial sea. During this flooding, critically important rituals, probably mediated through postmortem and even lethal human sacrifice, could be performed, possibly in all the mound groups lining Cahokia Creek but particularly in Monks Mound and the Kunnemann Group, both directly overlooking the Creek Bottom Group. The receding of the floodwaters, revealing the Creek Bottom mounds (which would appear to be rising from the sacred waters), would be recognized and count as the rebirth and renewal of the land.[3]

The postulated regrowing-of-the-earth ritual is perfectly consistent with the earlier discussion of the dual male-based fertility and female-based fecundity cults. Furthermore, given the unique nature of the floodplain zones, it is also consistent with the view that the traditional ritual practices relating to the heavens, the middle world, and the underworld(s) would be modified in the American Bottom by the emulation or innovation of platform mounds. Finding that many of these mounds contain significant mortuary residues (such as the postulated dual lethal sacrifices of Burials 13/14 and 117/118 in Mound 72, along with the multiple mass lethal sacrifices) also ties into what we would expect under the Mourning/World Renewal Mortuary model. That is, if an immanentist cosmology was held by a people who were intensifying subsistence and settlement practices to the practical degree required to meet their expanding demographic needs, then postmortem and even lethal human sacrifice would be consistent with the postulated regrowing-of-the-earth ritual.

This is speculative, of course, but it can be given considerable weight by being rephrased as a series of empirical expectations. In a social world where mound construction and the constructions themselves have a critical warranting role as constitutive media of world renewal ritual, we could expect that they would be situated so as to be perceived by all relevant parties as being congruent with the sacred structural energies immanent in the natural order. We can test this hypothesis in two ways: (1) by showing how the patterning of mounds can be accounted for in these terms, as I do in the following chapter, and (2) by showing how this eliminates the anomalies that are generated by alternative models—as I have just done here in respect to Milner's objectivist accounting of the same pattering.

Even further testing can be proposed. Of course, it is hard to second-guess the form of the symbolic pragmatic media that the people of the past would innovate to satisfy their practical ritual needs. However, when we consider the mounds in the above terms, we can infer that those charged with realizing these iconic symbols would be concerned that these Creek Bottom mounds were built in such a manner as to be able to resist a rushing flood. Therefore, if the mounds were excavated—and no one has done this yet (Pauketat and Lopinot 1997, 107)—we would expect their matrix from the bottom up to be made of heavy, sticky soils, such as the various gumbos (black, brown, and so on) that we know were used to cap certain extant mounds. This use of gumbo would have not only practical but also symbolic pragmatic use. These gumbos would have been good candidates for the production of iconic symbols, since they quite plausibly might have been associated with below-surface waters and treated as having the same nature as the original muds brought up by the Earth Diver. Also, possibly a layering of limestone or the equivalent was used to help prevent erosion. According to Pauketat's (1993, 138) research, black gumbo was used in Cahokia as a means of "topping off" several of the major mounds (see also Smith 1969, 86–87), and Melvin Fowler (Fowler et al. 1999, 170) reports similar selective usage of gumbos in constructing primary mound 72Sub1. Pauketat suggests that this usage of the black gumbo on major mounds would have been a ritual of closure, since no evidence in the form of rebuilt templelike structures has been found on these platforms once the water- and erosion-resistant material was placed. Thus, while gumbo would have been used to "close" the mounds built on the ridge, the same material may have been used not to close but to build the Creek Bottom mounds. If this turns out to be the case, then we would understand the use of gumbos for closing the large mounds of Cahokia. These were being built to be permanent, as permanent as the sacred earth that they represented could be.

Is this the truth? Can it now be said that we know the mounds were built for this purpose? According to the hermeneutic spiral method, this is a contingent truth—or, as I prefer to describe it, it is an approximation. As this approximation now stands, some may see it as better than the alternative explanations because it eliminates empirical anomalies and puzzles that these generated and could not adequately resolve (for example, that ranking determined the placement of the Creek Bottom Group) and also because it opens up new areas for research. Therefore, accepting this account for the moment and setting the others aside is rational but also contingently commits those who accept it to the theoretical scheme that resolves the anomalies. Since this is only an approximation of the prehistoric reality that is manifested by these earthworks, this scheme is bound to generate its own anomalies and, therefore, be subjected to the same process of critique and modification. That is what this book is all about.

I can now develop the spiral by turning to a fuller examination of the internal layout of Cahokia in terms that are consistent with the World Renewal Cult Heterarchy model. This will require an in-depth exploration of the phenomenon of ideological cult factions and the role played by ideologically informed construction in a politically factious religious process. To initiate this analysis, I must elucidate a relevant model, which I term the *Ideological Cult Faction model,* by returning first to the original premises of deontic ecology to review briefly how they apply to world renewal and then to the Autonomous Cult model to elucidate the structural conditions promoting the partisan dimension of cults that characterizes factionalism, particularly as it applies to the ecclesiastic-communal cult type.

THE IDEOLOGICAL CULT FACTION MODEL

Elizabeth Brumfiel has explored factionalism as a causal factor in the formation of the patterning of the archaeological record. She recognizes the importance of cultural traditions in the political dynamics of factions but only partially in the way I view them. For her, cosmology, ideology, worldview, and so on, are largely aspects of a single undifferentiated or, as I refer to it in chapter 3, fused cultural tradition. Different and even opposed factional groupings share a (fused) cultural tradition, and therefore the tradition acts as a stabilizing force that prevents factional competition from becoming revolutionary. As Brumfiel explains factional competition,

> [W]hile factions compete for resources, *their structural similarity insures that they will hold similar ideas about what the world is like and what it should be like.* Factional competition tends to be non-revolutionary in interest. The objective of factional competition is to achieve a favourable allocation of existing benefits; each faction hopes to gain more while its competitors gain less. Participants conceptualize factional competition as a zero-sum game in which one party's gain is another's loss. Thus, in factional competition debate generally centers upon the relative legitimacy of each faction's claim rather than the merits of substantively different social programs. (Brumfiel 1994, 5, emphasis added)

She admits, however, that factional competition may become socially transformative or even revolutionary. However, this could only be an unwitting consequence of factional competition since (for her) factions share the same fused tradition and therefore are socially conservative in nature. She explains, "Factional competition has been regarded as non-revolutionary, . . . a temporary response to changing conditions . . . or as an impediment to constructive, meaningful social action. However, given the proper environmental and social context, factional competition expands in scale and intensity until it transforms the conditions of its own existence. It can then be a major force in social transformation" (Brumfiel 1989, 127–28).

While Brumfiel locates the dynamics of factionalism in the pursuit of power with the claims of competing leaders being the main legitimizing factor in competitive interaction, my model of factions and factionalism locates this dynamism both in the existence of competing ideologies and in the social structural contradictions of the social system (Byers 2004, 497–501). Since, in the view that I have developed, cultural traditions are integrated structures of relatively autonomous forms of collective intentionality—cosmology, ethos, worldview, and ideology—related differentially as deep and surface cultural structures, they act both as stabilizing and as dynamizing forces. Therefore, while the cults that made up Cahokia would have had a largely shared cosmology and ethos as cultural background, there would have been a range of alternative ideologies. The factions of each cult would be partly constituted by identifying and being identified with one or another these ideologies. The representational contents of the ideological strategy to which a faction was committed would define the range of practices and their material warrants that this faction would recognize as most felicitous in transforming the cult's collective behavioral interventions into the type of ritual activities by which to discharge its sacred duties. These would differ from the representational contents of the strategies of competing factions. What would make these alternatives intelligible to each faction, despite the differences, is that not only would there be overlap among the ideologies, but also (and more importantly) the cosmology and ethos of each faction would be the same as or very similar to those of the other factions. Indeed, if the cults and their factions did not largely share a cosmology and an ethos, not only would they be unable to agree to compete, but also there would be no point to competing since these deep structures would define what is at stake. So basic is this sharing, that it would have operated for the most part at the largely taken-for-granted deep structural background level.

This perspective allows pinpointing the difficulty I have with Brumfiel's view of the structural similarity of factions. While it is valid at the deep structural level, her fused view of cultural traditions largely collapses the surface structures of ideology into the deep structures of cosmology. For example, as noted above, she treats factions as structurally similar because they hold "similar ideas [cosmology] about what the world is like and what it should be like [ideology]" (Brumfiel 1994, 5). Therefore, she must find the locus of factional competition outside the cultural traditions, as such. In my treatment, because cultural traditions are integrated, factional competition has two sources, both cultural and social. The relatively autonomous nature of ideology and cosmology is what sets the possibility of a cult dividing into factions while sustaining unity, and the social structural contradictions of ecclesiastic-communal cults are the causal source generating such factions and their competition.

The Ideological Continuum

The Sacred Earth principle—the collective belief that the world is immanently sacred—grounds the essential contradiction of human existence. In my discussion of deontic ecology, I point out that because of this principle, the natural order would be taken to be immanently sacred so that material behavioral interventions (for example, hunting, gathering, gardening, and even everyday settlement occupation) necessarily had an impact on the sacred natural order. My discussion of midwifery ritual characterizes it as a set of prescriptive and proscriptive rules built into the economic-ecological practices and by which the intrinsic pollution of such exploitative interventions could be minimized and actually transformed into forms of species reproduction. However, public ritual and ceremony are no less subject to the Sacred Earth principle. Carrying out ritual that materially intervenes in the natural order necessarily has an impact on the sacred order. Indeed, this perception of the causal transitivity of materially mediated human-cosmos relations characteristic of immanentist cosmologies grounds the intelligibility of world renewal ritual. If human material intervention is believed to have no causal effect on the essential sacredness of the world, there would be no sense to human sacrifice, either postmortem or lethal. However, if all material intervention in the natural order—even when inspired by serving the achieving of renewal duties—amounts to intervening in the sacred order, then its forms, magnitude, and timing also become a source of ideological dispute, and this dispute would typically be couched in proscriptive and prescriptive deontic terms.

Therefore, the deontic ecological perspective logically provides two alternative extremes with respect to the material dimension of world renewal ritual. I will refer to them as the proscriptive and prescriptive extremes; these constitute the proscriptive-prescriptive ideological continuum. It is ideological because the strategic postures that can be organized relative to each other are constituted of sets of rules, protocols, and their rationales that govern the range, quality, and quantity of material forms that will count as the most appropriate medium and context for constituting felicitous world renewal ritual. It is a continuum because different forms and degrees of material intervention would count as lesser or greater in their polluting-sanctifying effects. In general, the lesser the degree of material intervention required in performing rituals, the more proscriptive the ideological strategy; the greater the degree of material intervention, the more prescriptive the ideological strategy. Proscriptive orientations emphasize the avoidance ethos attitude so that tactics minimizing the material component are favored. Thus, the range, variation, quality, and quantity of the features, facilities, and artifacts are constrained to what is viewed as essential. The rationale for this is that the polluting costs entailed in producing symbolic pragmatic icons should not be greater than the sanctifying benefits of the ritual performatives. Prescriptive orientations favor maximizing tactics, deploying the ideological rationale that the polluting costs arising from expanding the material media and context are easily warranted and reversed by the enhanced sanctifying effect they have on the ritual performatives.

A critical part of this debate would hinge on the actual sacred power that the ritual is able to materially transfer to the cosmos. That is, the focus of world renewal ritual is always the sacrificial giving of spiritual energy by which the cosmos is renewed. Hence, the forms and contents of the sacrificial moment are always part of the ideological negotiations. This is particularly important in terms of the Mourning/World Renewal Mortuary model, which argues that the core of the mortuary process is sacrificial. Clearly, it becomes logical for postmortem sacrifice and lethal human sacrifice to become ideological issues with the proscriptive ideological orientation being partly defined by minimizing lethal sacrifice and favoring postmortem sacrifice and, of course, the converse priority characterizing the prescriptive ideological orientation.

Ideological Cult Factions

The ecclesiastic-communal cult is the most complex of the cult types. This is because it is based on a permanent congregation structured into a dual-sectored junior and senior age-grade laity and a clergy. The less complex communal cult could also have a permanent congregation. However, it did not have the laity/clergy structure, as such, and, often, it would lack or have only a minor form of senior/junior age structuring.[4] As I note in chapter 5, the leaders of the communal cult organized both the secular and the sacred activities of the cult and, when required, would "contract" a local religious specialist (such as a shaman or a member of a collegial priestly cult, that is, a specialized communal cult) for expert ritual services. The shaman would not be concerned with the general operations of the communal cult, but only with the particular ritual over which she/he had responsibility for its performance. This condition would have promoted stability within the communal cult since there would be a clear division of labor and responsibility among the participants.

I postulate that an integrated settlement articulation mode would be one possible condition that would promote and sustain the formation of a communal cult system. Stability would probably arise from the overlapping responsibilities of dual participation in clan and cult affairs in the same integrated community. This dual clan-cult relation would promote a generational division of labor with persons in the senior age-grade tending to opt out of active cult participation in favor of focusing on clan and lineage duties. Thus, for example, the Dohack and Range phase village clan and cult leadership would tend to be generationally specialized, with the cults being staffed primarily by persons in the junior male and female age-grades with their peer-selected leaders, and the clans would be under the leadership of the senior men and women. This generational specialization would promote the spatial and formal sectoring of the settlement as a means of reinforcing the arm's-length relation between clans and cults.[5]

However, the postulated coalescence manifested in the compound plaza-periphery integrated communities of the later Terminal Late Woodland George

Reeves/Merrell phase and the early and middle Lindeman/Edelhardt phase would have promoted a series of structural innovations bringing about an ecclesiastic-communal cult organization. Shamans would have started insisting on being part of the cult organizational structure. This is largely because, as I point out in chapter 8, these later Terminal Late Woodland settlements were likely brought about by the cults and clans of two or more villages forming alliances. Initially, neighboring settlements might have allied, and the shamans of these settlements (who previously may have travelled among the villages to serve as ad hoc ritual specialists when needed) would have been brought together in the same settlement as a single "college." It would be in their interest to form close relations with the cult alliances. Thus, the congregations would incorporate the shamans as specialized members, and this relation would quickly stabilize into the laity/clergy structure.

Furthermore, with the larger numbers involved in a cult alliance, there would be increasing opportunities and need for more senior members to remain active in the cults. This would promote an enlarged senior age-grade sector and an expansion of the laity leadership. Two sources of structural contradiction would be enhanced that would promote intracult stress: a tendency for the junior age-grade to perceive the senior age-grades as constraining their autonomy, and competition between laity and shamanic clergy for overall cult leadership.[6] Therefore, as more and more senior age-grade members remained active in the cult instead of retiring and focusing on clan and lineage affairs, the members of the junior age-grade sector would become frustrated and would promote strategies that enhanced their opportunities to gain reputation while remaining autonomous with respect to the senior age-grade sector. Similarly, the laity/clergy structure would promote ongoing competition between the leadership of these two sectors for managing the cult. Under these conditions, a cult would begin to fluctuate along the congregationalist↔presbyterian↔episcopalian continuum (C↔P↔E), as discussed in chapter 5.

This cross-cutting of structures constituting the ecclesiastic-communal cult type would tend to generate contradictory interests that would be the basis for the formation of ideological factions. The shamanic priests and the junior age-grade sector leadership would tend to have parallel interests, both generally pursuing a prescriptive ceremonial strategy of expanding the material cultural media of world renewal ritual. Why a prescriptive ritual strategy would benefit clergy and junior laity leadership alike is that it would promote expanding both the material media of world renewal ritual and the long-distance expeditions to procure the valued exotic materials that this ideological posture favors for enhancing world renewal ritual. These activities would enhance the value of the junior age-grade and promote the autonomy of this group relative to the senior age-grade. Also, a prescriptive stance would enhance the role of the clergy leadership. For example, as pointed out above, a logical orientation of a prescriptive strategy would be to push for expanding the lethal sacrificial component, again claiming that it would be the most effective way of renewing the sacred components of the cosmos that were the intended recipients. Thus, the two groups would have a certain degree of converging (while not completely congruent) interests. The shamanic priests would push for prescriptive programs, thereby gaining a greater say in the affairs of the cult, and the junior laity leaders would see this same strategy as expanding their opportunity for the pursuit of both personal and cult reputation and maintaining their age-grade autonomy. The conjunction of these two interest groups would be the basis for the formation and development of the prescriptive factional orientation; because of the convergence or overlap of some of the clergy and junior age-grade interests, should the prescriptive factions start to prevail, the cult would tend toward the episcopalian pole. (This tendency follows from the characterization A. F. C. Wallace made of the episcopalian cult as one being under the dominance of the priests or clergy.)

The primary source of resistance to this junior age-grade/priestly hegemony would be the senior laity members. While the major motive for this resistance would arise from the competition between laity and clergy leadership for overall management of the cult, the fact that junior laity would tend to identify their interests with the clergy would lead the senior laity to tend to promote a proscriptive orientation. On the grounds of minimizing risk, they would push to minimize the requisite amount of disordering of the natural order that ritual required. Traditional construction practices would be promoted as the standard setters. Calls to escalate lethal human sacrifice would be resisted and postmortem sacrifice favored. Long-distance exchange beyond the traditional routes would be resisted, and so on. Should the proscriptive factions under the leadership of the senior laity prevail, the overall cult posture would shift toward the congregationalist pole of the C↔P↔E continuum. (This tendency follows from the characterization by Wallace that the congregationalist cult is under the dominance of the laity leaders.) Should it shift too far, however, the stability of the cult would be endangered since the senior laity leadership would be perceived as a major impediment to the autonomy of the junior laity. Under these circumstances, the cult would quite possibly lose membership and fracture.

In chapter 12 I argue that because of increasing population and a concomitant intensifying of subsistence- and settlement-generated pollution, a moral imperative would develop in the American Bottom that would promote the harmonizing of the clan mortuary practices and goals with those of the cult. For this reason, there would be a general tendency for the prescriptive orientation to prevail, unless there were countervailing forces. This prescriptive tendency does not mean that laity/clergy and senior/junior age-grade structuring would not generate contradictions promoting a tendency for proscriptive and prescriptive factions to develop. However, these contradictions would be manifested in a different way, as I discuss below.

Centralist and Autonomist Factions

According to the World Renewal Cult Heterarchy model, with respect to Cahokia, the cult heterarchy council would be responsible for the collective facilities that the affiliation of cult alliances cooperatively constructed and used. These would most likely be the central precinct and its associated mounds, including, of course, Monks Mound, the Grand Plaza, possibly the Creek Bottom plaza-mound complex and the Kunnemann Group, and, starting in the late Stirling phase, the great timber curtain wall or sacred C-form palisade—but not the woodhenges. As I suggest in chapter 13, while the collective mounds and temples would require the same sort of ritual know-how and expertise as realized in one of the ordinary mound-plaza complexes (simply magnified in significance), the woodhenges would require specialized and esoteric ritual know-how, the type that shamanic priests could monopolize and pass on as part of the apprenticeship training of novices.

Therefore, I postulate that the woodhenge complex would entail a collegial priestly cult, or presbytery. As discussed in chapter 13, the earliest known of these cults would be the custodians of Woodhenge 72. As a collegial priestly cult, it would not be structured in the same way as the ordinary ecclesiastic-communal cult, in that there would be a priest/novice type rather than a clergy/laity type of structure. While the novices would not be priests, they would also not be a quasi-laity or secular body since, as novices, they would not have the same autonomy with respect to the master or initiated priests that the laity would have in the regular cults with respect to the clergy. This priestly order would probably have provided shamanic priests for the ordinary cults. Above all, however, they would be custodians of the woodhenges and would be expected to train their own replacements. Since their power base would be in the world renewal cult heterarchy, and since many shamanic priests making up the clergy of the ordinary cults would have been trained by this cultic order and would probably retain a sort of "dual" membership, it would have considerable and quite widespread influence, in particular, among the junior age-set membership of the autonomous regular cults.

Thus, the formation of a world renewal cult heterarchy would generate its own unique structural contradictions. The constituent cults within their cult alliances would be mutually autonomous such that the world renewal cult heterarchy would be their mutualistic collective creation. At the same time, the world renewal cult heterarchy would promote the development of one or more organizations that derived their standing from the nature of the specialized facilities for which they were the chief custodians, namely, the woodhenges (or equivalent facilities). As members of a specialized cult, these custodial priests would be in a position to challenge the autonomy of the constituent cult alliances. Therefore, despite the postulated conditions of harmonized clan and cult mortuary practices and goals, the combination of monumental construction and laity/clergy and senior/junior competition discussed above would promote two competing ideological postures, what I will term the *autonomist ideological posture* and the *centralist ideological posture*.

In relative terms, the autonomist ideological posture would have a strong proscriptivist coloration, promoting a minimizing of the level of intervention into the natural order, including the cycling of human life. That is, while not denying the validity of lethal sacrifice, it would argue that greater benefits arise from postmortem than lethal sacrifice since the former is not a deliberate intervention into the immanently sacred natural ordering of human life. Through promoting postmortem rituals as fully discussed earlier, this posture would cultivate and ensure effective recycling of human sacred energy. In contrast, the centralist ideological posture would promote a greater interventionist orientation, and therefore, while certainly not denying the validity of postmortem sacrifice, it would give priority to lethal human sacrifice, arguing that—performed in the proper iconic context and under the proper convergence of astronomical events—lethal human sacrifice would have a far greater sanctifying than a polluting effect, the latter being the primary result of deliberately terminating a human life.

In organizational terms, a proscriptive posture would emphasize the value of autonomy, promoting programs that all the participating cults and cult alliances could share consensually. Factions supporting a prescriptive posture certainly could not deny the value of autonomy central to the squatter ethos. However, they would promote programs that by their nature required not only strong centralized planning but also the exercise of esoteric know-how that was not available to the ordinary cults. Because the specialized group monopolized the know-how required for these programs, decision making in these programs would tend to become a process of nominal consensus construction. Hence, the successful realization of these programs, such as lethal sacrifice performed in accordance with specialized astronomical ritual know-how, would promote a form of consultation among the cult alliances that, while mimicking the type of consensus building that is required for the reproduction of organizational autonomy, would, in fact, ensure that the interests and goals of a select group (for example, the ritual specialists) would tend to prevail.

Because the interests of the junior age-grade leadership and the leadership of the collegial priestly cult would tend to be congruent (both leaning toward the promotion of prescriptive ideological postures), each regular ecclesiastic-communal cult would have a centralist faction rooted in the junior laity and clergy sectors, and of course, each would also have an autonomist faction, primarily headed by the senior age-grade leadership. Importantly, of course, because of the particular history of each cult, the proscriptive faction of one cult might be less or more proscriptive than that of another, and the same would apply to the cross-cult prescriptive factions. Therefore, a broad range of ideological positions would exist that would be greater than the actual position manifested in the total set of ritual activities that was being performed. Hence, while the primary inspirational source of the prescriptive ideological tendencies would be located in the specialized woodhenge collegial priestly cult, it would have significant but always fluctuating support in all the ordinary cults. Furthermore, this support would always be buffered by the fact that, no less than the senior age-grade members, the junior age-grade members would be strongly committed to the traditional values of personal and organizational autonomy. Indeed, it would be precisely because they would perceive the senior laity as encroaching on their autonomy that they would tend to resist such encroachment through promoting a more prescriptive program of ritual. Therefore, while inclined toward the prescriptivism of lethal human sacrifice, long-distance warfare, resource procurement, and exchange expeditions (all of which would be excellent vehicles for the pursuit of reputation), they would be reluctant to follow too closely the advice of the woodhenge collegial priestly cult leaders. This combination of social and cultural structural contradictions would underwrite the dynamism of world renewal cult heterarchies, and these would be subject to strong autonomist and centralist factional formation and competition.

In general, then, autonomist factions would support projects that promoted nonspecialized ritual know-how (the type that every autonomous cult would have available), even if these projects may have been quite expansive materially. The centralist factions would support projects that promoted the use of the specialized ritual know-how of the shamanic-priestly clergy, particularly as it was embodied in the Woodhenge cult. Since the realization of these two bodies of ideological know-how would be embodied in the collective monumental facilities outlined above, the trajectory of the autonomist-centralist ideological factional negotiations and competition would be mapped by modifications through time of these facilities. I postulate that the woodhenge priestly cult would promote projects that enhanced its interests by leveraging consensual council decisions to favor these projects. Therefore, these ritual projects would be tied more tightly to the woodhenge facilities than to the facilities located in and constituting the central precinct. Of course, these latter facilities could not be ignored by the centralist factions, since they were important (indeed, critical) monumental iconic warrants of world renewal ritual. However, the Woodhenge cult would more actively support central precinct–enhancing projects that also enhanced woodhenge-related projects than those that would be neutral or would subtract from the woodhenge facilities. Therefore, centralist factions in the cult alliances would tailor their support in negotiations in these terms. The reverse would be the case for the autonomist factions in the cults. They could not ignore the woodhenges, since these also were monumental iconic warrants. However, they would more actively promote and/or support woodhenge-related cult projects that also enhanced the central precinct ritual than those that would be neutral or would subtract from these central facilities.

Therefore, it is important to postulate the possible symbolic nature of these two categories of monumental facilities to identify patterns that would suggest enhancing woodhenge over central precinct, or vice versa, since these facilities would determine whether the developmental changes were the signature of the centralist or autonomist factions. This should not be too difficult to do since, as iconic warrants, monumental constructions would be both the medium and the outcome of iconic congruency strategies. That is, monumental constructions usually derive their symbolic pragmatic meanings (their action-constitutive powers) from perceived real, expressively mediated connection with cosmic elements. These congruency strategies can include the total set of properties that make up the tangible aspect of the monument: its form (circle, square, platform, ridge top), size, layout (plaza-platform pattern), orientation (celestial turning points or mythical directions), spacing from each other or from some central focus, and even material constituents (surface or deep soil, black gumbo/brown loam, limestone/sand), and so on. We cannot predict precisely what material properties will become central expressive components for any cultural set. However, repeated patterning of different properties—in particular, spatial, directional, or linear alignments with landmarks or basic components of the landscape or celestial bodies—can provide crucial keys. The premise here is that, as expressive symbols, monumental structures have tangible properties that would have been designed to ensure that they constitute an iconic linkage of the expressive symbol to its source-object, thereby presencing the essential nature of that source-object or aspect of the sacred world in the monument itself.

Since the woodhenges and Mound 72 figure prominently in this discussion as manifesting esoteric know-how concerning the cosmos (and clearly associated with lethal human sacrifice) while the central precinct manifests widely held ritual know-how, these two monumental complexes would seem to mediate contrasting although complementary types of world renewal ritual. Therefore, examining these two to discover systematic congruency contrasts between them would give the clues required to pin down the probable differences in the nature of the ritual for which each was primarily used. Clearly, there would be overlap since, as monumental icons of the same cosmos, both might have to manifest certain critical components of the cosmos. Therefore, the relative or changing emphases as visible in the patterning of the monuments may be the most important factors. These possible properties and their relevance for defining different types of ritual focus are explored in the following chapter.

This completes the elucidation of the Ideological Cult Faction model, which argues that the material development of Cahokia and similar world renewal cult heterarchies traces the dynamic history of ideological negotiations between autonomist and centralist factions. Should the autonomist factions become hegemonic, as marked by development of the central precinct over woodhenge monumentalism, the cult heterarchy would shift toward the congregationalist-proscriptive orientation; by contrast, should the centralist factions become hegemonic, as marked by the prevalence of the woodhenge over central-precinct monumentalism, the opposite, or episcopalian-prescriptive, orientation would emerge as hegemonic. Either extreme would tend to destabilize the world renewal cult heterarchy. However, as long as the factions compromise and retain the presbyterian center on the C↔P↔E continuum, the cult heterarchy could maintain viability. Should the compromise break down and the autonomists prevail, however, this would destabilize the cult heterarchy since the junior age-grade laity sector would start to feel its autonomy being constrained by the senior age-grade laity sector. Under these circumstances, a given cult heterarchy could be quite rapidly abandoned. If similar congregationalist-proscriptive orientations occurred in other heterarchies, the rapid abandonment of one major heterarchy could instigate a cascading effect, generating the widespread abandonment of all or most of the cult heterarchies. Should the centralist factions prevail, however, the shift to an episcopalian-prescriptive orientation could be equally destabilizing since the laity, both senior and junior, would perceive the autonomy of their cults as being seriously compromised. I explore these alternative possibilities in the final chapter.

17

The Layout of Cahokia

The Material Media and Outcome of Factionalism

In the analysis of Mound 72 and its role in Woodhenge 72 (chapter 13), I point out that a line joining the large post pit under the southeastern end of the mound (PP1) and a large post pit found on the southwest corner of the first terrace of Monks Mound constituted the north-south axis of Cahokia. Clay Sherrod and Martha Rolingson (1987, 91–92) treat the latter post pit as the primary focal point of Cahokia and refer to it as Point A, or Fowler's point, in honor of its discoverer, Melvin Fowler. They note that Point A delineates the locus of a series of superimposed post pits: "It is possible that the series of superimposed postmolds continues through these earlier levels and would indicate adherence to this point in the earliest construction phases" (Sherrod and Rolingson 1987, 95; also see Reed 1969, 31–42). Presumably, therefore, as part of each addition to the platform terrace, the old post would have been removed and a new post installed, possibly along with a new earth stratum as a renewal rite.

Although Monks Mound participates in the north-south axis through Point A (as I comment in chapter 13), Sherrod and Rolingson (1987, 91) note that its own axis is oriented 5° east of north. This axis is defined by three positions on the mound: Point B in the top-center of the first terrace ramp; Point D, being the central position on the south edge of the fourth terrace; and Point F, a large post pit in the center of the fourth terrace (Reed 1969, 33). Importantly, a line drawn through these three points and extended south intersects PP1 at the southeastern end of Mound 72. Therefore, PP1 is at the conjunction of two axes anchored by Monks Mound, the 5° east-of-north axis through Points B-F-D, and the north-south axis through Point A, which Sherrod and Rolingson suggest might also indicate that the polar star alignment was critical to the layout of Cahokia. As was pointed out earlier, Mound 72 is located halfway between Monks Mound and Rattlesnake Mound (Mound 66), which is the southernmost Cahokian mound known and is also on the same north-south axis. Sherrod and Rolingson also note that a line drawn from the Powell Mound, marking the conventionally deemed western extreme of Cahokia, through Point A and to Mound 27 east of Monks Mound forms the due east-west axis of the site. Finally, as discussed earlier, Fowler (1991, 3–9; Fowler et al. 1999, 141–52) has established that PP1 is an important perimeter post of Woodhenge 72 marking the summer solstice rising point when observed from the postulated center post of this woodhenge.

There would appear to be little question, therefore, that Point A was a critical datum point of this site in that it is the juncture of the north-south/east-west cardinal axes of the cosmos, and it participates in the solstitial turning points through being congruently integrated into PP1 and Woodhenge 72. In fact, it may have been experienced by the knowledgeable population as the primary *axis mundi* of the cosmos since, in an immanently sacred world, aligning major constructions with the azimuth turning points of prominent celestial bodies would be a standard form of iconic congruency construction (Byers 2004, 70, 91). In short, the builders would experience these alignments as fitting Cahokia to the structural axes of the cosmos or, alternatively, expressively embedding the essential powers of the cosmos into Cahokia. Thus their construction practices constituted Cahokia as an iconic microcosm of the cosmos.

As a result of their research on possible celestial alignments embedded in mound locales in both the lower Mississippi Valley and the American Bottom, Sherrod and Rolingson conclude that two sets of solar alignments—the equinoctial and the solstitial—were paramount in the Midcontinent and Southeast. They note, however, that these alignments were not equally recognized across these regions. In the lower Mississippi Valley locales, such as the Toltec Mounds site in Arkansas, the solstitial azimuth alignments were emphasized. In contrast, Sherrod and Rolingson claim that at Cahokia the equinoctial azimuth alignments were emphasized. While noting Wittry's claim that several woodhenges had been built on Tract 15A, they argue in their 1987 publication that the empirical data do not support this conclusion. Instead, they claim that the post pits identified by Wittry were used for the typical marker posts and, in some instances, were simply large support posts of structures distributed throughout the dense settlement of Tract 15A during the Lohmann phase (Sherrod and Rolingson 1987, 107–12).[1] Therefore, in discounting Wittry's (1969, 44–45) claims that there were any Tract 15A woodhenges, they also discount his claims that there were solstitial alignments embedded in these structures. Instead, because of the significance of Point A as the focal point of the cardinal axes and the fact that the east-west axis through Point A intersected Mound 27, Mound 31, Mound 41, Mound 44, Feature 452 (see below), and Mound 87 (that is, the far western Powell Mound)—and may reach even farther east, to Mounds 1 and 2, thereby embracing the full east-west extent of Cahokia—they claim that Cahokia was primarily laid out to be congruent with and embody the equinoxes, and possibly the polar star alignment.

The post pit of the central viewing post of Woodhenge III (Circle 2) is referred to as Feature 452, and it is on this east-west axis (Wittry 1996, 26). Therefore, despite rejecting the claim by Wittry that this was part of a woodhenge, Sherrod and Rolingson treat Feature 452 as a very important focal point, not only because it was on the east-west equinoctial axis through Point A, but also, they claim, because it was used as the primary "aligner post" for determining the siting of the Cahokian mounds. Indeed, they state, "Viewed from Feature 452, there was an alignment of large posts having insertion pits with mounds on the site. These alignments suggested that there might be a correlation between the posts and the mound locations" (Sherrod and Rolingson 1987, 112). To verify this possibility they mapped a series of lines linking Feature 452 to forty-two large post pits:

> Lines radiating from Feature 452 were drawn across 42 large post pits of the excavation plan of Tract 15A and their corresponding angles measured. Only posts of large diameter . . . with long insertion pits indicative of large, tall posts were considered. These angles were then reproduced in the surveyed portion of Feature 452 on the UWM map and the lines extended towards the central mound complex. Particular angles, notably the 90° equinox and the summer and winter solstice sunrise angles, verified the accuracy of the constructed angles. (Sherrod and Rolingson 1987, 112)

They postulate that these Feature 452/post-pit alignments served to position mounds in Cahokia relative to the east-west axis anchored through Feature 452 and Point A of Monks Mound. To demonstrate this postulate, they mapped ninety-one mounds and note that forty-five fall on these Feature 452/large post-pit alignments (Figure 17.1) while forty-six do not (Figure 17.2). They particularly note that nine of the latter mounds were west of Feature 452, and they recognize that, because of the clear line of sight between these western mounds and Feature 452, the builders could have easily aligned them.

They leave this puzzle unanswered while arguing that, for many of the other thirty-seven mounds that were unaligned, there were simple practical impediments to effecting the expected alignments. For example, lines of sight from Feature 452 to some of these unaligned mounds may have been blocked either because some were too far away from Feature 452 or else because they were located in the eastern shadow of Monks Mound, thereby being unobservable from this feature (Figure 17.2). The seven mounds in the far southeastern quadrant of Cahokia are another example. These formed "two clusters that are so distant that they might not have been visible" (Sherrod and Rolingson 1987, 115). However, Sherrod and Rolingson also note that near these there was a mound that was aligned with Feature 452. Similarly, while a number of mounds in the northeastern quadrant, more or less in the shadow of Monks Mound, were not aligned with Feature 452, ten were (Figure 17.1). While most of the mounds in the Kunnemann Group on the far north side of Cahokia Creek were not aligned, Sherrod and Rolingson note that two of them (Mounds 9 and 10) were. Their explanation for this apparent discrepancy is that the mounds making up the Kunnemann Group "may not have been part of the original community plan but were a subcommunity" (Sherrod and Rolingson 1987, 117). Finally, they suggest that other mounds that were not on the Feature 452 post-pit alignments may have been aligned with an equivalent aligner-post feature near Mound 27 on the eastern end of the east-west axis. Although such a feature has not been identified, they postulate its possibility. In sum, allowing for excessive distances, the blocking effect of Monks Mound, and the possibility of at least one other alignment post, as well as the likelihood that some of the most distant mound groups were only subcommunities, Sherrod and Rolingson conclude that aligning mounds anchored on Feature 452 post-pit alignments was a basic mode underwriting mound placement. Notably, this account still leaves unresolved the puzzle of the nine nonaligned posts west of Feature 452, these being in easy line of sight of Feature 452.

In any case, Sherrod and Rolingson note that the Feature 452/marker-post-pit alignments only account for the positioning of a mound relative to Feature 452 and one or more intervening marker posts, not for the particular distance a mound was placed from Feature 452. To account for spatial distancing, they postulate a mode of triangulation. A mound could be placed at the point where a Feature 452/post-pit axis junctures with an axis of determinate length anchored to a position on Monks Mound. On the basis of their research of the spacing of mounds in the earthwork sites of the lower Mississippi Valley, they postulate that any particular mound would be located according to a multiple increment of what they term the Toltec Module (TM). They specify the TM as being 47.5 meters in length. They arrived at this measurement by noting that the relative spacing of many of the mounds in sites in the lower Mississippi Valley are distanced from each other in terms of whole multiple increments of the

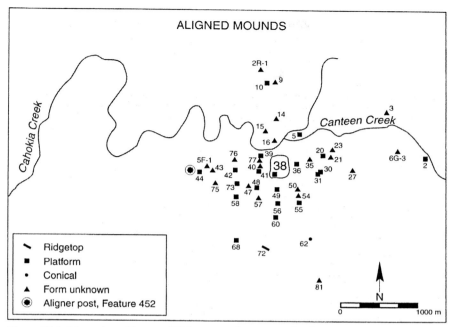

Figure 17.1. Mounds on Feature 452/post-pit alignments. (Rolingson 1996, fig. 7.1, p. 86. Reproduced by permission of the Wisconsin Archeological Society from *The Wisconsin Archeologist* 77[3/4], 1996.)

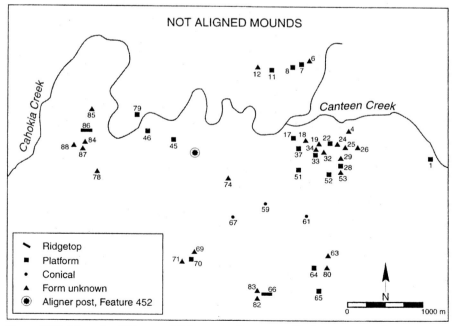

Figure 17.2. Mounds off Feature 452/post-pit alignments. (Rolingson 1996, fig. 7.2, p. 87. Reproduced by permission of the Wisconsin Archeological Society from *The Wisconsin Archeologist* 77[3/4], 1996.)

Table 17.1. Placement of Mounds on Toltec Module

	Fowler's Point (A)				Center Point (D)		
Mound Number	Distance (m)	Module (× 47.5)	Percent of Error*	Mound Number	Distance (m)	Module (× 47.5)	Percent of Error*
1	1,960	41.3	0.6	7	1,096	23.1	0.3
2	1,960	41.3	0.6	9	1,050	22.1	0.3
3	1,755	36.9	0.2	10	1,050	22.1	0.5
4	1,004	21.1	0.7	11	1,048	22.1	0.3
5	572	12.0	0.4	12	1,100	23.2	0.7
13	668	14.0	0.5	17	192	4.0	1.1
14	660	13.9	0.8	18	292	6.1	2.4
15	532	11.2	1.8	20	570	12.0	0.0
16	388	8.2	2.1	21	620	13.1	0.4
27	958	20.2	0.8	24	745	15.7	2.0
36	285	6.0	0.0	25	808	17.0	0.1
37	285	6.0	0.0	26	916	19.3	1.5
39	285	6.0	0.0	28	760	16.0	0.0
40	191	4.0	0.5	29	744	15.7	2.1
41	191	4.0	0.5	30	525	11.1	0.5
42	516	10.9	1.3	31	460	9.7	3.2
43	770	16.2	1.3	32	460	9.7	3.2
44	912	19.2	1.1	34	470	9.9	1.1
45	1,230	25.9	0.4	35	376	7.9	1.1
46	1,665	35.1	0.2	50	376	7.9	1.1
47	380	8.0	0.0	51	288	6.1	1.1
48	285	6.0	0.0	52	672	14.1	1.1
49	236	5.0	0.6	53	768	16.2	1.1
57	576	12.1	1.1	54	476	10.0	0.2
58	625	13.2	1.2	55	428	9.0	0.1
60	575	12.1	0.9	56	515	10.8	1.4
61	808	17.0	0.1	59	528	11.1	1.1
62	948	20.0	0.2	63	1,432	30.1	0.5
66	1,715	36.1	0.3	64	1,530	32.2	0.7
67	904	19.0	0.2	65	1,855	39.1	0.1
68	960	20.2	1.1	73	615	12.9	0.4
69	1,570	33.1	0.2	77	240	5.1	1.1
70	1,620	34.1	0.3	79	1,810	38.1	0.3
71	1,760	37.1	0.2	80	1,570	33.4	0.2
72	936	19.7	1.5	81	1,620	34.1	0.3
76	522	11.0	0.0	84	2,483	52.3	0.5
78	2,192	46.1	0.3	85	2,368	49.9	0.3
82	1,765	37.2	0.4	86	2,480	52.2	0.4
83	1,715	36.1	0.3	87	2,480	52.2	0.4
2R-1	1,330	28.0	0.0				
5F-1	860	18.1	0.6				

Source: Sherrod and Rolingson 1987, Table 12, p. 101. Courtesy of Arkansas Archeological Survey.

Note: No modules: 6, 8, 19, 22, 23, 33, 74, 75, 88, 6G-3

* The percent of error is the percentage that the measured distance of each mound differs from the actual distance of the module factor.

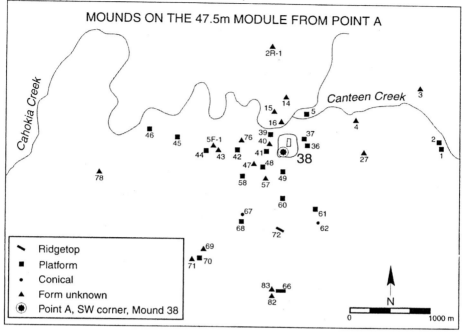

Figure 17.3. Mounds on Toltec Module increment from Point A. (Rolingson 1996, fig. 7.6, p. 91. Reproduced by permission of the Wisconsin Archeological Society from *The Wisconsin Archeologist* 77[3/4], 1996.)

TM. They decided to apply the TM to Cahokia, using Point A as the anchor from which to measure. The assumption here is that each mound should be located at a point formed by the conjunction of a Feature 452/post-pit axis with an axis extended from Point A having a length equal to a whole multiple of the TM: for example, 20 increments of 1 TM (20 × 47.5 meters) would place a mound at 950 meters from Point A. They allow for a 2 percent error, pointing out that archaeologists should not apply Western notions of precision to a prehistoric society.

They measured the distances of ninety mounds and established that forty-one of these are located in increments of the TM from Point A (Table 17.1; Figure 17.3). Of course, while these forty-one mounds conform to increments of TM from Point A, the other forty-nine mounds do not. Picking up the earlier point that many mounds may have deviated from a Feature 452/post-pit alignment because of excessive distances and/or blocking of clear lines of sight, Sherrod and Rolingson reasoned that one explanation could be that the

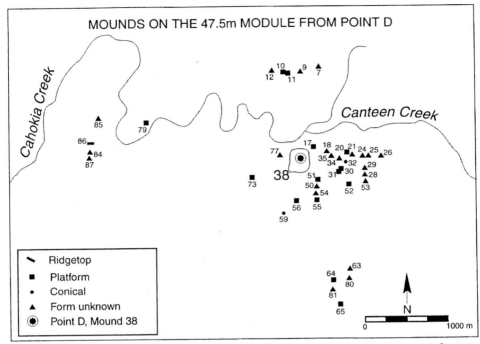

Figure 17.4. Mounds on Toltec Module increment from Point D. (Rolingson 1996, fig. 7.7, p. 92. Reproduced by permission of the Wisconsin Archeological Society from *The Wisconsin Archeologist* 77[3/4], 1996.)

mounds not on the Point A/TM increment may conform to TM increments if measured from a higher point on Monks Mound where clearer lines of sight would be established. They chose Point D, the midpoint of the south side of the fourth terrace. Thirty-nine mounds (Table 17.1; Figure 17.4) conform to increments of TM from Point D. Therefore, of the ninety mounds that made up Sherrod and Rolingson's database, eighty (that is, all but ten) fall on increments of TM measured from Points A and D. To account for the extraneous ten mounds, Sherrod and Rolingson suggest that some if not most of them were probably ancillary to the mounds that are spaced according to the TM from either Point A or Point D. Interestingly, of these ten, three are also on Feature 452 post-pit alignments.[2]

CRITIQUE

Can these failures to align mounds on the Feature 452/post-pit alignments and the shift in triangulation mode from Point A to Point D be accounted for in the practical terms that Sherrod and Rolingson suggest? There may be some cases that could be accounted for in this way. For example, with the increasing bulk of Monks Mound, the line of sight from Point A to the Kunnemann Mound Group on the far northern side of Cahokia Creek would likely be blocked or partially obscured, accounting for the incremental TM spacing of these mounds through Point D on the top terrace of Monks Mound. In fact, Sherrod and Rolingson suggest that Mounds 7, 11, and 12 of the Kunnemann Group, while conforming to the incremental TM through Point D, are not aligned with Feature 452 because, while visual line-of-sight would be allowed from Point D, both distance and undergrowth would obscure or block these mounds from being seen from Feature 452. However, as mentioned above, Mounds 9 and 10 of the Kunnemann Group are aligned with Feature 452, and they are also, like their neighbors (Mounds 7, 11, and 12), on the Point D TM increment. A similar puzzle arises with Mounds 66, 82, and 83. These are on the Point A TM increment but are not located on a Feature 452/post-pit alignment; this discrepancy is likewise attributed to distance and undergrowth. However, Mound 81 is even farther southeast than these mounds and therefore is farther from Feature 452. Yet it is on a Feature 452/post-pit alignment. If increasing distance from Monks Mound is invoked to account for the move from Point A to Point D in order to lay out increments of the TM for placing distant mounds, then, along with Mound 81 (which is aligned through Point D), Mounds 66, 82, and 83 should also have been oriented through Point D instead of Point A.

In short, there are too many exceptions to justify accepting the practicality claim as credible. Furthermore, in practical terms, the "surveyors" were clearly quite capable of overcoming these line-of-sight problems by using auxiliary datum points that would allow them to overcome distance, vegetational growth, the bulky mass and height of Monks Mound, and so on. Indeed, Sherrod and Rolingson point out that a line connecting Mounds 58, 48, 18, and 3 aligns with the summer solstice sunrise and winter solstice sunset, an alignment that is quite consistent with the notion of iconic congruency. However, they note that Monks Mound breaks the line of sight between these mounds. According to them, auxiliary points were constructed on Monks Mound to sustain the continuity of the alignment (see Sherrod and Rolingson 1987, fig. 23, p. 94).

Therefore, auxiliary posts and other simple devices could have been used to overcome the obstacles that they speak of, and indeed, some of the exceptions I note above could easily be the result of using such auxiliary surveying devices.

The upshot of this is that distance, vegetational overgrowth, and the blocking effect of Monks Mound do not explain these deviations from either Feature 452/post-pit alignments or the Point A to Point D shift. Through the use of a few simple practical aids, all the mounds could have been oriented and spaced using Feature 452 and Point A—except those that were built before Feature 452 (such as Mound 72, or, more accurately stated, PP1 under this mound). The conclusion, therefore, is that the variation is not a response to practical concerns but is the result of changes of the rules by which the appropriate positioning of a mound was determined. This means ideological changes and, of course, negotiations and shifts of influence between and among factions. Using Feature 452 or choosing not to use this feature, or selecting Point A or Point D while using Feature 452, therefore, would have had ideological implications. In effect, it would have been a declaration in favor of a certain ideological position. In the context of the preceding discussion of the autonomist and centralist factions, changes arising from ideological negotiations would mark shifting power relations over time. Can these alternatives be identified with one faction or another, and is there a time factor involved?

IDEOLOGY, FACTIONS, AND TIME: AN ALTERNATIVE ACCOUNT

I have taken the eighty mounds listed in the Point A (forty-one) and Point D (thirty-nine) TM increment columns in Table 17.1 and cross-sorted them according to whether a mound does or does not conform to the Feature 452/post-pit alignment. As shown in Table 17.2, this analysis generated four categories. Of the forty-one mounds in the Point A TM increment column, twenty-six fall on the Feature 452/post-pit alignment, while fifteen do not. Of the thirty-nine mounds in the Point D TM increment column, twenty-five do not fall on the Feature 452/post-pit alignment, and fourteen do. That is, an inverse pattern is apparent between Point A and Point D with respect to being on or off a Feature 452/post-pit alignment (Figure 17.3 and Figure 17.4). Assuming that the modifications outlined above map ideological negotiations and combining that premise with a few simple assumptions concerning construction and time, I used Table 17.2 to postulate an approximate chronology on which a historical account of Cahokian factional dynamics can be outlined.

As I clarify in an earlier chapter, Woodhenge 72 was probably the earli-

Table 17.2. Mound Correlations of Feature 452 Alignment and Point A/Toltec Module and Point D/Toltec Module

On Point A	On Point D
On Feature 452 Alignment	
2R-1, 5F-1, 2, 3, 5, 14,	9, 10, 20, 21, 30, 31,
15, 16, 27, 36, 39, 40,	35, 50, 54, 55, 56, 73,
41, 42, 43, 44, 47, 48,	77, 81 [*N* = 14]
49, 57, 58, 60, 62, 68,	
72, 76 [*N* = 26]	
Off Feature 452 Alignment	
1, 4, 13, 37, 45, 46, 61,	7, 11, 12, 17, 18, 24,
66, 67, 69, 70, 71, 78, 82,	25, 26, 28, 29, 32, 34,
83 [*N* = 15]	51, 52, 53, 59, 63, 64,
	65, 79, 80, 84, 85, 86,
	87 [*N* = 25]

est of the woodhenges. This means that its central viewing post would likely have operated as the original "aligner," similar to the postulated use of Feature 452/Woodhenge III (Circle 2) for this purpose after Woodhenge 72 was abandoned. Therefore, alignments made through this post would have preceded alignments made through Feature 452. Similarly, since Point A is on the first and lowest terrace of Monks Mound and Point D is on the fourth and highest terrace, we might reasonably assume that mounds based on the TM increments measured through Point D were probably built in most cases after most of those measured through Point A. This assumption suggests that mounds on the TM increment through Point A and having no association with Feature 452 (namely, the fifteen listed in the lower left panel of Table 17.2) would be the earliest mounds. That is to say, they would have been initiated and built during the same period as Woodhenge 72, namely, pre-Lohmann and early Lohmann phase times.[3] It is particularly notable in this regard that these mounds are distributed across the total expanse of Cahokia, even in areas that Sherrod and Rolingson claim would have been out of the line of sight from Feature 452 (although all of them would be within reasonable line of sight from Woodhenge 72): for example, Mounds 1 and 4 are the farthest east of Feature 452; Mound 37 is in the "eastern shadow" of Monks Mound; Mounds 66, 82, and 83 are far south of Feature 452, but all are within easy line of sight of Woodhenge 72.

From this it follows that the mounds grouped in the upper left panel of Table 17.2, based on Feature 452/Point A TM increments, would tend to fall within the Lohmann/Stirling phase transition as well as the early Stirling phase. The mounds in the upper right panel are based on Feature 452/Point D TM increments. Therefore, they would tend to fall within the middle to late Stirling phase. The mounds in the lower right panel, based on Point D TM increments but having no association with Feature 452 probably would fall within the Moorehead phase.[4] Of course, all this stands as a hypothesis that requires further verification. However, if a general validity to this chronological scheme is assumed, then it can be used to ground the claim that the variation in the mode of the distribution of these mounds is most reasonably explained as the result of changing ideological rules of preferred mound placement and, therefore, that it is useful for mapping historical tendencies in the relative influence of ideological factions in the affairs of Cahokia. What this amounts to is the claim that the two dominant factional positions—autonomist and centralist—would be committed differentially to the range of world renewal rituals performed in Cahokia. To work out the factional history that this postulated chronology implicates, therefore, I must relate these monumental constructions to the different possible rituals they mediated and also relate these ritual complexes to the two cult factional postures postulated as centralist and autonomist.

Centralist and Autonomist Factions

My argument to this effect takes as basic the two associations I outline under the Ideological Cult Faction model in the preceding chapter. First, Woodhenge 72 and the other known woodhenges would have been under the custodial responsibility of the specialized collegial priestly Woodhenge cult. Second, the central precinct of Monks Mound and its associated features and facilities would have been under the collective custodial responsibility of the affiliation of cult alliances that constituted Cahokia. In these terms, modifications and the nature of these modifications in the woodhenges would tend to reflect the degree and nature of the influence of the centralist factions in the operations of Cahokia and the modifications, and the nature of the modifications in the central precinct of Monks Mound and its associated features (the Grand Plaza, the perimeter mounds, the palisade, and so on) would tend to reflect the degree and nature of the influence of the autonomist factions in the operation of Cahokia. Therefore, the initial position and modification of Woodhenge 72, the historical modification of the placement of the woodhenges, and the corresponding history of modification of the central precinct would map the changing balancing of powers between the centralist and autonomist factions.

As I point out above, Sherrod and Rolingson did not treat Feature 452 as the central viewing post of a woodhenge. Given Timothy Pauketat's (1996, 73–74) recent work confirming the existence and the Stirling phase timing of the Tract 15A woodhenges, Rolingson (1996, 84–85) now acknowledges the earlier error (see note 1). However, in denying the existence of Tract 15A woodhenges at that time, Sherrod and Rolingson also denied the potential for solstitial alignments, so that the only significant celestial orientation that Feature 452 would embody is the equinoctial alignment. Partly for this reason, they conclude that Cahokia—unlike the mound sites in the lower Mississippi Valley, which emphasized solstitial alignments—emphasized equinoctial alignments.[5] However, we now know not only that Tract 15A was the locale of major Stirling phase woodhenges, but also that the building of Woodhenge 72 was probably initiated in pre-Mississippian times and marked both the equinoctial alignment and the solstitial alignment. However, the positioning of primary mound 72Sub1 over PP1, which is the solstitial sunrise marker post (Locus V-NE; Figure 13.2 and Figure 13.4), and the northwest-southeast orientation of Mound 72—marking the winter solstice sunrise and the summer solstice sunset—indicate that solstitial alignments may have been the primary concern of the Woodhenge 72 cult. It is also likely that all these alignments embedded in Woodhenge 72 were ritually important and would add to the influence of the Woodhenge cult in the affairs of Cahokia. Thus, at Cahokia there were at least two major alignment congruencies: solstitial and equinoctial. Both would have had legitimacy since, of course, both could be fitted within the same general cosmology.

There would appear to be a third alignment possibility, however, this being the 5° east-of-north axis of Monks Mound (or, viewed differently, the 5° south-of-east axis). As I comment in an earlier chapter, this skewing seems to have been important in the layout of the earliest mass lethal sacrificial burial pits, Features 205 and 237 (Figure 13.1). A similar skewing from the cardinal points seems to have been the case in pre-Columbian Mesoamerica. For example, Teotihuacan, Tikal, Tenochtitlan, Palenque, and so on, seem to have embedded in them both equinoctial and solstitial alignments while simultaneously having major constructions that do not conform to either. Sometimes this may be a result of lunar alignments or of mapping turning points of the Milky Way or constellations. The point is, however, there often seem to be cosmological congruency requirements that work against one another; therefore, compromises are required.[6] In this regard, a significant compromise at Cahokia might have been the 5° east-of-north alignment since this would have meant that Monks Mound, the largest earthwork, could not have its major axes aligned with either the equinoctial or the solstitial alignment. Instead, it had to be tied into these through auxiliary media, such as Points A, B, D, F, PP1 and Woodhenge 72, Mounds 27, 67, and, later, the Tract 15A woodhenges.

While equinoctial and solstitial alignments appear to have both been significant at Cahokia, I postulate that these two sets of alignments were not treated equally by all Cahokian parties and, furthermore, that the priority of one over the other may have changed through time. If this is so, as suggested above, then favoring one set of alignments over the other would probably have been the result of factional differences; therefore, changes indicative of shifting preferences would map changing factional dominance. It is not that the significance of establishing equinoctial alignments, for example, could be dismissed by one cult faction in favor of the significance of establishing solstitial alignments, or vice versa. It would not be so simple. Rather, as stated above, the significance of both was recognized. The question would be how to best combine the two, along with the 5° east-of-north skewing from the cardinal points. Of course, this means that every proposal would be seen as not fully realizing the priority of alignments that competing factions would promote. Therefore, central to my argument is the assertion that the layout of Cahokia, precisely where plaza-mound complexes should be placed, and precisely how they should be keyed into the solstitial and equinoctial alignments (and possibly other celestial orientations such as the 5° east-of-north and other alignments about which we have no current empirical evidence) would be the subject of ongoing and possibly, at times, quite acrimonious debates and factious negotiations.

Of course, in any given instance, negotiations must terminate—and as I argue in earlier chapters, among autonomous parties, consensus is necessary or else no fully felicitous collective activity is possible. In many cases, the consensus arrived at will be satisfactory-for-the-moment to all parties. In such cases, it will be a strained consensus that, in time, will require reciprocal fine-tuning if the collective reality of a world renewal cult heterarchy is to be sustained. Failure in such a case is always possible; indeed, in the American Bottom, it seems to have occurred several times (probably following the Stirling phase), leading to a series of disaffiliations of cult alliances, first between the upper and lower American Bottom cult alliances, and ultimately leading to the abandonment of the world renewal cult heterarchies in favor of more localized cult activities in the terminal Moorehead phase and into the Sand Prairie phase.

In any case, as noted above, Woodhenge 72 seems likely to have been the primary medium of solstitial-related world renewal ritual when it was in active use. This assertion does not deny that Woodhenge 72 also had equinoctial alignments embedded in it. However, primary mound 72Sub1 incorporated PP1, the summer solstice sunrise marking post. No equivalent specialized treatment was given to the postulated east-west equinoctial alignment posts. Furthermore, the total ridge-top Mound 72 was oriented to the southeast winter solstice sunrise and northwest summer solstice sunset. In contrast, Monks Mound seems likely to have been the primary medium of equinoctial-related ritual, as well as the primary integrative medium of the solstitial-, equinoctial-, and 5° east-of-north-related ritual. This would clearly constitute the central precinct with Monks Mound and its associated mounds and the Grand Plaza as the core of Cahokian ritual practices during the Lohmann phase. In the previous chapter, I argue that the probable nature of these collective practices might be adequately characterized as a form of regrowing-of-the-earth ritual, and the most important of these world renewal rituals would tend to be equated with the spring equinox and the major flood period.

Since Woodhenge 72 is now dated as initially constructed in the later pre-Lohmann and early Lohmann phases and was probably used to the end of this latter phase, this woodhenge clearly would have been an important part of the emergence and initial development of Cahokia as a world renewal cult heterarchy. Because PP1 of Woodhenge 72 marks the convergence of the north-south axis through Point A and the 5° east-of-north axis through Points B-D-F, this woodhenge would have been laid out after the initial construction of all or of a substantial part of the first terrace of Monks Mound. However, this woodhenge was placed well south of the series of mound-plaza complexes that were or came to be aligned along the east-west axis through Point A. This suggests an arm's-length relation between Woodhenge 72 and Monks Mound, the latter manifesting the affiliation of autonomous cult alliances responsible for but based outside Cahokia and the former, the emerging Cahokian-based Woodhenge cult.

For this reason, the mortuary contents of Mound 72 are particularly germane. These are described and discussed in detail in chapter 13. In terms of the sacrificial ritual interpretation given, they strongly manifest the prevalence of lethal over postmortem human sacrifice. While both forms of sacrifice would be valued, the lethal form has been postulated as the most interventionist in nature and, therefore, likely to be a primary trait of a prescriptive ideological posture. In this regard, it is notable that these mortuary deposits were carried out sequentially. The proportion of deposits marking postmortem compared to lethal sacrifice, correlated with any indication of favoring solstitial over equi-noctial directional alignments, could be used to map shifts in factional position in the Woodhenge cult. In this regard, a relatively balanced situation between the equinoctial- and solstitial-related ritual focus at Woodhenge 72 appears to have been probable in the earlier Lohmann or even pre-Lohmann phase. While the summer solstitial sunrise turning point was marked very early by Post Pit 1, both primary mounds 72Sub1 and 72Sub2 were initially built with their axes oriented to the cardinal directions, implicating the equinoctial turning points. In particular, Feature 225 (the charnel structure under 72Sub2) and the paired extended burials (Burials 117/118 and 119/120) placed on the first stage of this primary mound were all oriented north-south. Therefore, important compo-nents of the initial stages of Mound 72 incorporated both equinoctial and sol-stitial alignments.

In fact, it could be said that the 5° east-of-north axis is also recognized. It may be significant that what might be the two earliest of the mass lethal sacrificial burials in Mound 72—Feature 205 and Feature 237, the former be-ing constructed over PP2 (Feature 204) and the latter on the south slope of 72Sub2—have their north-south axes actually oriented slightly east of north, essentially congruent with this 5° east-of-north axis of Monks Mound (Figure 13.1). The latter axis probably relates to ritual that all Cahokian groups could equally respect and, therefore, favors neither the solstitial- nor the equinoctial-related rituals. However, the fact that Feature 205 and Feature 237 are lethal human sacrificial mortuary deposits also points to a shift toward favoring the prescriptive ideological orientation by the Woodhenge cult and therefore is quite indicative of the rising influence of the prescriptive factions and, of course, of the Woodhenge cult itself. Confirming this is the fact that after the mortu-ary deposits of Features 205 and 237 were completed the cardinal orientation of 72Sub2 was modified (as discussed in chapter 13) by the addition of the large lethal human sacrificial deposits of Feature 214, forming the content of the northwest-southeast ramp of 72Sub2. This shift changed the original com-bined north-south/east-west and 5° east-of-north orientation of 72Sub2—and, in all likelihood, the orientation of the total complex—by tying these primary mounds into a northwest-southeast orientation, which favored marking the summer solstice setting/winter solstice rising turning points (and the Locus III-NE marker post). Apparently, the very well known Beaded Burials (Burials 13/14) as well as all the subsequent mass lethal sacrificial deposits were oriented in the same manner.

Seen overall, therefore, the initial construction of primary mounds 72Sub1 and 72Sub2 could be said to have incorporated a rather balanced assimilation of both solstitial- and equinoctial-related world renewal ritual, and the early mortuary deposits also apparently incorporated 5° east-of-north ritual. This suggests that during the initial construction and use of Woodhenge 72, a rather neutral or middle-of-the-road presbyterian position with regard to autonomist and centralist factionalism prevailed. In fact, it might be more correct to say that at this early date, the factions were primarily opposed only in standard proscriptive/prescriptive terms. However, as Cahokia developed and the Woodhenge cult become more important, its intrinsic tendency to support a prescriptive orientation—a tendency immanent in its specialized capacities to lead in world renewal ritual—may have become the primary source challenging the mutualistic autonomy of regular cults and cult alliances. Thus, the prescriptive factions came to be centralist promoters, and the proscriptive factions, autonomist promoters.

However, the later deposits on the first stage of 72Sub2 combined both post-mortem and lethal human sacrificial deposits, the former represented by the bone pile and bundle burials and the latter by the two pairs of extended burials, Burials 117/118 and 119/120. When the latter are combined with Feature 205, the large lethal human sacrificial deposit in the insertion pit of PP2, a clear shift toward the prescriptive ideological posture is indicated. Thus the Feature 205 lethal sacrificial deposit would also probably represent the growing centralist tendencies that the Woodhenge cult would favor as a means of achieving their prescriptive ideological posture. This suggests that by about the mid-Lohmann phase not only was the Woodhenge 72 cult having a strong impact on the world renewal ritual program of Cahokia, but also it was the major support of the centralist-prescriptive factions in the regular cult alliances. This suggests that centralism was in ascendance. This ascendancy is mapped by the subsequent development of the major later lethal sacrificial events, first of Feature 101 (the Beaded Burials) and associated features, and then of Features 105, 106, 229, and so on.

The precise timing of this shift from an initially balanced posture with an emphasis on postmortem sacrifice to a more prescriptive posture can be disputed. However, the empirical data seem clearly to support that this shift did occur. Reinforcing this claim is the fact that the lethal sacrificial victims were young people, the majority being young women, as well as several young males who clearly were killed in situ, which implicates probably long-distance military procurement of victims, another indicator of the rise of the prescriptive orientation. Confirming this rising long-distance-oriented militarism is the large deposit of projectile points associated with the burials of Feature 102, under primary mound 72Sub1 (probably collective contributions of packages of arrows seized as battle rewards, some made of exotic cherts and displaying lower Mississippi Valley styles), and in the large artifact deposit of Feature 236, associated with primary mound 72Sub2. Therefore, by the mid-Lohmann phase, the Woodhenge 72 cult was doubtless a major player in promoting military ventures for the procuring of lethal sacrificial victims, consistent with the above claim that, while initially this cult manifested a balanced proscriptive-prescriptive ideological posture balancing between solstitial and equinoctial rituals, it quickly developed a strong prescriptivist orientation focusing on the solstitial and Locus 111-NE marker-post-related lethal sacrificial rituals and therefore would have had a strong influence with the junior age-grades of the ordinary cults, which were probably the major source of young men who would pursue reputation through being warriors and also undertaking long-distance expeditions for exotics used to produce potent iconic warranting artifacts.

The building of Mound 72 clearly marks the abandonment of Woodhenge 72. It also is usually taken as marking the termination of the Lohmann phase (or, at least, it is among the markers that indicate the transition). The other major marker would appear to be the razing of the plaza-based settlement in Tract 15A. This settlement had a significant history. Pauketat (1998, 135) has shown that during the Terminal Late Woodland Edelhardt phase, it was occupied as a complex village, probably similar to the compound plaza–periphery-type village of the George Reeves and Lindeman phase occupations at the Range site. This complex Cahokian village was then dismantled, marking the beginning of the Lohmann phase, and the area transformed into a major plaza with associated structures and marker posts, although apparently no mound construction occurred at that time. The Tract 15A plaza complex was probably the locale of one of the original founding cult alliances of Cahokia. In terms of the Upland Nucleated Village thesis discussed in the preceding chapter, the emergence of a major plaza suggests that the clans of this village may have been among those that moved to the upland zone. Therefore, the relation between the abandonment of Woodhenge 72, the razing of the structures of Tract 15A, and the building of a woodhenge and its related plaza could easily be interpreted as the continuity of the influence of the Woodhenge cult and the centralist factions.

However, there seems to be an anomaly here. Clearly, the mortuary and artifactual deposits of Mound 72 represent the Woodhenge cult as being highly influential and a source of support among the centralist factions of the regular cult alliances. But the construction of this mound and the abandonment of

Woodhenge 72 may also mark the zenith and the subsequent, drawn-out waning of the influence of the Woodhenge cult. The anomaly suggesting this possibility is the absence in Tract 15A of any ridge-top mounds similar to Mound 72. Since we know that at least four woodhenges (probably more) were sequentially built in Tract 15A during the Stirling phase, why are there no indicators of equivalent cyclic abandonment? That is, where are the other mortuary mounds that we might legitimately expect an influential prescriptive-centralist Woodhenge cult to generate? In radical contrast to the large-scale mortuary associations of Woodhenge 72, and with the possible exception of a few Stirling phase post-pit-associated human remains, the only mortuary residues found in Tract 15A were in association with Lohmann phase features, and (as I fully discuss in an earlier chapter) all of these latter are claimed to be incidental additions to refuse.

It has been noted that there is a series of quite impressive timber structures associated with the Tract 15A woodhenges. One of them, House 3, is larger than most mound summit structures and second only in size to the great structure built on the summit of the fourth terrace of Monks Mound, the largest known in the American Bottom of the Mississippian period (Pauketat 1996, 75; 1998, 114). Nevertheless, in relative terms, what is suggested by the absence in the Tract 15A woodhenges of any special treatment of perimeter posts equivalent to primary mounds 72Sub1, 72Sub2, and 72Sub3, by the absence of any mortuary deposits marking either postmortem or lethal human sacrificial rites, and by the apparent prevalence of postmortem over lethal human sacrificial deposits in the Stirling phase mounds of Cahokia, such as the Wilson Mound (Milner 1984, 484) and the Powell Mound (Ahler and DePuydt 1987, 21), is that rather than this move to Tract 15A manifesting the increasing influence of the Woodhenge cult, it would appear to manifest a waning of the cult's influence. Furthermore, Tract 15A is directly west of Monks Mound; therefore, it is on the east-west axis. Indeed, as I comment above, Feature 452—the center post of Woodhenge III (Circle 2)—is aligned on the east-west axis through Point A. This suggests that the solstitial-related marker posts of these Tract 15A woodhenges and the ritual they implicate were subsumed within the more dominant equinoctial ritual of Monks Mound. Therefore, the razing of the Lohmann phase plaza complex so as to build a new woodhenge may not at all mark the rising power of the Woodhenge cult. Instead, it probably marked the reemerging power of the Cahokian council of cult alliances (or, more precisely stated, the reemerging influence of the autonomist factions of the cult alliances making up that council).

In short, the decision to remove the Lohmann phase plaza complex of Tract 15A so that a new woodhenge could be built, and the subsequent rebuilding and expanding of the woodhenge in this zone, would appear to be a partial realization of the strategy of the autonomist factions, one condition of satisfaction of this strategy (that is, one goal) being to reduce the influence of the Woodhenge cult and therefore of the centralist factions in the Cahokian council of autonomous cult alliances. This claim may appear somewhat counterintuitive because apparently at the same time Cahokia shifted into the major Stirling phase expansionary mode that clearly required the allotting of increased labor resources to the cult heterarchy from the cults distributed across the American Bottom and probably also in the adjacent uplands. However, centralist factionalism should not be confused with the pooling and centering of resources. How this pooling and centering is brought about is what is critical in defining the factional power that it manifests. If it is done as a result of a Cahokian-based organization (for example, the Woodhenge cult) successfully promoting projects that commit the autonomous cult alliances to encourage their constituent cults to allocate greater resources to the heterarchy, it would be a sign of the continuing and growing influence of the centralist factions. As such, the autonomy principle would be strongly strained, and in all probability, the regular cults would start to abandon Cahokia by moving to another world renewal cult heterarchy where their autonomy would not be or, at least, would be less compromised. However, I interpret the razing of the Lohmann phase Tract 15A plaza complex in favor of building a new woodhenge to be a strategy designed to rein in the Woodhenge cult and the supporting centralist factions. The cult alliance that surrendered Tract 15A probably would have acquiesced because its own autonomist faction promoted it. This sacrifice on their part may have swung sufficient support toward the autonomist factions of the other cult alliances to effect a consensus in the council. This decision, therefore, would have placed the Woodhenge cult in a position where it would have to align itself with the consensus or risk losing credibility as an altruistic collegial priestly cult.

Furthermore, this move is likely to have been only part of a broader strategy. The overall and overt aspect of the strategy would have been to create a program that would be perceived even by the centralist factions as a win-win situation. This means that the Woodhenge cult move would have been part of a broader plan, possibly provoked by competition arising from a neighboring cult heterarchy, such as East St. Louis or St. Louis. The reputation of the affiliation of the cult alliances that made up Cahokia would be challenged, and the response would be to expand the world renewal capacity of Cahokia through initiating a major reconstruction program. Hence, by autonomist factions promoting the woodhenge/Tract 15A move as part of this larger plan, the centralist factions and the Woodhenge 72 cult would not be able to resist. At the same time, however, by agreeing to abandon Woodhenge 72 and its sacred primary mounds 72Sub1, 72Sub2, and 72Sub3, the Woodhenge 72 cult also necessarily became more closely integrated into the east-west ritual practices anchored by Monks Mound. Of course, the Woodhenge cult would also have the face-saving role of assigning Feature 452 as a major aligner for many of the mounds—those in the upper left panel of Table 17.2—even though the TM increments would be determined from Point A of Monks Mound, under the prevailing influence of the autonomist factions. Above all, by aligning the new woodhenge on this east-west axis through Point A, the solstice orientation and its associated ritual would be subsumed to the equinoctial-related world renewal ritual, the latter probably being closely tied to the postulated regrowing-of-the-earth ritual, itself primarily identified with the autonomist factions since, of course, the central precinct with Monks Mound, the Grand Plaza, the Creek Bottom mound group, the late Stirling phase palisade, and so on, was oriented to being the core medium of this ritual program.

Once the construction implementing this strategy was started, there was probably no credible reason for turning back. In fact, it is even possible that this move was justified on the grounds of inaugurating the completion of the Grand Plaza. Much of the refilling of the borrow pit south of Monks Mound and the building of the Grand Plaza are known to have been completed by the end of the Lohmann phase (Dalan 1997, 98), and the building of Mounds 50, 51, and 55 on the new plaza may have marked the initial Stirling phase.[7] I postulate that these latter mounds were under the custodial responsibility of different cult alliances. Therefore, the razing of the Lohmann-phase plaza and related structures of Tract 15A at about the same time may have been related, thereby marking the Lohmann-Stirling transition.

It is important to strengthen the validity of the Ideological Cult Faction model by completing my critique of the sequential settlement articulation mode account in chapter 11. At that time, I summarize and critiqued two arguments that Thomas Emerson and Timothy Pauketat put forward to confirm their claim that the Stirling phase marked the full emergence of the sacralized paramountcy. In their view, both the rapid appearance and widespread distribution of Ramey-Incised ceramics, on the one hand, and, on the other, the significant drop-off and very limited distribution of many exotics marked the successful rise of this paramountcy at Cahokia. Instead, I argue that these opposing trends were fully explicable as demarcating the success of the autonomist factions in their competition with the centralist factions. With the Ideological Cult Faction model elucidated and with the completion of its initial empirical grounding, I can now review these arguments and show precisely how the factional account serves as the preferred one.

CONFIRMING THE IDEOLOGICAL CULT FACTION MODEL

Part of the revitalization of the central precinct core of the Cahokian heterarchy would have been the promotion of several artifactual innovations and/or emulations that replaced older artifact traditions. The appearance of Ramey-Incised ceramics is generally recognized as a major marker of the Stirling phase. Emerson (1997a, 209–13) and Pauketat (Pauketat and Emerson 1991, 931–35) argue that the iconography of these ceramics represents the sky and earth deities, as well as the four sacred directions (rain, wind, and so on). Because of its standardization, they also argue for its centralized production and use in ritual contexts. Indeed, this centralized production not only marks specialized craftsmen, according to Pauketat (1994, 100, 161–62, 175), but also marks the elite patrons of these craftsmen as deriving their authority from the "divine chief" (Pauketat 1994, 184–85).[8] In short, centralized production is used by both scholars as grounds for their claim that the Stirling phase marks the full emergence of the sacred paramountcy.

I certainly accept that the Ramey-Incised pottery would have had ritual meaning; no doubt, it would have been understood as presencing the cosmic powers through the medium of their representation in the iconography. Understood in terms of the symbolic pragmatic view, the use of this pottery was not simply a means of "preaching the message." Its use would be promoted as an essential part of the conditions of satisfaction by which the behavioral interventions of those using it were constituted as the types of ritual acts intended and required. This goes beyond the claim that the symbolic meaning of the ceramics was vested in the motifs and forms of these ceramics. Those who participated in the activity that they were used to mediate would also recognize that these ceramics had been animated by the specialist artisans whose know-how would include both the technical arts and the ritual arts and thus that the ceramics had been produced in the appropriate iconic contexts.

In fact, specifying the conditions of production as having a critical role to play in constituting the efficacy of the ceramics is quite consistent with Emerson's and Pauketat's views as noted above. They also argue that it is by those using the ceramics knowing that they were made under the sacred patronage of the ruling elite that they would be identified as sacred. However, where I differ from Emerson and Pauketat is in my interpretation of the nature of these conditions of production. For Emerson and Pauketat, what constituted the ceramics as sacred was not the specialized form of know-how, its application, and the context of production, as such, but that the specialist artisans producing it would have been under the control and direction of the powerful and sacred elite patrons. Thus, the patrons and not the artisans were the source of the special powers of the ceramics. This is a critical part of their ideological thesis, namely, that elites were able to control the population through controlling the production and distribution of this and other critical ritual resources.[9]

However, I have already noted in chapter 9 that the Autonomous Cult model fully allows for specialized ritual production; by coupling this with the World Renewal Cult Heterarchy model, I have also argued that this specialized production would be carried out in the appropriate context (Cahokia as an *axis mundi*) and, of course, that it would be centralized in the appropriate structures built as part of the plaza-mound complexes of the producers' cult alliances. Therefore, its production would be regularized, promoted, standardized, and performed under the appropriate conditions as part of the ongoing responsibilities of the various cult alliances making up Cahokia. Hence, under these models I can interpret the production of this specialized nature as not requiring and therefore as not marking a dominance-type hierarchical elite order, as postulated by Emerson and Pauketat, but the enabling hierarchical context of the autonomous cult alliances.

Of course, the emergence of Ramey-Incised pottery is an important marker of the Stirling phase and therefore suggests a significant and rather abrupt break with the prior Lohmann phase. Also, since this break is marked by symbolic iconography, it is clearly ideological. Hence, it would also be part of the postulated shifts in factional power. Given the above argument that the abandoning of Woodhenge 72 and the razing of the Tract 15A Lohmann phase plaza complex to build a new woodhenge map the renewed vitality and influence of the autonomist factions in the Cahokian council, we can infer that Ramey-Incised ceramics would have been an innovation promoted by the autonomist factions by which the shamanic-ritual craft production by the regular or ordinary ecclesiastic-communal cults was recruited to express and simultaneously enhance the autonomy of the constituent cult alliances. The transient nature of occupancy of Cahokia (that is, the cult members' regular cycling between the cult locales and their domestic dwellings) would easily account for the widespread distribution of these ceramics during the Stirling phase. While at Cahokia, members would participate in cult rites mediated by Ramey-Incised pottery, and then they would return to their kinship-based countryside household dwellings with some of the pottery so that appropriate storage of sacred maize seed and so forth might be effected.

Thus, the point of the autonomist factions promoting this standardization of style and centralizing the management of its production in the world renewal cult heterarchies would be twofold: ensuring that they could effectively discharge their duties to the clans, namely, assisting them in reducing sacred pollution levels; and, without contradiction, enhancing the autonomy of the cults by controlling this production and distribution. In short, Ramey-Incised pottery marks a centralized management of a specialized ceramic production by which cult autonomy was promoted through regular widespread distribution of this style across the American Bottom, which simultaneously enhanced the discharging of cult members' duties to the cosmos and the clans.

As mentioned above, correlated with Ramey-Incised pottery is another characteristic of the Stirling phase: the significant reduction in exotics that has been noted by a number of archaeologists. In particular, Pauketat (1994, 162–67) has noted that only a few of the exotic material resources "stand out against a standardized background" (Pauketat 1994, 163) during the later Terminal Late Woodland phases and early Lohmann phase but that, rather suddenly during the middle and into the later Lohmann phase, the debris becomes dense with many exotic items having high ubiquity values, such as hematite, galena, mica, and copper; exotic cherts such as Cobden, Fort Payne, Mill Creek, and Kaolin; silicified sediments; igneous stone, in particular basalt; marine shell; and important artifacts such as fine Type-A projectile points, "fineware," and ground adzes. Indeed, during the later Lohmann subphases, which Pauketat labels as L-2 and L-3, respectively, he notes that feature fills "all exceed the mean values for these items by more than one standard deviation" (Pauketat 1994, 163). In stark contrast to this patterning, Pauketat comments, only "a limited array of items (mica and fineware vessels) stands out as Stirling-phase high-density items" (Pauketat 1994, 163).

He accounts for the rapid expansion of exotics during the Lohmann phase at Cahokia as marking the greater intensification of patron-client tribute and corvée relations and long-distance interelite exchange practices that he claims would characterize a quickly emerging paramount chiefdom out of the simple chiefdoms of the later Terminal Late Woodland period (Pauketat 1994, 171). He includes the possibility of warfare being encouraged by the chiefly system, as marked by the rather sudden appearance of the classic trinotched Cahokia point, that is, the Type-A projectile points, and he particularly points to the large caches of projectile points found in Mound 72 (Ahler 1999, 104–5; Fowler et al. 1999, 168; Pauketat 1994, 172). In Pauketat's view, this rather abrupt rise in exotics is the mark of a dominance-oriented political hierarchy based on a prestige economy in which the elite leaders successfully generated patron-client relations and subordinated the rural peoples as the source of corvée labor and surplus produce as tribute.

The fall-off of these materials during the Stirling phase seems to contradict Pauketat's model. However (as I note in chapter 11), he argues to the contrary. For him, this fall-off in exotica and the sudden appearance of Ramey-Incised pottery and its distribution are both simply the marks of a sacralized para-mountcy. He claims that by successfully endowing the persons of the chiefs—if not the elites more generally—with the sacred powers of the cosmos, thereby constituting them as the intermediaries between the gods and the commoners, elites no longer had to manipulate subelites with exotic goods but could rely simply on the enhanced sanctity of their positions to ensure the constant flow of wealth (as witnessed by the expansion of the monumentalism of Cahokia that occurred during the Stirling phase):

> Given this sort of sacral authority, it can be assumed that Stirling-phase officeholders would have been entitled to tribute and corvée simply by virtue of the sanctity of chiefly office. There might have been little incentive for the sort of collaborative tactics suspected to have characterized Lohmann-phase political arenas, and, in fact, the density and diversity of exotic goods in the refuse of [Tract 15A-Dunham Tract] and other Stirling-phase central and rural samples do appear to decrease. (Pauketat 1994, 185)

In contrast, I interpret this reduction of exotics (along with the appearance and widespread distribution of Ramey-Incised ceramics) as the expression of the failure of the centralist factions to maintain their position and the success of the autonomist factions to reassert their control of the world renewal cult heterarchies through the councils that were responsible to the constituent cults in the countryside and thereby to reassert their individual autonomy. In this regard, the history of the development of exotics as mapped in the Tract 15A and Dunham Tract archaeological assemblage is fully consistent with the autonomist/centralist factional negotiation and the ultimate success of the autonomist factions. The richest but not the only known deposits of exotics are found in association with Features 102 and 236 of Mound 72 (Fowler et al. 1999, 168–70; also see Winters 1974, 36–39 for a summary of the Mitchell site exotic deposits). The two large mortuary-related deposits of arrow points (caches 1550 and 1551) found under 72Sub1 would indicate warfare as an important institution, as Pauketat has also pointed out, and since many of these points were made of exotic cherts from the lower Mississippi Valley, long-distance warfare is suggested, in association with equally long-distance procuring of exotic resources, such as copper and mica.

As I suggest in the preceding chapter, promoting this long-distance warfare and associated long-distance procurement processes would be expected of the Woodhenge cult since its strong prescriptive tendencies would push it to surpass the traditional postmortem human sacrificial world renewal ritual by arguing for and practicing lethal human sacrifice. Such an explanation would also argue for the effectiveness of exotic materials over local equivalent materials in the production of ritual warrants. All this would also attract the junior age-grade laity sector. At the same time, the Woodhenge cult would probably be minimalist in terms of monumental earthwork construction, although it would not be able to prevent the construction of monumental earthworks. Earthworks would be important symbolic warrants of the postulated male-based fertility and female-based fecundity world renewal ritual spheres (as I suggest in earlier chapters), probably focused on regrowing-the-earth rites tied up with the fertility of rains and floods by which the cosmic powers of fecundity were revitalized. Since Monks Mound would be the primary locus of this important ritual, it would be the focus of the autonomous cult alliances, and the ritual related to it would take much of the attention and resources of these cults. Mound construction, of course, would be menial labor performed by the younger junior age-sets. Warfare, probably a much more esteemed task (although also having self-polluting consequences for those occupying the warrior position), would be associated with the older junior age-sets, clearly being promoted by the Woodhenge cult. Hence, the rather contradictory processes of the proliferation of exotics and, relative to the subsequent Stirling phase, the moderate level of earthwork construction as characterizing the middle and later Lohmann phase together suggest that the ideological posture of the centralist factions tended to prevail over that of the autonomist factions.

The reduction in exotics and the expansion of monumental construction following the abandoning and dismantling of Woodhenge 72, the razing of the Tract 15A plaza complex, and the building of the first of a series of new woodhenges (as I suggest above) would therefore mark the rather sudden turning point of the influence of the Woodhenge cult and its supporting centralist factions in the regular cults and the reaffirming of the hegemony of the autonomy of the cults making up the Cahokia world renewal cult heterarchy council. The procuring of long-distance exotics could not be entirely eliminated, since the centralist factions would argue that exotics were a stronger or more effective ritual medium than local materials. However, the counterargument could be that long-distance procurement generated significant pollution caused by the crossing of sacred natural boundaries by those responsible for procuring exotics. Therefore, we could anticipate a compromise, namely, the procuring of exotic materials in the medium distance, such as the rather easily available Missouri flint clay that was quite prolifically used for the type of iconic figurines found in the Stirling phase BBB Motor and Sponemann cult locales, as discussed earlier. Indeed, as Emerson and colleagues (2002, 313) point out, correlated with this drop-off of exotics during the late Lohmann and Stirling phases was the enhancing of "lesser" exotic resource procurement within the 150-kilometer range of Cahokia, a far cry from the more far-reaching exotic procurement zone of the Lohmann phase. This reduction in long-distance procurement, however, is fully consistent with the Ideological Cult Faction model, in this case as a reflection of a shift to the proscriptive-autonomist ideological posture. Finally, I wish to note that the innovation, development, and distribution of the Ramey-Incised pottery and its strong iconography of the sky or heavens, rain, thunder, the underworld, and so on, would neatly correlate with the resurgence of the Monks Mound regrowing-of-the-earth ritual during Stirling phase times.

However, the reduced level of exotics may not have simply been to spite the centralist factions and the Woodhenge cult. Once long-distance warfare is instigated, especially if lethal human sacrifice is involved, it can become a viciously self-entrenching cyclic process that cannot be stopped unilaterally, even if the autonomist factions may have wished to do so. Thus the enmity that may have been built up against Cahokia, postulated as a result of the centralist factions' promotion of long-distance warfare during the Lohmann phase to procure lethal human sacrificial victims, may have escalated to the point that the Cahokian affiliation of cult alliances under the hegemony of the autonomist factions may not have been able to eliminate the warfare, only to control it. One possible way to control it would be to shift from an offensive to a defensive stance. Initiated with the Stirling phase, promoted during this phase, and finally effectively realized through this promotion would be a project that, while costly in labor, would be both ritually enhancing and militarily effective, namely, the late Stirling phase building of the sacred C-form palisade. Consistent with this greater defensive posture, of course, would be the constraining of exotic resource procurement within the 150-kilometer-radius zone around Cahokia (Emerson et al. 2002, 313).

As I argue in chapter 10, since the sacred C-form palisade feature lacks a "fourth" wall, it would make for a very unusual fortress (which is apparently also the case for the multiple-mound Mississippian period sites of Aztalan in Wisconsin, Linn-Heilig and Kincaid in southwestern and southeastern Illinois, respectively, Angel in southwestern Indiana, and so on). Still, the defensive military stance, consistent with the posture of the autonomist factions, seems to be clearly indicated by the multiple bastions and L-shaped gates, which certainly would appear to be designed for defense, as well as allowing effective forays outside the curtain wall to engage the attacking enemy. Indeed, this may have been the point. That is, the claim that the curtain wall was both a monumental icon of the cosmos that presenced the essential creative powers of the heavens and the underworld(s) and a defensive construction is not contradictory, as long as we interpret this combination of traits—a strong defensive wall with bastions, defendable L-shaped gates, and an open, undefendable side—as manifesting widely accepted military ideological rules that specify what forms of aggressive behaviors would count as proper forms of armed engagement.

To Westerners, given our strong commitment to exclusive territorialism, war is usually won through conquest of land, and it is rewarded by dominance of the victors over the defeated and the imposition of corvée labor and tribute on the conquered, who may even be enslaved. Therefore, building an open-sided defensive bastioned wall would be strange and even contradictory. However, in traditional Native North American societies, battle was rarely for land since domain was inclusive. Typically it was waged for vengeance and to save and/or gain reputation. Killing the enemy in one-to-one combat would bring esteem. Capturing the enemy would bring greater esteem. Indeed, counting coup on the enemy and escaping unharmed would bring the greatest esteem. In short, not only were there different purposes to combat, but also the purposes that it served could be achieved only if the combatants conducted themselves according to the acceptable ideological institutions of armed engagement.

War and combat are intensely rule governed. Indeed, the only differences between killing as combat and killing as murder, for example, are the forms of collective intentionality and sociosymbolic contexts in which these objectively similar behavioral interventions are performed. The symbolic pragmatics of combat conducted to procure lethal sacrificial victims would be particularly crucial. Of paramount importance is knowing and performing the correct procedure for physically seizing an enemy, since only by conforming to the recognized protocol would this event count as the procuring of a human to serve as the medium for lethal sacrifice. That is, a person improperly seized could not count as a captured victim for future lethal sacrifice. One subset of primary rules would specify the circumstances of armed engagement and combat. For example, location would be specific. Only if the attack was directed against the wall itself or against certain components of the wall (for example, a bastion, a defended gate) and at certain times (for example, sunrise or sunset), and so on, would the successful capture of an individual or of individuals count as procuring one or more future victims. This does not mean that all combats were for this purpose. Attacking by shooting arrows at the defending enemy standing on the bastion support platform would likely count as proper combat. However, the deaths, if any, would count as simple although successful acts of vengeance.

All of the foregoing can be used to reinforce the point I make in chapter 10 concerning why there is no apparent wall "defending" the north side of the central precinct. In terms of the ritualized warfare outlined above, not only would there be no defensive need for such a wall, if it were to be constructed, it would probably have constituted the whole construction as an infelicitous sacred cosmic structure since it would close Cahokia from the underworld(s), as presenced in the Creek Bottom plaza. This means that any attack from the floodplain would not count as proper warfare combat. Therefore, there would be little or no point for an enemy to make such an attack. Furthermore, if an attack was attempted and Cahokian deaths occurred, the attackers would not gain esteem or discharge debts of vengeance. Instead, they would become pariahs, notorious and scorned for staining and weakening the sacred powers of the cosmos.

All these indicators of the autonomist faction's prevalence would go some distance toward accounting for the characteristics marking the Stirling phase: (1) the curtain timber wall as a great sacred C-form palisade marking a successful shift to a defensive military posture from the preceding centralist-promoted offensive military posture; (2) the expansion of monumental earthworks as the enhancing of the autonomy of the cult alliance at the cost of the Woodhenge cult and the centralist factions; (3) the innovation, production, and distribution of Ramey-Incised ceramics as the work of autonomous cults fulfilling their world renewal duties to the cosmos and the clans, largely mediated through the regrowing-of-the-earth ritual; (4) the availability of foreign exotics being seriously diminished as marking a reduced level of long-distance interaction, while simultaneously the exotics that are available being from within the 150-kilometer zone around Cahokia; and (5) the apparent shift away from lethal human sacrifice as manifested in Mound 72 and the repromotion of postmortem human sacrifice as manifested in Wilson Mound and Powell Mound (Ahler and DePuydt 1987, 18–21; Milner 1984, 484; 1998, 106).[10]

Therefore, the observed reduction in the quantity and range of exotics would be not only the result of the proscriptive tendencies of the autonomist factions, but also the consequence of their shifting from the offensive stance to a defensive military stance. In this regard, it might be relevant that David Anderson (1997, 257–58) has argued that residents of the American Bottom during the Lohmann and Stirling phases may have carried on long-distance warfare against the societies in the Cairo Bottom, a possibility that would be consistent with George Milner's (1998, 53–63) identifying in the ceramic data the probable existence of distinctly separate cultural traditions marked by a thirty-mile stretch on the eastern side of the Mississippi without any significant settlement. This discontinuity of cultural traits would be consistent with the above premise. As Milner describes the settlement pattern, "These sites serve as a crude estimate of the distribution of late prehistoric people who interacted with one another enough to share the same pottery tradition. Sites and pottery from the American Bottom south to Thebes Gap indicate that the margins of at least some ceramic style zones were sharp and long lasting, suggesting the existence of discontinuities in interaction among neighboring peoples" (Milner 1998, 53). Also notable is that the postulated hostile relations between the populations of the Cairo Bottom and the American Bottom regions and their immediate areas would confront the Linn-Heilig, Ware, and other multiple-mound locales of the former region with Cahokia and its neighboring world renewal cult heterarchy locales, such as East St. Louis, Mitchell, and so on.

This postulated interregional warfare raises a puzzle that I have not seen adequately addressed or resolved. Noted in the literature is the consistent presence, starting in the Terminal Late Woodland and continuing through the whole Mississippian period, of Mill Creek and Kaolin chert hoes and spades in the American Bottom. These were brought in as finished products from the same zone that Anderson and Milner claim would have held long-term hostile relations with Cahokia and the American Bottom. How could this be possible since, in terms of the hierarchical account, the enemies would be monistic modular polities? All direct exchange between enemy chiefdoms should be suspended, thereby making ongoing procurement of Mill Creek chert hoes and spades possible only through neutral intermediaries. Since these artifacts are recognized as utilitarian tools (although I suspect important warranting symbolic pragmatics are involved), intermediary exchange is unlikely to be capable of sustaining the sheer volume required.

Under the World Renewal Cult Heterarchy model, however, there is no difficulty in accounting for the appearance of such extralocal chert artifacts, since this would be consistent with the bifurcated settlement articulation mode of the Mississippian period American Bottom and the rules of armed engagement. Since clan and cult organizations would be autonomous, when occupying the dispersed clan-based villages, these persons would be neutral parties in any military confrontation between or among world renewal cults and cult heterarchies. In a social system having the bifurcated settlement articulation mode, seizing individuals from isolated farm fields or farmsteads would probably not count as procuring lethal sacrificial victims. Of course, the very same people when occupying a world renewal cult heterarchy locale, or even a cult nodal locale, would no longer be neutral under the rules of engagement and could be treated by the invading warrior party of an enemy cult or cult alliance as legitimate targets.

This also suggests that populations maintaining the more traditional integrated settlement articulation mode would be living in dually structured nucleatted villages. Since the cult would be an integral part of the village, no one in the village would be perceived by the enemy as neutral. The rules of engagement might lead to construing the total village as an actual or potential enemy; thus, the kidnapping of one or two women tilling in the fields who should be under the guard of cult warriors would count as a successful coup for this purpose.[11] Mill Creek and Kaolin hoes and spades are utilitarian and ubiquitous. Therefore, during periods of long-distance intercult enmity, the procurement links would likely be sustained through clan alliances, and, as clan members, those travelling on the traditional routes would be treated by armed cult parties as neutral. Thus, even at the height of warfare among distant world renewal cult heterarchies, parties involved in clan-based exchange would probably be immune to cult-based attacks.

The recent analysis of the distribution of Mill Creek hoes in the central Mississippi Valley by Jon Muller (1997, 368–70) can be cited in support of this possibility. Muller has analyzed the gravity decay fall-off curve of Mill Creek hoes as mapped from Union County in southwestern Illinois, the well-known primary source of Mill Creek and Kaolin chert hoes, to the American Bottom and points north. His purpose was to determine whether the fall-off distribution curve would correspond to long-distance down-the-line or centralized-control exchange processes. He notes that a large concentration of hoes and their residue is found in the American Bottom, particularly the northern expanse, but notes that if this "bump" on the curve is analytically removed from his distribution plot, the fall-off line from Union County to points north of Cahokia conforms quite neatly to the down-the-line exchange expectations. In terms of Mill Creek hoes, he concludes that "Cahokia . . . [was] a way station and a populous locality, but . . . [it was not] a center of *control* of distribution. The distribution of Mill Creek hoes even a little way from Cahokia is clearly more related to their distance from Union County than they are to St. Clair County" (Muller 1997, 370, emphasis in original). To confirm his observations he notes that "if one leaves out the American Bottom locations and looks at the adjoining points . . . [of his graph], these fit a gravity decay distribution *from Union County* better than they do a secondary source at Cahokia. . . . Taken altogether, the distributions of hoes of all kinds from the likely sources are strong indicators either of direct access or simply down-the-line exchange" (Muller 1997, 370, emphasis in original). Of course, in terms of the Dual Clan-Cult and World Renewal Cult Heterarchy models, this conclusion could be restated as strong support for the claim that the distribution of Mill Creek hoes was mediated by a domestic clan-based network and not by a cult-based network, which would probably have been caught up in long-distance enmities.

This completes the elucidation and empirical grounding of the Ideological Cult Faction model. I can now complete applying it by presenting an overall summary of the history of the factional competition that strongly influenced the development and, finally, the abandonment of Cahokia. Some redundancy will be required to do this, although I will keep it to the necessary minimum. I turn to this task in the next and final chapter.

The History and Outcome
of Factional Competition in Cahokia

As discussed in the previous chapter, while the abandoning of Woodhenge 72 by means of constructing Mound 72, razing the Tract 15A structures built around the Lohmann phase plaza, and building a new woodhenge in this place constitutes clear evidence of the continuing importance of the Woodhenge cult, I suggest that it also marks the weakening of the prescriptivist influence of this cult, since the series of new Tract 15A woodhenges, built sequentially in the shadow of Monks Mound, indicates the subsuming of solstitial ritual to the equinoctial and 5° east-of-north rituals. All of this indicates that the autonomist factions were gaining—or regaining—control of council consensus. As I also comment in the previous chapter, along with the reduction of the exotic procurement zone to a radius of 150 kilometers around Cahokia, this equinoctial focus means that planning for and, in late Stirling phase times, the construction of the sacred C-form palisade was an autonomist factional project. While certainly serving several purposes, in strategic terms, the most important achievement the C-form palisade may have initially served was reducing the focus on long-distance offensive warfare (which had been dominant in the Lohmann phase as part of the centralist factions' promoting of lethal human sacrifice) and replacing it with a more defensive warfare posture (which would have been more amenable to the interests and goals of the autonomist factions).

In addition, while Feature 452 continued to be used as the aligner, the postulated shift from Point A to Point D as the TM incremental anchoring point also displays the hand of the autonomist factions. This is because Point D also was part of the 5° east-of-north axis, and this had been an important factor in the laying out of Monks Mound when the original affiliated cult alliances initiated the construction program, probably in the Terminal Late Woodland–Mississippian transition period. Therefore, this 5° east-of-north axis was probably related to the primary ritual focus of Monks Mound. In chronological terms, this shift to using the Feature 452 alignment along with the Point D TM increment is postulated to have occurred in the mid-Stirling phase. Although the Creek Bottom Group correlates with the Feature 452 alignment/Point A TM incremental period, postulated to have occurred in the early Stirling phase, its being built during this time frame may again display the hand of the autonomist factions since the location of this mound-plaza complex on the floodplain of Cahokia Creek strongly argues that it would also be tightly linked to the regrowing-of-the-earth rites. Therefore, the Creek Bottom mound-plaza complex may have figured importantly in the strategy of the autonomist factions, since its postulated early Stirling phase construction logically links up with the later Stirling phase construction of the sacred C-form palisade in its symbolic pragmatic capacity as a monumental icon representing and presencing the essential properties of cosmic frame.

Conceived in these terms, this massive sacred C-form palisade construction would mark not only a defensive military posture prevailing over an offensive posture, but also the enhancing of the spring equinoctial-related regrowing-of-the-earth ritual in which the Creek Bottom Group would have played a critical role; both goals would be strongly identified with the autonomist factions. Interestingly, Mounds 9 and 10 of the Kunnemann Group also fall within the Feature 452 alignment/Point D TM incremental period (see Table 17.1). However, since the construction of the rest of the Kunnemann Group conforms only to the Point D TM incremental association—that is to say, the Feature 452 alignment does not apply—the construction of these mounds probably occurred during the later Stirling period. The exclusive use of Point D (while ignoring Feature 452) to establish construction alignments, therefore, seems to indicate that the autonomist factions prevailed at Cahokia into the Moorehead phase.

I postulate that by this time the solstitial alignment rituals were well incorporated into the Monks Mound–related ritual, suggesting that the Woodhenge cult had also been integrated into these ritual practices. The centralist factions, therefore, would have lost most of their influence, and prescriptivist proposals would have started to fall on deaf ears. The cult alliances would have come under a strong autonomist-proscriptive orientation. This also means that, in terms of the congregationalist↔presbyterian↔episcopalian continuum, the governance of the cults would be shifting from the more presbyterian, middle-of-the-road laity/clergy posture toward the congregationalist, laity-dominance posture. This would stimulate internal strains between the junior and senior age-grade sets as the latter started to exert greater influence in cult affairs. Therefore, as the cults moved into the Moorehead phase, internal strains would have increased.

I argue in chapter 12 that the Moorehead phase at Cahokia might be best treated as a world renewal cult heterarchy in maintenance or "boot camp" mode. This maintenance mode is indicated by the disappearance of the wood-henges and minimal mound construction. Instead, cult focus was possibly di-rected largely to training new cult members, primarily young bachelors, who would build and occupy larger barracklike quarters, as indicated by the appear-ance of large structures rather distantly spaced from each other and framing the plazas. If I add to this interpretation Thomas Emerson and Eva Hargrave's (2000, 5–7; also see Hedman and Hargrave 1999, ix, 87) claim that the East St. Louis Stone Quarry and related sites in the lower sector of the northern expanse of the American Bottom are actually dated to the terminal Moorehead phase and are contemporary with the later occupation of the Kane Mounds CBL site, then what this maintenance mode might be revealing is a revival of the traditional north-south division, as originally marked in the Terminal Late Woodland Pulcher/Late Bluff ceramic traditions (Kelly 1982, 35; 1990a, 77–78; 1990b, 117).

As Emerson and Hargrave (2000, 18) argue, by Moorehead times, strong indications of mortuary attributes in the upland CBLs near Cahokia mark these as quite distinct from the floodplain CBLs in the lower sector of the northern expanse of the floodplain. Rather than this manifesting (in Emerson and Hargrave's terminology) a form of ethnogenesis based on immigrant resi-dential communities, it may be the revival of the arm's-length relation between autonomous cults descended from the northern upland Late Bluff ceramic tradition and those descended from the southeastern Ozark upland Pulcher ceramic tradition, itself exacerbated by ideological differences over what would count as the most felicitous form of postmortem world renewal sacrifice. In the case of the East St. Louis Stone Quarry site and the related mortuary compo-nents of the nearby Florence Street and Range sites, maintaining the traditional Mississippian and probably pre-Mississippian postmortem cycling process was paramount, while in the upland CBLs near Cahokia, the promotion of crema-tion or fire-related postmortem manipulation (borrowed from more northern world renewal cults) became prominent.

I suggest in chapter 14 that this borrowing may have been mediated through the recruiting of cohorts of same-age companions from the more northern upland regions in the lower and central Illinois Valley and neighboring sectors of the upper Mississippi Valley. If so, these sources of new manpower for cult alliances of the upper sector of the northern expanse of the American Bottom may have allowed for the ongoing occupation of Cahokia in this new Moorehead phase "boot camp" mode. This would also, however, increasingly discourage the cults from the lower sector of the northern expanse of the American Bottom from continuing their participation. Instead (as I suggest in chapter 12), they may have disaffiliated from the latter to form a much more localized southern set of cult alliances, sharing their deceased among a network of autonomous cult CBLs characterized by stone-box mortuary pits and charnel structures. This tendency for heterarchies to disaffiliate is also characteristic of a congregationalist orientation since one way that the senior age-grade can maintain its strong influence is to reduce the level of interaction among the junior age-sets across autonomous cults.

Recruiting from a greater distance or distancing cult alliances from each other would be alternative or even mutually reinforcing tactics, thereby promoting the postulated reemergence of the north-south/upper-lower sector arm's-length relation. This may also raise the spectre of aggression between these sectors of the northern expanse. This possibility can be added to the above factional account for the rebuilding of the sacred C-form palisade during the Moorehead phase—at least three times—while mound construction apparently was largely terminated. Thus, the maintenance mode may have been quickly transforming into a literal boot-camp mode, enhancing and being enhanced by a growing north-south intra–American Bottom aggressive posture among autonomous cults and cult alliances.

If this is the case, the cult alliances could be expected to start to modify their material cultural media, limiting long-distance procurement expeditions even more to focus their members' activities closer to the cult locales while intensifying world renewal ritual to rectify the ongoing pollution of agriculture. The dispersed village order would persist as a proscriptive settlement posture, thereby minimizing settlement-induced pollution as well as ensuring neutrality for the domestic locales in the postulated conditions of rising interalliance cult hostilities. This shift in emphasis should show up in the countryside nodal locales of autonomous cults as these expanded their material makeup and reduced their material investment in the world renewal cult heterarchies while emphasizing the more aggressive boot-camp posture. For example, Emerson (1997c, 141–44) reports on the Moorehead phase Julien cult nodal site, pointing out the unusual size of Structure 31 and effectively recognizing it as a men's house. This structure was 7.5 meters by 5.6 meters, with internal room divisions or benches, hearths, quantities of ritual as well as military-related debris in pits, trinotched arrow points, storage pits, and so on. Emerson argues that a small structure nearby may have been a storage facility.

In broad terms, the Moorehead phase Julien cult nodal site could easily represent part of the material facilities of an autonomous world renewal cult that was shifting its emphasis from cult heterarchy investment to more local ritual concerns with a growing influence of intercult aggression, enhancing the religious role of the senior age-sets and the military role of the junior age-sets. Furthermore, since it is likely that flood levels were increasing as the water tables were rising during the late Moorehead and Sand Prairie phases, these floodplain cult CBLs may have begun to realize that, despite their best efforts, this area of the cosmos—the American Bottom—was suffering from human occupation of the land and that its abandonment might ultimately become necessary.[1] As Emerson observes,

> The chronological relationship between elevation and the placement of structures affiliated with the different Mississippian components has been documented at a number of sites. At the Julien site . . . structures belonging to the later Mississippian Moorehead . . . and Sand Prairie . . . phases were located high on the ridge, with a mean elevation of ca. 126.1 m above mean sea level (amsl). The earlier Stirling phase structures were located on the ridge crest and its flanks near an adjacent swale. Their average elevation was 125.9 m amsl. (Emerson 1992, 208)

THE POST-CAHOKIAN ERA: SPECULATIVE POSSIBILITIES

If my historical account of the development of world renewal cult heterarchies caused by the combination of ideological cult factionalism and heterarchical disaffiliation is adequate, it suggests that the late Mississippian period social system of the American Bottom not only was manifesting strong trends toward reestablishing an integrated settlement articulation mode of villages, but also that this was occurring in a milieu characterized by growing intercult hostility promoting the joint and specialized leadership of the senior and junior age-grades, the former focusing largely on the religious role and the latter on the military role. With the tendency toward disaffiliation aggravated by growing hostilities as outlined above, the shamanic priests of the Woodhenge cult would also probably have tended to become localized within their respective dispersed villages. As part of this process, the ecclesiastic-communal cult structure would also have dissipated, returning the cult system to a dual communal cult level based on mutually autonomous junior and senior age-grades sodalities. In fact, the above postulated specialization of senior and junior age-grades would have encouraged the senior age-grade cults to preserve and, in some cases, monopolize the type of regular and esoteric know-how and ritual that had previously been distributed across both the regular and specialized cults, while the junior age-grade communal sodalities reduced their cultic world renewal role and took on more defensive and long-distance foraging roles.

The perceived need to abandon the American Bottom under the above conditions of increasing water levels and intensifying hostilities may well have promoted the reformulation of these social systems into singular ethnic groups based on the integrated settlement articulation mode. This would have simply promoted the junior cult sodalities to reduce their world renewal role and enhance their specialized foraging (hunting) and military role. Simultaneously, the senior cult sodalities would have specialized in the area of world and social renewal ritual. The historic Osage social system could serve as an analogical illustration of this process. Melvin Fowler (Fowler et al. 1999, 183) drew on what we know of the Osage cosmology to illustrate the type of possible collective world belief system presupposed in the layout of Woodhenge 72 and Mound 72 (see chapter 13 for a review and critique). While he cautions that we cannot precisely link known Native American peoples to Cahokia, we can use the more abstract and widespread aspects of their culture tradition and social system to model the probable parallels with Cahokia. I quite agree with him on this, while cautioning that the least likely component of the cultural tradition on which to draw parallels would be ideology, since this is the component of a cultural tradition that is most subject to change. However, for this very reason, given the postulated nature of the termination of the Mississippian period in the American Bottom, I suggest that the social system of the historically known Osage might quite nicely conform to one possible direction of post-Mississippian social transformation that some of the postulated ethnic communities might have followed.

As I note above, abandoning the American Bottom as the end point of disaffiliation in conditions of rising hostilities and increasing pollution manifested by rising water levels would probably promote the reintegration of the cults and clans to form integrated village systems similar to those of the pre-Mississippian times. However, as I suggest above, this reintegration would not see the dissolution of the dual clan-cult structure. As a deep social structural property of the community, this duality would persist but be realized in new spatial re-engaging of clan and cult facilities akin to the type of plaza-periphery pattern I have outlined for the Terminal Late Woodland period (chapters 8 and 15). This would be particularly the case if, in fact, the junior age-grade reformed into a communal cult organization, leaving the clan organization under the responsibility of the senior age-grade leadership. Certainly, the latter was quite common in historical Native American social systems, with the junior age-grades constituting the military sodalities (having combined hunting and warfare responsibilities) and the senior age-grades taking on clan and villagewide responsibilities through conducting community and world renewal activities and having primary responsibility for village governance through providing civil peace chiefs drawn from the senior age-grade.

However, the historical conditions of this re-engaging of clans and cults would play an important role; as I note above, since the termination of the Mississippian period in the American Bottom meant that the communities involved were reformulating into the integrated settlement articulation mode in the context of the dissolution of the largest and most complex of the known social systems in the bifurcated settlement articulation mode, it would not be surprising to find the multiple cults and their equally multiple complementary clan systems generating a range of different forms of integrated village systems. One possibility, as I suggest above, would be for the Cahokian experience to generate autonomous junior and senior communal cults, with the latter specializing to become the primary custodians of esoteric and secret world renewal and community renewal ritual know-how.

The Osage seem to nicely fit this possibility. Although the ancestors of this historically known Siouan-speaking people did not necessarily participate in the American Bottom Mississippian period social system, they are known to have migrated prehistorically from the lower Ohio drainage, and by historic times settling in the Osage Valley of the lower Missouri drainage, not too distant from Cahokia (Bailey 1995, 27–29). Therefore, we might plausibly assume that the Osage ancestors could have been caught up in a Mississippian-type bifurcated social system, in the lower Ohio Valley and/or the middle Mississippi Valley, in particular, the American Bottom. Certainly this would partly account for the particular nature of the dual clan-cult structure of the typical Osage village.

I outline the layout of the traditional historic Osage villages in chapter 13. However, I do not explore the nature of the cult system in that chapter. Each village (traditionally, five) had its own priestly cult, referred to as the *non-hon'-zhin-ga* (the "little old men"), and the cults of all the villages, along with three tribal priests, were termed the *ni'-ka xo'-be* (the "holy men"). In this case, the cults were constituted of senior age-grade Osage males who achieved their position by becoming initiated into the cult, which was a collegial priestly organization. That is, all members were recognized as priests, although the actual membership was divided between those who were the real experts, having learned the requisite cosmology and ideology by heart, and those who relied on the former for primary guidance in ritual, thereby effectively generating the equivalent of a laity/clergy structure (Bailey 1995, 78).[2] The initiation was effected by a senior male becoming the custodian of the primary sacred icon, or *wa-xo'-be*, of his clan (Bailey 1995, 44–45).

Although the parallel clan structure did change over time, at the maximum, the Osage village was constituted of twenty-four patrilineal clans subdivided into Sky and Earth moieties (Rollings 1992, 46–51). The Sky moiety was constituted of nine clans associated with the sacred powers of the heavens and divided into two phratries: seven clans of the Sky People, and two clans forming a phratry known as "Those who came last." The Earth moiety was also divided into phratries: seven clans constituting the Water People phratry; another seven clans, the Land People phratry; and a single clan referred to as the "Isolated Earth People" (Bailey 1995, 35–41).

As I read the Osage literature, however, being a member of a particular clan did not ensure membership in the priestly cult. Rather, those who chose and were accepted into the priestly cult did so by sponsoring and materially supporting the ritual and festival costs of initiation by which they became the custodians of the iconic symbols of their clans. Hence, while both the cults and the clans had structures that embodied the same range of symbolic properties, they were relatively autonomous organizations. The cults' responsibilities were related to the rituals mediated through the iconic symbols of the clans (the sacred bundles, which collectively embodied the total range of powers of the cosmos); although the rituals performed are reported by Francis La Flesche as constituting supplications to the supreme god to actively help the Osage, maintain their health, and protect their lives, since the total know-how content of the action intentions realized in these rituals was esoteric and secret, to be revealed only to the initiates (Bailey 1995, 56), in my view (although this point is not mentioned by La Flesche), a major focus on renewal very likely underwrote these rituals. For example, initiates had to supply the range of raw materials necessary to reproduce the sacred bundles for which they would become the custodians. Such ritually sanctioned reproduction probably was a form of world renewal ritual with the bundles participating in the essential powers of what they were taken to represent, namely, the sacred powers of the cosmic components associated with the clans of the initiates.

In contrast (as noted in chapter 13), the clan organization of the village came under the leadership of the dual chiefs—*tsi-zhu ga-hi'-ge* (Sky Chief) and *hon-ga ga-hi'-ge* (Earth Chief)—and their assistants, known as *a-ki-da* (Rollings 1992, 50–53). These were chosen from select clans and had the responsibility for the running of the village, organizing the villagewide hunts, maintaining good order in the village, and so on (Bailey 1995, 42–44). In an important sense, these were the secular leaders of the clan structure, and the priestly collegial cults constituted the sacred leaders. The relations between these two groupings was arm's-length, in terms of spheres of responsibilities and spatial arrangements.

Their spatial relations neatly replicated the structural relations underwriting the plaza-periphery pattern that I outline for the Dohack and Range occupations of the early Terminal Late Woodland period Range site, but in a unique material manner. As described in chapter 13, the physical layout of the Osage village, at least in ideal terms, had the village divided into two halves, north and south, with the houses of members of the Sky moiety clans making up the northern half and the houses of members of the Earth moiety clans making up the southern half. In both cases, these clan-based residences were spatially organized relative to each other in a precise manner as stipulated by traditional know-how so as to fit each clan to its place in the cosmos. The central east-west avenue separating the two moieties was conceived of as the path of the sun, and all the houses were oriented in the same direction. The two houses of the village co-chiefs with their assistants were located in the center of this "avenue of the sun."

While the clan-based organization of the village was embodied in more or less fixed lodges, in quite a contrasting manner, the cult-based organization was more a virtual patterning. When the senior age-grade priestly cult of the village gathered, it formed what is referred to as the "House of Mysteries," or *tsi' wa-kon-da-gi*. This "house" had no fixed physical presence. Rather, it was constituted by the seating arrangement of the aggregation of the priestly cult members. Therefore, the "House of Mysteries" was not the place where they were gathered but the order in which the priestly members sat whenever they formally gathered. They arranged their seating in two parallel north-south rows, again according to the relative position of their clan lodges, except in an inverted west-east manner so that priests from the clans that occupied the eastern end of the village sat at the western end of the "House of Mysteries" and vice versa (Bailey 1995, 57–58, Figure 3.5, 59). Furthermore, in principle, this gathering could occur anywhere; typically, it did not occur in the actual central-village "avenue of the sun." In fact, if the "House of Mysteries" was to be constituted in a particular spot, it would probably occur in the house of the peer-selected cult leader, the *non-hon'-zhin-ga wa-thin*. This person was chosen by consensus by the total cult membership, and since the individual could come from any of the clans, the location of the meeting house could vary over time.

Although my interpretation of the relations of the priestly cults and the clans in the village does not accord with the one presented by Garrick Bailey (1995, 44) and Willard Rollings (1992, 50), both of whom treat the relation of the clans to the cult in deferential dominance-based hierarchical terms, I believe that these relations are more adequately understood as a particular but identifiable expression of the dual clan-cult arm's-length relation that I have fully explored in this book. To illustrate, in his outline of the Osage village social system, Bailey (1995, 44) concludes that "the priests were the ultimate power and authority within the tribe. Every major and most minor decisions and actions required a ritual and the formal sanction of the priests." In a similar vein, Rollings (1992, 50) specifically interprets the priestly cult as dominant: "The Osage village was dominated by the *Non-hon-zhin-ga,* who established rules of behavior which were in turn enforced by the two *Ga-hi-ge* and their *A-ki-da.*" However, this comment quite radically contrasts with a later statement of his that apparently "little coercive power existed among the Osage. They had several band chiefs, although those chiefs had little authority" (Rollings 1992, 52).

The apparent lack of coercive authority is quite consistent, however, when viewed under the notions of autonomy and heterarchy. As I argue in earlier chapters, when autonomous groups are unequal in powers and capacities and relate together hierarchically, these will be enabling hierarchies; therefore, not only are they often complementary in terms of functions and authority, but also decisions made that require collective action must be arrived at by consensus. This is clear when Rollings notes that "if a number of the [priestly] council opposed a particular act or decision it could not take place" (Rollings 1992, 54). This necessity for consensus was not only within the cult but also between the cult and the clans. Indeed, should the principle of autonomy and the pursuit of consensus not be respected, its violation could promote the disaffiliation of the disaffected parties. As Rollings notes, "In 1840, Victor Tixier, a Frenchman who spent the summer hunting with the Osage, noted that a group of young warriors had formed a separate village and called themselves *Bande-des-Chiens.* . . . [It] is likely that they were the beginning of an Osage warrior society"

(Rollings 1992, 36). All this is perfectly consistent with the Dual Clan-Cult model.

Therefore, the dual clan-cult spatial patterning of the Osage village was a unique expression of the arm's-length relation. In this case it was achieved by producing a dual actual/virtual spatial ordering. The clan lodges were actually organized physically and spatially so as to manifest the sacred structure of the cosmos, thereby embedding their clan structure into the cosmic structure, while the cults were virtually organized by their membership's inverted seating plan. This inverted order virtually peripheralized the cult from the clan-village layout, while embodying the cosmos in a pattern unique to the cult. Complementing this arm's-length relation was the division of labor between the village chiefs and the cult, the former dealing with the practicalities of everyday life (however, with built-in midwifery ritual) and the latter with the immanent powers that sustained the world. When the practicalities required modification, while both Bailey and Rollings stress the dominant role of the priestly cults, an alternative reading of the same data can claim that the cults would be called on to perform their duty by generating new ideological rules and associated ritual to legitimize what the village members were already doing.[3] That is, the clan-cult relation constituted an enabling hierarchy that, while recognizing the great esteem of the priestly cult leaders, nevertheless required ongoing negotiated consensus among the leadership for decisions and effective social changes to be carried out.

What is particularly interesting is that the cult was constituted of senior age-grade members of the community. This reverses the age-grade makeup of the cults that has been postulated for the Late Woodland and Terminal Late Woodland world renewal communal cults. In the latter case, I have suggested that these groupings would be based on the junior age-grade and that part of the uniqueness of the Mississippian period would arise from the formation of the ecclesiastic-communal cult system in which senior and junior age-grades would constitute mutualistic arm's-length sectors organized as an enabling hierarchy. However, as suggested above, with the particular historical experience of the world renewal cult heterarchies, the senior age-grade leadership would promote autonomist-proscriptive orientations, and with the disaffiliation of cults from these heterarchies (the so-called collapse of Cahokia), an Osage-type system might very well emerge in certain cases. Thus, the senior age-grade leadership would come to sustain the cult formations, while the junior age-grades would pursue more "secular" concerns, particularly of a collective foraging and military nature, both of which would also be richly shot through with ritual prescriptions and proscriptions.

Of course, this historical developmental scheme is both incomplete and incompletely demonstrated. It stands as a hypothesis that can be built upon and used to guide research and interpretive analyses of the empirical data. Nevertheless, when combined with the account of the Terminal Late Woodland–Mississippian transition under the Integrated-to-Bifurcated Settlement Articulation model and the World Renewal Cult Heterarchy model, the empirical basis of this speculative historical interpretation strengthens the validity of the Ideological Cult Faction model and the characterization of Cahokia as a world renewal cult heterarchy that ultimately disaffiliated. To complete this upward loop of the hermeneutic spiral, I will show how the theoretical scheme that I have presented can be used to address and resolve a set of puzzles that a major scholarly proponent of the hierarchical monistic modular polity account has noted and analyzed in detail. I summarize the anomalous data, critique his account, and present the alternatives below.

COMPLETING (FOR NOW) THE CAHOKIAN SPIRAL LOOP

In accordance with the hermeneutic spiral method, an important part of testing alternative models is done by addressing the empirical anomalies that each raises and assessing which model most effectively and reasonably resolves them. I have been resolving anomalies raised by the heterarchical polyistic localecentric account throughout this book, recursively modifying my original models in the light of the data and even generating new ones, while at the same time maintaining the core premises as applied to the archaeological record, such as the notion of an immanentist cosmology, a squatter ethos, the Sacred Earth principle, the essential contradiction of human existence that this implicates, the inclusive territorial and custodial domain perspective, the dual clan-cult structure, and so on. The result is that the current account that I present in this volume is considerably different from my original working models while still sustaining a fundamental continuity with their core premises. Therefore, it is up to others who wish to challenge my account to zero in on and critique any empirical anomalies and theoretical weaknesses that they note, and then show how their alternative accounts can rectify these theoretical infelicities and dissolve the anomalies.[4]

Some might despair over this method, claiming that it presumes that we can never achieve "the truth." However, that is precisely the point I have been stressing in this book. My position is that we can never generate notions or models of the prehistoric world that fully fit it as it really was. However, we can generate "best-fit truths," these being the rationally closest approximations of the ways of that world that we can make now, given our current state of empirical and theoretical knowledge. That is, we can choose rationally among the alternative approximations that are presented, basing our choice on both the reasoned assessment of the validity of the theory and theoretical presuppositions used to construct these approximations (that is, the alternative models) and then assessing the fit of these models by showing how one enhances our understanding of the relevant empirical data more fully and adequately than do the others. In this way, the hermeneutic spiral is an ongoing critique and production of our theoretically elucidated and empirically grounded knowledge.

Empirical Anomalies and Theoretical Infelicities

I will now focus on several important empirical anomalies of and quite high level theoretical infelicities that arise from the hierarchical monistic modular polity account of the American Bottom archaeological record. I did not choose these anomalies myself; they have already been recognized and discussed in depth by Vernon James Knight Jr., one of the major proponents of the hierarchical monistic modular polity account of the Mississippian period (1997, 231–34). Recently he has given a detailed comparison of the developmental histories of Cahokia and Moundville, arguing that these were two paramount chiefdoms that were mutually independent expressions of the Mississippian-type social system. While he finds that the parallels are striking, he comments that because Cahokia "was built on a uniquely grand scale, and the timing of its rise as a unified polity also appears to be singularly precocious in relation to counterparts such as Lake George, Etowah, or Moundville, . . . Cahokia is an awkward beast," and in fact, "its untidy bulk tugs forcefully at the seams of textbook-variety generalizations by which its lesser counterparts might be accommodated." He even comments that it is not "geographically in the Southeast," adding that "the story of southeastern prehistory might be more comfortably told if Cahokia did not exist" (Knight 1997, 229–30).

With these initial comments, we might expect that he would proceed to emphasize the differences between Cahokia and the other later mound locales of the Southeast, thereby, as he says, making their prehistory "more comfortably told." Instead he emphasizes that Cahokia is simply an unusually precocious development of the very same type of social system that evolved later and independently at Moundville. Indeed, the fact that both were hierarchical monistic modular polities is simply the result of separate populations having similar cultures facing the same constraints and pursuing similar paths. He reinforces this claim by asserting that, since Cahokia had already gone through its expansionary Stirling phase when Moundville was just entering its equivalent period, the histories of these two social systems were actually out of temporal phase. Therefore, we "may be justified in treating any developmental similarities as the consequence of parallel stimulations to generally similar cultural and natural systems, without the complication of factoring out mutual interactions" (Knight 1997, 235).[5]

Nevertheless, while emphasizing that some of the resemblances between the two multiple-mound sites "are comparatively unremarkable," Knight comments that other resemblances "are relatively unanticipated and therefore pose intriguing questions to be answered in our ongoing attempts to build satisfactory theoretical accounts" (Knight 1997, 242). Drawing from historical and ethnographic analogy, he recognizes several parallels that he initially treats as anomalies under his hierarchical account. He goes on to attempt to resolve these but, in my view, without success. First, he accepts the ruptural view of late prehistoric times that I have shown is currently prominent in the work of many American Bottom archaeologists. In this regard, he argues that the settlements of both regions experienced a rather rapid transformation from being egalitarian agricultural villages to being full-fledged paramount chiefdoms in which noble classes subordinated rural commoners. The transformation took only about 125 to 150 years in each case. Furthermore, the intermediary stage of simple chiefdoms that this transformation normally requires, according to the theory that Knight favors, was unusually brief, only decades, or, as he describes it, "a phase reduced to near archaeological invisibility, an eye-blink of no more than a few generations" (Knight 1997, 243). He also recognizes a trend that is an even more significant anomaly in my view. According to demographic and construction data, both paramount chiefdoms experienced a rapid, almost explosive expansion and political consolidation lasting for about half the period of each respective occupation, followed in both cases by a long, drawn-out period of diminishing activity, with each of the dominance-based hierarchies fading out from the archaeological record. Knight puts it very well: "These polities lasted three hundred to four hundred years, nearly half of which time, in each case, was in an apparently devolved and decentralized condition following an earlier spurt of aristocratic exorbitance and focus on paramountcy. The late stage is characterized by erratic new construction of public architecture, generally low levels of traffic in foreign luxuries, and, perhaps surprisingly, the total absence of military defense" (Knight 1997, 244). He particularly notes the drawn-out nature of this second half of their social existence: "Of special interest is the length of time each polity was able to survive in this manner before finally withering away. This merely raises unanswerable questions, pointing to the need for more data on how aristocracy was functioning during this interval" (Knight 1997, 244).

Although he notes that these anomalies raise "unanswerable questions" in the absence of adequate data, he nevertheless attempts to answer them by speculating that both Cahokia and Moundville had become mature or, as he calls them, structural paramountcies. For him, this type of paramountcy is intrinsically stable, having the attribute of "culturally encoded ... inertia": "Our prehistoric exemplars had become, by contrast, *structural* paramountcies, with culturally encoded hierarchical properties whose inertia alone could carry them forward" (Knight 1997, 246, emphasis in original). This is essentially the same explanation that was given by Timothy Pauketat and Thomas Emerson with regard to the claimed long, drawn-out dissolution of Cahokia, except for their implication that the fact that Cahokia lasted as long as it did is something of a miracle: "Cahokia's dissolution and the scattering of its residents to the four winds likewise may have been a process generated from within.... Given the well-known instability of chiefdoms, Cahokia stood little chance of lasting beyond a couple of centuries. The significance of its drawn-out ending, however, lies in the transformation of central Cahokia from a political capital to a sacred center and cemetery" (Pauketat and Emerson 1997b, 277–78).[6]

In short, Knight notes three puzzles that, he claims, are common to the developmental histories of both Cahokia and Moundville: (1) the rapidity of the radical, deep-structural transformations of the two social systems from egalitarianism to hierarchical aristocratic dominance while passing through an almost archaeologically invisible and certainly short transitional period of simple chiefdoms; (2) a period of rapid expansion and political-military consolidation of aristocratic paramountcies manifested in massive monumental constructions as well as economic wealth and concentration; (3) a long, drawn-out period of decentralization and ceremonialism, during which each system finally faded into prehistoric oblivion.

In terms of the hierarchical monistic modular polity account, are any of these expected? Instead of a rapid transformation from an egalitarian to a hierarchical system, should there not be a slow, gradual historical development? Knight notes this possibility. However, instead of treating the shortness of the transformation period as a problem that reflects unfavorably on the hierarchical monistic modular polity account, he treats it as a factual finding that undermines the "gradualist" hierarchical monistic modular polity versions of Cahokia and/or Moundville: "Only 125 to 150 years separates egalitarian, village-level societies from their maize-growing offspring who lived as tributaries to quite large regionally centralized polities. This accelerated timing will fly against any gradualist model of the development of complexity" (Knight 1997, 243). Therefore, the puzzle is dissolved by declaring that it is not a puzzle. Instead, the postulated rapid social transition is taken to be an archaeological fact, the discovery of which adds to archaeological knowledge about the dynamism of the Mississippian period cultures. The even briefer transition from simple chiefdoms to regional paramountcies is treated in the same manner, as an additional archaeological fact that can be added to our knowledge. However, this fact needs some extra theoretical bolstering because, as illustrated in the above quotation of Pauketat and Emerson's 1997 views, the theory that most or many proponents of the hierarchical account use is that a dominant chiefdom is rent by intraelite factionalism and breaks into constituent elements, after which one of these elements or a neighboring chiefdom expands by conquest to fill the power vacuum, becoming dominant and then in turn destabilizing and collapsing, and so the cycle goes, while the basic social structure is reproduced. That is, chiefdoms are famously unstable, and this attribute results in a rather rapid cycling of growth, competition, collapse, but typically no structural changes.

In this regard, Knight comments on the same paper by Hally and colleagues that I note in an earlier chapter was cited by David Anderson (1997, 256–57). In this case, in their paper on the Coosa complex chiefdom, David Hally and colleagues (1990, 133) conclude that "Little Egypt and the Carters site cluster may have been the politically most important town and chiefdom in the region in A.D. 1450, but it is difficult to tell this from the available archaeological evidence." Anderson recognizes this as a problem, but he is not led to wonder whether, in fact, Cahokia might not be a paramountcy at all but quite a different type of social entity. In contrast, Knight (1997, 245) recognizes that "this is a very important discrepancy." While noting that this discrepancy cannot be fully resolved at this time, he does hazard two suggestions. First, he suggests that these historical paramountcies were in their first century of existence and, but for the European intrusion, some of these "could have achieved the scale and stability of a Moundville or even a Cahokia" (Knight 1997, 245). However, apparently not fully satisfied with this possibility, he then, as I note above, postulates that unlike the mature or "structural" types, such as Cahokia, these unstable historical types were "*opportunistic* paramountcies" (Knight 1997, 246, emphasis in original). In this view, opportunistic chiefdoms have too brief an existence to generate the type of archaeological record that structural chiefdoms can and must generate.

I will accept the method Knight has used here. When puzzles or anomalies are recognized, if patterns exist that do not fit the model, then the model should be changed to fit the empirical data. In this case, Knight theorizes that we may be dealing not with fundamentally different types of social systems but simply with different types of chiefdoms (for example, opportunistic and structural) that have essentially the same social structural axes.[7] However, there are two problems with his model modification: one substantive, the other theoretical. While it might be the case that chiefdoms can be differentiated in this way, Knight does not present any historical chiefdom of this structural type by which a material cultural comparison with Cahokia and Moundville could be effected. Therefore, as it stands, this is an account by means of speculative typology. Of course, this absence of data could be corrected by further research, and therefore Knight's account can stand as a hypothesis. The theoretical problem, however, is more serious. The changes modify but do not reject the old model; therefore, this modification cannot contradict other claims made under the original model without undermining its validity. Furthermore, the new or modified version of the model must be based on sound theory. Of course, Knight does admit that these are simply suggestions, but in making them he has committed himself to some significant theoretical claims. First, he claims that mature or structural chiefdoms persist past their prime through inertia. This notion is borrowed from physics: in physics, inertia means that X will continue in the same manner unless some countervailing force is applied. Therefore, if X continues, then no countervailing force has intervened.

Is this analogy relevant or is it possibly misleading, obscuring where it should illuminate? In social systems terms, precisely what is culturally encoded and induced hierarchical inertia? Hierarchy must be continually reproduced through the ongoing activities that it makes possible, because these activities reproduce the hierarchy. These activities are defined and fully discussed under the hierarchical account (chapters 1, 10 , and 11) as the whole panoply of collective practices: ritual construction, wealth burials, military defense, and so on. These activities are claimed to have generated and characterized both Cahokia and Moundville, and, of course, all the exploitative corvée labor and tribute that elite dominance entails would be included. Surely what is meant by the term *inertia* in this case is the continuation of all this exploitative activity and its structural entailments, by which elites reproduced their power only to exercise it in the same or equivalent ways again and again and again. Is there any sense, therefore, in saying that this dominance-based "power-over" hierarchy persists in the absence of the very type of activity that dominance generates and must continue to generate if it is to survive? Is it not more exact to note that when the power differentials immanent in a dominance hierarchy are no longer manifested in the material activity or in its tangible material residue, they no longer exist? Hence, to characterize the absence of major construction, the absence of exotics, and the absence of centralized population at Cahokia (and Moundville) as the continuation of the same social power that generated these components but by means of sacred inertia is simply to obfuscate in order to rescue the model.

This conclusion can also be applied to Pauketat and Emerson's invoking the same argument. As they assert (Pauketat and Emerson 1997b, 277–78), the "significance of its drawn-out ending . . . lies in the transformation of central Cahokia from a political capital to a sacred center and cemetery." This is not to deny that both Cahokia and Moundville, as paramountcies, could have become places specialized for sacred ritual, as such. However, the implications of the hierarchical monistic modular polity account entail that transforming Cahokia into a "sacred center and cemetery" would simply mean that the political power was displaced and relocated in total; therefore, there should be a second "Cahokia." However, there is none—at least, none of which I am aware that has been targeted in the American Bottom archaeological literature. Instead, all parties admit that from A.D. 1250 on, the American Bottom experienced population reduction, small-scale and local dispersed villages, and the absence of indicators of the type of chiefly power that was supposedly the cause of Cahokia of the Lohmann and Stirling phases or of Moundville of the Moundville I phase (Knight and Steponaitis 1998, 13).

The second theoretical commitment to this opportunistic-structural distinction relates back to the later Terminal Late Woodland period Lindeman/Edelhardt phase. The settlements of this phase would seem to fit the opportunistic type. However, according to this scheme, which recognizes that such small opportunistic chiefdoms are unstable, the cycle of rising and falling should have been at least one hundred years, and the overall extension of this cyclical period leading up to a structural paramountcy should have been several centuries. This is, in fact, noted by Knight when he comments that "David Hally's data from the Georgia area, dealing mainly with simple Mississippian chiefdoms rather than regional paramountcies, show that they seldom lasted for more than a century. These small chiefdoms rose and fell with steady regularity for several hundred years across a volatile political landscape" (Knight 1997, 244). Instead, as Knight notes, the era of small chiefdoms in the American Bottom was "an eye-blink of no more than a few generations" (Knight 1997, 243). However, he treats this anomaly as factual and uses this "fact," along with the very short Terminal Late Woodland period of about 150 years between the supposed egalitarianism of the Late Woodland kinship-based village and the hierarchical "Big Bang" of Cahokia, to counter gradualist arguments.

Discussion

I have made it clear on theoretical grounds that I am very skeptical of the claims that abrupt and radical material cultural changes necessarily mark the type of abrupt and radical sociocultural changes that this historical processualist version of the hierarchical monistic modular polity account makes (Fortier and McElrath 2002, 203; Pauketat 2000, 34–35; 2002, 152–54). In the social and cultural terms that I have developed in this book, social systems are characterized by both deep and surface structures. Hence, through the direct intentional perceptual/action engagements we have with the world (as mediated by our worldview/ideology), the deep structures of cosmology/ethos and the basic social structures are realized and largely unwittingly but necessarily reproduced. This dual structuring is the basis for my claim that the actual, observable social patterns of dispersed village and cult heterarchy constituting the bifurcated settlement articulation mode of the Mississippian period are, in fact, surface structural expressions of the same deep social structures of clan and cult that were manifested in the integrated settlement articulation mode that I refer to as the compound plaza-periphery village system of the later Terminal Late Woodland period. This dual surface structure/deep structure perspective dissolves the gradualism/rupturalism debate that Andrew Fortier and Dale McElrath (2002, 173–74) have outlined as occurring among the proponents of the hierarchical monistic modular polity account by allowing for the fact that historical development can systematically occur without deep evolutionary change. Hence, my perspective recognizes that the *longue durée* of sociocultural systems resides in the durability of deep structures while the variability of human-scaled everyday time is largely the transformation of surface structures of sociocultural systems, the latter being clearly prone to modify quickly while the deep structures, as the very condition of possibility of this modifying, remain largely untouched and are reproduced.[8]

This is the theoretical approach to social and cultural systems that I have promoted and developed in this book. Therefore, in these terms, despite the radical material modifications of the settlement system that generated Cahokia and similar multiple-mound locales, I deny that these mark deep structural transformations of the sort that Knight, Emerson, and Pauketat perceive. Rather, they are largely the medium and outcome of surface structural changes, a shift from one settlement articulation mode to another that left the deep cultural and social structures largely but certainly not completely untouched. The immanentist cosmology and squatter ethos constituting the deep structures of the local cultural tradition and the deep structure of the clan-cult social relation remained intact. What was modified was the manner in which these were manifested; this means that it was the ideological rules underwriting ritual innovations, themselves motivated by the perception of increasing subsistence- and settlement-generated sacred pollution (such perception presupposing an immanentist cosmology and squatter ethos), that promoted the strategic spatial disengaging of cults and clans from the compound plaza-periphery integrated village and the formation of the bifurcated settlement articulation mode. Of course, this disengagement had unforeseen consequences.[9] However, these also were responded to largely by negotiated surface structural ideological changes, inspired by the history of changing conditions that I outline above (for example, prevalence of the autonomist factions, trends toward disaffiliation, long-distance recruiting of new cult alliances located in the northern upland regions, introduction of new mortuary rituals, and so on), while the deep structures remained largely intact since the latter constituted the conditions of possibility of such ideological changes.

This approach can account for the anomalies that Knight has noted without requiring further modification of my basic model. Therefore, I treat the puzzles that he raises (namely, the deep structural transformations of a kinship-based egalitarianism to a ranked kinship-based hierarchy occurring in a mere 150 years or so) as simply products of the hierarchical account; therefore, the validity of the postulated radical structural transformation hinges on the adequacy of that account. That is, I deny his claim of radical change—and much of the discussion in this book from chapter 8 onward constitutes the empirical and theoretical grounds for this rejection. Therefore, in terms of the heterarchical polyistic locale-centric account, the process of settlement change that occurred during this period (as fully analyzed in chapters 6, 7, and 8) was the developing of the peripheral-integrated settlement articulation mode typical of the later Late Woodland period through several innovative plaza-periphery types of integrated settlement articulation modes, as well as mortuary/world renewal ritual modifications (specified in chapter 14 and chapter 15 in the light of the upland mortuary data). In the latter part of this period, illustrated by the George Reeves–mid-Lindeman phase complex village at the Range site, the settlement pattern manifests early cult alliances straining the fabric of this compound plaza-periphery integrated settlement articulation mode because of the degree of perceived settlement- and subsistence-generated sacred/natural pollution that it was causing. An innovative step was to spatially disengage the clans and cults. Thus, the "Big Bang" that Pauketat (1997, 31–32) characterizes as the abrupt emergence of a collaborative paramountcy that quickly developed on the southern bank of Cahokia Creek is accounted for by the World Renewal Cult Heterarchy model as the material consequence of these disengaged cults in their alliances forming their own sacred mound locales and quite quickly transforming their traditional upland mortuary locales into auxiliary CBLs and shifting much of the terminal postmortem mortuary/world renewal ritual to the floodplain, all this being the process whereby cult alliances cooperatively and competitively generated the multiple-mound world renewal cult heterarchies. None of these world renewal cult heterarchies were chiefdoms, in the sense of being hierarchical monistic modular polities. However, they were distinctly different forms of places from anything that had existed previously in the American Bottom. Importantly, none of this distinction entailed significant deep structural changes.

The "inertia" anomaly of a long, drawn-out Moorehead and (possibly) Sand Prairie phase fading of the "sacred" powers of the "mighty chiefs" of Cahokia—the latter claimed to be manifested in the Lohmann and Stirling phases—is similarly dissolved by the World Renewal Cult Heterarchy model. In its terms, the social powers that were manifested in Cahokia and similar multiple-mound cult heterarchy sites never resided there. Despite the tensions and shifts caused by the postulated centralist-autonomist cult factional competition, these social powers pretty well always resided in the base locales of the autonomous cults distributed across the countryside. Hence, social powers were manifested but not vested in Cahokia. The World Renewal Cult Heterarchy model, therefore, can very easily account for both the perceived decentralization and the apparent reduction of the Cahokian population, a process described in the preceding chapter that started in the Stirling phase with the developing success of the autonomist factions over the centralist factions, even though this marked the time of the major expansion of construction. This model can also account for the apparently long, drawn-out nature of Cahokia's so-called collapse during the later Mississippian period, explaining this as the consequence of the autonomist factions succeeding at last in fettering the centralist factions while simultaneously shifting more resources to local concerns.

More to the point, however, as I have noted several times in this chapter, the most current data now indicate that there probably was no long, drawn-out demise of Cahokia. Rather, as Pauketat notes, "the Moorehead phase was seemingly short lived, and the best dates now suggest a potentially rapid political-economic decline between A.D. 1275 and 1300. Cemetery evidence and a lack of significant Sand Prairie phase habitation remains from greater Cahokia bear this out" (Pauketat 2002, 162–63). As I discuss below, while the World Renewal Cult Heterarchy model can accommodate either the long, drawn-out or the abrupt demise scenario, it would postulate quite different conditions for each.

In short, both this centralized expansion of Cahokia and either its drawn-out or its abrupt demise would be the expression of the ongoing strength of the autonomist factions coupled with a shifting emphasis toward proscriptive ceremonialism, probably further exacerbated, as I note above, by a growing disaffiliation among cult alliances caused by ideological disputes about what would count as felicitous world renewal/mortuary practices. This complex trend would promote the reemergence of the traditional arm's-length relation between the upper and lower sectors of the northern expanse of the American Bottom that may have been originally manifested in the early Terminal Late Woodland Pulcher/Late Bluff ceramic tradition.

The Demise of Cahokia

As noted above, recent work by Emerson and colleagues that they refer to as the Cahokian Collapse Project has resulted in some serious reassessment of the twilight-of-the-sacred-chiefdom view. First (as I note in chapter 12 and discuss in detail in chapter 14), on the basis of a new suite of radiocarbon dates, Emerson has established that the East St. Louis Stone Quarry mortuary data are not properly dated to the Sand Prairie phase. Instead, they relate to the late or terminal Moorehead phase, which he dates to A.D. 1275–1300 (Emerson 2002, 137–38). These dates overlap with the Kane Mounds dates. As I further noted, he and his colleagues have also argued that the two mortuary records (the Kane Mounds site representing the northern sector of the American Bottom, particularly the bluff ridge and upland region, and the East St. Louis Stone Quarry site representing the more southern sector) are not fully congruent and, in fact, display some significant differences. On these bases, they postulate a cultural rupture within the region. Interestingly, as a result of this new dating, Emerson (2002, 138) has also commented that there are currently no Sand Prairie phase mortuary data in the American Bottom and very little Sand Prairie cultural material at all in Cahokia. The upshot of this reconsideration is a major reversal of their original claim about the mode of Cahokian demise. As Emerson comments, "In 1991 I stated confidently that Cahokia did not go out with a bang but a fizzle. Today I would be much more hesitant regarding that statement. Whereas our understanding of the Cahokian coalescence has increased dramatically, the same cannot be said for our understanding of Cahokia's end" (Emerson 2002, 137). Indeed, he now concludes that the hegemony of Cahokia terminated rapidly by or shortly after A.D. 1300, which he also stipulates to be the end of the Moorehead phase. He states, "Reexamining the available data, the precipitous and abrupt decline of the Cahokian polity about A.D. 1300 seems most likely due to political and social collapse. We now know that Cahokia started with a 'bang'—we suspect it may have ended the same way" (Emerson 2002, 138–39).

It is notable that he characterizes this rapid demise in both political and social terms, since this would seem to preserve the basic premises of the hierarchical monistic modular polity account by according with the claim that paramount chiefdoms are famously unstable. However, it does not. As I note above, according to the hierarchical account, the demise of Cahokia as a paramount chiefdom should be followed by either the emergence of a second "Cahokia" or, just as likely, the rapid development of multiple although smaller "Cahokias" competing for dominance. None of this happens. Rather, the rapid demise of Cahokia was followed by a rather rapid abandonment of the American Bottom. In this regard, therefore, I would point out that the rapidity of the demise of Cahokia and the abandonment of the American Bottom are fully consistent with the heterarchical polyistic locale-centric account (as noted above). In addition, this account could also accommodate the slow demise view, while postulating a different range of conditions promoting it. However, since the data seem clearly to indicate a rapid demise, I will simply review how the World Renewal Cult Heterarchy model would account for a rapid demise.

In these terms, Cahokia was an affiliation of autonomous cult alliances. Except for a small core of permanent administrators representing the different cult alliances, it would have been occupied mostly by transient members of the constituent autonomous cults that were the building blocks of the alliances. Therefore, transient residency was a function of cult participation, and the latter was a function of commitments made and changed by autonomous cults in their deliberations carried out in the cult nodal sites dispersed across the countryside, both in the American Bottom and, at least until the end of the Stirling phase, in the nearby upland regions. Just as Cahokia and the other world renewal cult heterarchies were brought into existence by decision-making processes that were performed in multiple cult locales dispersed across the countryside, so also would their demise be determined by decisions made in similar multiple autonomous cult locales. The continuity, expansion, and/or demise of the cult heterarchies, therefore, would be a function of the balance of power among the ideological factions. Should this power remain toward the presbyterian center, representing a balancing of the proscriptive and pre-scriptive factions, the overall status of cult heterarchies would remain constant, with the reputation of individual cult heterarchies varying according to their competitive success or failure in respect to each other. Should there be a shift toward the episcopalian pole, we would anticipate a radical expansion of the cult heterarchies as the prescriptive centralist factions began to centralize pow-er at the cost of the proscriptive autonomous factions.

However, a shift toward the congregationalist pole would indicate that the proscriptive factions were prevailing; although one or two of the cult heterar-chies might at first expand at the cost of the others, later a rather rapid decline of even these heterarchies would be expected. This decline would result from the demise of the centralist factions and the working out of the pursuits of cults under the influence of ideological strategies of the proscriptive autonomist fac-tions. The latter would be very sensitive to any attempt of one or two alliances to develop alternative ritual forms, since this would be taken as constraining cult autonomy. The result could be expected: the innovation of new forms of traditional mortuary-mediated ritual could rapidly lead to disaffiliations of those cults that were more traditionalist. A rapid abandonment of the world renewal cult heterarchies would occur and, ultimately, the reestablishment of an integrated settlement articulation mode and the abandonment of the Amer-ican Bottom. Indeed, this postulated trajectory neatly fits Emerson's discussion of the emerging variation in the mortuary residue in the late Moorehead phase as outlined above (and more fully discussed in chapter 15) and summarizes the historical developmental scenario that I provide at the beginning of this chapter.

Appendix A

Sponemann Site, Sponemann Phase, Sitewide Ubiquity, and Exclusivity Indices

The empirical demonstration of the mixing-prohibition hypothesis requires determining the distribution of archaeobotanical remains across the Sponemann site. The question this appendix addresses is how to compute both the ubiquity index (UI) and the exclusivity index (EI) of each of the targeted species of the Sponemann phase of the Sponemann site. (Appendix B repeats this process for Community/Cluster 3 of the same site.)

The EI is the proportion of exclusive-to-shared features in which a given species is found. For example, of the 143 features in which maize is found in the Sponemann phase of the Sponemann site, there are 35 in which it is an isolate, that is, in which there were no identifiable representatives of any of the other four targeted species. The exclusivity index (EI) for each of the targeted species is defined here, therefore, as the total number of features in which the particular targeted species is found as an isolate in proportion to the total set of features having identifiable remains of the five species. In this case, the targeted species are maize, chenopodium, maygrass, erect knotweed, and little barley. If there are significant differences in the UIs of these five species, then we may assume that the species with the highest UI will be the most widely dispersed (that is, it will be found in the greatest proportion of the available features). For this reason, it should be found to be an isolate in a fairly large proportion of these features. Since the species with the highest UI will occupy a disproportionately large number of the available features, those species with lower UIs will have a more narrow span of distribution, and there will be disproportionately fewer features in which they could be isolates. Hence, under the null hypothesis we can expect that the EIs of species having lower UIs will be disproportionately lower than the EIs of species having higher UIs. Should a given species have an EI that is greater than would be expected given its UI, this would suggest that it was treated during processing in such a manner as to increase its normal chances of being an isolate. If alternative explanations for this reversal can be analyzed and dismissed, the null hypothesis can be rejected. From this we can infer that care was likely taken in the processing of this species to ensure its separation from the others. If the species that was treated in this manner was maize, this finding would be considered as supporting the mixing-prohibition hypothesis and, by extension, would be support for the Sacred Maize model (chapter 6).

Procedure

First it was necessary to sort out the total number of features into those containing identifiable residue of one or more of the targeted species from those not having any. The latter features were not included in this analysis. Therefore, all UIs and EIs were based on only the total of the sampled features having identifiable residues of one or more of these five targeted species. These features then were sorted into groupings so as to permit computation of both the UIs and the EIs of each category of species.

Table Descriptions

Table A.1 is a two-by-two table used to first separate those sampled features containing residue of one or more of the five targeted species from those features that have no such residue. It is based on two dimensions: (1) seed crops: present/absent; and (2) maize: present/absent. From this the UI and EI of maize were directly determined since, as shown in Table A.1, panels A and B display the total set of features with maize, subdivided between maize and seeds mixed (panel A) and maize only (panel B). Panel C displays all those features that have seed present but no maize, and it is internally divided into four subpanels according to the presence or absence of chenopodium and maygrass: subpanels C-1, C-2, C-3, and C-4. Panel D, of course, displays all those sampled features that had no identifiable residues of any of the five targeted species.

Table A.2 subdivides panel A of Table A.1, that is, those features having maize and seeds mixed, and Table A.3 subdivides panel C of Table A.1. Table A.2 is based on two dimensions: (1) maygrass: present/absent; and (2) chenopodium: present/absent. This generated four panels: E, F, G, and H. Panel E displays all those maize features with seeds that included both chenopodium and maygrass, along with erect knotweed and/or little barley. I then sorted out the features containing the latter two seed species and placed these immediately beneath in the same panel. I did the same for those features containing maize along with either maygrass or chenopodium in panels F and G, respectively. All those features in Panel H, of course, were maize features having no chenopodium or maygrass but having erect knotweed and/or little barley.

Table A.3 displays all those sampled features having one or more representations of the four seed species but no maize. It is also based on two dimensions:

(1) maygrass: present/absent; and (2) chenopodium: present/absent. Thus, in effect it reproduces the contents of panel C of Table A.1; these are shown in Table A.3 as panels C-1, C-2, C-3, and C-4. Each panel was further subdivided on the basis of presence/absence of erect knotweed and/or little barley. Determining the UIs for each of the seed species was then simply a matter of totaling all those features in each panel in which each seed species was represented and dividing these totals by the total number of features having identifiable representation of the five targeted species. The UIs/EIs of each of the targeted species were individually computed (see Tables A.4 through A.9). In each case, the EI of a targeted species was computed by using only the number of features in which the species was found as an isolate and dividing this by the total number of sampled features having representation of one or more of the five targeted species. (The sitewide UIs and EIs for all five targeted species are displayed in Table 6.1.) Included for comparison are the EI/UI ratios for each of the targeted species.

I computed the modified EI for each of the targeted species (shown in Tables A.4 through A.9). The modified EI of each species is computed using only the total number of sampled features with representation of the given targeted species. The modified EI neutralizes to some degree the influence of the UI, thereby allowing for a direct comparison of the EI/UI ratio. For example, while maize has a sitewide UI of only 0.39, it has a modified EI of 0.24, indicating that maize was an isolate in effectively one-quarter of the features containing it. In comparison, while maygrass has a much higher sitewide UI of 0.72, almost double the UI of maize, its modified EI of 0.30 is only marginally higher than the modified EI of maize. In fact, proportionally, the modified EI/UI ratio—in the tables, shown as EI(M)/UI—of maize is the highest of all the targeted species. This highlights the likelihood that maize was given special treatment in processing to ensure that it was minimally mixed with the other targeted species, thereby giving strong grounds to reject the null hypothesis and accept the mixing-prohibition hypothesis. (Table 6.2 displays the sitewide modified EIs for the five targeted species, as well as the EI(M)/UI ratio.)

Table A.1. Sitewide Distribution of Maize- and Seed-Containing Features

Seed Present	Seed Absent

Maize Present

A	B
9 19 23 56 66 69 77 80 92 106 134	7 21 40 131 192 213 228 240 242 256
155 156 168 191 203 216 217 218	309 335 348 350 378 408 411 414 424
223 233 236 244 257 258 264 268	461 474 476 481 483 493 495 507 531
271 272 276 280 281 283 284 293	572 591 659 678 793 876 879 [$N = 35$]
296 299 303 316 318 319 320 322	
329 336 346 353 366 372 373 375	
386 390 395 399 406 413 425 433	
439 440 444 445 463 464 466 470	
477 479 482 485 487 488 500 504	
508 511 512 542 557 561 592 599	
606 649 655 673 680 685 688 730	
740 751 762 823 824 825 829 839	
842 845 848 853 859 874 875 882	
894 [$N = 108$]	

Maize Absent

C	D
C-1. Maygrass and chenopod: 11 13	6 10 12 18 24 25 30 37 62 63 87
26 28 31 32 33 51 71 82 86 95 98	88 97 99 107 109 117 123 125
112 137 149 150 151 159 176 182	131 161 162 164 167 170 189 245
184 188 290 291 300 307 314 355	265 273 277 279 317 340 352 357
358 359 360 362 368 374 387 393	371 384 398 417 428 429 435 438
397 400 401 402 405 410 426 432	443 452 455 460 472 484 497 499
473 513 522 523 524 535 560 585	501 536 540 541 543 547 555 558
625 650 700 738 773 861 864 869	567 577 581 596 597 607 799 800
900 [$N = 62$]	857 870 [$N = 69$]
C-2. Maygrass only: 14 29 34 38	
39 41 42 44 45 49 50 52 53 64 67	
70 73 76 79 83 85 94 101 104 111	
115 116 119 120 122 128 132 133	
139 140 141 145 146 147 148 152	
153 160 163 165 179 186 200 207	
221 225 234 238 241 243 252 262	
269 275 278 285 289 292 294 295	
304 310 321 330 334 345 354 361	
369 379 380 382 383 385 391 392	
403 407 415 416 418 419 430 434	
441 447 448 451 454 458 468 471	
475 480 489 490 510 515 516 520	
530 534 544 548 553 565 593 731	
790 852 865 871 872 [$N = 118$]	

continued

C-3. Chenopod and erect knotweed
and/or little barley: 4 5 36 74 75
102 157 158 181 205 226 230 286
338 363 370 389 404 509 566 590
594 595 743 851 880 [*N* = 26]
C-4. Erect knotweed and/or
little barley: 61 65 126 202
220 266 267 297 333 356 394 431
437 462 496 562 586 598 628 877
881 [*N* = 21]

Table A.2. Distribution of Panel A of Table A.1: All Features Containing Maize and Seeds

Chenopodium Present	Chenopodium Absent
Maygrass Present	
E	F
9 19 56 134 168 233 236 244	66 92 106 155 156 191 203 216
271 280 281 283 303 316 319 346	217 218 223 264 268 272 284 318
375 390 395 406 413 425 433 470	320 322 329 353 366 372 373 386
482 487 488 504 508 557 655 680	399 439 440 444 445 463 466 477
685 730 740 762 823 824 839 848	485 500 542 599 606 649 673 751
853 859 874 [*N* = 43]	829 845 875 882 894 [*N* = 45]
Erect knotweed and little	Erect knotweed and little
barley: 134 271 346 375 390 395	barley: [*N* = 0]
762 874 [*N* = 8]	Erect knotweed: 320 606 829 875 [*N* = 4]
Erect knotweed: 280 406 433 470	Little barley: 191 [*N* = 1]
482 487 504 508 685 730 823 824	
839 848 859 [*N* = 15]	
Little barley: 9 56 236 244 316	
319 853 [*N* = 7]	
Maygrass Absent	
G	H
69 77 80 293 299 464 512 592 688	Erect knotweed and/or little barley: 23
825 842 [*N* = 11]	257 258 276 296 336 479 511 561 [*N* = 9]
Chenopod 69 77 80 293 464 512	Erect knotweed and little
688 825: [*N* = 8]	barley: 479 [*N* = 1]
Erect knotweed and little	Erect knotweed: 257 276 336
barley: [*N* = 0]	511 [*N* = 4]
Erect knotweed: 592* 842 [*N* = 2]	Little barley: 23 258 296
Little barley: 299 [*N* = 1]	561 [*N* = 4]

* Large deposit of erect knotweed—burned, 15,223 seeds.

Table A.3. Distribution of Panel C of Table A.1: All Features with Seeds and without Maize

Chenopodium Present	Chenopodium Absent

Maygrass Present

C-1

11 13 26 28 31 32 33 51 71 82
86 95 98 112 137 149 150 151 159
176 182 184 188 290 291 300 307
314 355 358 359 360 362 368 374
387 393 397 400 401 402 405 410
426 432 473 513 522 523 524 535
560 585 625 650 700 738 773 861
864 869 900 [*N* = 62]
Erect knotweed and little barley:
26 33 51 82 405 864 900 [*N* = 7]
Erect knotweed: 149 150 151 176
182 290 291 358 362 368 387 401
426 432 585 625 700 738 861 869
[*N* = 20]
Little barley: 31 112 188 355
402 473 513 524 560 650 773
[*N* = 11]

C-2

14 29 34 38 39 41 42 44 45 49
50 52 53 64 67 70 73 76 79 83
85 94 101 104 111 115 116 119
120 122 128 132 133 139 140 141
145 146 147 148 152 153 160 163
165 179 186 200 207 221 225 234
238 241 243 252 262 269 275 278
285 289 292 294 295 304 310 321
330 334 345 354 361 369 379 380
382 383 385 391 392 403 407 415
416 418 419 430 434 441 447 448
451 454 458 468 471 475 480 489
490 510 515 516 520 530 534 544
548 553 565 593 731 790 852 865
871 872 [*N* = 118]
Erect knotweed and little barley:
38 116 415 418 419 865 [*N* = 6]
Erect knotweed: 34 120 133 153
179 294 330 361 369 383 407 468
471 480 510 548 565 731 871 872 [*N* = 20]
Little barley: 39 45 49 94 115
122 140 292 354 430 458 [*N* = 11]

Maygrass Absent

C-3

4 5 36 74 75 102 157 158 181
205 226 230 286 338 363 370 389
404 509 566 590 594 595 743 851
880 [*N* = 26]
Chenopod: 4 36 74 75 102 158 226
286 338 389 509 590 595 743
[*N* = 14]
Erect knotweed and little barley:
157 [*N* = 1]
Erect knotweed: 181 205 230 370
404 566 594 851 [*N* = 8]
Little barley: 5 363 880 [*N* = 3]

C-4

Erect knotweed and/or little barley:
61 65 126 202 220 266 267 297
333 356 394 431 437 462 496 562
586 598 628 877 881 [*N* = 21]
Erect knotweed and little barley:
356 [*N* = 1]
Erect knotweed: 61 65 220 266 297
394 431 437 562 586 598 628 877
881 [*N* = 14]
Little barley: 126 202 267 333
462 496 [*N* = 6]

Table A.4. Set of Sampled Features Used as Basis for Sitewide UI/EI Analysis of Targeted Species

Species Presence	Number of Sampled Features
Table A.1 Panel	
A maize and seed	108
B maize only	35
C seed only	227
D no maize or seeds	69
Total sampled features	439
Less features with no maize or seeds	- 69
Total features with maize and seeds	370

Table A.5. Computation of Maygrass UI, EI, and Modified EI with EI(M)/UI Ratio

Maygrass	Number of Sampled Features
Table A.2 Panel	
E maize and maygrass and chenopod	43
F maize and maygrass, no chenopod	45
Table A.3 Panel	
C-1 maygrass and chenopod, no maize	62
C-2 maygrass, no chenopod, no maize	118
Total maygrass	268
Maygrass, no chenopod, no maize	118
Less maygrass with knotweed and/or barley	- 37
Total maygrass only	81

UI: 268/370 = 0.72
EI: 81/370 = 0.22
Modified EI: 81/268 = 0.30
EI(M)/UI: 0.30/0.72 = 0.42

Table A.6. Computation of Maize UI, EI, and Modified EI with EI(M)/UI Ratio

Maize	Number of Sampled Features
Table A.1 Panel	
A maize and seeds	108
B maize only	35
Total maize	143

UI: 143/370 = 0.39
EI: 35/370 = 0.09
Modified EI: 35/143 = 0.24
EI(M)/UI: 0.25/0.39 = 0.64

Table A.7. Computation of Chenopodium UI, EI, and Modified EI with EI(M)/UI Ratio

Chenopodium	Number of Sampled Features
Table A.2 Panel	
E chenopod and maize and maygrass	43
G chenopod and maize, no maygrass	11
Table A.3 Panel	
C-1 maygrass and chenopod, no maize	62
C-3 chenopod, no maygrass, no maize	26
Total chenopod	142
Chenopod, no maygrass, no maize	26
Less chenopod with barley and/or knotweed only	- 12
Total chenopod only	14

UI: 142/370 = 0.38
EI: 14/370 = 0.04
Modified EI: 14/142 = 0.10
EI(M)/UI: 0.10/0.38 = 0.26

Table A.8. Computation of Erect Knotweed UI, EI, and Modified EI with EI(M)/UI Ratio

Erect Knotweed	Number of Sampled Features
Table A.2 Panel	
E Erect knotweed and little barley and chenopod and maygrass and maize	23
F Erect knotweed and maygrass and maize	4
G Erect knotweed and chenopod and maize	2
H Erect knotweed and maize	5
Table A.3 Panel	
C-1 Erect knotweed and little barley and chenopod and maygrass	27
C-2 Erect knotweed and little barley and maygrass	26
C-3 Erect knotweed and little barley and chenopod	9
C-4 Erect knotweed and little barley	1
C-4 Erect knotweed only	14
Total erect knotweed	111

UI: 111/370 = 0.30
EI: 14/370 = 0.04
Modified EI: 14/111 = 0.13
EI(M)/UI: 0.13/0.30 = 0.43

Table A.9. Computation of Little Barley UI, EI, and Modified EI with EI(M)/UI Ratio

Little Barley	Number of Sampled Features
Table A.2 Panel	
E Little barley and erect knotweed and chenopod and maygrass and maize	15
F Little barley and erect knotweed and maygrass and maize	1
G Little barley and erect knotweed and chenopod and maize	1
H Little barley and maize	5
Table A.3 Panel	
C-1 Little barley and chenopod and maygrass, no maize	18
C-2 Little barley and maygrass, no chenopod, no maize	17
C-3 Little barley and chenopod, no maygrass, no maize	4
C-4 Little barley and erect knotweed, no maize	1
C-4 Little barley only	6
Total little barley	68

UI: 68/370 = 0.18
EI: 6/370 = 0.02
Modified EI: 6/68 = 0.09
EI(M)/UI: 0.09/0.19 = 0.50

Appendix B

Sponemann Site, Sponemann Phase, Community 3 Ubiquity, and Exclusivity Indices

To analyze the UIs and EIs of Community 3, I listed and analytically marked and extracted from the sitewide features all the sampled features from Cluster 3 (constituting Community 3) and then subdivided these into the northwestern sector (3b) and the southeastern sector (3a), following the division made by the excavators of the site. The same procedure as outlined in Appendix A for the sitewide analysis of UIs and EIs was then carried out, except that it was limited to Cluster 3 of the Community 3 boundaries. Because the clusterwide EI and UI patterning was similar to the sitewide patterning, I decided that it was not necessary to compute the EI/UI ratios or the modified EIs. Since I compared the distribution of seeds and maize in Community 3 to that of the total site and also compared their distribution between the northwestern and southeastern sectors, I had to prepare one overall table, Table B.1 (with sector distribution distinguished by boldface and italics).

To generate the UIs and EIs for Community 3, I followed the same procedure as I used for the sitewide analysis. However, the UI and EI for each species in Community 3 also have beside them the UIs and EIs for the northwestern and southeastern sectors. Table B.2 is similar to Table A.2 in that it sorts out all the features containing maize in Community 3, subdivided between sectors 3a and 3b (and again distinguished by boldface and italics). Table B.3 focuses on only the seed-containing features in Community 3, subdivided between sectors 3a and 3b. The UIs and EIs for all five targeted species of Community 3, clusterwide, were then computed individually (as shown in Tables B.4 through B.9). (The overall Community 3 UIs and EIs are shown in Table 6.3, and UIs and EIs for sectors 3a and 3b are displayed in Table 6.4.)

Table B.1. Community 3 Distribution of Maize- and Seed-Containing Features by Cluster Sector

Seed Present	Seed Absent

Maize Present

A	B
203 223 236 244 257 258 264 268	228 242 256 309 **335 348 350 378**
271 272 280 281 283 284 293 296	**411 424** 461 **474** 476 481 483 **493**
299 303 **316** 318 319 320 322 **329**	**495** 507 531 572 659 876 879
336 346 353 372 373 375 386 390	[N = 23 (**10** + 13)]
395 425 433 439 440 444 445 463	
464 466 470 477 479 482 485 487	
488 **500** 504 508 511 **839 853 882**	
[N = 56 (**17** + 39)]	

Maize Absent

C	D
C-1. Maygrass and chenopod: **137**	245 265 273 279 317 **340 352 357**
290 291 300 307 **314 355 358 359**	371 384 398 417 **428 435** 443 455
360 362 368 374 387 393 397 401	460 472 **497 499 501** 536 577 596
402 410 426 432 473 **535 625** 861	597 857 [N = 26 (**13** + 13)]
864 [N = 26 (**19** + 7)]	
C-2. Maygrass only: **133** 221 234	
241 262 269 275 278 285 289 292	
294 295 304 **310** 321 330 **334 345**	
354 361 369 379 380 382 383 385	
392 415 416 419 430 434 447 448	
451 454 458 468 471 **475** 480 **489**	
490 510 548 **852 865 871**	
[N=49 (**24** + 25)]	
C-3. Chenopod and erect knotweed	
and/or little barley: 226 230	
286 **338 363 370 389 404 851 880**	
[N = 10 (**7** + 3)]	
C-4. Erect knotweed and/or little	
barley: 202 220 266 267 297	
333 356 431 462 **496 628 877** 881	
[N = 13 (**6** + 7)]	

Note: Boldface indicates features and totals associated with the northwestern sector, while italics indicate features and totals associated with the southeastern sector.

Table B.2. Distribution of Panel A of Table B.1: All Features Containing Maize and Seeds

Chenopodium Present	Chenopodium Absent

Maygrass Present

E

236 244 271 280 281 283 303 **316**
319 **346 375 390 395 425 433** *470*
482 487 488 504 508 **839 853**
[*N* = 23 (**9** + *14*)]
Erect knotweed and little
barley: *271* **346 375 390 395**
[*N* = 5 (**4** + *1*)]
Erect knotweed: *280* **433** *470 482
487 504 508* **839** [*N* = 8 (**2** + *6*)]
Little barley: *244* **316** *319* **853**
[*N* = 4 (**2** + *2*)]

F

*203 223 264 268 272 284 318 320
322* **329 353** *372 373* **386** *439 440
444 445 463 466 477 485* **500 882**
[*N* = 24 (**7** + *17*)]
Erect knotweed: *320* [*N* = 1 [**0** + *1*]
Little barley: [*N* = 0]

Maygrass Absent

G

293 299 464 [*N* = 3 (**0** + *3*)]
Chenopod: *293 464* [*N* = 2 (**0** + *2*)]
Little barley: *299* [*N* = 1 (**0** + *1*)]

H

Erect knotweed and/or little barley: *257
258 296* **336** *479 511* [*N* = 6 (**1** + *5*)]
Erect knotweed and little barley:
479 [*N* = 1 (**0** + *1*)]
Erect knotweed: *257* **336** *511*
[*N* = 3 (**1** + *2*)]
Little barley: *258 296* [*N* = 2 (**0** + *2*)]

Note: Boldface indicates features and totals associated with the northwestern sector, while italics indicate features and totals associated with the southeastern sector.

Table B.3. Distribution of Panel C of Table B.1: All Features with Seeds and without Maize

Chenopodium Present	Chenopodium Absent
Maygrass Present	

C-1

137 *290 291 300 307* **314 355 358 359 360 362 368** *374* **387** *393 397* **401 402 410 426 432** *473 535* **625** *861* **864** [N = 26 (19 + *7*)]

Erect knotweed and little barley:
864 [*N* = 1 (**1** + *0*)]

Erect knotweed: *290 291* **358 362 368 387 401 426 432** *625 861* [*N* = 11 (**8** + *3*)]

Little barley: **355 402** *473* [*N* = 3 (**2** + *1*)]

C-2

133 221 234 241 262 269 275 278 285 289 292 294 295 304 **310** *321 330 334* **345** *354* **361 369 379 380 382 383 385 392 415 416 419 430 434** *447 448 451 454 458 468 471 475 480* **489 490** *510 548* **852 865 871** [*N* = 49 (**24** + *25*)

Erect knotweed and little barley:
415 419 865 [*N* = 3 (**3** + *0*)]

Erect knotweed: **133** *294 330* **361 369 383** *468 471 480 510 548* **871** [*N* = 12 (**5** + *7*)]

Little barley: *292* **354 430** *458* [*N* = 4 (**2** + *2*)]

Maygrass Absent

C-3	C-4
Chenopod and erect knotweed and little barley: *226 230 286* **338 363 370 389 404 851 880** [*N* = 10 (**7** + *3*)]	Erect knotweed and/or little barley: *202 220 266 267 297* **333 356 431** *462* **496 628 877** *881* [*N* = 13 (**6** + *7*)]
Chenopod: *226* **286 338 389** [*N* = 4 (**2** + *2*)]	Erect knotweed and little barley: **356** [*N* = 1 (**1** + *0*)]
Erect knotweed: *230* **370 404 851** [*N* = 4 (**3** + *1*)]	Erect knotweed: *220 266 297* **431 628 877** *881* [*N* = 7 (**3** + *4*)]
Little barley: **363 880** [*N* = 2 (**2** + *0*)]	Little barley: *202* **267 333** *462* **496** [*N* = 5 (**2** + *3*)]

Note: Boldface indicates features and totals associated with the northwestern sector, while italics indicate features and totals associated with the southeastern sector.

Table B.4. Set of Sampled Features Used as Basis for UI and EI Analysis of Targeted Species

Species Presence	Number of Sampled Features		
	Clusterwide	Sector	
		3b	*3a*
Table B.1 Panel			
A maize and seed	56	**17**	*39*
B maize only	23	**10**	*13*
C seed only	98	**56**	*42*
D no maize or seeds	26	**13**	*13*
Total sampled features	203	**96**	*107*
Less features with no maize or seeds	- 26	**- 13**	*- 13*
Total features with maize and seeds	177	**83**	*94*

Note: Boldface indicates features and totals associated with the northwestern sector (**3b**), while italics indicate features and totals associated with the southeastern sector *(3a)*.

Table B.5. Computation of Maygrass UIs and EIs, Clusterwide and by Cluster Sector

Maygrass	Clusterwide	Sector	
		3	*3a*
Table B.2 Panel			
E maize and maygrass and chenopod	23	**9**	*14*
F maize and maygrass, no chenopod	24	**7**	*17*
Table B.3 Panel			
C-1 maygrass and chenopod, no maize	26	**19**	*7*
C-2 maygrass, no chenopod, no maize	49	**24**	*25*
Total maygrass	122	**59**	*63*
Maygrass, no chenopod, no maize	49	**24**	*25*
Less maygrass with knotweed and/or barley	- 19	**- 10**	*- 9*
Total maygrass only	30	**14**	*16*
UI:	122/177 = 0.69	**59/83 = 0.71**	*63/94 = 0.67*
EI:	30/177 = 0.17	**14/83 = 0.17**	*16/94 = 0.17*

Note: Boldface indicates features and totals associated with the northwestern sector, while italics indicate features and totals associated with the southeastern sector.

Table B.6. Computation of Maize UIs and EIs, Clusterwide and by Cluster Sector

Maize	Clusterwide	Sector	
		3	3a
Table B.1 Panel			
A maize and seeds	56	**17**	*39*
B maize only	23	**10**	*13*
Total maize	79	**27**	*52*
UI:	79/177 = 0.45	**27/83 = 0.33**	*52/94 = 0.55*
EI:	23/177 = 0.13	**10/83 = 0.12**	*13/94 = 0.14*

Note: Boldface indicates features and totals associated with the northwestern sector, while italics indicate features and totals associated with the southeastern sector.

Table B.7. Computation of Chenopodium UIs and EIs, Clusterwide and by Cluster Sector

Chenopodium	Clusterwide	Sector	
		3b	3a
Table B.2 Panel			
E chenopod and maize and maygrass	23	**9**	*14*
G chenopod and maize, no maygrass	3	**0**	*3*
Table B.3 Panel			
C-1 maygrass and chenopod, no maize	26	**19**	*7*
C-3 chenopod, no maygrass, no maize	10	**7**	*3*
Total chenopod	62	**35**	*27*
Chenopod, no maygrass, no maize	10	**7**	*3*
Less chenopod with barley and/or knotweed only	- 6	**- 5**	*- 1*
Chenopod only	4	**2**	*2*
UI:	62/177 = 0.35	**35/83 = 0.42**	*27/94 = 0.29*
EI:	4/177 = 0.02	**2/83 = 0.02**	*2/94 = 0.02*

Note: Boldface indicates features and totals associated with the northwestern sector, while italics indicate features and totals associated with the southeastern sector.

Table B.8. Computation of Erect Knotweed UIs and EIs, Clusterwide and by Cluster Sector

Erect Knotweed	Clusterwide	Sector	
		3	*3a*
Table B.2 Panel			
E Erect knotweed and little barley and chenopod and maygrass and maize	13	**6**	*7*
F Erect knotweed and little barley and maygrass and maize	1	**0**	*1*
G Erect knotweed and chenopod and maize	0		
H Erect knotweed and maize	4	**1**	*3*
Table B.3 Panel			
C-1 Erect knotweed and little barley and chenopod and maygrass	12	**9**	*3*
C-2 Erect knotweed and little barley and maygrass	15	**8**	*7*
C-3 Erect knotweed and little barley and chenopod	4	**3**	*1*
C-4 Erect knotweed and little barley	1	**1**	*0*
C-4 Erect knotweed only	7	**3**	*4*
Total erect knotweed	57	**31**	*26*
UI:	57/177 = 0.32	**31/83 = 0.37**	*26/94 = 0.28*
EI:	7/177 = 0.04	**3/83 = 0.04**	*4/94 = 0.04*

Note: Boldface indicates features and totals associated with the northwestern sector, while italics indicate features and totals associated with the southeastern sector.

Table B.9. Computation of Little Barley UIs and EIs, Clusterwide and by Cluster Sector

Little Barley	Clusterwide	Sector	
		3b	3a
Table B.2 Panel			
E Little barley and erect knotweed and chenopod and maygrass and maize	9	6	3
F Little barley and erect knotweed and maygrass and maize	0		
G Little barley and erect knotweed and chenopod and maize	1	0	1
H Little barley and maize	3	1	2
Table B.3 Panel			
C-1 Little barley and chenopod and maygrass, no maize	4	3	1
C-2 Little barley and maygrass, no chenopod, no maize	7	5	2
C-3 Little barley and chenopod, no maize	2	2	0
C-4 Little barley and erect knotweed, no maize	1	1	0
C-4 Little barley only	5	2	3
Total little barley	32	20	12
UI:	32/177 = 0.18	20/83 = 0.24	12/94 = 0.13
EI:	5/177 = 0.03	2/83 = 0.02	3/94 = 0.03

Notes

Chapter 1. Introduction

1. Fortier and McElrath (2002, 174) make reference to McElrath's coining the term "Little Bang" as "presaging the 'Big Bang' . . . denoting the appearance of Mississippian culture in this area." This terminology is in keeping with their modeling the development of the social systems of the American Bottom in ruptural terms. I recognize the importance of the developments that they outline but wish to reserve for later developing the view that the material changes they note may be more adequately characterized as manifesting surface rather than deep structural changes constituting cultural and social ruptures.

2. Recently, Fowler (in Fowler et al. 1999, 59–60) has presented radiocarbon dates suggesting that monumental construction started at Cahokia in the later days of the Emergent Mississippian period.

3. This region is recognized as the outstanding and early expression of what is often referred to as the Southeastern Mississippian way of life. Because the primary focus of this book is the Mississippian period of the American Bottom, while I do touch on other examples of this way of life located primarily south and east of Cahokia, I will leave an in-depth study of the Southeast and its relations to the rest of the midcontinental region for another book.

4. Bhaskar (1978, chapter 3; 1979, 164–69) speaks of the hermeneutic spiral as the RRRE methodology. He takes this method as necessary when dealing with social systems because of their open nature (i.e., because of the impossibility of performing any realistic experimentation). The RRRE method is summed up in the following four phases: "(1) *Resolution* of a complex event into its components (causal analysis); (2) *Redescription* of component causes; (3) *Retrodiction* to possible (antecedent) causes of components via independently validated normic statements; and (4) *Elimination* of alternative possible causes of components" (Bhaskar 1979, 165, emphases in original).

5. In his attempt to deflate what he considers to be the more extreme claims about Cahokian-based power and size, Milner (1998, 148) minimizes labor requirements and population numbers: "It would have been a simple matter for a population of modest size to build the mounds. For example, it could have been accomplished by 470, 490, 310, and 68 laborers who worked 10 five-hour days each year during the Lohmann, Stirling, Moorehouse, and Sand Prairie phases, using durations of 100, 100, 50, and 125 years." He reiterates these points in a later paper. For him, mound "building could easily have been accomplished during events of some social ritual significance, when large numbers of people might have been gathered together. It would not be surpris-

ing if certain people regularly sponsored festivals that simultaneously augmented their reputations and provided an opportunity to construct earthen mounds, large wooden buildings, and the like" (Milner 2003, 140).

Chapter 2. The Deontic Ecological Perspective

1. Given the premise that stable access to resources will promote cemeteries as a form of legitimization of proprietorial domain and exclusive territories (a mortuary position that is well entrenched in all the versions of the hierarchical monistic modular polity account), it is particularly intriguing that, until the emergence of the Mississippian period, there is essentially an absence of any indicators of mortuary ritual across the American Bottom. This puzzle or anomaly, generated by the assumption that exclusive territories prevailed, is fully addressed later and resolved under the heterarchical polyistic locale-centric account.

2. Of course, Ingold is correct to speak of poaching, understood in terms of exclusive territorial/proprietorial domain, as non-existent in this type of world. However, I note earlier and argue in more detail in later chapters that foragers also recognize the difference between appropriate and transgressive exploitation.

3. In a world of proprietorial domains, of course, tool styles are proprietorial warrants. Knowing and having the right to use the proper tools bearing the appropriate (i.e., recognized) styles endows the users with the same right to occupy the territory as those who share these styles and, therefore, the right to exploit the resources. Indeed, in an important sense, the tools are as much "certificates of birth rights" as they are hunting "licenses" (Byers 1994, 375–76; 1999b, 30–31; 2004, 68–79).

4. Bhaskar (1978, 113) expresses this view as a general ontological observation extremely well: "Living creatures qua causal agents determine the conditions under which physical laws apply; they cannot therefore already be manifest in the latter. Sentience determines the conditions of applicability of physical laws, but it is also subject to them."

5. Irwin (1994, 62) characterizes the symbolic pragmatics of the culturally creative moment of visions very aptly here:

[T]he topology of dreaming is unified through a movement between discrete, structured events—a certain repetitive formal pacing. The vision unfolds as if it were a ritual, particularly the central events involving pragmatic instructions or teachings. The journey through the dream-space culminates in a ritual enactment that is unfolded and elaborated in visionary time. *In this sense the vision is a kind of pre-performative, or prototypical enactment through which the visionary receives a potential sanction and instruction for later social, ceremonial behavior.* Although the subjective experience of time is contracted or expanded, the actual unfolding of events follows a memorable pattern that can be recreated with varying degrees of modification. (Emphasis added.)

Chapter 3. Cultural Traditions and Prehistoric Archaeology

1. I am taking some liberties with the terms *intensional* and *extensional*. According to Searle (1983, 180–96), they are used to characterize the way in which a proposition is used. If it is used to refer to a mental state by saying "John believes that Caesar crossed the Rubicon," then the utterance is intensional in that it is referring to a state of mind of John, namely, that he has this belief. Archaeologists might also say that this is an emic statement. If I say "Caesar crossed the Rubicon," then this usage of the same proposition is extensional in that it is referring to a historic event. Of course, this would probably count as an etic statement in archaeology. I am using these two terms to differentiate between our tendency to perceive the world around us extensionally (i.e., discursive consciousness), while monitoring our extensional or discursive awareness, this monitoring being a form of intensional consciousness and, in Giddens's terms (1979, 24–25), constituting the practical level of awareness. Our ability to maintain both states is reflexivity, and our ability to be effortlessly reflexive is simply our ability to shift our explicit or discursive awareness effortlessly to our intensional states. However, our effortless reflexivity hinges on our expressive capacity, since, as I note earlier, typically we mediate this shift by self-articulation, e.g., "speaking" or visually imagining to ourselves (Taylor 1985b, 256–58).

2. I discuss intentions below. But briefly stated, prior intentions are intentions "stretched out," if you wish. They are the basis of our planning, or strategizing, and all strategies to be fulfilled must be implemented in actions. In this sense, a group or collective strategy (i.e., an ideology) is a form of commissive in that it commits the group to a preferred or even an imperative course of action. Importantly, *intension* (with an *s*) and *intention* (with a *t*) must not be confused. The former properly refers to emic statements, although I have extended it to refer to the agent's monitoring of her/his conscious states, while the latter refers to that form of consciousness that, when exercised, is always fulfilled by an action. More on this shortly.

3. This is an ontological characterization of intentionality, in this case, of Bel(r). How we can come to know whether a belief is true (epistemology) is not the problem I am addressing here. However, there is an important epistemological implication to this ontological view, in that, while the state of the world is what determines whether a belief (or a hypothesis) is true or false, the content of a belief (or hypothesis) is what specifies what state the world must be in—or, for archaeology, must have been in—to constitute the belief as true or false. Truth is a property not of the world but of our claims about it.

4. Retroduction is a form of transcendental logic (Bhaskar 1979, 24–28): within the framework of our general knowledge about the way the world is, what must the conditions have been to make X possible? Thus, given that we know that this residue is the outcome of the exercise of past intentions—according to the theory of Intentionality—we ask ourselves what the contents of these intentions must have been and, given these intentions, what type of duties and beliefs must have been entailed, and so on.

5. As I discuss later in the text, those who share the same ideology typically also are aware that there are alternative ideologies, often in the same community.

6. I address this problem in my interpretive analysis of the Sponemann phase of the Sponemann site (chapter 6), arguing that, indeed, this patterning can be easily accommodated to the symbolic pragmatic perspective.

7. Of course, I could be wrong—not in the sense that the experience of sacredness is part of the phenomenology of the experience itself but in the sense that there really is a property termed *sacredness* in the world. That is, the immanentist cosmology could be true, in that the world really may be immanently sacred. However, this is not the point I am making. Whether the cosmology is true or not, by virtue of the existence of a cosmology, the worldview and ideological experiences of the prehistoric peoples would have the phenomenal property associated with the sense of sacredness, namely, awe, reverence, and other such strong emotions.

Chapter 4. Deontic Ecology, Cultural Traditions, and Social Systems

1. The transcendentalist/immanentist dichotomy might appear to be overly rigid. This is a danger since such a dichotomy can generate a theory that becomes inflexible. In fact, speaking in more nuanced terms is easily done. For example, many immanentist cosmologies may be organized in a hierarchical manner, with the deities and spirits ranked in terms of their relation to humans. Hence, an immanentist cosmology might have otiose creator gods or creative forces that are immanent in the make-up of the world but totally indifferent to worldly affairs. The deities emerge out of these forces and take on the creator roles, dealing only with the basic components of time, space, and motion. Then, at a "lower" level, there may be "managerial deities," or in a more directly immanent position, there may be nature deities in the form of guardian spirits with whom humans more directly interact. Humans can also take on specialized mediation roles, and so on (Ingold 1987, 267–69). I postulate that Native North American cosmologies tend to be radically immanentist. By this I mean that the sacred powers take on many forms and roles, from creators to custodians to managers, and, of course, they might instigate encounters with individuals and groups, not to dominate but to enable these groups to realize themselves. This radical type of immanentist cosmology strongly correlates with inclusive territorialism, custodial tenure, and personal human-deity relations.

2. Since special needs also must be recognized as essential to sustaining agentive autonomy, these could situationally modify the "first come–first served" principle. Thus, those with special needs are bumped to the head of the queue. Should a rather permanent form of queuing emerge, a permanent rank-ordered hierarchy based on the principle of the "founder" would probably emerge. This would endow a particular group with real power, itself parasitic on the "first come–first served" principle. But this social power would be based on the duty of this higher-ranking group to ensure the discharging of autonomy-based entitlements. Because of the central value of au-

tonomy, such a hierarchy, I suggest, would emphasize enablement over dominance. I discuss this in more detail in the next chapter.

3. This claim is empirically testable, of course. However, the focus of this book makes pursuing such empirical testing unworkable. Therefore, my claim in this regard stands as a hypothesis to be tested.

4. That is to say, there can be gradations between the two extremes. For example, in the case of the integrated settlement articulation mode, while the clans and cults can maintain a single village, both could also sustain ancillary locales. The constituent units of the clans, such as extended families, might maintain temporary habitation sites near gardens that are distant from the village, while the cults might have small locales for rituals separate from the domestic dwellings. Even when a settlement system has a strongly bifurcated articulation, this use of ancillary or auxiliary locales might be sustained, especially for the cults, as I discuss later.

5. I have explored this matter in considerable detail elsewhere (Byers 2004, chapters 6 and 9).

6. As I note in a previous section, among cult allies, the exchange of exotics to be used to produce ritual warrants would figure strongly, and between enemy cults, warfare for procuring these resources (possibly including victims for lethal human sacrifice) would figure strongly.

Chapter 5. Mortuary Practices, Cults, and Social Systems

1. In a recent paper on Mound 72, Brown (2003, 82) has significantly advanced mortuary studies over the funerary paradigm by giving quite a different interpretation from the standard one, one that is largely consistent with the perspective that I develop here. I comment in greater detail on this paper in chapter 13.

2. Hall's view presupposes the notion that the human person is a complex of multiple spiritual components and that these relate together in multiple ways to constitute the person. This perspective is very close to Chris Fowler's (2004, 24–48, 130–40) notions of personhood and the way in which these govern human interaction and, in particular, the mortuary practices. The approach I develop, however, adds the symbolic pragmatic dimension to characterize the social nature and purpose of the mortuary practices in terms that I believe are relevant to understanding the Native American practices, namely, as both social and world renewal rituals.

3. Characterizing an action in terms of its objective appearances and outcomes is a form of behaviorism that is largely assumed in archaeology. As I argue in an earlier chapter when presenting the deontic ecological framework, hunting and poaching can be objectively identical, and yet, from the perspective of the participants in a society, these two behaviors are experienced and therefore are recognized as two different and opposite actions. This means, of course, that we are really dealing with a dual- or even a tri-level reality when interpreting the archaeological record: behavior-action-act. The social act of greeting in society A requires performing the complex action B by

a rule-governed behavioral process of nodding, smiling, shaking hands, and making the appropriate utterance of X. Similarly, the behavioral intervention of the pursuing and killing of game (predation) is constituted as the social activity of hunting by manifesting through the expressive symbolic moment (e.g., hunting gear style, bodily posture and kinesics, and so on) the appropriate action intentions and social positions, and a successful completion of a hunting episode counts as the complex social act of renewing the species being exploited, sacrificing to the animal's spirit custodian, and discharging reciprocal duties to one's brothers and brothers-in-law, and so on.

4. In this regard it is interesting to note that the mortuary treatment of the deceased Natchez Great Sun had a strong lethal sacrificial world renewal ritual component. According to Swanton (1911, 169), the Natchez chief was believed to be a direct descendant of the Sun. Therefore, the mortuary treatment of the chief was as much a renewal as a funerary rite, since the event was perceived as critically important to ensure the ongoing balancing of the cosmos. This would explain why selected persons were sacrificed at his "funeral/rebirth"; they were perceived as serving the Sun (Swanton 1911, 140–46). Hence, by these killings being constituted as lethal sacrifices, they endowed the mortuary event with a strong world renewal nature. Interestingly, selected victims could even in certain cases be substituted by relatives, if these volunteered. As described by Swanton (1911, 147), after a prospective victim was released from the obligation of being sacrificed at the mortuary ritual of the Great Sun, "in the afternoon three old women were brought, two of whom were his relatives, who, being extremely aged and wearied of life, offered themselves to pay his debt."

5. See Emerson 2003b (135–38) for an extended discussion of shamanism.

6. In chapter 1, I briefly discussed the use of this term, *Emergent Mississippian,* and the alternative that has recently been proposed to replace it, the *Terminal Late Woodland,* and the related theoretical debate (Fortier and McElrath 2002, 173, 186–87). In the following chapter, I switch to using the latter terminology and the associated chronology, specifying my position in regard to the theoretical aspect.

7. In fact, this hierarchical structuring of the age-sets of an age-grade might be much more relevant in the junior than in the senior age-grades since, in the latter, differential age would become less important within the age-grade, while social standing would probably come to be determined by overall experience and reputation of the individuals.

8. A number of archaeologists is attempting to escape the traditional typology of band, tribe, chiefdom, and state—and the various dichotomies that these might generate (e.g., egalitarian/non-egalitarian)—by using the concept of a heterarchy (Crumley 1995, 1; Rautman 1998, 325–26; Rogers 1995, 7–8). Indeed, the premises on which my notion of a polyistic locale-centric social system is based have been used by Rogers (1995, 9–15) to characterize the Late Woodland upper Yadkin River valley social systems. In this case, she emphasizes a heterarchical system as being based on residential villages whose occupants had juridically unfettered access to nonlocal resources and

to lands in other regions. In effect, she characterizes this social system in what I have called heterarchical polyistic locale-centric terms, along with inclusive territorialism, although she does not use this terminology. In any case, Crumley's (1995, 3) notion of heterarchy equivocates between equality and inequality: "Heterarchy may be defined as the relation of elements to one another where they are unranked or when they possess the potential for being ranked in a number of different ways." While Brumfiel (1995, 125) notes this equivocation, she summarizes several other current views of the notion of heterarchy, showing that there is, overall, a tendency to equate heterarchy with equality and, therefore, hierarchy with inequality. For example, she has noted one definition of a heterarchy as being "an array of independent, homogeneous elements," and another, also emphasizing equality, as being "the membership of elements in many different unranked interaction systems." Another takes a functional-differential view so that two or more components relate as "discrete but unranked systems that interact as equals." I believe substituting the term "autonomy" for the range of terms, "equality," "unranked," or "independent, homogeneous elements," captures the intended sense and the notion that autonomous groups can be organized in enabling hierarchies resolves this equivocation.

9. Seen in terms of the Mourning/World Renewal Mortuary model, an important resource that would mediate clan-cult relations would be the deceased. Clans might willingly hand over their deceased members, or the deceased dependents of one of their members, to the cult of this member to contribute to the cult's capacity to discharge its world renewal tasks through performing postmortem sacrificial rites. This willingness would arise from perceiving that the cult's mortuary rites would assist in eliminating the clan's debt to the cosmos, this debt being the cumulation of pollution that clan's agricultural activities necessary generated.

Chapter 6. The Sacred Maize Model and the Sponemann Site

1. Because people with an immanentist cosmology and squatter ethos are very sensitive to the sacred nature of their material relations with the environment, the unwitting consequences would not go unnoticed for long. When these consequences are noted, a community could innovate renewal ritual, as suggested under the Sacred Maize model, or could simply reverse course and stop using maize in this new manner, reserving it for only traditional ritual. Therefore, the Sacred Maize model, while recognizing the contingency of historical processes, does not claim that once the process was started, the outcome of expanding population and settlement was inevitable. Rather, the model is being used retroductively to explain what must have happened given the empirical data that we have (which are outlined below). Quite possibly, then, there may be many cases of Sponemann phase communities abandoning these innovations, a point made by Fortier and Jackson (2000, 132) and Fortier and McElrath (2002, 182) in noting that other Sponemann phase sites lack significant maize residue. However, since we in fact know that maize became ubiquitous in the American Bottom within fifty years of

the first known appearance of maize as a subsistence crop at the Sponemann site, we can conclude that the majority of communities chose to innovate or emulate rather than to surrender maize as a warranting mode for opening new lands and producing subsistence crops, thereby promoting further demographic expansion, and so on.

2. Some minor lip and rim decorative treatments exist in the Patrick phase ceramics, and also effigy rim lugs occur, albeit these are rare. Of particular distinction, however, is the emergence of the bowl (including effigy bowls), usually associated with communal events involving feasting, as discussed by Koldehoff (2002, 93) in some detail. His argument that the Woodland Ridge site was probably used for special seasonally related aggregation events having a strong focus on feasting—given that the proportion of bowls there is among the largest of the known smaller sites of the Patrick phase—correlates with the notion that the later Late Woodland population expansion would have stimulated ritual renewal events. As Koldehoff (2002, 4) argues,

> The common occurrence of large ceramic bowls and charred masses of starchy seeds supports the notion that Woodland Ridge was a periodic aggregation site and that individual feature clusters were probably reused by individual families or larger social groups. The great number of large bowls is especially significant— that is, proportionally, more bowls and more large bowls have been recovered from Woodland Ridge than from any previously reported Patrick phase site. The common occurrence of charred seeds from a number of medicinal and/or ritual plants (e.g., tobacco, nodding spurge, and pokeweed) lends further support to the aggregation hypothesis.

3. While Bruce Smith (1992b, 110) notes the empirical difficulties involved in a cost-benefit comparative analysis of indigenous and tropical (maize) grain production, he points out that indigenous plants not only had high nutritional content but also had potential for even more development in these terms: "[It] is important to emphasize that plant husbandry systems focused on indigenous seed-bearing plants have both impressive nutritional profiles and substantial, potential harvest yield values, and [these] had been established over a broad area of the eastern United States prior to the initial introduction of maize in the Eastern Woodlands."

4. Although the absence of hearths or fire pits in the small later Late Woodland and Terminal Late Woodland structures indicates that cooking fires were not made within these structures, day-to-day storage and precooking preparation of comestibles using this pottery would probably have been done there. Also, much of the cooking in pots may have been done through the use of fire-heated stones; while the heating of the stones would have occurred in outside fire hearths, the actual cooking could very well have been carried out in these small residential structures.

5. Indeed, this possibility could justify an experimental research project. Visually normal persons having the same degree of fine tactile perception could be recruited to test whether they could learn to discriminate by touch between accurate facsimiles of

these two types of pottery under different conditions of light and darkness and, if so, how easily and quickly this discrimination could be learned.

6. It is interesting to note that (as recorded in Swanton 1911, 113–23) the historic Natchez of Louisiana set aside a special field for the maize that was to be used for their busk world renewal/thanksgiving ceremonies. The preparation of the field, the planting of the corn, its cultivation and harvest, and even the building and filling of the storage facility were all done by the junior male warrior age-sets of the community. They were also responsible for the distribution of the maize during the busk ritual. However, the women were responsible for its cooking—and all, of course, participated in consuming it. No maize could be left unconsumed, so the feast would continue until all the maize from that special field had been distributed and consumed.

7. Metal was identified by many Native peoples with the Thunder God, who was a god of war and destruction and also a male power. Maize, of course, was identified with the Earth Mother. Prohibitions ensured that the tools representing each complementary power were kept separate.

8. The only other crop that the mobile Cheyenne regularly cultivated was tobacco, another special crop that was essential for both public tribal ceremony and private midwifery subsistence ritual. Importantly, there were strong prescriptions to keep these two crops separate. The women were responsible for the maize, and the men for the tobacco (Will and Hyde 1964, 44).

9. The required data are summarized in Fortier et al. 1991, table 11.1, 380–403.

Chapter 7. The Early Terminal Late Woodland Period Sponemann Community Development

1. As I argue in the previous chapter, however, this attribute reinforces the Sacred Maize model, since the mixing of the two types is consistent with the postulated proscription ensuring that maize and indigenous seed crops were kept separate during processing, especially cooking and storing.

2. In chapter 6, I note that 71 percent of the sitewide features were sampled for archaeobotanical content, and I comment there that Cluster 3 had the largest sampling. Of the total 274 features making up this cluster, I counted 203 features as having been sampled, or 74 percent, which is the highest across the total site.

3. As Fortier and Jackson (2000, 138) put it, "Regardless of how [keyhole] . . . structures were used, they were a relatively short-lived innovation in the American Bottom. They continue to serve as an important chronological marker of both the Patrick and Sponemann phases there and possibly for the late Late Woodland period/ stage throughout a large portion of the Midwest." In fact, Fortier and Jackson specify the keyhole structure as the primary chronological marker of the Patrick phase.

4. Fortier comments that there may have been other keyhole structures that they were unable to identify, largely because the ramps and distal basins were shallow and subject to damage from plowing and erosion (Fortier et al. 1991, 89). Therefore, al-

though identified as residences, one or more rectangular structures of the same size as the typical keyhole structure may have actually been keyhole structures, the ramps of which had been obliterated or not noted during excavation.

Chapter 8. The Development of Terminal Late Woodland Period American Bottom Settlement: The Range Site

1. If the four phases of the Terminal Late Woodland period, dated ca. cal A.D. 900–1050, are given equal weight, this allows for roughly 40 years each. Therefore, the Dohack phase can be conventionally dated ca. cal A.D. 900–940.

2. I point out in more detail shortly that the two types of structures actually seem to form two different and overlapping patterns: the keyhole structures are linearly oriented following the northeast–southwest axis of the ridge, whereas the small rectangular structures are oriented in a semicircle facing west.

3. More dog skeletons than identifiable human remains were found in association with keyhole structures, rectangular structures, and pits. Furthermore, these canine skeletons were in quite a good state of preservation, while almost all of the human remains were very poorly preserved, clearly indicative of incidental "burial" (Milner in Kelly et al. 1987, 402–3). I argue later that this type of mortuary data is consistent with the Mourning/World Renewal Mortuary model.

4. At the Fish Lake site, Fortier and colleagues (1984, 30) note a similar spatial relation between a keyhole structure and a large single-post structure; given the superpositioning pattern, they conclude that the latter predated the former.

5. Indeed, Kelly (1996, 106) makes this presumed consolidation even more explicit in a later article on the symbolic meaning of Cahokia, emphasizing that the three structural principles that underwrite the organizational layout of Cahokia, namely, "dualism, quadrilateralism, and centrality . . . are the basic principles . . . of Cahokia's configuration as a paramount community" and that these are clearly entailed in the Late Terminal Woodland patterning of the Range site. The problem I have with this statement is not the continuity argument—after all, the principles Kelly specifies would be deep structures of the cosmology—but that he identifies these with elite-based hierarchy. Indeed, he later claims that "Monks Mound and the paramount person on its summit are the center of this ritual universe, and it is his or her role that serves to mediate this balance in Cahokian society" (Kelly 1996, 109).

6. It seems that it could as well be described as seven pits forming two quadripartite-pits patterns by sharing a common connecting corner pit.

Chapter 9. Cahokia as a World Renewal Cult Heterarchy

1. The term *acropolis* certainly has the religious connotations I prefer. However, since the ancient Greek acropolis was the religious core of a polis, a city-state, it could easily be assimilated to the "paramount chiefdom" notion that plays a central role in

the conceptualization of Cahokia under the hierarchical monistic modular polity account, which is precisely the opposite connotation that I want to evoke. Using the term *center* also connotes the monistic modular polity view.

2. In this case, I am particularly attracted to Saitta's (1994, 214) use of the notion of entitlements as the means of discharging duties of an economic nature to members in social systems that are based on what he calls subsumed classes. I summarize his argument in an earlier chapter, where I note that it is presented in the context of the monistic modular polity perspective. However, I think it is even more relevant in understanding the economic and social structuring of a heterarchical polyistic locale-centric social system constituted of autonomous kinship and sodality groups, as promoted in this book.

3. Alt (2001, 146–55) has noted a number of similarities and differences in residential architecture, community layout, ceramics, and lithics between the upland sites of Knoebel, Halliday, and Hal Smith in comparison to Cahokia and the dispersed village system of the American Bottom; she attributes these similarities and differences to the occupants of these upland areas both emulating and resisting cultural practices in the American Bottom. Her argument is that these upland immigrants were attracted to and participated in Cahokian life by adopting only "those changes that maintained an affiliation with the current changes at Cahokia," while they simultaneously "resisted those changes that would have altered social life" (Alt 2001, 155). These are very insightful observations. However, she makes them with the assumption that Cahokia was a dominant paramount chiefdom, and, therefore, she concludes that the "upland people apparently rejected the sociopolitical authority of Cahokia and retained more traditional patterns of living and doing" (Alt 2001, 155). I address these same data later and show how they can be understood in terms consistent with the heterarchical polyistic locale-centric view, thereby expanding this alternative understanding of Cahokia and the upland regions.

Chapter 10. Cahokia as a Hierarchical Monistic Modular Polity: A Critical View

1. According to Trubitt (2003, 155), she and John Kelly commenced a project in 1998 "to locate the west and north walls of Cahokia's Central Palisade." She reports that the remains of at least three and possibly four separate western wall remnants were found overlapping. I comment later on the fact that she did not report any evidence of a northern wall.

2. In fact, Pauketat and Barker's (2000, 128) recent review of Jay Taylor's 1927 work on Mounds 66 and 64 has definitively established that Mound 66 had a large number of bundle burials, probably very similar to those that Milner (1984, 480–82) has established were deposited in the Wilson Mound, as I discuss later.

3. I examine his analysis of these mounds and their contents in more detail later, as they figure importantly in clarifying the social nature of Cahokia.

4. Milner (1998, 114) specifically comments on the difficulty of drawing a boundary in this regard, since not only the mounds but also the settlement debris were "strung out" along Cahokia Creek:

> [I]t is safe to say that nothing has been identified that departs from the general Cahokia pattern. Mounds and dense areas of habitation debris in the other mound centers tend to be strung out along prominent floodplain ridges, often those bordering deep wetlands. Widely dispersed debris scatters frustrate attempts to define the limits of these settlements. For example, mounds and habitation areas are distributed along high ridges far beyond the various site limits used to define the Lunsford-Pulcher mound group. Much like the situation at Cahokia, mounds outside the boundaries of Lunsford-Pulcher are omitted from the conventional four-tiered American Bottom settlement model where supposedly discrete settlements are ranked by the number of mounds they encompassed.

5. Milner specifically recognizes a difference between the upper northern expanse of the American Bottom and the more narrow extension south of Lunsford-Pulcher to the mouth of Kaskaskia River. He suggests that the mound locales in this region were truly autonomous with regard to each other and quasi-autonomous with regard to Cahokia. He observes,

> The distribution and occupational histories of multiple and single-mound centers from Lunsford-Pulcher south to the mouth of the Kaskaskia River, many of which were identified during the early 1970s, . . . have yet to be systematically examined. . . . It is unlikely that the settlement system was as strictly hierarchical as the existing model suggests. Although more work is needed to clarify the principal components at the mound centers, the occupational histories of these sites appear to have been highly varied. (Milner 1990, 20–21)

6. I could ask this question of Muller's (1997, 279) comment also. In a manner similar to Anderson's, Muller claims that, except that it is obviously larger, Cahokia is much like the other "Mississippian centers." However, he does qualify this claim by noting one important difference, this being that "its postulated 3-tier social system literally elevated its midrange elite . . . as well as the top-rank elite upon mounds." However, this recognition of a midrange elite begs the question of why, if the Cahokian social structure was of the same nature as other Mississippian centers, it had a midrange elite? Indeed, this multitiered social system actually highlights the likelihood that Cahokia was different. In the terms that I am developing, of course, Cahokia was a very large heterarchy of affiliated alliances of autonomous cults, organized as ecclesiastic-communal cults internally structured as enabling hierarchies of senior and junior age-sets crosscut by clergy.

7. Muller cites Anderson (1994) as making this argument "at length." An added value of this quotation is that it reinforces my point that proponents of the hierarchical

monistic modular polity account of the Mississippian period rely on the funerary view for support, and of course, this claim presupposes the exclusive territorial/proprietorial domain paradigm. Muller's characterization of "the assertion to authority" as being "nearly universally" represented by the association of funerary mortuary practices with mounds supports my point quite neatly.

8. Later in its construction history, the open side of the Hopewell site C-form overlooking the bottomland was closed with a stone wall, and an embankment "square" was added to its east wall.

Chapter 11. The "Rural" Settlement Pattern

1. However, men's houses do not have to be based on kinship, and, in fact, the constitutive structure of most such "clubs" is companionship, i.e., same-age/same-gender, bachelors who may be only incidentally related by kinship (as brothers and/or brothers-in-law). I return to this point shortly, since, of course, it suggests the direction that I pursue in reinterpreting this same set of data.

2. Here Emerson equivocates. On the one hand, he specifically notes that the two sites are different in that the Stirling phase occupation of the BBB Motor site has a mortuary component, while the Sponemann site does not. At Sponemann, he observes, "we find a rich accompanying assemblage of ritual plants, vessels, cult figurines, exotic artifacts, and so forth. It is similar to the BBB Motor site temple area but with *a complete absence of mortuary facilities*" (Emerson 1997a, 225, emphasis added). However, on the other hand, he comments (near the end of the same page) that "a highly organized and specialized mortuary and cult priesthood appeared at sites such as BBB Motor and Sponemann," implying that these were the same type of cult, despite recognizing the absence of direct mortuary evidence at the Sponemann site.

3. The complementary male-female nature of these cult identifications would suggest characterizing the heterarchical relation as complementary rather than mutualistic. However, I will retain the latter characterization since I am emphasizing the fact that they are both world renewal cults, and therefore they would recognize each other as such so that their heterarchical relations would be mutualistic, even though the formal content of the ritual they performed and interactions they carried out would be complementary.

4. This division into two types of autonomous cults, clearly apparent in both the Lohmann and the Stirling phases, suggests a deep structural continuity; this duality can legitimately be projected onto the archaeological record of the Terminal Late Woodland period, for example, the duality that was apparent in the George Reeves and Lindeman phases, and even back to the Sponemann phase dual keyhole structures of the Sponemann site and of the Patrick phase occupation of the Range site.

Chapter 12. Cahokian Mortuary Practices: The Media of World Renewal Ritual

1. There have been a number of comments concerning the prevalence of mound and

nonmound burials along the bluffs overlooking the American Bottom. Milner (1984, 470) quotes Moorehead's comment that the bluff line was "one vast ancient cemetery." Munson (1971, 10) also comments on the large number of Late Bluff or Terminal Late Woodland burial mounds on the bluffs overlooking the American Bottom. I discuss this matter in more detail in chapter 14.

2. Milner (1983, 123) specifically comments on the absence of any known habitation data that might represent the community that the Cemetery model claims would have used the East St. Louis Stone Quarry site. He explains this lacuna by suggesting that the community would have been widely dispersed.

3. Emerson and Hargrave (2000, 17–18) claim that by this time the mortuary practices of the upland region (as represented by the later Kane Mounds site data) and the southern sector of the northern expanse of the American Bottom (as represented at the mortuary components of the Florence Street, Range, and East St. Louis Stone Quarry sites) constituted two contrasting and contemporary mortuary programs. I think their argument for contrasting mortuary programs is well founded, and I discuss it in detail in chapter 14.

4. Milner (1982, 299–300) does comment on the signs of burning to which some of the Kane Mounds bone bundles and extended burials were subjected. He suggests, however, that this was the by-product of the abandoning of a possible charnel structure by ritually burning it. Emerson and Hargrave (2000, 12), however, note that there were many signs of cremation or partial cremation and treat this, along with the absence of stone-pit features, as a major difference from the mortuary practices of the lower or southern sector of the northern expanse.

5. Klepinger (1993, 423) favors treating this Cahokian mortuary locale as that of "simple peasant folk," a position that is partly supported by Witty (1993, 432).

6. However, I have already noted that a number of early Mississippian upland CBLs have recently been reported that add to our Lohmann phase data; these are discussed in detail in chapter 14.

Chapter 13. Mound 72: Funerary Monument or World Renewal Icon?

1. Brown (2003, 83–84) has written a comprehensive treatment of some of the burials of Mound 72 that clearly breaks with this perspective and, in fact, is very close to the view that I present in this chapter. I address his very valuable and insightful paper later.

2. In fact, Fowler (1996, 45) has noted that the reorientation of Mound 72 involved removing part of the northeast and southeast sides of 72Sub2 and 72Sub1 and that this was done in the early Stirling phase: "The final mound form was oriented on an azimuth of 300°, or 30° north of the E-W axis if viewed from the southeast. To achieve this final orientation, the SE portions of 72Sub1 and the NE portions of 72Sub2 were removed during the Stirling phase."

3. Fowler draws a direct parallel between this raptorial beaded mortuary shroud

with Burial 13 on top and the raptor/dead-human motif found in several examples of Southeastern ceremonial icons. He postulates that this iconography expresses the significance of the personage of Burial 13. But he rejects the view that this person would have been the "great leader," or paramount chief. Instead, he suggests that this personage, "and his associated burials, were powerful early Mississippian chiefs, but, they were probably leaders of only one of the many communities that made up early Cahokia" (Fowler et al. 1999, 188).

4. Fowler has analytically sectored the assumed forty-eight posts of the postulated Woodhenge 72 into northeast, southeast, southwest, and northwest quarters. Starting with the northeast quarter as NE, he numbers the posts from I to XIII, starting with the equinoctial post pit as locus I-NE and the northernmost post pit as locus XIII-NE. PP1 under 72Sub1 marks the summer solstice and is locus V-NE. PP2 under 72Sub2 is locus IX-NE (Figures 13.2 and 13.4).

5. At a later date, just west of Feature 102, Burials 1, 2, and 3 were deposited in a pit dug into 72Sub1, constituting Feature 104 (Rose 1999, 65).

6. Fowler comments that the Feature 214 pit "was 5 by 2 m and was excavated about 1 m below the original ground surface. After the burials were placed in this pit, it was covered with a ramplike structure, sometimes referred to as an 'altar' in the field notes" (Fowler et al. 1999, 28). However, he also adds that this was oriented at 135° azimuth, although Rose comments that it was only azimuth 120°.

7. The term *lethal* used with *sacrifice* is not redundant since, as I discuss earlier, I postulate contrasting forms of human sacrifice—lethal and postmortem. The former is characterized by killing being figured in as a constitutive behavior of the ritual itself, while in the latter case, the sacrificial component is realized as a series of postmortem treatments of the deceased who died for reasons unrelated to these treatments.

8. For example, in the Eastern Orthodox churches, the icons of the saints are taken to be presencing the sanctity of the saints that they represent, and it is by this sanctity being present that the behavioral streams termed *prayer* and *exhortation* count as such.

9. This explanation raises an interesting question for the skeptic: if people having an immanentist cosmology actually experience monuments in this manner, why did monumental mound construction not occur earlier and everywhere that such traditions prevailed? That is, have I not painted myself into a corner? I answer this question in much more detail later, but a brief answer can be given by recalling the earlier claim that beliefs do not determine but enable actions. Thus, while neighboring peoples can share the same immanentist cosmology, they can strongly disagree ideologically over the most effective form of material interventions that should be taken to rectify the pollution that their very similar levels of subsistence exploitation and settlement occupation generate.

10. However, in this regard, Goldstein (2000, 201) presents a cautionary note: "[Secondary] disposal of the dead is not really a mortuary treatment in the same way

as primary burial because the secondary treatment is triggered by something independent of the death of the individual . . . [such that] in a secondary disposal context, the bones are used to symbolize something else, and it is the symbolism of these bones that is important to understand." While I can fully agree with her emphasis on the special meaning of bones, there is no reason to radically separate primary and secondary treatments by claiming that only the first is a "real" mortuary treatment. Instead, as I argue in earlier chapters, funerary ritual is only part of the total possible range of mortuary activities for which the dead are critical media.

11. Fowler also recognizes this southwest sector as important. But he notes that the importance arises from the fact that all these burials were inside the northeast sector of the circle of posts that constituted Woodhenge 72: "Another important relationship of Mound 72 to Woodhenge 72 is that all of the burials in Mound 72 are inside the arc or circumference of the circle of Woodhenge 72 between Loci IV-NE and X-NE" (1996, 49).

12. Of course, this number of mixed primary extended and bone bundle burials excludes the 161 extended burials making up the lethal human sacrificial burials.

13. Krupp (1996, 65) has noted the possibility that Locus III-NE marks the time of the year, August 20–21, when the new fire ceremony or green corn rite might have been performed.

14. This statement has to be qualified. Fowler (1999, 167) comments that, in some cases, bone preservation of extended burials that he and Rose categorize as "retainers" in association with the Beaded Burials was so poor that not all of these burials could be definitively identified as in situ burials; instead, some may have been curated prior to final burial. More emphatically, Goldstein suggests that possibly none of the Mound 72 burials is primary in nature and that all could be secondary: "Many of the burials in Mound 72, including those in the mass graves, may represent secondary disposal treatments" (2000, 198). While she does not deny that any were the result of lethal acts, she does state that "rather than massive human sacrifice on-site, it seems equally possible that the bodies of individuals who had died or were killed in their own communities were shipped to Cahokia for inclusion in the ceremonies that resulted in these mass graves" (Goldstein 2000, 198). In the following section of the text, I present arguments to the contrary.

15. Hall (2000, 247–49) discusses the role of the goddess-pretender in Aztec lethal sacrifice and relates the latter to similar Pawnee Evening Star sacrifice. The god-pretender institution is widely known to ground Mesoamerican lethal human sacrifice. The individual who is selected by the leadership of a cult to represent its particular god or goddess is required to participate in ritual as an iconic representation of the god/goddess, and, usually after one year, he/she is sacrificed in an act of death and rebirth of the god/goddess (Fagan 1984, 228–33; Townsend 1992, 136–37). This would be consistent with Brown's view that Feature 101 is the outcome of a major performative reenactment of the death and rebirth of the culture-hero creator.

Chapter 14. Integrating the Floodplain and Upland Mortuary Records

1. However, as pointed out above, Emerson and colleagues (2003, 172) also comment on the possibility that much of the Stemler Bluff mortuary component could be placed in the later Terminal Late Woodland period. If attributed to the early Mississippian period, the size of this component would require a significantly large dispersed population, since there are only three wall-trench structures in the total set of residential structures of this site (the others display typical Terminal Late Woodland period attributes). But if the mortuary component is recognized as primarily pre-Mississippian, it would be, as they say, "truly unique and would represent the only known cemetery from that time period" (Emerson et al. 2003, 172). It would also lead to countering their claim that mortuary practices involving burial were a Mississippian period innovation in this region. I discuss and critique this claim in more detail shortly.

2. See Wittry et al. 1994, 139–40, for Wittry's discussion of the Patrick phase mortuary feature implicated by the two sets of unusual pit features that he terms *truss trenches* at the Holdener site in the bluff-top area about ten kilometers north of the Stemler Bluff site. In his view, these truss trenches were built to hold trussed or crossed poles that would have supported two large wooden platforms used for curating the deceased.

3. I exclude the mortuary component of the Halliday site, and other sites like it, from this assessment. As I discuss in the next chapter, this mortuary component presents some very interesting differences from the Center Grove site and the Knoebel/Knoebel South site and may be best treated as the CBL of a nucleated village displaying the residue of strong funerary as well as mourning and clan-related renewal ritual.

4. Koldehoff (personal communication, August 2004) has suggested that the most likely dating would be the Patrick phase.

5. Wittry, in his reporting on the possible Patrick phase mortuary practices of the Holdener site (Wittry et al. 1994, 139), comments on a personal communication from Gregory Perino (1993), who reported uncovering "bone beds . . . on the bluff edge about 7.4 kilometers . . . southwest of the Holdener site." While not suggesting that these mortuary remains were from the Holdener site, Wittry is suggesting that these may have been the residue of the type of scaffold-based mortuary treatment that he argues occurred at Holdener and other Patrick phase upland sites.

6. Of course, strictly speaking, the Meyer Cave site does not constitute a CBL. However, if we accept that most of the pottery and human skeletal materials were systematically removed for final world renewal postmortem sacrificial ritual deposit prior to the woodrats doing their job, then the site certainly implicates the existence of one or more nearby CBLs.

7. As Walz and colleagues report, "[w]hile evidence for these native cultigens was recovered, the low overall seed density, 1.03 per liter of processed sediments, makes a fuller interpretation of their dietary contribution difficult. These differences in the

ubiquity and relative abundance of spring and fall-harvested starchy-seeded plants are subtle and may simply reflect sampling or preservational biases rather than differences in the intensity of their use at Stemler Bluff with respect to contemporaneous groups in the American Bottom region" (Walz et al. 1997, 197). They comment on the fragmentary nature of the maize and give a cautious interpretation that preserves their basic claim that this site was, at base, a residential village: "Given the fragmentary nature of the maize, it is not possible to make inferences regarding the nature of its use at the site without a large degree of speculation. It is possible that the fragmentary charred kernels serves as evidence for the roasting of maize in a green or immature state. No statement regarding the possible storage and subsequent usage of dried maize, however, is attempted given the nature of the remains" (Walz et al. 1997, 196–97).

8. For example, Emerson and Hargrave (2000, 16) note the burial of an elite elder in the Kane Mounds site. Since they took the Kane Mounds site to be a commoner cemetery, this presence of a burial deemed to be elite suggests a discontinuity with the floodplain sites, which are also called commoner cemeteries by them but lack isolated elite burials.

9. In fact, Emerson (2002, 137–38) now argues for a much earlier and more rapid "collapse" of Cahokia. I comment on and discuss this change of position in more detail in my closing chapter.

Chapter 15. The Terminal Late Woodland–Mississippian Transition: Alternative Accounts

1. By saying the "rural aspect," I am implying that this settlement dispersal is only one part of the transition. That is, as I discuss shortly, under this view there was also an "urban aspect" to the Lohmann phase. It is this aspect that particularly defines the emergence of the Mississippian under this view, namely, the abrupt consolidation of Cahokia termed the "Big Bang," ca. cal A.D. 1050.

2. For example, as noted earlier, Fowler argues that Woodhenge 72 was likely constructed shortly prior to the Mississippian period (Fowler et al. 1999, 59–60).

3. Milner's (1998, fig. 6.1, 124) estimate of the maximum Lohmann phase population numbers is quite moderate, by comparison. Using essentially the same data, he argues for a maximum Cahokian population of about 8,200, with a minimum population of 3,200. I suspect that his estimate is the better approximation. However, as noted above, since the World Renewal Cult Heterarchy model claims that, at any given time, the majority of the population of Cahokia was made up of transient residents, Milner's more conservative population estimate of between 15,000 and 50,000 for the total American Bottom, which includes his Cahokian estimate, would have to be reduced by his minimum and maximum estimates for Cahokia, since most of those residing at any time in Cahokia would also have had permanent countryside residences. This would suggest a maximum Lohmann phase American Bottom population of about 12,000 to 42,000.

4. This concern to allow for the time needed for the modification of the deep struc-

tures of the Late Woodland so that the transition to the paramount chiefdom type of Mississippian period social system can be explained is expressed by Fortier and Jackson (2000, 124). They note that dating the end of the Patrick phase to A.D. 900 or even A.D. 1000 and the beginning of the Lohmann phase to A.D. 1050 would leave only 50 to 150 years for the Terminal Late Woodland period. Therefore, they opt for terminating the Patrick phase at A.D. 900 rather than the more radical A.D. 1000. While this might be taken by some as evidence that the model is influencing their choice, as justification, they argue "that radiometric dating techniques, calibrated or not, simply cannot provide the kind of resolution needed to establish absolute sequential parameters in an area such as the American Bottom, which exhibits so much cultural diversity in so short a time frame."

5. Of course, it is also possible that the clans and cults of a community shared custodianship for a given CBL. However, given the rather abrupt emergence of the Mississippian multiple-mound CBLs, I am inclined toward the view that these upland CBLs were under the custodianship of cults. These alternatives will have to be left for future research.

6. However, the Lab Woofie site, located on the lower slope of the bluffs, could possibly be an auxiliary CBL of a floodplain autonomous cult.

7. Ingold (1987, 246–47) elaborates on this notion of hunting as sacrifice and, at the same time, effectively grounds what I have termed the essential contradiction of human existence:

[W]hilst life depends on the harmonious integration of the various components or levels of being, this can only be achieved at one locus by breaking things up at another. Thus, the hunter lives by killing and eating animals, which inevitably entails their dismemberment. Much of the ritual surrounding the treatment of slaughtered beasts, particularly concerning the careful preservation of bones and other inedible parts, and their deposition in the correct medium and in the precise order that they occur in the skeleton, is designed to assist the reconstitution of the animals from the pieces into which they have been broken for the purposes of consumption, thus ensuring the regeneration of that on which human life depends. . . . Above all, nothing should be wasted, for this would indicate a casually destructive attitude to nature which would only offend the animal guardians. . . . So as he conducts himself through life, a man must tread with caution, breaking as little as possible, doing what he can to mend what in nature must of necessity be broken, and warding off the equally inevitable and ultimate disintegration of his own person.

8. This possibility of curated bodies is also consistent with Goldstein's argument that human bones were used ritually because they were perceived as powerful media (2000, 200–202). She develops this argument in the context of the funerary paradigm and even suggests that because human bones were curated and used for nonfunerary

ritual purpose, such ritual should not be properly treated as mortuary in nature (i.e., only funerals were properly mortuary practices): "[S]econdary disposal of the dead is not really a mortuary treatment in the same way as primary burial because the secondary treatment is triggered by something independent of the death of the individual" (Goldstein 2000, 201).

Chapter 16. The Organizational Principles of Multiple-Mound Locales

1. Of course, the deontic ecological approach would definitely not deny Milner's claim that a multiple-mound locale treated as the center of a monistic modular polity required significant combinations of land and resources. Where disagreement arises is his basic assumption that mound construction, as such, is only contingently related to subsistence and settlement and that this can result in generating ecologically irrational earthwork settings. In my treatment, the mounds and their construction figure centrally in the ecological strategy of this social world, with the proviso being that this is an ecological strategy grounded on a cultural tradition that has an immanentist cosmology and a squatter ethos as core components. Because of these deep cultural structures, mounds figured as important—indeed, critical—iconic warranting devices of ecological renewal.

2. Of course, since the St. Louis and Creek Bottom Groups actually exist, Milner would have to allow that there must have been a few abnormal leaders in charge, those who would allow the pursuit of personal esteem override the practical needs of her/his people.

3. Interestingly, in referring to the opposing St. Louis and East St. Louis sites, Emerson has noted that in "early historic times it appears that there may have been a crossing point on the Mississippi between these two centers" (2002, 133). If this also were the case in prehistoric times, then it would go some way to explaining this parallelism between Cahokia/Kunnemann and East St. Louis/St. Louis. Because of the smaller magnitude of the Cahokia Creek system, an actual mound complex—the Creek Bottom Group—could be built on the floodplain. While the greater magnitude of the Mississippi River system might make this floodplain construction impossible, there may have been a small or narrow floodplain in the "middle" of the Mississippi where ritual could be performed just prior to the seasonal flooding or, if the waters were still too high, could be performed from boats anchored in the appropriate spots. Performing water-related world renewal rituals from boats is not unknown in pre-Columbian cultures, and they were an important part of the annual sacred cycle of the Lake of the Moon surrounding Tenochtitlan (Townsend 1992, 136–37).

4. I have argued elsewhere (Byers 2004, 241–77) that while communal cults have a less complex structure than ecclesiastic-communal cults do, the system of communal cults can be quite complex. For example, in my analysis of the Adena of the middle Ohio Valley, I argued that the organization and distribution of the archaeological record of earthworks marks a dual set of mutually autonomous communal cult networks,

one based on the senior age-grade and one on the junior age-grade. From this I postulated that the Ohio Hopewell, particularly in the Chillicothe and Newark areas, might be best understood as a network of ecclesiastic-communal cults that emerged by the integration of the preexisting senior and junior Adena-type communal cult networks.

5. However, an integrated settlement articulation mode could also promote both senior and junior generational communal cults, with the former constituting an autonomous, largely exclusive collegial priestly cult whose members, belonging to the senior generation, were drawn into the cult by special initiation rituals. This type of collegial cult would have strong shamanic tendencies with its members being both selected by older members and attracted to joining by their intrinsic spiritual capacities. Under certain conditions this type of cult could become extremely influential in an integrated village social system, much like the Osage priesthood (the *Non-hon'-zhin-ga*) that drew its members from the senior age-grades of the twenty-four clans (Bailey 1995, 44–45). While clearly these (mostly) men were members of clans, it was by being initiated that they became members of this autonomous collegial priestly cult. I must point out, however, that Bailey would not characterize the relation between the *Non-hon'-zhin-ga* and the Osage community in these terms, since he claims that this priesthood was essentially the ruling authority of the community (Bailey 1995, 44). However, in a social system where agentive autonomy is a central ethos value, there is no contradiction between "ruling authority" and autonomy, since the relation between the "rulers" and the "ruled" is based on mutual responsibilities and not rights dominating duties. Therefore, the relational network would constitute an enabling hierarchy with the levels sustained by a mutually recognized arm's-length respect. This would entail consensus among the leadership at each level.

6. As I note in chapter 5, cults are homogeneous organizations. Same-gender/same-age interaction is the basis of companionship, the relationship that would be central to the cults. Of course, an alliance could possibly combine male- and female-based cults. However, these would probably remain distinct and autonomous constituent sectors of the alliance.

Chapter 17. The Layout of Cahokia: The Material Media and Outcome of Factionalism

1. Their 1987 work predated Pauketat's published work on Tract 15A (1996, 73–74; 1998, 5–6), in which he definitively demonstrated that, whereas during the Lohmann phase this area included a large plaza with both large and small structures surrounding it (as discussed in chapter 15), during the Stirling phase all of the latter had been cleared away, a large plaza constructed, and a series of woodhenges (or as he called them, post-circle monuments) dominated this zone. Rolingson (1996, 84–85) has acknowledged this fact. In my view, Pauketat's work in this regard is commendable and, indeed, has simply strengthened the validity of Sherrod and Rolingson's work on the placement of the mounds of Cahokia.

2. In fact, Rolingson (1996, 91–92) notes that of the ninety mounds, seventeen (or 19 percent) were not on the TM increment. However, while the seven extra would appear to slightly exceed the 2 percent margin of error, they can be interpreted as generally within the ±2 percent. In any case, I do not believe that these few extra mounds make any difference to the following analysis. As with the other ten, their not being on the TM increment could simply be because they were placed in accordance with nearby primary mounds that were on the TM module.

3. This could be independently empirically verified, of course. For example, given the probable late Terminal Late Woodland construction of Woodhenge 72, since PP1 of Mound 72 is on the Point A TM increment, we should not be surprised that it is also on the Feature 452 alignment. However, in this case, a more correct description would probably be to say that Feature 452 is on the Woodhenge 72 alignment, that is, Feature 452 would have been positioned by the conjunction of axes measured from Point A and either the center viewing post of Woodhenge 72 or PP1.

4. At the end of the Stirling phase, the Tract 15A woodhenges were dismantled and Moorehead phase structures were constructed. Therefore, Feature 452 would probably have been abandoned.

5. Of course, as I comment earlier in this chapter, Sherrod and Rolingson note that the solstitial alignments were not ignored at Cahokia. However, the mode of marking (as they report these alignments) seems to treat these solstitial alignments as having lesser importance than the equinoctial alignments, since Point A of Monks Mound, for example, was directly tied into equinoctial alignments while only auxiliary points on Monks Mound allowed for mediating the solstitial alignments in tandem with several other mounds. Therefore, the latter seemed to have been tacked on to this mound's more basic involvement with the equinoctial alignments.

6. There may be a fourth major alignment, of course. As discussed in chapter 13, all the mass lethal human sacrificial deposits were oriented toward the Woodhenge 72 Locus III-NE post, and Krupp (1996, 65) has commented on the possibility that Locus III-NE marks the time of the year, August 20–21, when the new fire ceremony or green corn rite might have been performed.

7. Mounds 50 and 55 are listed in the upper right panel of Table 17.2, while Mound 51 is in the lower right. In terms of the relative chronology postulated for this distribution, the former two would fit the early Stirling phase timing. Mound 51, however, would be late Stirling. Interestingly, Rolingson (1996, 92–93) comments that radiocarbon dating places all these in the Stirling phase, along with Mounds 54 and 56, which are also in the upper right panel.

8. Ramey-Incised pottery, along with other distinctive artifacts and features, has been used by Pauketat (2000, 33) to further his argument that the Cahokia elite recruited symbolism in order to dominate. In this case, he claims that these are the symbols representing the community and that by centralizing this symbolic production and use in Cahokia, the elite also appropriated community as group-identity forma-

tion: "These were symbols with interrelated, multivocalic meanings that defined the cosmos, kinship, gender, and the domestic rhythms of everyday life. . . . In this respect, the entire ritual grounds of Mississippian centers themselves were constructions and reconstructions of community as meaning and identity . . . with the other material symbols and meaningful practices simply being parts of this whole."

9. For example, as I point out in chapter 11, Emerson and Pauketat put forward a similar argument to account for the fall-off of the quantity and distribution of exotica.

10. According to Table 17.2, Rattlesnake Mound (Mound 66), located in the lower left panel, would be a Lohmann phase feature; its paired mound (Mound 65), in the lower right panel, would be a late Stirling or Moorehead phase mound. Rattlesnake Mound, a large ridge-top mound, would probably be contemporary with the smaller ridge-top Mound 72, even though the latter is located in the upper left panel since, as I argue earlier in this chapter, the position of Feature 452 was likely fixed by using PP1 under Mound 72. The known mortuary deposit contents of Rattlesnake Mound appear to be primarily bundle burials, in contrast to the primary extended burials and mass lethal sacrificial deposits that form the majority of the contents of Mound 72. This pattern of treatment of the deceased would suggest a prevalence of postmortem human sacrifice in the former and, in contrast, of lethal human sacrifice in the latter. If this is the case, then the two contrasts could be manifesting the centralist-autonomist competition. While Mound 72 is clearly associated with the solstitial ritual, the east-west orientation of Rattlesnake Mound suggests that this mound may be associated with equinoctial ritual. However, since Taylor did not carry out a comprehensive excavation of Mound 66, it could still contain much more mortuary data (Pauketat and Barker 2000, 128, 139), and therefore, this interpretation must remain hypothetical for now.

11. Emerson (1991, 235–36) argues that the rather abrupt "Mississippianization" of the lower Illinois Valley during the Stirling phase can be seen as the result of the migration of disaffected chiefs from the American Bottom who lost out in the competitive infighting. The alternative view would be to argue that this "Mississippianization" was the result of the preexisting integrated villages in this area adopting the bifurcated settlement articulation mode. Previously, as integrated villages, they could have been subjected to ongoing attacks from the cult alliances of the American Bottom. By shifting to the bifurcated mode, the cults could pursue their vengeance warfare while the dispersed villages would become neutral. Alternatively, the cults could also be in a position that would enhance their joining with and participating in the American Bottom cult heterarchies, thereby accounting for the emergence in the late Moorehead phase of the Kane Mounds CBL site Illinois Valley mortuary traits (Emerson and Hargrave 2000, 17–18). Of course, this is merely a suggestion that requires much further research.

Chapter 18. The History and Outcome of Factional Competition in Cahokia

1. I am alluding to the Vacant Quarter thesis of Williams (1990, 173), of course, in which he postulates that much of the bottomlands of the central Mississippi Valley drainage became essentially vacated by A.D. 1400. This is consistent with the rather rapid collapse of Cahokia following A.D. 1300, as recently acknowledged by Emerson (2002, 137). I discuss this collapse in more detail later in the chapter.

2. There were seven degrees of esoteric knowledge and know-how associated with each sector of the cosmos. Since each clan was identified with one sector or aspect of the cosmos, this meant a total of 168 (24 × 7) bodies of cosmological knowledge and ritual know-how to learn. A priestly initiate was always started at the first degree level and could proceed to each of the higher degree levels in his sector. Only a small group of members ever achieved full knowledge in their areas, and they became the experts who would actually conduct the rituals that were under their competence (Bailey 1995, 49–58). In fact, Bailey characterizes them as the "leaders of the Osage priesthoods [who] formed the intellectual elite of the tribe— what in Western society would be called the theologians, philosophers, and scholars," and he contrasts them with "the less intellectually oriented priests, as well as the common people, [who] viewed rituals quite differently. To many of these people, rituals possessed mystical potency. Embodied within the *wa-xo'-be* were supernatural forces that were potentially dangerous and could be used for good or evil" (Bailey 1995, 278).

3. For example, Bailey (1995, 44–45) asserts,

> Together the priests were the ultimate power and authority within the tribe. Every major and most minor decisions and actions required a ritual and the formal sanction of the priests. It is they alone who determined policies or war and peace. Only priests could authorize a war party or award war honors. Only the priests could perform the necessary farming, hunting, and other rituals. . . . [T]he whole tribal structure and even the offices of the chiefs were creations of the priests. Ritual and the concurrent authority of the priests permeated every aspect of Osage life.

However, I suggest that it is one thing to note that many practices required the blessing of the priests and another to conclude that the latter were the dominant force in the social structure. Instead I detect a strong element of custodial duty involved, with the priests being urged to discharge their duties and they, in turn, continually urging that the junior age-grade warriors, for example, uphold the value of Osage unity while, at the same time, enacting modifications to standing practices that they could see that the young were ready to carry out in any case.

4. Some of the anomalies that I address and resolve through applying premises of the heterarchical polyistic locale-centric account are (1) the claimed concurrent/subsequent demographic nucleation/dispersal characterizing the emergence and development of the Lohmann phase, (2) the material permeability of the postulated elite/

commoner division as marked by the distribution of exotics and ceramic fineware and other so-called elite items, (3) the fall-off in exotics marking the Stirling phase, (4) the anomalous position of the St. Louis site and the Creek Bottom Group of Cahokia arising from Milner's objectivist account, (5) the contradiction revealed in the mortuary data between the claim that it manifests an elite/commoner structure and simultaneously an egalitarian distribution of health and nutrition, (6) the simultaneous presence of two contrasting mortuary programs caught up in the same Mound 72 CBL, (7) the existence of a palisade with an open side, (8) the apparent "trashing" of human remains in a social system that clearly valued mortuary remains, and (9) the absence of mortuary remains in many of the upland "graves," to note a few. Even the Sacred Maize model, as a fundamental component of the overall deontic ecological framework of the heterarchical polyistic locale-centric account can be added here, accounting for the puzzle of the rather rapid emergence of maize as a subsistence food after generations of limited ritual use and the equally rapid emergence of the Z-twist/S-twist duality.

5. According to Knight and Steponaitis (1998, fig. 1.2, p. 8; also see Steponaitis 1998, 39–40), the occupation of Moundville reached its zenith between the later early Moundville I, when its three-sided palisade overlooking the Black Warrior River may also have been first built, and the end of Moundville I. This would date it between ca. A.D. 1100/1125 and ca. A.D. 1250. According to Pauketat (1991, 59), this would be almost the equivalent of the Stirling phase at Cahokia, with the latter terminating a little earlier, ca. A.D. 1200. Of note, however, is the rebuilding of the Cahokia palisade at least twice and possibly three times in the Moorehead phase. This would also mean that both Cahokia and Moundville built and maintained palisades during the same time period. In fact, Knight argues that the total Moundville mound-plaza system was in use between A.D. 1250 and 1300. Clearly this means that it would have reached its zenith by A.D. 1250 (Knight 1998, 52). I will not pursue this point here except to note that this timing would seem to contradict Knight's claim that two historical trajectories were out of temporal phase. In fact, given his claim that Moundville I was initiated ca. A.D. 1050, and given that this is the currently accepted date for the initiation of the Lohmann phase, we might more logically see this as quite a close and synchronous rather than an out-of-phase development history of these two multiple-mound locales.

6. However, as I note earlier in note 1 of this chapter, both Emerson (2002, 138–39) and Pauketat (2002, 162–63) have recently modified their position, now recognizing that Cahokia and the American Bottom regional system probably "collapsed" as rapidly as it emerged. They even mention this possibility in the same paper from which the quotation in the text associated with this note is taken: "In fact, ongoing research by Emerson may point toward a more abrupt ending of the Moorehead-phase Cahokian-Mississippian world" (Pauketat and Emerson 1997b, 278). I analyze this new position in the critique that follows this description of the anomalies.

7. This is very close to the tactic used by King (2003, 5–6) in comparing Etowah and

Cahokia. He claims that the latter is a paramount chiefdom based on the corporate political economic strategy and the former is based on the network political economic strategy (King 2003, 17). Knight's structural-chiefdom and opportunistic-chiefdom categories would appear to fit King's view, the former being based on the corporate strategy (stable) and the latter on the network strategy (unstable).

8. In addition to Searle's theory of intentionality, Bhaskar's view of society and action forms the theoretical background for my deep/surface structural distinction. Bhaskar characterizes the agent-structure relation as a double duality by noting that society "is both the ever-present *condition* (material cause) and the continually repro-duced *outcome* of human agency. And praxis is both work, that is, conscious *production*, and (normally unconscious) *reproduction* of the conditions of production, that is soci-ety. One could refer to the former as the *duality of structure,* and the latter as the *duality of praxis*" (43–44, emphases in original). In my view, the deep/surface structural dis-tinction is a necessary addition to Bhaskar's double duality of agency and structure.

9. I hope, by my discussion of the particular social and cultural nature of the his-toric Osage as possibly the result of their prehistoric Mississippian-related collective experience, to illustrate the degree to which deep structures can be both modified and reproduced. For example, the immanentist cosmology and squatter ethos constituting the deep structures of the Osage cultural tradition, as well as their dual clan-cult social relations, must have remained largely intact.

Bibliography

Ahler, Steven R. 1999. Projectile Point Caches. Chapter 8 in *The Mound 72 Area: Dedicated and Sacred Space in Early Cahokia,* by Melvin L. Fowler, Jerome Rose, Barbara Vander Leest, and Steven R. Ahler, 101–15. Illinois State Museum Reports of Investigations 54. Springfield.

Ahler, Steven R., and Peter J. DePuydt. 1987. *A Report on the 1931 Powell Mound Excavations, Madison County, Illinois.* Illinois State Museum Reports of Investigations 43. Springfield.

Alt, Susan M. 2001. Cahokian Change and the Authority of Tradition. In *The Archaeology of Traditions: Agency and History before and after Columbus,* ed. Timothy R. Pauketat, 141–56. Gainesville: University Press of Florida.

Anderson, David G. 1997. The Role of Cahokia in the Evolution of Southeastern Society. In *Cahokia: Domination and Ideology in the Mississippian World,* ed. Timothy Pauketat and Thomas E. Emerson, 248–68. Lincoln: University of Nebraska Press.

Anderson, James. 1969. A Cahokia Palisade Sequence. In *Explorations in Cahokian Archaeology,* ed. Melvin L. Fowler, 89–99. Illinois Archaeological Survey Bulletin 7. Urbana: University of Illinois Press.

Bailey, Garrick A. 1995. *The Osage and the Invisible World: From the Works of Francis La Flesche.* Norman: University of Oklahoma Press.

Bell, Robert E. 1972. *The Harlan Site, Ck-6, a Prehistoric Mound Center in Cherokee County, Eastern Oklahoma.* Memoir 2. Norman: Oklahoma Anthropological Society.

Bhaskar, Roy. 1978. *A Realist Theory of Science.* Hassocks, Sussex: Harvester Press.

———. 1979. *The Possibility of Naturalism.* Atlantic Highlands, N.J.: Humanities Press.

Black, Glenn A. 1967. *Angel Site: An Archaeological, Historical, and Ethnological Study,* vol. 1. Indianapolis: Indiana Historical Society.

Booth, Donald L. 2001. The Center Grove Site: A Nearly Invisible Early Mississippian Mortuary Facility in the Uplands of Madison County, Illinois. *Illinois Archaeology* 13(1–2):36–56.

Bradley, Richard. 1993. *Altering the Earth.* Edinburgh: Society of Antiquaries of Scotland.

Brown, James A. 1975. Spiro Art and Its Mortuary Context. In *Death and the Afterlife in Pre-Columbian America,* ed. Elizabeth P. Benson, 1–32. Washington, D.C.: Dunbarton Oaks.

———. 1985. Long-Term Trends to Sedentism and the Emergence of Complexity in the American Midwest. In *Prehistoric Hunters-Gatherers,* ed. T. Douglas Price and James A. Brown, 201–31. New York: Academic Press.

————. 1986. Food for Thought: Where Has Subsistence Analysis Gotten Us? In *Foraging, Collecting, and Harvesting: Archaic Period Subsistence and Settlement in the Eastern Woodlands,* ed. Sarah W. Neusius, 315–30. Center for Archaeological Investigations, Occasional Paper 6. Carbondale: University of Illinois Press.

————. 1995. Andean Mortuary Practices in Perspective. In *Tombs for the Living: Andean Mortuary Practices,* ed. Tom D. Dillehay, 391–405. Washington, D.C.: Dunbarton Oaks Research Library and Collections.

————. 2003. The Cahokia Mound 72-Sub 1 Burials. In *A Deep-Time Perspective: Studies in Symbols, Meaning, and the Archaeological Record,* ed. John D. Richards and Melvin L. Fowler. *Wisconsin Archaeologist* 84(1–2):81–97.

Brown, James A., and Robert K. Vierra. 1983. What Happened in the Middle Archaic? Introduction to an Ecological Approach to Koster Site Archaeology. In *Archaic Hunters and Gatherers in the American Midwest,* ed. James L. Phillips and James A. Brown, 165–95. New York: Academic Press.

Brumfiel, Elizabeth M. 1989. Factional Competition in Complex Society. In *Domination and Resistance,* ed. Daniel Miller, Michael Rowlands, and Christopher Tilley, 127–39. London: Unwin Hyman.

————. 1994. Introduction. In *Factional Competition and Political Development in the New World,* ed. Elizabeth M. Brumfiel and John W. Fox, 3–14. Cambridge: Cambridge University Press.

————. 1995. Comments. In *Heterarchy and the Analysis of Complex Societies,* ed. Robert M. Ehrenreich, Carole L. Crumley, and Janet E. Levy, 125–31. Archaeological Papers of the American Anthropological Association 6. Arlington, Va.

Byers, A. Martin. 1987. *The Earthwork Enclosures of the Central Ohio Valley: A Temporal and Structural Analysis of Woodland Society and Culture.* Ph.D. dissertation, State University of New York at Albany. Ann Arbor, Mich.: University Microfilms.

————. 1994. Symboling and the Middle-Upper Palaeolithic Transition. *Current Anthropology* 35(4):369–99.

————. 1999a. Intentionality, Symbolic Pragmatics, and Material Culture: Revisiting Binford's View of the Old Copper Complex. *American Antiquity* 64(2):265–87.

————. 1999b. Communication and Material Culture: Pleistocene Tools as Action Cues. *Cambridge Journal of Archaeology* 9(1):23–41.

————. 2004. *The Ohio Hopewell Episode: Paradigm Lost, Paradigm Gained.* Akron, Ohio: University of Akron Press.

Charles, Douglas K. 1985. *Corporate Symbols: An Interpretive Prehistory of Indian Burial Mounds in West-Central Illinois.* Ph.D. dissertation, Northwestern University. Ann Arbor, Mich.: University Microfilms.

————. 1995. Diachronic Regional Social Dynamics: Mortuary Sites in the Illinois Valley/American Bottom Region. In *Regional Approaches to Mortuary Analysis,* ed. Lane Anderson Beck, 77–99. New York: Plenum Press.

Charles, Douglas K., and Jane E. Buikstra. 1983. Archaic Mortuary Sites in the Central Mississippi Drainage: Distribution, Structure and Behavioral Implications. In *Archaic Hunters and Gatherers in the American Midwest*, ed. James L. Phillips and James A. Brown, 117–45. New York: Academic Press.

Charles, Douglas K., Jane E. Buikstra, and Lyle W. Konigsberg. 1986. Behavioral Implications of Terminal Archaic and Early Woodland Mortuary Practices in the Lower Illinois Valley. In *Early Woodland Archaeology*, ed. Kenneth B. Farnsworth and Thomas E. Emerson, 458–74. Kampsville Seminar 2. Kampsville, Ill.: Center for American Archaeology.

Cheney, Dorothy L., and Robert M. Seyfarth. 1990. *How Monkeys See the World: Inside the Mind of Another Species*. Chicago: University of Chicago Press.

Cobb, Charles R. 1989. An Appraisal of the Role of Mill Creek Chert Hoes in Mississippian Exchange Systems. *Southeastern Archaeology* 8(2):79–92.

———. 1991. One Hundred Years of Investigations at the Linn Site in Southern Illinois. *Illinois Archaeology* 3(1):56–76.

Conrad, Geoffrey W., and Arthur A. Demarest. 1984. *Religion and Empire: The Dynamics of Aztec and Inca Expansion*. Cambridge: Cambridge University Press.

Crumley, Carole L. 1995. Heterarchy and the Analysis of Complex Societies. In *Heterarchy and the Analysis of Complex Societies*, ed. Robert M. Ehrenreich, Carole L. Crumley, and Jane E. Levy, 1–5. Archaeological Papers of the American Anthropological Association 6. Arlington, Va.

Dalan, Rinita A. 1997. Cahokian Food Production Reconsidered. In *Cahokia: Dominance and Ideology in the Mississippian World*, ed. Timothy R. Pauketat and Thomas E. Emerson, 89–102. Lincoln: University of Nebraska Press.

Drooker, Penelope Ballard. 1992. *Mississippian Village Textiles at Wickliffe*. Tuscaloosa: University of Alabama Press.

Emerson, Thomas E. 1984. Water, Serpents, and the Underworld: An Exploration into Cahokia Symbolism. In *The Southeastern Ceremonial Complex: Artifacts and Analysis*, ed. Patricia Galloway, 45–92. Lincoln: University of Nebraska Press.

———. 1991. Some Perspectives on Cahokia and the Northern Mississippian Expansion. In *Cahokia and the Hinterlands: Middle Mississippian Cultures of the Midwest*, ed. Thomas E. Emerson and R. Barry Lewis, 221–36. Urbana: University of Illinois Press.

———. 1992. The Mississippian Dispersed Village as a Social and Environmental Strategy. In *Late Prehistoric Agriculture: Observations from the Midwest*, ed. William I. Wood, 198–216. Studies in Illinois Archaeology 8. Springfield: Illinois Historic Preservation Agency.

———. 1997a. Cahokian Elite Ideology and the Mississippian Cosmos. In *Cahokia: Domination and Ideology in the Mississippian World*, ed. Timothy R. Pauketat and Thomas E. Emerson, 190–228. Lincoln: University of Nebraska Press.

———. 1997b. Reflections from the Countryside on Cahokian Hegemony. In *Cahokia:*

Domination and Ideology in the Mississippian World, ed. Timothy R. Pauketat and Thomas E. Emerson, 167–89. Lincoln: University of Nebraska Press.

———. 1997c. *Cahokia and the Archaeology of Power.* Tuscaloosa: University of Alabama Press.

———. 2002. An Introduction to Cahokia, 2002: Diversity, Complexity, and History. *Midcontinental Journal of Archaeology* 27(2):127–48.

———. 2003a. Crossing Boundaries between Worlds: Changing Beliefs and Mortuary Practices at Cahokia. In *A Deep-Time Perspective: Studies in Symbols, Meaning, and the Archaeological Record,* ed. John D. Richards and Melvin L. Fowler. *Wisconsin Archaeologist* 84(1–2):73–80.

———. 2003b. Materializing Cahokia Shamans. *Southeastern Archaeology* 22(2):135–53.

Emerson, Thomas E., and Eva A. Hargrave. 2000. Strangers in Paradise? Recognizing Ethnic Mortuary Diversity on the Fringes of Cahokia. *Southeastern Archaeology* 19(1):1–23.

Emerson, Thomas E., Eva A. Hargrave, and Kristin Hedman. 2003. Death and Ritual in Early Rural Cahokia. In *Theory, Method, and Practice in Modern Archaeology,* ed. Robert J. Jeske and Douglas K. Charles, 163–81. Westport, Conn.: Praeger.

Emerson, Thomas E., Randall E. Hughes, Mary R. Hynes, and Sarah U. Wisseman. 2002. Implications of Sourcing Cahokia-Style Flint Clay Figurines in the American Bottom and the Upper Mississippi River Valley. *Midcontinental Journal of Archaeology* 27(2):309–38.

Emerson, Thomas E., and Douglas K. Jackson. 1984. *The BBB Motor Site (11-Ms-595).* Illinois Department of Transportation. American Bottom Archaeology FAI-270 Site Reports. Vol. 6. University of Illinois Press, Urbana.

Emerson, Thomas E., George R. Milner, and Douglas K. Jackson. 1983. *The Florence Street Site (11-S-458).* Illinois Department of Transportation. Urbana: University of Illinois Press.

Emerson, Thomas E., and Timothy Pauketat. 2002. Embodying Power and Resistance at Cahokia. In *The Dynamics of Power,* ed. Maria O'Donovan, 105–25. Center for Archaeological Investigations, Occasional Papers 30. Carbondale: Southern Illinois University Press.

Esarey, Duane, and Timothy R. Pauketat. 1992. *The Lohmann Site: An Early Mississippian Center in the American Bottom (11-S-49).* Illinois Department of Transportation. Urbana: University of Illinois Press.

Fagan, Brian M. 1984. *The Aztecs.* New York: W. H. Freeman and Company.

Fortier, Andrew C., and Douglas K. Jackson. 2000. The Formation of a Late Woodland Heartland in the American Bottom, Illinois cal. A.D. 650–900. In *Late Woodland Societies: Tradition and Transformation across the Midcontinent,* ed. Thomas E. Emerson, Dale L. McElrath, and Andrew C. Fortier, 123–47. Lincoln: University of Nebraska Press.

Fortier, Andrew C., Richard B. Lacampagne, and Fred A. Finney. 1984. *The Fish Lake Site (11-Mo-608)*. American Bottom Archaeology FAI-270 Site Reports 8. Urbana: University of Illinois Press.

Fortier, Andrew C., Thomas O. Maher, and Joyce A. Williams. 1991. *The Sponemann Site: The Formative Emergent Mississippian Sponemann Phase Occupation (11-Ms-517)*. Illinois Department of Transportation. Urbana: University of Illinois Press.

Fortier, Andrew C., and Dale L. McElrath. 2002. Deconstructing the Emergent Mississippian Concept: The Case for the Terminal Late Woodland. *Midcontinental Journal of Archaeology* 27(2):171–215.

Fowler, Chris. 2004. *The Archaeology of Personhood: An Anthropological Approach*. London: Routledge.

Fowler, Melvin L. 1974. Cahokia: Ancient Capitol of the Midwest. *Addison-Wesley Module in Archaeology*. 48:3–38.

———. 1978. Cahokia and the American Bottom: Settlement Archaeology. In *Mississippian Settlement Patterns*, ed. Bruce D. Smith, 455–78. New York: Academic Press.

———. 1991. Mound 72 and the Early Mississippian of Cahokia. In *New Perspectives on Cahokia: Views from the Periphery*, ed. James B. Stoltman, 1–28. Monographs in World Archaeology 2. Madison, Wis.: Prehistory Press.

———. 1992. The Eastern Horticultural Complex and Mississippian Agricultural Fields: Studies and Hypotheses. In *Late Prehistoric Agriculture: Observations from the Midwest*, ed. William I. Woods, 1–18. Studies in Illinois Archaeology 8. Springfield: Illinois Historic Preservation Agency.

———. 1996. The Mound 72 and Woodhenge 72 Area of Cahokia. In *Ancient Skies and Sky Watchers of Cahokia: Woodhenges, Eclipses, and Cahokian Cosmology*, ed. Melvin L. Fowler. *Wisconsin Archaeologist* 77(3/4):36–59.

———. 1997. *The Cahokia Atlas: A Historical Atlas of Cahokia Archaeology*. Rev. ed. Illinois Transportation Archaeological Research Program. Urbana: University of Illinois Press.

Fowler, Melvin L., Jerome Rose, Barbara Vander Leest, and Steven R. Ahler. 1999. *The Mound 72 Area: Dedicated and Sacred Space in Early Cahokia*. Illinois State Museum Reports of Investigations 54. Springfield.

Fritz, Gayle J. 1992. "Newer," "Better" Maize and the Mississippian Emergence: A Critique of Prime Mover Explanations. In *Late Prehistoric Agriculture: Observations from the Midwest*, ed. William I. Woods, 19–43. Studies in Illinois Archaeology 8. Springfield: Illinois Historic Preservation Agency.

Giddens, Anthony. 1979. *Central Problems in Social Theory: Action, Structure and Contradiction in Social Analysis*. London: MacMillan Press.

———. 1984. *The Constitution of Society*. Berkeley: University of California Press.

Goldstein, Lynne G. 1980. *Mississippian Mortuary Practices: A Case Study of Two Cemeteries in the Lower Illinois Valley*. : Northwestern University Archeological Program, Scientific Papers 4. Evanston, Ill.

———. 1981. One-Dimensional Archaeology and Multi-Dimensional People: Spatial Organisation and Mortuary Analysis. In *The Archaeology of Death,* ed. Robert Chapman, Ian Kinnes, and Klavs Randsborg, 53–69. London: Cambridge University Press.

———. 1995. Landscape and Mortuary Practices: A Case Study for Regional Perspectives. In *Regional Approaches to Mortuary Analysis,* ed. Lane Anderson Beck, 101–21. New York: Plenum Press.

———. 2000. Mississippian Ritual as Viewed through the Practice of Secondary Disposal of the Dead. In *Modoc, Monuments, Mesoamerica: Papers in Honor of Melvin L. Fowler,* ed. Steven R. Ahler, 193–204. Scientific Papers 28. Springfield: Illinois State Museum.

Goldstein, Lynne G., and John D. Richards. 1991. Ancient Aztalan: The Cultural and Ecological Context of a Late Prehistoric Site in the Midwest. In *Cahokia and the Hinterlands: Middle Mississippian Cultures of the Midwest,* ed. Thomas E. Emerson and R. Barry Lewis, 193–206. Urbana: University of Illinois Press.

Green, Thomas J., and Cheryl A. Munson. 1978. Mississippian Settlement Patterns in Southwestern Indiana. In *Mississippian Settlement Patterns,* ed. Bruce D. Smith, 293–330. New York: Academic Press.

Hall, Robert L. 1977. An Anthropocentric Perspective for Eastern United States Prehistory. *American Antiquity* 42(4):499–518.

———. 1980. The Two-Climax Model of Illinois Prehistory. In *Early Native Americans: Prehistoric Demography, Economy and Technology,* ed. David L. Browman, 401–62. The Hague: Mouton Press.

———. 1984. The Cultural Background of Mississippian Symbolism. In *The Southeastern Ceremonial Complex: Artifacts and Analysis—The Cottonlandia Conference,* ed. Patricia Galloway, 239–278. Lincoln: University of Nebraska Press.

———. 1996. American Indian Worlds, World Quarters, World Centers, and Their Shrines. In *The Ancient Skies and Sky Watchers of Cahokia: Woodhenges, Eclipses, and Cosmology,* ed. Marvin L. Fowler. *Wisconsin Archaeologist* 77(3–4):120–27.

———. 1997. *An Archaeology of the Soul: North American Indian Belief and Ritual.* Urbana: University of Illinois Press.

———. 2000. Sacrificed Foursomes and Green Corn Ceremonialism. In *Mounds, Modoc, and Mesoamerica: Papers in Honor of Melvin L. Fowler,* ed. Steven R. Ahler, 245–53. Scientific Papers 28. Springfield: Illinois State Museum.

Hally, David J., Marvin T. Smith, and James B. Langford. 1990. The Archaeological Reality of de Soto's Coosa. In *Columbian Consequences: Archaeological and Historical Perspectives on the Spanish Hinterlands East,* ed. David Hurst Thomas, 121–38. Washington, D.C.: Smithsonian Institution Press.

Harré, Rom. 1979. *Social Being: A Theory of Social Psychology.* Oxford: Basil Blackwell.

Hedman, Kristin, and Eva A. Hargrave. 1999. *Hill Prairie Mounds: The Osteology of a Late Middle Mississippian Mortuary Population.* Illinois Transportation Archaeological Research Reports 6. University of Illinois Department of Anthropology. Urbana-Champaign: University of Illinois Press.

Holly, George R., William I. Woods, Renita A. Dalan, and Harold W. Walters. 1997. Appendix 6, Current Research. In *The Cahokia Atlas: A Historical Atlas of Cahokia Archaeology,* rev. ed., by Melvin L. Fowler, 231–35. Illinois Transportation Archaeological Research Program. Urbana: University of Illinois Press.

Hurt, R. Douglas. 1987. *Indian Agriculture in America: Prehistory to the Present.* Lawrence: University Press of Kansas.

Ingold, Tim. 1987. *The Appropriation of Nature: Essays on Human Ecology and Social Relations.* Iowa City: University of Iowa Press.

Irwin, Lee. 1994. *The Dream Seekers: Native American Visionary Traditions of the Great Plains.* Norman: University of Oklahoma Press.

Iseminger, William R., Timothy R. Pauketat, Brad Koldehoff, Lucretia S. Kelly, and Leonard Blake. 1990. *East Palisade Investigations,* 1–197. Illinois Cultural Resources 14. Illinois Historic Preservation Agency. Urbana: University of Illinois Press.

Jackson, Douglas J., Andrew Fortier, and Joyce A. Williams. 1992. *The Sponemann Site,* vol. 2, *The Mississippian and Oneota Occupations.* American Bottom Archaeology FAI-270 Site Reports 24. Urbana: University of Illinois Press.

Johannessen, Sissel. 1993a. Farmers of the Late Woodland. In *Foraging and Farming in the Eastern Woodlands,* ed. C. Margaret Scarry, 57–77. Gainesville: University Press of Florida.

———. 1993b. Food, Dishes, and Society in the Mississippi Valley. In *Foraging and Farming in the Eastern Woodlands,* ed. C. Margaret Scarry, 182–205. Gainesville: University Press of Florida.

Kelly, John Edward. 1982. *Formative Development at Cahokia and the Adjacent American Bottom: A Merrell Tract Perspective,* vols. 1 and 2. Archaeological Research Laboratory. Macomb: Western Illinois University Press.

———. 1990a. Range Site Community Patterns. In *The Mississippian Emergence,* ed. Bruce D. Smith, 67–112. Washington, D.C.: Smithsonian Institution Press.

———. 1990b. The Emergence of Mississippian Culture in the American Bottom Region. In *The Mississippian Emergence,* ed. Bruce D. Smith, 113–52. Washington, D.C.: Smithsonian Institution Press.

———. 1992. The Impact of Maize on the Development of Nucleated Settlements: An American Bottom Example. In *Late Prehistoric Agriculture: Observations from the Midwest,* ed. William I. Woods, 167–97. Studies in Illinois Archaeology 8. Springfield: Illinois Historic Preservation Agency.

———. 1993. The Pulcher Site: An Archaeological and Historical Overview. *Illinois Archaeology* 5(1–2):434–51.

———. 1994. The Archaeology of the East St. Louis Mound Center: Past and Present. *Illinois Archaeology* 6:1–57.

———. 1996. Redefining Cahokia: Principles and Elements of Community Organization. In *Ancient Skies and Sky Watchers of Cahokia: Woodhenges, Eclipses, and Cahokian Cosmology*, ed. Melvin L. Fowler. *Wisconsin Archaeologist* 77(3–4):97–119.

———. 1997. Stirling-Phase Sociopolitical Activity at East St. Louis and Cahokia. In *Cahokia: Domination and Ideology in the Mississippian World*, ed. Timothy R. Pauketat and Thomas E. Emerson, 141–66. Lincoln: University of Nebraska Press.

———. 2000. The Nature and Context of Emergent Mississippian Cultural Dynamics in the Greater American Bottom. In *Late Woodland Societies: Tradition and Transformation over the Midcontinent*, ed. Thomas E. Emerson, Dale L. McElrath, and Andrew C. Fortier, 163–75. Lincoln: University of Nebraska Press.

Kelly, John E., Andrew C. Fortier, Steven J. Ozuk, and Joyce A. Williams. 1987. *The Range Site: Archaic through Late Woodland Occupations (11-S-47)*. American Bottom Archaeology FAI-270 Site Reports 16. Urbana: University of Illinois Press.

Kelly, John E., Steven J. Ozuk, Douglas K. Jackson, Dale L. McElrath, Fred A. Finney, and Duane Esarey. 1984. Emergent Mississippian Period. In *American Bottom Archaeology*, ed. Charles J. Bareis and James W. Porter, 128–57. Illinois Department of Transportation. Urbana: University of Illinois Press.

Kelly, John E., Steven J. Ozuk, and Joyce A. Williams. 1990. *The Range Site, vol. 2, The Emergent Mississippian Dohack and Range Phase Occupations (11-S-47)*. American Bottom Archaeology FAI-270 Site Reports 20. Illinois Department of Transportation. Urbana: University of Illinois Press.

Kelly, Lucretia S. 1997. Patterns of Faunal Exploitation. In *Cahokia: Dominance and Ideology in the Mississippian World*, ed. Timothy R. Pauketat and Thomas E. Emerson, 69–88. Lincoln: University of Nebraska Press.

King, Adam. 2003. *Etowah: The Political History of a Chiefdom Capital*. Tuscaloosa: University of Alabama Press.

Klepinger, Linda L. 1993. The Skeletons of Fingerhut: An Early Cahokian Cemetery. *Illinois Archaeology* (1–2):421–24.

Knight, Vernon James, Jr. 1990. Social Organization and the Evolution of Hierarchy in Southeastern Chiefdoms. *Journal of Anthropological Research* 46(1):1–23.

———. 1997. Some Developmental Parallels between Cahokia and Moundville. In *Cahokia: Domination and Ideology in the Mississippian World*, ed. Timothy R. Pauketat and Thomas E. Emerson, pp. 229–47. Lincoln: University of Nebraska Press.

———. 1998. Moundville as a Diagrammatic Ceremonial Center. In *Archaeology of the Moundville Chiefdom*, ed. Vernon James Knight Jr. and Vincas Steponaitis, 44–62. Washington, D.C.: Smithsonian Institution Press.

Knight, Vernon James Jr. and Vincas P. Steponaitis. 1998. A New History of Moundville. In *Archaeology of the Moundville Chiefdom*, ed. Vernon James Knight Jr. and Vincas P. Steponaitis, 1–25. Washington, D.C.: Smithsonian Institution Press.

Koldehoff, Brad. 2002. *The Woodland Ridge Site and Late Woodland Use in the Southern*

American Bottom. Illinois Transportation Archaeological Research Program. Archaeological Report 15. Urbana-Champaign: University of Illinois Press.

Koldehoff, Brad, Dawn E. Cobb, and Jack R. Nawrot. 2002. The Eastern Woodrat (*Neotoma floridana*) and Its Archaeological Significance: A Southern Illinois Case Study. *Illinois Archaeology* 14:1–19.

Koldehoff, Brad, Timothy R. Pauketat, and John E. Kelly. 1993. The Emerald Site and the Mississippian Occupation of the Central Silver Creek Valley. *Illinois Archaeology* 5(1–2):331–43.

Krupp, E. C. 1996. How Much Sun Can a Woodhenge Catch? In *The Ancient Skies and Sky Watchers of Cahokia: Woodhenges, Eclipses, and Cahokian Cosmology*, ed. Melvin L. Fowler, *Wisconsin Archaeologists* 77(3/4):60–72.

Lopinot, Neal H. 1992. Spatial and Temporal Variability in Mississippian Subsistence: The Archaeobotanical Record. In *Late Prehistoric Agriculture: Observations from the Midwest*, ed. William I. Woods, 44–94. Studies in Illinois Archaeology Number 8, Illinois Historic Preservation Agency, Springfield, Illinois.

Mehrer, Mark W. 1995. *Cahokia's Countryside: Household Archaeology, Settlement Pattern, and Social Power*. Dekalb: Illinois University Press.

———. 2000. Heterarchy and Hierarchy: The Community as Institution in Cahokia's Polity. In *The Archaeology of Communities: A Household Perspective*, ed. Marcello A. Canuto and Jason Yaeger, 44–59. London: Routledge.

Melbye, F. Jerome. 1963. *The Kane Burial Mounds*. Archaeology Salvage Report 15. Carbondale: Southern Illinois University Museum.

Milner, George R. 1982. *Measuring Prehistoric Levels of Health: A Study of Mississippian Period Skeletal Remains from the American Bottom, Illinois*. Ph.D. dissertation, Northwestern University.

———. 1983. *The East St. Louis Stone Quarry Site Cemetery (11-S-468)*. American Bottom Archaeology FAI 270 Site Reports 1. Illinois Department of Transportation. Urbana: University of Illinois Press.

———. 1984. Social and Temporal Implications of Variation among American Bottom Mississippian Cemeteries. *American Antiquity* 49(3):468–88.

———. 1990. The Late Prehistoric Cahokia Cultural System of the Mississippi River Valley. *Journal of World Archaeology* 4(1):1–43.

———. 1992. Morbidity, Mortality, and the Adaptive Success of an Oneota Population from West-Central Illinois. In *Late Prehistoric Agriculture: Observations from the Midwest*, ed. William I. Woods, 136–66. Studies in Illinois Archaeology 8. Springfield: Illinois Historic Preservation Agency.

———. 1998. *The Cahokia Chiefdom: The Archaeology of a Mississippian Society*. Washington, D.C.: Smithsonian Institution Press.

———. 2003. Archaeological Indicators of Rank in the Cahokian Chiefdom. In *Theory, Method, and Practice in Modern Archaeology*, ed. Robert J. Jeske and Douglas K. Charles, 133–48. Westport, Conn.: Praeger.

Muller, Jon. 1978. The Kincaid System: Mississippian Settlement in the Environs of a Large Site. In *Mississippian Settlement Patterns,* ed. Bruce D. Smith, 269–92. New York: Academic Press.

———. 1997. *Mississippian Political Economy.* New York: Plenum Press.

Munson, Patrick J. 1971. *An Archaeological Survey of the Wood Terrace and Adjacent Bottoms and Bluffs in Madison County, Illinois.* Illinois State Museum Reports of Investigations no. 21, part 1, 3–17. Springfield.

O'Brien, Patricia J. 1989. Cahokia: The Political Capital of the "Ramey" State? *North American Archaeologist* 10(4):275–92.

Pauketat, Timothy R. 1991. *The Dynamics of Pre-State Political Centralization in the North American Midcontinent.* Ph.D. dissertation, University of Michigan.

———. 1992. The Reign and Ruin of the Lords of Cahokia: A Dialectic of Dominance. In *Lords of the Southeast: Social Inequality and the Native Elites of Southeastern North America,* ed. Alex W. Barker and Timothy R. Pauketat, 31–51. Archaeology Papers of the American Anthropological Association Number 3.

———. 1993. *Temples for Cahokia Lords: Preston Holder's 1955–1956 Excavations of Kunnemann Mound.* University of Michigan, Memoirs of the Museum of Anthropology 26. Ann Arbor, Mich.: Museum of Anthropology.

———. 1994. *The Ascent of Chiefs: Cahokia and Mississippian Politics in Native North America.* Tuscaloosa: University of Alabama Press.

———. 1996. The Place of Post-Circle Monuments in Cahokian Political History. In *The Ancient Skies and Sky Watchers of Cahokia: Woodhenges, Eclipses, and Cahokian Cosmology,* ed. Melvin L. Fowler. *Wisconsin Archaeologist* 77(3–4):73–83.

———. 1997. Cahokian Political Economy. In *Cahokia: Domination and Ideology in the Mississippian World,* ed. Timothy R. Pauketat and Thomas E. Emerson, 30–51. Lincoln: University of Nebraska Press.

———. 1998. *The Archaeology of Downtown Cahokia: The Tract 15A and Dunham Tract Excavation.* Studies in Archaeology 1. Illinois Transportation Archaeological Research Program. Urbana: University of Illinois Press.

———. 2000. Politicization and Community in the Pre-Columbian Mississippi Valley. In *The Archaeology of Communities: A New World Perspective,* ed. Marcello A. Canuto and Jaron Yaeger, 16–43. London: Routledge.

———. 2002. A Fourth-Generation Synthesis of Cahokia and Mississippianization. *Midcontinental Journal of Archaeology* 27(2):149–70.

———. 2003. Resettled Farmers and the Making of a Mississippian Polity. *American Antiquity* 68(1):39–66.

Pauketat, Timothy R., and Alex W. Barker. 2000. Mounds 85 and 66 at Cahokia: Additional Details of the 1927 Excavations. In *Modoc, Monuments, Mesoamerica: Papers in Honor of Melvin L. Fowler,* ed. Steven R. Ahler, 125–40. Scientific Papers 28. Springfield: Illinois State Museum.

Pauketat, Timothy R., and Thomas E. Emerson. 1991. The Ideology of Authority and the Power of the Pot. *American Anthropologist* 93:919–41.

———. 1997a. Introduction. In *Cahokia: Domination and Ideology in the Mississippian World,* ed. Timothy R. Pauketat and Thomas E. Emerson, 1–29. Lincoln: University of Nebraska Press.

———. 1997b. Conclusion: Cahokia and the Four Winds. In *Cahokia: Domination and Ideology in the Mississippian World,* ed. Timothy R. Pauketat and Thomas E. Emerson, 269–78. Lincoln: University of Nebraska Press.

———. 1999. Representations of Hegemony as Community at Cahokia. In *Material Symbols: Culture and Economy in Prehistory,* ed. John E. Robb, 302–17. Center for Archaeological Investigations, Occasional Paper 26. Carbondale: Southern Illinois University Press.

Pauketat, Timothy R., and Neal H. Lopinot. 1997. Cahokian Population Dynamics. In *Cahokia: Dominance and Ideology in the Mississippian World,* ed. Timothy R. Pauketat and Thomas E. Emerson, 103–23. Lincoln: University of Nebraska Press.

Porubcan, Paula J. 2000. Human and Nonhuman Surplus Display at Mound 72, Cahokia. In *Modoc, Monuments, Mesoamerica: Papers in Honor of Melvin L. Fowler,* ed. Steven R. Ahler, 207–16. Scientific Papers 28. Springfield: Illinois State Museum.

Porter, James Warren. 1969. The Mitchell Site and Prehistoric Exchange Systems. In *Explorations into Cahokia Archaeology,* ed. Melvin L. Fowler, 137–64. Illinois Archaeological Survey Bulletin 7. Urbana: University of Illinois Press.

Prentice, Guy, and Mark Mehrer. 1981. The Lab Woofie Site (11-S-346). *Midcontinental Journal of Archaeology* 6(1): 33–55.

Rautman, Alison E. 1998. Hierarchy and Heterarchy in the American Southwest: A Comment on McGuire and Saitta. *American Antiquity* 63(2):325–33.

Reed, Nelson A. 1969. Monks and Other Mississippian Mounds. In *Explorations in Cahokian Archaeology,* ed. Melvin L. Fowler, 31–42. Illinois Archaeological Survey Bulletin No. 7. Urbana: University of Illinois.

Rindos, David, and Sissel Johannessen. 1991. Human-Plant Interactions and Cultural Change in the American Bottom. In *Cahokia and the Hinterlands: Middle Mississippian Cultures of the Midwest,* ed. Thomas E. Emerson and R. Barry Lewis, 35–45. Urbana: University of Illinois Press.

Rogers, Rhea J. 1995. Tribes in Heterarchy: A Case Study from the Prehistoric Southeastern United States. In *Heterarchy and the Analysis of Complex Societies,* ed. Robert M. Ehrenreich, Carole L. Crumley, and Jane E. Levy, pp. 7–16. Archaeological Papers of the American Anthropological Association 6. Arlington, Va.

Rolingson, Martha Ann. 1996. Elements of Community Design at Cahokia. In *The Ancient Skies and Sky Watchers of Cahokia: Woodhenges, Eclipses, and Cahokian Cosmology,* ed. Melvin L. Fowler. *Wisconsin Archaeologist* 77(3–4):84–96.

Rollings, Willard H. 1992. *The Osage: An Ethnohistorical Study of Hegemony on the Prairie-Plains*. Columbia: University of Missouri Press.

Rose, Jerome C. 1999. Mortuary Data and Analysis. In *The Mound 72 Area: Dedicated and Sacred Space in Early Cahokia*, by Melvin L. Fowler, Jerome Rose, Barbara Vander Leest, and Steven R. Ahler, 63–82. Illinois State Museum Reports of Investigations 54. Springfield.

Saitta, Dean J. 1994. Agency, Class, and Interpretation. *Journal of Anthropological Archaeology* 13:201–27.

Scarry, C. Margaret. 1993. Variability in Mississippi Crop Production Strategies. In *Foraging and Farming in the Eastern Woodlands*, ed. C. Margaret Scarry, 78–90. Gainesville: University Press of Florida.

Searle, John R. 1983. *Intentionality*. Cambridge: Cambridge University Press.

———. 1995. *The Construction of Social Reality*. New York: Free Press.

Seeman, Mark F., and William S. Dancey. 2000. The Late Woodland Period in Southern Ohio: Basic Issues and Prospects. In *Late Woodland Societies: Tradition and Transformation across the Midcontinent*, ed. Thomas E. Emerson, Dale L. McElrath, and Andrew C. Fortier, 583–611. Lincoln: University of Nebraska Press.

Sherrod, P. Clay, and Martha Ann Rolingson. 1987. *Surveyors of the Ancient Mississippi Valley: Modules and Alignments in Prehistoric Mound Sites*. Research Series 28. Fayetteville: Arkansas Archaeological Survey.

Smith, Bruce D. 1987. The Independent Domestication of Indigenous Seed-Bearing Plants in Eastern North America. In *Emergent Horticultural Economies of the Eastern Woodlands*, ed. William F. Keegan, 3–47. Center for Archaeological Investigations Occasional Paper 7. Carbondale: Southern Illinois University Press.

———. 1992a. *Rivers of Change: Essays on Early Agriculturalists in Eastern North America*. Washington, D.C.: Smithsonian Institution Press.

———. 1992b. Prehistoric Plant Husbandry in Eastern North America. In *The Origins of Agriculture: An International Perspective*, ed. C. Wesley Cowan and Patty Jo Watson, 101–19. Washington, D.C.: Smithsonian Institution Press.

———. 1995. Seed Plant Domestication in Eastern North America. In *The Last Hunters–First Farmers*, ed. T. Douglas Price and Anne Birgitte Gebauer, 193–214. Santa Fe, N.Mex.: New School of American Research Press.

Smith, Harriet. 1969. The Murdoch Mound, Cahokia Site. In *Explorations into Cahokia Archaeology*, ed. Melvin L. Fowler, 49–88. Illinois Archaeological Survey Bulletin 7. Urbana: University of Illinois Press.

Stahl, Ann Brower. 1985. *The Dohack Site (11-S-642)*. American Bottom Archaeology FAI-270 Site Report 12. Illinois Department of Transportation. Urbana: Illinois University Press.

Steponaitis, Vincas P. 1998. Population Trends at Moundville. In *Archaeology of the Moundville Chiefdom*, ed. Vernon James Knight Jr. and Vincas P. Steponaitis, 26–43. Washington, D.C.: Smithsonian Institution Press.

Sugiyama, Saburo. 1989. Burials Dedicated to the Old Temple of Quetzalcoatl at Teoti-huacan, Mexico. *American Antiquity* 54:85–106.

Swanton, John W. 1911. *Indians of the Lower Mississippi Valley and the Adjacent Coast of the Gulf of Mexico.* Bureau of American Ethnology. Washington, D.C.: Smithsonian Institution.

Taylor, Charles. 1985a. What Is Human Agency? In *Human Agency and Language: Philosophical Papers,* 15–44. Cambridge: Cambridge University Press.

———. 1985b. Theories of Meaning. In *Human Agency and Language: Philosophical Papers,* 248–92. Cambridge: Cambridge University Press.

———. 1985c. Language and Human Nature. In *Human Agency and Language: Philosophical Papers,* 215–47. Cambridge: Cambridge University Press.

Thomas, Cyrus. 1894. Report on the Mound Explorations of the Bureau of Ethnology. *Twelfth Annual Report of the Bureau of Ethnology.* Washington, D.C.: Smithsonian Institution.

Townsend, Richard F. 1979. *State and Cosmos in the Art of Tenochtitlan.* Studies in Pre-Columbian Art and Archaeology 20. Washington, D.C.: Dunbarton Oaks Research Library and Collections.

———. 1992. *The Aztecs.* London: Thames and Hudson.

Trubitt, Mary Beth D. 2003. Mississippi Period Warfare and Palisade Construction at Cahokia. In *Theory, Method, and Practice in Modern Archaeology,* ed. Robert J. Jeske and Douglas K. Charles, 149–62. Westport, Conn.: Praeger.

Van Zantwijk, Rudolf. 1985. *The Aztec Arrangement: The Social History of Pre-Spanish Mexico.* Norman: University of Oklahoma Press.

Wallace, A. F. C. 1966. *Religion: An Anthropological View.* New York: Random House.

Walz, Gregory R., Brian Adams, Jacqueline M. McDowell, Paula P. Kreisa, Kevin P. Mc-Gowan, Kristin Hedman, and Cynthia L. Balek. 1997. *Archaeological Investigations for the Relocation of Valmeyer, Monroe County, Illinois,* vol. 3, *The Stemler Bluff Site.* Public Service Archaeology Program Research Report 28. University of Illinois Department of Anthropology. Urbana-Champaign: University of Illinois Press.

Watson, Robert J. 2000. Sacred Landscapes at Cahokia: Mound 72 and the Mound 72 Precinct. In *Modoc, Monuments, Mesoamerica: Papers in Honor of Melvin L. Fowler,* ed. Steven R. Ahler, 228–41. Scientific Papers 28. Springfield: Illinois State Museum.

Weissner, Polly. 1983. Style and Social Information in Kalahari San Projectile Points. *American Antiquity* 48:253–76.

Will, George F., and George E. Hyde. 1964. *Corn among the Indians of the Upper Missouri.* Originally published 1917, William H. Miner Co. Reprint, Lincoln: University of Nebraska Press.

Williams, Stephen. 1990. The Vacant Quarter and Other Late Events in the Lower Valley. In *Towns and Temples along the Mississippi,* ed. D. H. Dye, 170–80. Tuscaloosa: University of Alabama Press.

Wilson, Monica. 1963. *Good Company: A Study of Nyakyusa Age Villages.* Boston: Beacon Press.

Winters, Howard D. 1974. Some Unusual Grave Goods from a Mississippian Burial Mound. *Indian Notes* [Museum of the American Indian] 2:34–46.

Wittry, Warren L. 1969. The American Woodhenge. In *Explorations into Cahokia Archaeology,* ed. Melvin L. Fowler, 43–48. Illinois Archaeological Survey Bulletin 7. Urbana: University of Illinois Press.

———. 1996. Discovering and Interpreting the Cahokia Woodhenges. In *The Ancient Skies and Sky Watchers of Cahokia: Woodhenges, Eclipses, and Cahokian Cosmology,* ed. Melvin L. Fowler. *Wisconsin Archaeologist* 77(3–4):26–35.

Wittry, Warren L., John C. Arnold, Charles O. Witty, and Timothy R. Pauketat. 1994. *The Holdener Site: Late Woodland, Emergent Mississippian, and Mississippian Occupations in the American Bottom Uplands (11-S-685).* American Bottom Archaeology FAI-270 Site Reports 26. Urbana: University of Illinois Press.

Witty, Charles O. 1993. The Fingerhut (11S34/7) Cemetery Three Decades Later. *Illinois Archaeologist* (1–2):425–33.

Wymer, Dee Anne. 1993. Cultural Change and Subsistence: The Middle and Late Woodland Transition in the Mid-Ohio Valley. In *Foraging and Farming in the Eastern Woodlands,* ed. C. Margaret Scarry, 138–56. Gainesville: University Press of Florida.

Index

A. Martin Byers recently retired from a lifetime of teaching at Vanier College, Montreal, and holds a research associate position with the Department of Anthropology, McGill University. He has published a number of papers on the symbolic interpretation of material culture. He is the author of *The Ohio Hopewell Episode: Paradigm Lost and Paradigm Gained* (2004), which interprets the symbolic and social meaning of the well-known geometrical earthworks of this region.